HOW TO COOK INDIAN

How to Cook Indian

More than 500 Classic Recipes for the Modern Kitchen

SANJEEV KAPOOR

STEWART, TABORI & CHANG ~ NEW YORK

Published in 2011 by Stewart, Tabori & Chang
An imprint of ABRAMS

Library of Congress Cataloging-in-Publication Data

Kapoor, Sanjeev, 1964-
  How to cook Indian : more than 500 classic recipes for the modern kitchen
/ Sanjeev Kapoor.
      p. cm.
  Includes index.
  ISBN 978-1-58479-913-9 (alk. paper)
  1. Cooking, Indic. 2. Cookbooks. I. Title.
  TX724.5.I4K2964 2011
  641.5954—dc22
                        2010050496

EDITOR: Natalie Kaire
DESIGNERS: Galen Smith and Danielle Young
PRODUCTION MANAGER: Anet Sirna-Bruder

The text of this book was composed in Filosofia and Bureau Grotesque.

Printed and bound in U.S.A.
10 9 8 7 6 5 4 3 2 1

Stewart, Tabori & Chang books are available at special discounts when purchased in quantity for
premiums and promotions as well as fundraising or educational use. Special editions can also be
created to specification. For details, contact specialsales@abramsbooks.com or the address below.

THE ART OF BOOKS SINCE 1949

115 West 18th Street
New York, NY 10011
www.abramsbooks.com

CONTENTS

INTRODUCTION

I WAS BORN IN A SMALL TOWN CALLED AMBALA, which is in the state of Haryana, in North India. I spent most of my childhood in Delhi, but my father's job took him from city to city, so we moved a lot. My mother has family in Meerut, in Uttar Pradesh, and my paternal aunt lives in Kolkata, and I traveled around India visiting them when I was young. Wherever my parents set up house, my mother exchanged food and recipes with neighbors from other states and regions, and those dishes made their way onto our table. Eventually I married Alyona, who is a Kutchi from the western Indian state of Gujarat. Her sister is a chef and her mother is a very inspirational cook. These accomplished women have greatly influenced my own way of cooking.

As an adult, I traveled to all the major cities in the south and the northeast of India. I have vacationed on the beautiful beaches that line India's extensive coasts and enjoyed the fresh catch from the sea. I have driven the coconut-lined roads of the Konkan coast and feasted on the robust food found there. All my travels, all my experiences, and all my research into the history and origins of Indian cuisine have been instrumental in making me the chef that I am. And so this book is filled with pieces of my heart: some personal stories, a bit of history, and, of course, hundreds of new and classic recipes, many of them modern and simplified adaptations of dishes that have been enjoyed in India for centuries.

India has long been a favorite destination for travelers, in part because of its astonishingly varied culture, geography, and rich history. It is a country of contrasts and extremes. India has the world's most recently formed (and still rising) mountains—the Himalayas—as well as the world's most ancient rocks. The country also has the world's wettest place—at Chirapunji—and the hottest desert—at Thar. There are stretches of permanent snow in the Himalayas and Karakoram, and tropical rain forests in Kerala. If geography has any impact on the development of a people's food, India has surely benefitted from this, as it has come up with one of the richest and most diverse cuisines in the world. You could taste a new dish every day, and it would take more than a few lifetimes before you would exhaust the entire repertoire of Indian food.

When traveling south from the northernmost states or from east to west, you will encounter a distinct diversity of tastes and spices. While wheat is a staple in the northern, western, and central states, rice predominates in the south and east. While heady aromas of saffron and anise welcome you to Kashmir, a whiff of curry leaves being tempered in oil makes you feel at home in Tamil Nadu. If a diverse presentation of pulses interests you in Rajasthan, the magnificent variety of fish in the Bengal will enthrall you.

But while regional cuisines vary tremendously, they share some common threads. Indian food is healthy, featuring grains, pulses, and loads of vegetables at every meal; the dishes highlight hot, tart, sweet, and tangy flavors in exquisite balance; and they are much easier to cook than you might expect. In this book, I try to put to rest the myth that Indian food has to be elaborately prepared. Many of the ingredient lists are long, it's true, but once you have the basic spices on hand, it's just a matter of tossing them into your pan. And while some of the recipes are composed of many separate steps, each one is simple and straightforward. Use the best-quality ingredients you can find, as good ingredients are essential to good cooking. Measure, chop, and set out the ingredients before you start heating your pan. Taste each dish before serving and adjust the seasoning if necessary.

Indian food is very popular because of its wide variety of vegetarian dishes. The world is turning toward vegetarianism, and I can say emphatically that the best guide to vegetarian cooking is Indian cuisine, with its vast array of vegetable-based main courses and the lentil stews called *dals*, the many yogurt and vegetable medleys called *raitas*, and the hot and sweet pickles that accompany them. That said, fish (both from the rivers and the sea), chicken, goat, and lamb are abundant, and as you'll see in these pages. there are many dishes that use them to their best advantage.

Whether you've been cooking Indian food for years or you're just beginning, these recipes—some of them titled in Hindi, some in Hindi-English, some in regional languages to honor the spirit of where the dishes originated—will take you on an amazing journey. This book is very important to me, and through it I hope to share my passion for Indian food and life with you. The only things missing here are the sound of spices crackling in oil and the singular aroma that rises from the pan as they sputter and sizzle. But that is something you can provide.

Happy cooking!

SANJEEV KAPOOR

·······{ IN YOUR KITCHEN }·······

COMMONLY USED INGREDIENTS TO HAVE ON HAND

If you keep these staple ingredients in your cupboard and refrigerator, a delicious Indian meal is a simple matter of picking up a couple fresh vegetables or some meat and diving right into any of the recipes in this book.

Dals: If you have one or two types of *dal* (lentils) in your pantry, you're never more than a few steps from a hearty and satisfying meal. Keep them in glass jars or airtight plastic containers to keep them fresh. See the glossary (page 587) for descriptions of the varieties of *dal* used in this book.

Garlic and red onions: Keep plenty of alliums handy in a cool, dry pantry or in a basket on the countertop, as they're used in most of the savory dishes in this book. Also, see the instructions for making and freezing garlic paste on page 12 and onion paste on page 11.

Ghee: Keep a jar of ghee in the pantry or in the refrigerator; it should keep for several months either way. Just be sure to use a dry spoon each time you take ghee from the jar.

Ginger: Wrap unpeeled fresh ginger in a paper towel and keep it in the fridge, where it will stay usable for weeks. Or peel, slice, and submerge in a clean jar of dry sherry for longer refrigerator storage. See page 12 for instructions on making and freezing ginger paste.

Green chiles: Fresh green chiles are used extensively in Indian cooking, either whole, split, minced, or puréed with other ingredients depending on, aside from textural considerations, the amount of heat desired: Whole chiles lend their flavor without imparting too much heat to a curry, for example. The best substitute for the long, slender Indian green chiles are serranos, which are about the size and thickness of your finger, medium-dark green, and a bit hotter than jalapeños. To store chiles, pull off and discard the stems, rinse them, then pat them dry (or let them sit on a sunny countertop on a clean towel to air-dry for an hour or so), wrap in paper towels, and store in an open plastic bag in the refrigerator; they'll keep for several weeks. Alternatively, store them whole or minced in the freezer for several months, thawing only as many as you need at a time.

Red chiles: In this book, where red chile powder is indicated, a powder made from a milder variety like Kashmiri red chiles is my preferred chile type, though New Mexico chiles, or even paprika, can be used as a substitute. The quantity can be adjusted to taste. Many different varieties of dried chiles are sold in Indian grocery stores; check the package label or ask the store's proprietor for guidance. In some recipes I indicate that the very mild and deep-red Kashmiri red chile powder is most appropriate, and in some cases *deghi mirch*, which is very similar to Hungarian paprika, is best; in these dishes you could use paprika instead, but don't be tempted to substitute cayenne, which would be far too hot. Note, too, that U.S. "chili powder" (with an "i") is a mixture of different spices and herbs for making chili, and should not be used for these recipes. When whole dried red chiles are called for, the thin, finger-length hot cayenne peppers (or a milder type) can be used.

Rice: Fragrant, long-grained basmati rice is generally used in India for special occasions and to make biryanis. There are many other types of rice, including jasmine and short-grain rice and parboiled rice, available at Indian grocers and regular supermarkets. Indian markets sell basmati rices at different price points depending on the length of the grains, the percentage of broken grains, and overall quality. For more variety, stock brown basmati rice in your pantry as well—it's becoming more available in regular supermarkets.

Spices: Indian cooking relies on spices in a way unlike any other world cuisine, and staring down a typically long ingredient list can be intimidating if you are just starting to learn to cook Indian. However, once you have the basic spices, the recipes become infinitely more manageable. Whole spices, and many preground spices, will keep for ages in airtight containers in a dark cupboard (claims that they'll lose all potency after a mere twelve months to the contrary). A convenient way to store your most-used spices is in a *masala dhabba*, a round stainless-steel container with seven smaller compartments for different spices. The best models will have two lids, one of them very tight-fitting to keep the spices from mingling. When you begin to cook, simply pull the whole container from the cupboard and spoon out the spices you need. To start, I'd recommend filling a *masala dhabba* with ground cumin, ground coriander, turmeric, whole mustard seeds, whole cumin seeds, whole green cardamom, and ground *garam masala*.

Tamarind: Tamarind is available in several different forms: as whole ripe pods, which you can shell, soak, and push through a sieve to remove the seeds and fibers; as blocks of stiff tamarind pulp, which also need to be soaked and strained; and as tamarind concentrate, sold in squat plastic jars. If you're using concentrate rather than the reconstituted pulp, reduce the amount in the recipe by half.

Vegetable oil: Any kind of vegetable oil will do for most of these recipes—peanut and mustard oils are traditional in different regions (see page 589 for more about choosing an edible mustard oil), but canola or safflower or a blend of oils can also be used.

Yogurt: Plain yogurt is a very common ingredient in this book and is useful to have on hand—it keeps for weeks in the refrigerator. Use full-fat varieties, if possible.

EVERYDAY TOOLS AND KITCHENWARES

You don't need a vast arsenal of special kitchen equipment to make the recipes in this book. Here are the basics. (You'll find a list of specialty equipment on page 591.)

Double boiler: A double boiler is used to melt chocolate gently without burning or seizing, and to cook sauces or thick liquids that might burn if cooked over direct heat. It consists of an upper vessel (containing the food to be cooked) situated above a lower pot of water. When the water is heated, the steam produced transfers heat to the upper vessel. If you don't have a double boiler, use a regular saucepan and set a heatproof metal or glass bowl on top of it; make sure the water in the saucepan does not touch the bottom of the bowl.

Griddle: Making Indian griddle breads such as *roti* and *paratha* is easiest with a heavy cast-iron or nonstick Indian griddle, or *tawa*, which is either flat or slightly concave (for shallow frying), but a large cast-iron skillet will do in a pinch.

Mini food processor, blender, spice grinder: Many households in India rely on an appliance called a "mixie" or "mixer-blender," a combination food processor, blender, and wet-and-dry spice grinder for the various puréeing and grinding required in some recipes. A mini food processor, blender, and/or electric spice grinder can handle all of these tasks just as well—and there's always the simple mortar and pestle for quickly grinding small batches of whole spices. If you're short

on space, you might consider using a regular countertop blender with a one-cup "food processor" jar attachment for blending batters and puréeing small quantities of wet ingredients (chiles, cilantro, ginger, and so on) for seasoning pastes, and a coffee grinder for spices.

Saucepans and soup pots: Have a variety of saucepans and soup or stock pots ready for simmering small quantities of sauce components and larger batches of soups and *dal*.

Sauté pans: You'll need a heavy nonstick or well-seasoned sauté pan or skillet for most of the curries in this book. A twelve-inch or larger one would be useful.

Steamer: All-purpose Indian steamers are made of stainless steel with stacked trays that can be fit into grooves inside the main vessel; the lid is vented to allow some of the steam to escape. Food to be steamed is put on plates that are then set on top of the trays. A bamboo steamer will work for these recipes if you put the food on a plate before putting it in the steamer tray. For *idlis*, steamed rice cakes, you'll need an *idli* stand to fit into a steamer pot (see page 591).

Tempering pan: Many of the *dal* and curry recipes in this book feature a uniquely Indian final step: tempering. A bit of vegetable oil or ghee is heated and various spices are added and cooked until they sputter and release their distinctive aromas. The mixture is then drizzled into the *dal* and the pot is covered and left to stand for a couple minutes while the sizzling oil and spices meld with the lentils and vegetables. An Indian tempering pan is a small cup-shaped pan with a rounded bottom and a long handle; a very small, heavy sauté pan or skillet is a fine substitute.

Utensils: A **slotted spoon** or **wire skimmer** is used extensively throughout this book to stir and scoop frying foods out of hot oil. **Tongs** are used to turn griddled breads as they cook, lift pot lids, and gently transfer delicate ground-meat kabobs from skillet to serving plates—a **thin metal spatula** is helpful here as well. A **mortar and pestle** can be useful for grinding spices and making chutneys. **Muslin cloth** or **cheesecloth** is used to drain yogurt and fresh *paneer* cheese. A **fine-mesh sieve** and a good **colander** are handy for draining and straining as well. **Skewers**—either bamboo or metal, thin or wide and flat—are used to make kabobs.

Wok: The *kadai*, or Indian wok, is a deep, flat-bottomed pan with curved sides and, usually, a looped handle on either side. It's used for quick deep-frying and also for *dals* and curries. A nonstick or well-seasoned Chinese-style wok or even a wide, deep sauté pan or saucepan would work fine for most dishes.

Basics

Indian cooking is known for its use of spices and spice combinations (commonly called masalas). Our affinity with spices can be traced back to ancient times and is still a trademark of contemporary Indian cuisine. In my childhood days, there was always a flurry of activity with the advent of summer, when family and friends prepared various masalas and other preserves. Good-quality spices would be cleaned and sun-dried or roasted before being pounded in various combinations to create the variety of masalas to be used throughout the year.

Most masalas can be bought ready-made these days. But people who like to make their own masalas, or those for whom packaged masalas are not easily available, will find most of the basic recipes that are used widely in Indian cooking in this chapter. Be it *chholay masala* or *garam masala*, *dhansak masala* or *sambhar masala*, fresh garlic paste or fresh ginger paste, these are the go-to recipes for every home cook. I think you'll find that these masalas are worth the preparation, and that they're sure to please the most discerning palates.

Also in this chapter you'll find recipes for the making of *roti*, *paratha*, *naan*, *appam*, and other favorites, which are key in rounding out these meals.

Almond Paste

Makes 3½ tablespoons.

15 almonds

1. Place a small nonstick saucepan over high heat and add ½ cup (100 ml) water. When the water comes to a boil, add the almonds and remove from the heat.

2. Let the almonds soak in the hot water for 5 minutes. Drain and peel. Transfer to a spice grinder, add 2 tablespoons water, and grind to a smooth paste. Use immediately or store for up to a day, covered in the refrigerator.

Boiled-Onion Paste

Makes ¾ cup (190 grams).

3 medium onions, peeled and quartered

1. Place a nonstick saucepan over high heat and add 3 cups (600 ml) water. When the water comes to a boil, lower the heat to medium, add the onions, cover, and cook for 20 minutes.

2. Drain and transfer the onions to a food processor. Process to a smooth paste.

Cashew Paste

Makes ½ cup (150 grams).

½ cup raw cashews

1. Soak the cashews in a bowl with 1 cup (200 ml) water for 30 minutes.
2. Drain and transfer to a spice grinder. Add ⅓ cup (65 ml) water and grind to a smooth paste.

Garlic Paste

Makes 6 tablespoons (100 grams).

25 cloves garlic, peeled

1. Put the garlic in a food processor. Add ½ cup (100 ml) water and process to a smooth paste.
2. Store in an airtight container in the refrigerator for up to a week.

Ginger Paste

Makes 6 tablespoons (90 grams).

7-inch (18-cm) piece fresh ginger, peeled and roughly chopped

1. Put the ginger in a food processor. Add 3 tablespoons water and process to a smooth paste.
2. Store in an airtight container in the refrigerator for up to a week.

Ginger-Garlic Paste

Makes 7 tablespoons (80 grams).

3-inch (7½-cm) piece fresh ginger, peeled and roughly chopped
10 cloves garlic, peeled and roughly chopped

1. Put the ginger and garlic in a food processor. Add ¼ cup (50 ml) water and process to a smooth paste.

2. Store in an airtight container in the refrigerator for up to a week.

Green Chile Paste

Makes 3 tablespoons (40 grams).

12 green chiles, stemmed and roughly chopped

1. Put the chiles in a food processor. Add 2 tablespoons water and process to a smooth paste.

2. Store in an airtight container in the refrigerator for up to a week.

Note To make red chile paste, replace the green chiles with 12 fresh red chiles and follow the recipe above.

Appam

Traditionally, fresh toddy (an alcohol made from the sap of palm trees) is used to ferment the batter for *appams*. A special type of cast-iron wok called an *appam kadai* is used to cook these pancakes from the south, but any small nonstick wok will work as well. Just make sure it has a heavy lid. Serve these with *kaikari ishtew* (page 269), lamb *ishtew* (page 387), or *kozhi ishtew* (page 427).

Makes 8.

1 cup (200 grams) short-grain rice
3 slices white bread
½ cup (75 grams) cooked rice
½ cup (60 grams) grated fresh coconut (or frozen unsweetened coconut)
1 teaspoon table salt
½ teaspoon vegetable oil

1. Put the raw rice in a bowl, wash in plenty of water 2 or 3 times, and drain. Add 3 cups (600 ml) water and soak for 3 to 4 hours. Drain.

2. Soak the bread in 1 cup (200 ml) water for 15 minutes. Take the slices out and squeeze to remove the excess water.

3. Put the raw rice in a spice grinder, add ¼ cup (50 ml) water, and grind to a smooth paste. Transfer to a large bowl.

4. Put the cooked rice, coconut, and bread in a food processor. Add 2 tablespoons water and process to a smooth batter. Add to the rice paste in the bowl and stir well.

5. Cover the bowl with plastic wrap and set aside in a warm place to ferment overnight.

6. Add the salt and 2 tablespoons water and stir well.

7. Place a small cast-iron or nonstick wok over medium heat, add the oil and 1 tablespoon water, and rotate the wok so that the oil-water mixture coats the entire wok. Pour out the excess oil and water.

8. Pour in 2 ladlefuls of batter and tilt the wok to spread the batter. The edges should be thin and the excess batter should collect at the center. Cover with a heavy lid and cook for 2 to 3 minutes or until the edges of the *appam* start to leave the wok and are crisp and thin and the center is soft and spongy. Repeat with the remaining batter.

9. Serve hot.

Brown Rice

Serve this with *dhansaak* (page 295).

Serves 4.

2 tablespoons ghee (page 37)
2 (1-inch/2½-cm) cinnamon sticks
2 star anise
6 to 8 whole cloves
2 large red onions, sliced
2 teaspoons sugar
1½ cups (300 grams) basmati rice, soaked
1 teaspoon table salt

1. Place a nonstick saucepan over medium heat and add the ghee. When the ghee melts and small bubbles appear at the bottom of the pan, add the cinnamon, star anise, and cloves, and sauté for 30 seconds. Add the onions and sauté for 7 to 8 minutes or until well browned.

2. Add the sugar and sauté until it dissolves. Add the rice and stir. Add 5 cups (1 liter) water and the salt, and bring to a boil. Lower the heat to medium, cover, and cook for 15 minutes or until done.

3. Serve hot.

Dahi

····∗{ Perfect yogurt }∗·······················

Makes 2½ cups (600 grams).

2½ cups (500 ml) whole milk
1 teaspoon good-quality plain yogurt

1. Place a nonstick saucepan over high heat and add the milk. Bring to a boil. Remove from the heat and set aside to cool.

2. When the milk has cooled to 114°F/45°C or is lukewarm, add the yogurt and stir gently with a spoon or whisk.

3. Transfer to an earthenware pot and set aside in a warm place overnight until the mixture thickens. Do not jostle the pot. In the winter or at higher altitudes, wrap the pot in a blanket or towel to keep it warm.

4. When the yogurt has thickened, transfer to the refrigerator. Remember to save 1 teaspoon of the yogurt to make the next batch.

Ganthia

····∗{ Gram-flour snack }∗·······················

This is a simple snack that looks like a small, stout stick. It is easily prepared using a *ganthia* press (page 591), which can be found at most Indian grocery stores. The prepared dough is pushed through the holes in the mold and the small sticks of the dough that come out are deep-fried.

Makes 3 cups (230 grams).

2 cups (200 grams) *besan* (chickpea/gram flour)
1½ teaspoons table salt
¼ teaspoon ground turmeric
1 teaspoon red chile powder
½ teaspoon *ajwain*
¼ cup (50 ml) plus 1 quart (800 ml) vegetable oil

1. Put the *besan* in a bowl. Add the salt, turmeric, chile powder, and *ajwain*, and stir.

2. Heat ¼ cup (50 ml) oil in a small saucepan and add it to the *besan* mixture. Add ½ cup (100 ml) water and knead to make a stiff dough. Set the dough aside to rest for 30 minutes.

3. Place a nonstick wok over high heat and add 1 quart (800 ml) oil. When small bubbles appear at the bottom of the wok, put some of the dough in a *ganthia* mold and press it directly into the hot oil. Cook, stirring occasionally with a slotted spoon, until deep golden brown. Remove with the slotted spoon and drain on paper towels. Repeat with the remaining dough.

4. Let cool and store in an airtight container.

Paneer

······⸬⟫ **Pressed fresh cheese** ⟨⸬··

Makes 7 ounces (200 grams).

5 cups (1 liter) whole milk
1 cup (200 ml) heavy cream
1 tablespoon vinegar

1. Place a deep nonstick saucepan over high heat and add the milk. Stir in the cream and bring to a boil. Lower the heat to medium, add the vinegar, and stir until the mixture curdles. The solids will separate from the whey. Remove from the heat.

2. Place a double layer of cheesecloth over a strainer and pour in the *paneer*. Gather the edges of the muslin and dip the wrapped *paneer* in a bowl of cold water. Tie up the muslin and hang it over a bowl for 15 to 20 minutes or until most of the whey has drained; reserve the whey for another use.

3. Place the wrapped *paneer* on a plate and put a heavy weight on it for 10 minutes or until firm. Unwrap and cut the *paneer* into slices or cubes.

······⸬⟫ **Chef's Tip** ⟨⸬ You will get about 3½ cups (650 ml) whey, which contains a lot of nutrients. It can be used instead of water in *roti* dough or even in soup.

Basic Paratha

·······⊱{ Indian griddle bread with ghee }⊰···

Makes 6.

1 cup plus 2 tablespoons (165 grams) *atta* (whole-wheat flour)
¾ teaspoon table salt
6 teaspoons ghee (page 37), melted

1. Combine the *atta* and salt in a bowl. Add ½ cup (100 ml) water and knead to make a medium-soft dough. Cover with a damp cloth and set aside for 15 minutes.

2. Divide the dough into 6 portions and shape into balls. Roll out into 3-inch (7½-cm) rounds. Brush the surface of each with ¼ teaspoon ghee, then fold in half and then again in half to make a triangle. Roll out these triangles to bigger triangles with each side measuring 5 to 6 inches.

3. Place a nonstick griddle over medium heat and let it heat for 2 minutes. Place a dough triangle on it and cook for 1 minute, turn it over, and drizzle ¼ teaspoon ghee all around the edges. Turn again and drizzle ½ teaspoon ghee all around. Cook until both sides are light golden brown. Repeat with the remaining dough triangles.

4. Serve hot.

Basic Roti

·······⊱{ Basic Indian bread }⊰···

Makes 8.

1 cup plus 2 tablespoons (165 grams) *atta* (whole-wheat flour)
¾ teaspoon table salt
Ghee (page 37)

1. Combine the *atta* and salt in a bowl. Add ½ cup (100 ml) water and knead to make a medium-soft dough. Cover with a damp cloth and set aside for 15 minutes.

2. Divide the dough into 8 portions and shape into balls. Dust with a little flour and roll out into 5-inch rounds.

3. Place a nonstick griddle over medium heat and let it heat for 2 minutes. Place a dough round on it and cook for 30 seconds. Turn over and cook on the other side for 15 seconds, then, if you are using a gas burner, hold it with tongs over the open flame and cook until it puffs. Turn and cook the other side. Repeat with the remaining dough rounds.

4. Serve hot, topped with ghee.

Luchi

Deep-fried bread

Makes 16.

> 2 cups (240 grams) *maida* (refined flour) or pastry flour
> 1 teaspoon table salt
> 1 tablespoon ghee (page 37), softened
> 1 quart (800 ml) vegetable oil

1. Sift the *maida* with the salt into a large bowl. Add the ghee and ⅔ cup (135 ml) water and knead to make a soft dough. Cover with a damp cloth and set aside for 30 minutes.

2. Divide the dough into 16 portions and shape into small balls. Roll out into 3-inch (7½-cm) rounds.

3. Place a nonstick wok over high heat and add the oil. When small bubbles appear at the bottom of the wok, gently slide in one dough round at a time and cook, turning with a slotted spoon, until puffed up and pale cream in color. Remove with the slotted spoon and drain on paper towels.

4. Serve immediately.

Naan

Makes 8.

4 cups (480 grams) *maida* (refined flour) or pastry flour
1 teaspoon baking powder
½ teaspoon baking soda
1 teaspoon table salt
2 teaspoons sugar
1 whole egg (optional; see Notes)
1 cup (200 ml) milk
2 tablespoons plain yogurt
2 tablespoons vegetable oil
2 teaspoons *kalonji* (nigella; see Notes)
2 teaspoons butter

1. Sift the flour, baking powder, baking soda, and salt together into a large bowl. Add the sugar, egg (if using), milk, yogurt, and 3 tablespoons water, and knead for about 10 minutes to make a medium-soft dough. Apply a little oil to the dough, cover with a damp cloth, and set aside for 1 hour in a warm place.

2. Preheat the oven to 400°F/200°C.

3. Divide the dough into 8 portions and shape into balls. Apply a little oil to each ball and sprinkle the *kalonji* on top. Flatten each ball of dough into a 6-inch round. Stretch the dough on one side to make a triangular shape. Place the *naans* on a lightly greased baking sheet and bake for 15 to 18 minutes or until crisp and brown on both sides.

4. Serve hot, topped with the butter.

······· ⋇} **Notes** {⋇ You can omit the egg in this recipe. It will not affect the taste or texture of the *naan* at all.

Kalonji (nigella) is available in Indian grocery stores and is sometimes called onion seeds.

Papdis

Small, crisp flat wafers made with dough, often used in Indian street food.

Makes 18.

1 cup (120 grams) *maida* (refined flour) or pastry flour
½ teaspoon cumin seeds (optional)
5 teaspoons ghee (page 37), melted
1 teaspoon table salt
1 quart (800 ml) vegetable oil

1. Put the *maida* in a bowl. Add the cumin (if using), ghee, and salt, and stir. Gradually add ¼ cup (50 ml) water and knead to make a stiff dough. Cover with a damp cloth and set aside to rest for 10 to 15 minutes.

2. Divide the dough into 18 portions and shape into balls. Roll out into 2½-inch (6½-cm) rounds. Prick with a fork all over the surface.

3. Place a nonstick wok over high heat and add the oil. When small bubbles appear at the bottom of the wok, gently slide in the dough rounds, two at a time, and cook, stirring with a slotted spoon, until golden brown and crisp. Remove with the slotted spoon and drain on paper towels.

4. Let cool to room temperature, then store in an airtight container.

Khajoor Aur Imli Ki Chutney

{ Sweet date-and-tamarind chutney }

Makes 2 cups (600 grams).

15 to 20 dates, pitted
2 teaspoons cumin seeds
¼ teaspoon fennel seeds
1 cup (200 grams) grated cane jaggery
1 cup (340 grams) tamarind pulp
2 teaspoons red chile powder
1 teaspoon ground ginger
1 teaspoon black salt
1 teaspoon table salt

1. Roughly chop the dates.

2. Place a small nonstick sauté pan over medium heat. Add the cumin and fennel, and dry-roast until fragrant. Cool slightly, then transfer to a spice grinder and grind to a powder.

3. In a nonstick saucepan, combine the dates, jaggery, tamarind pulp, cumin and fennel powder, red chile powder, ginger, black salt, table salt, and 1 cup (200 ml) water. Place over medium heat and bring to a boil. Lower the heat and continue to cook for 6 to 8 minutes.

4. Let cool to room temperature and serve, or store in an airtight container in the refrigerator for up to a month.

Pudina Aur Dhaniya Chutney

Mint-and-cilantro chutney

Makes ½ cup (110 grams).

1 cup roughly chopped fresh cilantro
½ cup roughly chopped fresh mint
2 to 3 green chiles, stemmed and chopped
½ teaspoon black salt
¼ teaspoon sugar
1 teaspoon freshly squeezed lemon juice

1. Put the cilantro, mint, and chiles in a food processor. Add ¼ cup (50 ml) water and process to a smooth paste.

2. Add the black salt and sugar, and process to combine.

3. Transfer to a bowl and stir in the lemon juice.

········⸘ **Chef's Tip** ⸙ To add sourness, you can use crushed *anardana* (dried pomegranate seeds) or *amchur* (dried mango powder) instead of the lemon juice. In season, a bit of green mango is a good substitute too.

Sichuan Sauce

········⸘ **Spicy Chile Sauce** ⸙ ···

Makes 1 cup (240 grams).

10 to 12 dried red chiles, stemmed and finely chopped
10 cloves garlic, peeled
2 scallions with green tops
½ cup (100 ml) vegetable oil
2 green chiles, stemmed
1-inch (2½-cm) piece fresh ginger, grated
½ cup (100 ml) vegetable stock (page 36)
2- to 3-inch (5- to 7½-cm) rib celery, chopped
1 tablespoon tomato ketchup
1½ teaspoons table salt
2 teaspoons white vinegar

1. Boil the red chiles in 1 cup (200 ml) water for 5 to 7 minutes. Drain.

2. Finely chop 2 cloves of the garlic. Finely chop the scallion whites and greens separately.

3. Put the chiles and the remaining 8 cloves garlic in a mini food processor, add 2 tablespoons water, and grind to a fine paste.

4. Place a nonstick sauté pan over medium heat and add the oil. When small bubbles appear at the bottom of the pan, add the chopped garlic, green chiles, scallion whites, and ginger, and sauté for 1 minute.

5. Add the chile-garlic paste and sauté for 5 minutes.

6. Add the stock, celery, ketchup, and salt, and stir to blend well. Add the vinegar and stir well. Simmer for 5 minutes and remove from the heat.

7. Add the scallion greens and stir. Let cool and store in an airtight container in the refrigerator for up to 2 days.

Chaat Masala

A spicy and tangy mix used in *chaats*, salads, and savory dishes like fritters, to enhance their taste.

Makes ½ cup (55 grams).

¼ cup (20 grams) coriander seeds
2 teaspoons cumin seeds
1 teaspoon *ajwain*
2 or 3 dried red chiles, stemmed
3 tablespoons black salt
½ teaspoon citric acid
1 teaspoon *amchur* (dried mango powder)
1 tablespoon table salt
1 teaspoon ground black pepper

1. Place a small nonstick sauté pan over medium heat. Add the coriander and dry-roast until lightly browned and fragrant. Transfer to a bowl.

2. One spice at a time, dry-roast the cumin and *ajwain*, and add them to the coriander. Stir and set aside to cool completely.

3. Transfer to a spice grinder. Add the chiles, black salt, citric acid, *amchur*, table salt, and pepper. Grind to a fine powder.

4. Store in an airtight container.

Chai Masala

⁕⟩ Spice mix for tea ⟨⁕

Makes ¼ cup (20 grams).

¾ tablespoon whole black peppercorns
4 (1-inch/2½-cm) cinnamon sticks, broken
16 whole cloves
16 green cardamom pods
4 teaspoons ground ginger

1. Put the peppercorns, cinnamon, cloves, and cardamom in a spice grinder, and grind to a fine powder.

2. Sift the powder into a bowl. Add the ginger and stir well.

3. Store in an airtight container.

Chholay Masala

⁕⟩ Spice mix for making *chole (chholay)* ⟨⁕

Makes ¾ cup (100 grams).

2 tablespoons cumin seeds
3 tablespoons coriander seeds
2 (1-inch/2½-cm) cinnamon sticks
8 to 10 whole cloves
1 black cardamom pod
½ teaspoon *ajwain*
2½ teaspoons whole black peppercorns
1 teaspoon *kasoori methi* (dried fenugreek leaves)
3 to 5 *tirphal* (optional; see Note)
2 tablespoons *anardana* (dried pomegranate seeds)
8 to 10 bay leaves
8 to 10 dried red chiles, stemmed
1 teaspoon *amchur* (dried mango powder)
½ teaspoon ground ginger
1 teaspoon table salt
2 teaspoons black salt

1. Place a small nonstick sauté pan over medium heat. Add the cumin, coriander, cinnamon, cloves, cardamom, *ajwain*, peppercorns, *kasoori methi*, *tirphal* (if using), *anardana*, bay leaves, and chiles, and dry-roast until fragrant.

2. Transfer the mixture to a plate and set aside to cool completely.

3. Transfer to a spice grinder and add the *amchur*, ginger, table salt, and black salt. Grind to a fine powder.

4. Store in an airtight container.

········≈} **Note** }⊛ *Tirphal* (not to be confused with *triphala*, a combination of herbs used in Ayurvedic medicine) is a spice from a tree that grows deep in the rain forests of western India. The berries are dried, and the seeds are removed and discarded. *Tirphal*, which strongly resembles Sichuan peppercorns in appearance, has a strong woody aroma and a sharp flavor.

Dhansaak Masala

········≈} **Spice mix for *dhansaak*** }⊛ ··

Makes ¾ cup (70 grams).

10 dried red chiles, stemmed
2-inch (5-cm) cinnamon stick, broken
3 bay leaves
1 tablespoon cumin seeds
2 tablespoons coriander seeds
4 to 6 black cardamom pods
2 teaspoons whole black peppercorns
½ tablespoon whole cloves
1 teaspoon fenugreek seeds
1 tablespoon black mustard seeds
2 or 3 blades mace
½ tablespoon ground turmeric

1. Place a small nonstick sauté pan over medium heat. Add all the ingredients except the turmeric, lower the heat, and dry-roast for 5 minutes. Add the turmeric, stir, and remove from the heat. Set aside to cool completely.

2. Transfer to a spice grinder and grind to a fine powder.

3. Store in an airtight container.

Garam Masala

A flavor-enhancing blend of spices used widely in Indian cuisine.

Makes 1 cup (75 grams).

10 to 12 blades mace
8 to 10 (1-inch/2½-cm) cinnamon sticks
25 whole cloves
25 green cardamom pods
10 to 12 black cardamom pods
8 to 10 bay leaves
8 teaspoons cumin seeds
4 teaspoons whole black peppercorns
½ teaspoon grated nutmeg

1. Place a small nonstick sauté pan over medium heat. Add the mace and dry-roast until fragrant. Transfer to a bowl.

2. One spice at a time, dry-roast the cinnamon, cloves, green cardamom, black cardamom, bay leaves, cumin, and peppercorns, and transfer to the bowl. Set aside to cool completely.

3. Transfer to a spice grinder and grind to a fine powder. Add the grated nutmeg. Store in an airtight container.

Goda Masala

A highly flavorful blend of spices typically used in Maharashtrian food (native to the western Indian state of Maharastia).

Makes 1½ cups (135 grams).

Vegetable oil
1 cup (80 grams) coriander seeds
2 tablespoons cumin seeds
¼ cup (5 grams) *dagad phool* (lichen stone flower; optional; see Notes)
6 (2-inch/5-cm) cinnamon sticks
16 green cardamom pods
25 whole cloves
¾ teaspoon caraway seeds
25 whole black peppercorns
10 to 12 bay leaves
1 teaspoon dried *nagkeshar* (cobra saffron; optional; see Notes)
2 blades mace
3 tablespoons grated dried coconut
1 teaspoon white sesame seeds
3 dried red chiles, stemmed
1 teaspoon asafetida

1. Place a small nonstick sauté pan over medium heat. Add a couple drops of oil, and, one at a time, roast all the ingredients until fragrant. Transfer to a bowl and let cool completely.

2. Transfer to a spice grinder and grind to a fine powder.

3. Store in an airtight container.

·····❖{ Notes }❖ *Dagad phool* (sometimes labeled *patthar ke phool*) is a fungus, a lichen that grows on rocks in the Himalayas and mountainous regions of western and central India. Used in small quantities, it lends a dark color and musky flavor to dishes.

Nagkeshar, or cobra saffron, is an herb with a mild, slightly sweet flavor.

Nihari Masala

This mix is used specifically to make a dish called *nalli nihari* (page 391).

Makes 1 cup (160 grams).

¼ cup (35 grams) cumin seeds
¼ cup (35 grams) fennel seeds
12 to 15 dried red chiles, stemmed
20 whole cloves
5 green cardamom pods
3 black cardamom pods
25 to 30 whole black peppercorns
¼ cup (50 grams) white poppy seeds
2 bay leaves
1 blade mace
2 tablespoons ground ginger
½ tablespoon freshly grated nutmeg
4 or 5 (1-inch/2½-cm) cinnamon sticks
5 tablespoons ground *dalia* (roasted *chana dal*)

1. Place a nonstick sauté pan over medium heat. Add the cumin, fennel, chiles, cloves, green and black cardamom, peppercorns, poppy seeds, bay leaves, mace, ginger, nutmeg, and cinnamon, and dry-roast for 5 minutes or until fragrant.

2. Add the *dalia* and dry-roast for 2 minutes. Remove from the heat and set aside to cool. Transfer to a spice grinder and grind to a fine powder.

3. Sift through a fine sieve and store in an airtight container in the refrigerator.

Pav Bhaji Masala

Spice mix for *pav bhaji*

A special blend of spices added to vegetables to make a dish called *pav bhaji* (page 90).

Makes 5 tablespoons (75 grams).

1½ tablespoons *amchur* (dried mango powder)
½ teaspoon whole black peppercorns
12 Kashmiri dried red chiles, stemmed
2 tablespoons cumin seeds
2½ tablespoons coriander seeds
6 (1-inch/2½-cm) cinnamon sticks
1 teaspoon table salt
¼ teaspoon black salt
25 whole cloves
1 black cardamom pod
6 to 8 fresh curry leaves
2 bay leaves
1 tablespoon fennel seeds

1. Place a small nonstick sauté pan over medium heat. Add all the ingredients, one by one in the order listed, lower the heat, and dry-roast for 5 minutes.

2. Set aside to cool completely. Transfer to a spice grinder and grind to a fine powder.

3. Store in an airtight container.

Punjabi Garam Masala

Spice mix

Another variety of *garam masala*, more popular in Punjabi homes.

Makes 1¾ cups (200 grams).

1 cup (100 grams) whole black peppercorns
¾ cup plus 1 tablespoon (120 grams) cumin seeds
11 black cardamom pods
4 or 5 whole cloves
1-inch (2½-cm) cinnamon stick

1. Place a small nonstick sauté pan over medium heat. Add the peppercorns and dry-roast for 4 minutes. Transfer to a plate.

2. One spice at a time, dry-roast the cumin, cardamom, cloves, and cinnamon, and add them to the peppercorns. Set aside to cool completely.

3. Transfer to a spice grinder and grind to a fine powder. Store in an airtight container.

Rasam Powder

·······⊰ Spice mix ⊱···

A spice blend used to make *rasam*, a South Indian soup.

Makes 2¼ cups (250 grams).

1 cup (80 grams) coriander seeds
½ cup (100 grams) *toor dal/arhar dal* (split pigeon peas)
¼ cup (35 grams) cumin seeds
¼ cup (25 grams) whole black peppercorns
10 to 12 fresh curry leaves
15 dried red chiles, stemmed

1. Place a medium nonstick sauté pan over medium heat. Add the coriander, *dals*, cumin, peppercorns, curry leaves, and chiles, and dry-roast for 3 to 4 minutes or until fragrant. Let cool completely.

2. Transfer to a spice grinder and grind to a fine powder.

3. Store in an airtight container in the refrigerator or in a cool, dry place for up to 6 months.

Ground Roasted Cumin

This is an excellent topping for *raitas* (yogurt sauces; page 65) or *chaats* (page 81).

Makes 6 tablespoons (30 grams).

4½ tablespoons cumin seeds

1. Place a small nonstick sauté pan over medium heat. Add the cumin and dry-roast until lightly colored. Set aside to cool completely.

2. Transfer to a spice grinder and grind to a fine powder.

3. Store in an airtight container.

Sambhar

Basic masala for South Indian lentil dishes

Makes 1¾ cups (180 grams).

½ cup (40 grams) coriander seeds
1 tablespoon cumin seeds
2 tablespoons *chana dal* (split Bengal gram)
2 tablespoons *dhuli moong dal* (split skinless green gram)
2 tablespoons *toor dal/arhar dal* (split pigeon peas)
1 tablespoon brown mustard seeds
1 tablespoon fenugreek seeds
10 to 12 whole black peppercorns
25 to 30 dried red chiles, stemmed
2 to 3 tablespoons ground turmeric

1. Place a medium nonstick sauté pan over medium heat. Add the coriander, cumin, *dals*, mustard seeds, fenugreek, peppercorns, and chiles, and dry-roast for 3 to 4 minutes or until fragrant. Transfer to a bowl and set aside to cool completely.

2. Transfer to a spice grinder. Add the turmeric and grind to a fine powder.

3. Store in an airtight container in the refrigerator or in a cool, dry place for up to 6 months.

Ver

Makes ¼ cup plus 2 tablespoons (45 grams).

1½ tablespoons fennel seeds
1½ tablespoons caraway seeds
2 bay leaves
1 tablespoon black cardamom seeds
¼ teaspoon green cardamom seeds
2½-inch cinnamon stick
8 to 10 whole cloves
1 teaspoon fenugreek seeds
8 to 10 whole black peppercorns
1 large blade mace
1 star anise
¼ teaspoon freshly grated nutmeg

1. Place a small nonstick sauté pan over medium heat. Add the fennel, caraway, bay leaves, black cardamom, green cardamom, cinnamon, cloves, fenugreek, peppercorns, mace, and star anise, and dry-roast until fragrant. Set aside to cool completely.

2. Transfer to a spice grinder. Add the nutmeg and grind to a fine powder.

3. Store in an airtight container in the refrigerator or in a cool, dry place.

Chicken Stock

Makes 3¼ cups (650 ml).

7 ounces (200 grams) chicken bones, such as wing tips, neck, or other bones
1 medium red onion, quartered
1 medium carrot, roughly chopped
2 or 3 sprigs fresh parsley, roughly chopped
1 rib celery, roughly chopped
1 leek with top, roughly chopped (optional)
6 or 7 whole black peppercorns
5 or 6 whole cloves
1 bay leaf

1. Remove any excess fat from the bones.

2. Place a nonstick saucepan over high heat and add 2 cups (400 ml) water. Add the bones and boil for 5 minutes. Drain off the water.

3. Add the remaining ingredients and 10 cups (2 liters) water. Place over high heat and bring to a boil. Lower the heat to low. Spoon off any scum that rises to the top and replace it with cold water. Simmer for at least 1 hour and up to 1½ hours.

4. Pour through a strainer into a large bowl; discard the solids. Let the stock cool to room temperature, then cover and store in the refrigerator.

Lamb Stock

Makes 3 cups (600 ml).

7 ounces (200 grams) lamb bones
1 medium red onion, quartered
1 medium carrot, cut into 8 pieces
1 rib celery, cut into 1-inch (2½-cm) pieces
2 or 3 sprigs fresh parsley
6 or 7 whole black peppercorns
1 bay leaf

1. Remove any excess fat from the bones.

2. Place a nonstick saucepan over high heat and add 2 cups (400 ml) water. Add the bones and boil for 5 minutes. Drain.

3. Add the onion, carrot, celery, parsley, peppercorns, bay leaf, and 12 cups (2.4 liters) water. Place over high heat and bring to a boil. Lower the heat to low. Spoon off any scum that rises to the top and replace it with cold water. Simmer for at least 2 hours and up to 2½ hours.

4. Pour through a strainer into a large bowl; discard the solids. Let the stock cool to room temperature, then cover and store in the refrigerator.

Vegetable Stock

Makes 2¼ cups (450 ml).

1 medium red onion, sliced
½ medium carrot, sliced
½ rib celery, chopped
2 cloves garlic, crushed
1 bay leaf
5 or 6 whole black peppercorns
2 or 3 whole cloves

1. Place a nonstick saucepan over high heat and add 5 cups (1 liter) water. Add the onion, carrot, celery, garlic, bay leaf, peppercorns, and cloves and bring to a boil. Lower the heat to medium and simmer for 30 minutes.

2. Pour through a strainer into a large bowl; discard the solids. Let the stock cool to room temperature, then cover and store in the refrigerator.

Atta Dough

For sealing a pan and lid while cooking *biryani*

Makes 1½ cups (200 grams).

1 cup (150 grams) *atta* (whole-wheat flour)

1. Combine the *atta* and ¾ cup (150 ml) water in a bowl and knead to make a soft dough.

2. Roll the dough into a long rope. Place it around the edge of the pan that needs to be sealed. Place the lid over the dough and press down hard. As the *biryani* cooks, the dough will dry up. When you remove the pan from the heat, peel the dough off to open the lid. (Since it will be totally dried up, it should peel off easily.)

Ghee

Makes 1⅔ cups (325 grams).

2 cups (500 grams) unsalted butter

1. Place a nonstick saucepan over medium heat and add the butter. When the butter is melted, lower the heat to low and cook, stirring frequently so that it does not scorch, for 30 minutes or until the liquid is light brown and the residue settles to the bottom. There will be some milk solids that rise to the top as foam and these should be skimmed off.

2. Set aside to cool slightly. Strain into a clean jar and let cool completely. Cover with an airtight lid and store in the refrigerator for up to 2 weeks.

Khoya

Unsweetened solid condensed milk

Makes 1 cup (155 grams).

5 cups (1 liter) full-fat buffalo or cow's milk

1. Place a heavy-bottomed saucepan over high heat and add the milk. When it comes to a boil, lower the heat to medium and cook, stirring continuously, for about 30 minutes or until the milk is reduced and forms a thick lump. It is very important to stir continuously and not allow a cream to form on the surface because this will affect the texture of the *khoya*.

2. Let cool completely, then store in an airtight container in the refrigerator for up to 3 days.

Beverages

For centuries, a potter's wheel was used in India to make earthenware pots called *matkas* that kept drinking water cool. Surprisingly, even with refrigeration and electricity, traditional *matkas* are still used in many Indian homes.

Indians love cool drinks and cooling foods when the weather is hot, and they enjoy warming drinks in the winter. In Delhi, the dry summer wind called *lu* not only dehydrates you but also saps all of your energy, and a glass of chilled watermelon juice hits the spot on those hot days. In Punjab, a tall glass of chilled *lassi* (page 44) is most welcome in the summer, and spice-laden drinks such as *jal jeera* (page 41) are served as aperitifs. And a cool *kokum sharbat* (page 43) is served to welcome guests and is essential at weddings.

During the winter months, a saffron-enriched milkshake called *zafrani sharbat* (page 46) is popular in Kashmir, and even though it's a cold drink, the spice is wintry and warming.

The drinks that follow will enhance your appetite, refresh your palate, fill in those little gaps between meals, or cool your parched throat.

Adrak Navratan

This drink is an excellent digestive. It can be kept in the refrigerator for up to a week. Dried dates and raisins impart natural sweetness to the drink, but if you wish to make it sweeter you can add 1 teaspoon sugar to each glass of *adrak navratan*.

Serves 4.

10 to 12 dried dates
1½ teaspoons julienned tender fresh ginger
½ cup (90 grams) raisins
5 or 6 hot green chiles, stemmed and cut in half
½ cup (100 ml) freshly squeezed lemon juice
1½ teaspoons table salt
1 teaspoon black salt

1. Pit the dates and thinly slice them lengthwise.

2. Combine the dates, ginger, raisins, chiles, lemon juice, salt, black salt, and 1 cup (200 ml) water in a bowl and stir well. Transfer the mixture into a wide-mouthed glass jar. Shake well and set aside for 7 days or until the juice turns pink.

3. To serve, put 1 tablespoon of the juice and 1 tablespoon of the julienned dates and ginger in a glass. Fill the glass with cold water and serve.

Gulab-E-Aab

This rose drink has a layer of a special type of dessert called *malai burfi* on top. You can find the dessert at any Indian store. As a variation, you can top the drink with a scoop of vanilla ice cream instead.

Serves 4.

$7\frac{1}{2}$ cups (1.5 liters) whole milk
$\frac{1}{2}$ cup (125 grams) sugar
A few saffron threads
$\frac{1}{2}$ teaspoon ground green cardamom
2 tablespoons rose syrup
4 *malai burfi* (condensed-milk *mithai*, store-bought)
10 almonds, blanched (see Note), peeled, and slivered
20 pistachios, blanched (see Note), peeled, and slivered

1. Place a deep nonstick saucepan over high heat and add the milk. Lower the heat to medium, add the sugar, and cook, stirring, until the sugar dissolves. Transfer to a bowl. Add the saffron and stir until it dissolves.

2. Add the cardamom to the milk and stir. Set aside to cool to room temperature.

3. Add the rose syrup and stir. Place the bowl in the refrigerator to chill.

4. Ladle into individual glasses. Crush the *malai burfi* and sprinkle it over the top of the milk in each glass. Garnish with almonds and pistachios and serve cold.

······ ⋇{ **Notes** }⋇ *Malai burfi:* This delicious Indian dessert is prepared by boiling milk and reducing it until most of the moisture evaporates. Once the milk thickens to a solid mass, it is flavored with sugar and other ingredients. It is then shaped into small pieces.

To blanch almonds or pistachios, put them in 1 cup (200 ml) boiling water for 5 minutes. Drain and rub off the skins.

Jal Jeera

······⁑} **Refreshing spicy drink** }⁑······

This drink is very popular in Indian homes. Be sure to use fresh cumin. Check with your nose: If the cumin is aromatic, then the spice is active and hasn't lost its flavor.

Serves 4.

2 tablespoons ground roasted cumin (page 32)
2 tablespoons fresh mint-leaf paste (50 leaves)
½ teaspoon fresh cilantro-leaf paste (¼ cup leaves)
1½ tablespoons *amchur* (dried mango powder)
1 tablespoon black salt
3 tablespoons freshly squeezed lemon juice
1 teaspoon sugar
Fresh mint leaves

1. In a large jug, combine the cumin, mint paste, cilantro paste, *amchur*, black salt, lemon juice, and sugar.

2. Add 5 cups (1 liter) cold water and stir until all the ingredients are well blended.

3. Pour into individual glasses, garnish with mint leaves, and serve cold.

Kairi Panna

This tart mango drink is the perfect chiller for summer. You can add mint leaves for garnish if you like.

Serves 4.

1 large green mango
1 teaspoon ground roasted cumin (page 32)
8 to 10 whole black peppercorns, crushed
¾ teaspoon black salt
Small pinch of asafetida
½ cup (125 grams) sugar

1. Wash the mango well under running water.

2. Place a nonstick saucepan over high heat and add 4 cups (800 ml) water. When it comes to a boil, add the mango and lower the heat to medium. Cook for 25 minutes or until the mango is soft and the skin begins to peel off. Let cool to room temperature.

3. Drain off the water and peel and pit the mango; mash and strain the pulp into a deep bowl.

4. Add the cumin, pepper, black salt, asafetida, and sugar. Stir until the sugar is dissolved.

5. Divide the mixture between 4 tall glasses, then fill them with cold water. Stir well and serve immediately.

······◦〉 **Chef's Tip** 〈◦ You can make the pulp in bulk and store it in the refrigerator. It will keep for up to a week.

Kale Angoor Ka Sharbat

········❁{ **Black grape drink** }❁··

This delightful tangy and strong-tasting drink is very popular during hot Indian summers. You can also prepare it a few hours before serving. Chill it and then serve over crushed ice.

Serves 4.

¾ teaspoon cumin seeds
½ teaspoon *ajwain*
1 teaspoon fennel seeds
1 tablespoon black salt
4 cups (800 ml) black grape juice
1½ tablespoons tamarind pulp
Crushed ice

1. Place a shallow pan over medium heat, add the cumin, *ajwain*, and fennel, and roast for 2 minutes or until fragrant. Let cool and transfer to a spice grinder. Add the black salt and grind to a fine powder.

2. Pour the black grape juice into a jug; add the ground spices and tamarind pulp and stir well.

3. Add crushed ice and stir. Pour into individual glasses and serve cold.

Kokum Sharbat

········❁{ **Ruby-red cooler** }❁··

Kokum (Garcinia indica), also known as gamboge in English, is a native fruit of India and is grown abundantly in Konkan, Karnataka, and Kerala along the western coast of India due to the availability of adequate rainfall, good sunshine, and fertile soil in these regions. It is found in the United States in Indian grocery stores in dried form. This drink is a healthy substitute for carbonated and caffeinated drinks. *Kokum* also aids digestion and fights acidity. You can replace the conventional *pani* in the *pani puris* (page 88) with this.

Serves 4.

¾ cup (190 grams) sugar
4 or 5 fresh *kokum* petals, or 8 to 10 dried pieces (see Notes)
¼ teaspoon table salt
½ teaspoon ground roasted cumin (page 32)

1. Place a nonstick saucepan over high heat and add 1 cup (200 ml) water. Add the sugar, bring to a boil, then lower the heat to medium. Cook, stirring frequently, until you get a syrup of one-string consistency (see Notes).

2. Meanwhile, put the *kokum* in a mini food processor, add ¼ cup (50 ml) water, and process to make a purée. Add the purée to the sugar syrup and boil for 2 to 3 minutes.

3. Remove from the heat and add the salt and cumin. Stir well and set aside to cool to room temperature.

4. To serve, pour ¼ cup (50 ml) of the *kokum* syrup into each glass, fill it with cold water, and stir. Serve immediately.

Notes If using dried *kokum*, soak it in ½ cup (100 ml) boiling water for about 20 minutes to soften, then blend it in the same water.

To test if the sugar syrup has reached one-string consistency, place a drop of the slightly cooled syrup between your thumb and forefinger and pull them apart. If the syrup forms a single string, it is ready.

Lassi with Honey

Sweet yogurt drink with honey

This is a perfect drink to help you cool off during a hot summer day.

Serves 4.

1½ cups (375 grams) plain yogurt
7 tablespoons honey
Pinch of table salt
2 teaspoons freshly squeezed lemon juice
Ice

1. Put the yogurt, honey, salt, and lemon juice in a blender and blend until smooth. Add ½ cup (100 ml) water and blend again.

2. Fill individual glasses with ice and pour in the *lassi*. Serve immediately.

Majjika

Rosewater and yogurt drink

Rosewater, known as *gulab jal* in India, is commonly used to add heady fragrance to recipes. Here it is paired with yogurt for a delightful summer drink.

Serves 4.

½ cup (125 grams) plain yogurt
2 to 3 tablespoons sugar
1 teaspoon rosewater
4 scoops vanilla ice cream
1 teaspoon dried or fresh untreated rose petals

1. Put the yogurt, 1½ cups (300 ml) water, the sugar, and rosewater in a blender and blend for 1 to 2 minutes, until frothy.

2. Transfer to a deep bowl and refrigerate until very cold.

3. Pour into 4 individual glasses, top each with a scoop of ice cream, and sprinkle with the rose petals. Serve immediately.

Masala Soda

Spiced soda

This superb spiced drink makes a great mocktail. I first fell in love with it on the streets of the city of Meerut and would always make a point to try it whenever I saw it.

Serves 4.

6 tablespoons (90 ml) *kokum sharbat* (page 43)
½ tablespoon black salt
5 or 6 whole black peppercorns, crushed
1 tablespoon freshly squeezed lemon juice
Crushed ice
1 quart (800 ml) cold seltzer
10 to 12 fresh mint leaves, torn

1. Combine the *kokum sharbat*, black salt, pepper, lemon juice, and about 2 cups crushed ice in a glass jar and stir well.

2. Pour into 4 individual glasses. Fill with soda and stir well. Garnish with the mint and serve immediately.

Masala Taak

·······⊹⟨ **Spiced buttermilk** ⟩⊹··

This simple spiced buttermilk is a perfect cooler on a hot summer day.

Serves 4.

1 teaspoon cumin seeds
1 cup (250 grams) plain yogurt
1 green chile, stemmed and chopped
½-inch (1¾-cm) piece fresh ginger, chopped
1 tablespoon chopped fresh cilantro
1½ teaspoons black salt

1. Place a small nonstick sauté pan over medium heat. Add the cumin seeds and roast until they turn slightly brown. Let cool and grind to a coarse powder.

2. Whisk the yogurt thoroughly in a large bowl. Gradually add about 5 cups (1 liter) cold water and whisk thoroughly.

3. Add the chile, ginger, cilantro, black salt, and cumin and stir thoroughly. Pour into individual tall glasses and serve cold.

Zafrani Sharbat

·······⊹⟨ **Cold saffron-flavored drink** ⟩⊹···

Saffron is known as *zafran* in Urdu. Here we use saffron to prepare a delightful cold drink. Look for saffron ice cream (*kesar*) at Indian grocery stores; if you can't find it, plain vanilla works well.

Serves 4.

10 to 12 saffron threads
7½ cups (1.5 liters) milk, plus 2 tablespoons warmed
¼ cup (60 grams) sugar
Pinch of ground green cardamom
10 to 12 almonds, blanched (see Note, page 40) and slivered
6 to 8 pistachios, blanched (see Note, page 40) and slivered
4 scoops saffron ice cream

1. Soak the saffron in the 2 tablespoons warm milk and set aside.

2. Place a nonstick saucepan over high heat, add the remaining milk, and bring to a boil. Lower the heat to medium and simmer, stirring frequently, for 10 minutes.

3. Add the sugar, cardamom, and saffron milk and simmer for another 5 to 6 minutes, until thick and creamy.

4. Remove from the heat, add the almonds and pistachios, and stir well. Let cool to room temperature, then place in the refrigerator to chill.

5. Pour the milk into 4 glasses, top each with a scoop of ice cream, and serve immediately.

Masala Chai with Lemongrass

········*⟩ **Hot lemongrass-flavored tea** ⟨*········

This recipe comes from the west coast of India: The Gujaratis love it! Serve it on a rainy day with a plate of *pakoras* (fritters)—it is simply heavenly.

Serves 4.

2 cups (400 ml) milk
4 to 5 small stalks fresh lemongrass, chopped
4 teaspoons black tea leaves
½ teaspoon *chai masala* (spice mix for tea; page 25)
8 teaspoons sugar

1. Put the milk and 2 cups (400 ml) water in a nonstick saucepan. Place over high heat and bring to a boil.

2. Lower the heat to medium, add the lemongrass, tea leaves, and *chai masala*, and boil for 1 minute. Add the sugar. When it comes to a boil again, lower the heat to low and simmer for 2 to 3 minutes.

3. Strain into individual cups and serve piping hot.

Pannagam

····◦{ Cane Jaggery–flavored drink }◦····································

In South India, the birth of the Hindu god Lord Rama is celebrated during the festival of Rama Navami, and this drink is served to the devotees. It is served in small portions after the prayers are over. In some places, lemon juice is used instead of tamarind.

Serves 4.

¾ cup (150 grams) grated cane jaggery
2-inch (5-cm) piece dried ginger
6 green cardamom pods
18 to 20 whole black peppercorns
1½ tablespoons tamarind pulp
1¼ teaspoons black salt
5 or 6 fresh mint leaves

1. Put the jaggery in a bowl, add 1½ cups (300 ml) water, and soak for 10 to 15 minutes. Stir until the jaggery dissolves. Strain the mixture through a fine sieve into another bowl.

2. Put the dried ginger, cardamom, and peppercorns in a spice grinder and grind to a fine powder. Sift through a fine sieve to remove any large pieces.

3. Put the tamarind pulp in a small bowl, add the spice powder, and stir well. Add to the jaggery water along with the black salt and stir well.

4. Finely shred the mint and add it to the jaggery mixture. Stir and let stand for 10 to 15 minutes.

5. Strain into small glasses and serve warm.

Ukala

····◦{ Hot *chai masala*–flavored milk }◦····································

Serves 4.

2 cups (400 ml) milk
8 teaspoons sugar
1 teaspoon *chai masala* (spice mix for tea; page 25)

1. Combine the milk, 2½ cups (500 ml) water, and the sugar in a nonstick saucepan, place over high heat, and bring to a boil. Lower the heat to low, add the *chai masala*, and simmer for 5 to 7 minutes, until the flavors are well combined.

2. Strain into individual teacups and serve hot.

Kali Mirch Ka Drink

This drink soothes a sore throat—or will at least clear your sinuses.

Serves 4.

1 teaspoon table salt
20 whole black peppercorns
¼ teaspoon fenugreek seeds
¼ teaspoon cumin seeds
1½ teaspoons coriander seeds
4 cloves garlic
6 dried red chiles, stemmed
1 tablespoon tamarind pulp
1 teaspoon coconut oil
½ teaspoon mustard seeds
8 to 10 fresh curry leaves
2 green chiles, stemmed and slit
6 pearl onions, peeled and blanched

1. Place a nonstick saucepan over high heat. Add 5 cups (1 liter) water and the salt and bring to a boil.

2. Put the peppercorns, fenugreek, cumin, coriander, garlic, and red chiles in a mortar and crush them with a pestle. Add the crushed spices and garlic to the boiling water in the pan and stir. Add the tamarind pulp, lower the heat to medium, cover, and simmer for 15 to 20 minutes.

3. Remove from the heat. Strain through a fine sieve and set aside.

4. Place a small nonstick sauté pan over high heat and add the coconut oil. When small bubbles appear at the bottom of the pan, add the mustard seeds and let them sputter. Add the curry leaves, green chiles, and onions, and sauté for 4 to 5 minutes. Add this to the prepared drink and cover immediately to trap the flavors.

5. Ladle into individual bowls and serve warm.

CHAPTER 3

Soups and *Shorbas*

The idea of starting a meal with a soup to whet the appetite is not widely popular in traditional Indian homes, where meals are not served in courses. With the exception of the Anglo-Indian standby *mulligatawny* (page 56), soups—at least the brothy ones served in the West—are still uncommon here, and we have miles to go before we can boast of a huge repertoire.

There is not much historical documentation, but in this chapter I present some of the classic *shorbas* (soups) from the royal kitchens of yore. Take, for example, the chicken *shorba* (page 61) from northern India, a dish that will rejuvenate just like your own mother's chicken soup did. One of my favorite soups is the *paya shorba* (page 63), made from lamb trotters. It is very soothing and warming in winter. The southern states offer thin, spicy *rasam* (page 59) that clear up the sinuses and a terrific soup called tomato *saar* (page 60), which is excellent on its own or ladled over rice.

There are plenty of vegetarian options here: The *sabz makai kali mirch ka shorba* (page 58) is like a garden in a bowl.

Anarkali Shorba

This dish is named after a legendary and beautiful dancer from the court of the Mughal emperor Akbar. It can be prepared up to a day in advance and reheated gently before serving.

Serves 4.

1½ tablespoons butter, at room temperature
1½-inch (4-cm) piece fresh ginger, chopped
2 bay leaves
3 or 4 whole cloves
1-inch (2½-cm) cinnamon stick
1 green cardamom pod
1 medium onion, chopped
2 tablespoons *toor dal/arhar dal* (split pigeon peas)
¼ cup (50 grams) *masoor dal* (split red lentils)
2 tablespoons raw rice
1½ teaspoons table salt
½ teaspoon ground black pepper
1 bunch fresh cilantro with stems, chopped
1 bunch spinach leaves, finely chopped
1 cup (200 ml) fresh pomegranate juice
1 tablespoon crushed black peppercorns
Arils from half a medium pomegranate

1. Place a nonstick sauté pan over medium heat, add the butter, and let it melt. Add the ginger, bay leaves, cloves, cinnamon, and cardamom, and sauté for 1 to 2 minutes or until fragrant. Add the onion and sauté for 4 to 5 minutes or until the onion is light golden brown.

2. Add the *dals* and rice, and cook, stirring, for 1 to 2 minutes. Add 9 cups (1.8 liters) water and bring to a boil. Lower the heat to low and simmer for 15 minutes.

3. Add the salt, ground black pepper, cilantro, and spinach. Simmer gently for 10 minutes.

4. Pour into a sieve set over a bowl, transfer the liquid to a deep nonstick saucepan, and place over low heat.

5. Remove and discard the cinnamon stick. Transfer the remaining solids to a blender and blend until smooth. Add the purée to the liquid in the pan and stir well. Add the pomegranate juice and simmer gently for 10 minutes.

6. Ladle into individual soup bowls, garnish with the crushed peppercorns and pomegranate arils, and serve hot.

Badam Shorba

·······⊰ **Almond soup** ⊱⊱··

This rich soup tastes best when it is freshly made. Blanching the almonds first softens them a little and makes grinding them a lot easier. If your almonds have been sitting around in the pantry for a while, be sure to taste them and make sure that they are not rancid.

Serves 4.

1½ cups (150 grams) almonds
1¾ cups (350 ml) milk
2 teaspoons butter, at room temperature
1¼ teaspoons *maida* (refined flour) or pastry flour
½ teaspoon sugar
1 teaspoon table salt
½ teaspoon ground white pepper
1½ tablespoons heavy cream

1. Soak the almonds in hot water for 4 to 5 minutes. Drain and peel them. Slice 10 to 12 almonds and set them aside for garnish. Put the remaining almonds and ¾ cup (150 ml) of the milk in a food processor, and process to a smooth paste.

2. Place a nonstick saucepan over high heat, add the butter, and let it melt. Add the *maida*, lower the heat to medium, and sauté for 1 minute, stirring continuously to ensure that the color of the flour does not change. Gradually add the remaining 1 cup (200 ml) milk and stir continuously so that lumps do not form.

3. Add the sugar, salt, and white pepper, and cook, stirring continuously, until the mixture comes to a boil. Lower the heat and simmer for 5 minutes, stirring occasionally.

4. Add the almond and milk paste and 2 cups (400 ml) hot water, and simmer for 10 to 15 minutes, stirring occasionally, until the soup thickens. Ladle into individual soup bowls.

5. Place a small nonstick sauté pan over high heat. When it is hot, lower the heat to medium, add the reserved sliced almonds, and toast until they just begin to change color. Sprinkle the toasted almonds over the soup in each bowl and drizzle with the cream. Serve immediately.

Hare Moong Ka Shorba

This is one of the best Indian soups I have ever tasted. It is loaded with protein, has a fantastic mouth-feel, and gives you a burst of energy. My wife, Alyona, is an expert at making it, and we worked on this recipe together.

Serves 4.

1 cup (240 grams) *sabut moong* (whole green gram)
1 tablespoon table salt
2 bay leaves
2 green cardamom pods
1 whole clove
1-inch (2½ -cm) cinnamon stick
3 green chiles, stemmed and chopped
2 or 3 scallions with green tops
1 tablespoon vegetable oil
½ teaspoon cumin seeds
4 cloves garlic, minced
1-inch (2½ -cm) piece fresh ginger, chopped
1½ tablespoons freshly squeezed lemon juice
2 cups (275 grams) cooked rice vermicelli

1. Put the *sabut moong* in a large bowl, wash in plenty of water 2 or 3 times, and drain. Add 3 cups (600 ml) water and soak overnight. Drain in a colander.

2. Place a nonstick saucepan over medium heat and add 1 quart (800 ml) water. Add 1 teaspoon of the salt, the bay leaves, cardamom, clove, cinnamon, chiles, and the *sabut moong*. Cook over medium heat for 20 minutes or until the *sabut moong* is soft and all the water has been absorbed or evaporated. Set aside to cool completely.

3. Purée with an immersion blender. Push the mixture through a sieve into a large bowl. Add 5 cups (1 liter) water and stir. Set aside.

4. Chop the scallion bulbs and greens separately.

5. Place a nonstick saucepan over medium heat and add the oil. Add the cumin and when it begins to change color, add the scallion bulbs, garlic, and ginger, and sauté for 30 seconds.

6. Stir in the *sabut moong* mixture and bring to a boil. Lower the heat, add the lemon juice, and simmer, uncovered, for 5 minutes. Add the scallion tops and the remaining 2 teaspoons salt.

7. Add the vermicelli and simmer for 1 minute. Ladle into individual soup bowls and serve hot.

Laganshaala

This is a hearty vegetable soup with a Western influence brought in by the Parsi community of Mumbai. Parsis came to India from Iran and settled in the state of Gujarat.

Serves 4.

2 tablespoons vegetable oil
1 teaspoon cumin seeds
2 or 3 dried red chiles, stemmed and broken in half
2 small onions, sliced
5 cloves garlic, sliced
2 or 3 green chiles, stemmed and slit
2 small potatoes, cut into ½-inch (1-cm) cubes
1 medium sweet potato, cut into ½-inch (1-cm) cubes
1 medium carrot, cut into ½-inch (1-cm) cubes
½ head cauliflower, separated into small florets
1 medium tomato, quartered
½ teaspoon table salt
1 tablespoon Worcestershire sauce
1 teaspoon white vinegar
1 teaspoon sugar

1. Place a nonstick saucepan over medium heat and add the oil. When small bubbles appear at the bottom of the pan, add the cumin and dried chiles. When they begin to change color, add the onions and sauté for 2 to 3 minutes or until lightly browned. Add the garlic and green chiles, and sauté for 1 minute.

2. Add the potatoes, sweet potato, carrot, cauliflower, tomato, salt, and 2 to 3 cups (400 to 600 ml) water, and stir. Lower the heat to low, cover, and cook for 5 minutes or until all the vegetables are almost cooked.

3. Add the Worcestershire sauce, vinegar, and sugar, stir, and cook for 5 to 10 minutes or until the vegetables are completely soft and the liquid has reduced by about half.

4. Ladle into individual soup bowls and serve hot.

Matar Ka Shorba

§ Green pea soup §

This simple yet luscious dish is the creation of my brother, Rajeev. When he made it for me, I fell in love with it at first sip.

Serves 4.

3¼ cups (500 grams) shelled fresh or frozen green peas
2-inch (5-cm) piece fresh ginger, roughly chopped
10 cloves garlic, roughly chopped
2 green chiles, stemmed and roughly chopped
3 tablespoons ghee (page 37) or vegetable oil
½ teaspoon cumin seeds
2 bay leaves
1 medium onion, minced
3 cups (600 ml) vegetable stock (page 36)
1½ teaspoons table salt
8 fresh mint leaves

1. Place a medium nonstick saucepan over high heat, add 2 cups (400 ml) water, and bring to a boil. Add the peas and cook for 7 minutes or until tender. Let cool, then transfer the peas and liquid to a blender, and blend to a smooth purée. Transfer to a deep bowl and set aside.

2. Put the ginger, garlic, chiles, and 3 tablespoons water in a spice grinder, and grind to a smooth paste.

3. Place the saucepan over high heat, add the ghee, and heat until small bubbles appear at the bottom of the pan. Lower the heat to medium, add the cumin and bay leaves, and sauté for 30 seconds. Add the onion and sauté until light golden. Add the ginger-garlic-chile paste and sauté for 1 minute.

4. Add the green pea purée, stir, and cook for 5 minutes, stirring continuously. Add the stock, stir well, and bring to a boil.

5. Add the salt and stir. Remove and discard the bay leaves. Lower the heat to low and cook for 5 minutes.

6. This soup will be thick; if you prefer a thinner soup, add more water until you reach the consistency you want.

7. Ladle into individual soup bowls. Garnish with the mint leaves and serve hot.

Mulligatawny Soup

A flavorful red lentil and vegetable soup

An Anglo-Indian preparation, this soup is also known as "pepper water" because the Tamil word *mulligu* means "pepper" and *thanni* means "water." But it doesn't stop at pepper, for the variations on this soup are many. The recipe here is what is made in my home; I sip this warm concoction when I feel a cold coming on.

Serves 4.

1 tablespoon *besan* (chickpea/gram flour)
1 tablespoon vegetable oil
2 or 3 dried red chiles, stemmed
2 (1-inch/2½-cm) cinnamon sticks
4 whole cloves
4 green cardamom pods
2 bay leaves
12 to 15 whole black peppercorns
1-inch (2½-cm) piece fresh ginger, chopped
4 to 6 cloves garlic
1 medium onion, quartered
1 medium carrot, roughly chopped
16 to 20 fresh curry leaves
1 tablespoon coriander seeds
1 teaspoon cumin seeds
½ small green apple, cored and sliced
½ small potato, diced
6 tablespoons *masoor dal* (split red lentil)
1 teaspoon ground turmeric
1 teaspoon table salt
5 cups (1 liter) vegetable stock (page 36)
¼ cup (30 grams) grated fresh coconut (or frozen unsweetened coconut)
1 tablespoon cooked white rice

1. Place a nonstick sauté pan over medium heat. Add the *besan* and roast over low heat, stirring continuously, for 4 to 5 minutes or until lightly browned and fragrant. Set aside.

2. Place a nonstick saucepan over medium heat and add the oil. When small bubbles appear at the bottom of the pan, add the chiles, cinnamon, cloves, cardamom, bay leaves, peppercorns, ginger, and garlic, and sauté for 1 minute. Add the onion, carrot, curry leaves, coriander, cumin, apple, and potato, and sauté for 2 minutes. Add the *dal*, turmeric, salt, and stock, and bring to a boil. Add the *besan* and coconut, and cook for 15 to 20 minutes or until the *dal* and potato are cooked.

3. Pour into a strainer set over a bowl and ladle the liquid into individual soup bowls. Garnish with the rice and serve hot.

Palak Shorba

······ ❊❴ **Spinach soup** ❵❊ ···

I love spinach so much that friends often joke that I would make a dessert with it. This soup, rich with butter and fragrant with cinnamon and cloves, will have to do for now.

Serves 4.

2 medium bunches spinach, washed and stemmed
2 tablespoons butter, at room temperature
3 black cardamom pods
2 whole cloves
1-inch (2½-cm) cinnamon stick
2 tablespoons *maida* (refined flour) or pastry flour
3-inch (7½-cm) piece fresh ginger, minced
2 cloves garlic, minced
1 medium onion, finely chopped
4 or 5 whole black peppercorns
4 bay leaves
1 teaspoon table salt
¼ teaspoon ground white pepper
1 teaspoon ground roasted cumin (page 32)

1. Place a deep nonstick saucepan over high heat, add 2 cups (400 ml) water, and bring to a boil. Add the spinach and blanch for 2 to 3 minutes. Drain, refresh in cold water, and drain again. Transfer to a food processor and process to a smooth purée. Set aside.

2. Place the same deep nonstick saucepan over medium heat, add the butter, and let it melt. Add the cardamom, cloves, cinnamon, and *maida,* and sauté for 2 to 3 minutes.

3. Add the ginger, garlic, and onion, and sauté for about 5 minutes.

4. Add the peppercorns, bay leaves, salt, white pepper, cumin, and 5 cups (1 liter) water, and stir. Bring to a boil over high heat. Lower the heat to medium and simmer for 10 minutes, stirring occasionally.

5. Pour into a strainer set over another deep nonstick saucepan; discard the solids. Add the spinach purée to the strained liquid and stir well.

6. Place over medium heat and cook for 4 to 5 minutes.

7. Ladle into individual soup bowls and serve piping hot.

Sabz Makai Kali Mirch Ka Shorba

····⊰※{ **Mixed vegetable soup with corn and peppers** }※⊱·······················

I always say that it is a challenge to get Indians to eat soup—they would rather start right in on the main course. This soup, rich with vegetables and spices, is my way of trying to change that.

Serves 4.

~ **For the vegetable stock:**
2 whole cloves
1 bay leaf
7 or 8 black peppercorns, crushed
½ teaspoon table salt
½ carrot, roughly chopped
3 or 4 cauliflower stems
1 medium onion, roughly chopped
1-inch (2½-cm) piece fresh ginger, roughly chopped

~ **For the soup:**
1 tablespoon vegetable oil
5 or 6 cloves garlic, minced
1 cup (150 grams) corn kernels, crushed
½ carrot, diced and blanched
4 or 5 small florets of broccoli
4 or 5 haricots verts or green beans, diced
¼ medium red bell pepper, seeded and diced
¼ medium yellow bell pepper, seeded and diced
1 teaspoon table salt
5 or 6 black peppercorns, crushed

1. Make the vegetable stock: Place a nonstick saucepan over high heat, add 5 cups (1 liter) water, and bring to a boil. Add the cloves, bay leaf, peppercorns, salt, carrot, cauliflower stems, onion, and ginger, and bring to a boil. Lower the heat to medium and simmer for 30 minutes. Pour into a strainer set over a bowl; discard the solids. Set the stock aside.

2. Make the soup: Place a nonstick saucepan over medium heat and add the oil. When small bubbles appear at the bottom of the pan, add the garlic and sauté for 5 seconds. Add the stock and bring to a boil.

3. Lower the heat to medium, add the corn, and cook, stirring continuously, for 2 to 3 minutes.

4. Add the carrot, broccoli, haricots verts, and red and yellow bell peppers, and stir. Add the salt and half of the peppercorns, and cook for 2 to 3 minutes.

5. Ladle the soup into individual soup bowls, sprinkle with the remaining peppercorns, and serve piping hot.

Tomato Rasam

Called by various names in South India—*rasam*, *chaaru*, or *saaru*—this dish will always have the imprint of the cook, since everyone makes it differently. This version relies heavily on tomatoes and tamarind for the essential sour flavor. *Rasam* is traditionally served with rice, but I like to serve it as an appetizer. I strain it, pour it into small glasses, and garnish it with lemon wedges. It makes a lovely warm drink.

Serves 4.

¼ cup (60 grams) *toor dal/arhar dal* (split pigeon peas)
1¾ teaspoons ground turmeric
2½ tablespoons tamarind pulp
2 medium tomatoes, chopped
1½ teaspoons table salt
1½ teaspoons *rasam* powder (spice mix; page 31)
¼ teaspoon asafetida
¼ cup (15 grams) chopped fresh cilantro
2 tablespoons ghee (page 37)
½ teaspoon black mustard seeds
½ teaspoon cumin seeds
5 or 6 fresh curry leaves
¼ teaspoon ground black pepper

1. Put the *dal* in a bowl, wash in plenty of water 2 or 3 times, and drain. Add 2 cups (400 ml) water and soak for 30 minutes. Drain the *dal* in a colander.

2. Place a nonstick saucepan over high heat, add 4½ cups (900 ml) water and 1 teaspoon of the turmeric, and bring to a boil. Add the *dal*, lower the heat to medium, and cook for 15 minutes or until soft. Pour into a strainer set over a bowl. Discard the solids and use only the liquid.

3. Place another nonstick saucepan over high heat and add the tamarind pulp, the liquid collected in step 2, the tomatoes, salt, the remaining turmeric, the *rasam* powder, and ⅛ teaspoon of the asafetida. Bring to a boil, then lower the heat to medium and simmer for 10 to 15 minutes or until reduced by half.

4. Add the *dal* cooking water and the cilantro, and simmer for 3 to 5 minutes. Remove from the heat. This is the *rasam*.

5. Place a nonstick tempering pan or small sauté pan over high heat and add the ghee. When small bubbles appear at the bottom of the pan, add the mustard seeds. When they sputter, add the cumin, curry leaves, the remaining ⅛ teaspoon asafetida, and the black pepper. Add this tempering to the *rasam* and cover immediately to trap the flavors.

6. Serve hot with steamed rice.

Tomato Saar

Though this dish is typically eaten with rice, I prefer to sip it as a soup.

Serves 4.

2 tablespoons vegetable oil
5 or 6 cloves garlic, chopped
2 bay leaves
15 whole black peppercorns
1-inch (2½-cm) piece fresh ginger, chopped
9 medium tomatoes, roughly chopped
1 teaspoon black mustard seeds
8 to 10 fresh curry leaves
1 teaspoon cumin seeds
3 or 4 green chiles, stemmed and slit
¼ teaspoon asafetida
1 teaspoon table salt
1 tablespoon grated fresh coconut (or frozen unsweetened coconut)
1 tablespoon chopped fresh cilantro

1. Place a nonstick saucepan over high heat and add 1 tablespoon of the oil. When small bubbles appear at the bottom of the pan, add the garlic, bay leaves, 10 of the peppercorns, and the ginger, and sauté for 1 minute.

2. Add the tomatoes and cook for 10 minutes. Add 1 quart (800 ml) water and bring to a boil. Pour into a strainer set over a bowl; reserve the liquid and let the solids cool.

3. Transfer the solids to a blender and blend to a smooth purée. Set aside.

4. Crush the remaining 5 peppercorns.

5. Place a nonstick saucepan over medium heat and add the remaining 1 tablespoon oil. When small bubbles appear at the bottom of the pan, add the mustard seeds, curry leaves, crushed peppercorns, cumin, chiles, asafetida, and salt, and sauté for 1 minute.

6. Add the purée and the strained stock, and stir well. Bring to a boil. Add the coconut and cilantro.

7. Ladle into individual soup bowls and serve hot.

Chicken Shorba

The aromatic chicken stock that we prepare in this recipe makes a great base for many other dishes. You can use this stock instead of water when making rice or couscous. It will add great depth and flavor to your dishes. The stock keeps well in the refrigerator for up to a week.

Serves 4.

1 pound (500 grams) chicken bones
1 medium onion, roughly chopped
1 medium carrot, roughly chopped
1 bay leaf
4 whole black peppercorns
2 whole cloves
4 green cardamom pods
1 black cardamom pod
1-inch (2½-cm) cinnamon stick
2 tablespoons butter, at room temperature
4 ounces (125 grams) boneless chicken, cut into ½-inch (1-cm) cubes
2 tablespoons *maida* (refined flour) or pastry flour
1 tablespoon vegetable oil
½ teaspoon cumin seeds
1 teaspoon crushed fennel seeds
10 cloves garlic, chopped
½ teaspoon ground white pepper
¾ teaspoon table salt

1. Place a medium nonstick saucepan over high heat and add 4¼ cups (900 ml) water. Add the chicken bones, onion, carrot, bay leaf, peppercorns, cloves, green and black cardamom, and cinnamon, and bring to a boil. Boil for 20 minutes or until the liquid is reduced to 2½ cups (500 ml). Pour into a strainer set over a bowl; discard the solids and set the stock aside.

2. Place the same medium saucepan over high heat, add 1 tablespoon of the butter, and let it melt. Add the chicken and sauté until cooked through and tender. Remove from the heat and set aside.

3. Put the remaining 1 tablespoon butter in the same pan over medium heat. Add the *maida* and sauté for 1 to 2 minutes. Set aside.

4. Place a nonstick saucepan over high heat, add the oil, and heat. When small bubbles appear at the bottom, add the cumin, fennel, and garlic. Sauté for 1 minute, lower the heat to medium, and add the *maida* mixture, the reduced chicken stock, white pepper, and salt. Cook over high heat, stirring continuously, until the mixture comes to a boil. Lower the heat to medium, add the chicken, and simmer for 3 to 4 minutes. Ladle into individual soup bowls and serve hot.

Kozhi Karuveppalai Soup

·······≈{ **Chicken and curry-leaf soup** }≈··

This comes as a refreshing change from regular chicken soup. Curry leaves are used extensively in the food of South India, and in this soup they lend such a dominant flavor that they are the star. I sometimes skip the coconut garnish because the little bits of chicken suffice.

Serves 4.

30 fresh curry leaves
1 pound (500 grams) chicken bones
1 medium onion, roughly chopped
4 to 6 cloves garlic, roughly chopped
2 tablespoons tamarind pulp
1 small tomato, diced
4 ounces (125 grams) boneless, skinless chicken thigh
1 teaspoon table salt, or more as needed
½ teaspoon ground turmeric
1 teaspoon red chile powder
¼ teaspoon asafetida
2 tablespoons *besan* (chickpea/gram flour)
½ cup (60 grams) shaved fresh coconut (or frozen unsweetened coconut slivers, thawed)
1 tablespoon freshly squeezed lemon juice

1. Roughly chop 25 of the curry leaves.

2. Place a nonstick saucepan over high heat, add 7 to 8 cups (1800 ml) water and the chicken bones, and bring to a boil. Lower the heat to medium, skim the scum from the surface, and simmer for 10 minutes.

3. Add the onion, garlic, tamarind pulp, tomato, chicken, salt, turmeric, chile powder, asafetida, and chopped curry leaves. Simmer over medium heat for 15 minutes. Remove the chicken and let the soup continue to simmer. Cool the chicken to room temperature, then chop into bite-size pieces.

4. Stir the *besan* into ¼ cup (50 ml) water and add it into the simmering soup. Add half of the coconut and stir well. Cover and simmer for 10 to 12 minutes.

5. Pour the soup into a strainer set over a bowl, pressing the solids to extract their flavor.

6. Transfer the stock to a clean nonstick saucepan and place over medium heat. Add the chopped chicken and adjust the seasoning. Bring to a boil, then stir in the lemon juice and the remaining coconut.

7. Ladle into individual soup bowls, garnish with the remaining curry leaves, and serve piping hot.

Paya Shorba

If you are in Delhi in wintertime, you will be surprised by the carts that sprout up from nowhere to sell this soup. I am not sure which tastes better: the homemade version or the roadside version. Add more red or green chiles if you'd like a spicier soup, or use fewer if you prefer it mild.

Serves 4.

8 (3½-ounce/100-gram) lamb trotters
½ teaspoon ground turmeric
1 tablespoon table salt, or more as needed
4 dried red chiles, stemmed
1 tablespoon fennel seeds
1 teaspoon cumin seeds
1 tablespoon coriander seeds
4 or 5 whole black peppercorns
½ cup (100 ml) coconut milk
3 tablespoons sesame oil
2 star anise
2 bay leaves
1-inch (2½-cm) cinnamon stick
1-inch (2½-cm) piece fresh ginger, roughly chopped
4 to 6 cloves garlic, roughly chopped
10 pearl onions, peeled
2 green chiles, stemmed and slit
10 to 12 fresh curry leaves, finely chopped
¼ teaspoon asafetida
1 medium tomato, roughly chopped
½ medium bunch fresh cilantro, finely chopped
1 lemon, cut into 4 wedges

1. Place a nonstick saucepan over high heat, add 1 quart (800 ml) water, and bring to a boil. Add the trotters, ¼ teaspoon of the turmeric, and 1 teaspoon of the salt. Bring to a boil and cook for 5 minutes. Drain and wash the trotters under running water. This will remove any dirt from the trotters.

2. Place a small nonstick pan over high heat. After 2 minutes, lower the heat to medium and add the dried chiles, fennel, cumin, coriander, and peppercorns. Dry-roast the spices for 2 to 3 minutes or until fragrant. Transfer to a bowl and set aside to cool to room temperature. Transfer to a spice grinder and grind to a coarse powder.

3. Place a nonstick saucepan over high heat and add the oil. When small bubbles appear at the bottom of the pan, add the star anise, bay leaves, and cinnamon, and sauté for 1 to 2 minutes or until fragrant.

5. Add the trotters and sauté for 3 to 4 minutes, or until lightly browned. Add the ginger, garlic, onions, green chiles, and curry leaves. Keep stirring. Sprinkle the ground spice mixture, the remaining ¼ teaspoon turmeric, and the asafetida over the trotters, and cook for 10 minutes, turning frequently.

6. Add the tomato, cilantro, the remaining 2 teaspoons salt, and about 10 cups (2 liters) water. Bring to a boil, then lower the heat and simmer for 3 to 4 hours or until the soup has reduced by half. Remove the trotters carefully and set aside.

7. Pour the soup through a fine sieve set over another nonstick saucepan, pressing on the solids to extract their flavor. Discard the solids.

8. Place the broth over high heat and bring to a boil. Adjust the seasoning as needed.

9. Place the trotters in individual soup bowls, ladle the broth over them, and serve piping hot with the lemon wedges.

·······⟩ **Chef's Tip** ⟨⁕ The blanching of the trotters should be done quickly to avoid loss of flavor and gelatin. Add some peeled potatoes to the soup in step 6 if you want a thicker soup.

CHAPTER 4

Salads and *Raitas*

The traditional combination of *dal*, *chawal*, *roti*, and *sabzi* (lentils, rice, Indian bread, and vegetables) arrayed on an Indian *thali*—a serving platter—often includes two more types of dishes that serve as perfect accompaniments: fresh salads and yogurt relishes called *raitas*.

An Indian salad may be as simple as an onion thinly sliced into rings and sprinkled with salt and lemon juice that accompanies a heavy meat or chicken dish, a beet *raita* (page 67) that brightens up a plate of *burani*, a roasted-eggplant yogurt used as a dip or spread (page 68), or cubes of spiced mango tossed with fresh coconut (page 66). Or it may be more complex, like the tandoori *murgh* salad (page 80), a lovely dish of shredded chicken and chopped vegetables that is one of my favorite "TV dinners."

Ambe Sasam

······⊰ Ripe mangoes and coconut with mustard seeds ⊱······························

The Gawandes, very dear friends of ours, urged me to try this dish, and while I believe that ripe mango is best consumed plain, *ambe sasam* (with the right variety of mango) is an exception.

When mangoes are not in season, you can make the *sasam* with other fruits, such as ripe banana, orange, pineapple, apple, and grapes.

Serves 4.

3 medium mangoes, ripe
¾ cup (90 grams) grated fresh coconut (or frozen unsweetened coconut)
2 dried red chiles, preferably *bedgi* (see Note page 234), seeded and dry-roasted
¼ teaspoon brown mustard seeds
1 teaspoon tamarind pulp
2 tablespoons grated cane jaggery
½ teaspoon table salt

1. Peel and pit the mangoes and cut the flesh into ½-inch (1-cm) cubes. You should have about 1½ cups (375 grams) mango.

2. Put the coconut, chiles, mustard seeds, tamarind pulp, and ¼ cup (50 ml) water in a food processor and process to a coarse paste. Add the jaggery and a few of the mango pieces, and process.

3. Put the mangoes in a medium bowl. Add the ground mixture and salt, and stir well. Cover the bowl with plastic wrap and put in the refrigerator to chill for about 30 minutes.

4. Serve cold.

Beet Raita

You can use yellow or red beets for this cooling side dish.

Serves 4.

2 medium beets, tops removed
3 cups (750 grams) plain yogurt
1 teaspoon ground roasted cumin (page 32)
1 teaspoon red chile powder
1 teaspoon table salt

1. Wash the beets thoroughly under running water to remove any mud.

2. Place a nonstick saucepan over high heat and add 4 cups (800 ml) water. When the water comes to a boil, add the beets. Bring to a boil, then lower the heat to medium and cook for 35 to 40 minutes or until the beets are tender. Drain and set aside to cool to room temperature.

3. Peel the beets and dice them. Set aside.

4. Put the yogurt in a large bowl and beat with an immersion blender until very smooth. (You can also strain the yogurt through a double layer of cheesecloth to get a perfectly smooth consistency.)

5. Add the beets to the yogurt. Add the cumin, chile powder, and salt. Stir well. Put in the refrigerator to chill for at least 30 minutes before serving.

Chef's Tip Red beets will bleed and change the color of the yogurt to dark pink. Plan the rest of your meal accordingly so that the colors are well coordinated.

Burani

Use Greek yogurt to prepare this tangy, garlicky side dish. It is usually served alongside *biryani* (pages 467–487).

Serves 4.

2 cups (550 grams) plain Greek yogurt
25 to 30 cloves garlic, puréed
½ teaspoon table salt
1 teaspoon black salt
½ teaspoon red chile powder
¼ cup (50 ml) milk

1. Put the yogurt in a bowl. Add the garlic, table salt, black salt, and chile powder, and whisk until well blended. Add the milk and whisk again.

2. Spread a double layer of cheesecloth over another deep bowl, pour the *raita* over the cloth, gather the edges, and squeeze the mixture through the cloth to get a smooth *raita*. Discard the solids.

3. Put in the refrigerator to chill for at least 30 minutes before serving.

Buz Vangun

·······{ Roasted-eggplant yogurt }······································

Serve this roasted-eggplant-and-yogurt dish as a dip or use it as a spread for crackers or bread.

Serves 4.

1 large eggplant
1 teaspoon vegetable oil
1 cup (250 grams) plain yogurt
¼ teaspoon red chile powder
½ teaspoon ground roasted cumin (page 32)
2 green chiles, stemmed and minced
Pinch of asafetida
¾ teaspoon table salt

1. Wash the eggplant and rub it with the oil. Make long slits in it and roast over a medium gas flame or a charcoal grill, turning it with tongs, for 15 minutes or until the inside is soft and the skin is completely charred.

2. Put the eggplant in a bowl of cold water to cool to room temperature. Peel and mash the eggplant in a medium bowl.

3. Whisk the yogurt until smooth.

4. Add the yogurt, chile powder, cumin, chiles, asafetida, and salt to the eggplant. Stir well.

5. Put in the refrigerator to chill for at least 30 minutes before serving.

Cauliflower Koshimbir

······· Cauliflower salad ·······

This savory dish can be served as a side or as a warm salad. If you don't have a steamer, you can cook the grated cauliflower in a microwave oven.

Serves 4.

1 medium head cauliflower, grated
1 green chile, stemmed and chopped
1 tablespoon chopped fresh cilantro
1 tablespoon grated fresh coconut (or frozen unsweetened coconut)
2 teaspoons freshly squeezed lemon juice
½ teaspoon table salt
½ teaspoon sugar
2 teaspoons vegetable oil
½ teaspoon black mustard seeds
Pinch of asafetida

1. Place a steamer with 2 cups (400 ml) water over high heat. Put the grated cauliflower in a stainless-steel bowl and place it in the top of the steamer. Cover and steam for 10 minutes. Remove from the steamer and let cool to room temperature.

2. In a deep bowl, combine the cauliflower, chile, cilantro, coconut, lemon juice, salt, and sugar.

3. Place a small nonstick sauté pan over medium-high heat and add the oil. When small bubbles appear at the bottom of the pan, add the mustard seeds. When they sputter, add the asafetida and immediately pour this tempering over the cauliflower mixture. Cover immediately to trap the flavors and let stand for 5 minutes.

4. Stir well and serve.

Chile, Pineapple, and Anar Raita

……❃❴ Chile, pineapple, and pomegranate in yogurt ❵❃……

This cooling side dish is perfect with tandoori chicken (page 208).

Serves 4.

2 cups (500 grams) plain yogurt
½ teaspoon sea salt
4 fresh or canned pineapple slices, cut into chunks
½ cup (80 grams) fresh pomegranate arils
¼ teaspoon red chile flakes
10 to 12 fresh mint leaves, chopped, plus 1 sprig for garnish
½ teaspoon ground roasted cumin (page 32)

1. Put the yogurt in a bowl and whisk until smooth. Add the sea salt and whisk again.

2. Add the pineapple, pomegranate arils, chile flakes, and chopped mint, and stir.

3. Sprinkle with the cumin and garnish with the mint sprig. Serve chilled.

Gajarachi Pachadi

This lovely salad from the western Indian state of Maharashtra makes a great side to any grilled dish.

Serves 4.

2 tablespoons *dhuli moong dal* (split skinless green gram)
2 medium carrots, grated
2 or 3 green chiles, stemmed and finely chopped
½ teaspoon red chile powder
1 teaspoon table salt
1 teaspoon freshly squeezed lemon juice
2 teaspoons ghee (page 37)
½ teaspoon black mustard seeds
Pinch of asafetida
½ teaspoon ground turmeric
2 tablespoons chopped fresh cilantro
1 tablespoon grated fresh coconut (or frozen unsweetened coconut)

1. Put the *dal* in a medium bowl, wash in plenty of water 2 or 3 times, and drain. Add 1 cup (200 ml) water and soak for 1 hour. Drain the *dal* in a colander.

2. Put the *dal*, carrot, chiles, chile powder, and salt in a medium bowl, and stir well. Transfer to a food processor and process coarsely. Add the lemon juice and process. Return the mixture to the bowl.

3. Place a small sauté pan over medium heat and add the ghee. Add the mustard seeds. When they sputter, add the asafetida and turmeric, and stir. Add this tempering to the carrot mixture and stir well.

4. Garnish with the cilantro and coconut, and serve.

Gulmarg Salad

This delightful salad in a lemony dressing should be prepared just before serving; otherwise the apples will begin to brown.

Serves 4.

2 tablespoons freshly squeezed lemon juice
2 medium apples, cored, quartered, and thinly sliced
8 to 10 fresh button mushrooms, sliced
1 medium orange
8 lettuce leaves
1 tablespoon salad oil
2 dried red chiles, seeded and chopped
2 tablespoons chopped fresh cilantro
2 tablespoons chopped fresh mint
½ teaspoon table salt, or to taste
¾ cup (100 grams) bean sprouts
1 medium carrot, halved lengthwise and thinly sliced
2 medium tomatoes, quartered and sliced
2 medium scallions, white and green parts, sliced

1. Sprinkle ½ tablespoon of the lemon juice on the apple and mushroom slices, and stir gently.

2. Peel the orange and discard the seeds and pith. Separate into segments and cut each of the segments in half.

3. Trim the lettuce leaves, wash under running water, and set aside in a bowl of ice water to keep them fresh and crisp.

4. Combine the remaining 1½ tablespoons lemon juice, the oil, chiles, cilantro, and mint in a medium bowl. Add the salt and stir well.

5. Drain the lettuce leaves and tear them into bite-size pieces. Make a bed of the leaves on a serving dish. Drizzle with one quarter of the dressing.

6. Combine the apples, mushrooms, orange, bean sprouts, carrot, tomatoes, and scallions in a large bowl. Add the remaining dressing, toss to combine, and arrange the mixture on the lettuce. Serve immediately.

Kela Anar Raita

···❧{ Banana and pomegranate in yogurt }❧······························

A delicious *raita* of pomegranates and bananas served chilled and garnished with mint leaves. Serve alongside your favorite spicy curry or grilled foods.

Serves 4.

2 medium ripe bananas
1 teaspoon freshly squeezed lemon juice
10 to 12 fresh mint leaves
1 cup (120 grams) fresh pomegranate arils
1½ cups (375 grams) plain yogurt, whisked
1 teaspoon ground roasted cumin (page 32)
1 teaspoon sugar
1 teaspoon black salt

1. Peel the bananas and cut into ½-inch (1-cm) cubes. Sprinkle with the lemon juice to prevent discoloration.

2. Reserve 4 or 5 mint leaves for garnish and finely chop the rest.

3. In a large bowl, combine the bananas, pomegranate arils, yogurt, chopped mint, cumin, sugar, and black salt. Stir well and put in the refrigerator to chill for about 30 minutes.

4. Garnish with the reserved mint and serve cold.

Kelyache Koshimbir

···❧{ Spicy banana salad }❧·······························

This typical southern Indian salad or side should be prepared just before it is to be eaten. It does not keep long, not even in the refrigerator.

Serves 4.

1½ cups (375 grams) plain yogurt
1 tablespoon sugar
2 green chiles, stemmed and minced
2 tablespoons chopped fresh cilantro
4 medium ripe bananas, peeled and cut into cubes
1 teaspoon table salt

1. Put the yogurt in a medium bowl and beat until smooth.

2. Add the sugar, chiles, and cilantro, and stir well with a spoon. Add the banana and salt, and stir well. Serve immediately.

Khamang Kakdi

······· ✤{ Cucumber salad }✤ ···

Cucumber salads are very popular in India, and this is one of my favorites. Be sure to make this just before serving, otherwise it will become too watery.

Serves 4.

3 medium cucumbers
2 green chiles, stemmed and minced
½ cup (75 grams) roasted peanuts, coarsely ground
⅓ cup (40 grams) grated fresh coconut (or frozen unsweetened coconut)
1 tablespoon freshly squeezed lemon juice
1 teaspoon sugar
1 tablespoon ghee (page 37)
½ teaspoon black mustard seeds
¼ teaspoon cumin seeds
1 teaspoon table salt
2 tablespoons chopped fresh cilantro

1. Peel, wash, and halve the cucumbers lengthwise. Remove the seeds and finely chop the flesh. Put in a bowl and add the chiles, peanuts, coconut, lemon juice, and sugar, and stir well.

2. Place a small nonstick sauté pan over medium heat and add the ghee. When small bubbles appear at the bottom of the pan, add the mustard seeds. When they sputter, add the cumin seeds and sauté for 30 seconds. Immediately add this tempering to the cucumber mixture and stir well. Add the salt and stir.

3. Garnish with the cilantro and serve immediately.

Kosumali

This healthy cold salad is very popular in South India, where it's usually prepared with just carrots. Here I add cucumbers and green mangoes for more variety.

Serves 4.

¼ cup (50 grams) *dhuli moong dal* (split skinless green gram)
¼ cup (25 grams) sprouted *moong* (sprouted green gram)
1 medium carrot, grated
½ medium cucumber, diced
2 green chiles, stemmed and minced
½ medium green mango, peeled and chopped
1 tablespoon chopped fresh cilantro
1 teaspoon freshly squeezed lemon juice
1 teaspoon table salt
1 teaspoon vegetable oil
½ teaspoon black mustard seeds
5 fresh curry leaves
2 tablespoons grated fresh coconut (or frozen unsweetened coconut)

1. Put the *dhuli dal* in a bowl, wash in plenty of water 2 or 3 times, and drain. Add 1 cup (200 ml) water and soak for 30 minutes. Drain the *dal* in a colander and set aside in a bowl.

2. Place a nonstick saucepan over high heat, add 1 cup (200 ml) water, and bring to a boil. Lower the heat to medium, add the sprouted *moong*, cover, and cook for 20 minutes. Drain well and set aside to cool to room temperature.

3. Add the sprouted *moong* to the *dal*, along with the carrot, cucumber, chiles, green mango, and cilantro, and stir well. Add the lemon juice and salt, and stir well.

4. Place a small nonstick sauté pan over medium heat and add the oil. When small bubbles appear at the bottom of the pan, add the mustard seeds. When they sputter, add the curry leaves, then immediately pour this tempering into the *dal* mixture and stir well.

5. Garnish with the coconut. Chill for about 20 minutes and serve cold.

······❧ **Note** ❧ Sprouting beans: Soak the beans in water for a few hours. Then drain and place them on a moist cheesecloth. Leave at room temperature. Make sure the cloth stays moist. The beans should sprout in a day or two.

Ladyfinger Pachidi

······⋇{ **Okra with yogurt** }⋇··

In India, okra is commonly referred to as "ladyfingers," not to be confused with the Italian cookies of that name. Be sure to crisp up the okra well or it will become mushy after you add it to the yogurt. You can add grated fresh coconut to the yogurt and okra if you'd like. This cooling side dish is very refreshing in the summer.

Serves 4.

15 to 20 okra pods
1 quart (800 ml) vegetable oil
1½ cups (375 grams) plain yogurt
¼ teaspoon table salt
¼ teaspoon asafetida
1 tablespoon sesame oil
½ teaspoon black mustard seeds
¼ teaspoon fenugreek seeds
2 dried red chiles, stemmed and broken in half
10 to 12 fresh curry leaves

1. Wash the okra and pat dry with paper towels. Thinly slice the okra and spread out on paper towels for about 10 minutes.

2. Place a nonstick deep wok over high heat and add the oil. When small bubbles appear at the bottom of the wok, slide in the okra and fry until lightly browned and crisp. Remove with a slotted spoon and drain on paper towels. Let cool to room temperature.

3. Put the yogurt in a bowl and whisk until smooth. Add the salt and asafetida, and whisk. Stir in the okra.

4. Place a small nonstick sauté pan over medium heat and add the sesame oil. When small bubbles appear at the bottom of the pan, add the mustard seeds. When they sputter, add the fenugreek, chiles, and curry leaves. Pour this tempering over the okra and immediately cover the bowl to trap the flavors.

5. Stir and serve.

Lauki Raita

This simple dish pairs mild-tasting bottle gourd with seasoned yogurt. As a variation, you can garnish the dish with dried mint. This gourd can be substituted with red pumpkin.

Serves 4.

9 ounces (250 grams) *lauki* (bottle gourd)
1¾ teaspoons table salt
1 cup (250 grams) plain yogurt, chilled
½ teaspoon red chile powder
1 teaspoon ground roasted cumin (page 32)

1. Peel and grate the *lauki.* Drain any liquid.

2. Transfer to a nonstick saucepan. Add 1 teaspoon of the salt and cook over medium heat for 5 minutes. Drain off the water released by the *lauki* and transfer the cooked gourd to a plate to cool.

3. Put the yogurt in a bowl and whisk until smooth. Add the remaining ¾ teaspoon salt and the chile powder, and stir well. Add the *lauki* and stir well. Put in the refrigerator to chill for at least 30 minutes.

4. Sprinkle with the cumin and serve cold.

Moong Moth Ka Anokha Salad

······⁕{ **Salad of mixed sprouts** }⁕······

Sprouts are not a common ingredient in North Indian cuisine, but as we become more health conscious, these protein-laden little pulses have made their presence felt. I have adopted sprouts in a big way in my cooking, and one of the finer offerings is this salad.

Serves 4.

½ cup (75 grams) sprouted *moong* (sprouted green gram; see Note page 75)
½ cup (70 grams) sprouted *moth/matki* (see Note)
1 teaspoon table salt
1 green chile, stemmed and minced
½ medium orange
1 medium red onion, cut into ½-inch (1-cm) cubes, layers separated
½ medium apple, cored and cut into ½-inch (1-cm) cubes
1 medium green bell pepper, seeded and cut into ½-inch (1-cm) cubes
1 medium cucumber, seeded and cut into ½-inch (1-cm) cubes
2 medium tomatoes, cut into ½-inch (1-cm) cubes
½ teaspoon *chaat masala* (spice mix for *chaat*; page 24)
1 tablespoon freshly squeezed lemon juice

1. Place the sprouts in 2 separate bowls. Add ¼ teaspoon of the salt and ½ cup (100 ml) water to each bowl and cook in a microwave oven on high power for 2 minutes. Drain and transfer the sprouts to a large bowl. Add the chile.

2. Halve the orange and remove the skin, pith, and seeds. Cut into small cubes.

3. Add the orange, onion, apple, bell pepper, cucumber, tomatoes, and remaining ½ teaspoon salt to the sprouts and stir. Add the *chaat masala* and lemon juice, and stir.

4. Arrange the salad on a platter and serve.

······⁕{ **Note** }⁕ *Moth* is a brown gram that is a little smaller in size than green gram (*moong*).

Palak Raita

This is a very popular accompaniment in North India. Puréed spinach is combined with yogurt spiced with mineral-rich black salt. The strong-smelling salt is an acquired taste; you can use regular salt if you wish.

Serves 4.

> **2 medium bunches fresh spinach leaves**
> **1 teaspoon table salt**
> **1½ cups (375 grams) plain yogurt**
> **½ teaspoon black salt**
> **2 green chiles, stemmed**
> **2 teaspoons cumin seeds**
> **6 to 8 whole black peppercorns**
> **2 tablespoons vegetable oil**

1. Wash the spinach leaves well. Roughly chop one bunch and put in a microwave-safe bowl. Add ½ teaspoon salt and cook in a microwave oven on high power for 1½ minutes. Alternatively, you can boil 2 cups (400 ml) water with ½ teaspoon salt in a saucepan over high heat and blanch the spinach leaves for 1 to 2 minutes. Drain in a colander and shock in cold water. Let the spinach remain in the colander so that all the water drains away.

2. Whisk the yogurt and the remaining ½ teaspoon salt together in a deep bowl. Add the black salt and whisk again.

3. Put the cooked spinach and chiles in a food processor, and process to a smooth paste.

4. Place a small nonstick sauté pan over medium heat. Add the cumin seeds and peppercorns, and dry-roast over medium heat for 1 minute or until fragrant. Let cool slightly, then put the spices in a mortar and pound them to a coarse powder with a pestle.

5. Add the puréed spinach to the whisked yogurt and stir well. Put in the refrigerator to chill for 2 to 3 hours.

6. Shred the remaining spinach leaves.

7. Place a nonstick saucepan over medium heat and add the oil. When small bubbles appear at the bottom of the pan, add the shredded spinach and sauté for 1 to 2 minutes. Drain and set aside.

8. Add some of the pounded cumin seeds and peppercorns to the yogurt mixture, and stir. Sprinkle some on top. Garnish with the sautéed spinach and serve.

·······⁂{ **Chef's Tip** }⁂ Here I suggest pounding the roasted cumin seeds and peppercorns in a mortar with a pestle, because the amount may not be enough to grind in a blender.

Tandoori Murgh Salad

Tandoori chicken salad

This dish (also considered a *chaat*) is a tangy mixture of grilled marinated chicken with colorful peppers. This is a great way to use leftover tandoori chicken, and makes a delightful light lunch.

Serves 4.

2 (5-ounce/150-gram) boneless, skinless chicken breasts
1 teaspoon Kashmiri red chile powder or paprika
1 teaspoon fresh ginger paste (page 12)
1 teaspoon fresh garlic paste (page 12)
½ cup (135 grams) drained plain yogurt (see Note)
1 teaspoon table salt
1 tablespoon freshly squeezed lemon juice
½ teaspoon *garam masala* (spice mix; page 27)
1½ tablespoons vegetable oil
1 green bell pepper, cut into thin strips
½ red bell pepper, cut into thin strips
½ yellow bell pepper, cut into thin strips
1 onion, sliced
2 green chiles, stemmed and chopped
2 tablespoons chopped fresh cilantro
1 tablespoon freshly squeezed lemon juice
1 teaspoon *chaat masala* (spice mix for *chaat*; page 24)
½ small green mango, peeled and chopped (optional)
Salt to taste

1. With a sharp knife, make incisions in the chicken breasts and set aside.

2. Put the chile powder, ginger paste, garlic paste, yogurt, salt, lemon juice, *garam masala*, and 2 teaspoons of the oil in a large bowl, and stir well. Add the chicken and stir well so that all the pieces are well covered with the mixture. Cover the bowl and place it in the refrigerator to marinate for 3 to 4 hours.

3. Preheat the oven to 400°F/200°C. Thread the chicken pieces onto metal skewers, arrange on a rimmed baking sheet, and bake for 20 to 25 minutes, until almost done. Baste with the remaining oil and cook for 4 minutes more. When cooled, remove the chicken from the skewers and shred it.

4. In a large bowl, combine the shredded chicken, bell peppers, onion, chiles, half of the cilantro, the lemon juice, *chaat masala*, mango (if using), and salt and toss to mix well.

5. Transfer to a serving plate, garnish with the remaining cilantro, and serve.

Note ❋ To get ½ cup (135 grams) drained yogurt, pour ¾ cup (200 grams) plain yogurt into a square of muslin or several layers of cheesecloth, gather up the ends, and tie. Hang until all the water is drained, 30 to 40 minutes.

Aloo Kachalu Chaat

When we were kids we used to sing a silly Hindi rhyme that began, "Aloo kachalu" (potatoes and sweet potatoes) and then went on about them being put in the basket with an eggplant that kicked them out. Anyway, I think the potatoes and sweet potatoes are wonderful where they are here: in a *chaat*, with no eggplant within miles of them!

Serves 4.

1-inch (2½-cm) piece fresh ginger, cut into thin strips
1½ tablespoons freshly squeezed lemon juice
½ teaspoon table salt
1 large ripe banana
2 medium potatoes, boiled, peeled, and cut into 1-inch (2½-cm) cubes
1 large sweet potato, boiled, peeled, and cut into 1-inch (2½-cm) cubes
1 teaspoon tamarind pulp
2 green chiles, stemmed and minced
1 teaspoon *chaat masala* (spice mix for *chaat*; page 24)
¼ cup (40 grams) fresh pomegranate arils
2 tablespoons chopped fresh cilantro

1. Put the ginger in a small bowl, add ½ teaspoon of the lemon juice and a pinch of the salt, and set aside in the refrigerator.

2. Peel and cut the banana into 1-inch (2½-cm) pieces. Put them in a large bowl and drizzle with 1 teaspoon of the lemon juice.

3. Add the potatoes and sweet potato, the remaining 1 tablespoon lemon juice, the tamarind pulp, chiles, *chaat masala*, the remaining salt, the pomegranate arils, and cilantro. Toss gently to combine.

4. Serve garnished with the ginger.

CHAPTER 5

Chaats

A *chaat* is a snack that features the tastes of Indian cuisine—*khatta* (sour), *meetha* (sweet), *teekha* (spicy), and *chatpata* (tangy)—all on one plate. Embedded in Indian culture, *chaat* is a street food that is eaten at any time of the day. There are food carts, tea stalls, and mobile snack vendors on almost every street corner. The *chaat* vendor will mix up a treat for you—such as a *dahi papdi chaat* (page 86)—and then sprinkle it with chiles for heat, or drizzle on some tamarind chutney for sourness, or dollop it with some yogurt for a cooling effect, or dust it with more *chaat masala* (page 24) for flavor—all according to your specifications.

Chaats are complete sensory experiences, so when the *bhel puri* (page 84) is tossed and mixed and served to you on a little plate, do not eat it immediately: Take a deep breath and savor the mouthwatering aromas, take a few seconds to listen to the light crackling sound as the chutneys make their way into the spongy puffed rice . . . and then start eating!

Aloo Chaat Dilli Style

······⊰ **A tangy potato snack** ⊱···

This recipe will transport you to the capital of India. Delhi, known as "Dilli" in the local dialect, has two sections: Old Delhi and New Delhi. Old Delhi is still the stronghold of eateries that boast the old style of Mughal cooking. New Delhi is replete with contemporary restaurants and street food. This snack, sold on the roadside, is best eaten just after the potatoes are cooked, while they're still crisp.

Serves 4.

1-inch (2½-cm) piece fresh ginger, julienned
1 tablespoon freshly squeezed lemon juice
⅝ teaspoon table salt
3 medium potatoes, cut into ½-inch (1-cm) cubes
1 quart (800 ml) vegetable oil
1 large red onion, chopped
⅛ teaspoon black salt (page 586)
½ teaspoon *chaat masala* (spice mix for *chaat*; page 24)
½ teaspoon red chile powder
¼ teaspoon ground roasted cumin (page 32)
2 green chiles, stemmed and diced
3 tablespoons chopped fresh cilantro

1. Put the ginger in a small bowl, add 1 teaspoon of the lemon juice and ⅛ teaspoon of the table salt, and stir well. Set aside in the refrigerator.

2. Put the potatoes in a bowl and toss with ¼ teaspoon of the table salt.

3. Place a nonstick wok over medium heat and add the oil. When small bubbles appear at the bottom of the wok, add the potatoes, a few pieces at a time. Cook, stirring with a slotted spoon, for 5 to 6 minutes or until crisp and golden brown. Remove with a slotted spoon and drain on paper towels.

4. Transfer the potatoes to a large bowl. Add the onion, the remaining ¼ teaspoon table salt, the black salt, *chaat masala*, chile powder, cumin, chiles, cilantro, and the remaining 2 teaspoons lemon juice, and stir well.

5. Transfer to a serving bowl, garnish with the ginger, and serve immediately.

Bhel Puri

······ ⊰ **Puffed rice *chaat*** ⊱ ··

A very popular Mumbai street food that is famous both in India and abroad. Puffed rice, chickpea vermicelli, and crisp *puris* (Indian flour wafers) come together with a zesty mix of chutneys to create the ultimate snack.

As you mix the chutneys with the puffed rice, place your ear next to the bowl and you will be able to hear a light crackle and pop. That is the sound of the *kurmura* absorbing the chutneys. If it makes the sound, your puffed rice is fresh. If it doesn't, you need a new bag.

The puffed rice, *masala chana dal*, vermicelli, and wafers used here are all readily available at Indian grocery stores.

Serves 4.

4 cups (80 grams) *kurmura* (puffed rice)
1 medium red onion, chopped
¼ cup (50 grams) roasted *masala chana dal* (store-bought spiced lentils)
¼ cup (40 grams) roasted peanuts
2 medium potatoes, boiled, peeled, and diced
2 or 3 green chiles, stemmed and minced
½ cup (20 grams) *sev* (chickpea-flour vermicelli)
8 crisp *puris* (flour wafers; page 21)
Table salt
½ cup (120 grams) *pudina aur dhaniya* chutney (mint-and-cilantro chutney; page 22)
6 tablespoons *khajoor aur imli ki* chutney (sweet date-and-tamarind chutney; page 22)
1 teaspoon chile garlic chutney (page 519)
1 teaspoon freshly squeezed lemon juice
2 tablespoons chopped fresh cilantro

1. Put the *kurmura*, onion, *masala chana dal*, peanuts, potatoes, chiles, and half of the *sev* in a large bowl and toss to combine.

2. Add 4 crushed *puris* and toss. Add salt to taste.

3. Add the three chutneys and stir well.

4. Add the lemon juice and stir. Garnish with cilantro and the remaining *sev*.

5. Serve immediately with the remaining *puris*.

Dahi Batata Puri

Puffed flour crisps with potatoes and chutneys

This is a typical street food from the northern part of India: Puffed flour crisps are stuffed with potatoes, sprouts, and assorted chutneys. Prepare this just before serving or the crisps will lose their texture and become soggy.

Serves 4.

1½ cups (375 grams) plain yogurt, whisked
½ teaspoon table salt
1 tablespoon sugar
2 small potatoes, boiled, peeled, and chopped
½ cup (50 grams) sprouted *moong* beans, blanched (see Note)
1 teaspoon red chile powder
½ teaspoon *chaat masala* (spice mix for *chaat*; page 24)
24 puffed crisp *puris* (deep-fried flour balloons; page 21)
¼ cup (50 grams) *pudina aur dhaniya* chutney (mint-and-cilantro chutney; page 22)
¼ cup (60 grams) *khajoor aur imli ki* chutney (sweet date-and-tamarind chutney; page 22)
¼ cup (10 grams) *sev* (chickpea-flour vermicelli)
1 teaspoon ground roasted cumin (page 32)
2 tablespoons chopped fresh cilantro
2 tablespoons fresh pomegranate arils (optional)

1. Put the yogurt in a bowl, add ¼ teaspoon of the salt and the sugar, and whisk until smooth. Set aside in the refrigerator.

2. In a large bowl, combine the potatoes, sprouted *moong* beans, the remaining ¼ teaspoon salt, ½ teaspoon of the chile powder, and the *chaat masala*.

3. Puncture a hole on one side of each *puri*, fill it with the potato mixture, dip in the yogurt, and place on a plate. Alternatively, you can arrange the *puris* on the plate and then pour the yogurt over, reserving some for topping at the end.

4. Drizzle the two chutneys over the *puris*. Sprinkle with the *sev*, the remaining ¼ teaspoon chile powder, the cumin, cilantro, and pomegranate arils. Drizzle the remaining yogurt on top. Serve immediately.

Note ❄ To blanch sprouted *moong* beans: Place a nonstick saucepan over high heat, add 2 cups (400 ml) water, and bring to a boil. As the water starts boiling, add the sprouted *moong* beans, lower the heat to medium, and simmer for 2 to 3 minutes. Drain in a colander and refresh in cold water. Drain thoroughly and use.

Dahi Papdi Chaat

Flour crisps topped with sprouts, chutney, yogurt, and *sev*

I grew up in Delhi, where eating *chaat* at the roadside was—and still is—the thing to do. This dish is easy to make and, as with most *chaats*, is great for feeding a large group.

Serves 4.

1½ cups (375 grams) plain yogurt, whisked
½ teaspoon table salt
1 tablespoon sugar
24 small flat crisp *papdis* (flat flour wafers; page 21)
2 medium potatoes, boiled, peeled, and chopped
½ cup (50 grams) sprouted *moong* beans, blanched (page 75)
1 teaspoon chile garlic chutney (page 519)
3 tablespoons *pudina aur dhaniya* chutney (mint-and-cilantro chutney; page 22)
¼ cup (60 grams) *khajoor aur imli ki* chutney (sweet date-and-tamarind chutney; page 22)
1 teaspoon ground roasted cumin (page 32)
½ teaspoon *chaat masala* (spice mix for *chaat*; page 24)
½ teaspoon red chile powder
2 tablespoons chopped fresh cilantro
¼ cup (10 grams) *sev* (chickpea-flour vermicelli)
2 tablespoons fresh pomegranate arils (optional)

1. Place the yogurt in a bowl, add ¼ teaspoon of the salt and the sugar, and whisk until smooth. Set aside in the refrigerator.

2. Arrange 6 *papdis* on each of 4 serving plates. Place some potatoes on each *papdi*. Top with some sprouted *moong* beans.

3. Drizzle with a little of each chutney.

4. Sprinkle with the cumin, *chaat masala*, a little chile powder, and the remaining ¼ teaspoon salt.

5. Spoon the yogurt on top, then drizzle with the rest of the chutneys and sprinkle with the cilantro, *sev*, and pomegranate arils. Serve immediately.

Jhaal Muri

This street food of puffed rice, also called *kurmura* in India, and fresh vegetables tossed with spices should be prepared just before serving or the puffed rice will become soggy.

Serves 4.

3 cups (60 grams) *kurmura* (puffed rice)
1 medium red onion, chopped
¼ cup (40 grams) sprouted *kala chana* (sprouted black Bengal gram), blanched (page 75)
1 small cucumber, peeled and cut into ½-inch (1-cm) pieces
1 small tomato, seeded and cut into ½-inch (1-cm) pieces
2 green chiles, stemmed and chopped
2 tablespoons roasted peanuts, skins removed
2 tablespoons chopped fresh cilantro
2 tablespoons mustard oil, taken from a jar of store-bought pickle (see Notes)
¼ teaspoon table salt
2 tablespoons *jhaal muri masala* (see Notes)
2 tablespoons sliced fresh coconut

1. In a large bowl, combine the *kurmura*, onion, *kala chana*, cucumber, tomato, chiles, peanuts, and cilantro, and toss to stir well.

2. Add the oil, salt, and *jhaal muri masala*, and toss again to stir well. Garnish with the coconut and serve immediately.

⋯⋯⋅⋗ **Notes** ⋖⋅ If you do not have a jar of store-bought Indian pickle containing mustard oil, heat 2 tablespoons refined mustard oil (see below) to the smoking point. Remove from the heat, add ½ teaspoon mustard seeds, ¼ teaspoon fenugreek seeds, ¼ teaspoon fennel seeds, ½ teaspoon red chile powder, and a pinch of asafetida. Let it stand for 1 hour, strain to remove the solids, and use. All these ingredients are readily available in Indian grocery stores.

To make *jhaal muri masala*, combine 1 teaspoon black salt, 1 tablespoon roasted ground cumin, 1 teaspoon *chaat masala*, and ½ teaspoon ground white pepper. This masala is used to make the dish tangy.

Mustard oil is available in two varieties, filtered and refined. If you are using filtered mustard oil, you will need to first heat it until it reaches the smoking point, then let it cool completely before using. If you are using the refined variety, you can use it right away. In either case, please use mustard oil that is labeled specifically for cooking. If you cannot find it, regular vegetable oil will work as well.

Pani Puri

······❋⟩ A flour crisp stuffed with peas and served with spiced water ⟨❋······

This famed street food has many names: *golgappe* in the north, *puchka* in Bengal, and *pani puri* in Maharashtra. It is sold from large earthenware pots covered with damp red cloths and glass cases filled with *puris* (small deep-fried breads that look like crisp, hollow balloons). All one has to do is hold a *patrel*, a flat roll made of dried *colocassia* leaves, and the vendor will take one *puri*, crack it open on the top to make a small hole, and fill it with peas and chutney, and then dip it into the spicy water and place it on your bowl, dripping with the aromatic water. You have to eat them as fast as the vendor can assemble them—these guys are speedy and can manage three or four customers at a time! When you've eaten as many as you'd like, you hold up your hand and signal him to stop. He knows how much to charge you for what you've eaten even though you will likely have lost count.

Serves 4.

~ For the *ragda:*
1¼ cups (250 grams) *vatana* (dried white peas)
¼ teaspoon ground turmeric
Pinch of asafetida
1 teaspoon table salt
4 teaspoons *chaat masala* (spice mix for *chaat*; page 24)
3 to 4 tablespoons *khajoor aur imli ki* chutney (sweet date-and-tamarind chutney; page 22)

~ For the spicy water:
1 cup (60 grams) chopped fresh mint
1 cup (60 grams) chopped fresh cilantro
5 green chiles, stemmed and cut in half
½ teaspoon table salt
2 teaspoons black salt
1 tablespoon ground roasted cumin (page 32)
2 tablespoons freshly squeezed lemon juice

24 crisp *puris* (meant for *pani puri*; store-bought)

1. Make the *ragda:* Put the *vatana* in a large bowl, wash in plenty of water 2 or 3 times, and drain. Add 4 cups (800 ml) water and soak overnight. Drain the peas in a colander.

2. Place a nonstick saucepan over high heat and add 4 cups (800 ml) water. Add the turmeric, asafetida, and salt. When the water begins to boil, add the peas. When the water comes to a boil again, lower the heat to medium, cover, and cook for 30 to 35 minutes or until the peas are soft.

3. Mash the peas slightly. Add the *chaat masala* and chutney, and simmer for 10 minutes. Keep the *ragda* hot.

4. Make the spicy water: Put the mint, cilantro, and chiles in a blender, and blend to a smooth paste. Transfer the paste to a large bowl, add 6 cups (1.2 liters) water, the table salt, black salt, cumin, and lemon juice. Stir well, adjust the seasoning, and place in the refrigerator to chill.

5. To serve, fill each *puri* with a little *ragda*, then pour in some spicy water. Serve immediately.

Papdi Chaat

·······⊰ **Flour crisp and potato snack** ⊱···

One of the many popular *chaats* of the north—crisp flat *puris* topped with potato and chutneys. Prepare this just before serving or the *puris* will become soggy.

Serves 4.

20 small crisp flat *puris* (flour wafers; page 21)
2 medium boiled potatoes, peeled and thinly sliced
1 large onion, finely chopped
2 tablespoons *khajoor aur imli ki* chutney (sweet date-and-tamarind chutney; page 22)
2 tablespoons *pudina aur dhaniya* chutney (mint-and-cilantro chutney; page 22)
½ tablespoon freshly squeezed lemon juice
1 teaspoon ground roasted cumin (page 32)
½ teaspoon black salt
¼ cup (10 grams) *sev* (chickpea-flour vermicelli)
1 tablespoon *boondi* (see Note)
2 tablespoons fresh pomegranate arils
2 tablespoons minced fresh cilantro

1. Arrange the *puris* on a serving dish. Spread the potatoes over them neatly and top with the onion.

2. Drizzle a little of both chutneys on each *puri*.

3. Sprinkle with the lemon juice, cumin, and black salt.

4. Top with the *sev*, *boondi*, pomegranate arils, and cilantro and serve immediately.

·······⊰ **Note** ⊱· *Boondi* are small, crisp *besan* dumplings available at Indian grocery stores.

Pav Bhaji

······{ Mixed vegetables with bread }······

Say the words *pav bhaji* to anyone in Mumbai and his or her face will light up. It's a popular fast food that is categorized by nutritionists as junk food because the vegetables are usually overcooked and there is *a lot* of butter involved. Still, if you don't overcook the vegetables and go easy on the butter, this dish is a great way to introduce vegetables to a fussy kid. To keep it fresh, change the vegetables each time you make it. My daughters love it sprinkled with some lemon juice and chopped onions.

Serves 4.

3 tablespoons plus 8 teaspoons unsalted butter, plus ½ teaspoon for the griddle
2 medium red onions, diced
1 teaspoon fresh ginger paste (page 12)
2 teaspoons fresh garlic paste (page 12)
3 tablespoons red chile paste (see Note page 13)
1 medium green bell pepper, seeded and chopped
¼ cup (40 grams) shelled green peas, boiled and mashed lightly
¼ small head cauliflower, grated
1½ tablespoons *pav bhaji masala* (spice mix for *pav bhaji*; page 30)
8 medium tomatoes, diced
1½ teaspoons table salt
3 medium potatoes, boiled, peeled, and grated
8 *pavs* (breads; store-bought dinner rolls can be substituted)
2 tablespoons minced fresh cilantro
2 lemons, cut into wedges

1. Place a nonstick saucepan over medium heat and add 3 tablespoons of the butter. When the butter melts, add three quarters of the onions and sauté for 2 to 3 minutes or until lightly browned.

2. Add the ginger paste and garlic paste, and stir-fry for 30 seconds. Add the chile paste and sauté for 1 minute. Add the bell pepper, peas, and cauliflower, and sauté for 1 minute. Add the *pav bhaji masala* and cook for 1 minute.

3. Add the tomatoes and salt. Cover and cook for 5 minutes or until the tomatoes are pulpy. Mash the mixture with a potato masher. Add the potatoes and stir. Add 1 cup (200 ml) water and stir well. Cook for 5 minutes. Add ½ cup (100 ml) water and cook for 5 minutes. Transfer the *bhaji* to a serving bowl.

4. Place a nonstick griddle over medium heat and add ½ teaspoon butter. Slit one *pav* and cook it in the butter, pressing down on it with a spatula 2 or 3 times, for 30 seconds or until crisp and lightly browned. Cook the remaining *pavs*.

5. Sprinkle the *bhaji* with the cilantro. Divide into 4 individual servings and drop 1 teaspoon butter on each serving. Serve hot with the *pavs*, the remaining onions, and lemon wedges.

Ragda Pattice

······❊} Potato cutlets topped with white peas and chutneys {❊······

One of the best-selling foods on the streets of Mumbai is *pattice*, small potato cutlets, dunked in *ragda*, a white pea sauce, and garnished with chutneys and chopped onions. It's delicious and filling, and in many Gujarati homes it is served as a meal by itself.

Serves 4.

~ For the *ragda*:
1¼ cups (250 grams) *vatana* (dried white peas)
¼ teaspoon ground turmeric
Pinch of asafetida
1 teaspoon table salt

~ For the *pattice*:
4 small potatoes, boiled, peeled, and mashed
2 tablespoons cornstarch
3 green chiles, stemmed and chopped
½ teaspoon table salt
1 tablespoon vegetable oil
2 tablespoons *pudina aur dhaniya* chutney (mint-and-cilantro chutney; page 22)
2 tablespoons *khajoor aur imli ki* chutney (sweet date-and-tamarind chutney; page 22)
2 medium red onions, chopped
2 teaspoons *chaat masala* (spice mix for *chaat*; page 24)
2 tablespoons chopped fresh cilantro

1. Make the *ragda*: Put the *vatana* in a large bowl, wash in plenty of water 2 or 3 times, and drain. Add 4 cups (800 ml) water and soak overnight. Drain the peas in a colander.

2. Place a nonstick saucepan over high heat and add 4 cups (800 ml) water. Add the turmeric, asafetida, and salt. When the water begins to boil, add the peas. When the water comes to a boil again, lower the heat to medium, cover, and cook for 30 to 35 minutes or until the peas are soft. Keep hot.

3. Make the *pattice*: In a deep bowl, stir together the potatoes, cornstarch, chiles, and salt.

4. Divide into 8 portions and shape into balls. Flatten each ball by pressing it gently between your palms to make 1-inch (2½-cm) thick *pattice*.

5. Place a medium nonstick sauté pan over medium heat and add the oil. When the oil begins to smoke slightly, place the *pattice* in the pan, with a little space between each one. Cook, turning once or twice, until both sides are golden brown. Keep the *pattice* warm.

6. For each serving, place 2 *pattice* on a plate and pour some *ragda* over them so that it covers the *pattice*. Drizzle with the chutneys; sprinkle onions, *chaat masala*, and cilantro on top.

7. Serve immediately.

Sev Batata Puri

······•❖{ Crisp flour–wafer–and–potato snack }❖ ·······························

You just won't be able to stop eating these delicious crisp *puris* topped with potato, chutneys, and *sev*. I certainly can't! Some people in India also refer to these crisp, flat, store-bought *puris* as *papdis*. In Indian stores they are sold under both names and are the same.

Makes 24.

1 small green mango
2 large potatoes, boiled, peeled, and diced
½ teaspoon table salt
¼ teaspoon red chile powder
24 small, crisp, flat *puris* (flour wafers; page 21)
2 medium red onions, chopped
3 tablespoons *pudina aur dhaniya* chutney (mint-and-cilantro chutney; page 22)
1 teaspoon chile garlic chutney (page 519)
¼ cup (60 grams) *khajoor aur imli ki* chutney (sweet date-and-tamarind chutney; page 22)
1 cup (40 grams) *sev* (chickpea-flour vermicelli)
1½ teaspoons *chaat masala* (spice mix for *chaat*; page 24)
2 tablespoons chopped fresh cilantro

1. Wash the mango. Peel and halve it lengthwise. Scoop out the pit and dice the mango flesh.

2. Put the potatoes in a bowl and add the mango, salt, and chile powder. Stir well.

3. Arrange the *puris* in a single layer on a large plate.

4. Put a spoonful of the potato mixture on each *puri*. Sprinkle the onions over the *puris*. Drizzle with a little of each chutney.

5. Sprinkle the *sev* generously over the chutneys to completely cover them.

6. Sprinkle with the *chaat masala* and then with the cilantro. Serve immediately.

Peanut Chaat

This unique snack is prepared by boiling peanuts, along with turmeric, and then tossing them with onions and tomatoes. In a pinch, you can also use roasted peanuts.

Serves 4.

2 cups (300 grams) raw peanuts
1 tablespoon sea salt
1 teaspoon ground turmeric
½ teaspoon table salt
¼ teaspoon *chaat masala* (spice mix for *chaat*; page 24)
½ teaspoon red chile powder
1 teaspoon ground roasted cumin (page 32)
1 medium red onion, chopped
1 medium tomato, chopped
2 green chiles, stemmed and chopped
2 tablespoons chopped fresh cilantro
2 tablespoons freshly squeezed lemon juice

1. Place a nonstick saucepan over high heat and add 5 cups (1 liter) water. When the water comes to a boil, add the peanuts, sea salt, and turmeric, and cook for 20 minutes. Drain.

2. Transfer the peanuts to a deep serving bowl. Add the table salt, *chaat masala*, chile powder, cumin, onion, tomato, chiles, cilantro, and lemon juice, and stir well. Serve hot or at room temperature.

Urad Dal Kachori

These dumplings are stuffed with a spicy split-black-gram mixture. They are a very popular snack in India. These taste best when warm.

Serves 4.

2 cups (240 grams) *maida* (refined flour) or pastry flour
¾ teaspoon table salt
½ teaspoon baking soda
5 tablespoons vegetable oil

~ For the filling:
½ cup (100 grams) *dhuli urad dal* (split skinless black gram)
3 tablespoons ghee (page 37)
1-inch (2½-cm) piece fresh ginger, peeled and minced
1 green chile, stemmed and chopped
Pinch of asafetida
1 teaspoon ground coriander powder
½ teaspoon ground roasted cumin (page 32)
1 teaspoon red chile powder
¼ teaspoon ground fennel seeds
6 to 8 cashews, roughly chopped
1 tablespoon raisins
½ teaspoon sugar
½ teaspoon table salt
1 tablespoon freshly squeezed lemon juice
1 quart (800 ml) vegetable oil
Khajoor aur imli ki chutney (sweet date-and-tamarind chutney; page 22)

1. Sift the flour with the salt and baking soda into a deep bowl. Add the 5 tablespoons oil and combine well. Add ½ cup (100 ml) water and knead to make a soft dough. Cover the bowl with a dampened cloth and set aside for 1 hour.

2. Make the filling: Wash the *dhuli urad dal* well 2 or 3 times, then drain and soak in 2 cups (400 ml) water for 2 hours. Drain in a colander. Put the soaked *dal* in a mini food processor, add ¼ cup (50 ml) water, and process to a coarse paste.

3. Heat a small nonstick wok over high heat, then lower the heat to medium and add the ghee. When small bubbles appear at the bottom of the wok, add the gram paste, ginger, chile, asafetida, coriander, cumin, chile powder, fennel, cashews, and raisins. Sauté for 5 to 6 minutes or until the mixture is completely dry and begins to stick to the bottom of the pan.

4. Add the sugar, salt, and lemon juice. Stir well and remove from the heat. Transfer to a bowl and let cool completely.

5. Divide the dough into 16 portions and shape each into a ball. Place a ball on a flat surface and, using a rolling pin, roll it out into a small round about 2 inches (5 centimeters) in diameter. Roll it so it is thinner around the edges and thicker in the center. Place a portion of the filling in the center of the round and bring the edges together. Pinch them tightly together to seal. Pick up the dumpling in your palm and gently reshape it into a ball with a light hand. Use the remaining dough and filling to make 15 more *kachoris*.

6. Place a large nonstick wok over high heat and add the 1 quart (800 ml) oil. When small bubbles appear at the bottom of the wok, gently slide in half of the *kachoris* and fry them over low heat for 10 to 15 minutes or until the crusts are golden brown and crisp. Using a slotted spoon, transfer the *kachoris* to paper towels to drain. Repeat with the remaining *kachoris*.

7. Serve immediately with the chutney.

CHAPTER 6

Kebabs, Snacks, and Starters

The Indian counterpart to the Western barbecue grill is the tandoor, a clay oven fired with charcoal. Also known as a *sanjha choolha* ("common cooking place"), the tandoor literally brings people together. Women gather at the communal village tandoors at sundown, bringing dough with them from home. They chat and socialize while cooking their bread in the tandoor.

Tandoori cooking is one of the oldest ways of cooking food in India and can be traced back to the nomadic tribes of the northwest frontier who cooked their food in fires of charcoal and cow dung that they built in holes dug in the ground. Today, of course, the tandoor is used not only for the daily bread—*naan* (page 20) or *tandoori roti*—but also more exotic fare like kebabs and *tikkas*. Even *dals* and sauces can be cooked slowly to flavorful perfection in a tandoor. The most distinctive thing about cooking in a tandoor is the smoky flavor that it imparts to the food, and it is perhaps no accident that tandoori dishes were the first from India to gain international popularity.

Tandoori cooking is not only exceptionally flavorful—the food is usually cooked in its own juices and thus retains its natural flavors—but it is also healthier than other methods of cooking because it requires minimal additional fat.

Be sure to try the tandoori chicken recipe (page 208) I have included here. It is possibly one of the most popular tandoori dishes in the world, and perhaps the most popular Indian dish period. You don't have to have a clay oven to make these dishes: The tandoori style is quite adaptable to modern ovens.

Many of the kebab and meat recipes in this chapter are classics, and the *chandi kaliyan* (page 188), covered in edible silver foil, is a wonderful example of old-school decadence. Try the *chaap fry Amritsari* (page 211), which brings northern seasonings into play with breaded lamb chops, and then do a complete turnaround and make the *chettinaad* fried chicken (page 190), which takes you to the southern states.

These dishes are perfect served as appetizers or hors d'oeuvres or as parts of more elaborate Indian meals, but I've also included here a selection of snacks—like Punjabi samosas (page 154) and *peethiwali aloo tikki* (page 151)—that are best enjoyed as fillers between meals. *Dahi wada* (page 110) captures the essence of Indian *raitas* and is served as a special side dish at weddings and auspicious occasions, or as a filling but light meal on its own.

Aloo Nazakat

······⁊{ **A spectacular deep-fried potato dish** }⁊···

This dish takes some time and effort to prepare, but the results are outstanding: a deep-fried potato stuffed with cheese and lentil wafers.

Serves 4.

4 medium potatoes
3 tablespoons *chana dal* (split Bengal gram)
2 tablespoons plus 1 quart (800 ml) vegetable oil
2 small *urad dal papads* (see Note)
1½ teaspoons fresh ginger paste (page 12)
1½ teaspoons fresh garlic paste (page 12)
1½ teaspoons table salt
1 cup (250 grams) plain yogurt, whisked
½ teaspoon black salt
1 teaspoon *garam masala* (spice mix; page 27)
1 teaspoon red chile powder
3 tablespoons chopped fresh cilantro
2 tablespoons refined mustard oil (see Note page 87)
½ cup (70 grams) grated *paneer* (pressed fresh cheese; page 17)
2 teaspoons *chaat masala* (spice mix for *chaat*; page 24)
2 green chiles, stemmed and chopped

1. Peel the potatoes and cut them in half horizontally. Using a spoon, scoop out the insides of the potato halves, leaving a ¼-inch-thick (½-cm-thick) shell all around. Chop the scooped-out flesh and set aside.

2. Place a nonstick griddle over medium heat. Add the *dal*, lower the heat to low, and dry-roast until fragrant and golden. Transfer to a plate and set aside to cool to room temperature. Transfer to a spice grinder and grind to a powder. Set aside.

3. Place a nonstick wok over high heat and add 1 quart (800 ml) vegetable oil. When small bubbles appear at the bottom of the wok, lower the heat to medium and gently slide the potato shells into the oil and fry for 2 to 3 minutes or until the outer surface of the potato shells is golden brown. Remove with a slotted spoon and drain on paper towels.

4. In the same oil, fry the *papads* one at a time for 5 seconds. Remove with a slotted spoon and drain on paper towels.

5. Place a medium nonstick sauté pan over medium heat and add the remaining 2 tablespoons vegetable oil. When small bubbles appear at the bottom of the pan, add ½ teaspoon of the ginger paste and ½ teaspoon of the garlic paste. Sauté for 30 seconds or until fragrant.

6. Add the chopped potatoes and ½ teaspoon of the salt and sauté over medium heat for 5 to 6 minutes.

7. To make the marinade, put the yogurt in a bowl and add ½ teaspoon of the salt, the black salt, *garam masala*, chile powder, 2 tablespoons of the cilantro, the roasted *dal*, the remaining 1 teaspoon ginger paste, and the remaining 1 teaspoon garlic paste. Stir well. Add the mustard oil and stir again. Set aside.

8. To make the filling, put the *paneer* in a bowl. Add the remaining ½ teaspoon salt, the *chaat masala*, the remaining 1 tablespoon cilantro, the chiles, and the sautéed potato mixture.

9. Crush the fried *papads* to a coarse powder and add to the stuffing ingredients. Stir well.

10. Take each potato shell and fill it up to the brim with the filling. Put the potatoes in the yogurt marinade and stir gently to coat them. Cover the bowl and let the potatoes marinate for about 30 minutes.

11. Preheat the oven to 350°F/180°C. Grease a baking sheet.

12. Arrange the potatoes on the baking sheet and bake for 15 to 20 minutes. Serve immediately.

> **Note** *Urad dal papads* are *poppadums* made with *urad dal* (black gram) flour. Packages of these are available in Indian stores.

Amla Aur Beetroot Ki Tikki

Indian gooseberry-and-beet patties

Two very nutritious ingredients make this little patty: *amla*, or Indian gooseberry, which is high in vitamin C, and beets, which are a rich source of easily digestible carbohydrates. If *amlas* are unavailable, substitute an equal weight of raw green mango.

Serves 4.

5 tablespoons vegetable oil
1 medium red onion, chopped
3 medium beets, boiled, peeled, and grated
1 teaspoon table salt
½ tablespoon red chile powder
¼ teaspoon *chaat masala* (spice mix for *chaat*; page 24)
1 tablespoon freshly squeezed lemon juice
3 medium potatoes, boiled, peeled, and mashed
6 medium *amlas* (Indian gooseberries), grated
5 tablespoons cornstarch

1. Place a nonstick sauté pan over medium heat and add 1 tablespoon of the oil. When small bubbles appear at the bottom of the pan, add the onion and sauté for 3 to 4 minutes or until lightly browned.

2. Add the beets and salt, and sauté for 7 minutes or until all the excess moisture has evaporated. Add the chile powder and *chaat masala,* and stir well. Add the lemon juice and stir well.

3. In a large bowl, combine the beet mixture with the potatoes and stir well. Add the *amlas* and 2 tablespoons of the cornstarch, and stir well. Let cool, then put in the refrigerator to chill for 30 minutes.

4. Grease your hands, then divide the beet-potato mixture into 8 portions. Shape each portion into a thick 2½-inch (6½-cm) patty.

5. Dredge the patties in the remaining cornstarch and set aside.

6. Place a nonstick griddle over medium heat. Place a patty on the griddle, drizzle ½ tablespoon of the oil all around it, and cook for 2 minutes on each side or until both sides are evenly cooked. Cook the remaining patties using the remaining oil.

7. Transfer to a serving platter and serve hot.

Batata Vada

········⟨⟫ **Batter-fried potato dumplings** ⟨⟫···

I am not sure which sells more in Mumbai—*batata vadas* or McDonald's hamburgers. But given a choice I would go for *batata vadas* laced with dry red garlic chutney.

Serves 4.

6 small potatoes
1-inch (2½-cm) piece fresh ginger, chopped
6 cloves garlic
4 or 5 green chiles, stemmed and chopped
1½ cups (150 grams) *besan* (chickpea/gram flour)
1 teaspoon red chile powder
1 tablespoon table salt
Pinch of baking soda
4 teaspoons plus 1 quart (800 ml) vegetable oil
¼ teaspoon ground turmeric
2 tablespoons chopped fresh cilantro
½ teaspoon mustard seeds
Pinch of asafetida
10 to 12 fresh curry leaves

1. Wash and scrub the potatoes well. Put 4 cups (800 ml) water in a deep saucepan and place over medium heat. When the water begins to boil, add the potatoes and cook, covered, for 25 minutes or until the potatoes are tender. Drain in a colander and let cool to room temperature. Once cooled, peel the potatoes, then mash them using a potato masher. Set aside.

2. Put the ginger, garlic, and chiles in a mini food processor with 2 tablespoons water, and process to a smooth paste. Transfer the paste to a small bowl and set aside.

3. Place the *besan* in a deep bowl. Add the chile powder, 1 teaspoon of the salt, and the baking soda. Add ½ cup plus 6 tablespoons (190 ml) water and whisk well to make a smooth, lump-free batter. It should not be too thick.

4. Place a medium nonstick sauté pan over medium heat and add 3 teaspoons of the oil. When small bubbles appear at the bottom of the pan, add the ginger-garlic-chile paste and sauté for 1 minute. Add the mashed potatoes and the turmeric, and sauté for 5 to 6 minutes. Add the cilantro and the remaining 2 teaspoons salt. Stir well and sauté for 2 to 3 minutes. Transfer the mixture to a bowl.

5. Place a small nonstick sauté pan over medium heat and add 1 teaspoon of the oil. When small bubbles appear at the bottom of the pan, add the mustard seeds. When they sputter, add the asafetida and curry leaves. Immediately pour the spices over the potato mixture and stir well. Let cool to room temperature.

6. Once cooled, divide the mixture into 16 portions and shape each into a smooth ball.

7. Place a wok over high heat and add the remaining 1 quart (800 ml) oil. When small bubbles appear at the bottom of the wok, dip 4 of the potato balls in the *besan* batter, one at a time, and gently slide them into the hot oil; do not overcrowd the wok. Lower the heat to medium and fry, spooning a little oil over the balls with a slotted spoon, until they are light golden brown. Remove with the slotted spoon and drain on paper towels. Repeat with the remaining potato balls.

8. Serve immediately with a chutney of your choice.

Chef's tip If you have leftover *besan* batter, you can dip thin, round slices of potato or green pepper in the batter and deep-fry until golden. These are called *bhajias*.

Bedvin Kachori

······· A crisp whole-wheat pastry with lentils ·······

Kachoris are typical snacks from the west of India. As one travels from region to region, the *kachori* changes in size and stuffing. When cooking *kachoris*, have patience and be sure to control the temperature of the oil: If it is too hot, they will brown too fast and the flaky pastry will remain chewy and uncooked; if it is not hot enough, they will harden and absorb too much oil.

Makes 16.

¼ cup (50 grams) *chilkewali moong dal* (split green gram with skin)
1½ teaspoons ground coriander
1 teaspoon red chile powder
1-inch (2½-cm) piece fresh ginger, roughly chopped
1 teaspoon ground black pepper
½ teaspoon *garam masala* (spice mix; page 27)
½ teaspoon asafetida
2 cups (300 grams) *atta* (whole-wheat flour)
1½ teaspoons table salt
1 tablespoon plus 1 quart (800 ml) vegetable oil

1. Put the *dal* in a bowl, wash in plenty of water 2 or 3 times, and drain. Add ¾ cup (150 ml) water and soak for 30 minutes. Drain the *dal* in a colander and transfer to a food processor.

2. Add the coriander, chile powder, ginger, black pepper, *garam masala*, asafetida, and ¼ cup (50 ml) water, and process to a fine paste. Set aside.

3. Put the *atta* in a large bowl. Add the *dal* paste, salt, 1 tablespoon of the oil, and ½ cup (100 ml) water, and knead to make a semistiff dough. Cover with a damp cloth and let rest for 20 minutes.

4. Divide the dough into 16 portions and spread out each portion into a small disk with your fingertips.

5. Place a nonstick wok over high heat and add the remaining 1 quart (800 ml) oil. When small bubbles appear at the bottom of the wok, lower the heat to medium and gently slide in the *kachoris*, one at a time, and press gently with a slotted spoon until they puff up. Turn and cook for a few minutes or until both sides are golden and crisp. Remove with the slotted spoon and drain on paper towels.

6. Serve hot.

······· Chef's tip ······· You can use *chilkewali urad dal* (split black gram with skin) instead of the *chilkewali moong dal*.

Begun Bhaja

······◈{ Eggplant with white poppy seeds }◈······

This fried eggplant dish comes from the eastern part of India, where poppy seeds are used often. Eggplant tends to absorb oil, so you may need a little more to finish frying all the eggplant pieces.

Makes 16 pieces.

2 medium round eggplants
2 teaspoons ground turmeric
1½ teaspoons red chile powder
1 teaspoon table salt
1 teaspoon freshly squeezed lemon juice
¼ cup (50 grams) white poppy seeds
2 tablespoons vegetable oil, or more if needed

1. Remove the stems from the eggplants, wash them, and cut each in half lengthwise. Cut horizontally into ½-inch-thick (1-cm-thick) slices.

2. Combine the turmeric, chile powder, and salt in a small bowl. Sprinkle the mixture on both sides of the eggplant slices. Sprinkle with the lemon juice.

3. Put the poppy seeds in a shallow dish and roll the eggplant slices in them to coat both sides of the slices well. Set aside for 15 minutes.

4. Heat a nonstick sauté pan over medium heat and add the oil. When small bubbles appear at the bottom of the pan, gently slide in the eggplant slices, four at a time, and fry until golden. Turn and fry until the other side is golden. Remove with a slotted spoon and drain on paper towels. Add more oil to the pan for each batch, if needed.

5. Serve immediately.

Bhindi Kurkuri

·······❧{ **Crisp and tangy okra** }※···

Kurkuri means "crisp and crunchy"—and okra is one vegetable that truly benefits from being cooked until crisp. This versatile snack can be served anytime.

Serves 4.

1 pound (500 grams) okra
1½ teaspoons table salt
1 teaspoon red chile powder
¾ teaspoon *garam masala* (spice mix; page 27)
½ teaspoon *amchur* (dried mango powder)
½ teaspoon *chaat masala* (spice mix for *chaat*; page 24)
¼ cup (20 grams) *besan* (chickpea/gram flour)
1 quart (800 ml) vegetable oil
½ tablespoon freshly squeezed lemon juice

1. Wash the okra and pat dry with a kitchen towel. Trim off the ends, then thinly slice lengthwise.

2. Spread the okra slices on a flat dish and sprinkle with the salt, chile powder, *garam masala*, *amchur*, and *chaat masala*. Toss well and set aside for 10 minutes.

3. Sprinkle the *besan* over the okra and stir so that the slices are coated evenly.

4. Place a nonstick wok over high heat and add the oil. When small bubbles appear at the bottom of the wok, lower the heat to low, add the okra in small batches, separating the pieces as you drop them into the oil, and cook, stirring with a slotted spoon, for 2 to 3 minutes or until crisp and lightly browned. Remove with a slotted spoon and drain on paper towels.

5. Sprinkle with the lemon juice and serve immediately.

Bread Ke Pakode

This is a favorite hot snack at our house. You can refrigerate any leftover chutney to use for *chaats* or to serve with *samosas* or *dhoklas*.

Makes 16.

~ For the batter:
1½ cups (150 grams) *besan* (chickpea/gram flour)
1 teaspoon *ajwain*
¼ teaspoon ground turmeric
½ teaspoon red chile powder
2 teaspoons table salt
1 tablespoon chopped fresh cilantro

~ For the chutney:
10 to 15 pitted dates
2 teaspoons cumin seeds
1 teaspoon fennel seeds
2 tablespoons grated cane jaggery
5 tablespoons tamarind pulp
5 tablespoons red chile powder
1 teaspoon ground ginger
1 teaspoon black salt
½ teaspoon table salt

~ For the sandwiches:
1 (7-ounce/200-gram) block *paneer* (pressed fresh cheese; page 17)
8 slices white bread
1 quart (800 ml) vegetable oil
Pudina aur dhaniya chutney (mint-and-cilantro chutney; page 22)

1. Make the batter: Put the *besan*, *ajwain*, turmeric, chile powder, salt, and cilantro in a deep bowl. Stir well and add ½ cup plus 6 tablespoons (190 ml) water and whisk until smooth and lump-free. Set aside.

2. Make the chutney: Put the dates, cumin, fennel, jaggery, tamarind pulp, chile powder, and ground ginger in a deep nonstick saucepan. Add 1 cup (200 ml) water and place over medium heat. Cook for 10 minutes, then lower the heat to low and cook for 10 minutes more or until the dates are tender. Remove from the heat and let cool to room temperature. Transfer to a food processor and process until smooth; the chutney should be thick. Transfer to a bowl and add the black salt and table salt, and stir well.

3. Make the sandwiches: Place the block of *paneer* on a cutting board and cut into ½-inch-thick (1-cm-thick) slices.

4. Place 4 slices of bread on a work surface. Arrange the *paneer* slices over them, taking care that they do not overlap. Spread 1 tablespoon of the chutney on the *paneer*. Cover with more *paneer* slices, again taking care that they do not overlap. Cover with the remaining bread slices to make 4 thick *paneer-* and chutney-stuffed sandwiches. Cut each sandwich into 4 pieces.

5. Place a nonstick wok over high heat and add the oil. When small bubbles appear at the bottom of the wok, lower the heat to medium. Working in batches, carefully dip each sandwich piece in the batter and gently slide it into the hot oil. Fry a few pieces at a time until golden brown. Turn with a slotted spoon once or twice. Drain on paper towels. Serve with the chutney.

Bread Upma

·······⧫{ **Bread stir-fry** }⧫·······

This is a wonderful way to use up stale bread. This dish is served at breakfast or snacktime in India. It tastes best when served immediately. Be sure to stir-fry quickly, or the bread may absorb too much oil.

Serves 4.

¼ cup (50 ml) vegetable oil
Pinch of asafetida
½ teaspoon cumin seeds
¼ teaspoon brown mustard seeds
1 medium red onion, peeled and chopped
1 medium potato, boiled, peeled, and diced
¼ teaspoon ground turmeric
½ teaspoon red chile powder
8 slices day-old white bread, cut into small pieces
2 green chiles, stemmed and chopped
2 tablespoons chopped fresh cilantro
1 teaspoon freshly squeezed lemon juice
½ teaspoon table salt

1. Place a nonstick wok over high heat and add the oil. When small bubbles appear at the bottom of the wok, lower the heat to medium and add the asafetida, cumin seeds, and mustard seeds. When the cumin changes color and the mustard seeds begin to sputter, add the onion and sauté for 2 minutes or until translucent.

2. Add the potato and sauté for 1 minute. Add the turmeric and chile powder, and stir well. Sauté for 1 minute. Add the bread, chiles, cilantro, lemon juice, salt, and 3 tablespoons water, and toss well. Serve immediately.

Broken-Wheat Upma

······⟨ **A healthy version of the popular breakfast snack** ⟩······

Upma is a wholesome Indian snack traditionally made with semolina, but some regions use broken wheat, which tastes quite different from the finer semolina. Broken wheat is sold as *lapsi* in Indian grocery stores.

You could use diced broccoli instead of the carrot and blanched sweet corn instead of peas—experiment with your favorite combinations of vegetables.

Serves 4.

1 medium carrot, peeled and chopped
¼ cup (40 grams) frozen green peas
¼ cup (65 grams) low-fat plain yogurt
¼ teaspoon black mustard seeds
1 teaspoon *dhuli urad dal* (split skinless black gram)
10 to 12 fresh curry leaves
1 medium red onion, chopped
1 cup (200 grams) *lapsi* (fine broken wheat)
1-inch (2½-cm) piece fresh ginger, chopped
3 or 4 green chiles, stemmed and chopped
1 teaspoon table salt, or more if necessary
1 teaspoon freshly squeezed lemon juice
2 tablespoons chopped fresh cilantro

1. Place a small nonstick saucepan over high heat, add 1 cup (200 ml) water, and bring to a boil. Add the carrot and green peas and cook for 3 to 4 minutes. Drain in a colander. Refresh under running water and drain well. Alternatively, you can microwave the vegetables until they are tender.

2. Put the yogurt in a deep bowl, add 3½ cups (700 ml) water, and whisk until smooth. Set aside.

3. Place a medium nonstick saucepan over low heat. After 2 minutes, add the mustard seeds and *urad dal*. When the mustard seeds sputter, add the curry leaves and onion, and cook, stirring occasionally, for 4 to 5 minutes or until the onion is lightly browned.

4. Stir in the *lapsi* and cook for 2 minutes. Add the ginger and chiles, and cook for 5 minutes more or until the mixture has a roasted aroma.

5. Add the yogurt mixture and salt. Increase the heat to medium and bring to a boil. Lower the heat to low and cook, stirring continuously, for 7 to 8 minutes or until all the water is absorbed.

6. Add the carrot and peas, along with the lemon juice. Stir gently and taste for salt; add more if necessary. If the *upma* is too dry, add 2 to 3 tablespoons water. Cover and cook over low heat for 8 minutes.

7. Transfer to a serving bowl, garnish with the cilantro, and serve immediately.

Bendekaya Vepudu

One vegetable my two girls love is okra, which we call *bhindi* in Hindi. This is one of the dishes they often demand.

Serves 4.

2¼ pounds (1 kg) okra
1 quart (800 ml) vegetable oil
4 or 5 cloves garlic, thinly sliced
2 teaspoons roasted cumin seeds (page 32)
2 teaspoons coriander seeds
4 or 5 whole cloves
1-inch (2½-cm) cinnamon stick
3 green cardamom pods
6 to 8 whole black peppercorns
4 dried red chiles, stemmed and broken in half
1 teaspoon table salt

1. Wash and drain the okra. Pat dry with a kitchen towel. Trim off the two ends and cut the okra into ½-inch (1-cm) pieces.

2. Place a nonstick sauté pan over medium heat and add 2 tablespoons of the oil. When small bubbles appear at the bottom of the pan, lower the heat to low, add the garlic, and cook until golden brown. Remove with a slotted spoon and drain on paper towels.

3. Place a nonstick wok over high heat and add the remaining oil. When small bubbles appear at the bottom of the wok, lower the heat to medium and add the okra, in two or three batches, and cook until the okra is crisp and browned. Remove with a slotted spoon and drain on paper towels.

4. Put the cumin, coriander, cloves, cinnamon, cardamom, peppercorns, chiles, garlic flakes, and salt in a spice grinder, and grind to a powder.

5. Sprinkle the spice mix on the fried okra and toss well. Serve immediately.

····•❦ **Chef's tip** ❧•❈ Garnish with some crushed roasted peanuts for extra flavor.

Chukandar Ki Galouti

·····{ Beet kebabs }···

Take care when handling the beet mixture; all the ingredients are delicate and require just the right amount of pressure when you are forming the patties. *Charoli* seeds, called for here, are tiny almond-flavored seeds commonly used to garnish desserts and in meat dishes.

Serves 4.

½ cup (100 grams) ghee (page 37)
2¾ pounds (1.3 kg) beets, peeled and grated
¾ teaspoon table salt
1 tablespoon freshly squeezed lemon juice
5 cloves garlic, chopped
1-inch (2½-cm) piece fresh ginger, chopped
4 green chiles, stemmed and chopped
½ cup (60 grams) finely ground cashews
½ cup (90 grams) grated *khoya/mawa* (unsweetened solid condensed milk; page 37)
¼ cup (50 grams) roasted *chana dal* (split Bengal gram), finely ground
½ teaspoon caraway seeds
¼ teaspoon *garam masala* (spice mix; page 27)
¼ teaspoon ground green cardamom
¼ teaspoon ground black pepper
2 tablespoons *charoli/chironji* (melon seeds) optional
2 tablespoons *kewra* (screw pine) water
Vegetable oil

1. Place a nonstick saucepan over medium heat and add 2 tablespoons of the ghee. When small bubbles appear at the bottom of the pan, lower the heat to low and add the beets and salt, and sauté for 5 to 6 minutes, stirring frequently. Add the lemon juice and stir. Sauté for 15 minutes or until all the moisture dries up and the beets are thoroughly cooked and mashed.

2. Add the garlic and ginger, and stir. Add the chiles and sauté for 3 to 4 minutes.

3. Transfer the mixture to a bowl. Add the cashews, *khoya*, *dal*, caraway, *garam masala*, cardamom, black pepper, *charoli*, and *kewra* water, and stir well.

4. Divide the beet mixture into 8 portions. Grease your palms with a little oil, take each portion of the mixture in your hands, and shape into a thick, round 2-inch (5-cm) patty.

5. Place a nonstick sauté pan over medium heat and add the remaining 4 tablespoons ghee. When small bubbles appear at the bottom of the pan, lower the heat to low and gently slide 4 patties into the hot ghee and cook for 30 seconds or until the undersides are done. Turn and cook for 30 seconds or until the other sides are done. Do not turn the patties too often, as they are very delicate and may break. Remove with a slotted spoon and drain on paper towels. Repeat with the remaining patties. Serve immediately.

Dahi Wada

·······•·{ Deep-fried lentil dumplings served in spicy yogurt }·•······································

The results when making this Punjabi dish can be hit or miss—the dumplings can become hard if you don't whisk to add air to them as indicated in step 1. The solution is to follow the recipe instructions diligently.

Serves 4.

1 cup (200 grams) *dhuli urad dal* (split skinless black gram)
1 teaspoon cumin seeds
1 ½ teaspoons table salt
Pinch of asafetida
1 quart (800 ml) vegetable oil
3 cups (750 grams) plain yogurt
1 teaspoon ground roasted cumin (page 32)
1 teaspoon red chile powder
1 tablespoon chopped fresh cilantro
Khajoor aur imli ki chutney (sweet date-and-tamarind chutney; page 22)

1. Wash the *dhuli urad dal* and soak it in 3 cups water (600 ml) for 2 hours. Drain and place in a food processor with 1 ¼ cups (250 ml) water. Process to a smooth and fluffy paste. Transfer to a bowl, add the cumin, 1 teaspoon of the salt, and the asafetida, then whisk to incorporate air into the batter.

2. Place a wok or a heavy saucepan over medium heat and add the oil. When small bubbles appear at the bottom of the wok, shape the batter into small dumplings and slide them, a few at a time, into the hot oil; do not overcrowd the wok. Cook the *wadas*, turning them over frequently with a slotted spoon, for 12 minutes or until golden brown. Remove with a slotted spoon and transfer them to a bowl of hot water.

3. Put the yogurt in a deep serving bowl and whisk until smooth. Add the remaining ½ teaspoon salt and stir well.

4. Squeeze the *wadas* gently between your palms to remove excess water. Add them to the yogurt and let soak for 15 to 20 minutes.

5. Sprinkle with the cumin, chile powder, and cilantro. Drizzle with the chutney and serve.

Dal Pakwan

······· **A crisp bread served with flavorful lentils** *·······*

In Mumbai, long queues form outside shops selling this *dal* and bread on Sunday mornings; it's a popular breakfast dish in the Sindhi community. The best *pakwans* are made fresh at home right before mealtime. Just break off the crisp, golden-brown pieces and spoon up the *dal* with them.

Serves 4.

~ For the *dal*:
1 cup (200 grams) *chana dal* (split Bengal gram)
½ teaspoon table salt, or more to taste
¼ teaspoon ground turmeric
½ teaspoon red chile powder
¼ teaspoon *garam masala* (spice mix; page 27)
¾ teaspoon *amchur* (dried mango powder)
3 tablespoons vegetable oil
1 teaspoon cumin seeds
4 or 5 green chiles, stemmed and slit
8 to 10 fresh curry leaves
1 medium red onion, peeled and diced
½ cup (30 grams) chopped fresh cilantro

~ For the *pakwan*:
1 quart (800 ml) vegetable oil
1 cup (120 grams) *maida* (refined flour) or pastry flour
2 tablespoons *atta* (whole-wheat flour)
1 tablespoon fine semolina flour
¼ teaspoon cumin seeds
10 to 12 black peppercorns, crushed
½ teaspoon table salt

1. Make the *dal*: Put the *dal* in a bowl, wash in plenty of water 2 or 3 times, and drain. Add 3 cups (600 ml) water and soak for about 1 hour. Drain the *dal* in a strainer.

2. Place a nonstick saucepan over high heat and add 3 cups (600 ml) water. When it comes to a rapid boil, add the *dal*, salt, and turmeric. When the mixture comes to a boil again, lower the heat to medium, cover, and cook for 25 minutes. Add ½ cup (100 ml) water and cook until soft.

3. Add ¼ teaspoon of the chile powder, ⅛ teaspoon of the *garam masala*, and half of the *amchur*. Taste for salt and add more if needed. Cook over low heat for 10 minutes.

4. Place a small nonstick pan over medium heat and add the oil. When small bubbles appear at the bottom of the pan, add the cumin seeds. When they begin to change color, add the chiles, curry leaves, the remaining ⅛ teaspoon *garam masala*, and the remaining ¼ teaspoon chile powder. Stir and pour the mixture over the *dal*, stir well, remove from the heat, cover, and set aside.

5. Place a nonstick wok over medium heat and add 1 quart (800 ml) oil.

6. While the oil heats, make the *pakwan*: Sift the *maida* and *atta* into a large bowl. Add the semolina, cumin, peppercorns, 2 tablespoons of the hot oil, and the salt. Add ¼ cup (50 ml) water and knead to make a medium-soft dough.

7. Divide the dough into 8 portions and roll each portion out into a 4-inch (10-cm) round. Prick lightly with a fork.

8. Check the oil. When small bubbles appear at the bottom of the wok, lower the heat to low and add the dough rounds, one by one, and cook until golden and crisp on both sides, pressing the *pakwan* down into the oil with a slotted spoon so they become very crisp. Remove with the slotted spoon and drain on paper towels. Let them cool to room temperature.

9. Garnish the *dal* with the onion and cilantro and serve with the *pakwan*.

Dudhi Na Muthia

······⊰ **Bottle gourd dumplings with mustard seeds and curry leaves** ⊱······

Being a Punjabi, I did not have much experience with Gujarati food until I got married. This snack gets its name from the fact that the dough is placed on the palm and pressed into shape by clenching the fist (*muthi* in Gujarati). I like to eat the *muthia* plain, right after they've been steamed; this saves calories, but in most homes the tempering is considered essential.

Serves 4.

14 ounces (400 grams) bottle gourd (substitute: red pumpkin)
1 tablespoon ginger paste (page 12)
1 tablespoons green chile paste (page 13)
¾ cup plus 2 tablespoons (85 grams) *besan* (chickpea/gram flour)
1¼ cups (190 grams) *atta* (whole-wheat flour)
1 teaspoon table salt
½ teaspoon ground turmeric
⅛ teaspoon asafetida
2 tablespoons chopped fresh cilantro
1½ tablespoons sesame seeds
1 teaspoon sugar
1 teaspoon freshly squeezed lemon juice
1 tablespoon sour plain yogurt (see page 513)
3 tablespoons vegetable oil
1 teaspoon brown mustard seeds
1 teaspoon cumin seeds
20 fresh curry leaves

1. Peel the bottle gourd and grate it. Put it in a large bowl and add the ginger paste, green chile paste, *besan*, *atta*, salt, turmeric, asafetida, cilantro, 1 tablespoon of the sesame seeds, the sugar, lemon juice, and yogurt. Combine well and knead to make a sticky dough.

2. Grease your palms with a little oil. Divide the dough into 4 portions and shape each portion into a ½-inch (1-cm) diameter cylinder.

3. Place a steamer over high heat and add 2 cups (400 ml) water. When the water comes to a boil, put the rolls on a steaming tray and place the tray in the steamer. Steam for 15 minutes or until a skewer inserted into one of the pieces comes out clean. Remove from the steamer and let cool completely. Cut into 1-inch (2½-cm) pieces.

4. Place a nonstick wok over medium heat and add the oil. When small bubbles appear at the bottom of the wok, add the mustard seeds, cumin, curry leaves, and the remaining ½ tablespoon sesame seeds. When the seeds sputter, add the dumpling pieces and toss well. Lower the heat to low and sauté, tossing occasionally, for 3 to 4 minutes or until the *muthia* are lightly browned on all sides.

5. Serve hot.

Green Pea Kachori

····· ⊰ **A crisp bread stuffed with spicy green peas** ⊱ ···

Getting a flaky but crisp crust here is rather tricky: If the heat is too high, the *kachoris* will brown on the outside but remain raw and chewy inside. If the oil isn't hot enough, the crust will not be flaky and you will have hard *kachoris* on hand. It takes time to cook them at the right temperature, but if you do, the flat, stuffed disks will puff up and look spectacular. Serve them with *khajoor aur imli ki* chutney (sweet date-and-tamarind chutney; page 22).

Serves 4.

1 cup (120 grams) *maida* (refined flour) or pastry flour
¼ teaspoon *ajwain*
¼ teaspoon table salt
2 tablespoons ghee (page 37), melted
1 tablespoon plus 1 quart (800 ml) vegetable oil
Pinch of asafetida
½ teaspoon cumin seeds
1-inch (2½-cm) piece fresh ginger, chopped
3 or 4 green chiles, stemmed and chopped
1 cup (150 grams) fresh or frozen green peas, crushed
½ teaspoon table salt
½ teaspoon *garam masala* (spice mix; page 27)
¼ cup (30 grams) grated fresh coconut (or frozen unsweetened coconut)
¼ cup (40 grams) roasted peanuts, crushed

1. Put the *maida*, *ajwain*, ¼ teaspoon of the salt, and the ghee in a bowl, and stir. Add ⅓ cup (65 ml) cold water and knead to make a stiff dough. Cover with a double layer of damp cheesecloth and set aside for 30 minutes.

2. Place a medium nonstick sauté pan over medium heat and add 1 tablespoon of the oil. When small bubbles appear at the bottom of the pan, lower the heat to low and add the asafetida and cumin. When the cumin begins to change color, add the ginger, chiles, peas, and the remaining ½ teaspoon salt. Stir and cook for 2 to 3 minutes. Remove from the heat and add the *garam masala*. Stir and set aside to cool completely.

3. When cooled, add the coconut and peanuts, and stir well.

4. Divide the dough into 8 portions. Shape each portion into a ball and then roll out into a thick 4-inch (10-cm) round. Place a portion of the pea filling in the center and gather the edges to enclose the filling; pinch hard to seal. Using your fingers, pat the *kachori* into a flat 3-inch (7½-cm) round.

5. Place a nonstick wok over high heat and add 1 quart (800 ml) oil. When small bubbles appear at the bottom of the wok, lower the heat to medium and gently slide in 2 *kachoris*. Fry, spooning hot oil over them and turning with a slotted spoon frequently, for 8 to 10 minutes or until golden. Remove with the slotted spoon and drain on paper towels. Repeat with the remaining kachoris. Serve hot.

Handvo

····· *A pan-fried savory rice, *dal*, and vegetable cake* *·····

In Ahmedabad, in Gujarat, you are likely to see home kitchens equipped with special steamers to make *dhoklas* and a special cooker that is used solely to make *handvo*. Yes, it's such an important dish that cooks invest in a special gadget to make it. The cooker has a large dome with a perforated lid that covers a container with a tube in the center. The *handvo* batter is poured into the well-greased container, which is placed in a tray filled with sand. The cooker with the container and tray is put over the heat and the *handvo* batter is cooked slowly and steadily into a ring-shaped cake with a very crisp, dark crust. You can also use a regular nonstick sauté pan, as I describe below. Enjoy a freshly cooked *handvo* for dinner accompanied by loads of mint-and-cilantro chutney (page 22).

Serves 4.

1 cup (200 grams) raw rice
¼ cup (50 grams) *dhuli moong dal* (split skinless green gram)
¼ cup (50 grams) *chana dal* (split Bengal gram)
¼ cup (50 grams) *dhuli urad dal* (split skinless black gram)
½ cup (125 grams) sour plain yogurt (see page 513)
2 tablespoons vegetable oil
1 teaspoon ginger paste (page 12)
1 teaspoon green chile paste (page 13)
½ teaspoon red chile powder
⅛ teaspoon ground turmeric
2 teaspoons table salt
½ small red onion, thinly sliced
2 tablespoons grated bottle gourd (substitute: red pumpkin)
2 tablespoons shredded cabbage
1 tablespoon grated carrot
Small pinch of asafetida
½ teaspoon brown mustard seeds
4 fresh curry leaves
1 dried red chile, stemmed and broken in half
½ teaspoon sesame seeds
¼ teaspoon baking soda

1. Put the rice and *dals* in a bowl, wash in plenty of water 2 or 3 times, and drain. Add 3 cups (600 ml) water and soak for 5 hours. Drain, transfer to a food processor with 5 tablespoons water, and process coarsely.

2. Transfer to a deep bowl. Add the yogurt, 1 tablespoon of the oil, and 2 tablespoons lukewarm water, and whisk to make a thick batter. Cover the bowl and set aside in a warm place to ferment overnight.

3. Add the ginger paste, green chile paste, chile powder, turmeric, and salt, and stir well. Add the onion, bottle gourd, cabbage, and carrot, and stir well. Set the batter aside.

4. Place a small nonstick sauté pan over medium heat and add ¾ tablespoon of the oil. When small bubbles appear at the bottom of the pan, add the asafetida and mustard seeds. When the seeds sputter, add the curry leaves, red chile, and sesame seeds. Add this tempering to the batter and stir well. Add the baking soda and stir well.

5. Place a large nonstick sauté pan over medium heat and add the remaining ¼ tablespoon oil. When small bubbles appear at the bottom of the pan, lower the heat to low, add the batter, and let it spread evenly. Cover and cook for 20 minutes. Flip it over. Cover and cook for 15 minutes or until both sides are evenly browned. Cut into wedges and serve.

Hara Bhara Kabab

········{ **Fresh spinach and potato kebabs** }···

This vegetarian appetizer is very popular in restaurants in India. At my Yellow Chilli restaurants, we add a layer of depth and complexity by stuffing the kebabs with yogurt.

Makes 24 kebabs.

7 ounces (200 grams) spinach leaves, blanched and chopped (see Note)
¾ cup (110 grams) fresh or frozen green peas, boiled and mashed
3 medium potatoes, boiled, peeled, and grated
2 green chiles, stemmed and chopped
2 tablespoons chopped fresh cilantro
1-inch (2½-cm) piece fresh ginger, chopped
1 teaspoon *chaat masala* (spice mix for *chaat*; page 24)
1 teaspoon table salt
2 tablespoons cornstarch
2 tablespoons vegetable oil

1. Put the spinach, peas, and potatoes in a deep bowl, and stir well. Add the chiles, cilantro, ginger, *chaat masala*, and salt, and stir well. Add the cornstarch and stir to a smooth, soft dough. Divide the spinach mixture into 12 equal portions. Shape each portion into a ball and then press it between your palms to form it into a flat, round shape that looks like a thick disk.

2. Place a nonstick sauté pan over medium-high heat and add 1 teaspoon of the oil. Put 6 kebabs in the pan, with space between them. Drizzle 1 teaspoon of the oil all around the kebabs and cook for 2 to 3 minutes or until the underside is golden brown. Using a spatula, turn them over, drizzle 1 teaspoon of the oil all around them, and cook for 2 to 3 minutes more or until golden brown. Drain on paper towels. Cook the remaining 6 kebabs with the remaining oil. Serve immediately.

········{ **Note** }··· You can also use frozen chopped spinach (just thaw and squeeze out the excess water). To blanch fresh spinach leaves, boil 2 cups (60 ml) of water, add the leaves, and boil for 2 to 3 minutes. Drain and refresh in cold water. Drain again, squeeze out excess water, and finely chop.

Hare Masale Ka Bhuna Paneer

······❋{ *Paneer* with mint and cilantro }❋·······································

Paneer and vegetables are coated in a spicy green marinade and broiled. Tart, juicy, fresh pomegranate seeds and the distinctive flavor of mustard oil make the dish special.

Serves 4.

4 ounces (125 grams) *paneer* (pressed fresh cheese; page 17)

~ For the first marinade:
1 tablespoon fresh ginger paste (page 12)
1 tablespoon fresh garlic paste (page 12)
2 tablespoons freshly squeezed lemon juice
1 teaspoon table salt

~ For the second marinade:
1 cup (25 grams) fresh cilantro leaves
½ cup (12 grams) fresh mint leaves
2 tablespoons fresh pomegranate arils
¾-inch piece fresh ginger, chopped
5 cloves garlic
6 green chiles, stemmed and chopped
1 cup (270 grams) drained plain yogurt
½ teaspoon table salt
½ teaspoon *garam masala* (spice mix; page 27)
2 teaspoons ground roasted cumin (page 32)
¼ cup (25 grams) *besan* (chickpea/gram flour), roasted (see Note)
1 tablespoon *kasoori methi* (dried fenugreek leaves), ground
1 tablespoon filtered mustard oil (see Note page 87)
10 fresh curry leaves
1 large tomato, seeded and cut into 1-inch (2½-cm) cubes
1 medium green bell pepper, cut into 1-inch (2½-cm) cubes
1 medium red onion, cut into 1-inch (2½-cm) cubes
5 tablespoons butter, melted
1 tablespoon freshly squeezed lemon juice
2 teaspoons *chaat masala* (spice mix for *chaat*; page 24)

1. Cut the *paneer* into 8 (1-inch/2½-cm) cubes and set aside.

2. Make the first marinade: Put all the ingredients in a large bowl and stir well. Add the *paneer* and stir gently to coat. Set aside for 30 minutes.

3. Make the second marinade: Blanch the cilantro and mint in boiling water for 1 minute, then drain in a colander. Wash under cold running water for 30 seconds, then let drain for 30 minutes. Put the cilantro and mint, the pomegranate arils, ginger, garlic, chiles, and 2 tablespoons water in a food processor. Process to a paste. Transfer to a large bowl.

4. Add the yogurt, ½ teaspoon salt, the *garam masala*, cumin, *besan*, and *kasoori methi*, and stir well.

5. Put the mustard oil in small saucepan and place over low heat. Tear the curry leaves into small bits. When the oil begins to smoke, add the curry leaves and immediately remove from the heat and pour into the second marinade.

6. Add the *paneer* pieces (along with the first marinade) and the tomato, bell pepper, and onion. Cover the bowl with plastic wrap and put in the refrigerator to marinate for 3 to 4 hours.

7. Preheat the broiler to high.

8. String the *paneer* alternately with the tomato, pepper, and onion onto skewers. Put the skewers on a baking sheet and broil for 3 to 4 minutes. Baste with 2 tablespoons of the butter, then broil for 2 to 3 minutes more.

9. Put the remaining 3 tablespoons melted butter in a nonstick sauté pan and place over medium heat. Remove the grilled paneer and vegetables from the skewers and add them to the hot butter. Stir-fry for 30 seconds over high heat.

10. Transfer to a serving bowl and sprinkle with the lemon juice and *chaat masala*.

11. Serve immediately.

··········⋛ **Note** ⋚⁂ To roast *besan*, place a small nonstick sauté pan over medium heat and add the *besan*. Roast, stirring continuously, until the *besan* is fragrant and lightly browned.

Idiappam

Four simple ingredients—rice, water, oil, and salt—result in a masterpiece of a dish. Although it is not commonly made in modern households in South India, this airy treat does come into the limelight on special occasions. Whenever I am in Kerala, I make a point of having this for breakfast at least once. Serve the *idiappam* sprinkled with fresh coconut and drizzled with coconut milk or a chutney.

This recipe requires an *idiappam* press. It is made of wood or metal and has a fine mesh through which the dough is pushed to form thin, noodlelike strings. You can find them at many Indian grocery stores and online.

Serves 4.

2½ cups (300 grams) short-grain rice
2 tablespoons vegetable oil
1½ teaspoons table salt

1. Wash the rice, drain, and soak in 3 cups (600 ml) water for about 2 hours. Drain well and spread out on a clean, dry, absorbent cloth in an airy place for 30 minutes. Put in a mini food processor and process to a smooth powder. Shake the rice through a fine sieve and discard the large bits in the sieve. Measure the volume of ground rice and pour an equal volume of water into a saucepan.

2. Place the water over high heat, bring to a rapid boil, and add the oil and salt. Lower the heat to low. Gradually add the rice flour in a continuous stream, stirring constantly to prevent lumps from forming.

3. Add ¼ cup (50 ml) water if the mixture seems too thick. Cook for 5 minutes, remove from the heat, and let rest, covered, for about 5 minutes.

4. When cool enough to handle, transfer the dough to a flat plate and knead well with damp hands for 5 minutes.

5. Divide the dough into 12 balls that will fit into an *idiappam* press.

6. Heat 2 cups (400 ml) water in a steamer. Arrange the balls on a perforated plate and place it in the steamer. Steam for about 15 minutes or until cooked. Cover and keep warm.

7. Put the steamed rice-flour balls one by one into the *idiappam* press and press them onto a plate and let cool.

8. Serve at room temperature.

Idlis

Soft and spongy *idlis* (rice dumplings) are always served with *sambhar* (page 32) and coconut cilantro chutney (page 520). It is not difficult to make *idlis* at home. This hot, healthy snack is probably the lightest—but also the most filling—snack in the South Indian repertoire.

You will need an *idli* steamer for this (page 591); they are readily available at Indian grocery stores.

Makes 20.

1 cup (200 grams) parboiled rice
¼ cup (50 grams) raw short-grain rice
½ cup (100 grams) *dhuli urad dal* (split skinless black gram)
½ teaspoon fenugreek seeds
1 teaspoon table salt
Vegetable oil for the *idli* trays

1. Put the parboiled rice and raw rice in a large bowl, wash in plenty of water 2 or 3 times, and drain. Add 3 cups (600 ml) water and soak for 2 to 3 hours.

2. Wash and soak the *dal* and fenugreek seeds in 1 cup (200 ml) water for 2 to 3 hours.

3. Drain the *dal* and fenugreek, and put in a food processor with ½ cup (100 ml) water. Process to a smooth and spongy batter. Transfer to a nonstick saucepan.

4. Drain the rices and put in the same food processor with 1 cup (200 ml) water. Process to a slightly coarse mixture. Transfer to the saucepan with the *dal* mixture.

5. Add the salt and stir thoroughly in brisk whipping motions so as to aerate the batter well. It should have a pancake batter consistency.

6. Cover the pan with a tight lid and set aside in a warm place overnight to ferment.

7. Heat 2 cups (400 ml) water in a steamer and lightly oil the *idli* trays. Gently stir the batter and pour it into the trays, taking care not to fill the indentations to the brim. Fit the trays onto the stand and put in the steamer. Cover and steam for about 10 minutes or until a toothpick inserted in an *idli* comes out clean.

8. Take the *idli* stand out of the steamer and set aside to cool slightly. Spoon the *idlis* out and keep them covered with a double layer of damp cheesecloth until it is time to serve.

9. Serve warm.

Kachche Kele Ke Cutlet

········⟩ **Green banana patties with sweet tamarind chutney** ⟨········

Marwaris of the princely Indian state of Rajasthan are followers of a religion called Jainism. Jains do not eat any root vegetables, so in most homes the use of potatoes is taboo, along with onion and garlic. So what do they do to make potato cutlets, which are a very typical snack around the rest of the country? They use green bananas! Unless they are told, guests would never know that potatoes are missing from these cutlets. Marwari food is replete with surprises like this.

Serves 4.

3 medium unripe bananas, unpeeled
¼ cup (40 grams) green peas, fresh or frozen
2 green chiles, stemmed and minced
Pinch of asafetida
¼ teaspoon red chile powder
¼ teaspoon *amchur* (dried mango powder)
½ teaspoon *garam masala* (spice mix; page 27)
2 tablespoons chopped fresh cilantro
1 teaspoon table salt
About 1 cup (200 ml) vegetable oil
½ cup *khajoor aur imli ki* chutney (sweet date-and-tamarind chutney; page 22)

1. Wash the bananas and pat dry; do not peel them. Cut each one into 3 pieces.

2. Put a steamer with water in the bottom over high heat and place the banana pieces in the top. Cover and steam for 10 minutes. Open the lid. If the peel of the bananas is dark and the flesh is soft, they are done. Remove from the heat and carefully spoon the banana pieces into a large dish. Let cool to room temperature.

3. Pour 2 cups (400 ml) water in a small saucepan and bring to a boil over medium heat. Add the peas and cook for 2 minutes or until soft and tender. Drain in a colander.

4. Peel the steamed banana pieces and place them in a deep bowl. Add the peas and mash them together using a potato masher or fork. Add the chiles, asafetida, chile powder, *amchur*, *garam masala*, cilantro, and salt. Combine the mixture well, preferably with your hand. Divide the mixture into 16 portions. Apply ½ teaspoon of the oil to your palms and shape each portion into a round cutlet about ½ inch (1 cm) thick.

5. Place a large nonstick sauté pan over high heat and add 2 to 3 tablespoons oil. When small bubbles appear at the bottom of the pan, reduce the heat to medium. Using a spatula, lift up a cutlet and place it in the hot oil. Cook three or four cutlets at a time for 3 to 4 minutes or until the underside is light golden. Turn over with the spatula and drizzle some more oil around the edges of the cutlets. Cook for 3 to 4 minutes more or until the other side is light golden. Remove with a slotted spoon and drain on paper towels; transfer to a serving dish. Cook the remaining cutlets.

6. Serve the cutlets with the chutney as a dip.

Kalla Dosas

I admit that my wife, Alyona, is more deft than I am at making thin *dosas* that cook just right and are perfectly crisp. Luckily, this *dosa* doesn't need to be paper thin and is a lot easier to make than most. These are usually cooked on a griddle called a *kalla* (hence the name), a flat, heavy cast-iron griddle.

Makes 8.

1¼ cups (250 grams) raw *sona masoori* rice (see Note)
½ cup plus 2 tablespoons (125 grams) parboiled rice
2 tablespoons *dhuli urad dal* (split skinless black gram)
1 teaspoon *chana dal* (split Bengal gram)
¼ teaspoon fenugreek seeds
1 tablespoon table salt
4 teaspoons vegetable oil

1. Put both the rices in a bowl, wash in plenty of water 2 or 3 times, and drain. Add 1 quart (800 ml) water and soak for 3 to 4 hours.

2. Put the *dals* and fenugreek seeds in another bowl, wash 2 or 3 times, and drain. Add 2 cups (400 ml) water and soak for 3 to 4 hours.

3. Drain the rice and transfer to a food processor with 1 cup (200 ml) water. Process until smooth. Transfer to a large bowl.

4. Drain the *dals* and fenugreek, and transfer to the food processor with ½ cup (100 ml) water. Process until smooth, then add to the ground rice. Whisk the batter well. Add the salt and ½ cup (100 ml) water, and whisk again.

5. Cover the bowl with plastic wrap and set aside in a warm place overnight to ferment.

6. Add 5 tablespoons (75 ml) water and whisk to make a batter of pouring consistency.

7. Place a nonstick griddle over medium heat. Grease it with ½ teaspoon of the oil. Lower the heat to low. Pour a ladleful of the batter onto the griddle and do not spread it. Cover with a dome-shaped lid and cook for 5 minutes or until the underside is lightly browned and the top side is perforated by bubbles. Repeat with the remaining batter and oil.

8. Serve hot.

·······❈{ **Note** }❈ *Sona masoori* is a medium-grain rice. It is lightweight and aromatic and is considered to be healthier than regular rice, as it has less starch.

Kanchipuram Idlis

Spiced steamed rice dumplings

Kanchipuram, where this snack is popular, is a city in South India known for its resplendent silk saris that come in gorgeous colors and feature woven-gold borders. The steamed rice cakes have a color tinted by turmeric, and they have some crunch and texture from the *dal* and peppercorns. Serve the *idlis* with coconut cilantro chutney (page 520) and *sambhar* (page 32).

You'll need an *idli* steamer to make this (page 591).

Serves 4.

1 cup (200 grams) short-grain rice
½ cup (100 grams) *dhuli urad dal* (split skinless black gram)
¾ teaspoon fenugreek seeds
1 teaspoon ground turmeric
30 black peppercorns, coarsely crushed
2 teaspoons *chana dal* (split Bengal gram)
Pinch of asafetida
1 cup (250 grams) plain yogurt
½ cup (100 grams) ghee (page 37)
1 teaspoon table salt
A few tender banana leaves

1. Put the rice and *urad dal* in a bowl, wash in plenty of water 2 or 3 times, and drain. Add the fenugreek and 3 cups (600 ml) water, and soak for 3 to 4 hours. Drain and transfer to a food processor with ½ cup (100 ml) water. Process to a smooth paste of pouring consistency. Transfer to a large bowl.

2. Add the turmeric, peppercorns, *chana dal*, asafetida, yogurt, ghee, and salt. Stir well, cover, and set aside to ferment overnight.

3. Whisk the batter to aerate it and add ¼ cup (50 ml) water to adjust the consistency. It should be fairly thick.

4. Heat 3 to 4 cups (600 to 800 ml) water in a steamer.

5. Line the indentations in the *idli* trays with the banana leaves and pour the batter into them. Place in the steamer and steam for about 20 minutes or until cooked through.

6. Serve hot.

Kand Ke Pattice

····⋅⋅*{ **Purple yam and potato patties** }*·································

Kand, or purple yam, is an exotic tuber with a lovely smooth texture, which I capitalize on here in stuffed patties that are not only beautiful after you cut into them but also delicious. Serve them with sweetened yogurt or *pudina aur dhaniya* chutney (mint-and-cilantro chutney; page 22).

Serves 4.

2 medium purple yams, peeled and boiled
1 ¼ teaspoons table salt
7 tablespoons arrowroot powder
2 medium potatoes, cooked and peeled
½ cup (60 grams) grated fresh coconut (or frozen unsweetened coconut)
5 or 6 black peppercorns, crushed
7 or 8 cashews, finely chopped
2 green chiles, stemmed and chopped
½-inch (1-cm) piece fresh ginger, chopped
1 tablespoon raisins
1 tablespoon chopped fresh cilantro
½ cup (100 ml) vegetable oil

1. Grate the yams into a bowl. Add ½ teaspoon of the salt and 5 tablespoons (30 ml) of the arrowroot powder, and knead well. Divide into 8 portions.

2. Grate the potatoes into another bowl. Add ½ teaspoon of the salt and ½ tablespoon of the arrowroot powder, and knead well. Divide into 8 portions. Spread the remaining arrowroot powder on a plate.

3. Make the stuffing: Put the coconut in a third bowl. Add the peppercorns, cashews, chiles, ginger, raisins, and the remaining ¼ teaspoon salt, and combine well. Add the cilantro and combine well. Divide into 8 portions.

4. Take one portion of potato, roll lightly in the arrowroot powder, and spread it on your palm. Place a portion of the stuffing over the potato, gather the edges, and shape into a ball. Take a portion of the yam mixture, roll lightly in the arrowroot powder, and spread it on your palm. Place the stuffed potato ball in the center, gather the edges, and shape into a ball. Place the ball on a flat surface and gently flatten it into a 3-inch patty. Gently roll the sides so that they are even and smooth. Repeat with the remaining stuffing, potato, and yam mixtures. Note that you can make these in advance and refrigerate them until you are ready to cook and serve.

5. Sprinkle the remaining arrowroot powder over the patties.

6. Place a nonstick sauté pan over medium heat and add 1 tablespoon of the oil. When small bubbles appear at the bottom of the pan, add one patty and cook for 1 minute on each side, or until crisp and lightly browned. Remove with a slotted spoon and drain on paper towels. Repeat with the remaining patties and oil. Serve hot.

Kanda Bhajia

·····•⟨ **Crisp onion fritters** ⟩•··

Street food in Mumbai does not stop at *bhel puri* (page 84). In fact, one vendor may offer three or four different freshly made snacks. There is always a huge crowd waiting for these cooked fritters that, indeed, sell like hotcakes.

Makes 30.

4 large red onions, sliced
1 teaspoon table salt
¾ cup (75 grams) *besan* (chickpea/gram flour)
3 tablespoons rice flour
1½ teaspoons red chile powder
½ teaspoon ground roasted cumin (page 32)
1 teaspoon ground coriander
¼ teaspoon ground turmeric
½ teaspoon *ajwain*
2 tablespoons chopped fresh cilantro
1 quart (800 ml) vegetable oil

1. Put the onions in a bowl and toss with the salt. Set aside for 10 minutes.

2. Add the *besan*, rice flour, chile powder, cumin, coriander, turmeric, *ajwain*, and cilantro, and stir well.

3. Place a nonstick wok over high heat and add the oil. When small bubbles appear at the bottom of the wok, lower the heat to medium. Drop teaspoonfuls of the onion mixture into the hot oil, taking care not to crowd them. Cook, stirring occasionally with a slotted spoon, until golden brown and crisp. Remove with the slotted spoon and drain on paper towels.

4. Serve hot.

Kanda Poha

·······⊰ **Onions and pressed rice** ⊱···

When in Maharashtra, eat as the locals do: *Kanda poha* is an inexpensive, easy-to-prepare dish that is great for breakfast or as an afternoon snack. *Kanda* is the Marathi word for "onions," and *poha* is pressed rice (available at Indian grocery stores). You can add fresh pomegranate arils or corn kernels, you can omit the potato and peas, you can garnish this dish with thin chickpea-flour *sev*, you can serve it drizzled with ketchup . . . this is a very flexible recipe!

Serves 4.

3½ cups (400 grams) thick *poha* (pressed rice)
1½ teaspoons table salt
½ teaspoon sugar
1 quart (800 ml) plus ¼ cup (50 ml) vegetable oil
¼ cup (40 grams) raw peanuts
1 teaspoon brown mustard seeds
1 teaspoon cumin seeds
Pinch of asafetida
6 or 7 fresh curry leaves
4 medium red onions, chopped
6 green chiles, stemmed and chopped
½ teaspoon ground turmeric
¼ teaspoon red chile powder
1 medium potato, cut into ½-inch (1-cm) cubes
¼ cup (40 grams) blanched green peas (optional)
1 teaspoon freshly squeezed lemon juice
2 tablespoons chopped fresh cilantro

1. Put the *poha* in a colander and wash it under running water. The *poha* should be moist but not mashed. Drain well. Add the salt and sugar, and toss gently. Set aside.

2. Place a nonstick wok over high heat and add 1 quart (800 ml) of the oil. When small bubbles appear at the bottom of the wok, lower the heat to medium and add the peanuts. Cook for 3 to 4 minutes or until lightly browned and crisp. Remove with a slotted spoon and drain on paper towels.

3. Place a nonstick sauté pan over medium heat and add the remaining oil. When small bubbles appear at the bottom of the pan, add the mustard seeds. When they begin to sputter, add the cumin, asafetida, and curry leaves, and sauté for 30 seconds.

4. Add the onions and sauté for 8 minutes or until the onions are lightly browned.

5. Add the chiles and sauté for 30 seconds. Add the turmeric and chile powder, and stir well. Add the potato and stir. Cook for 7 minutes or until the potato is tender.

6. Add the peanuts and peas, and stir. Add the *poha* and stir gently. Lower the heat to low, cover, and cook for 7 minutes or until the *poha* is heated through.

7. Add the lemon juice and stir gently.

8. Transfer the *poha* to a serving bowl, garnish with the cilantro, and serve hot.

Kanji Bada

······⟨ Lentil dumplings soaked in sour water ⟩·······················

I have eaten this dish so many times, and yet whenever it is served to me, I wonder if it is a drink or a snack. Whichever way you look at it, this is a sour preparation that really whets the appetite. The *badas* are made of lentils ground with spices, shaped into small balls, and deep-fried. They are then soaked in *kanji*, a fermented water spiced with ground mustard and red chile powder.

Serves 4.

~ **For the *kanji*:**
1½ tablespoons black mustard seeds, coarsely ground
½ teaspoon red chile powder
1½ teaspoons black salt

~ **For the *badas*:**
½ cup plus 2 tablespoons (125 grams) *dhuli moong dal* (split skinless green gram)
⅛ teaspoon asafetida
½ teaspoon coriander seeds, coarsely ground
½ teaspoon fennel seeds, coarsely ground
½ teaspoon fresh green chile paste (page 13)
1½ tablespoons chopped fresh cilantro
Pinch of baking powder
¾ teaspoon table salt
8 black peppercorns, crushed
1 quart (800 ml) vegetable oil

1. Make the *kanji*: Combine the mustard seeds, chile powder, and black salt in a large bowl. Add 2½ cups (500 ml) water and stir well. Cover and set aside for about 2 days to ferment. Taste to see if it has turned sour. When the water is sour, put it in the refrigerator.

2. Make the *badas*: Put the *dal* in a bowl, wash in plenty of water 2 or 3 times, and drain. Add 1½ cups (300 ml) water and soak for 3 hours. Drain the *dal* and put in a spice grinder. Grind to a smooth paste without adding any extra water.

3. Transfer the paste to a large bowl. Add the asafetida, coriander, fennel, chile paste, cilantro, baking powder, salt, and peppercorns, and stir well. Whisk the batter with your hands for 10 to 15 minutes to make it light.

4. Place a nonstick wok over high heat and add the oil. When small bubbles appear at the bottom of the wok, drop the batter, a tablespoon at a time, into the hot oil. Cook over medium heat until golden brown, turning frequently with a slotted spoon. Remove with the slotted spoon and drain on paper towels. Let the *badas* cool completely.

5. Soak the *badas* in 1½ cups (300 ml) plain water for 5 minutes. Squeeze gently, then submerge them in the *kanji*. Cover the bowl with the lid and chill in the refrigerator for at least 2 hours. Serve cold.

Kasoori Paneer Tikka

·····❧ *Paneer* marinated in spicy yogurt and grilled ❧·····

Dried fenugreek leaves, called *kasoori methi*, are believed to have first been used in a province in Pakistan, and perhaps this is where the versatile herb gets its name. In India, it is inexpensive and a must-have for the spice shelf. Roast it and crush it to release the maximum flavor. It is best added during the last stages of cooking. It marries well with onions, tomatoes, chicken, cream, and *paneer*.

Serves 4.

9 ounces (250 grams) *paneer* (pressed fresh cheese; page 17)
1 medium green bell pepper, seeded
1 medium red onion
1 medium tomato, seeded
1 cup (250 grams) plain yogurt
2 tablespoons *pudina aur dhaniya* chutney (mint-and-cilantro chutney; page 22)
1 teaspoon fresh green chile paste (page 13)
1 teaspoon fresh ginger paste (page 12)
1 teaspoon fresh garlic paste (page 12)
¼ teaspoon ground turmeric
1 teaspoon *garam masala* (spice mix; page 27)
1 teaspoon *chaat masala* (spice mix for *chaat*; page 24)
2 tablespoons *kasoori methi* (dried fenugreek leaves), roasted and crushed
2 tablespoons roasted *chana dal*, finely ground
¼ cup (50 ml) heavy cream
1 teaspoon table salt
2 tablespoons filtered mustard oil (see Note page 87)
2 tablespoons vegetable oil
2 tablespoons freshly squeezed lemon juice

1. Cut the *paneer*, bell pepper, onion, and tomato into 1½-inch (4-cm) pieces. Separate the layers of the onion pieces.

2. Stir together the yogurt, chutney, chile paste, ginger paste, garlic paste, turmeric, *garam masala*, ½ teaspoon of the *chaat masala*, the *kasoori methi*, *dal*, cream, and salt in a large bowl. Add the *paneer* and stir gently. Let marinate for about 15 minutes.

3. Put the mustard oil in a nonstick wok and place over medium heat. When it begins to smoke, remove from the heat and let cool completely. Stir the mustard oil into the *paneer*.

4. Soak a few wooden skewers in water for 15 minutes.

5. Thread the bell pepper, *paneer*, tomato, and onion onto the skewers.

6. Place a nonstick sauté pan over medium heat and add the vegetable oil. When small bubbles appear at the bottom of the pan, place the skewers on it and cook, turning a few times so that the *tikkas* cook evenly on all sides until the *paneer* is golden.

7. Arrange on a plate, sprinkle with the remaining ½ teaspoon *chaat masala* and the lemon juice, and serve immediately.

Khakhra

······❄{ **Crisp flatbreads** }❄···

In a typical Gujarati home, leftover *rotis* (griddle breads) are roasted until crisp to make *khakhra*. Today these are commercially available in many flavors. I always keep a snack box full of *khakhras* in my office to munch on. They make a great snack instead of potato chips.

Makes 15.

2 cups (150 grams) *atta* (whole-wheat flour)
1 teaspoon table salt
2 teaspoons crushed *kasoori methi* (dried fenugreek leaves)
About 5 tablespoons vegetable oil

1. Put the flour and salt in a deep bowl. Add the *kasoori methi* and 3 tablespoons of the oil. Add 1 cup (200 ml) water and knead to make a stiff dough. Cover with a double layer of damp cheesecloth and let rest for 15 minutes.

2. Divide the dough into 15 equal portions and shape into balls. Roll out into thin 6-inch (15-cm) rounds, using a few drops of oil on the rolling pin to ease the rolling, as the dough tends to be sticky.

3. Place a nonstick griddle over low heat. After 2 minutes, place 1 dough round on it and cook over low heat, holding it down for 30 seconds at a time using a potato masher. (In India they use a wooden press, but a masher will work well.) Turn the round over and cook using the pressure of the masher. At this stage it helps to drizzle a few drops of oil around the edges of the dough. Cook until crisp, with tiny brown flecks on both sides.

4. Let cool to room temperature, then store in an airtight container for up to 4 weeks.

······⦊ **Chef's tip** ⦉······ *Khakhras* can be made with different flavors—garlic, *pav bhaji masala*, *chaat masala*, fresh fenugreek leaves, fresh spinach leaves, tomato, and so on.

Khaman Dhokla

······⦊ Fermented *besan* batter, steamed and tempered ⦉······

When it comes to choosing my favorite Gujarati snack, I would put this one right after *khandvi* (page 131). When I married Alyona, she introduced me to these savories from her home state.

Serves 4.

1 cup (100 grams) *besan* (chickpea/gram flour)
½ cup (125 grams) plain yogurt, whisked
1 teaspoon table salt
1 green chile, stemmed and chopped
¾-inch (1½-cm) piece fresh ginger, chopped
¼ teaspoon ground turmeric
1 tablespoon vegetable oil
½ teaspoon baking soda
½ tablespoon freshly squeezed lemon juice
½ teaspoon brown mustard seeds
1 tablespoon chopped fresh cilantro
2 tablespoons scraped fresh coconut

1. Put the *besan* in a bowl. Add the yogurt and 6 tablespoons warm water and whisk well so that there are no lumps. The mixture should have a slightly thick consistency. Add the salt, stir, and cover the bowl with a lid. Set aside to ferment for 3 to 4 hours.

2. Put the chiles, ginger, and 1 tablespoon water in a spice grinder, and grind to a paste.

3. To the *besan* mixture, add the turmeric and chile-ginger paste, and stir well.

4. Place a steamer over high heat and add 2 cups (400 ml) water. Grease a *dhokla* plate or a shallow cake pan with 1 teaspoon of the oil.

5. Stir the baking soda, 1 teaspoon of the oil, and the lemon juice together in a small bowl. Add to the *besan* mixture and whisk briskly.

6. Pour the batter into the greased plate or cake pan and place it in the steamer. Cover and steam for 10 to 12 minutes or until a skewer inserted in the center of the cake comes out clean.

7. Remove the plate or cake pan from the steamer and set aside to cool slightly. Cut the cake into 1½-inch (4-cm) squares and place these *dhoklas* in a serving bowl or plate.

8. Place a small nonstick sauté pan over medium heat and add the remaining 2 teaspoons oil. When small bubbles appear at the bottom of the pan, add the mustard seeds. When the seeds begin to sputter, remove from the heat and pour over the *dhoklas*.

9. Garnish with the cilantro and coconut, and serve warm.

Khandvi

······ ❋❵ *Besan* roll-ups ❴❋ ···

This is a delicious, beautiful, bright yellow savory roll-up dish from Gujarat, in the western part of India. I learned to make this dish from my wife, who makes it better than anyone I know. Making *khandvi* is an art: It takes some practice to know when the *besan* batter is cooked to the correct consistency. The roll-ups can be refrigerated for 4 to 6 hours before the tempering and garnishes are added, but are best served immediately.

Serves 4.

1¼ cups (125 grams) *besan* (chickpea/gram flour)
1-inch (2½-cm) piece fresh ginger, chopped
2 green chiles, stemmed and halved
¼ cup (50 ml) vegetable oil
½ cup (125 grams) plain yogurt
½ teaspoon table salt
½ teaspoon ground turmeric
1 tablespoon freshly squeezed lemon juice
Pinch of asafetida
1 teaspoon black mustard seeds
2 tablespoons grated fresh coconut (or frozen unsweetened coconut)
2 tablespoons chopped fresh cilantro

1. Sift the *besan* into a deep bowl and set aside.

2. Put the ginger and the chiles in a spice grinder with 1 teaspoon water, and grind to a smooth paste.

3. Using 1 tablespoon of the oil for each, grease the reverse sides of 2 large stainless-steel *thalis* (plates). Instead, you may grease a marble tabletop.

4. Put the yogurt in a small bowl and add ½ cup (100 ml) water. Whisk until smooth. Set aside.

5. Add the ginger-chile paste to the *besan* along with the salt, turmeric, lemon juice, yogurt mixture, and asafetida. Whisk to make a smooth batter with no lumps.

6. Pour the *besan* mixture into a large nonstick sauté pan. Place it over medium heat and cook for 5 to 8 minutes, stirring continuously, then lower the heat to low. Cook, stirring continuously, for 8 minutes or until the mixture is thick. To check if the batter is cooked, take about ½ teaspoonful of it and spread it thinly on the oiled surface. Let it cool for 1 minute. Then lift it off the surface by rolling it up. If the batter comes off the surface it means that it is cooked enough.

7. Remove from the heat and, working quickly, spread half of the batter over the greased reverse side of one *thali* and the remaining half over the other *thali*, as thinly as possible, while the batter is still hot. Let cool completely.

8. Cut into strips 2 inches wide and roll them up tightly. Pick up each roll gently and place in a serving dish.

9. Place a small nonstick sauté pan over medium heat and add the remaining 2 tablespoons oil. When small bubbles begin to appear at the bottom of the pan, add the mustard seeds. When they sputter, pour this tempering over the rolled-up pieces.

10. Sprinkle with the coconut and cilantro, and serve immediately.

Khubani Ke Shammi

······⟨ **Apricot-stuffed potatoes** ⟩······

These kebabs have a soft heart because of the stuffing in the center. The chiles and pepper balance the sweetness of the apricot.

Makes 12.

¼ cup (50 grams) dried apricots
¼ cup (50 grams) *khoya/mawa* (unsweetened solid condensed milk; page 37), crumbled
¼ cup (50 ml) plus 2 teaspoons vegetable oil
1 teaspoon cumin seeds
½-inch (1-cm) piece fresh ginger, chopped
3 green chiles, stemmed and chopped
1 teaspoon *garam masala* (spice mix; page 27)
¼ teaspoon ground black pepper
3 tablespoons chopped fresh cilantro
1 teaspoon table salt
4 medium potatoes, boiled, peeled, and mashed
¼ cup cornstarch

1. Soak the apricots in 1 cup (200 ml) water for 1 hour. Drain and finely chop. Transfer to a bowl, add the *khoya*, and stir.

2. Place a shallow nonstick sauté pan over medium heat and add 2 teaspoons of the oil. When small bubbles appear at the bottom of the pan, add the cumin. When it begins to change color, add the ginger, chiles, *garam masala*, and pepper. Stir well and remove from the heat. Set aside to cool.

3. Add the ginger-chile mixture to the apricot-*khoya* mixture. Add the cilantro and ½ teaspoon of the salt, and stir well. Divide into 12 portions.

4. Put the mashed potatoes in another bowl. Add the remaining ½ teaspoon salt and stir well. Divide into 12 portions.

5. Roll each portion of potato into a ball and flatten into a round disk. Place a portion of apricot-*khoya* mixture in the center, gather the edges to enclose the filling, and seal well. Gently roll into a ball again and flatten slightly.

6. Put the cornstarch on a plate and roll the kebabs in it. Shake off the excess and set aside on another plate.

7. Place a nonstick sauté pan over medium heat and add the remaining ¼ cup (50 ml) oil. When small bubbles appear at the bottom of the pan, gently slide in the kebabs, a few at a time, and cook, turning continuously, for 4 to 5 minutes or until golden brown on both sides.

8. Serve hot.

Lehsuni Tandoori Aloo

······· *❊{ **Crisp stuffed potatoes** }❊* ··

This recipe may seem a little elaborate on first reading, but the actual preparation is quite simple. This unusual, beautifully presented vegetarian dish is very popular in my Yellow Chilli restaurants.

Serves 6.

~ For the potato shells and filling:
8 small potatoes
1 quart (800 ml) plus 2 tablespoons vegetable oil
1 teaspoon caraway seeds
10 to 12 cloves garlic, chopped
1 medium red onion, chopped
1 teaspoon table salt
1-inch (2½-cm) piece fresh ginger, chopped
3 green chiles, stemmed and chopped
4 ounces (100 grams) *paneer* (pressed fresh cheese; page 17), grated
½ cup (40 grams) grated mild white cheese
2 tablespoons chopped fresh cilantro

~ For the marinade:
1 cup (275 grams) plain Greek yogurt
2 teaspoons fresh ginger paste (page 12)
2½ teaspoons fresh garlic paste (page 12)
2 tablespoons freshly squeezed lemon juice
1 teaspoon table salt
1 tablespoon red chile powder
2 teaspoons *garam masala* (spice mix; page 27)
¼ cup (35 grams) ground *dalia* (roasted *chana dal*, store-bought)
1 tablespoon filtered mustard oil (see Note page 87)

~ For baking and serving:
2 tablespoons vegetable oil
Melted butter for basting
2 teaspoons *chaat masala* (spice mix for *chaat*; page 24)

1. Make the potato shells and filling: Peel the potatoes. With a sharp knife or the peeler, scoop out the flesh from the center of one side of each potato to make a hollow. Mince the trimmings.

2. Place a nonstick wok over high heat and add 1 quart (800 ml) of the vegetable oil. When small bubbles appear at the bottom of the wok, lower the heat to medium, add the hollowed potatoes, and cook, stirring occasionally with a slotted spoon, for 3 minutes or until lightly browned. Remove with the slotted spoon and drain on paper towels.

3. Place a nonstick sauté pan over medium heat and add the remaining 2 tablespoons oil. When small bubbles appear at the bottom of the pan, add the caraway, garlic, and onion, and sauté for 2 to 3 minutes.

4. Add the chopped potato trimmings and sauté for 8 minutes. Add the salt and stir well.

5. Add the ginger and chiles, and cook for 2 minutes. Remove from the heat and transfer the mixture to a bowl.

6. Add the *paneer*, cheese, and cilantro. Stir well and set aside.

7. Make the marinade: Combine the yogurt, ginger paste, garlic paste, lemon juice, salt, chile powder, *garam masala*, *dalia*, and mustard oil in a large bowl.

8. Bake and serve the potatoes: Preheat the oven to 425°F/220°C. Grease a baking sheet with 1 tablespoon of the oil.

9. Stuff the filling into the hollowed potatoes. Put the stuffed potatoes in the marinade and turn to coat them well on all sides.

10. Place them upright on the baking sheet. Drizzle with the remaining 1 tablespoon oil and bake in the preheated oven for about 15 minutes.

11. Baste with butter and bake for 5 minutes.

12. Halve each potato and place on a serving platter. Sprinkle with the *chaat masala* and serve hot.

Makai, Badam, Aur Akhrot Ki Tikki

······❈⟩ Corn, almond, and walnut patties ⟨❈·······

Hyderabadi food is the royal cuisine of India—and royalty indulges in rich foods. This probably explains the nuts and cheese in this dish, and also the exotic lotus root and sweet corn. It takes time to prepare and assemble all the ingredients, but the payoff is worth it! Serve the patties accompanied by *pudina aur dhaniya* chutney (mint-and-cilantro chutney; page 22).

Makes 20.

7 ounces (200 grams) canned lotus root (see Note)
1½ cups (225 grams) fresh or canned corn kernels
20 almonds, blanched and peeled (page 40)
About 2 cups (400 ml) vegetable oil
1 teaspoon caraway seeds
1 teaspoon red chile powder
1 teaspoon ground black pepper
1 teaspoon ground fennel
1 teaspoon *garam masala* (spice mix; page 27)
1 teaspoon *chaat masala* (spice mix for *chaat*; page 24)
3½ ounces (100 grams) *paneer* (pressed fresh cheese; page 17), grated
1 teaspoon table salt
½ cup (40 grams) grated mild white cheddar cheese
1 tablespoon freshly squeezed lemon juice
1-inch (2½-cm) piece fresh ginger, chopped
2 tablespoons chopped fresh cilantro
16 walnut halves, chopped
24 raisins, chopped

1. Drain the lotus root, transfer to a food processor, and process to a paste. Set aside in a bowl.

2. Drain the corn if using canned, transfer to the processor, and process to a paste. Set aside in a bowl.

3. Put the almonds in the food processor, process to a paste, and set aside.

4. Place a nonstick wok over medium heat and add 2 tablespoons of the oil. When small bubbles appear at the bottom of the wok, add the caraway and sauté for 30 seconds or until fragrant. Add the lotus root paste, corn paste, and almond paste, and sauté for 10 minutes or until the mixture is very thick.

5. Add the chile powder, pepper, fennel, *garam masala*, and *chaat masala*, and stir well. Add the *paneer* and salt, and stir well. Cook until the mixture leaves the sides of the wok and looks well combined.

6. Remove from the heat, and add the cheddar cheese, lemon juice, ginger, and cilantro. Let cool.

7. Divide the mixture into 20 portions and shape into smooth balls. Stuff the balls with walnuts and raisins and roll into balls again. Flatten them slightly into patties.

8. Place a large nonstick sauté pan over medium heat and add 2 to 3 tablespoons of the oil. When small bubbles appear at the bottom of the pan, place 4 patties in the pan and cook for 3 to 4 minutes or until the undersides are lightly golden. Turn with a spatula and drizzle some more oil around the edges of the patties. Cook for 3 to 4 minutes or until the other side is lightly golden. Drain on paper towels. Repeat with the remaining patties.

9. Serve immediately.

> **Note** If using fresh lotus roots, clean them thoroughly by scrubbing them well under running water. Peel them and then chop roughly. Boil in 2 cups (400 ml) water in a nonstick saucepan over medium heat for 10 minutes or until soft. Drain and let cool.

Masala Dosas

Lentil and rice pancakes stuffed with spicy potatoes

This has got to be one of the most popular snacks in India, and I think that learning to make this dish is the perfect introduction to South Indian cuisine. Don't be intimidated, because the *dosas* take some practice to get right: The key lies in the proper seasoning of the griddle. Often the first couple of *dosas* don't work out, so keep trying—the rest will likely go more smoothly. Serve with coconut cilantro chutney (page 520) and *sambhar* (page 32).

Makes 8.

~ **For the *dosa* batter:**
1 cup plus 5 tablespoons (275 grams) parboiled rice
2 tablespoons raw short-grain rice
½ cup (100 grams) *dhuli urad dal* (split skinless black gram)
½ teaspoon fenugreek seeds (optional)
1¼ teaspoons table salt
4 teaspoons vegetable oil

~ **For the potato *bhaji*:**
¼ cup (50 ml) vegetable oil
1 teaspoon black mustard seeds
½ teaspoon asafetida
2 teaspoons *chana dal* (split Bengal gram)
4 green chiles, stemmed and chopped
15 fresh curry leaves
2 large red onions, chopped
6 large potatoes, boiled, peeled, and cubed
1 teaspoon ground turmeric
2 teaspoons table salt
¼ cup (15 grams) chopped fresh cilantro
2 tablespoons freshly squeezed lemon juice

1. Make the *dosa* batter: Put the parboiled and raw rices in a bowl, wash in plenty of water 2 or 3 times, and drain. Add 3 cups (600 ml) water and soak for at least 4 hours. Wash the *dal* and fenugreek seeds, and soak in 1½ cups (300 ml) water for 4 hours.

2. Drain the rices and *dal* separately. Put the rices in a food processor with 1½ cups (300 ml) water and process until smooth. Transfer to a large bowl. Put the *dal* and fenugreek in the food processor with ¼ cup (50 ml) water and grind to a smooth paste. Add to the rice paste.

3. Add the salt and stir the batter thoroughly with your hand in a whipping motion to aerate the mixture. Cover the bowl tightly and set aside to ferment for 6 hours or up to overnight.

4. Make the potato *bhaji*: Place a nonstick wok over medium heat and add the oil. When small bubbles appear at the bottom of the wok, add the mustard seeds. When the seeds begin to sputter, add the asafetida and *dal*, and sauté until lightly browned. Add the chiles, curry leaves, and onions, and sauté until the onions are lightly browned. Add the potatoes, turmeric, and salt. Stir well. Sprinkle with 2 tablespoons water and cook until the potatoes are heated through. Add the cilantro and lemon juice, and stir well.

5. Place a flat nonstick griddle over medium heat and grease with a little oil. Pour in a ladleful of batter and spread the *dosa* batter as thinly as possible.

6. Pour ½ teaspoon oil around the *dosa* and cook until crisp on the edges and golden brown. Repeat with the remaining batter and oil.

7. Place about 4 tablespoons of the potato *bhaji* in the center of the *dosa*, fold the two ends over the *bhaji*, and serve immediately.

Medu Wadas

······*{ **Savory doughnuts** }···

We rarely deep-fry at our home, but the desire for these crisp yet spongy lentil fritters makes us get the wok out! In Bangalore restaurants, *medu wadas* are served for breakfast alongside soft *idlis* (page 120), all dunked in fragrant *sambhar* (page 32) and accompanied with coconut cilantro chutney (page 520). To get the spongiest *wadas* possible, it is important to make the paste without adding water and to whisk it well in order to aerate it before frying.

Serves 4.

½ cup (100 grams) *dhuli urad dal* (split skinless black gram)
1½ teaspoons table salt
¼ teaspoon asafetida
8 to 10 fresh curry leaves, chopped
3 green chiles, stemmed and chopped
1 tablespoon chopped fresh cilantro
1 quart (800 ml) vegetable oil

1. Put the *dal* in a bowl, wash in plenty of water 2 or 3 times, and drain. Add 2 cups (400 ml) water and soak for 3 to 4 hours. Drain well.

2. Put the *dal* in a food processor. Add the salt, asafetida, curry leaves, green chiles, and ¼ cup (50 ml) water, and process to a thick, smooth paste.

3. Transfer the paste to a bowl. Add the cilantro and stir well.

4. Place a nonstick wok over high heat and add the oil. When small bubbles appear at the bottom of the wok, lower the heat to medium.

5. Dampen your palms and take a little of the paste in one palm. Shape into a ball and make a hole in the center with your thumb (like a doughnut). Repeat with the remaining paste.

6. Gently lower these *wadas*, a few at a time, into the hot oil and cook, turning frequently with a slotted spoon, until crisp and golden brown. Remove with the slotted spoon and drain on paper towels.

7. Serve hot.

······*{ **Chef's tip** }·* The *wadas* should not be fried over high heat or they will brown on the outside but remain uncooked inside. They should be crisp on the outside and cooked and fluffy inside.

Mirchi Bhajiya

········· Batter-fried stuffed green chiles ·········

Here is the key to this recipe: Remove the seeds and white pith inside the chiles, for that innocuous little white fleshy part is even hotter than the seeds. This simple step will tame the chile and make it more palate-friendly.

Makes 8.

¾ cup (75 grams) *besan* (chickpea/gram flour)
¾ teaspoon baking powder
¼ teaspoon asafetida
¾ teaspoon red chile powder
1½ teaspoons table salt
1 quart (800 ml) vegetable oil
½ teaspoon brown mustard seeds
4 or 5 cloves garlic, crushed
¼ teaspoon ground turmeric
2 large potatoes, boiled, peeled, and mashed
8 large green chiles, slit and seeded

1. Put the *besan*, baking powder, asafetida, chile powder, ¾ teaspoon of the salt, and 1 cup (200 ml) water in a large bowl and whisk well to make a smooth batter. Set the batter aside for about 10 minutes.

2. Place a medium nonstick sauté pan over medium heat and add 1 tablespoon of the oil. When small bubbles appear at the bottom of the pan, add the mustard seeds. When they begin to sputter, add the garlic and sauté over medium heat until fragrant. Add the turmeric and mashed potatoes and stir well. Add the remaining ¾ teaspoon salt and stir. Remove from the heat and set aside to cool.

3. Divide the mixture into 8 portions and stuff each portion into a slit chile.

4. Place a nonstick wok over high heat and add the remaining oil. When small bubbles appear at the bottom of the wok, lower the heat to medium. Dip each chile in the batter and gently slide it into the hot oil. Cook 4 chiles at a time, turning with a slotted spoon a few times, for 4 to 5 minutes or until golden and crisp. Remove with the slotted spoon and drain on paper towels.

5. Serve immediately.

Mysore Masala Dosas

······{ Crisp and spicy rice pancakes, Mysore style }···

In this recipe, a thin pancake of lightly fermented rice batter is stuffed with a garlicky red chutney and potato *bhaji* (spiced mashed potatoes). While there is no dearth of *dosa* variations in the traditional regional cuisines of India, modern twists on the classic *dosa*-chutney-vegetable combination are showing up in urban eateries, where you'll find concoctions like American chop suey *dosa* and Chinese chow mein *dosa*.

Makes 8.

~ For the *dosa* batter:
1 cup plus 5 tablespoons (275 grams) parboiled rice
2 tablespoons raw short-grain rice
½ cup (100 grams) *dhuli urad dal* (split skinless black gram)
½ teaspoon fenugreek seeds (optional)
1¼ teaspoons table salt

~ For the red chutney:
½ cup (100 grams) roasted *chana dal* (split Bengal gram)
8 cloves garlic
5 or 6 dried red chiles, stemmed and broken
1 tablespoon freshly squeezed lemon juice
½ teaspoon table salt

~ For the potato *bhaji*:
2 tablespoons vegetable oil
½ teaspoon brown mustard seeds
¼ teaspoon asafetida
1 teaspoon *chana dal* (split Bengal gram)
2 green chiles, stemmed and chopped
8 fresh curry leaves
1 large red onion, chopped
3 small potatoes, boiled, peeled, and cubed
½ teaspoon ground turmeric
1 teaspoon table salt
2 tablespoons chopped fresh cilantro
1 tablespoon freshly squeezed lemon juice

~ **For cooking and serving:**
1 cup (200 ml) vegetable oil
2 medium red onions, chopped
1 large green bell pepper, seeded and chopped
2 large tomatoes, chopped
1 teaspoon red chile powder
2 teaspoons *chaat masala* **(spice mix for** *chaat*; **page 24)**
¼ cup (60 grams) butter

1. Make the *dosa* batter: Put the parboiled and raw rices in a bowl, wash in plenty of water 2 or 3 times, and drain. Add 3 cups (600 ml) water and soak for at least 4 and up to 8 hours. In a separate bowl, wash the *dal* and fenugreek (if using), drain, and soak in 1½ cups (300 ml) water for 4 hours.

2. Drain the rice and *dal* separately. Put the rice in a food processor with 1½ cups (300 ml) water and process until smooth. Transfer to a large bowl. Transfer the *dal* and fenugreek to the food processor with ¼ cup (50 ml) water, and process to a smooth paste. Add to the rice paste.

3. Add the salt and stir well with your hand in a whisking motion to aerate the batter. Cover the bowl tightly and set aside to ferment for 6 hours or up to overnight.

4. Make the red chutney: Put the *dal*, garlic, red chiles, lemon juice, salt, and cumin in a spice grinder, and grind to a smooth paste. Transfer to a bowl and set aside.

5. Make the potato *bhaji*: Place a nonstick wok over medium heat and add the oil. When small bubbles appear at the bottom of the wok, add the mustard seeds. When the seeds begin to sputter, add the asafetida and *chana dal*, and sauté until lightly browned.

6. Add the chiles, curry leaves, and onions, and sauté until the onions are lightly browned. Add the potatoes, turmeric, and salt. Stir well. Sprinkle with 2 tablespoons water and cook until the potatoes are heated through. Add the cilantro and lemon juice, and stir well.

7. Place a nonstick griddle over medium heat. Drizzle 2 or 3 drops of oil on the griddle, then wipe it clean with a cloth. Let the griddle heat for 2 to 3 minutes over medium heat.

8. Pour a small ladleful of the batter onto the griddle and spread evenly with the back of the ladle to make an 8-inch *dosa*. Drizzle ½ teaspoon oil around the *dosa* and cook over low heat for 30 seconds.

9. Spread 1 teaspoon of the chutney over the *dosa*. Put some of the potato *bhaji* in the center of the *dosa* and top with some of the onions, bell peppers, and tomatoes. Sprinkle ⅛ teaspoon of the chile powder and ½ teaspoon of the *chaat masala* over the potato mixture and stir gently. Drop ½ tablespoon of the butter over the potato mixture and stir and mash lightly with a potato masher, taking care not to damage the *dosa*. Spread the mixture over the *dosa*.

10. Cook the *dosa* over low heat until the underside is golden and crisp.

11. Gently fold over one side of the *dosa* and transfer it to a serving plate. Repeat with the remaining batter and filling. Cut into pieces and serve immediately.

Namakpara

These salty biscuits are served at teatime in India. Traditionally they are deep-fried, but I present a healthier alternative here.

Serves 4.

½ cup (75 grams) *atta* (whole-wheat flour)
½ cup (60 grams) *maida* (refined flour) or pastry flour, plus extra for dusting
½ teaspoon baking powder
3 tablespoons ghee (page 37), softened
¾ teaspoon table salt
½ teaspoon *ajwain*, crushed
Vegetable oil for greasing the baking sheet

1. Put the two flours and baking powder in a bowl, and stir to combine. Add the ghee and rub it in with your fingertips until the mixture resembles bread crumbs.

2. Add the salt and *ajwain*. Add ¼ cup plus 2 tablespoons (80 ml) cold water and knead to make a stiff dough. Cover the dough and let it rest for 15 minutes.

3. Sprinkle some flour on a flat surface and roll out the dough into a ¼-inch-thick (½-cm-thick) disk.

4. Preheat the oven to 400°F/200°C. Grease a baking sheet with a little oil and sprinkle some more flour on it.

5. Cut the dough into diamond-shaped pieces. Place them on the baking sheet and bake in the middle of the oven for 15 to 20 minutes.

6. Let cool to room temperature before serving, or store in an airtight container for up to 7 days.

······❳ **Chef's tip** ❲❋ To fry the biscuits, heat 1 quart (800 ml) oil in a nonstick wok. When small bubbles appear at the bottom of the wok, slide in the diamond-shaped dough pieces and cook until golden brown. Remove with a slotted spoon, drain on paper towels until cool, and serve.

Palak Dhoklas

····· ⦕ Steamed spinach pancakes ⦖ ···

My mother-in-law, who lives in Pune, in the state of Maharashtra, is an innovative cook; this is her recipe. I often visit Pune for work, and I love to stop by my in-laws' house to see them and try all of my mother-in-law's tasty treats.

You will need a special *dhokla* steamer for this (see Note page 164 for details). Serve these *dhoklas* with chutney.

Serves 4.

1 cup (200 grams) *toor dal/arhar dal* (split pigeon peas)
2 cups (500 grams) plain yogurt
1 pound (450 grams) fresh spinach leaves
3 green chiles, stemmed and chopped
1 teaspoon table salt
1 teaspoon sugar
¼ teaspoon asafetida
1 teaspoon fruit salt (such as Eno brand, or use baking soda)
1 tablespoon freshly squeezed lemon juice
2 teaspoons vegetable oil, plus more for greasing the steamer plates

1. Place the *dal* in a bowl, wash in plenty of water 1 or 2 times, and drain. Add 3 cups (600 ml) water and soak for 4 to 6 hours. Drain and place in a food processor with the yogurt. Process to a smooth paste. Transfer to a large bowl.

2. Thoroughly wash the spinach leaves under running water and drain well.

3. Place a nonstick saucepan over high heat and add 1 quart (800 ml) water. When it comes to a rapid boil, add the spinach and cook for 1 minute. Drain in a colander and refresh under running water. Let drain for 30 minutes. Chop coarsely and put in a food processor. Process to a paste and add to the *dal*.

4. Add the chiles, table salt, sugar, and asafetida, and stir well.

5. Grease the *dhokla* steamer plates with oil. Heat 2 cups (400 ml) water in the steamer pot.

6. Stir the fruit salt and lemon juice together, add the mixture to the batter, and stir. Add 2 teaspoons oil and stir.

7. Pour the batter into the plates, fit them on the stand, and place the stand in the steamer. Cover and steam for 15 minutes or until the moisture has dried and the mixture has cooked through.

8. Let cool slightly, cut into pieces, and serve.

Palak Ke Pakora

Batter-fried spinach leaves

Pakoras are fritters that know no boundaries. If it's a vegetable, you can make a *pakora* out of it. Slice it, dip it in a batter of chickpea flour, and then deep-fry it.

I first tasted these spinach *pakoras* at my sister's house. She would painstakingly pick up one leaf at a time, dip it in the batter, and fry it.

Makes 16.

16 fresh spinach leaves with stems
2 cups (200 grams) *besan* (chickpea/gram flour)
½ teaspoon table salt
1 teaspoon red chile powder
¼ teaspoon ground turmeric
1 teaspoon fresh green chile paste (page 13)
½ teaspoon *ajwain*
Pinch of asafetida
1 quart (800 ml) vegetable oil

1. Pat the spinach dry.

2. Put the *besan* in a bowl and add the salt, chile powder, turmeric, chile paste, *ajwain*, and asafetida. Add 1 cup (200 ml) water and whisk well to make a thin batter without any lumps.

3. Place a nonstick wok over high heat and add the oil. When small bubbles appear at the bottom of the wok, lower the heat to medium. Dip each spinach leaf in the batter and gently slide it into the hot oil, two or three at a time. Cook, turning with a slotted spoon a few times, for 5 minutes or until golden brown and crisp. Remove with the slotted spoon and drain on paper towels.

4. Serve immediately.

Paneer Chutney Pakora

········•⟨ Spicy batter-fried *paneer* ⟩•········

The effort in assembling this *pakora* (fritter) is worth it. Make these in large quantities when you have your friends over because they will disappear fast. If you'd like, you can replace the green chutney used here with chile garlic chutney (page 519).

Makes 20.

9 ounces (250 grams) *paneer* (pressed fresh cheese; page 17)
1 medium bunch fresh cilantro
1 medium bunch fresh mint
6 green chiles, stemmed
½-inch (1-cm) piece fresh ginger, peeled
2 cloves garlic
2 tablespoons freshly squeezed lemon juice
1½ teaspoons table salt
1 cup (200 grams) *besan* (chickpea/gram flour)
¼ teaspoon ground turmeric
1 to 2 dried red chiles, stemmed and crushed
1 quart (800 ml) vegetable oil
1 teaspoon red chile powder
2 teaspoons *chaat masala* (spice mix for *chaat*; page 24)

1. Cut the *paneer* into 1-inch (2½-cm) cubes.

2. Roughly chop the cilantro, mint, 4 of the green chiles, half of the ginger, and 1 clove of garlic. Put them in a food processor with 1 tablespoon of the lemon juice and 1 teaspoon of the salt, and process to make a smooth chutney.

3. Separately process the remaining ginger, garlic, and 2 green chiles to a smooth paste.

4. Put the *besan*, turmeric, red chiles, ginger-garlic–green chile paste, and the remaining ½ teaspoon salt in a large bowl. Add the remaining 1 tablespoon lemon juice and 1 tablespoon of the oil, and stir. Add ½ cup (100 ml) water to make a thick batter. Set aside.

5. Spread the chutney on either side of the *paneer* pieces.

6. Place a nonstick wok over high heat and add the remaining oil. When small bubbles appear at the bottom of the wok, lower the heat to medium. Dip the *paneer* in the batter and gently slide them into the hot oil, one or two at a time. Cook, turning with a slotted spoon a few times, for 2 to 3 minutes or until golden brown and crisp. Remove with the slotted spoon and drain on paper towels.

7. Stir together the chile powder and *chaat masala*, and sprinkle the mixture over the *pakoras*. Serve immediately.

Paneer Di Soti Boti

······{ **Batter-fried *paneer* skewers** }·····································

Paneer di soti boti means "paneer on a stick." To keep the skewered foods together, make sure the batter is quite thin so it doesn't weigh down the loaded wooden skewer when you dip it in the oil. Serve these with *pudina aur dhaniya* chutney (mint-and-cilantro chutney; page 22).

Makes 16.

7 ounces (200 grams) *paneer* (pressed fresh cheese; page 17), cut into ½-inch (1-cm) cubes
1 large onion, cut into ½-inch (1-cm) squares
1 large tomato, cut into ½-inch (1-cm) squares
1 large green bell pepper, seeded and cut into ½-inch (1-cm) squares
2 teaspoons red chile powder
1 tablespoon freshly squeezed lemon juice
2 teaspoons fresh ginger paste (page 12)
2 teaspoons fresh garlic paste (page 12)
1½ teaspoons table salt
1 cup (100 grams) *besan* (chickpea/gram flour)
½ teaspoon ground turmeric
½ teaspoon *chaat masala* (spice mix for *chaat*; page 24)
¼ cup (65 grams) plain yogurt
1 quart (800 ml) vegetable oil

1. Put the *paneer*, onion, tomato, and bell pepper in a deep bowl. Add 1 teaspoon of the chile powder, the lemon juice, 1 teaspoon of the ginger paste, 1 teaspoon of the garlic paste, and ½ teaspoon of the salt, and stir gently. Set aside to marinate for 15 minutes.

2. Thread the *paneer* and vegetables onto wooden skewers in the following order: onion, *paneer*, tomato, bell pepper, *paneer*, and bell pepper. Set the skewers aside on a plate.

3. Put the *besan*, the remaining 1 teaspoon salt, remaining 1 teaspoon chile powder, the turmeric, *chaat masala*, remaining 1 teaspoon ginger paste, and remaining 1 teaspoon garlic paste in a bowl. Stir well.

4. Add ½ cup (100 ml) water and stir. Add the yogurt and stir again. Add more water to adjust the consistency of the batter if necessary.

5. Place a nonstick wok over high heat and add the oil. When small bubbles appear at the bottom of the wok, lower the heat to medium. Dip the skewers into the batter and slide them into the hot oil, one or two at a time. Cook until golden and crisp, turning frequently with a slotted spoon. Remove with the slotted spoon and drain on paper towels.

6. Serve immediately.

Paneer Rolls

This is a recipe that my wife, Alyona, and I created a while ago. We were having a party at home and were reasonably sure that there were some *paneer* fans on our guest list. Now we have even more *paneer* fans among our circle of friends!

Makes 12.

¾ tablespoon raisins
7 ounces (200 grams) *paneer* (pressed fresh cheese; page 17), grated
2 medium potatoes, peeled, boiled, and mashed
3 green chiles, stemmed and chopped
2 tablespoons chopped fresh cilantro
½ teaspoon red chile powder
¾ teaspoon *garam masala* (spice mix; page 27)
¾ teaspoon *chaat masala* (spice mix for *chaat*; page 24)
1 teaspoon table salt
3 tablespoons *maida* (refined flour) or pastry flour
¾ cup (80 grams) bread crumbs
1 large egg
1 quart (800 ml) vegetable oil

1. Soak the raisins in ½ cup (100 ml) warm water for 15 minutes. Drain.

2. Combine the *paneer*, mashed potatoes, chiles, cilantro, chile powder, *garam masala*, *chaat masala*, salt, and raisins in a bowl.

3. Divide into 12 portions and shape each into a cylindrical croquette.

4. Spread out the *maida* and bread crumbs on two separate plates.

5. Put the egg in a bowl and whisk until smooth. Roll the croquettes in the flour, then dip in the egg, then roll in the bread crumbs.

6. Place a nonstick wok over high heat and add the oil. When small bubbles appear at the bottom of the wok, lower the heat to medium. Gently slide the croquettes into the hot oil, two or three at a time. Cook, turning with a slotted spoon a few times, until golden brown and crisp. Remove with the slotted spoon and drain on paper towels.

7. Serve immediately.

Paneer Tikka Kathi Rolls

·······⋛ Spicy cheese cubes wrapped in whole-wheat griddle bread ⋚·······

In Kolkata, *kathi* rolls (*rotis* filled with a variety of stuffings) are a street food that sells like hotcakes. But I like to make this special *paneer* version at home.

Makes 4.

¼ cup (65 grams) plain yogurt, whisked
1 teaspoon red chile powder
¼ teaspoon ground turmeric
½ teaspoon fresh ginger paste (page 12)
¼ teaspoon fresh garlic paste (page 12)
1 tablespoon *besan* (chickpea/gram flour)
¾ teaspoon *chaat masala* (spice mix for *chaat*; page 24)
½ teaspoon *kasoori methi* (dried fenugreek leaves)
½ teaspoon *garam masala* (spice mix; page 27)
1½ teaspoons table salt
1 cup (140 grams) *paneer* cubes (pressed fresh cheese; page 17)
2 medium tomatoes, seeded and chopped
2 tablespoons vegetable oil
1 medium green bell pepper, seeded and chopped
1 cup (150 grams) *atta* (whole-wheat flour)
¼ cup (50 ml) milk
4 teaspoons *pudina aur dhaniya* chutney (mint-and-cilantro chutney; page 22)
2 small red onions, cut into round slices

1. Put the yogurt, chile powder, turmeric, ginger paste, garlic paste, *besan*, ½ teaspoon of the *chaat masala*, the *kasoori methi*, *garam masala*, and ½ teaspoon of the salt in a large bowl. Stir and add the *paneer* and tomatoes. Toss gently. Set aside to marinate for 10 minutes.

2. Place a nonstick sauté pan over medium heat and add the oil. When small bubbles appear at the bottom of the pan, add the bell peppers and sauté for 2 minutes. Add the *paneer* with the marinade, and sauté over high heat for 2 minutes, stirring occasionally, or until dry. Divide the mixture into 4 portions and set aside.

3. To make the *rotis*, combine the *atta*, milk, the remaining 1 teaspoon salt, and 2½ tablespoons water, and knead to make a soft dough. Divide the dough into 4 portions. Roll out each portion into a thin round.

4. Place a nonstick griddle over medium heat and cook each *roti* lightly on both sides. Spread 1 teaspoon of the chutney on each *roti* and top with some onion slices.

5. Place a portion of the *paneer* mixture in the center of each *roti* over the onions, sprinkle with a little of the remaining *chaat masala*, and roll up tightly.

6. Heat the griddle and cook the *roti* rolls until warmed through. Cut into 2-inch-long (5-cm-long) pieces and serve immediately.

Papaya Chi Wadi

Steamed papaya dumplings

I discovered this snack when I moved to Mumbai and began exploring the local Maharashtrian food. Up until that time, I had thought of ripe papaya as only a table fruit.

Makes 12.

1 small ripe papaya
2 or 3 fresh cloves garlic, chopped
½-inch (1-cm) piece fresh ginger, chopped
2 green chiles, stemmed and chopped
½ teaspoon red chile powder
½ teaspoon ground turmeric
½ teaspoon ground roasted cumin (page 32)
1 teaspoon table salt
1 teaspoon freshly squeezed lemon juice
½ cup (50 grams) *besan* (chickpea/gram flour)
1 cup (60 grams) chopped fresh cilantro
Pinch of baking soda
1 teaspoon plus 1 quart (800 ml) vegetable oil
1 teaspoon *chaat masala* (spice mix for *chaat*; page 24)

1. Wash, peel, and seed the papaya, and grate it into a large bowl.

2. Put the garlic, ginger, and chiles in a spice grinder with 1 tablespoon water and grind to a paste.

3. Add the paste to the papaya, along with the chile powder, turmeric, cumin, salt, lemon juice, *besan*, cilantro, baking soda, and ¼ cup (50 ml) water. Stir well.

4. Place a steamer over high heat. Add 2½ cups (500 ml) water and bring to a boil.

5. Grease a ridged plate (that can be placed in the steamer) with 1 teaspoon oil. Put the papaya mixture into it and smooth the surface. Place the plate in the steamer and steam for 12 minutes or until well set.

6. Remove the plate from the steamer and let cool slightly. Cut the steamed patty into ½-inch (1-cm) squares.

7. Place a nonstick wok over high heat and add 1 quart (800 ml) oil. When small bubbles appear at the bottom of the wok, gently slide in the steamed pieces, in small batches, and cook until golden brown all over. Remove with a slotted spoon and drain on paper towels.

8. Sprinkle with the *chaat masala* and serve hot.

Peethiwali Aloo Tikki

····· ❊{ **Potato-crusted spicy** *dal* }❊ ··

I wish I could take you to the famous *tikki* center in Amritsar, where vendors do a brisk business over huge iron griddles covered with dozens of *tikkis* bubbling in oil. I tasted this *tikki* there many years ago.

Makes 8.

¼ cup (50 grams) *dhuli urad dal* (split skinless black gram)
¼ teaspoon ground turmeric
3 tablespoons ghee (page 37)
Pinch of asafetida
1½ teaspoons fennel seeds
½ teaspoon crushed black peppercorns
½ teaspoon red chile powder
½ teaspoon *garam masala* (spice mix; page 27)
1 teaspoon *amchur* (dried mango powder)
1-inch (2½-cm) cinnamon stick
½ teaspoon table salt
4 small potatoes, boiled, peeled, and grated
1 quart (800 ml) vegetable oil
¼ cup (30 grams) cornstarch

1. Put the *dal* in a bowl, wash in plenty of water 2 or 3 times, and drain. Add 1 cup (200 ml) water and soak for 2 hours. Drain.

2. Place a nonstick saucepan over high heat and add 1 cup (200 ml) water. Add the turmeric and *dal*, and cook for 18 minutes or until soft. Drain.

3. Place a nonstick sauté pan over medium heat and add the ghee. When the ghee melts and small bubbles appear at the bottom of the pan, add the asafetida, fennel, and peppercorns, and sauté for 30 seconds. Add the *dal* and sauté for 30 seconds. Add the chile powder, *garam masala*, and *amchur*, and stir.

4. Crush the cinnamon coarsely in a mortar with a pestle. Add it along with the salt to the *dal* mixture and stir well. Let cool to room temperature. Divide into 8 portions. Put the potatoes in a large bowl and knead them well. Divide the potatoes into 8 portions.

5. Grease your palms with a little of the oil, take a portion of the potatoes in your hand, and make a dent in the center. Place a portion of the *dal* stuffing in the dent and gather the edges to enclose the *dal*. Shape into a thick round patty, or *tikki*. Repeat with the remaining potatoes and *dal* mixture. Spread the cornstarch on a plate and roll the *tikkis* in it.

6. Place a nonstick wok over high heat and add the remaining oil. When small bubbles appear at the bottom of the wok, lower the heat to medium and gently slide in 4 *tikkis*. Cook, turning with a slotted spoon a few times, until golden and crisp. Remove with the slotted spoon and drain on paper towels. Repeat with the remaining *tikkis*. Serve hot.

Phal-Sabz Seekh

······◦}⟨ **Fruit-and-vegetable kebabs** ⟩{◦······

This kebab recipe comes from Hyderabad. The banana gives it a firm foundation, and I have added some contemporary touches like broccoli and prunes.

Makes 6.

2 large unripe, raw bananas, halved
1½ tablespoons butter, plus ¼ cup (60 grams) melted butter
¾ teaspoon *ajwain*
7 ounces (200 grams) white button mushrooms, chopped
1 small carrot, grated
4 broccoli florets, chopped
¾ tablespoon chopped fresh cilantro
¾-inch (1½-cm) piece fresh ginger, chopped
1½ fresh red chiles, stemmed and chopped
1 teaspoon table salt
8 pitted prunes, chopped
½ teaspoon black salt
¾ teaspoon ground black pepper
½ teaspoon ground green cardamom
Pinch of ground edible sandalwood powder (optional)
Pinch of ground dried untreated rose petals
2 medium potatoes, boiled, peeled, and mashed
½ cup (55 grams) bread crumbs
1½ tablespoons vegetable oil

1. Place a nonstick saucepan over high heat and add 1 quart (800 ml) water. When the water comes to a boil, add the bananas and cook for 15 minutes or until tender. Drain in a colander and set aside to cool. When cooled, peel the bananas and grate them into a bowl.

2. Place a medium nonstick sauté pan over medium heat and add 1½ tablespoons butter. When the butter melts, add the *ajwain* and sauté for 10 seconds. Add the mushrooms, carrot, and broccoli, and sauté until the moisture evaporates. Add the cilantro, ginger, chiles, and table salt. Stir and set aside to cool.

3. Preheat the oven to 350°F/180°C.

4. Put the cooled mixture in a food processor. Add the prunes, black salt, pepper, cardamom, edible sandalwood (if using), rose petals, potatoes, bananas, and bread crumbs, and process until smooth.

5. Transfer the mixture to a bowl and divide into 6 portions. Wrap each portion around a wooden skewer.

6. Arrange the skewers on a greased baking sheet, brush with the melted butter, and bake for 6 to 7 minutes. Gently slide the kebabs from the skewers onto a plate. Cut each into 4 pieces and serve immediately.

Poha Cutlets

I have always been fascinated by *poha*. I visited the city of Roha (rhymes with *poha*), a two-hour drive from Mumbai, and saw how *poha* is made from paddy rice that is steamed, pressed, rolled, and dried. When it is soaked in liquids such as water or milk, it tends to absorb the water and swell up. Here I use it to prepare one of my favorite snacks. This simple dish can be made quickly and easily, and makes a delicious appetizer.

Makes 12 pieces.

1 cup (120 grams) *poha* (pressed rice)
1 quart (800 ml) vegetable oil
½ teaspoon cumin seeds
½ teaspoon black mustard seeds
1 medium red onion, diced
2 tablespoons *maida* (refined flour) or pastry flour
1 teaspoon red chile powder
2 green chiles, stemmed and minced
¼ teaspoon ground turmeric
3 medium potatoes, boiled and mashed
1½ teaspoons table salt
2 tablespoons chopped fresh cilantro
10 cashews, chopped
1 tablespoon freshly squeezed lemon juice
1 teaspoon *chaat masala* (spice mix for *chaat*; page 24)
Pudina aur dhaniya chutney (mint-and-cilantro chutney; page 22)

1. Put the *poha* in a colander and wash it under running water until the water runs clear. Let the *poha* drain for 5 to 6 minutes.

2. Place a small nonstick sauté pan over high heat and add 2 tablespoons of the oil. When small bubbles appear at the bottom of the pan, add the cumin seeds, mustard seeds, onion, and *maida*, and cook for 2 to 3 minutes. Add the chile powder, chiles, and turmeric, stir well, and cook for 1 minute. Transfer the mixture to a deep bowl and let cool to room temperature.

3. Add the *poha*, mashed potatoes, salt, cilantro, cashews, lemon juice, and *chaat masala*. Combine to make a smooth dough. Divide the mixture into 12 portions and shape each into a round or oblong patty ½ inch (1 cm) thick.

4. Put the remaining oil in a deep-fryer and heat to 375°F/190°C. Gently slide the patties, a few at a time, into the hot oil and cook until golden on all sides, turning with a slotted spoon. Remove with the slotted spoon and drain on paper towels. Serve immediately with the chutney.

Punjabi Samosa

······※} **Popular cone-shaped, deep-fried snack with spicy stuffing** {※······

If potatoes have to be deep-fried, they should be inside a *samosa*—much better than French fries! Making a good *samosa* is an art, particularly when working with the dough, and takes practice to perfect.

Serves 4.

~ For the dough:
1 cup (120 grams) *maida* (refined flour) or pastry flour
½ teaspoon *ajwain* (optional)
5 teaspoons ghee (page 37), melted
1 teaspoon table salt

~ For the filling:
1 tablespoon coriander seeds
1 teaspoon *anardana* (dried pomegranate seeds)
2 tablespoons vegetable oil
1 teaspoon cumin seeds
1-inch (2½-cm) piece fresh ginger, chopped
3 or 4 green chiles, stemmed and chopped
1 teaspoon red chile powder
1 teaspoon *amchur* (dried mango powder)
1 teaspoon *garam masala* (spice mix; page 27)
¾ teaspoon table salt
½ cup (75 grams) green peas, boiled (optional)
4 small potatoes, boiled, peeled, and coarsely mashed
2 tablespoons chopped fresh cilantro

~ To cook and serve:
1 quart (800 ml) vegetable oil
Khajoor aur imli ki chutney (sweet date-and-tamarind chutney; page 22)

1. Make the dough: Put the *maida* in a bowl. Add the *ajwain* (if using), ghee, and salt, and stir. Add ¼ cup (50 ml) water, little by little, and knead to make a stiff dough. Cover with a damp cloth and set aside to rest for 10 to 15 minutes.

2. Make the filling: Place a small nonstick pan over medium heat. Let it heat for 2 minutes, then add the coriander and *anardana*, and dry-roast for 1 minute or until fragrant. Set aside to cool to room temperature, then transfer the seed mixture into a mortar. Pound with a pestle to a coarse powder.

3. Place a nonstick sauté pan over medium heat and add the oil. When small bubbles appear at the bottom of the pan, add the cumin seeds. When the cumin is lightly browned, add the ginger and chiles, and stir well. Add the chile powder, *amchur*, *garam masala*, and salt. Add the spices from step 2. Stir well to mix.

4. Lower the heat to low, add the peas (if using) and potatoes, and cook for 5 minutes. Add the cilantro and stir well. Remove from the heat and set aside to cool to room temperature. Divide the cooled filling into 16 portions.

5. Divide the dough into 8 equal portions and shape them into balls. Dust each ball with a little flour and roll out into ovals 4 inches (10 cm) wide in the center. Cut each oval in half horizontally and dampen the edges with water. Place one half over the fingers of your left hand with the straight edge resting over your forefinger. Fold over one end of the straight edge and bring it to the middle of the rounded edge. Now fold over the other end and bring it over to the middle of the rounded edge to rest over the first end to make a seam. Press gently to seal the seam. Now you should have a cone. Open the cone and make a small pleat directly opposite the seam and press gently. Fill the cone with one portion of the stuffing. Bring the seam and the pleat together on the rounded edge and gently press the entire open end of the cone closed. Repeat with the remaining dough and filling.

6. Cook the *samosas*: Place a nonstick wok over high heat and add the oil. When small bubbles appear at the bottom of the wok, lower the heat to medium and gently slide the *samosas*, two at time, into the hot oil. Fry for 7 minutes or until crisp and golden brown. While they are frying, gently spoon hot oil over the *samosas* with a slotted spoon.

7. Remove with the slotted spoon and drain on paper towels.

8. Serve hot with the chutney.

Rajma Galouti Kabab

····· ❧{ Delicately flavored kidney bean kebabs }❧ ···

A vegetarian version of the famous lamb *galouti kabab* can be made with yams, peas, or spinach, but these, which use red kidney beans, come closest to the original delicacy. Kidney beans, like all beans, are a very good source of cholesterol-lowering fiber. In addition, their high fiber content prevents blood sugar levels from rising too rapidly after a meal, making these beans an especially good choice for individuals with diabetes, insulin resistance, or hypoglycemia.

Makes 8.

½ teaspoon caraway seeds
2 green cardamom pods
1 black cardamom pod
1 whole clove
½-inch (1-cm) cinnamon stick
8 cashews
1 tablespoon *chironji* or *charoli* (melon seeds)
Generous pinch of saffron threads
¼ teaspoon *kewra* (screw pine) water
4 teaspoons vegetable oil
½-inch (1-cm) piece fresh ginger, chopped
3 cloves garlic, chopped
3 green chiles, stemmed and chopped
2 cups (450 grams) canned red kidney beans
2 tablespoons grated *khoya/mawa* (unsweetened solid condensed milk; page 37)
½ teaspoon ground white pepper
½ teaspoon table salt
½ tablespoon freshly squeezed lemon juice
1 sprig fresh mint
1 medium red onion, cut into thin rings

1. Place a small nonstick sauté pan over medium heat. Add the caraway, green and black cardamom, clove, and cinnamon stick, and dry-roast until fragrant. Let cool, then transfer to a spice grinder and grind to a fine powder.

2. Place a small nonstick sauté pan over medium heat. Add the cashews and melon seeds and dry-roast until lightly colored. Let cool, then transfer to a clean spice grinder or mini food processor with ¼ cup (50 ml) water and grind to a fine paste.

3. Soak the saffron in the *kewra* water in a small bowl.

4. Place a nonstick sauté pan over medium heat and add the oil. When small bubbles appear at the bottom of the pan, add the ginger and garlic, and sauté for 1 minute. Add the chiles and sauté for 1 minute.

5. Add the beans and sauté for 3 to 4 minutes. Add the cashew paste and sauté for 4 to 5 minutes. Add the *khoya*, white pepper, and salt. Sauté for 4 to 5 minutes. Remove from the heat and let cool.

6. Mash the bean mixture to a smooth paste. (If the paste is not firm, cook it further in a nonstick pan to thicken it.) Sprinkle with the roasted and ground spices and soaked saffron. Add the lemon juice and stir well. Divide the mixture into 8 portions. Roll each portion into a ball and then lightly press into patties.

7. Place another nonstick sauté pan over medium heat and grease it lightly. Put the patties in the pan and cook for 2 minutes or until lightly colored on both sides.

8. Garnish with the mint and onion and serve immediately.

Posto Boda

······⊹❴ **Poppy-seed fritters** ❵··

White poppy seeds have a mild nutty flavor that is enhanced by crushing; when ground to a paste, they provide creaminess in curries. This typical Bengali preparation is the simplest and easiest way to become familiar with poppy seeds as an ingredient. Serve the fritters with rice and *dal*.

Serves 4.

½ cup (100 grams) white poppy seeds
3 or 4 green chiles, stemmed and chopped
5 or 6 cloves garlic
1 teaspoon table salt
3 tablespoons vegetable oil

1. Soak the poppy seeds in 1 cup (200 ml) water for 1 hour. Drain off the water and put the soaked seeds in a mini food processor. Add the chiles, garlic, salt, and 3 tablespoons water, and process to a smooth paste.

2. Transfer the paste to a bowl. Divide into 8 portions and shape them into flat patties.

3. Place a nonstick sauté pan over medium heat and add the oil. When small bubbles appear at the bottom of the pan, add the patties and cook, turning gently, until both sides are lightly browned. Remove with a slotted spoon and drain on paper towels.

4. Serve hot.

Raunaq-E-Seekh

······⟨ **Vegetable kebabs** ⟩··

Raunaq-e-seekh is an Urdu word that refers to a glamorous kebab. Kebabs, a gift of the Mughal era, are considered high quality if the meat practically melts in your mouth in a perfectly balanced mix of spices. Vegetable kebabs are a challenge, but this popular version lives up to its name.

Makes 8.

5 tablespoons vegetable oil
1 teaspoon caraway seeds
6 green chiles, stemmed and minced
1 tablespoon fresh ginger paste (page 12)
1 tablespoon fresh garlic paste (page 12)
3 medium carrots, grated
12 thin green beans, strings removed and chopped
¼ cup (125 grams) grated cauliflower
1 medium green bell pepper, seeded and chopped
1 cup (150 grams) fresh or frozen green peas, blanched and mashed
⅔ cup (100 grams) fresh or frozen corn kernels, blanched and mashed
3 medium potatoes, boiled, peeled, and mashed
1 teaspoon *garam masala* (spice mix; page 27)
1 teaspoon table salt
1 teaspoon ground white pepper
¼ cup (35 grams) ground *dalia* (roasted *chana dal*, store-bought)
2 teaspoons freshly squeezed lemon juice
2 teaspoons *chaat masala* (spice mix for *chaat*; page 24)

1. Place a nonstick wok over medium heat and add 3 tablespoons of the oil. When small bubbles appear at the bottom of the pan, add the caraway. Sauté for 10 seconds. Add the chiles, ginger paste, and garlic paste, and sauté for 30 seconds. Add the carrots, beans, cauliflower, and bell pepper, and cook for 8 to 10 minutes or until all the excess moisture has evaporated.

2. Add the peas, corn, and potatoes, and stir well. Add the *garam masala*, salt, and white pepper, and stir. Add the *dalia* and lemon juice, and stir. Remove from the heat and let cool completely.

3. Divide the vegetable mixture into 8 portions. Take a portion of the vegetable mixture and shape it neatly around a satay stick or wooden skewer, making a long sausage shape. Repeat to make 8 kebabs.

4. Place a nonstick griddle over medium heat. Working in batches, and adding ½ tablespoon of the remaining oil to the pan for each batch, place the kebabs, two at a time, on the pan and cook for 5 to 6 minutes, turning, until light golden brown on all sides.

5. Slide the kebabs off the satay sticks and place them on a serving platter. Cut each in half on the diagonal. Sprinkle with the *chaat masala* and serve hot.

Rawa Dosas

When I was a child, crisp semolina *dosas* (thin pancakes) really fascinated me, especially at eateries where you could see the cooks making them. They would sprinkle the batter onto the hot skillet instead of pouring it, yet somehow it would all come together into a crisp—*really* crisp—savory pancake! I have long since learned that the secret lies in tempering the skillet before you begin: melting ghee on it and then wiping it clean before making each *dosa*. Serve each *dosa* as soon as it's cooked, ideally with *sambhar* (South Indian lentils; page 32) and *nariel aur dhaniya* chutney (coconut cilantro chutney; page 520).

Serves 4.

1 cup (200 grams) *rawa/suji* (semolina flour)
½ cup (75 grams) rice flour
¼ cup (30 grams) *maida* (refined flour) or pastry flour
1-inch (2½-cm) piece fresh ginger, minced
2 green chiles, stemmed and minced
12 to 15 black peppercorns, crushed
¼ cup (30 grams) grated fresh coconut
2 teaspoons table salt
8 cashews, crushed
2 tablespoons chopped fresh cilantro
4 teaspoons ghee (page 37), melted

1. Place the *rawa* in a deep bowl. Add the rice flour and *maida*, and stir well. Add 1 quart (800 ml) water and whisk until smooth. There should not be any lumps in the batter, and it should be quite thin and runny. Cover the bowl with a lid and let rest for 15 minutes.

2. Add the ginger, chiles, peppercorns, coconut, salt, cashews, and cilantro to the batter. Stir well.

3. Place a large nonstick sauté pan over low heat and let it heat for 5 minutes. Brush with ghee. Take a square piece of cheesecloth, dampen it with water, and use it to wipe the ghee from the sauté pan. Now the pan is "tempered" and ready for making the *dosas*.

4. Pour a ladleful of batter into the hot pan, in a circular motion, until it covers almost the entire pan. Cook over low heat, drizzling a few drops of the ghee around the edges of the *dosa*. After 2 minutes, flip the *dosa* using a spatula and cook the underside for 2 to 4 minutes or until it is crisp and golden and the edges of the *dosa* start to separate from the pan.

5. Using the spatula, transfer the *dosa* to a plate and serve immediately. Repeat with the remaining batter and ghee.

······◦⟨ **Chef's tip** ⟩◦ If you spread the batter thin enough, you need not cook the second side.

Rayalaseema Pesarettu

······· *{ Spicy green-gram pancakes }* ·······

Rayalaseema is in Andhra Pradesh and is the home of many temples. This *dosa* of whole green gram is spicy, but you can adjust the chiles according to your tolerance. Green gram is a good source of protein, and if you make the *dosas* with just a little oil, they can be considered health food. Serve them with your choice of chutney or *sambhar* (page 32).

Makes 12.

1 cup (240 grams) *sabut moong* (whole green gram)
1-inch (2½-cm) piece fresh ginger, chopped
4 green chiles, stemmed and chopped
1 medium red onion, chopped
2 teaspoons table salt
1 tablespoon rice flour
½ teaspoon ground roasted cumin seeds (page 32)
12½ teaspoons (65 ml) vegetable oil

1. Put the *sabut moong* in a bowl, wash in plenty of water 2 or 3 times, and drain. Add 3 cups (600 ml) water and soak overnight. Drain.

2. Put the *sabut moong*, ginger, chiles, and onion in a food processor with 1½ cups (300 ml) water and process to make a smooth batter.

3. Transfer the batter to a large bowl. Add the salt, rice flour, and cumin, and stir well.

4. Place a nonstick griddle over medium heat and grease it lightly with ½ teaspoon oil.

5. Spread a ladleful of the batter with a round spoon, about 6 inches in diameter or as thin as possible.

6. Drizzle ½ teaspoon of the oil around the edges, cover with a dome-shaped lid, and cook for 2 to 3 minutes over medium heat. Turn over, drizzle another ½ teaspoon oil around the edges, and cook the other side for 2 to 3 minutes or until golden and crisp. Repeat with the remaining batter and oil.

7. Serve hot.

Sannas

Reminiscent of the South Indian snack *idli* (steamed rice cakes; page 120), Goan *sannas* are enriched with coconut milk. Goans usually use toddy (fermented palm sap) to leaven the dough of this rice cake, but here I use yeast, which is much more available. When the batter becomes light and airy, it is ready to be poured into the molds and steamed. Stainless-steel molds called *vantleo* are traditional, but *idli* molds work just as well. (Page 591 for more about *idli* molds/steamers.) The rice has to soak overnight, so plan accordingly. Serve these with any spicy curry.

Makes 16.

½ cup (100 grams) parboiled white rice
½ cup (100 grams) raw short-grain rice
¼ cup (50 grams) *dhuli urad dal* (split skinless black gram)
1 teaspoon active dry yeast
¼ teaspoon sugar
¼ cup (50 ml) coconut milk
1 teaspoon table salt

1. Wash the parboiled rice and soak in 1½ cups (300 ml) water overnight. Wash the short-grain rice and soak in 1½ cups (300 ml) water overnight. Wash the *dal* and soak in 1 cup (200 ml) water overnight.

2. The following morning, drain the parboiled rice and put it in a spice grinder. Grind to a smooth, thick paste and transfer to a large bowl. Drain the short-grain rice and grind to a smooth, thick paste; transfer to the same bowl. Drain the *dal* and grind to a smooth, thick paste; transfer to the same bowl. Whisk until well blended.

3. Put the yeast in a small bowl with the sugar and 1 tablespoon warm water. When it begins to bubble, add it to the rice batter and whisk well. Add the coconut milk and salt, and stir. Cover the bowl and set aside in a warm place to ferment for about 5 hours or until the batter doubles in volume.

4. Place a steamer with 2 cups (400 ml) water in the bottom over high heat and bring to a boil. Grease the *idli* molds. Pour the batter into each indentation, fit the *idli* molds onto the stand, and place the stand in the steamer. Cover and steam over medium heat for about 15 minutes or until done (the fully cooked steamed cake will not have any moisture and will lift out easily from the steamer).

5. Serve hot.

Sindhi Aloo Tuk

.... **Baby potatoes with dried mango powder** ....

This dish comes from the Sindhi community of India. They also make this *tuk* with *colocassia*, but the potato version appeals more to me. (Also called taro, *colocassia* is a type of tuber. It has large leaves in the shape of an elephant's ear.) Sprinkle the spices over the potatoes while they are still hot so that the seasonings cling to the oily surface; the potatoes can then be served hot or at room temperature.

Serves 4.

13 ounces (375 grams) baby potatoes, peeled
1 quart (800 ml) vegetable oil
½ teaspoon red chile powder
½ teaspoon *amchur* (dried mango powder)
½ teaspoon ground coriander
½ teaspoon ground roasted cumin (page 32)
½ teaspoon table salt

1. Place a nonstick saucepan over high heat and add 3 cups (600 ml) water. When the water begins to boil, add the potatoes and cook for 15 minutes or until they are half cooked.

2. Drain the potatoes in a colander. Let cool, then press each between your palms to flatten them into thick disks.

3. Place a nonstick wok over high heat and add the oil. When small bubbles appear at the bottom of the wok, lower the heat to medium and gently slide in the potatoes in small batches. Cook each batch, turning with a slotted spoon a few times, for 8 minutes or until golden and crisp. Remove with the slotted spoon and drain on paper towels.

4. Sprinkle the chile powder, *amchur*, coriander, cumin, and salt over the hot potatoes, and toss to coat.

5. Serve hot or at room temperature.

Tiranga Paneer Tikka

····❊{ **Tricolor cheese bites** }❊···

I made this dish to represent India's tricolored flag, and my family demands that I make it every Indian Independence Day and Indian Republic Day.

Makes 8.

1 pound (450 grams) *paneer* (pressed fresh cheese; page 17)
½ teaspoon red chile powder
1½ teaspoons table salt
¼ cup (60 grams) *pudina aur dhaniya* chutney (mint-and-cilantro chutney; page 22)
1 cup (250 grams) plain yogurt
2 tablespoons *besan* (chickpea/gram flour)
½ tablespoon fresh ginger paste (page 12)
½ tablespoon fresh garlic paste (page 12)
¼ cup (20 grams) chopped fresh cilantro
4 green chiles, stemmed and chopped
1½ tablespoons freshly squeezed lemon juice
Melted butter for basting

1. Grate about 3½ ounces (100 grams) of the *paneer*. Cut the remaining *paneer* into 1½-inch (4-cm) cubes. Slice each cube twice (into three layers) without cutting all the way through. Set aside.

2. Put the grated *paneer*, chile powder, and ¼ teaspoon salt in a bowl, and stir well.

3. Take a cube of *paneer*. Spread some of the chutney in the first layer, and some of the grated *paneer* mixture in the second layer.

4. Put the yogurt, *besan*, ginger paste, garlic paste, cilantro, chiles, ¼ teaspoon of the salt, and the lemon juice in a large bowl. Stir well.

5. Add the stuffed *paneer* and stir gently so that all the cubes are evenly covered with the marinade. Set aside for about 1 hour.

6. Thread the *paneer* cubes onto wooden skewers, with space between them.

7. Preheat a charcoal fire to medium and grill the skewers for 5 to 6 minutes, basting with butter. (You can also cook them on the stovetop on a hot griddle.)

8. Serve immediately.

White Dhoklas

····· Steamed-rice-and-*dal* cakes ·····

The thickness of these popular Gujarati *dhoklas* (which can be paper-thin or as thick as a slice of bread) varies from cook to cook. These *dhoklas* will be about the size of a slice of bread. Serve with *pudina aur dhaniya* chutney (mint-and-cilantro chutney; page 22).

Serves 4.

1 cup (200 grams) raw, short-grain rice
¼ cup (50 grams) **dhuli urad dal** (split skinless black gram)
¼ cup (65 grams) sour plain yogurt (see page 513), whisked
1 teaspoon ginger paste (page 12)
1 teaspoon green chile paste (page 13)
½ teaspoon table salt
7 or 8 black peppercorns, crushed
1 teaspoon baking soda
1 tablespoon plus 2 teaspoons vegetable oil
2 teaspoons freshly squeezed lemon juice

1. Put the rice and *dal* in a bowl, wash in plenty of water 2 or 3 times, and drain. Add 3 cups (600 ml) water and soak for 4 hours. Drain.

2. Put the rice mixture in a mini food processor with ½ cup (100 ml) water and process until smooth. The mixture should be thick but of pouring consistency.

3. Transfer to a large bowl and whisk in the yogurt. There should not be any lumps in the batter. Cover the bowl with a lid and put in a warm place to ferment overnight.

4. Heat 2 cups (400 ml) water in a steamer.

5. To the batter, add the ginger paste, green chile paste, salt, peppercorns, and ½ teaspoon of the baking soda, and stir well.

6. Grease two round *dhokla* pans (see Note) with 1 tablespoon of the oil. Pour the batter into the pans until they are half full.

7. In a small bowl, combine the remaining 2 teaspoons oil, ½ teaspoon baking soda, and the lemon juice, and add half of this to each *dhokla* pan. Fit the pans onto the stand. Place the stand in the steamer. Cover and steam for 10 to 12 minutes or until a skewer inserted in a *dhokla* comes out clean.

8. Take the stand out of the steamer and remove the pans. Let cool slightly, then cut the *dhoklas* into cubes. Serve warm.

····· **Note** ⁕ A *dhokla* pan, or an Indian steamer, is a cylindrical stainless-steel container with 2 or 3 grooves and a tight-fitting dome-shaped lid. Water is put in the bottom of the container, a perforated plate is set into the lowest groove, and the container with the food that is to be steamed is placed over the perforated plate.

If you are steaming fish, you can use 2 or 3 perforated plates and place the fish right on them. For steaming *idlis* and *dhoklas*, you use a stand in which you can put 3 or 4 plates. For *idlis*, the plates have indentations; for *dhoklas*, the plates are flat. The plates are lightly greased and the batter is poured into them. The plates are then fitted into the stand and placed in the steamer. The steamer is covered with the lid and the food is steamed for the time specified in the recipe.

Tootak

········⸬{ Saffron-flavored Indian bread }⸬········

Tootak is a short-crust dough snack made from semolina and was a popular breakfast treat for the Nizams (royal rulers) of Hyderabad.

Serves 4.

1 cup (200 grams) *rawa/suji* (semolina flour)
2 teaspoons table salt
½ cup (100 grams) ghee (page 37)
½ cup (90 grams) grated *khoya/mawa* (unsweetened solid condensed milk; page 37)
½ cup (100 ml) milk
A few saffron threads
1 tablespoon rosewater
1 tablespoon vegetable oil
1 teaspoon cumin seeds
1-inch (2½-cm) piece fresh ginger, chopped
1 teaspoon red chile powder
1 teaspoon ground black pepper
2 teaspoons ground coriander
¼ teaspoon *garam masala* (spice mix; page 27)
1 cup (200 grams) grated *paneer* (pressed fresh cheese; page 17)
1 potato, boiled and mashed
20 cashews, chopped
15 raisins
1 tablespoon chopped fresh cilantro
1 tablespoon freshly squeezed lemon juice

1. Put the semolina, 1 teaspoon of the salt, the ghee, *khoya*, and milk in a bowl and knead to make a soft dough. Cover the dough with a damp cloth and set aside to rest for 2 to 3 hours. Knead the dough once again and let rest for 30 minutes.

2. In a small cup, combine the saffron and rosewater; set aside.

3. Place a medium nonstick sauté pan over high heat and add the oil. When small bubbles appear at the bottom of the pan, lower the heat to medium and add the cumin. When the cumin begins to change color, add the ginger and sauté until it is lightly browned.

4. Add the chile powder, black pepper, coriander, the remaining 1 teaspoon salt, and the *garam masala*. Cook for 2 to 3 minutes. Add the *paneer*, potatoes, cashews, and raisins. Stir and cook until completely dry.

5. Sprinkle with the cilantro and lemon juice. Stir well. Divide into 16 equal portions and set aside to cool.

6. Preheat the oven to 400°F/200°C. Take one portion of the dough, shape it into a *katori* (small bowl) with your fingers, put one portion of the paneer-potato mixture inside, gather the edges, and shape into a ball. Seal neatly, flatten slightly, and shape into an oval. Repeat with the remaining dough and filling.

7. Arrange on a baking sheet and let rest for 10 minutes.

8. Brush with the saffron-rosewater mixture and bake for 20 minutes. Serve hot.

Adraki Jhinga

······§ **Ginger-marinated sautéed shrimp** }······································

Adrak is Hindi for "ginger," and the name of this dish is apt: The shrimp are marinated in a sharp ginger mixture. Serve these with *pudina aur dhaniya* chutney (mint-and-cilantro chutney; page 22).

Serves 4.

20 large shrimp, cleaned, heads removed
1 teaspoon table salt
1 tablespoon freshly squeezed lemon juice
1 tablespoon fresh ginger paste (page 12)
1 tablespoon red chile paste (see Note page 13)
2 tablespoons *maida* (refined flour) or pastry flour
3 tablespoons vegetable oil

1. Peel and devein the shrimp, keeping the tails intact. Wash, pat dry, and put them in a bowl.

2. Add the salt, lemon juice, ginger paste, chile paste, and *maida*, and toss well. Set aside for 15 minutes.

3. Place a nonstick sauté pan over medium heat and add the oil. When small bubbles appear at the bottom of the pan, add the shrimp along with the marinade and cook for 2 minutes; do not overcook the shrimp, or they will become tough and rubbery. Remove with a slotted spoon and drain on paper towels.

4. Serve hot.

Amritsari Machchi

While I really like the caramel-hued malt vinegar that is used in this recipe, it is often hard to find. The closest substitute in look, flavor, and acidity (about 5%) is cider vinegar. *Rawas*, the fish used here, is called the Indian salmon. It is very different from American salmon. For this recipe, you can use rockfish or grouper if *rawas* is unavailable.

Serves 4.

1⅓ pounds (600 grams) boneless *rawas* (Indian salmon) fillets
¼ cup (50 ml) malt vinegar
½ cup (50 grams) *besan* (chickpea/gram flour)
2 tablespoons *maida* (refined flour) or pastry flour
1 tablespoon plain yogurt
1 large egg
1 teaspoon *ajwain*
1 teaspoon table salt
1 tablespoon freshly squeezed lemon juice
1 tablespoon red chile powder
2 tablespoons fresh ginger paste (page 12)
2 tablespoons fresh garlic paste (page 12)
1 quart (800 ml) vegetable oil
1 teaspoon *chaat masala* (spice mix for *chaat*; page 24)
2 lemons, cut in half

1. Cut the fish fillets into 1½-inch (4-cm) cubes and put them in a bowl. Add the vinegar and marinate for 20 minutes. Drain and pat dry with paper towels.

2. Put the *besan*, *maida*, yogurt, egg, *ajwain*, salt, lemon juice, chile powder, ginger paste, and garlic paste in a deep bowl. Add water a little at a time, whisking to make a smooth batter.

3. Put the fish cubes in the batter and marinate for about 20 minutes.

4. Put the oil in a deep-fryer and heat to 375°F/190°C.

5. Working in batches, spoon fish pieces from the batter and slide into the hot oil one at a time. Take care not to overcrowd the fryer, as this may lower the temperature of the oil and cause the fish to absorb too much oil and become soggy. Lower the heat to medium and fry until the fish is golden brown and crisp. Remove with a slotted spoon and drain on paper towels.

6. Sprinkle with the *chaat masala* and lemon juice. Serve immediately.

Angoori Shrimp

This easy and surprisingly delicious dish looks absolutely stunning. While on the griddle, the plump grapes share their sweetness generously with the shrimp, which take on a beautiful glaze as they cook. I first came up with this dish in California when I was doing a show about cooking with grapes.

Serves 4.

¼ cup (50 ml) honey
1½ teaspoons table salt
½ cup (100 ml) balsamic vinegar
1 teaspoon red chile flakes
16 jumbo shrimp, peeled and deveined
24 red grapes
2 tablespoons vegetable oil

1. Place a small nonstick saucepan over medium heat, add the honey, ½ teaspoon of the salt, and the vinegar, and cook for 3 to 4 minutes. Stir in the chile flakes and remove from the heat; cover to keep warm.

2. Thread the shrimp and grapes alternately onto 8 wooden skewers. Sprinkle the remaining 1 teaspoon salt over them.

3. Place a nonstick griddle over medium heat and brush with 1 teaspoon of the oil. Place the skewers on the griddle and cook, basting with the remaining oil and turning frequently, for 4 minutes, until the shrimp are cooked evenly on all sides.

4. Arrange the shrimp and grapes on a platter, pour the honey sauce over them, and serve hot.

Chingri Pakora

The state of Bengal can be easily divided into east and west by the style of cuisine. This is how the East Bengalis make these dumplings. In a Bengali home in the western part of the state, you would find egg and a little sugar in the batter, and the *pakoras* would also be less spicy. Whichever the case, these crisp dumplings are best enjoyed right out of the fryer as a snack or side dish.

Serves 4.

1 pound (500 grams) small shrimp
½ cup (50 grams) *besan* (chickpea/gram flour)
1 tablespoon rice flour
1 teaspoon chopped garlic
2 medium red onions, diced
½ teaspoon red chile powder
2 green chiles, stemmed and chopped
2 tablespoons chopped fresh cilantro
1¼ teaspoons salt
2 teaspoons freshly squeezed lemon juice
1 quart (800 ml) vegetable oil

1. Peel and devein the shrimp. Wash them thoroughly under running water. Drain in a colander and then pat them dry with a kitchen towel.

2. Put the shrimp in a bowl. Add the *besan*, rice flour, garlic, onions, chile powder, chiles, cilantro, salt, lemon juice, and 3 tablespoons of the oil. Stir well. Shape into ¾-inch (1½-cm) balls.

3. Place a nonstick wok over high heat and add the remaining oil. When small bubbles appear at the bottom of the wok, lower the heat to medium and gently slide in a few shrimp balls. Cook over medium heat, turning frequently with a slotted spoon, for 6 to 7 minutes or until golden brown. Remove with the slotted spoon and drain on paper towels.

4. Serve immediately.

Rawas Fish Fingers

····· ⁂{ Marinated boneless fish rolled in coarse rice flour and deep-fried }⁂ ·····

The crunchiness of the fish fingers is thanks to the coarse rice flour. You can use bread crumbs or semolina for dredging, but the effect will be different.

Serves 4.

11 ounces (300 grams) boneless *rawas* (Indian salmon) fillets (see page 167; you can use rockfish or grouper)
1 tablespoon fresh ginger paste (page 12)
1 tablespoon fresh garlic paste (page 12)
1 teaspoon table salt
2 tablespoons freshly squeezed lemon juice
¾ cup (115 grams) coarse rice flour (see Note)
2 teaspoons red chile powder
1 quart (800 ml) vegetable oil
Chile garlic chutney (page 519)

1. Wash the fillets thoroughly under running water. Drain them in a colander and pat dry with paper towels. Cut the fillets into 20 to 22 finger-size pieces.

2. Put the ginger paste, garlic paste, salt, and lemon juice in a deep bowl. Stir well and add the fish fingers. Marinate for 30 minutes.

3. Put the rice flour in a large shallow dish. Roll the fish fingers in the rice flour.

4. Place a nonstick wok over high heat and add the oil. When small bubbles appear at the bottom of the wok, lower the heat to medium, and gently slide in the fish fingers, a few at a time. Cook, turning frequently with a slotted spoon, until golden and crisp. Remove with the slotted spoon and drain on paper towels.

5. Serve immediately with chutney.

····· ⁂{ **Note** }⁂ To make coarse rice flour, soak raw short-grain rice in water for 20 minutes. Drain and spread the rice on a clean absorbent towel to dry. Transfer to a food processor and process to a coarse powder. Store in an airtight container for up to 3 months.

Karwari Shrimp

These batter-fried, lemony shrimp make an excellent appetizer or first course. Serve with your choice of dipping sauce.

Serves 4.

20 medium shrimp, shelled and deveined
3 tablespoons freshly squeezed lemon juice
1½ teaspoons ground turmeric
1 quart (800 ml) vegetable oil
1 teaspoon cumin seeds
10 dried red chiles, stemmed and broken in half
1½ teaspoons coriander seeds
½ teaspoon black mustard seeds
½ teaspoon fenugreek seeds
2 teaspoons table salt
1 onion, sliced
½ cup (100 grams) *rawa/suji* (semolina flour)

1. Place the shrimp, lemon juice, and turmeric in a deep glass bowl and stir well. Marinate for 30 minutes.

2. Place a deep, heavy-bottomed sauté pan over high heat and add 2 tablespoons of the oil. When small bubbles appear at the bottom of the pan, add the cumin, chiles, coriander, mustard seeds, fenugreek, and 1 teaspoon of the salt, and sauté for 1 minute or until the seeds are lightly browned.

3. Add the onion and sauté for 3 to 4 minutes or until the onion is golden brown. Transfer to a bowl and set aside to cool to room temperature. Transfer to a mini food processor with 3 tablespoons water and process to a smooth paste.

4. Transfer the paste to the bowl with the marinated shrimp and stir well. Put in the refrigerator to marinate for 15 minutes.

5. Put the semolina in a bowl and add the remaining 1 teaspoon salt. Sprinkle this mixture on the marinated shrimp and stir gently until well combined, making sure that the shrimp remain whole.

6. Put the remaining oil in a deep-fryer and heat to 375°F/190°C. Gently lower five or six shrimp, one at time, into the hot oil. Lower the heat to medium and fry until they are golden and crisp. Remove with a slotted spoon and drain on paper towels. Serve immediately.

Macher Chop

The Bengalis' passion for fish is legendary—they enjoy many different types (relishing all parts of them—even the head), and they have a huge repertoire of fish dishes. This great appetizer is very traditional. Shortcut cooks simply stir the potatoes and flakey fish together, but give me this version any day!

Makes 12.

1 pound (500 grams) whole whitefish, cleaned and cut into 4 or 5 pieces
2 tablespoons plus 1 quart (800 ml) vegetable oil
2 medium red onions, chopped
4 teaspoons fresh ginger-garlic paste (page 13)
3 green chiles, stemmed and chopped
1½ teaspoons table salt
2 tablespoons chopped fresh cilantro
4 large potatoes, boiled, peeled, and mashed
2 large eggs
1 cup (110 grams) bread crumbs

1. Pat the fish dry with an absorbent towel.

2. Place a nonstick saucepan over high heat and add 2 cups (400 ml) water. When the water comes to a boil, add the fish pieces and cook for 3 to 4 minutes or until the fish is cooked through. Drain and put the fish on a plate. Remove the bones and skin, and flake the flesh. Set aside in a bowl.

3. Place a nonstick sauté pan over medium heat and add 2 tablespoons of the oil. When small bubbles appear at the bottom of the pan, add the onions, ginger-garlic paste, chiles, 1 teaspoon of the salt, and the cilantro. Sauté for 3 minutes or until the onions are lightly browned. Add to the flaked fish, stir well, and set aside to cool. Divide into 12 portions.

4. Put the mashed potatoes in a bowl, add the remaining ½ teaspoon salt, and stir well. Divide into 12 portions.

5. Roll one portion of the potato mixture into a ball and flatten it slightly. Make a dent in the center and place one portion of the fish mixture in the center. Gather in the edges to enclose the filling and roll into a ball again. Flatten it slightly to make a patty. Repeat with the remaining potato mixture and fish mixture.

6. Put the eggs in a bowl and whisk well. Put the bread crumbs on a plate. Dip the patties into the egg, then roll in the bread crumbs, making sure they are well coated.

7. Place a nonstick wok over high heat and add 1 quart (800 ml) oil. When small bubbles appear at the bottom of the wok, gently slide in 3 patties. Cook, turning a few times with a slotted spoon, for 2 to 3 minutes or until golden brown on all sides. Remove with the slotted spoon and drain on paper towels.

8. Serve immediately.

Malvani Shrimp Fry

·······•❧ **Crisp shrimp with ginger and garlic** ❧•···

This specialty of the west-coast regions of India should be prepared just before it is served or the shrimp will lose their crispness.

Serves 4.

32 medium shrimp, shelled and deveined
1 teaspoon table salt
1½ tablespoons freshly squeezed lemon juice
¾ teaspoon ground turmeric
2 teaspoons red chile powder
1 teaspoon fresh ginger paste (page 12)
1 teaspoon fresh garlic paste (page 12)
2 tablespoons rice flour
2 tablespoons *rawa/suji* (semolina flour)
¼ cup (50 ml) vegetable oil

1. Wash the shrimp thoroughly under running water. Drain well and pat dry with paper towels. Put in a bowl and add ½ teaspoon of the salt and the lemon juice. Stir well, then marinate for 15 minutes.

2. Put the turmeric, chile powder, the remaining ½ teaspoon salt, the ginger paste, and garlic paste in a bowl, and stir well. Add to the marinated shrimp and stir well. Cover the bowl and put in the refrigerator to marinate for 30 minutes.

3. Put the rice flour and semolina in a flat dish and stir well. Dredge the shrimp in the mixture.

4. Place a medium nonstick sauté pan over medium heat. Add the oil. When small bubbles appear at the bottom of the pan, lower the heat to low. Slide one shrimp at a time into the hot oil and fry, turning often with a slotted spoon, until golden and crisp. Remove with the slotted spoon and drain on paper towels. Serve immediately.

Masala Fried Squid

······◦{ **Fried marinated squid** }◦···

Squid is so tender that it cooks fast. Serve these crisp rings as a side dish with *dal* and rice.

Serves 4.

6 medium squid bodies
2 teaspoons red chile powder
½ teaspoon ground turmeric
¾ teaspoon table salt
1 tablespoon ginger paste (page 12)
1 tablespoon garlic paste (page 12)
1 tablespoon chopped fresh cilantro
1 tablespoon freshly squeezed lemon juice
½ large egg, whisked
1 quart (800 ml) vegetable oil
½ cup rice flour

1. Clean, wash, and drain the squid in a colander. Cut into ¼-inch-thick (½-cm-thick) rings.

2. Combine the chile powder, turmeric, salt, ginger paste, garlic paste, cilantro, lemon juice, and egg in a bowl. Add the squid rings and stir to coat. Cover the bowl with plastic wrap and set aside to marinate for 30 minutes.

3. Place a nonstick wok over high heat and add the oil. Spread the rice flour on a plate. When small bubbles appear at the bottom of the wok, lower the heat to medium, roll the squid in the rice flour, and slide the rings into the hot oil. Cook, stirring with a slotted spoon, until golden and crisp. Remove with the slotted spoon and drain on paper towels.

4. Serve hot.

Meen Pathiris

··········{ Fried fish rolls }··

This traditional recipe from Kerala is, sadly, not so commonplace these days. In some homes, the snack is steamed rather than fried, but I find the crispness of the fried version more appealing.

Serves 4.

3½ ounces (100 grams) whitefish fillets
1 teaspoon red chile powder
1 teaspoon ground coriander
½ teaspoon ground turmeric
1¼ teaspoons table salt
5 tablespoons plus 1 quart (800 ml) vegetable oil
5 to 6 fresh curry leaves
5 shallots, sliced
½-inch (1-cm) piece fresh ginger, chopped
10 cloves garlic, chopped
1 green chile, stemmed and chopped
¼ teaspoon *garam masala* (spice mix; page 27)
¼ teaspoon ground fennel seeds
1 teaspoon freshly squeezed lemon juice
1⅔ cups (200 grams) *maida* (refined flour) or pastry flour
2 large eggs, well beaten

1. Pat the fish dry with an absorbent towel. Put in a bowl and sprinkle with the chile powder, coriander, turmeric, and ½ teaspoon of the salt. Toss once or twice. Cover the bowl and put in the refrigerator to marinate for 30 minutes.

2. Place a nonstick sauté pan over medium heat and add 2 tablespoons of the oil. When small bubbles appear at the bottom of the pan, add the curry leaves, shallots, ginger, garlic, and chile, and sauté until the shallots are golden brown.

3. Add the fish and stir. Lower the heat to low and cook for 6 to 7 minutes. Transfer the mixture to a plate and flake the fish into small pieces.

4. Sprinkle with the *garam masala*, fennel, and lemon juice. Set aside.

5. Sift the *maida* and the remaining ¾ teaspoon salt into a bowl. Rub in 3 tablespoons of the oil. Add ⅓ cup (70 ml) water and knead to make a stiff dough. Cover the dough with a damp cloth and let rest for 20 minutes. Divide into 4 portions.

6. Roll out each portion into a thick 6-inch (15-cm) round. Place a portion of the fish mixture in the center of each, gather the edges to enclose the filling, and seal the *pathiris*.

7. Place a nonstick wok over high heat and add 1 quart (800 ml) oil. When small bubbles appear at the bottom of the wok, slide in the *pathiris*, two at a time, and cook, gently stirring with a slotted spoon, until golden on all sides. Remove with the slotted spoon and drain on paper towels. Leave the wok on the heat.

8. Dip the *pathiris* in the eggs and return them to the hot oil. Remove when the egg is cooked. Drain on paper towels and serve immediately.

Patrani Machchi

·········⟨ **Fish fillets spread with green chutney, wrapped in banana leaves, and steamed** ⟩··········

Traditionally this dish is steamed, but you can also cook it in a sauté pan over medium heat, turning it frequently so that the banana leaf doesn't burn.

Serves 4.

8 (7-ounce/200-gram) boneless pomfret fillets (you can use pompano or butterfish)
1½ teaspoons table salt
2 tablespoons freshly squeezed lemon juice
1 cup (120 grams) grated fresh coconut (or frozen unsweetened coconut)
2 cups (120 grams) chopped fresh cilantro
5 green chiles, stemmed
4 teaspoons cumin seeds
12 cloves garlic
3 or 4 banana leaves

1. Cut each fish fillet into pieces 2 inches by 1½ inches (5 cm by 4 cm). Sprinkle with ½ teaspoon of the salt and 1 tablespoon of the lemon juice and put in the refrigerator to marinate for 30 minutes.

2. Put the coconut, cilantro, chiles, cumin, and garlic in a food processor with 2 to 3 tablespoons water and process until smooth. Add the remaining 1 teaspoon salt and the remaining 1 tablespoon lemon juice and blend. Spread the chutney on both sides of all the fish pieces and marinate for about 15 minutes.

3. Cut each banana leaf into 4 pieces. Holding them with tongs, singe the leaves one at a time over an open flame to make them malleable.

4. Place a few marinated fish pieces in the center of each piece of banana leaf and smear some of the chutney on them. Fold in the ends of the leaf to cover the fish pieces completely and shape into a parcel.

5. Put water in the bottom of a steamer over high heat. Place the fish parcels in the top of the steamer, lower the heat to medium, cover, and steam for 15 minutes.

6. Serve the fish in the leaf so that each guest can open the parcel and enjoy the fish hot.

Paturi Maach

This is a fantastic dish both in taste and in presentation. Serve the fish still wrapped in the leaf. As your guests open the parcels, the heady aroma of the fish and mustard will fill the air, getting the meal off to a spectacular start. In India, I would use *betki* fish, but you can use red snapper fillets.

Serves 4.

4 (6-inch-square) pieces tender banana leaf
4 (4-ounce/125-gram) *betki* or red snapper fillets
¼ cup (50 ml) filtered mustard oil (see Note page 87)
6 teaspoons *kalonji* (nigella; see Note page 231)
1 teaspoon ground turmeric
1 teaspoon red chile powder
1 teaspoon table salt
6 teaspoons black mustard seed paste (see Note)
¼ teaspoon sugar

1. Singe each banana-leaf piece over an open gas flame to make it malleable.

2. Wash the fish thoroughly under running water and drain well. Pat dry with paper towels and cut the fillets into 4-inch squares.

3. Put 2 tablespoons of the mustard oil in a large bowl. Add the *kalonji*, turmeric, chile powder, and salt. Stir well. Add the fish pieces and toss so that all of them are coated with the mixture. Cover the bowl with plastic wrap and put in the refrigerator to marinate for 1 hour.

4. Add the mustard paste, sugar, and remaining 2 tablespoons mustard oil, and stir. Cover the bowl again with plastic wrap and return to the refrigerator for 30 minutes more.

5. Wrap the individual fish pieces in the banana-leaf pieces. Secure the open edges of the banana packets with toothpicks so that they do not open during the steaming process.

6. Place a steamer over high heat, and add 1½ cups (300 ml) water, and bring it to a boil. Fit a perforated plate in the steamer and place the fish parcels on it. Lower the heat to medium, cover, and steam for 15 minutes.

7. Serve the fish in the leaf so that each guest can open the parcel and enjoy the fish hot.

···········❊{ **Note** }❊· To make the paste, combine 1 teaspoon ground mustard seeds with 2 teaspoons water.

Pomfret Reichado

·······*{ **Fish with red chiles** }*· ··································

This dish is a classic Goan fish recipe. It uses *reichado masala*, which includes Kashmiri red chiles and vinegar. This dish is best prepared just before serving; otherwise the fish will lose its crispness.

Serves 4.

4 (7½-ounce/220-gram) whole pomfret fish (you can use pompano or butterfish)
30 to 35 Kashmiri red chiles, stemmed and broken in half
1 tablespoon cumin seeds
4 to 6 cloves garlic
2-inch (5-cm) piece fresh ginger, chopped
10 to 12 whole black peppercorns
2 tablespoons tamarind pulp
¼ cup (50 ml) malt vinegar or cider vinegar
1 teaspoon table salt
2 cups (400 ml) vegetable oil

1. Clean and wash the fish thoroughly. Pat dry with paper towels. With a sharp knife, make 2 or 3 slits on either side of the center bone on both sides of the fish. Also make a slit in the side of each fish.

2. Soak the chiles, cumin, garlic, ginger, peppercorns, and tamarind pulp in the vinegar for 10 to 15 minutes. Transfer to a mini food processor with 2 tablespoons water and process to a smooth paste. Add the salt.

3. Using your fingertips, apply the ground spice paste all over the fish, coating it liberally and stuffing the paste inside the slits. The fish should be covered completely with the paste. Put the fish on a plate and put in the refrigerator for 30 minutes to marinate.

4. Place a wide nonstick sauté pan over high heat and add the oil. When small bubbles appear at the bottom of the pan, gently place one fish in the oil. Lower the heat to medium and fry, turning once, for 10 to 15 minutes or until both sides are golden brown. Fry the remaining fish and serve hot.

Poricha Konju

Shrimp fry well, but only if the tender meat is protected from the hot oil. I personally enjoy the soothing flavor of curry leaves in the crisp coating here. Serve the shrimp with a sauce or chutney of your choice.

Serves 4.

14 ounces (400 grams) medium shrimp, peeled and deveined
1 tablespoon freshly squeezed lemon juice
2 teaspoons table salt
25 fresh curry leaves
4 green chiles, stemmed and chopped
3 cloves garlic, chopped
½ teaspoon *ajwain*
2 teaspoons red chile powder
¼ cup plus 2 tablespoons (60 grams) rice flour
¼ cup (50 ml) vegetable oil

1. Wash and drain the shrimp. Pat them dry with an absorbent towel. Put them in a bowl, add the lemon juice and salt, and toss. Set aside to marinate for 15 minutes.

2. Put the curry leaves, chiles, and garlic in a spice grinder with 2 tablespoons water and grind to a smooth paste. Crush the *ajwain* lightly in a mortar and stir it into the paste along with the chile powder.

3. Add the paste to the marinated shrimp and stir well so that the shrimp are well coated. Set aside to marinate for 15 to 20 minutes. Sprinkle with the rice flour and stir well.

4. Place a medium nonstick sauté pan over medium heat and add the oil. When small bubbles appear at the bottom of the pan, add the shrimp and cook, stirring continuously, until golden brown and crisp. Remove with a slotted spoon and drain on paper towels.

5. Serve hot.

Chef's tip The paste here should be thick enough to adhere to the shrimp. You can substitute fish, crabmeat, squid, or even mussels for the shrimp.

Shrimp Idlis

···········❧ **Steamed rice cakes with shrimp** ❧···········

New snack ideas are always welcome. Luckily, you can add just about any chopped vegetable, nut, or spice to *idli* batter. Here, we add shrimp. Serve these *idlis* with coconut cilantro chutney (page 520). See page 591 for details about *idli* steamers.

Makes 12.

½ cup (100 grams) parboiled rice
¼ cup (50 grams) *dhuli urad dal* (split skinless black gram)
4 ounces (110 grams) small shrimp, peeled and deveined
1½ teaspoons table salt
¼ teaspoon crushed dried red chile
1 tablespoon chopped fresh cilantro
1 tablespoon vegetable oil

1. Put the rice in a bowl, wash in plenty of water 2 or 3 times, and drain. Add 1½ cups (300 ml) water and soak overnight. Wash the *dal* and soak in 1 cup (200 ml) water overnight.

2. Drain the rice and put in a spice grinder. Grind to a smooth, thick paste. Transfer to a large bowl. Drain the *dal* and grind to a smooth, thick paste. Add it to the rice and whisk well.

3. Add 1¼ cups (250 ml) water to the batter and whisk to get a smooth consistency (a little thicker than pancake batter).

4. Cover the bowl with plastic wrap and set in a warm place to ferment for 4 to 5 hours or overnight.

5. Wash the shrimp well under running water and drain in a colander. Chop them and put in a bowl.

6. Place a steamer over high heat and add 2 cups (400 ml) water. Bring to a boil.

7. Reserving a few shrimp, add the rest of the shrimp to the batter along with the salt, chile, and cilantro, and stir well.

8. Lightly grease an *idli* mold with oil. Pour a spoonful of batter into each indentation and place one of the remaining shrimp over the batter in each.

9. Fit the *idli* molds onto the stand, place the stand in the steamer, and steam for 12 to 15 minutes. Remove from the heat and let cool for 3 to 4 minutes.

10. Spoon out the *idlis* and serve immediately.

Shrimp Karanji

······§ Half moon–shaped pies stuffed with spicy shrimp §······

Karanji is a very popular snack in Maharashtra. It is stuffed with a sweet coconut filling and is often made during festivals and for special occasions. I do something different here by using a savory shrimp filling. These are best consumed fresh, on the spot!

Makes 12.

1 cup (120 grams) *maida* (refined flour) or pastry flour
1½ tablespoons coarse *rawa/suji* (semolina flour)
¼ cup (50 grams) ghee
¼ cup (50 ml) milk
10 ounces (300 grams) shrimp, peeled and deveined
1 teaspoon fresh ginger paste (page 12)
1 teaspoon fresh garlic paste (page 12)
2 teaspoons fresh green chile paste (page 13)
½ teaspoon table salt
1 tablespoon plus 1 quart (800 ml) vegetable oil
2 medium red onions, chopped
¼ cup (25 grams) grated fresh coconut (or frozen unsweetened coconut)
¼ cup (13 grams) chopped fresh cilantro

1. Make the dough: Sift the *maida* into a bowl. Add the semolina and rub in the ghee with your fingertips until the mixture resembles bread crumbs. Add the milk and knead in enough water to make a semisoft dough. Cover the dough with a damp cloth and set aside for 30 minutes.

2. Wash the shrimp well under running water and drain in a colander. Chop them and put in a bowl. Add the ginger paste, garlic paste, chile paste, and salt, and stir well.

3. Place a nonstick sauté pan over medium heat and add 1 tablespoon of the oil. When small bubbles appear at the bottom of the pan, add the onions and sauté until light golden.

4. Add the shrimp mixture and cook until all the moisture evaporates. Add the coconut and cilantro, and stir well. Set aside to cool.

5. Divide the dough into 12 portions and roll them out into 3-inch (7½-cm) rounds. Place each round on a work surface, place 1 portion of shrimp mixture on one half of each round, and fold over to make a half-moon shape. Press the edges to seal the *karanjis* well.

6. Place a nonstick wok over high heat and add the oil. When small bubbles appear at the bottom of the wok, slide in the *karanjis*, two at a time, and cook, stirring with a slotted spoon, until they puff up slightly. Turn and continue cooking until both sides are light golden. Remove with the slotted spoon and drain on paper towels.

7. Serve hot.

Shrimp Vadai

South Indian cuisine features many different fritters, and I like to serve this particular one to liven up a simple meal of lentils and rice.

Serves 4.

9 ounces (250 grams) small shrimp, peeled and deveined
1 medium red onion, minced
2 tablespoons grated fresh coconut (or frozen unsweetened coconut)
½ teaspoon ground turmeric
1½ teaspoons red chile powder
½ teaspoon *garam masala* (spice mix; page 27)
20 fresh curry leaves
1½ teaspoons table salt
¾ cup (75 grams) *besan* (chickpea/gram flour)
¼ cup (15 grams) chopped fresh cilantro
1 quart (800 ml) vegetable oil

1. Wash the shrimp well under running water. Pat them dry and put them in a food processor. Add the onion, coconut, turmeric, chile powder, *garam masala*, curry leaves, and salt, and pulse to make a coarse mixture.

2. Transfer to a bowl, add the *besan* and cilantro, and stir well.

3. Divide the mixture into 16 portions and roll them into balls.

4. Place a nonstick wok over high heat and add the oil. When small bubbles appear at the bottom of the wok, gently slide in the balls, eight at a time, and cook, stirring gently with a slotted spoon, for 3 to 4 minutes or until golden brown. Remove with the slotted spoon and drain on paper towels.

5. Serve hot.

Talela Rawas

······· *❈*{ Pan-fried marinated fish }*❈* ···

Rawas is Indian salmon, different from American salmon and quite big, with dark flesh. In the United States, you can substitute rockfish or grouper. This is a delicious but very simple dish, perfect for new cooks who don't have much experience with fish. Serve it with *dal* and rice.

Serves 4.

1 pound (500 grams) *rawas* (Indian salmon) or rockfish or grouper fillets
2 tablespoons freshly squeezed lemon juice
1 teaspoon table salt
1½ teaspoons red chile powder
½ teaspoon ground turmeric
½ tablespoon tamarind pulp
¾ cup (110 grams) coarsely ground raw rice
½ cup (100 ml) vegetable oil
1 tablespoon chopped fresh cilantro

1. Cut the fish into 1-inch-thick (2½-cm-thick) slices. Wash well under running water and drain in a colander. Press the slices between paper towels to remove any excess moisture.

2. Sprinkle with 1 tablespoon of the lemon juice and ½ teaspoon of the salt, and set aside.

3. Put the chile powder, turmeric, tamarind pulp, the remaining ½ teaspoon salt, and 2 tablespoons water in a bowl, and stir well. Add the fish and stir to coat. Set aside to marinate for 15 to 20 minutes.

4. Add the ground rice and toss to coat.

5. Place a nonstick sauté pan over medium heat and add the oil. When small bubbles appear at the bottom of the pan, add the fish pieces, a few at a time, and cook, turning once or twice, for a few minutes or until they are cooked through and both sides are light golden brown.

6. Transfer to a serving platter and garnish with the cilantro. Sprinkle with the remaining 1 tablespoon lemon juice and serve immediately.

Tandoori Pomfret

····**⋇**⟨ **Pomfret cooked tandoor style** ⟩**⋇**···

Pomfret cooked in a tandoor oven is the most popular fish dish in any good seafood restaurant in Mumbai. But for ease of preparation, I've given instructions for cooking it in a conventional oven. The best way to enjoy this fish is with lots of lemon juice and lemon wedges.

Serves 4.

4 (7½-ounce/220-gram) whole pomfret fish, (you can use pompano or butterfish)
1¾ teaspoons table salt
2 tablespoons freshly squeezed lemon juice
1 teaspoon fresh ginger paste (page 12)
1 teaspoon fresh garlic paste (page 12)
1½ cups (375 grams) plain yogurt
2½ teaspoons red chile powder
2 teaspoons *garam masala* (spice mix; page 27)
2 tablespoons vegetable oil
½ teaspoon *ajwain*
¼ cup (25 grams) *besan* (chickpea/gram flour)
¾ teaspoon ground turmeric
¼ cup (60 ml) melted butter

1. Clean and wash the fish thoroughly. Pat dry with paper towels. Make incisions on both sides of each fish. Combine 1 teaspoon of the salt, the lemon juice, ginger paste, and garlic paste, and rub it all over the fish. Put the fish on a platter, and set aside for 20 minutes.

2. Combine the yogurt, the remaining ¾ teaspoon salt, the chile powder, and the *garam masala* in a bowl and set aside.

3. Place a nonstick sauté pan over medium heat and add the oil. When small bubbles appear at the bottom of the pan, add the *ajwain* and *besan*, and sauté for 4 to 5 minutes or until fragrant. Remove from the heat and stir in the turmeric. Add to the yogurt mixture and whisk well. Rub this mixture all over the fish and into the incisions. Cover the platter with plastic wrap and put in the refrigerator to marinate for 1 hour.

4. Preheat the oven to 350°F/180°C.

5. Put the fish on a greased baking sheet and bake on the middle rack of the oven for 8 to 10 minutes, watching carefully that they do not overcook.

6. Baste with the butter and cook for another 5 minutes or until the fish have a crip and golden crust, again watching carefully that they do not overcook.

7. Serve hot.

Sungatache Bhaje

·······◦} **Crisp shrimp patties** {◦···

My wife, Alyona, loves *pulao* with shrimp, and the kids adore fried shrimp, so there is always something interesting happening with shrimp in our kitchen. And here is an example of just that: wonderfully spiced and crisp shrimp patties.

Makes 8.

7 ounces (200 grams) shrimp, peeled and deveined
3 cloves garlic, chopped
½-inch (1-cm) piece fresh ginger, chopped
½ teaspoon ground turmeric
1 teaspoon table salt
1 teaspoon red chile powder
3 tablespoons *maida* (refined flour) or pastry flour
2 tablespoons fine *rawa/suji* (semolina flour)
¼ cup (50 ml) vegetable oil

1. Wash the shrimp well under running water and pat dry with an absorbent cloth so that all the excess moisture is removed.

2. Put the shrimp in a bowl. Add the garlic, ginger, turmeric, salt, chile powder, *maida*, and semolina, and combine well.

3. Place a nonstick sauté pan over medium heat and add the oil. When small bubbles appear at the bottom of the pan, pour in a spoonful of the shrimp mixture and flatten it slightly. Cook, flipping sides a couple of times, for 2 minutes on each side or until the shrimp are cooked through and crisp on the outside. Remove with a slotted spoon and drain on paper towels.

4. Serve hot.

Yera Varuval

·······❊{ **Crisp sautéed hot-and-sour shrimp** }❊·····································

This dish from the northern part of Tamil Nadu is also called *eral varuval*—shrimp fry. The ginger and garlic balance out the flavor of the shrimp beautifully. I do not mind eating these on their own as a snack, but ideally they are accompanied with rice and *sambhar* (page 32).

Serves 4.

14 ounces (400 grams) medium shrimp, peeled and deveined
1 tablespoon fresh ginger paste (page 12)
1 tablespoon fresh garlic paste (page 12)
2½ teaspoons ground roasted cumin (page 32)
1 tablespoon tamarind pulp, or the juice of 1 lemon
1 tablespoon red chile powder
25 fresh curry leaves (5 chopped, 20 whole)
1 teaspoon ground turmeric
3½ tablespoons rice flour
2 teaspoons table salt
6 tablespoons (90 ml) vegetable oil
2 medium red onions, cut into rings
2 lemons, cut into wedges

1. Wash the shrimp and drain well. Pat dry with a kitchen towel.

2. Combine the ginger paste, garlic paste, cumin, tamarind pulp, chile powder, the 5 chopped curry leaves, turmeric, rice flour, salt, and 2 tablespoons of the oil in a bowl. Add the shrimp and toss well. Put in the refrigerator to marinate for 30 minutes.

3. Place a shallow nonstick sauté pan over medium heat and add the remaining 4 tablespoons oil. Add the 20 whole curry leaves and cook until dark green and crisp. Add the shrimp and cook until cooked through and golden brown and crisp. Remove with a slotted spoon and drain on paper towels.

4. Garnish with the onions and lemons, and serve immediately.

Andhra Chile Chicken

········-❧{ **Andhra-style spicy chicken** }❧··

Chiles are an integral part of the cooking of Andhra Pradesh, a state located in the southern part of India. You can vary the heat of this dish by reducing or increasing the number of chiles used. You can also try different varieties of red chiles for different flavors and heat levels.

Serves 4.

1¾ pounds (800 grams) skinless, boneless chicken pieces (white and dark meat)
4 tablespoons plus 1 teaspoon (65 ml) vegetable oil
1 teaspoon cumin seeds
1-inch (2½-cm) cinnamon stick
4 green cardamom pods
4 whole cloves
18 to 20 dried red chiles
1 medium onion, sliced
15 to 20 fresh curry leaves
4 green chiles, stemmed and slit
1 teaspoon table salt
1 tablespoon ground coriander

1. Cut the chicken into small pieces and put them in a bowl.

2. Place a small nonstick sauté pan over medium heat and add 1 teaspoon of the oil. When small bubbles begin to appear at the bottom of the pan, add the cumin seeds, cinnamon, cardamom, and cloves, and sauté for 1 minute. Set aside to cool.

3. Soak the red chiles in ¼ cup (50 ml) water for 30 minutes. Put the sautéed spices and the soaked chiles in a mini food processor with a little of the soaking water and process to a smooth paste.

4. Add the paste to the chicken pieces and toss to combine, cover the bowl, and put it in the refrigerator to marinate for 2 to 3 hours.

5. Place a medium nonstick sauté pan over high heat and add 2 tablespoons of the oil. When small bubbles begin to appear at the bottom of the pan, add the onion, curry leaves, green chiles, salt, and coriander, and sauté for 1 minute.

6. Add the chicken pieces and stir well. Add the remaining 2 tablespoons oil and cook, stirring frequently, for 10 minutes or until the chicken is cooked through. Serve hot.

Chandi Kaliyan

·······*§ **Chicken with silver foil** §*· ···························

The title of the dish means "buds of silver," and in this dish the chicken is cooked in a mild marinade until it is very tender, similar to the softness of a flower bud. Served on a bed of rice with a blanket of edible silver foil, this is a grand presentation that always impresses. It sells like hotcakes at our Yellow Chilli restaurants.

Most Indian grocers sell silver foil. You can also find it online.

Serves 4.

1¾ pounds (800 grams) boneless chicken, cut into 16 (1-inch/2½-cm) cubes

~ For the first marinade:
2 teaspoons fresh ginger paste (page 12)
2 teaspoons fresh garlic paste (page 12)
1 teaspoon table salt
1 teaspoon ground white pepper
1 tablespoon freshly squeezed lemon juice

~ For the second marinade:
¾ cup (60 grams) cream cheese
¼ cup (65 grams) plain yogurt
1 teaspoon cornstarch
½ teaspoon ground white pepper
½ teaspoon ground green cardamom
2 green chiles, stemmed and chopped
½ tablespoon chopped fresh cilantro
¼ cup (50 ml) heavy cream
¼ teaspoon freshly grated nutmeg
½ teaspoon table salt

~ For cooking and serving:
Melted butter
Steamed rice
1 teaspoon freshly squeezed lemon juice
1 teaspoon *chaat masala* (spice mix for *chaat*; page 24)
3 sheets *chandi ka varq* (edible silver foil; available at Indian grocery stores)

1. Place the chicken cubes in a large bowl.

2. Make the first marinade: Stir the ginger paste, garlic paste, salt, white pepper, and lemon juice together, and rub it all over the chicken. Cover the bowl with plastic wrap and put in the refrigerator for 30 minutes.

3. Make the second marinade: Put the cheese and yogurt on a plate and stir well with your palm until smooth and creamy. Add the cornstarch, white pepper, cardamom, chiles, cilantro, cream, nutmeg, and salt.

4. Add the second marinade to the chicken and stir well. Cover and put in the refrigerator to marinate for 4 hours.

5. Preheat the oven to 450°F/230°C.

6. String the chicken cubes, with the marinade, onto long, thin skewers. Place on a baking sheet and bake for 7 minutes, turning frequently and basting the chicken with the melted butter.

7. Baste with butter again and bake for 1 minute more.

8. Slide the chicken cubes off the skewers onto a bed of rice. Sprinkle with the lemon juice and *chaat masala* and cover with the *chandi ka varq*. Serve immediately.

Chettinaad Fried Chicken

Chettinaad cuisine originates in the deep southern region of Tamil Nadu. It has a strong character: Freshly ground spices like pepper and chiles mingle with garlic and ginger and liberal amounts of oil. Deeply flavored with curry leaves, this fried chicken needs some marinating time, so plan ahead. And I do recommend that you adjust the spice levels to your taste.

Serves 4.

1 (2-pound/1-kg) whole bone-in chicken
2 medium red onions, roughly chopped
1-inch (2½-cm) piece fresh ginger, roughly chopped
5 cloves garlic, roughly chopped
4 green chiles, stemmed and roughly chopped
6 dried red chiles, stemmed and broken in half
½ teaspoon ground turmeric
1 tablespoon freshly squeezed lemon juice
2 tablespoons rice flour
1½ teaspoons table salt
15 fresh curry leaves, finely shredded
1 cup (200 ml) vegetable oil

1. Split the chicken through the backbone and separate the breast into two equal halves. Make three or four ½-inch-deep (1-cm-deep) cuts on the breast and leg pieces.

2. Put the onions, ginger, garlic, green chiles, and red chiles in a food processor with 3 tablespoons water, and process to a smooth paste. Transfer to a deep bowl and stir in the turmeric, lemon juice, rice flour, and salt.

3. Add the chicken pieces and toss to coat them liberally with the paste. Add the curry leaves and stir. Cover the bowl with plastic wrap and put in the refrigerator for 2 to 3 hours to marinate. Remove from the refrigerator and remove the chicken pieces from the marinade. Reserve the marinade.

4. Place a deep nonstick wok over medium heat and add the oil. When small bubbles appear at the bottom of the wok, add the chicken and increase the heat to high. Sauté for 2 minutes on both sides. This helps to seal in the juices. Lower the heat to medium, cover, and cook for 15 to 20 minutes, turning over and basting frequently with the reserved marinade. Sprinkle with 2 to 3 tablespoons water if the chicken starts drying out and the marinade is all used up.

5. Cook over high heat for 6 to 7 minutes, so that the surface of the chicken is crisp and golden brown.

6. Cut into smaller pieces and serve immediately.

Chicken 65

There are many anecdotes about the origin of this dish's name, but nobody really knows for sure how it came to be coined. In any case, the name stuck, and the dish is one of the most popular chicken appetizers in Andhra Pradesh. Most places serve bone-in chicken, but I feel boneless chicken makes it more enjoyable.

Serves 4.

14 ounces (400 grams) boneless, skinless chicken, cut into 1½-inch (4-cm) pieces
1 tablespoon fresh ginger paste (page 12)
1 tablespoon fresh garlic paste (page 12)
1 teaspoon ground black pepper
1 teaspoon table salt
1 large egg, whisked
1 quart (800 ml) plus 2 tablespoons vegetable oil
½ cup (125 grams) plain yogurt
2 tablespoons red chile paste (see Note page 13)
1 teaspoon *maida* (refined flour) or pastry flour
½ teaspoon brown mustard seeds
4 dried red chiles, stemmed and broken in half
20 to 15 fresh curry leaves
¼ cup (30 grams) grated fresh coconut (or frozen unsweetened coconut)

1. Put the chicken in a bowl. Add the ginger paste, garlic paste, pepper, salt, and egg, and combine well. Add ½ tablespoon water and combine well.

2. Place a nonstick wok over high heat and add the 1 quart (800 ml) oil. When small bubbles appear at the bottom of the wok, lower the heat to medium and add the chicken pieces, a few at a time, and cook, stirring with a slotted spoon, for 3 to 4 minutes or until cooked through. Remove with the slotted spoon and drain on paper towels.

3. Place the yogurt, chile paste, and flour in a bowl and whisk well.

4. Place a nonstick sauté pan over medium heat and add the remaing 2 tablespoons oil. When small bubbles appear at the bottom of the pan, add the mustard seeds, chiles, and curry leaves. When the seeds sputter, add the yogurt mixture and stir well. Sauté for 1 to 2 minutes.

5. Add the chicken and cook for 5 to 7 minutes or until all the excess moisture evaporates.

6. Add the coconut and toss well. Serve hot.

Chicken Cafreal

······❧{ Chicken marinated in a green masala and cooked until dry }❧······

In my opinion, if there is a dish that can take tandoori chicken head-on, it is chicken *cafreal*, a dry dish from Goa.

Serves 4.

1 (2-pound/1-kg) whole bone-in chicken
3 tablespoons plus 2 cups (400 ml) vegetable oil
2 medium red onions, sliced
1 tablespoon coriander seeds
1 teaspoon cumin seeds
4 whole cloves
3 green cardamom pods
8 whole black peppercorns
1-inch (2½-cm) cinnamon stick
1 tablespoon white poppy seeds
1-inch (2½-cm) piece fresh ginger, roughly chopped
4 cloves garlic, roughly chopped
4 green chiles, stemmed and roughly chopped
⅔ cup (40 grams) chopped fresh cilantro
½ teaspoon ground turmeric
1 tablespoon tamarind pulp
1½ teaspoons table salt
3 tablespoons white vinegar

1. Remove the skin from the chicken, trim off excess fat, and cut the chicken into 8 pieces. Make deep incisions in the flesh using a sharp knife. Put the pieces in a bowl.

2. Place a nonstick wok over high heat and add the 2 cups oil. When small bubbles appear at the bottom of the wok, add the onions and cook until golden brown. Remove with a slotted spoon and drain on paper towels; set aside.

3. Place a small nonstick pan over medium heat. Let it heat for 2 minutes, then add the coriander, cumin, cloves, cardamom, peppercorns, cinnamon, and poppy seeds, and dry-roast for 1½ minutes or until fragrant. Set aside to cool to room temperature.

4. Transfer the cooled spices to a food processor. Add the ginger, garlic, chiles, cilantro, turmeric, tamarind pulp, and 6 tablespoons (90 ml) water, and process to a paste.

5. Transfer the paste to the bowl with the chicken pieces. Add the salt and stir well so that all the pieces are coated. Cover the bowl with plastic wrap and put it in the refrigerator for 2 to 3 hours to marinate.

6. Place a large nonstick sauté pan over medium heat and add the 3 tablespoons oil. When small bubbles appear at the bottom of the pan, add the marinated chicken pieces and stir. Cover and cook, stirring occasionally, for 8 to 10 minutes or until the chicken is cooked through.

7. Uncover and sauté for 2 to 3 minutes so that all the moisture evaporates and the *masala* coats the chicken pieces well.

8. Garnish with the onions and serve hot.

Chicken Kathi Roll

·······❊{ **Spiced boneless chicken pieces rolled in *roomali rotis*** }❊·······

Kolkata has the famous street food called *kathi* rolls, which are basically kebabs served rolled up in a flatbread spread with chutneys and a special *masala*. This is my home version, and it makes an ideal starter at a party when you serve it cut into bite-size pieces: Spear each piece with a toothpick to hold the roll together.

Roomali rotis, named for their resemblance to a handkerchief (*roomal*), are available at most Indian grocery stores. If you cannot find them, you can use soft flour tortillas or regular Indian *rotis* as a substitute.

Makes 4 rolls.

7 ounces (200 grams) boneless chicken, cut into thin strips
1½ teaspoons freshly squeezed lemon juice
1 teaspoon red chile powder
1 teaspoon fresh garlic paste (page 12)
1 teaspoon fresh ginger paste (page 12)
1 teaspoon *garam masala* (spice mix; page 27)
4 green chiles, stemmed and crushed
½ teaspoon table salt
2 tablespoons vegetable oil
1 teaspoon ground roasted cumin (page 32)
2 medium red onions, sliced
1 medium carrot, peeled and cut into thin strips
4 frozen *roomali rotis*
¼ cup (60 grams) *pudina aur dhaniya* chutney (mint-and-cilantro chutney; page 22)
2 tablespoons chopped fresh cilantro

1. Put the chicken in a bowl. Add the lemon juice, chile powder, garlic paste, ginger paste, *garam masala*, green chiles, and salt, and stir well. Cover the bowl with plastic wrap and put in the refrigerator for 1 hour to marinate.

2. Place a nonstick sauté pan over medium heat and add the oil. When small bubbles appear at the bottom of the pan, add the marinated chicken and sauté for 10 to 12 minutes, stirring frequently. Add the cumin and stir well. Divide into 4 portions.

3. In a separate bowl, combine the onions and carrot. Divide into 4 portions and set aside.

4. Put the frozen *roomali rotis* in a microwave oven and cook on high for 1 minute. Lay them out on a work surface. Spread 1 tablespoon of the chutney over each, arrange 1 portion of the cooked chicken in the center lengthwise, and sprinkle with ½ tablespoon cilantro. Next sprinkle with a portion of the onion-carrot mixture.

5. Fold one side of the *roti* over the filling, then fold the other side over it. Beginning from one end, roll up tightly. Repeat with the remaining *roti* and filling, and serve immediately.

Chicken Tikka

············*⟩ **Bite-size spicy chicken kebabs** ⟨*············

Chicken *tikka* is probably the first introduction to Indian food for most non-Indians. Boneless tandoori chicken is called a *tikka*—a small bite-size kebab. We make them all the time. And if you have leftovers, I would suggest you make a chicken *tikka chaat*: Toss warm *tikkas* with colored bell peppers and top with whisked plain yogurt and cilantro or mint chutney. It makes a great easy lunch.

Serves 4

1¾ pounds (800 grams) boneless, skinless chicken, cut into 1½-inch (4-cm) cubes
1 teaspoon Kashmiri chile powder or paprika powder
1 tablespoon freshly squeezed lemon juice
½ teaspoon table salt

~ For the marinade:
½ cup (125 grams) plain yogurt, drained until thick (see Note page 80)
1 teaspoon Kashmiri chile powder or paprika powder
1 teaspoon table salt
2 tablespoons fresh ginger paste (page 12)
2 tablespoons fresh garlic paste (page 12)
2 tablespoons freshly squeezed lemon juice
½ teaspoon *garam masala* (spice mix; page 27)
2 tablespoons refined mustard oil (see Note page 87)
2 tablespoons melted butter
½ teaspoon *chaat masala* (spice mix for *chaat*; page 24)
2 onions, cut into rings
1 medium lemon, cut into wedges

1. Put the chicken in a deep bowl.

2. Place the chile powder, lemon juice, and salt in a small bowl, and stir well. Rub this paste onto the chicken cubes so that they are evenly coated. Cover the bowl with plastic wrap and put in the refrigerator for 30 minutes to marinate.

3. Make the marinade: Put the yogurt in a bowl. Stir in the chile powder, salt, ginger paste, garlic paste, lemon juice, *garam masala*, and mustard oil. Whisk until smooth.

4. Rub the yogurt mixture into the chicken so that all the cubes are well coated. Cover the bowl and put it in the refrigerator for 3 to 4 hours to marinate.

5. Meanwhile, soak some wooden skewers in water. Preheat the oven to 400°F/200°C.

6. Thread the chicken cubes onto skewers. Arrange in a single layer on a rimmed baking sheet and bake for 10 to 12 minutes or until the chicken is cooked through. You can also cook them in a moderately hot tandoor for 10 to 12 minutes. Baste with the butter and cook for 2 minutes more.

7. Sprinkle with *chaat masala* and serve with onion rings and lemon wedges.

Egg Patties

If you like to serve surprises, then this is a recipe you should try. The soft egg center is a special touch.

Serves 4.

1 tablespoon ghee (page 37)
¼ teaspoon cumin seeds
1 teaspoon fresh garlic paste (page 12)
1-inch (2½-cm) piece fresh ginger, chopped
3 green chiles, stemmed and minced
1 small red onion, chopped
1 medium tomato, finely chopped
½ teaspoon red chile powder
¼ teaspoon ground turmeric
¼ teaspoon *garam masala* (spice mix; page 27)
1 teaspoon table salt
2 tablespoons chopped fresh cilantro
6 large eggs
4 medium potatoes, boiled, peeled, and mashed
2 cups (400 ml) vegetable oil
1½ cups (165 grams) bread crumbs
Tomato ketchup

1. Place a large nonstick sauté pan over medium heat and add the ghee. When small bubbles appear at the bottom of the pan, add the cumin seeds. When they begin to change color, add the garlic paste and ginger, and sauté for 30 seconds.

2. Add the green chiles and onion, and sauté until the onion is golden brown. Add the tomato and cook for 3 to 4 minutes. Add the chile powder, turmeric, and *garam masala*, and stir. Add ½ teaspoon of the salt and the cilantro, and stir well. Crack in 5 of the eggs one by one and cook, stirring continuously, for 5 to 6 minutes or until the mixture thickens and sets. Let cool to room temperature.

3. Crack the remaining egg in a bowl, whisk lightly, and set aside. Knead the mashed potatoes. Add the remaining ½ teaspoon salt and stir well. Divide into 8 portions. Take a portion in your palm and flatten it into a 3-inch disk. Place a heaping spoonful of the egg mixture in the center and fold in the sides to seal the stuffing. Seal by pressing the patty lightly.

4. Place a nonstick wok over high heat and add the oil. When small bubbles appear at the bottom of the wok, lower the heat to medium.

5. Put the bread crumbs on a plate. Dip each patty in the beaten egg, roll in the bread crumbs, and gently slide into the hot oil. Cook the patties over medium heat, two at a time, turning frequently with a slotted spoon, for 5 minutes or until they are golden brown all over. Remove with a slotted spoon and drain on paper towels. Serve hot with tomato ketchup.

Khaas Seekh

These are special skewered kebabs that require a little finesse to assemble, but the cooking is done in a jiffy. My wife, Alyona, prefers these kebabs when we are entertaining because she can prepare them in the early afternoon, keep them under plastic wrap in the refrigerator, and then cook them quickly just before serving the meal.

Makes 8.

½ cup (70 grams) grated *paneer* (pressed fresh cheese; page 17)
1½ teaspoons ground green cardamom
1 tablespoon *garam masala* (spice mix; page 27)
1 tablespoon chopped fresh mint
1⅓ pounds (620 grams) ground chicken
1 large egg
1½ teaspoons table salt
1 teaspoon ground white pepper
2 green chiles, stemmed and chopped
2 tablespoons vegetable oil

1. Soak 8 wooden skewers in water for 30 minutes. Drain and let dry.

2. Put the *paneer*, ¾ teaspoon of the cardamom, ½ tablespoon of the *garam masala*, and the mint in a large bowl. Stir, mashing well with your hands. Take a portion of this mixture and press it around a skewer in a thin layer. Press the ends firmly. Repeat with the remaining *paneer* mixture and skewers.

3. Put the chicken in another bowl. Add the egg, salt, the remaining ¾ teaspoon cardamom, the white pepper, the remaining ½ tablespoon *garam masala*, and the chiles, and stir well.

4. Take a portion of the chicken mixture and spread it over the *paneer* mixture on the skewers. Repeat with the remaining skewers. You can keep the *seekhs* in the refrigerator for at least an hour before cooking.

5. Place a shallow nonstick sauté pan over medium heat and add the oil. When small bubbles appear at the bottom of the pan, place the *seekhs* in the pan and cook, turning continuously, until they are golden brown all over and cooked through.

6. Drain on paper towels. When they are slightly cooled, gently slide the *seekhs* from the skewers, place them on a serving plate, and serve immediately.

Kozhi Milagu Varuval

······· ❊ ⧼ **Chicken pepper fry** ⧽ ❊ ···

This dry preparation can be served as a snack or an appetizer. The pepperiness is heady, so make plenty: Your guests will demand seconds.

Serves 4.

1¾ pounds (800 grams) boneless chicken, cut into small pieces
1 teaspoon red chile powder
1 teaspoon ground turmeric
1 teaspoon ground coriander
1½ teaspoons table salt
20 black peppercorns, crushed
2 tablespoons vegetable oil
1-inch (2½-cm) piece fresh ginger, chopped
10 cloves garlic, chopped
2 medium red onions, chopped
10 fresh curry leaves
1 large tomato, chopped

1. Put the chicken in a large bowl, add the chile powder, turmeric, coriander, 1 teaspoon of the salt, and the peppercorns, and stir well. Set aside to marinate for 30 minutes.

2. Place a nonstick saucepan over medium heat and add the oil. When small bubbles appear at the bottom of the pan, add the ginger, garlic, and onions, and sauté for 3 to 4 minutes or until the onions are golden.

3. Add the curry leaves and chicken, and sauté for 10 minutes or until well browned.

4. Add the tomato and the remaining ½ teaspoon salt, and sauté for 3 minutes or until the tomatoes are soft.

5. Cover and simmer for 10 minutes or until the chicken is cooked through. Uncover and cook until the mixture is almost dry.

6. Serve immediately.

Kuzhi Paniyaram

This is the smartest way to use up leftover *idli* batter. These are usually made in a *paniyaram tawa*, a special pan with little golf ball–sized indentations in it. If you don't have one, you can use a plain flat griddle and make five or six *paniyarams* at a time, dropping a tablespoon of batter for each and keeping a little space between them. *Paniyaram* is a popular tiffin (snack) item in the South Indian city of Chettinad and can be made either savory or sweet. Serve these with coconut cilantro chutney (page 520).

Makes 24.

½ cup (100 grams) raw short-grain rice
1 cup (200 grams) parboiled rice
¼ cup (50 grams) *dhuli urad dal* (split skinless black gram)
⅛ teaspoon fenugreek seeds
1 teaspoon table salt
5 teaspoons vegetable oil
⅛ teaspoon brown mustard seeds
⅛ teaspoon cumin seeds
5 or 6 fresh curry leaves, chopped
1 small red onion, finely chopped
1 green chile, stemmed and finely chopped

1. Put the raw rice, parboiled rice, and *dal* in a bowl, wash in plenty of water 2 or 3 times, and drain. Add the fenugreek seeds and 3 cups (600 ml) water, and soak for at least 5 hours.

2. Drain and place in a food processor with 1½ cups (300 ml) water. Process to a batter that has a grainy texture. Transfer to a large bowl. Add the salt and stir well. Cover the bowl with a lid and set aside in a warm place to ferment overnight.

3. Place a small nonstick sauté pan over medium heat and add 1 teaspoon of the oil. When small bubbles appear at the bottom of the pan, add the mustard seeds, cumin, curry leaves, onion, and chile. Sauté for 2 to 3 minutes. Add this tempering to the batter and stir well.

4. Place the *paniyaram tawa* (or a flat griddle) over medium heat and grease each indentation with a little oil. Pour a ladleful of batter in each, add a few drops of oil around the edges, and cook for 4 to 5 minutes or until the undersides are lightly browned.

5. Turn them over using a spoon, drizzle with a little more oil, and cook for 3 to 4 minutes or until the second side is lightly browned.

6. Serve immediately.

Lahsooni Dhania Murgh

The combined flavors of fresh cilantro and garlic in these succulent chicken kebabs make them one of my favorites.

Serves 4.

~ For the first marinade:
2 tablespoons fresh ginger-garlic paste (page 13)
½ teaspoon table salt
3 tablespoons freshly squeezed lemon juice
4 (4-ounce/125 gram) boneless, skinless chicken thighs

~ For the second marinade:
3 tablespoons *besan* (chickpea/gram flour)
1 teaspoon ground turmeric
3 tablespoons chopped garlic
1 cup (250 grams) plain yogurt, whisked
3 green chiles, stemmed and chopped
1 tablespoon fresh ginger-garlic paste (page 13)
5 tablespoons (35 grams) fresh cilantro-leaf paste (page 23)
2 tablespoons freshly squeezed lemon juice
1 teaspoon *garam masala* (spice mix; page 27)
1½ tablespoons vegetable oil

~ To cook and serve:
Melted butter
Chaat masala (spice mix for *chaat*; page 24)

1. Make the first marinade: Put the ginger-garlic paste, salt, and lemon juice in a large, deep bowl. Stir well and add the chicken. Stir again so that all the chicken pieces are coated. Cover and put in the refrigerator to marinate for 30 minutes.

2. Make the second marinade: Place a nonstick griddle over low heat. Add the *besan* and toast, stirring continuously, for 1 to 2 minutes or until it is fragrant and lightly browned. Add the turmeric. Toast over low heat for 2 minutes. Transfer to a dry bowl.

3. Return the griddle to low heat. Add the garlic and toast for 3 to 4 minutes or until lightly browned. Set aside.

4. Put the yogurt, chiles, ginger-garlic paste, roasted *besan* and turmeric, cilantro-leaf paste, browned garlic, lemon juice, *garam masala*, and oil in a bowl, and stir well.

5. Add to the chicken and stir well. Cover and put in the refrigerator to marinate for 3 hours.

6. Preheat the oven to 425°F/225°C.

7. Put the chicken pieces on metal skewers and arrange in a single layer on a rimmed baking sheet. Cook for 20 minutes, basting with butter every 5 minutes, until the chicken is cooked through.

8. Gently remove the chicken from the skewers. Sprinkle with the *chaat masala* and serve immediately.

Lal Murgh

···❈❴ Red chicken ❵❈··

This is an Indian version of fried chicken—and it has a kick. The presentation is spectacular, with the chicken hidden under a mound of shiny dried red chiles.

Serves 4.

1¾ pounds (800 grams) bone-in chicken, cut into 1-inch (2½-cm) pieces
1½ teaspoons table salt
1 tablespoon garlic paste (page 12)
1 tablespoon ginger paste (page 12)
1 tablespoon red chile paste (see Note page 13)
1 teaspoon *garam masala* (spice mix; page 27)
1 tablespoon *chaat masala* (spice mix for *chaat*; page 24)
1 large egg, beaten
3 tablespoons *maida* (refined flour) or pastry flour
¼ cup (20 grams) cornflakes
2 tablespoons freshly squeezed lemon juice
1 quart (800 ml) vegetable oil
1½ cups (75 grams) small, round red chiles or dried red chiles of your choice

1. Put the chicken in a bowl, add the salt, garlic paste, ginger paste, chile paste, *garam masala*, ½ tablespoon of the *chaat masala*, the egg, and *maida*, and stir.

2. Crush the cornflakes and add them to the chicken. Add the lemon juice and stir.

3. Put 3 tablespoons of the oil in a small wok. Add the chiles and sauté for 1 minute. Remove with a slotted spoon and set aside in a bowl.

4. Put the remaining oil in a large wok and place over medium heat. When small bubbles appear at the bottom of the wok, add the chicken pieces, a few at a time, and cook until crisp, turning frequently with a slotted spoon. Drain on paper towels.

5. Put the cooked chicken in a bowl. Sprinkle with the remaining ½ tablespoon *chaat masala* and toss. Transfer to a serving plate, cover with the sautéed chiles, and serve immediately.

Marghi Na Farcha

We love making this at home—it's a favorite with kids and adults alike.

Serves 4.

1 (1¾-pound/800-gram) whole chicken
1 teaspoon table salt
1½ tablespoons red chile powder
¾ teaspoon ground turmeric
1 tablespoon fresh ginger paste (page 12)
1 tablespoon fresh garlic paste (page 12)
2 tablespoons chopped fresh cilantro
2 tablespoons freshly squeezed lemon juice
2 large eggs
1 quart (800 ml) vegetable oil
1 cup (110 grams) bread crumbs
½ teaspoon *garam masala* (spice mix; page 27)

1. Put the chicken on a clean work surface and remove the skin. With a sharp knife, cut in half through the backbone and breastbone. Cut each breast half into 2 pieces. Separate the drumstick from the thigh. You now have 8 pieces of chicken.

2. Put the salt, chile powder, turmeric, ginger paste, garlic paste, cilantro, and lemon juice in a deep bowl and stir well.

3. Add the chicken and stir well. Cover the bowl and put in the refrigerator for at least 2 hours to marinate.

4. Crack the eggs into a small bowl and whisk. Put the bread crumbs in a large shallow dish.

5. Place a medium nonstick sauté pan over medium heat and add 1 tablespoon of the oil. Add the chicken and sauté for 2 to 3 minutes. Remove the chicken pieces from the pan and roll them in the bread crumbs, making sure they are well coated.

6. Put the remaining vegetable oil in a deep-fryer and heat to 375°F/190°C. Pick up 1 piece of crumb-coated chicken, dip it in the beaten eggs, and gently slide it into the hot oil. Deep-fry for 3 to 5 minutes or until golden and cooked through. Remove with a slotted spoon and drain on paper towels. Repeat with the remaining chicken.

7. Sprinkle with the *garam masala* and serve immediately.

Murgh Gilafi Tikka

······§ **Spiced grilled chicken in a yogurt sauce** §·······

Boneless chicken on skewers is always a hit—be it chicken *tikka*, *yakitori*, chicken satay, chicken shaslik, or chicken brochettes. But in my opinion *murgh gilafi tikka* beats those hands down because of the depth of flavors from the spices used. Once the *tikka* is cooked, it is simmered in a sauce before serving (unlike many other typical *tikka* preparations).

Serves 4.

4 (3½-ounce/100-gram) boneless chicken breasts, cut into 2-inch (5-cm) cubes
5 small red onions
1-inch (2½-cm) piece fresh ginger, peeled
5 cloves garlic
3 or 4 green chiles, stemmed and roughly chopped
2 tablespoons chopped fresh cilantro
¾ cup (200 grams) Greek yogurt
1 teaspoon red chile powder
1 teaspoon ground turmeric
1 teaspoon table salt
1 teaspoon *besan* (chickpea/gram flour)
3 medium tomatoes, seeded and cut into 2-inch (5-cm) pieces
2 medium green bell peppers, seeded and cut into 2-inch (5-cm) pieces
¼ cup plus 2 teaspoons (70 ml) vegetable oil, plus 2 tablespoons
6 to 8 whole cloves
2-inch (5-cm) cinnamon stick
2 bay leaves
5 or 6 green cardamom pods
2 tablespoons heavy cream

1. Pat the chicken dry with paper towels. Soak 10 (6-inch/15-cm) wooden skewers in water.

2. Chop 3 of the onions and set aside for the sauce. Cut the remaining 2 into 2-inch (5-cm) cubes and separate the layers.

3. Put the ginger, garlic, chiles, and cilantro in a mini food processor with 2 tablespoons water, and process to a fine paste.

4. Put the chicken in a large bowl. Add the yogurt, the ground paste, chile powder, turmeric, and salt, and stir so that all the chicken pieces are well coated with the marinade. Cover the bowl with plastic wrap and put in the refrigerator to marinate for 1 hour.

5. Remove the chicken from the marinade and reserve the marinade. Add the *besan* to the reserved marinade and stir well. Set aside.

6. On each skewer, string an onion piece, chicken piece, tomato piece, and bell pepper piece.

7. Place a nonstick sauté pan over high heat and add ¼ cup plus 2 teaspoons (70 ml) oil. When small bubbles appear at the bottom of the pan, place the skewers in and cook for 1 minute. Lower the heat to medium and cook, turning, for 5 to 6 minutes or until the chicken pieces are cooked through. Remove the chicken and vegetables from the skewers, and set aside.

8. Place a nonstick sauté pan over medium heat and add the remaining 2 tablespoons oil. Add the cloves, cinnamon, bay leaves, and cardamom, and sauté for 1 minute or until fragrant. Add the chopped onions and sauté for 3 to 4 minutes or until golden brown. Add the reserved marinade and cook, stirring, until the sauce thickens. Add the chicken and vegetables, and cook for 1 to 2 minutes.

9. Add the cream and stir gently. Serve hot.

Murgh Hazarvi

······╣ **Rich and delicately flavored chicken kebabs** ╠·······················

Chicken and cheese always taste good together. In India, yogurt is traditionally used for marinades, but here I have used cream, cheese, and egg. This appetizer is very popular in my restaurants.

Serves 4.

14 ounces (400 grams) boneless chicken breasts, cut into 2-inch (5-cm) cubes
2 tablespoons fresh ginger paste (page 12)
2 tablespoons fresh garlic paste (page 12)
1 teaspoon ground white pepper
¾ teaspoon table salt
½ cup (40 grams) cream cheese
4 green chiles, stemmed and chopped
¼ teaspoon ground mace
¼ teaspoon freshly grated nutmeg
2 tablespoons chopped fresh cilantro
1 large egg
¾ cup (150 ml) heavy cream
Melted butter

1. Put the chicken in a large bowl. Add the ginger paste, garlic paste, white pepper, and ½ teaspoon of the salt, and stir well so that all the chicken pieces are well coated.

2. Put the cream cheese in a large bowl. Add the chiles, mace, nutmeg, cilantro, and the remaining ¼ teaspoon salt, and stir well to make sure there are no lumps and all the ingredients are combined.

3. Add the egg and stir well. Add the chicken to the cream cheese mixture. Add the cream and stir gently.

4. Cover the bowl with plastic wrap and put in the refrigerator to marinate for 2 to 3 hours. While the chicken is marinating, soak the skewers in water.

5. Preheat the oven to 400°F/200°C.

6. String the chicken onto the wooden skewers and place on a baking sheet. Bake for 8 minutes or until almost cooked through and lightly browned.

7. Brush with butter and cook for another 2 minutes or until the chicken is cooked through. Remove from the skewers and serve hot.

Murgh Neza Kabab

····· **Baked chicken marinated in cream and spices** ·····

In this recipe from Hyderabad, a city in South India, the mixture of spices and herbs not only coats the drumsticks but also permeates deep into the meat so there's lots of flavor in every bite.

Serves 4.

1½ pounds (700 grams) chicken leg quarters
2 tablespoons fresh ginger paste (page 12)
2 tablespoons fresh garlic paste (page 12)
2 teaspoons table salt
½ teaspoon ground white pepper
½ teaspoon *garam masala* (spice mix; page 27)
¼ teaspoon crushed *kasoori methi* (dried fenugreek leaves)
1 tablespoon distilled white vinegar
2 tablespoons chopped fresh cilantro
½ teaspoon ground green cardamom
3 tablespoons vegetable oil
1 cup (100 grams) *besan* (chickpea/gram flour)
1 large egg
¼ cup (50 ml) heavy cream
2 tablespoons butter, melted
1 lemon, cut into wedges
1 large red onion, cut into rings
1 large tomato, sliced

1. Loosen the thighbone of each chicken leg quarter, but do not remove it fully.

2. Put the ginger paste, garlic paste, salt, white pepper, *garam masala*, *kasoori methi*, vinegar, cilantro, and cardamom in a large bowl, and stir well to combine. Add the chicken and turn to coat well. Set aside to marinate for 20 minutes.

3. Place a medium nonstick sauté pan over medium heat and add the oil. When small bubbles appear at the bottom of the pan, lower the heat to low, add the *besan*, and sauté until fragrant and lightly colored. Transfer to a bowl and let cool.

4. Add the egg to the *besan* and whisk to make a smooth paste. Add the cream and whisk again.

5. Coat the chicken with this paste and set aside for 20 minutes.

6. Preheat the oven to 400°F/200°C.

7. With a wooden skewer, skewer each chicken leg once along the drumstick bone and once through the thigh flesh. Place on a baking sheet and bake for 7 to 8 minutes. Baste each leg quarter with ½ tablespoon of the butter. Bake for 10 to 15 minutes more or until lightly colored and cooked through.

8. Remove the chicken from the skewers and placc on a serving dish. Garnish with the lemon, onion, and tomato, and serve hot.

Naadan Kozhi Roast

······❈{ **Country-style chicken** }❈·······

Naadan means "village," and *kozhi* means "chicken"—and this is a typical rural dish from Kerala, a verdant state in the south of India laced with palm-lined backwaters and hills carpeted with spice farms. The air is fragrant and the food replete with rustic charm. This chicken dish is simple to make, and it's a perfect example of everyday Keralan food.

Serves 4.

14 ounces (400 grams) boneless chicken, cut into 2-inch (5-cm) cubes
2 tablespoons thick yogurt
2 teaspoons fresh garlic paste (page 12)
½ teaspoon red chile powder
1½ tablespoons rice flour
¼ teaspoon ground turmeric
2 teaspoons ground coriander
1 teaspoon table salt
1 quart (800 ml) plus 1½ tablespoons vegetable oil
10 to 15 fresh curry leaves
10 shallots, peeled and halved
1-inch (2½-cm) piece fresh ginger, julienned
2 green chiles, stemmed and slit
6 to 8 black peppercorns, crushed

1. Clean the chicken cubes thoroughly under running water and drain well in a colander.

2. Put the yogurt in a large bowl. Add the garlic paste, chile powder, rice flour, turmeric, coriander, and salt, and whisk well.

3. Add the chicken and stir well to coat. Cover the bowl with plastic wrap and put in the refrigerator to marinate for 1 hour.

4. Place a nonstick wok over high heat and add 1 quart (800 ml) oil. When small bubbles appear at the bottom of the wok, lower the heat to medium, slide in the chicken cubes, a few at a time, and fry, turning frequently with a slotted spoon, for 5 to 7 minutes or until well browned and just cooked through. Remove with the slotted spoon and drain on paper towels.

5. Place another nonstick wok over medium heat and add 1½ tablespoons oil. When small bubbles appear at the bottom of the wok, add the curry leaves, shallots, ginger, chiles, and peppercorns. Sauté for 2 to 3 minutes.

6. Add the chicken and toss. Cook for 2 minutes, stirring continuously.

7. Serve immediately.

Nawabi Kalmi Kabab

······⊰⊱ **Chicken marinated in yogurt mixed with egg and spices** ⊰⊱······················

This dish originates from the northwest frontier of India and was popular with the Mughals during their rule.

Serves 4.

14 ounces (400 grams) boneless chicken, cut into 2-inch (5-cm) cubes
1-inch (2½-cm) cinnamon stick
½ teaspoon caraway seeds
2 whole cloves
8 to 10 saffron threads
1 teaspoon fresh ginger paste (page 12)
1 teaspoon fresh garlic paste (page 12)
½ cup (140 grams) plain Greek yogurt
2 tablespoons freshly squeezed lemon juice
1 large egg, whisked
¼ cup (30 grams) *maida* (refined flour) or pastry flour
¾ teaspoon table salt
Butter for basting
1 large red onion, cut into rings
A few sprigs fresh mint, chopped
1 lemon, cut into wedges

1. Prick each chicken piece with a fork in two or three places.

2. Place a small nonstick sauté pan over medium heat, add the cinnamon, caraway, cloves, and saffron, and dry-roast lightly. Let cool, then transfer to a spice grinder and grind to a fine powder.

3. Combine the ginger paste, garlic paste, yogurt, roasted spice powder, lemon juice, egg, *maida*, and salt in a large bowl. Add the chicken and toss to coat. Cover the bowl with plastic wrap and put it in the refrigerator to marinate for 2 to 3 hours.

4. Preheat the oven to 425°/220°C.

5. Arrange the chicken pieces on a baking sheet and bake for 8 minutes. Baste with butter and bake for 2 minutes more.

6. Garnish with the onion, mint, and lemon wedges, and serve hot.

Tandoori Chicken

·······⊰ **Chicken marinated in spicy yogurt and baked** ⊱···

This darling of the Indian palate, traditionally cooked in a clay oven called a tandoor, is one of my personal favorites. Leaving the bone in ensures that the final dish will be succulent and juicy.

Serves 4.

1 (1¾-pound/800-gram) whole bone-in chicken
1 teaspoon Kashmiri red chile powder or paprika powder
1 tablespoon freshly squeezed lemon juice
1 teaspoon table salt

~ For the marinade:
1 cup (250 grams) plain yogurt, drained until thick (see Note page 80)
2 tablespoons fresh ginger paste (page 12)
2 tablespoons fresh garlic paste (page 12)
1 teaspoon Kashmiri chile powder or paprika powder
½ teaspoon table salt
2 tablespoons freshly squeezed lemon juice
½ teaspoon *garam masala* (spice mix; page 27)
2 tablespoons filtered mustard oil (see Note page 87)

~ To cook and serve:
2 medium red onions
Melted butter
½ teaspoon *chaat masala* (spice mix for *chaat*; page 24)
2 lemons, cut into wedges

1. Cut the chicken into 4 pieces: 2 leg quarters and 2 breast halves. Make incisions in the flesh with a sharp knife. Put the chicken in a deep bowl.

2. In a small bowl, stir together the chile powder, lemon juice, and salt, and rub it onto the chicken pieces. Cover the bowl with plastic wrap and put in the refrigerator for 30 minutes to marinate.

3. Make the marinade: Put the yogurt in a bowl, add the ginger paste, garlic paste, chile powder, salt, lemon juice, *garam masala*, and mustard oil, and stir.

4. Add the marinade to the chicken pieces and toss so that all the pieces are well covered with it. Cover the bowl again and put it in the refrigerator for 3 to 4 hours to marinate.

5. Cut the onions into round slices and then separate the rings. Put in a bowl of iced water and soak for 30 minutes. Drain well and set aside in the refrigerator until needed. This will keep the onions crisp.

6. Preheat the oven to 400°F/200°C. Put the chicken pieces onto metal or presoaked wooden skewers, arrange in a single layer on a rimmed baking sheet, and cook for 10 to 12 minutes or until almost cooked through. Baste with butter and cook for 8 minutes more.

7. Sprinkle with *chaat masala* and serve hot with the onion rings and lemon wedges.

········⊰ **Chef's tip** ⊱· To make chicken *tikka*, use boneless chicken pieces cut into 1½-inch (4-cm) cubes and proceed as for tandoori chicken.

Tangdi Kabab

A favorite with my kids, who call it "chicken with a handle."

Serves 4.

1 pound (500 grams) chicken drumsticks
½ tablespoon freshly squeezed lemon juice
1 cup (250 grams) plain yogurt, drained until thick (see Note page 80)
2 tablespoons *besan* (chickpea/gram flour)
2 teaspoons fresh ginger paste (page 12)
2 teaspoons fresh garlic paste (page 12)
1 teaspoon ground turmeric
1 teaspoon *garam masala* (spice mix; page 27)
1 teaspoon red chile powder
½ teaspoon table salt
4 green chiles, stemmed and chopped
Vegetable oil for greasing
2 tablespoons melted butter
1 teaspoon *chaat masala* (spice mix for *chaat*; page 24)
1 lemon, cut into wedges

1. Trim off excess fat and skin from the drumsticks. Make 3 or 4 long, deep incisions on each drumstick. Rub with the lemon juice and put in the refrigerator for 30 minutes to marinate.

2. Put the yogurt in a bowl and set aside.

3. Place a medium nonstick sauté pan over low heat. Add the *besan* and roast over low heat, stirring continuously, for 4 to 5 minutes or until lightly browned and fragrant.

4. Let cool to room temperature and transfer to a deep bowl. Add the yogurt, ginger paste, garlic paste, turmeric, *garam masala*, chile powder, salt, and chiles.

5. Add the chicken drumsticks to this mixture and stir well so that the drumsticks are evenly coated. Cover the bowl and put in the refrigerator for 1 to 2 hours to marinate.

6. Preheat the oven to 425°F/220°C. Line a rimmed baking sheet with aluminum foil and oil the foil.

7. Arrange the drumsticks on the baking sheet and bake for 5 minutes. Lower the oven temperature to 390°F/200°C and bake for 15 to 20 minutes, basting every 5 minutes with the butter and turning the drumsticks to ensure even cooking and color.

8. Sprinkle with the *chaat masala* and garnish with lemon wedges. Serve immediately.

Chaap Fry Amritsari

Fried lamb chops from Amritsar

Chaap means "chop." When you make these chops at home, try to be generous with the bread-crumb coating: A thick and even layer ensures that the meat inside remains tender.

Serves 4.

1 pound (500 grams) lamb chops
2 tablespoons malt vinegar
2 tablespoons raw papaya paste (page 535)
1½ teaspoons table salt
1½ tablespoons red chile powder
¾ tablespoon *garam masala* (spice mix; page 27)
1 tablespoon fresh ginger paste (page 12)
1 tablespoon fresh garlic paste (page 12)
9 ounces (250 grams) ground lamb
1-inch (2½-cm) piece fresh ginger, peeled
2 green chiles, stemmed
15 to 20 fresh mint leaves
1 large egg
1 cup (110 grams) dried bread crumbs
¼ cup (50 ml) vegetable oil

1. Pat the chops dry with an absorbent towel. Use a meat mallet to flatten them.

2. Stir together the vinegar, papaya paste, 1 teaspoon of the salt, the chile powder, ½ tablespoon of the *garam masala*, the ginger paste, and garlic paste in a large bowl. Add the chops and stir so that all the chops are evenly covered with the mixture. Cover the bowl with plastic wrap and put in the refrigerator to marinate for 2 hours.

3. Put the ground lamb, remaining ¼ tablespoon *garam masala*, the ginger, chiles, mint, and the remaining ½ teaspoon salt in a food processor, and process until all the ingredients are well incorporated.

4. Coat the chops on one side with the ground lamb mixture and flatten them again with the meat mallet so they are evenly coated with the mixture.

5. Break the egg into a bowl and whisk it well. Spread the bread crumbs in a plate. Dip the chops in the egg and then roll in the bread crumbs until they are well covered on all sides.

6. Place a nonstick sauté pan over medium heat and add the oil. When small bubbles appear at the bottom of the pan, put the chops in the pan and cook for 10 to 12 minutes, turning once or twice so they are evenly cooked on all sides.

7. Serve hot.

Chops Kari Varuval

····· ·⁓{ **Lamb chops marinated in yogurt and cooked with southern spices** }⁓· ·····

Indian cooking is about amalgamating spices and then cooking them correctly. This recipe is a fine example of this. I suggest making this dish when you have plenty of time, as the cooking requires some care.

Serves 4.

1 pound (500 grams) lamb chops
1 teaspoon ground turmeric
3 tablespoons plain yogurt
2 tablespoons vegetable oil
3 medium red onions, sliced
1-inch (2½-cm) piece fresh ginger, chopped
10 cloves garlic, chopped
5 or 6 green chiles, stemmed and chopped
3 tablespoons chopped fresh cilantro
2½ teaspoons coriander seeds
30 whole black peppercorns
½ teaspoon fennel seeds
1-inch (2½-cm) cinnamon stick, broken in half
6 whole cloves
4 green cardamom pods
2 bay leaves
1½ teaspoons table salt
1½ tablespoons ghee (page 37)
1 tablespoon freshly squeezed lemon juice

1. Pat the chops dry with a kitchen towel and then flatten slightly by beating with the blunt side of a knife or with a meat mallet. Place them in a bowl. Stir the turmeric into the yogurt, rub the mixture on the chops, cover the bowl with plastic wrap, and put in the refrigerator to marinate for 1 hour.

2. Place a nonstick saucepan over medium heat and add 2 teaspoons of the oil. When small bubbles appear at the bottom of the pan, add one third of the onions, the ginger, garlic, chiles, cilantro, coriander, peppercorns, fennel, half the cinnamon, 4 of the cloves, and 2 of the cardamom pods, and sauté for 2 to 3 minutes or until fragrant. Cool and place in a food processor with 2 tablespoons water. Process to a fine paste.

3. Place another nonstick saucepan over medium heat and add the remaining oil. When small bubbles appear at the bottom of the pan, add the bay leaves, remaining cinnamon, remaining cloves, remaining cardamom pods, and remaining onions. Sauté for 4 to 5 minutes or until the onions are lightly browned.

4. Add the ground spice mixture and sauté for 2 to 3 minutes. Add the chops and continue to sauté for 8 minutes or until the chops are well covered with the spices and the oil comes to the top.

5. Add 1 cup (200 ml) water and the salt, and stir well.

6. Add the ghee and reduce the heat to low. Cover and cook for 15 to 20 minutes, stirring frequently. Add another ½ cup (100 ml) water if the lamb is not yet cooked through. Continue to cook for 1 hour or until the lamb is tender.

7. Uncover and simmer until the sauce is thick. Sprinkle with the lemon juice and serve immediately.

Dum Ke Kabab

······⟩{ Oven-baked lamb kebabs }⟨······································

These oven-baked kebabs are silky smooth in taste and get their great depth of flavor from all the spices that are dry-roasted and ground before being added to the meat.

Makes 24.

1 quart (800 ml) vegetable oil
2 onions, sliced
1-inch (2½-cm) cinnamon stick
4 green cardamom pods
3 whole cloves
½ teaspoon allspice berries
1 teaspoon *magaz* (melon seeds)
½ teaspoon white poppy seeds
3 dried red chiles, stemmed and broken in half
½ teaspoon caraway seeds
3 green chiles, stemmed and halved
2 tablespoons chopped fresh cilantro
4 cloves garlic
½-inch (1-cm) piece fresh ginger, chopped
1½ teaspoons *besan* (chickpea/gram flour)
1 pound (500 grams) ground lamb
1 tablespoon freshly squeezed lemon juice
1 teaspoon table salt
½ cup (125 grams) plain yogurt, whisked
½ teaspoon red chile powder
¼ teaspoon *garam masala* (spice mix; page 27)
1½ tablespoons ghee (page 37)

~ **For the garnish:**
1 medium onion, peeled and cut into rings
A few sprigs fresh mint
1 lemon, cut into wedges

1. Put the oil in a deep-fryer and heat to 375°F/190°C. Add the sliced onions and fry until golden. Remove with a slotted spoon and drain on paper towels. Set aside.

2. Place a medium nonstick pan over medium heat. Add the cinnamon, cardamom, and cloves, and dry-roast, stirring occasionally, for 2 to 3 minutes or until fragrant. Transfer to a dry bowl and let cool to room temperature.

3. Dry-roast the allspice in the same pan for 1 to 2 minutes or until fragrant. Transfer to the bowl with the other roasted spices and let cool to room temperature. Transfer to a spice grinder and grind to a fine powder. Set aside.

4. Place the same pan over medium heat. Add the *magaz* and roast over low heat for 1 to 2 minutes or until fragrant. Transfer to a dry bowl. Add the poppy seeds to the same pan and dry-roast for 1 to 2 minutes and add to the *magaz* in the bowl. Add the red chiles to same pan and dry-roast for 2 minutes or until little brown specks form on them. Transfer to the bowl with the other spices. Last, dry-roast the caraway over low heat for 1 to 2 minutes or until fragrant. Add to the collected spices and let cool to room temperature.

5. Put the spice mixture (from steps 2, 3, and 4), green chiles, cilantro, garlic, and ginger in a spice grinder with 2 tablespoons water and grind to a smooth paste. Transfer to a small bowl.

6. Place the same nonstick pan over low heat. Add the *besan* and roast, stirring continuously, for 4 to 5 minutes or until lightly browned and fragrant.

7. Put the lamb, fried onions, roasted *besan*, and ground spice paste in a food processor, and process until smooth. Transfer to a deep bowl.

8. Add the lemon juice and salt. Stir well. Cover and put in the refrigerator for 30 minutes.

9. Preheat the oven to 425°F/225°C. Whisk the yogurt, chile powder, and *garam masala* until well blended.

10. Divide the chilled lamb mixture into 24 equal portions and shape into balls. Grease your palms with a little oil and form each ball into a sausage shape 1½ inches (4 cm) long. Arrange them on a greased baking sheet and spoon a little of the yogurt mixture onto each. Bake in the center of the oven for 20 minutes, basting every 5 minutes with the ghee.

11. Garnish with the onion rings, mint sprigs, and lemon wedges, and serve immediately.

Kabargah

················{ Lamb ribs dipped in a spicy yogurt batter and deep-fried }················

While working with teams who served prime ministers like Mrs. Indira Gandhi and Mr. Rajiv Gandhi, I found that Kashmiri food was always favored at state banquets. It was during this time that I picked up little nuances of the region's cuisine and learned how to perfect this dish.

Serves 4.

1 pound (500 grams) lamb ribs, cut into pieces with 2 or 3 ribs in each
2 cups (400 ml) milk
3 green cardamom pods
1-inch (2½-cm) cinnamon stick
4 whole cloves
Generous pinch of saffron threads
2 teaspoons ground fennel seeds
1 teaspoon ground ginger
Pinch of asafetida
3 bay leaves
1½ teaspoons table salt
6 tablespoons plain yogurt
2 teaspoons red chile powder
1 quart (800 ml) vegetable oil

1. Place a deep nonstick saucepan over high heat and add the ribs, milk, 1 cup (200 ml) water, the cardamom, cinnamon, cloves, saffron, fennel, ground ginger, asafetida, bay leaves, and 1 teaspoon of the salt. When the mixture comes to a boil, lower the heat to medium, cover, and cook for 50 minutes or until the lamb is tender and most of the liquid has evaporated.

2. Put the yogurt in a bowl, and add the chile powder and the remaining ½ teaspoon salt. Add 2 teaspoons water and whisk to make a smooth batter.

3. Place a nonstick wok over high heat and add the oil. When small bubbles appear at the bottom of the wok, lower the heat to medium. Working in batches, dip the lamb ribs in the yogurt batter and slide into the hot oil. Cook for 2 to 3 minutes or until golden brown. Remove with a slotted spoon and drain on paper towels. Serve immediately.

Kakori Kabab

There are several stories that surround the creation of these succulent kebabs. Centuries ago, the Nawab of Kakori (in the province of Awadh, which is modern-day Uttar Pradesh) had a mishap in which he lost his teeth (another story has it that the Nawab was simply getting on in age). He loved lamb and still wanted to eat it, so his cooks created this special soft version for him.

Makes 8.

1 quart (800 ml) plus 8 teaspoons vegetable oil
1 large red onion, sliced
1 teaspoon white poppy seeds
½ cup (75 grams) cashews
5 or 6 whole cloves
2 green cardamom pods
¼ blade mace
½ tablespoon untreated dried rose petals
Pinch of freshly grated nutmeg
7 ounce (200 grams) ground lamb
2 tablespoons ground lamb fat
¼ tablespoon grated *khoya/mawa* (unsweetened solid condensed milk; page 37)
1 teaspoon ground white pepper
½ tablespoon yellow chile powder (optional)
8 or 9 saffron threads
½ tablespoon fresh ginger paste (page 12)
½ tablespoon fresh garlic paste (page 12)
1 teaspoon table salt

1. Place a nonstick wok over high heat and add the oil. When small bubbles appear at the bottom of the wok, add the onion and cook, stirring with a slotted spoon, until well browned. Remove with the slotted spoon and drain on paper towels.

2. Soak the poppy seeds in 2 tablespoons hot water in a small bowl for 30 minutes. Transfer the poppy seeds and water to a spice grinder and grind to a paste.

3. Place a small nonstick sauté pan over medium heat, add the cashews, and dry-roast until lightly browned. Let cool, then transfer to a spice grinder and grind to a powder.

4. Return the pan to medium heat and add the cloves, cardamom, mace, rose petals, and nutmeg, and dry-roast for 1 minute. Transfer to a spice grinder and grind to a powder.

5. Add the lamb, lamb fat, fried onion, poppy seed paste, cashew powder, spice powder, *khoya*, white pepper, yellow chile powder (if using), saffron, ginger paste, and garlic paste. Add 2 or 3 ice cubes and process until the mixture is smooth.

6. Transfer to a bowl, add the salt, and stir. Cover the bowl with plastic wrap and put in the refrigerator for 2 to 3 hours.

7. Divide into 8 portions. Heat a nonstick sauté pan over medium heat. Cook for a couple of minutes on each side until the lamb is completely cooked through, 3 to 4 minutes. Use about 1 teaspoon of oil per kebab to aid in the cooking process.

8. Serve immediately.

······∘⫸ **Note** ⫷∘ Yellow chiles are plump and sweet and have a waxy appearance. They can grow to an unusually large size and they have a mild peppery flavor. As with other chiles, the thinner and smaller the chile, the hotter it will be. Yellow chiles are often used for *chaats* and other exotic North Indian dishes.

Kheema Potli

······⚹{ Spicy ground lamb in a pastry shaped like a money bag }⚹ ··············

Stuffed savories like samosas are popular and much appreciated for their unique style. We go one step further here and package ground lamb in a pastry that looks as if you are serving little money bags—a fun presentation of a crisp pastry with a delicious filling. I have seen people use little bits of onion greens to tie up the *potlis*. Serve with *pudina aur dhaniya chutney* (mint-and-cilantro chutney; page 22).

Makes 20 pieces.

∼ For the pastry:
1 cup (120 grams) *maida* (refined flour) or pastry flour
2 tablespoons fine *rawa/suji* (semolina flour)
5 teaspoons ghee (page 37), melted
1 teaspoon table salt
1 quart (800 ml) vegetable oil

∼ For the filling:
2 tablespoons vegetable oil
1 teaspoon cumin seeds
10 ounces (300 grams) ground lamb
2-inch (5-cm) piece fresh ginger, peeled and chopped
3 green chiles, stemmed and chopped
1 teaspoon red chile powder
1 tablespoon ground coriander
1 teaspoon ground cumin
½ teaspoon table salt
¾ cup (185 grams) plain yogurt
1 teaspoon *garam masala* (spice mix; page 27)
2 tablespoons chopped fresh cilantro

1. To make the dough: Place the *maida* in a bowl. Add the semolina, ghee, and salt, and mix. Add ¼ cup (50 ml) water, little by little, and knead into a stiff dough. Cover with a damp cloth and set aside to rest for 10 to 15 minutes.

2. To make the filling: Place a medium nonstick sauté pan over medium heat and add the 2 tablespoons oil. When small bubbles appear at the bottom of the pan, add the cumin seeds. When they begin to change color, add the ground lamb and sauté for 5 minutes or until the lamb is half done.

3. Add the ginger, green chiles, red chile powder, ground coriander, ground cumin, and salt, and mix well. Reduce the heat to low, cover with a lid, and sauté for 5 minutes. Add the yogurt and stir. Increase the heat to high and sauté for 10 minutes, stirring continuously. Reduce the heat to medium and cook for 10 minutes or until the lamb is fully cooked and completely dry.

4. Add the *garam masala* and the cilantro, and mix well. Take the pan off the heat and allow the mixture to cool completely.

5. Divide the dough into 20 portions and shape into balls. Roll out a ball into a 3-inch-diameter (7½-cm-diameter) disk. Place a portion of the ground lamb mixture in the center. Sprinkle a little water between the edge of the disk and the filling. Gather the edges together in neat pleats and pinch the dough just above the filling to seal. Let the edges of the *potli* remain loose to imitate the shape of a money bag. Repeat with the remaining dough and filling.

6. Place a nonstick wok over high heat and add the 1 quart oil. When small bubbles appear at the bottom of the wok, reduce the heat to medium and gently slide in the *potlis*, a few at a time. Stir gently with a slotted spoon so that the *potlis* cook evenly. When they are golden brown, remove with the slotted spoon and drain on paper towels. Repeat with the remaining *potlis*.

Lamb Pepper Fry

········⋅⋅{ **Boneless lamb with peppercorns** }⋅⋅·····································

This is a traditional dish of the Syrian Christians of Kerala. They make it with beef, but this recipe uses lamb.

Serves 4.

3 tablespoons plus 1 teaspoon oil
2 medium onions, peeled and sliced
4 to 6 cloves garlic, peeled and chopped
1-inch (2½-cm) piece fresh ginger, peeled and chopped
20 whole black peppercorns
1 tablespoon coriander seeds
6 dried red chiles, stemmed and broken in half
1 teaspoon fennel seeds
1 star anise
1 teaspoon cumin seeds
½ cup (60 grams) grated fresh coconut (or frozen unsweetened coconut)
16 to 18 fresh curry leaves
1 pound (500 grams) boneless lamb, cut into 1-inch (2½-cm) pieces
1 teaspoon *garam masala* (spice mix; page 27)
1½ teaspoons ground coriander
1 teaspoon red chile powder
½ teaspoon ground turmeric
1 teaspoon table salt
1 tablespoon slivered coconut (see Note)
1 teaspoon black mustard seeds
2 green chiles, stemmed and slit

1. Place a medium nonstick sauté pan over medium heat and add 1 tablespoon oil. Add half the onions, the garlic, ginger, peppercorns, coriander seeds, 3 of the dried chiles, the fennel, star anise, cumin, and grated fresh coconut, and sauté for 2 to 3 minutes or until the onions are light golden brown. Set aside to cool to room temperature.

2. Transfer to a food processor with 6 tablespoons (90 ml) water and process to a smooth paste.

3. Place another medium nonstick sauté pan over medium heat and add 2 tablespoons of the oil. Add 10 to 12 of the curry leaves, the remaining 3 red chiles, and the remaining onions, and sauté for 1 minute or until the onions are translucent. Add the lamb and cook for 5 minutes.

4. Add the ground paste, *garam masala*, ground coriander, chile powder, turmeric, and salt, and cook for 2 to 3 minutes.

5. Add 1 quart (800 ml) water and cook over low heat for 30 to 35 minutes or until the lamb is tender and most of the water has evaporated.

6. Place a small nonstick pan over medium heat and add the remaining 1 teaspoon oil. Add the slivered coconut, mustard seeds, green chiles, and the remaining curry leaves, and sauté for 1 minute. Pour this mixture over the lamb and cover immediately to trap the flavors. Serve hot.

······⊰ **Note** ⊱· Slivered coconut is available in the freezer section at Indian grocery stores.

Lukhmi

······⊰ **Savory pastry with ground lamb stuffing** ⊱··

This flaky breakfast snack was an everyday must for the Nizams (royal rulers) of Hyderabad, and is available in the mornings from all the coffee houses in the region.

Serves 4.

8 ounces (250 grams) freshly ground lamb
1½ teaspoons table salt
Pinch of ground turmeric
½ teaspoon red chile powder
½ teaspoon fresh ginger paste (page 12)
½ teaspoon fresh garlic paste (page 12)
1 quart (800 ml) vegetable oil
2 tablespoons chopped fresh cilantro
2 or 3 green chiles, stemmed and chopped
½ tablespoon freshly squeezed lemon juice
1 cup (120 grams) *maida* (refined flour) or pastry flour, plus extra for dusting
2 tablespoons ghee (page 37), melted
1 tablespoon plain yogurt

1. Place the lamb, 1 teaspoon salt, turmeric, chile powder, ginger paste, and garlic paste in a nonstick saucepan. Add ½ cup (100 ml) water and place over medium heat. Bring to a boil, stirring occasionally. Cook, uncovered, for 15 to 20 minutes, until the lamb is tender.

2. Place a medium nonstick sauté pan over medium heat and add 1½ tablespoons of the oil. Add the cilantro and chiles and sauté for 1 minute. Add the lamb mixture and sauté for 1 to 2 minutes or until all the water has evaporated and the mixture is dry. Stir in the lemon juice. Set aside to cool to room temperature.

3. Put the *maida* in a deep bowl. Add the remaining ½ teaspoon salt, the ghee, yogurt, and 1 tablespoon water, and knead to make a soft dough. You might need to sprinkle with some more drops of water. Cover the dough with plastic wrap and refrigerate for 30 minutes.

4. Divide the chilled dough into 16 equal portions. Shape each portion into a ball, dust with *maida*, and roll out into a rectangle 5 inches (12.5 centimeters) long and ⅛ inch (3 mm) thick. Place 1 tablespoon of the lamb mixture in the center, moisten the edges with water, and fold the dough from the top down to cover the filling and seal the edges on all three sides. Fold one third of the stuffed rectangle to the center and bring the other third over to make a book fold. Repeat with the remaining dough and filling.

5. Put the remaining oil in a deep-fryer and heat to 375°F/190°C. Slide one *lukhmi* at a time into the hot oil and fry until golden brown. Remove with a slotted spoon and drain on paper towels. Serve immediately.

Parsi Lamb Cutlets

·······❧{ Crisp ground lamb or goat patties }❧·······································

These patties can be prepared a day in advance if you are planning a party. You can even shape the patties and freeze them with waxed paper between the layers. To serve, thaw them, dip them in the egg, and cook.

Makes 8.

3 slices white bread
8 ounces (250 grams) ground lamb or goat
1½ teaspoons table salt
1 teaspoon fresh ginger paste (page 12)
1 teaspoon fresh garlic paste (page 12)
4 green chiles, stemmed and diced
¾ teaspoon red chile powder
½ teaspoon ground coriander
½ teaspoon ground roasted cumin (page 32)
⅛ teaspoon ground turmeric
1 tablespoon chopped fresh mint
1 tablespoon chopped fresh cilantro
¾ cup (80 grams) bread crumbs
3 large eggs
½ cup (100 ml) vegetable oil
2 lemons, both cut into 4 wedges
1 medium red onion, thinly sliced and separated into rings

1. Soak the bread in 1 cup (200 ml) water for 30 seconds and squeeze to remove the excess water.

2. Put the meat, bread, 1 teaspoon of the salt, the ginger paste, garlic paste, chiles, chile powder, coriander, cumin, turmeric, mint, and cilantro in a large bowl. Combine well, cover the bowl with plastic wrap, and put in the refrigerator to marinate for 3 to 4 hours.

3. Divide the mixture into 8 portions, shape into balls, and roll in the bread crumbs. Place each ball on a flat surface and flatten with your fingers into a 4-inch (10-cm) patty, dusting with bread crumbs to prevent sticking. Put the patties on a plate and put in the refrigerator for 30 minutes.

4. Put the eggs in a bowl and beat them lightly with a fork. Add the remaining ½ teaspoon salt and 2 tablespoons of water and beat again.

5. Place a nonstick sauté pan over medium heat and add 1 tablespoon of the oil. When small bubbles appear at the bottom of the pan, dip a patty in the egg and place it in the pan. Cook, turning with a slotted spoon, for 2 to 3 minutes or until lightly browned on both sides. Remove with the slotted spoon and drain on paper towels. Repeat with the remaining patties and oil.

6. Serve hot with lemon wedges and onion rings.

Patthar Ka Gosht

·······⋙{ **Kebabs cooked on hot stones** }⋘·······················

Stone cooking is an art—but a dying one, unfortunately. You can use a granite stone here or cook the kebabs in a nonstick griddle. The beauty of this kebab is the tenderness of the meat. Serve it with hot *naan* (page 20).

Makes 16.

1¾ **pounds (800 grams) boneless lamb, cut into 1½-inch (4-cm) pieces**

~ **For the marinade:**
2-inch (5-cm) piece fresh ginger, peeled
10 cloves garlic
5 green chiles, stemmed
3-inch (7½-cm) piece green papaya (optional)
1 cup (200 ml) vegetable oil
2 medium red onions, sliced
2 tablespoons plain yogurt
1 teaspoon ground black pepper
1 teaspoon ground green cardamom
1 teaspoon *garam masala* (spice mix; page 27)
1 teaspoon ground *patthar ke phool* (lichen stone flower; optional)
1 tablespoon malt vinegar
2 teaspoons table salt
Vegetable oil and salt for seasoning the stone

1. Pound the lamb with a meat mallet or the flat side of a knife to a ¼-inch (½-cm) thickness. Put the pieces in a bowl.

2. Put the ginger, garlic, chiles, and papaya in a spice grinder with 3 tablespoons water, and grind to a fine paste.

3. Place a nonstick wok over medium heat and add the oil. When small bubbles appear at the bottom of the wok, add the onions and cook for 4 to 5 minutes or until browned. Remove with a slotted spoon and drain on paper towels; let cool. Transfer to a spice grinder, add the yogurt and 2 tablespoons water, and grind to a fine paste.

4. Combine the ginger-garlic–green chile paste, onion-yogurt paste, pepper, cardamom, *garam masala*, *patthar ke phool* (if using), vinegar, and ¼ cup of the oil from the wok in a small bowl. Spread this mixture over the lamb pieces. Cover the bowl with plastic wrap and put in the refrigerator overnight to marinate.

5. Take a flat piece of rough granite or a *kadappa* stone that is about 1½ feet (46 cm) long, 1 foot (30 cm) wide, and 2 inches (5 cm) thick. Wash the stone and prop either end on bricks over an outdoor fire pit, taking care that it is safely balanced. Light a charcoal fire underneath the stone and heat the stone well. Season the stone by applying oil when the stone is very hot, then sprinkle with a little salt and wipe the stone with a clean cloth. It's now ready to use.

6. Sprinkle a little oil on the stone and place the lamb pieces on it. Cook, turning the pieces a few times and basting occasionally with oil, until cooked through.

7. Serve immediately.

········⟨ **Note** ⟩⁂ *Kadappa* stone is a black limestone. It is very hard and can withstand extreme temperatures. The stone is quarried at Betamcherla, Andhra Pradesh. Granite can be used as a substitute.

Khubani Ke Shammi

····· Apricot-stuffed potatoes ·····

These kebabs have a soft heart because of the stuffing in the center. The chiles and pepper balance the sweetness of the apricot.

Makes 12.

¼ cup (50 grams) dried apricots
¼ cup (50 grams) *khoya/mawa* (unsweetened solid condensed milk; page 37), crumbled
¼ cup (50 ml) plus 2 teaspoons vegetable oil
1 teaspoon cumin seeds
½-inch (1-cm) piece fresh ginger, chopped
3 green chiles, stemmed and chopped
1 teaspoon *garam masala* (spice mix; page 27)
¼ teaspoon ground black pepper
3 tablespoons chopped fresh cilantro
1 teaspoon table salt
4 medium potatoes, boiled, peeled, and mashed
¼ cup cornstarch

1. Soak the apricots in 1 cup (200 ml) water for 1 hour. Drain and finely chop. Transfer to a bowl, add the *khoya*, and stir.

2. Place a shallow nonstick sauté pan over medium heat and add 2 teaspoons of the oil. When small bubbles appear at the bottom of the pan, add the cumin. When it begins to change color, add the ginger, chiles, *garam masala*, and pepper. Stir well and remove from the heat. Set aside to cool.

3. Add the ginger-chile mixture to the apricot-*khoya* mixture. Add the cilantro and ½ teaspoon of the salt, and stir well. Divide into 12 portions.

4. Put the mashed potatoes in another bowl. Add the remaining ½ teaspoon salt and stir well. Divide into 12 portions.

5. Roll each portion of potato into a ball and flatten into a round disk. Place a portion of apricot-*khoya* mixture in the center, gather the edges to enclose the filling, and seal well. Gently roll into a ball again and flatten slightly.

6. Put the cornstarch on a plate and roll the kebabs in it. Shake off the excess and set aside on another plate.

7. Place a nonstick sauté pan over medium heat and add the remaining oil. When small bubbles appear at the bottom of the pan, gently slide in the kebabs, a few at a time, and cook, turning continuously, for 4 to 5 minutes or until golden brown on both sides.

8. Serve hot.

Shikhampuri Kabab

······ { Ground lamb patties stuffed with thick spiced yogurt } ······

The name of these novel kebabs translates to "full belly," and I don't know if that refers to the fact that the kebabs are stuffed or that they are very filling. Either way, they are true to their name. Serve these with sliced onions separated into rings and *pudina aur dhaniya* chutney (mint-and-cilantro chutney; page 22).

Makes 8.

1 quart (800 ml) plus 8 teaspoons vegetable oil
1½ medium red onions, peeled and sliced
2 tablespoons ghee (page 37)
½ teaspoon caraway seeds
2 dried red chiles, stemmed and broken
½-inch (1-cm) piece fresh ginger, roughly chopped
5 cloves garlic, roughly chopped
9 ounces (250 grams) ground lamb
1 tablespoon *chana dal* (split Bengal gram), soaked for 30 minutes
¼ cup plus 1 tablespoon chopped fresh mint
¼ cup plus 1 tablespoon chopped fresh cilantro
½ tablespoon freshly squeezed lemon juice
1 teaspoon table salt
1 large egg

~ For the filling:
1 cup (250 grams) plain yogurt
1 green chile, stemmed and chopped
1 large red onion, peeled and chopped
2 tablespoons chopped fresh mint
½ teaspoon table salt
½ teaspoon roasted cumin seeds

1. Place a nonstick wok over high heat and add 1 quart (800 ml) of the oil. When small bubbles appear at the bottom of the wok, add the onions and cook, stirring with a slotted spoon, until the onions are well browned. Remove with the slotted spoon and drain on paper towels.

2. Place a nonstick sauté pan over medium heat and add the ghee. When small bubbles appear at the bottom of the pan, add the caraway, chiles, ginger, and garlic, and sauté for 1 minute.

3. Add the lamb and sauté for 5 minutes, stirring occasionally.

4. Drain the *dal* and add it to the pan. Stir and sauté for 1 minute.

5. Add the mint and cilantro, and stir well. Cook for 5 minutes. Remove from the heat and set aside to cool completely.

6. Transfer the mixture to a food processor. Add the onions, lemon juice, and salt, and process to a coarse paste. Transfer to a bowl.

7. Divide the lamb mixture into 8 portions.

8. Make the filling: Hang the yogurt in a double layer of cheesecloth for 1 hour or until most of the excess water has drained away. Transfer to a bowl, add the chile, onion, mint, salt, and cumin, and stir well. Divide into 8 portions.

9. Flatten one portion of the lamb mixture in the palm of your hand and place a portion of yogurt stuffing in the center. Gather the edges, shape into a ball, and flatten slightly. Repeat to make the remaining kebabs.

10. Beat the egg in a bowl.

11. Place a nonstick sauté pan over medium heat and add 2 teaspoons of the oil. Dip 2 kebabs in the egg, put them in the sauté pan, and cook, turning once, for 3 to 4 minutes or until both the sides are cooked and lightly browned. Drain on paper towels. Repeat with the remaining kebabs.

12. Serve hot.

CHAPTER 7

Main Courses: Vegetarian

At least 70 percent of the population of India does not eat meat or chicken, and many will not eat eggs. Included in this group are the Jains, who are not only vegetarians but also do not eat tubers, onions, or garlic; a Jain might not eat an *aloo tikki* (page 151), a patty made with potatoes, but will enjoy a *tikki* made with green banana (page 121). Indians have a deep respect for vegetables, and the repertoire of vegetarian recipes is huge.

It's only recently that a great variety of fruits and vegetables have become readily available (and still only in large metropolitan areas), but buying fresh produce daily has long been a passion of the Indian homemaker.

The recipes that follow are proof of how advanced vegetarian cooking is in India. The humble potato, for example, becomes the all-time favorite *aloo matar* (page 230) or the glowing red Kashmiri *dum aloo* (page 236). Okra, eggplant, gourds, peas, spinach, fenugreek greens, and mustard greens will find their way into your kitchen with much more regularity when you discover that you have so much to make with them! Included in this chapter is a wealth of *paneer* recipes—some everyday dishes and some more unusual ones. *Paneer* is a prime source of essential protein and calcium, and it's no coincidence that it is sold by fruit and vegetable vendors in India.

Aloo Chokha

········ Spicy potato dish ········

My initial working years in the kitchen were in Varanasi in the Indian state of Uttar Pradesh, and my cooks in the hotel kitchen used to make this often for their lunch. It is prepared in a similar way in the neighboring state of Bihar.

Serves 4 to 6.

2 tablespoons filtered mustard oil (see Note page 87)
1 teaspoon coriander seeds
2 dried red chiles, stemmed
3 medium red onions, chopped
3 or 4 cloves garlic, crushed
3 or 4 green chiles, stemmed and chopped
1 teaspoon ground coriander
1 teaspoon ground roasted cumin (page 32)
6 small potatoes, boiled, peeled, and mashed
1 teaspoon *amchur* (dried mango powder)
1 teaspoon table salt

1. Place a medium nonstick sauté pan over medium heat and add the mustard oil. When the oil starts smoking, remove from the heat and cool slightly.

2. Crush the coriander seeds in a mortar with a pestle. Cut the dried chiles into small pieces.

3. Return the pan with the oil to medium heat. When small bubbles appear at the bottom of the pan, add the dried chiles and onions, and sauté for 3 to 4 minutes or until the onions are golden brown.

4. Add the garlic and continue to sauté for 1 minute. Add the green chiles, crushed coriander seeds, ground coriander, and cumin powder, and stir. Add the potatoes and stir. Add the *amchur* and salt and stir well.

5. Transfer to a serving dish and serve hot.

Aloo Matar

····•≋{ Potatoes and green peas in an onion-tomato gravy }≋•····

Typically, Indians like at least two dishes with each meal, one wet curry like lentils and one dried *sabzi* (stir-fried vegetables). This dish comes in really handy when you do not wish to prepare two things: Make *aloo matar*, and things are simple. Serve with *parathas* (page 18).

Serves 4.

2 tablespoons vegetable oil
1 bay leaf
1 teaspoon cumin seeds
2 medium red onions, chopped
1½ teaspoons fresh ginger paste (page 12)
1½ teaspoons fresh garlic paste (page 12)
¼ teaspoon ground turmeric
1½ teaspoons ground coriander
1 teaspoon red chile powder
4 small potatoes, peeled and cut into ½-inch (1-cm) cubes
1 cup (235 grams) fresh tomato purée
1¼ cups (190 grams) green peas
1 teaspoon *garam masala* (spice mix; page 27)
1 teaspoon table salt
2 tablespoons chopped fresh cilantro

1. Place a medium nonstick saucepan over medium heat and add the oil. When small bubbles appear at the bottom of the pan, add the bay leaf and cumin. When the seeds begin to change color, add the onions and sauté for 3 to 4 minutes or until golden. Add the ginger paste and garlic paste, and sauté for 30 seconds.

2. Add the turmeric, coriander, and chile powder, and sauté for 30 seconds. Stir in the potatoes and 3 cups (600 ml) water. Cover and cook for 5 minutes or until the potatoes are half cooked.

3. Stir in the tomato purée, cover, and cook for 8 minutes or until the potatoes are tender.

4. Add the peas, *garam masala*, and salt, and stir. Cover and cook for about 15 minutes.

5. Garnish with the cilantro and serve hot.

Aloo Posto

Posto is the Bengali word for "poppy seeds," and while these seeds are very popular in Bengali cooking, this wasn't always the case. In fact, there is some evidence that poppy seeds were originally grown in this East Indian state only for making opium.

Serves 4.

¼ cup (50 grams) white poppy seeds
2 tablespoons refined mustard oil (see Note page 87)
½ teaspoon *kalonji* (nigella; see Note)
2 small green chiles, stemmed and slit
5 small potatoes, peeled and cut into 1-inch (2½-cm) cubes
2 teaspoons table salt
½ teaspoon sugar
1 teaspoon ghee (page 37), melted (optional)

1. Soak the poppy seeds in 1 cup (200 ml) warm water for 15 to 20 minutes. Drain off excess water and put the poppy seeds in a spice grinder. Grind to a smooth paste. Set aside.

2. Place a medium nonstick sauté pan over high heat, add the mustard oil, and heat almost to the smoking point. Remove from the heat and let cool completely.

3. Place the pan with the mustard oil over medium heat again. When small bubbles appear at the bottom of the pan, add the *kalonji* and chiles, and sauté for 10 to 12 seconds. Add the potatoes and salt and stir again. Sauté over medium heat for 5 minutes, stirring frequently.

4. Add the poppy seed paste, stir, and add ½ cup (100 ml) water. Lower the heat to low, cover, and cook for 10 to 12 minutes or until the potatoes are almost done. Remove from the heat, add the sugar, and stir.

5. Return the pan to low heat and cook for 1 minute or until the potatoes are soft. Stir in the ghee (if using) and serve immediately.

·······⚬{ **Note** }⚬ *Kalonji* (nigella) is available in Indian grocery stores and is sometimes called onion seeds.

Ambat Batata

Potatoes are an essential ingredient in the Indian kitchen, and I love learning new ways of serving them. *Ambat batata* is a sour potato curry from Malwan, which lies along the Konkan coast of Maharashtra. *Ambat* in Marathi means "sour," and here the flavor comes from yogurt and *kokum*. I love this dish with hot *rotis* (page 18).

Serves 4.

5 small potatoes, boiled and peeled
3 tablespoons vegetable oil
½ teaspoon brown mustard seeds
1 teaspoon cumin seeds
6 or 7 fresh curry leaves
3 green chiles, stemmed and chopped
3 medium red onions, chopped
½ teaspoon ground turmeric
½ cup (125 grams) plain yogurt
4 or 5 fresh *kokum* petals, or 2 or 3 dried (see Note page 44)
¼ cup (15 grams) chopped fresh cilantro
¼ cup (30 grams) grated fresh coconut (or frozen unsweetened coconut)
1 teaspoon table salt
2 teaspoons freshly squeezed lemon juice

1. Halve each potato and cut each half into 4 equal pieces.

2. Place a medium nonstick sauté pan over medium heat and add the oil. When small bubbles appear at the bottom of the pan, add the mustard seeds. When they begin to sputter, add the cumin, curry leaves, and chiles, and sauté for 1 minute.

3. Add the onions and sauté for 3 to 4 minutes or until golden brown. Add the turmeric and potatoes, and sauté for 1 to 2 minutes. Stir in the yogurt, *kokum*, half of the cilantro, half of the coconut, the salt, and lemon juice. Lower the heat and simmer for 1 to 2 minutes.

4. Transfer to a serving dish and garnish with the remaining cilantro and remaining coconut. Serve hot.

Bataka Nu Rassawala Shaak

I call this a quick-fix dish. In Gujarati homes this dish would be made to stretch a meal if there were more guests than anticipated—and it can be cooked at the last minute while the guests are being served the other food. Some people cook the potatoes in the sauce, but I think it's easier to precook them. Serve with any Indian bread.

Serves 4.

5 tablespoons vegetable oil
2 teaspoons brown mustard seeds
¼ teaspoon asafetida
10 fresh curry leaves
4 dried red chiles, stemmed and broken
1 teaspoon red chile powder
1 teaspoon ground turmeric
2 teaspoons ground coriander
1 teaspoon ground roasted cumin (page 32)
1¼ teaspoons table salt
3 tablespoons grated cane jaggery
5 tablespoons tamarind pulp
5 small potatoes, boiled and diced
3 tablespoons chopped fresh cilantro

1. Place a nonstick wok over medium heat and add the oil. When small bubbles appear at the bottom of the wok, add the mustard seeds. When they begin to sputter, add the asafetida, curry leaves, and chiles, and sauté for 15 seconds. Add the chile powder, turmeric, coriander, and cumin, and stir. Sprinkle with 3 tablespoons water to prevent scorching.

2. Add the salt, jaggery, and tamarind pulp along with 2 cups (400 ml) water, and bring to a boil.

3. Add the potatoes and simmer for 5 to 10 minutes.

4. Garnish with the cilantro and serve hot.

Batata Song

My colleague Neena Murdeshwar makes this dish extremely well, and if she cooks it at home, she's expected to bring a handsome portion of it for all of us in the office. Serve this dish with *puris* (page 21) or *chapatis* (page 438).

Serves 4.

8 to 10 dried red chiles, preferably *bedgi* (see Notes), stemmed, seeds removed
2 teaspoons tamarind paste
3 tablespoons coconut oil (see Notes)
2 large red onions, chopped
4 medium potatoes, boiled, peeled, and cut into ½-inch (1-cm) cubes
1 teaspoon table salt

1. Place a small nonstick sauté pan over medium heat. Let it heat for 2 minutes, then lower the heat to low and add the chiles; dry-roast for 30 seconds. Transfer to a mini food processor and add the tamarind along with ½ cup (100 ml) water and process to a fine paste.

2. Place a medium nonstick sauté pan over medium heat and add the oil. When small bubbles appear at the bottom of the pan, add the onions and cook for 4 to 5 minutes or until golden brown.

3. Add the ground paste and sauté for 2 to 3 minutes. Add the potatoes and stir well. Add 1½ cups (300 ml) water and the salt, and stir. Bring to a boil, then lower the heat to low and simmer for 5 to 7 minutes or until the sauce is thick. Serve hot.

·······⊰ **Notes** ⊱⁕ *Bedgi* is a variety of dried red chile. They are not very spicy but give a beautiful red color to the dish. The seeds are removed to further reduce the heat.

If you do not like the flavor of coconut oil, you can use any vegetable oil.

Batatya Cha Kachrya

······⟩ᕽ⟨ **Sautéed potatoes with curry leaves** ⟩ᕽ⟨ ·····················

Enter a home in Maharashtra or an urban Mumbai household, and this is the comfort food you probably will be served: a simple dry preparation of potatoes.

Serves 4.

5 small potatoes
2 tablespoons vegetable oil
¼ teaspoon brown mustard seeds
⅛ teaspoon asafetida
¼ teaspoon ground turmeric
8 to 10 fresh curry leaves
2 green chiles, stemmed and broken in half
½ teaspoon table salt
1 teaspoon red chile powder
¼ teaspoon sugar
2 tablespoons chopped fresh cilantro

1. Peel the potatoes, halve them lengthwise, and cut into thin semicircular slices. Soak them in 3 cups (600 ml) water in a large bowl.

2. Place a nonstick sauté pan over medium heat and add the oil. When small bubbles appear at the bottom of the pan, add the mustard seeds, asafetida, turmeric, curry leaves, and chiles, and sauté for 1 minute.

3. Drain and add the potatoes, and sauté for 2 minutes. Add the salt and stir. Cover and cook for 7 to 8 minutes.

4. Add the chile powder and sugar, and stir. Cover and cook for 2 to 3 minutes or until the potatoes are tender.

5. Garnish with the cilantro and serve hot as a side dish.

Kashmiri Dum Aloo

····· ◦❧ **Potato curry** ❧◦ ···

The typical *dum aloo* served in most restaurants, even in India, is very different from the Kashmiri recipe here. However, I prefer this version. I make it a point to find good-quality baby potatoes, as they will make or break the dish.

Serves 4.

20 small baby potatoes, peeled
2¼ teaspoons table salt
1 quart (800 ml) vegetable oil
5 or 6 Kashmiri red chiles, ground
2 cups (500 grams) plain yogurt
½ teaspoon ground green cardamom
1 teaspoon ground ginger
2 tablespoons ground fennel
¼ cup (50 ml) filtered mustard oil (see Note page 87)
Generous pinch of ground cloves
Pinch of asafetida
½ teaspoon ground roasted cumin (page 32)
½ teaspoon *garam masala* (spice mix; page 27)

1. Prick the potatoes all over with a fork.

2. Add 1 teaspoon of the salt to 2 cups (400 ml) water in a deep bowl and soak the potatoes for 15 minutes. Drain and pat dry.

3. Place a nonstick wok over high heat and add the oil. When small bubbles appear at the bottom of the wok, lower the heat to medium, add the potatoes, and cook for 10 minutes or until golden brown. Remove with a slotted spoon and drain on paper towels; set aside.

4. Soak the chiles in ½ cup (100 ml) water for 15 minutes. Drain and place them in a spice grinder with 2 tablespoons water and grind to a fine paste.

5. Put the yogurt in a bowl, add the chile paste, cardamom, ginger, and fennel, and whisk until well blended.

6. Place a nonstick saucepan over medium heat and add the mustard oil. Add the cloves and asafetida. Add ½ cup (100 ml) water and the remaining 1¼ teaspoons salt, and bring to a boil.

7. Stir in the yogurt mixture and bring to a boil again. Add the potatoes and cook for 12 minutes or until the potatoes absorb the sauce and the oil comes to the top.

8. Sprinkle with the cumin and *garam masala*, and serve hot.

Methi Aloo

····· { Fresh fenugreek with potatoes and spices } ···

This vegetable dish has a long history in our family—we call it our running "Dad joke." My father was a good cook and a good critic. Once my mother put this on the table and he said, "Ah, today it is real *methi aloo!*" She was a little puzzled, so he clarified: "You have more fenugreek and less potato; sometimes you make *aloo methi*." Punjabis, like me, love *methi aloo*, and Gujaratis, like my wife, Alyona, prefer *aloo methi*. Either way, the dish is great with fresh *roti* (page 18).

Serves 4.

2 medium bunches *methi* (fresh fenugreek leaves), stemmed
2 tablespoons vegetable oil
1 teaspoon cumin seeds
5 cloves garlic, chopped
½-inch (1-cm) piece fresh ginger, chopped
2 or 3 dried red chiles, stemmed and broken in half
2 large red onions, sliced
1 teaspoon red chile powder
½ teaspoon ground turmeric
3 small unpeeled potatoes, parboiled and cubed
1 teaspoon table salt
1 teaspoon freshly squeezed lemon juice

1. Wash the *methi* under running water. Drain well and chop coarsely. Set aside.

2. Place a nonstick sauté pan over medium heat and add the oil. When small bubbles appear at the bottom of the pan, add the cumin. When it begins to change color, add the garlic and ginger, and sauté for 30 seconds.

3. Add the chiles and sauté for 1 minute. Add the onions and sauté until translucent. Add the chile powder and turmeric, and sauté for 30 seconds. Add the potatoes and sauté for 2 to 3 minutes.

4. Add the *methi* and stir well. Cover and cook for 3 to 4 minutes or until the potatoes are tender.

5. Add the salt and lemon juice. Stir gently and cook for 1 minute.

6. Serve hot.

Urulai Chettinadu

Baby potatoes are cooked with a spicy *masala* in this South Indian specialty. Serve with hot *rotis* (page 18).

Serves 4.

18 ounces (500 grams) baby potatoes
4 dried red chiles, stemmed and broken in half
2 tablespoons *dhuli urad dal* (split skinless black gram)
10 to 12 whole black peppercorns
5 tablespoons vegetable oil
1 teaspoon black mustard seeds
20 fresh curry leaves
20 pearl onions, peeled
1 teaspoon table salt

1. Wash and scrub the potatoes. Do not peel them. Cut each in half.

2. Place a nonstick sauté pan over low heat. Add the chiles, *dal*, and peppercorns, and dry-roast, stirring continuously, for 4 to 5 minutes or until the *dal* is golden and fragrant. Remove from the heat and let cool completely.

3. Transfer to a mortar and pound with a pestle to a coarse powder. Set aside.

4. Place a nonstick wok over medium heat and add the oil. When small bubbles appear at the bottom of the wok, lower the heat to low and add the mustard seeds, curry leaves, and onions. Sauté, stirring occasionally, until the onions are lightly browned.

5. Add the potatoes and salt. Stir well. Cover and cook over low heat for 10 to 15 minutes, stirring occasionally, until the potatoes are almost done. You can test with a skewer or a fork for doneness.

6. Add the ground spice mixture and stir well so that all the potatoes are coated. Cover and cook over low heat for 3 to 4 minutes. Serve immediately.

Baghare Baingan

This famous Hyderabadi dish features a delicate interplay of different nuts and seeds. I like to serve it at parties because even though it takes some effort to prepare, it is always well appreciated. The sweet and sour notes added at the end tickle the palate. Serve with any Indian bread.

Serves 4.

9 ounces (250 grams) small purple eggplants
¼ cup (50 ml) plus 1 quart (800 ml) vegetable oil
2 medium red onions, sliced
1½ tablespoons sesame seeds
2 tablespoons peanuts
¾ teaspoon white poppy seeds
1 tablespoon dried grated coconut
½ teaspoon black mustard seeds
¼ teaspoon cumin seeds
¼ teaspoon fennel seeds
¼ teaspoon *kalonji* (nigella; see Note page 231)
Pinch of fenugreek seeds
10 to 12 fresh curry leaves
1 tablespoon fresh ginger paste (page 12)
1 tablespoon fresh garlic paste (page 12)
1 tablespoon fresh green chile paste (page 13)
½ teaspoon ground turmeric
1½ teaspoons ground coriander
½ teaspoon ground roasted cumin (page 32)
½ teaspoon red chile powder
¾ teaspoon table salt
2 tablespoons tamarind pulp
½ teaspoon grated cane jaggery

1. Wash the eggplants and make deep slits (all the way through) along the length, taking care that the stem ends remain intact.

2. Place a nonstick wok over high heat and add 1 quart (800 ml) oil. When small bubbles appear at the bottom of the wok, slide in the eggplants and cook for 3 to 4 minutes. Remove with a slotted spoon and drain on paper towels. Set aside.

3. Add the onions to the hot oil and cook until golden. Drain on paper towels and set aside.

4. Place a medium nonstick sauté pan over medium heat. Let it heat for 2 minutes. Add the sesame seeds and dry-roast until lightly browned. Transfer to a plate and set aside to cool. Dry-roast the peanuts, poppy seeds, and coconut separately and set aside to cool.

5. Transfer the roasted ingredients to a mini food processor with ½ cup (100 ml) water and process to a fine paste.

6. Place a nonstick sauté pan over medium heat and add ¼ cup (50 ml) oil. When small bubbles appear at the bottom of the pan, add the mustard seeds, cumin seeds, fennel, *kalonji*, and fenugreek, and sauté until lightly browned. Add the curry leaves, ginger paste, garlic paste, and green chile paste. Cook until the oil comes to the top. Add the fried onions, turmeric, coriander, ground cumin, chile powder, and salt, and cook for 3 to 4 minutes.

7. Add the tamarind and jaggery, and cook for 2 to 3 minutes. Add the coconut paste and cook until the oil comes to the top. Lower the heat to low, add 1 cup (200 ml) water, and bring to a boil. Add the fried eggplants and cook for 4 to 5 minutes.

8. Serve hot.

Baingan Ka Bharta

·······{ **Roasted eggplant** }··

This North Indian dish is as much about the sweetness of onions and the tanginess of tomatoes as it is about the smoky taste of roasted eggplant.

Serves 4.

1 large eggplant
3 tablespoons vegetable oil
5 large red onions, chopped
3 medium tomatoes, chopped
1½ teaspoons table salt
1 teaspoon red chile powder
2 tablespoons chopped fresh cilantro

1. Roast the eggplant over a medium gas flame or a charcoal grill, turning it frequently with tongs, until the inside is soft and the skin is completely charred on all sides. Let cool, then peel and mash. Put the eggplant in a bowl.

2. Place a medium nonstick sauté pan over medium heat and add the oil. When small bubbles appear at the bottom of the pan, add the onions and sauté for 3 to 4 minutes or until light golden.

3. Add the tomatoes, salt, and chile powder, and sauté until the oil comes to the top.

4. Add the eggplant and cilantro, and stir well. Serve hot.

·······{ **Chef's Tip** }※ It is easier to remove the charred skin of a roasted eggplant if it is dipped in water just after roasting.

Baingan Saaswe

Roasted eggplant with mustard seeds

This is an interesting combination of coconut, mustard seeds, and roasted eggplant. I fondly think of it as the South Indian version of the North Indian *baingan ka bharta* (page 240).

Serves 4.

1 large eggplant
5 dried red chiles, stemmed
1 teaspoon black mustard seeds
½ cup (60 grams) grated fresh coconut (or frozen unsweetened coconut)
3 or 4 cloves garlic
1½ teaspoons table salt
1 cup (200 ml) buttermilk
2 teaspoons vegetable oil

1. Roast the eggplant over a medium gas flame or a charcoal grill, turning it frequently with tongs, until the inside is soft and the skin is completely charred on all sides. Let cool, then peel and mash. Put the eggplant in a deep bowl.

2. Put 3 of the chiles, ½ teaspoon of the mustard seeds, the coconut, garlic, ½ teaspoon of the salt, and ½ cup (100 ml) water in a mini food processor and process to a fine paste.

3. Add the buttermilk and the remaining 1 teaspoon salt to the eggplant, and stir. Add the ground paste and stir.

4. Place a small nonstick sauté pan over medium heat and add the oil. When small bubbles appear at the bottom of the pan, add the remaining ½ teaspoon mustard seeds. When they sputter, break the remaining 2 chiles into small pieces and add them to the pan; sauté for 30 seconds. Add this tempering to the eggplant mixture and cover immediately to trap the flavors.

5. Stir well and serve as a side dish.

Bharli Vangi

Stuffed baby eggplants

This popular Maharashtrian dish of baby eggplants stuffed with an elaborate coconut and spice mixture is made on special occasions.

Serves 4.

8 to 10 baby eggplants
¾ cup (90 grams) grated fresh coconut (or frozen unsweetened coconut)
¼ cup (15 grams) finely chopped fresh cilantro
¼ cup (50 ml) vegetable oil
2 medium red onions, thinly sliced
¼ cup (20 grams) grated dried coconut
2 tablespoons sesame seeds
¼ cup (30 grams) roasted peanuts, skins removed
½ teaspoon cumin seeds
1 teaspoon coriander seeds
2 teaspoons *goda masala* (spice mix; page 28)
1½ teaspoons table salt
¼ teaspoon ground turmeric
1½ teaspoons red chile powder
1 teaspoon grated cane jaggery
½ teaspoon tamarind pulp
½ teaspoon brown mustard seeds
6 to 8 fresh curry leaves

1. Slit the eggplants from the bottom into 4 sections, keeping the stem end intact. Put in a bowl of water while you prepare the filling.

2. Reserve 1 tablespoon each of the fresh coconut and cilantro for garnish.

3. Place a medium nonstick sauté pan over medium heat and add 1 teaspoon of the oil. When small bubbles appear at the bottom of the pan, add the onions and sauté for 2 to 3 minutes or until lightly colored. Add the dried coconut, sesame seeds, peanuts, cumin, and coriander, and sauté, stirring continuously, for 2 minutes or until the coconut is light golden. Let cool, then transfer to a food processor with 1 cup (200 ml) water and process to a paste.

4. Transfer to a small bowl, add the *goda masala*, salt, turmeric, chile powder, the remaining fresh coconut, the remaining cilantro, the jaggery, and tamarind pulp, and stir well. Stuff this mixture into the eggplants.

5. Place a medium nonstick sauté pan over medium heat and add the remaining oil. When small bubbles appear at the bottom of the pan, add the mustard seeds. When they begin to sputter, add the curry leaves and, gently, the stuffed eggplants. Cook for 2 to 3 minutes, gently turning the eggplants once or twice to ensure even cooking. Add 1 cup (200 ml) water and bring to a boil. Lower the heat to low, cover, and cook for 8 to 10 minutes or until the eggplants are cooked and soft. (Most of the stuffing will fall out of the eggplant and form the sauce for the dish.)

6. Garnish with the reserved coconut and cilantro, and serve hot.

Methi Baingan

······❧{ **Fresh fenugreek leaves with small eggplants** }❧······

Serve this delicious dish with any Indian bread.

Serves 4.

¼ cup (50 ml) vegetable oil
10 to 12 small eggplants
1 teaspoon cumin seeds
2 medium red onions, chopped
1 teaspoon fresh ginger paste (page 12)
1 teaspoon fresh garlic paste (page 12)
2 medium tomatoes, puréed
1½ teaspoons table salt
1 teaspoon *deghi mirch* (red chile) powder (see Note)
½ teaspoon ground turmeric
1½ teaspoons ground coriander
½ cup (125 grams) plain yogurt, whisked
1½ pounds (700 grams) *methi* (fresh fenugreek leaves), trimmed, chopped, and blanched
¼ teaspoon ground *kasoori methi* (dried fenugreek leaves)
½ teaspoon *garam masala* (spice mix; page 27)

1. Take each eggplant and trim off portions of the crown, leaving the stems attached. Make two criss-cross slits at the bottom of each.

2. Place a nonstick sauté pan over medium heat and add 2 tablespoons of the oil. When small bubbles appear at the bottom of the pan, add the eggplants and sauté until well-browned. Remove with a slotted spoon and drain on paper towels.

3. Add the remaining 2 tablespoons oil to the same heated pan. When small bubbles appear at the bottom of the pan, add the cumin and sauté for 20 seconds. Add the onions and sauté for 5 minutes or until browned.

4. Add the ginger paste and garlic paste, and cook for 2 minutes. Add the tomatoes and cook for 5 minutes or until the oil comes to the top.

5. Add the salt, chile powder, turmeric, and coriander, and stir well. Cook for 1 minute or until the raw flavors disappear.

6. Add the yogurt and cook for 2 minutes or until all the ingredients are well blended. Add the *methi*, eggplants, and ½ cup (100 ml) water, and cook until the sauce thickens. As soon as the sauce thickens, the curry is ready.

7. Add the *kasoori methi* and *garam masala*, and stir well.

8. Serve hot.

·······⊰ **Note** ⊱· *Deghi mirch* is a mild, ground, dried Indian chile pepper powder that provides a gentle taste. Hungarian paprika powder can be used as a substitute.

Besanwali Bhindi

·······⊰ **Whole okra cooked with chickpea flour and spices** ⊱·······················

Baby okra is tender and cooks rather quickly. In this recipe, I love the sweetness of the shallots and the crispness that the *besan* imparts to the dish. I recommend serving this with *dal* and *roti* for a perfect everyday Indian meal.

Serves 4.

14 ounces (400 grams) small okra
1 teaspoon table salt
½ teaspoon ground turmeric
1 teaspoon *garam masala* (spice mix; page 27)
1½ teaspoons ground roasted cumin (page 32)
1 teaspoon *amchur* (dried mango powder)
1½ teaspoons fennel seeds, crushed
1 teaspoon red chile powder
1 tablespoon ground coriander
6 tablespoons vegetable oil
½ teaspoon *kalonji* (nigella; see Note page 231)
20 small shallots, sliced
¼ cup (25 grams) *besan* (chickpea/gram flour)

1. Trim off the ends of the okra and make a slit in one side of each okra pod without cutting through. Set aside in a bowl.

2. In a small bowl, combine the salt, turmeric, *garam masala*, cumin, *amchur*, fennel, chile powder, and coriander. Stuff the spice mixture into the slits in the okra. Sprinkle the remaining mixture (if any) over the okra and drizzle with 2 tablespoons of the oil. Stir and set aside.

3. Place a nonstick sauté pan over medium heat and add the remaining 4 tablespoons (50 ml) oil. When small bubbles appear at the bottom of the pan, add the *kalonji* and sauté for 30 seconds or until fragrant.

4. Add the shallots and sauté for 1 minute. Add the stuffed okra and sauté for 2 to 3 minutes. Add the besan and sauté for 1 to 2 minutes.

5. Lower the heat to low, cover, and cook, stirring occasionally, for 6 to 8 minutes or until the okra is tender.

6. Transfer to a serving bowl and serve hot as a side dish.

Vendakkai Mor Thalippu

Okra with yogurt and coconut

Okra and yogurt have a natural affinity that is perfectly demonstrated in this thick yogurt curry from South India, and in the okra *raita* (page 76) and okra *kadhi* from North India and western India.

Serves 4.

2 cups (500 grams) plain yogurt
½ teaspoon ground turmeric
2 tablespoons raw rice
¼ cup (30 grams) grated fresh coconut (or frozen unsweetened coconut)
2 tablespoons vegetable oil
½ teaspoon brown mustard seeds
¼ teaspoon fenugreek seeds
2 dried red chiles, stemmed and broken in half
10 to 12 fresh curry leaves
2 medium red onions, sliced
4 green chiles, stemmed and slit
8 ounces (225 grams) okra, cut into ½-inch-thick (1-cm-thick) rounds
1 teaspoon table salt
2 tablespoons coconut oil, melted

1. In a large bowl, whisk the yogurt together with the turmeric and set aside.

2. Soak the rice in 6 tablespoons (90 ml) water for 15 minutes. Transfer to a spice grinder, add the coconut, and grind to a smooth paste. Add to the yogurt and whisk well.

3. Place a nonstick sauté pan over medium heat and add the vegetable oil. When small bubbles appear at the bottom of the pan, add the mustard seeds, fenugreek, red chiles, and curry leaves. When the mustard seeds start to sputter, add the onion and green chiles, and sauté for 3 to 4 minutes or until the onion is translucent.

4. Increase the heat to high, add the okra, and sauté for 6 minutes or until half done. Lower the heat to low, add the yogurt-coconut mixture and salt, and cook for 3 minutes or until the curry is thick.

5. Drizzle with the coconut oil and serve hot.

Vendakkai Pachadi

⋯⋯⋯⋰⋅{ **Crisp okra in yogurt sauce** }⋅⋯⋯⋯⋯⋯⋯⋯⋯⋯⋯⋯⋯⋯⋯⋯⋯⋯⋯⋯⋯⋯⋯

Crisply cooked okra takes to yogurt rather well, which is why it's often served with *raita* in North India.

Serves 4.

3 tablespoons vegetable oil
9 ounces (250 grams) okra, trimmed and thinly sliced
1 teaspoon table salt
½ cup (60 grams) grated fresh coconut (or frozen unsweetened coconut)
1½ cups (375 grams) plain yogurt
5 green chiles, stemmed and chopped
½-inch (1-cm) piece fresh ginger, chopped
1 tablespoon coconut oil
½ teaspoon brown mustard seeds
1 dried red chile, stemmed and broken
10 to 12 fresh curry leaves

1. Place a nonstick sauté pan over medium heat and add the vegetable oil. When small bubbles appear at the bottom of the pan, add the okra and sauté for 5 to 6 minutes.

2. Transfer the okra to a large bowl and toss with the salt.

3. Put the coconut in a mini food processor with ¼ cup (50 ml) water and process to a fine paste.

4. Whisk the yogurt in a large bowl until smooth. Stir in the okra, coconut paste, green chiles, and ginger.

5. Place a small nonstick sauté pan over medium heat and add the coconut oil. When small bubbles appear at the bottom of the pan, add the mustard seeds, red chile, and curry leaves. When the mustard seeds sputter, add the mixture to the okra-yogurt mixture and stir well.

6. Put in the refrigerator to chill. Serve cold.

Ganthia Saag

The western region of India, particularly the states of Gujarat and Maharashtra, is rich in snacks made with gram (or chickpea) flour. This is an example of how the love of these snacks carries over into curries. Serve this with *thepla* (page 465) or *roti* (page 18).

Serves 4.

1½ teaspoons red chile powder
½ teaspoon *garam masala* (spice mix; page 27)
½ teaspoon *amchur* (dried mango powder)
2 teaspoons ground coriander
2 tablespoons vegetable oil
1 teaspoon cumin seeds
¼ teaspoon asafetida
1 teaspoon sugar
2 cups (150 grams) *ganthia* (see Note)
1¼ teaspoons table salt
1 tablespoon chopped fresh cilantro

1. Put the chile powder, *garam masala*, *amchur*, and coriander in a bowl, and add 2 cups (400 ml) water. Stir well.

2. Place a nonstick sauté pan over medium heat and add the oil. When small bubbles appear at the bottom of the pan, add the cumin and asafetida. When the seeds begin to change color, add the spice and water mixture, and simmer for 3 to 4 minutes.

3. Add the sugar and stir to dissolve. Lower the heat to low, add the *ganthia* and salt, and stir. Cook for 1 to 2 minutes.

4. Garnish with the cilantro and serve hot.

······❖⟨ **Note** ⟩❖ *Ganthia* are savory sticks made from *besan* (chickpea/gram flour) cooked in oil until crisp. They are available in Indian grocery stores.

Garlic Spinach Massiyal

······⊹{ **Spicy spinach and garlic** }⊹··

If you love your greens, this spinach stir-fry will win your heart.

Serves 4.

4 medium bunches spinach, stemmed and roughly chopped
2 teaspoons salt
½ lemon-size tamarind ball (taken from a tamarind brick) or 1 tablespoon tamarind pulp
¼ cup (50 ml) sesame oil
¼ teaspoon black mustard seeds
1 tablespoon *dhuli urad dal* (split skinless black gram)
3 or 4 dried red chiles, stemmed and broken in half
10 to 12 fresh curry leaves
12 to 15 cloves garlic, sliced
4 green chiles, stemmed and slit
¼ teaspoon asafetida
1 tablespoon rice flour, mixed with ¼ cup (50 ml) water

1. Pour 2 cups (400 ml) water in a deep pan, add 1 teaspoon of the salt, and soak the spinach leaves to remove the bitterness. Drain well in a colander.

2. Put the tamarind in a bowl, add ½ cup (100 ml) warm water, and soak for 15 minutes. Press and remove the pulp, push through a strainer, and set aside.

3. Place a nonstick sauté pan over medium heat and add the sesame oil. When small bubbles appear at the bottom of the pan, add the mustard seeds. When the seeds sputter, add the *dal*, red chiles, and curry leaves. Stir well, add the garlic and green chiles, and sauté for 1 minute.

4. Add the spinach and tamarind pulp, and cook over medium heat for 3 to 4 minutes, stirring frequently.

5. Sprinkle with the asafetida and stir in the rice-flour mixture. Add the remaining 1 teaspoon salt, cook for 2 minutes, and serve hot.

Hak

·······•⟩ Stir-fried spinach ⟨•···

Traditional Kashmiri cuisine veers heavily toward nonvegetarian dishes, so this light stir-fry of spinach comes as a surprise. *Ver* (page 33) is a special spice mix that is sold in a solid disk form. It can be used to make authentic Kashmiri food as well as to spice up regular *dal* or pulse dishes a little differently.

Serves 4.

4 medium bunches spinach, stemmed
3 tablespoons vegetable oil
1 teaspoon cumin seeds
½ teaspoon asafetida
2 teaspoons red chile powder
½ teaspoon ground turmeric
2 teaspoons table salt
2 teaspoons *ver* (page 33)

1. Wash the spinach thoroughly under running water. Drain well in a colander. Finely chop and set aside.

2. Place a nonstick sauté pan over medium heat and add the oil. When small bubbles appear at the bottom of the pan, add the cumin. When the cumin begins to change color, add the asafetida, chile powder, turmeric, spinach, salt, and 2 tablespoons water, and stir well.

3. Cook, uncovered, until all the water has evaporated and the oil comes to the top.

4. Sprinkle with the *ver* and serve hot.

Keerai Kozhambu

············ ·⟩ **A spinach and *dal* curry** ⟨· ············

This dish, popular in the north as well as in the south, has many variations. The greens and lentils used change from cook to cook. What a delight it is to know that this healthy dish, when eaten with *roti* (page 18) or rice, makes a fairly balanced meal.

Serves 4.

1 medium bunch spinach or green amaranth leaves, stemmed
½ cup (100 grams) *masoor dal* (split red lentils)
½ teaspoon ground turmeric
3 cloves garlic, crushed
⅛ teaspoon asafetida
2 tablespoons vegetable oil
1¾ teaspoons table salt
1 large red onion, diced
4 or 5 green chiles, stemmed and chopped
1 large tomato, chopped
3 tablespoons tamarind pulp
1 tablespoon coconut oil
¼ teaspoon brown mustard seeds
¼ teaspoon cumin seeds
¼ teaspoon fenugreek seeds
¼ teaspoon *dhuli urad dal* (split skinless black gram)
1 dried red chile, stemmed and broken in half
8 to 10 fresh curry leaves

1. Put the spinach in a colander and wash it 2 or 3 times under running water. Drain well, and chop it finely. Set aside in a bowl. Wash the *masoor dal* in running water and drain.

2. Place a nonstick saucepan over medium heat and add 2 cups (400 ml) water. When the water comes to a boil, add the *masoor dal*, turmeric, garlic, asafetida, ½ tablespoon of the vegetable oil, and ¼ teaspoon of the salt, and cook for 10 minutes or until the lentils are tender.

3. Place another nonstick saucepan over medium heat and add the remaining 1½ tablespoons of vegetable oil. When small bubbles appear at the bottom of the pan, add the onion and sauté for 2 minutes. Add the green chiles, tomato, and spinach, and sauté for 2 to 3 minutes. Add the tamarind pulp, the remaining 1½ teaspoons salt, and the cooked *dal*, and stir well. Add 1½ cups (300 ml) water, stir, and bring to a boil. Simmer for 8 to 10 minutes. In a small nonstick sauté pan, add the coconut oil. When small bubbles appear at the bottom of the pan, add the mustard seeds and cumin. When they sputter, add the fenugreek, *dhuli urad dal*, red chile, and curry leaves, and sauté for 30 seconds. Add this tempering to the *masoor dal* and stir well.

4. Transfer to a serving bowl and serve hot.

Makai Palak

My wife, Alyona, is a big fan of this spinach-and-corn dish, served with *rotis* (page 18) or *parathas* (page 18). In fact, she enjoys the leftovers on toast for breakfast!

Serves 4.

2 large bunches fresh spinach, chopped
1 tablespoon vegetable oil
2 medium red onions, chopped
1 tablespoon fresh garlic paste (page 12)
2 green chiles, stemmed and chopped
1-inch (2½-cm) piece ginger, julienned
½ teaspoon red chile powder
Pinch of ground turmeric
¾ teaspoon *amchur* (dried mango powder)
½ cup (75 grams) cooked corn kernels
1½ teaspoons table salt
½ cup (125 grams) plain yogurt, whisked
1 teaspoon *garam masala* (spice mix; page 27)
¼ teaspoon ground roasted *kasoori methi* (dried fenugreek leaves)

1. Place a nonstick saucepan over high heat and add 8 cups (1.6 liters) water. When it comes to a boil, add the spinach and blanch for 1 minute. Drain and refresh in cold water. Drain well in a colander. Transfer to a food processor and process to a purée. Transfer to a bowl.

2. Place a nonstick sauté pan over medium heat and add the oil. When small bubbles appear at the bottom of the pan, add the onions and sauté for 2 to 3 minutes or until lightly browned. Add the garlic paste and stir. Add the chiles and ginger, and sauté until browned.

3. Add the chile powder, turmeric, and *amchur*, and stir. Add the spinach purée and stir well.

4. Add the corn and salt, and stir. Add the yogurt, *garam masala*, and *kasoori methi*. Stir and remove from the heat.

5. Serve hot.

Mooli Saag

When I was a child in Delhi, vegetable vendors would pile their carts high with glistening white radishes during the winter. My mother huddled in a warm shawl while picking up enough radishes to last the week. She made radish *parathas* and used the leaves to make a quick stir-fry similar to this one. Serve this with *parathas* (page 18).

Serves 4.

4 medium white daikon radishes with leaves
2 teaspoons table salt
2 tablespoons vegetable oil
½ teaspoon brown mustard seeds
½ teaspoon cumin seeds
Pinch of asafetida
½ teaspoon ground turmeric
1 teaspoon red chile powder
1½ teaspoons sugar
1 teaspoon *amchur* (dried mango powder)

1. Wash the radishes and tops well under running water. Drain well in a colander.

2. Peel and dice the radishes. Shred the leaves. Sprinkle the salt on the radishes and set aside for 20 minutes. Drain off the liquid.

3. Place a medium nonstick sauté pan over medium heat and add the oil. When small bubbles appear at the bottom of the pan, add the mustard seeds. When they begin to sputter, add the cumin and asafetida, and sauté for 30 seconds. Add the turmeric and chile powder, and sauté for 10 seconds.

4. Add the radishes and leaves. Sauté for 1 minute. Add ¼ cup (50 ml) water, cover, and cook over medium heat for 10 minutes or until the radishes are tender.

5. Taste and add more salt if needed. Sprinkle with the sugar and *amchur*, and stir.

6. Serve hot.

Sai Bhaji

Sai bhaji is a popular vegetarian dish in Sindhi cuisine. The Sindhis originated from the province of Sindh, now in Pakistan, but they migrated to various states in India during Partition. A common Sindhi meal is *phulkas* (wheat-flour breads like *chapatis*) with *dal* and vegetables, either dry or with sauce. Serve this with steamed rice.

Serves 4.

½ cup (100 grams) *chana dal* (split Bengal gram)
¼ cup (50 ml) vegetable oil
2 teaspoons cumin seeds
1-inch (2½-cm) piece fresh ginger, chopped
5 cloves garlic, chopped
3 green chiles, stemmed and chopped
1 large red onion, roughly chopped
3 medium tomatoes, roughly chopped
3 small eggplants, cut into 8 pieces each
2 medium potatoes, cut into 1-inch (2½-cm) cubes
1½ teaspoons red chile powder
1 teaspoon ground turmeric
2 tablespoons ground coriander
2 teaspoons table salt
3 medium bunches fresh spinach, chopped
½ cup (50 grams) chopped fresh dill
1 cup (50 grams) chopped fresh sorrel
1 cup (50 grams) chopped *methi* (fresh fenugreek leaves)

1. Put the *dal* in a bowl, wash in plenty of water 2 or 3 times, and drain. Add 1 cup (200 ml) water and soak for 1 hour. Drain.

2. Place a nonstick saucepan over medium heat and add the oil. When small bubbles appear at the bottom of the pan, add the cumin and sauté for 30 seconds. Add the ginger and garlic, and sauté for 30 seconds. Add the chiles and sauté for 30 seconds.

3. Add the onion and sauté for 3 minutes. Add the tomatoes and sauté for 5 minutes. Add the *dal*, eggplant, and potatoes, and stir. Add the chile powder, turmeric, coriander, and salt, and sauté for 5 minutes.

4. Add the spinach, dill, sorrel, *khatta bhani*, and *methi*, and sauté for 2 minutes. Add 2½ cups (500 ml) water and simmer for 40 minutes or until the *dal* is soft.

5. Blend with an immersion blender for 1 to 2 minutes.

6. Transfer to a serving bowl and serve hot.

Sarson Ka Saag

·······⟨ **Mustard greens and spinach** ⟩···

Sarson ka saag is a fantastic winter meal from North India. Punjabis love this served with *makki di roti* (cornmeal bread; page 459)—each is incomplete without the other.

Serves 4.

2¼ pounds (1 kg) mustard greens, tough stems removed
1 bunch spinach, tough stems removed
1 bunch *bathua* (lamb's quarters), tough stems removed (see Note)
2 tablespoons cornmeal
¼ cup (50 grams) ghee (page 37)
2 medium red onions, diced
2 (1-inch/2½-cm) pieces fresh ginger, minced
6 to 8 cloves garlic, chopped
4 green chiles, stemmed and minced
1½ teaspoons table salt
Butter

1. Wash and drain the mustard greens, spinach, and *bathua*. Chop and set aside.

2. Place a nonstick saucepan over medium heat, add ¼ cup (50 ml) water, and bring to a boil. Add the greens and boil for 15 minutes or until very tender and yellowish. If there is any water left, drain and reserve. Let the greens cool, then transfer to a food processor and process to a smooth paste. Add the cornmeal and stir.

3. Place a nonstick sauté pan over medium heat and add the ghee. When small bubbles appear at the bottom of the pan, add the onions, ginger, garlic, and chiles, and sauté for 7 to 8 minutes or until lightly browned.

4. Add the greens and sauté for 5 to 6 minutes. Add the reserved water to adjust the consistency if necessary. Add the salt and cook, stirring, for 4 to 5 minutes or until well blended.

5. Serve hot with butter.

·······⟨ **Chef's Tip** ⟩⟨ Traditionally *sarson ka saag* is pounded to a paste with a wooden churner called a *mathni* or *ravai* while it is being cooked. The process is quite cumbersome and time consuming, but the result is delicious.

·······⟨ **Note** ⟩⟨ *Bathua* is an edible weed that is used in India especially during the winter months.

Beans Poriyal

This beautiful Kerala-style preparation brings out the best in green beans and coconut.

Serves 4.

2 tablespoons vegetable oil
½ teaspoon black mustard seeds
1 teaspoon *dhuli urad dal* (split skinless black gram)
Pinch of asafetida
2 dried red chiles, stemmed and broken
9 ounces (250 grams) haricots verts, cut into ¼-inch (½-cm) pieces
8 to 10 fresh curry leaves
½ teaspoon table salt
¼ cup (30 grams) grated fresh coconut (or frozen unsweetened coconut)

1. Place a medium nonstick sauté pan over medium heat and add the oil. Add the mustard seeds and *dal*, and sauté until the mustard sputters and the *dal* is lightly browned.

2. Add the asafetida and chiles, and sauté for 30 seconds. Add the haricots verts, curry leaves, and salt. Add half of the coconut and stir well.

3. Add 2 tablespoons water and cook for 10 to 15 minutes or until the haricots verts are tender.

4. Garnish with the remaining coconut and serve hot as a side dish.

Guar Ki Sabzi

·······❊{ **Cluster beans with dried mango** }❊···

Cluster beans have a slightly bitter aftertaste; hence the use of yogurt as a souring agent in this Rajasthani recipe.

Serves 4.

4 dried mango pieces
2 tablespoons vegetable oil
1 teaspoon cumin seeds
2 dried red chiles, stemmed and broken
Large pinch of asafetida
1 teaspoon dry mustard powder
7 ounces (200 grams) *guar* (cluster beans; see Note), stringed and broken into small pieces
1 teaspoon table salt
6 tablespoons plain yogurt, whisked
2 teaspoon red chile powder
1 teaspoon ground turmeric
2 tablespoons *garam masala* (spice mix; page 27)
2 teaspoons ground coriander

1. Soak the dried mango in ¼ cup (50 ml) water for 30 minutes.

2. Place a nonstick sauté pan over medium heat and add the oil. When small bubbles appear at the bottom of the pan, add the cumin, chiles, asafetida, and mustard powder, and sauté for 1 minute.

3. Add the beans and salt. Stir well and add the yogurt.

4. In a small bowl, stir together the chile powder, turmeric, *garam masala*, and coriander powder, add ¼ cup (50 ml) water, and stir to combine. Add this mixture to the pan and stir. Add the mango along with the water in which it was soaked and stir. Cook for 10 minutes or until most of the liquid has evaporated.

5. Serve hot.

·······❊{ **Note** }❊ *Guar* is a legume grown in India and the source of guar gum. Though if grows well in a wet climate, it can tolerate arid conditions pretty well. It is grown mostly in India. Also now you can find it in the United States in the freezer section of many Indian grocery stores.

Aviyal

⋯⋯⋅⊰ Mixed vegetables in coconut-and-yogurt gravy ⊱⋅⋯⋯⋯⋯⋯⋯⋯⋯⋯⋯⋯

Years ago when I cooked this popular South Indian dish for the first time on my show, I received more than fifty letters with recipes for *aviyal*—each different from the other, and each claiming to be the most authentic version. This is my version. If you can't find Indian broad beans, you can use green beans.

Serves 4.

1 medium carrot
8 haricots verts or thin green beans, strings removed
8 Indian broad beans (hyacinth beans), strings removed
7 ounces (200 grams) white pumpkin, peeled
1 medium green banana, peeled
1 drumstick vegetable (page 588), canned or frozen
1 small yam, peeled
1½ teaspoons table salt
½ cup (60 grams) grated fresh coconut (or frozen unsweetened coconut)
4 green chiles, stemmed
1½ teaspoons cumin seeds
1 tablespoon raw rice
1½ cups (375 grams) plain yogurt
10 to 12 fresh curry leaves
2 tablespoons coconut oil, melted

1. Cut the carrot, haricots verts, broad beans, pumpkin, banana, drumstick, and yam into thick, 2-inch-long (5-cm-long) fingers.

2. Place a nonstick saucepan over high heat and add 2 cups (400 ml) water. When it comes to a boil, add ½ teaspoon of the salt and the yam, and boil for 8 minutes or until almost cooked. Drain in a colander and set aside.

3. Put the coconut, green chiles, cumin, rice, and ⅓ cup (70 ml) water in a mini food processor and process to a fine paste. Transfer the paste to a bowl. Add the yogurt and whisk until well blended. Set aside.

4. Place the nonstick saucepan over high heat and add 1½ cups (300 ml) water. When it comes to a boil, add the carrot, haricots verts, broad beans, pumpkin, banana, drumstick, the remaining 1 teaspoon salt, and the curry leaves. Lower the heat to medium and cook for 10 minutes or until the vegetables are almost cooked.

5. Add the yogurt mixture and yam, and stir well. Bring to a simmer, then remove from the heat.

6. Transfer to a serving dish and drizzle with the coconut oil. Serve hot as a side dish.

⋯⋯⋅⊰ **Note** ⊱⋅ If you do not like the smell of raw coconut oil, heat up the oil, add the curry leaves, and temper the *aviyal*. But do avoid reheating the *aviyal*.

Cabbage Chana Dal

·······•⟨ **Cabbage with split Bengal gram** ⟩•···

In India, cabbage is very popular with vegetarians, who appreciate its lovely flavor and great versatility. Many regions have their own distinctive versions of this dish, and I have chosen the lightest preparation.

Serves 4.

¼ cup (50 grams) *chana dal* (split Bengal gram)
1 tablespoon vegetable oil
½ teaspoon brown mustard seeds
10 to 12 fresh curry leaves
4 dried red chiles, stemmed and broken
1-inch (2½-cm) piece fresh ginger, chopped
1 medium head cabbage, shredded
¼ teaspoon ground turmeric
¾ teaspoon table salt
1 teaspoon *garam masala* (spice mix; page 27)
2 tablespoons grated fresh coconut (or frozen unsweetened coconut)

1. Put the *dal* in a bowl, wash in plenty of water 2 or 3 times, and drain. Add 1 cup (200 ml) water and soak for 30 minutes. Drain in a colander.

2. Place a nonstick saucepan over medium heat and add 1 cup (200 ml) water. Bring to a boil and add the *dal*. Cook for 20 minutes or until the *dal* is very soft. Drain in a colander.

3. Place a nonstick sauté pan over medium heat and add the oil. When small bubbles appear at the bottom of the pan, add the mustard seeds. When they begin to sputter, add the curry leaves and chiles, and sauté for 15 seconds. Add the ginger and sauté for 15 seconds. Add the cabbage and toss well to coat it with the oil and spices. Add the turmeric and salt, and stir. Add the *dal* and stir well. Cook for 7 to 8 minutes.

4. Add the *garam masala* and stir well.

5. Garnish with the coconut and serve hot.

Chorchori

This dish originated in Bengal and is prepared with whatever uncooked vegetables are left over at the end of a week. Serve it with *dal* and steamed rice.

Serves 4.

2 tablespoons vegetable oil
1½ teaspoons *panch phoron* (page 589)
1 *turai* (ridge gourd), cut into 1½-inch (4-cm) fingers
2 eggplants, cut into 1½-inch (4-cm) fingers
4 ounces (100 grams) red or pie pumpkin, peeled, seeded, and cut into 1½-inch (4-cm) fingers
2 medium potatoes, peeled and cut into 1½-inch (4-cm) fingers
5 medium *parwars* (striped pear gourds; see Note), cut into 1½-inch (4-cm) fingers
1 drumstick vegetable (page 588), cut into 1½-inch (4-cm) pieces
¼ teaspoon ground turmeric
½ teaspoon ground roasted cumin (page 32)
2 or 3 green chiles, stemmed and slit
Pinch of sugar
2 teaspoons table salt

1. Place a medium nonstick sauté pan over medium heat and add the oil. When small bubbles appear at the bottom of the pan, add the *panch phoron,* and sauté for 30 seconds.

2. Add all the vegetables and toss well. Add the turmeric, cumin, chiles, sugar, and salt. Toss again.

3. Add ½ cup (100 ml) water and stir. Cook, uncovered, for 15 to 20 minutes or until the vegetables are tender and all the moisture has evaporated. Take care that the vegetables do not overcook.

4. Serve hot.

Note *Parwar* is a striped pear gourd. It has heart-shaped leaves and is grown on a trellis. It thrives in a hot to moderately warm and humid climate.

Dhokar Dalna

······· Bengali steamed *dal* dumplings in a spicy sauce ·······

This dish plays an important part in the Bengali *niramish* (vegetarian) repertoire. *Dhokar* literally means "to cheat," and as the texture of the lightly spiced lentil cakes resembles that of fish, the name is appropriate. If you see the mixture coming off the sides of the pan while you are steaming the lentil paste, it is a sign that it is cooked. If you oversteam it, the lentil cake will lose moisture and become hard.

Serve these with *luchi* (page 19).

Serves 4.

1 cup (200 grams) *chana dal* (split Bengal gram)
2 teaspoons cumin seeds
4 green chiles, stemmed
¾ teaspoon ground turmeric
2 teaspoons table salt
2½ tablespoons vegetable oil
2 medium potatoes, peeled and cut into 1-inch (2½-cm) cubes
3 medium red onions, grated
2 teaspoons fresh ginger paste (page 12)
2 teaspoons fresh garlic paste (page 12)
1 teaspoon red chile powder
1½ teaspoons ground roasted cumin (page 32)
4 medium tomatoes, grated

1. Put the *dal* in a large bowl, wash in plenty of water 2 or 3 times, and drain. Add 3 cups (600 ml) water and soak for 6 to 8 hours. Drain in a colander and transfer to a food processor. Add the cumin, chiles, ¼ teaspoon of the turmeric, and ¼ cup (50 ml) water, and process to a smooth paste. Add 1 teaspoon of the salt and process to combine the batter well.

2. Grease a 7-inch-diameter (18-cm-diameter), ½-inch-deep (1-cm-deep) plate. Pour the batter into it and level the surface.

3. Place a steamer over high heat and add 2 cups (400 ml) water. When the water comes to a boil, fit the plate into one of the grooves. Lower the heat to medium, cover, and steam for 12 minutes or until a skewer inserted in the center of the cake comes out clean.

4. Remove the plate from the steamer and let the cake cool slightly. Cut into 1-inch (2½-cm) diamond-shaped pieces.

5. Place a nonstick sauté pan over medium heat and add the oil. When small bubbles appear at the bottom of the pan, add the potatoes and sauté until the potatoes are light golden. Remove with a slotted spoon and place in a bowl.

6. To the hot oil in the pan, add the onions and sauté until golden brown. Add the ginger paste and garlic paste, and sauté for 2 minutes. Add the chile powder, the remaining ½ teaspoon turmeric, and the cumin, and sauté for 1 minute. Add the tomatoes and the remaining 1 teaspoon salt and sauté for 6 to 7 minutes.

7. Add the steamed lentil diamonds, potatoes, and 2 cups (400 ml) water. Lower the heat to low and cook for 20 minutes.

8. Serve hot.

Diwani Handi

·······❧ **Vegetables with fenugreek** ❧·····················

Hyderabadi cooks are experts at mixing and matching vegetables of contrasting textures and tastes, and this recipe uses strongly flavored fenugreek leaves with fleshy eggplant and a variety of beans. Very creative, very presentable, and very delicious, the dish has an honored spot on the menus of my Yellow Chilli restaurants. If you can't find Indian broad beans, you can use green beans. Serve it with any Indian bread.

Serves 4.

1 quart (800 ml) plus 3 tablespoons vegetable oil
4 medium red onions, sliced
2 or 3 green chiles, stemmed, seeded, and chopped
1 tablespoon fresh ginger paste (page 12)
1 tablespoon fresh garlic paste (page 12)
1 teaspoon red chile powder
½ teaspoon ground turmeric
1 teaspoon table salt
1 cup (250 grams) plain yogurt, whisked
3 medium potatoes, peeled and cut into ½-inch (1-cm) cubes
3 medium carrots, cut into ½-inch (1-cm) cubes
10 haricots verts, sliced on the bias
10 Indian broad beans (hyacinth beans), sliced on the bias (page 588)
6 small eggplants, slit in half with the stem ends intact
½ cup (75 grams) fresh or frozen green peas
½ medium bunch *methi* (fresh fenugreek leaves), chopped
2 tablespoons chopped fresh cilantro
½ teaspoon *garam masala* (spice mix; page 27)

1. Place a nonstick wok over high heat and add 1 quart (800 ml) oil. When small bubbles appear at the bottom of the wok, add the onions and cook, stirring with a slotted spoon, until the onions are well browned. Remove with the slotted spoon and drain on paper towels.

2. Place a nonstick saucepan over medium heat and add 3 tablespoons oil. Add the chiles, ginger paste, and garlic paste, and sauté for 1 minute. Add the chile powder, turmeric, and salt, and stir. Add the yogurt and sauté for 1 to 2 minutes.

3. Add the potatoes, carrots, haricots verts, broad beans, eggplants, peas, and browned onions, and stir well. Lower the heat to low, add ¾ cup (150 ml) water, cover, and cook for 10 minutes or until the vegetables are tender.

4. Add the *methi*, cilantro, and *garam masala*, and stir well. Cook for 3 to 4 minutes. Serve hot.

Dum Ki Arbi

········∗{ *Colocassia* roots in a yogurt-based sauce }∗········

Colocassia roots might be sticky to handle, but frying them in oil helps them hold their shape and reduces the stickiness, which makes it easier for the *colocassia* to be coated with rich, spicy *masalas*. This preparation has all the touches of the regal Hyderabadi cuisine.

Serves 4.

1 quart (800 ml) plus ¼ cup (50 ml) vegetable oil
1 pound (500 grams) *colocassia* (taro) roots, peeled and cut into 1-inch (2½-cm) pieces
3 medium red onions, peeled and quartered
3 tablespoons white poppy seeds
2 cups (500 grams) plain yogurt
½ teaspoon red chile powder
1 teaspoon ground roasted cumin (page 32)
½ teaspoon ground turmeric
4 to 6 green cardamom pods
1 tablespoon fresh ginger paste (page 12)
1 tablespoon fresh garlic paste (page 12)
1 teaspoon ground coriander
¼ teaspoon freshly grated nutmeg
½ teaspoon *garam masala* (spice mix; page 27)
1 teaspoon table salt
¼ cup (50 ml) heavy cream
1 tablespoon chopped fresh cilantro

1. Place a nonstick wok over high heat and add 1 quart (800 ml) oil. When small bubbles appear at the bottom of the wok, slide in the *colocassia* and cook until golden brown and crisp. Remove with a slotted spoon and drain on paper towels; set aside.

2. Place a nonstick saucepan over high heat and add 2 cups (400 ml) water. When it comes to a boil, add the onion quarters and cook until soft. Drain, let cool, and place in a food processor. Process to a smooth paste and set aside in a small bowl.

3. Place a small nonstick sauté pan over medium heat and add the poppy seeds. Dry-roast for 3 to 4 minutes. Transfer to a bowl with ¼ cup (50 ml) water and soak for 30 minutes. Transfer the poppy seeds along with the water to the spice grinder and grind to a smooth paste.

4. Put the yogurt in a bowl, add the chile powder, cumin, and turmeric, and whisk until well blended.

5. Place a nonstick saucepan over medium heat and add the remaining oil. Add the cardamom, and when it starts to change color, add the onion paste and sauté until light golden brown. Add the ginger paste, garlic paste, and coriander. Stir well. Stir in the poppy seed paste and cook for 1 minute.

6. Add the yogurt mixture and bring to a boil. Add the *colocassia*, nutmeg, *garam masala*, salt, and 1 cup (200 ml) water. Cover with a tight-fitting lid and simmer for 30 minutes. (Alternatively, cover the pan with aluminum foil or seal the lid with *atta* dough (see page 36), so that the aroma is contained in the pan and does not escape.)

7. Stir in the cream and garnish with the cilantro. Serve hot.

Eriseri

······∘⊰ **Keralite yams and green bananas** ⊱∘······························

Eriseri is a popular dish in Kerala and is made with various combinations of vegetables and pulses. It forms an important part of the "Sadya" meal that is served on special occasions such as weddings, birthdays, and the arrival of a new baby.

You can use any vegetables here and adjust the quantity of peppercorns to suit your taste. You can also use some red chiles in addition to the peppercorns.

Serves 4.

1 pound (500 grams) yams, peeled and cut into ½-inch (1-cm) cubes
1 medium unripe banana, peeled and cut into ½-inch (1-cm) cubes
¾ cup (90 grams) grated fresh coconut (or frozen unsweetened coconut)
15 whole black peppercorns
1 teaspoon cumin seeds
¼ teaspoon ground turmeric
2 teaspoons table salt
¼ cup (50 ml) coconut oil
1 teaspoon mustard seeds
10 to 12 fresh curry leaves

1. Wash the yams thoroughly under running water. Drain in a colander. Wash the banana and put in a bowl of water until ready to use.

2. Place a nonstick sauté pan over medium heat. Add ½ cup of the coconut and dry-roast until golden brown. Set aside to cool.

3. Put the roasted coconut, peppercorns, and cumin in a spice grinder with ¼ cup (50 ml) water and grind to a smooth paste.

4. Place a nonstick saucepan over high heat and add 2 cups (400 ml) water. Add the turmeric and salt. When the water comes to a boil, lower the heat to medium, add the yams, cover, and cook for 5 minutes. Add the banana and cook for 5 minutes.

5. Add the coconut paste and stir. Lower the heat to low and simmer for 5 minutes or until the sauce thickens.

6. Meanwhile, place a small nonstick sauté pan over medium heat and add the coconut oil. When small bubbles appear at the bottom of the pan, add the mustard seeds. When the seeds sputter, add the curry leaves and the remaining ¼ cup coconut, and sauté for 2 minutes. Add this tempering to the curry and cover immediately to trap the flavors.

7. Serve hot.

Feijoada

····❖⟨ Goan-style kidney beans ⟩❖···

Feijoada, considered Brazil's national dish, is a thick stew with heavy meats and beans. In Goa, where the cuisine is very much influenced by the Portuguese, the Indian version contains beans and Goan sausage. Personally, though, I find this vegetarian version to be just as tasty. Serve it with steamed rice.

Serves 4.

8 dried red chiles, broken
7 or 8 whole black peppercorns
10 whole cloves
1 tablespoon coriander seeds
1 teaspoon cumin seeds
1 cup (120 grams) grated fresh coconut (or frozen unsweetened coconut)
2 tablespoons vegetable oil
2 large red onions, chopped
2½ cups (560 grams) canned cooked red kidney beans
1 teaspoon table salt
1 tablespoon tamarind pulp

1. Place a small nonstick sauté pan over medium heat. Add the chiles, peppercorns, cloves, coriander, and cumin, and dry-roast for 2 to 3 minutes or until fragrant. Add the coconut and roast for 2 to 3 minutes. Cool slightly and transfer to a mini food processor. Add ¼ cup (50 ml) water and process to a smooth paste.

2. Place a nonstick saucepan over medium heat and add the oil. When small bubbles appear at the bottom of the pan, add the onions and sauté for 3 to 4 minutes or until lightly browned. Add the coconut paste and stir.

3. Add the beans and stir. Add the salt and tamarind pulp, and stir well. Add 1 cup (200 ml) water and bring to a boil. Lower the heat to low and simmer for 10 to 15 minutes.

4. Serve hot.

········⋇⟆ **Chef's Tip** ⟅⋇ If using dried kidney beans, soak 1½ cups (360 grams) beans in 1 quart (800 ml) water overnight. Drain and cook in 6 cups (1200 ml) water for 1 hour or until the beans are soft. Proceed with the recipe.

Gatta Curry

········⋇⟆ **Steamed *besan* dumplings in a yogurt-based spicy curry** ⟅⋇·····························

We had a neighbor in Delhi who was from Rajasthan. She and my mom used to swap recipes and food. This curry entered our home, and the recipe has stayed, courtesy of one of those exchanges. I think my mother still makes the best *gatta curry*; sometimes she fries the dumplings and puts them in a typical Punjabi-style thick onion-tomato *masala* instead of the traditional Rajasthani yogurt curry that we have here. Serve this curry with steamed rice.

Serves 4.

~ **For the *gatta*:**
1½ cups (150 grams) *besan* (chickpea/gram flour)
Pinch of asafetida
¼ teaspoon ground turmeric
1 teaspoon red chile powder
½ teaspoon table salt
Pinch of baking soda
½ teaspoon fresh ginger paste (page 12)
2 tablespoons plain yogurt
7 or 8 fresh mint leaves, chopped
1 quart (800 ml) vegetable oil

~ For the sauce:
1½ cups (375 grams) plain yogurt
1 teaspoon red chile powder
2 teaspoons ground coriander
1 teaspoon ground turmeric
1 tablespoon *besan* (chickpea/gram flour)
1 teaspoon table salt
2 tablespoons ghee (page 37)
1 teaspoon cumin seeds
4 whole cloves
Pinch of asafetida
2 medium red onions, grated
½ teaspoon *garam masala* (spice mix; page 27)

1. Make the *gatta*: Stir together the *besan*, asafetida, turmeric, chile powder, salt, baking soda, ginger paste, yogurt, and mint in a bowl. Add ¼ cup (50 ml) water and stir to make a stiff dough.

2. Divide the dough into 4 portions. Apply ½ teaspoon oil to your palms and roll each portion into a 6-inch-long (15-cm-long) cylinder.

3. Place a nonstick saucepan over high heat, add 2 cups (400 ml) water, and bring to a boil. Lower the dough cylinders into the water, lower the heat to medium, and cook for 10 to 15 minutes. Drain in a large colander set over a large bowl; reserve the water. Let the dumplings cool slightly, then cut into ½-inch-long (1-cm-long) pieces (the *gatta*).

4. Place a nonstick wok over high heat and add 1 quart (800 ml) oil. When small bubbles appear at the bottom of the wok, lower the heat to medium and gently slide in the *gatta*. Fry until golden. Remove with a slotted spoon and drain on paper towels. Set aside.

5. Make the sauce: Whisk the yogurt, chile powder, coriander, turmeric, *besan*, and salt together.

6. Place a nonstick saucepan over medium heat and add the ghee. When small bubbles appear at the bottom of the pan, add the cumin, cloves, and asafetida. Cook until the cumin starts to change color. Add the onions and cook over high heat for 3 to 4 minutes or until the onions are light golden.

7. Lower the heat to low, add the yogurt mixture, and cook for 5 minutes.

8. Add the *gatta* and the reserved cooking water. Cook over low heat for 7 minutes or until the sauce is thick. Add the *garam masala* and adjust the seasoning if necessary.

9. Serve hot.

Jhinge Posto

····················{ Ridged gourd cooked in a poppy-seed *masala* }····················

Bengalis use poppy seeds extensively. The seeds are usually soaked and then ground into a milky paste that helps thicken curries. Traditionally, the seeds are ground in a stone mortar with a pestle, but in the modern kitchen electric grinders are the norm.

Serves 4.

2 tablespoons white poppy seeds
3 green chiles, stemmed and chopped
¾ teaspoon table salt
2 tablespoons vegetable oil
2 whole cloves
2 medium red onions, diced
14 ounces (400 grams) ridged gourd (see Note), cut into 1-inch (2½-cm) cubes
½ teaspoon ground turmeric

1. Soak the poppy seeds in ½ cup (100 ml) water for 30 minutes. Drain and place in a spice grinder with the chiles and ¼ teaspoon of the salt, and grind to a smooth paste without adding any water. Transfer to a small bowl and set aside.

2. Place a nonstick sauté pan over medium heat and add the oil. When small bubbles appear at the bottom of the pan, add the cloves and onions, and sauté for 4 to 5 minutes or until the onions are golden brown.

3. Add the ridged gourd and sauté for 3 to 4 minutes. Add the turmeric and stir. Add the poppy seed paste and remaining ½ teaspoon salt, and stir. Cover and cook for 10 to 15 minutes or until the ridged gourd is tender.

4. Serve hot as a side dish.

····················{ **Note** }····················· Ridged gourd is also known as *loofah*, *luffa*, *tori*, *turiy*, and *turai*. It is believed to have originated in the Arabic deserts. It is dark green and ridged and has a white pulp with white seeds. There is no substitute for ridged gourd in this dish.

Kaalan

This is a vegetarian favorite from Kerala, whose cuisine is known for its yogurt curries and use of tubers. If you want, you can substitute vegetable oil for the coconut oil.

Serves 4.

11 ounces (300 grams) yams, peeled and cut into ½-inch (1-cm) fingers
2 medium green bananas, peeled and cut into ½-inch (1-cm) fingers
9 ounces (250 grams) white pumpkin (see Note), peeled and cut into ½-inch (1-cm) fingers
1 cup (120 grams) grated fresh coconut (or frozen unsweetened coconut)
2 teaspoons cumin seeds
8 to 10 whole black peppercorns
4 green chiles, stemmed
2 teaspoons table salt
½ teaspoon ground turmeric (optional)
1 cup (250 grams) plain yogurt, whisked
2 tablespoons coconut oil
1 teaspoon brown mustard seeds
¼ teaspoon fenugreek seeds
2 dried red chiles, stemmed and broken
10 to 12 fresh curry leaves

1. Wash the yams, bananas, and ash gourd well under running water and drain in a colander.

2. Put the coconut, 1 teaspoon of the cumin, the peppercorns, and green chiles in a mini food processor with ¼ cup (50 ml) water, and process to a smooth paste.

3. Place a nonstick saucepan over medium heat and add 2 cups (400 ml) water. Add the salt and turmeric, and bring to a boil. Add the vegetables and cook for 3 minutes or until half cooked. Add the yogurt and stir well. Bring to a boil, lower the heat to medium, and simmer for 5 minutes. Add the coconut paste, stir well, and cook for 2 minutes. Remove from the heat.

4. Place a small nonstick sauté pan over medium heat and add the coconut oil. When small bubbles appear at the bottom of the pan, add the mustard seeds, fenugreek, and the remaining 1 teaspoon cumin. When the seeds sputter, add the red chiles and curry leaves and add this tempering to the vegetables. Cover immediately to trap the aroma. Serve hot.

····•❧ **Note** ❧• White pumpkin is also known as ash gourd or winter melon. It is grown for its very large fruit. The mature melon has a thick, sweet flesh. In North India it is used to make a dessert called *petha*.

Kaikari Ishtew

······❧{ Mixed vegetables stewed in coconut milk with star anise }❧······

A traditional delight from the South Indian state of Kerala, this vegetable dish is traditionally served with a soft bread called *appam* (page 14). This is a real treat for coconut lovers. Be sure to use the star anise because without it, *ishtew* is simply not *ishtew*.

Serves 4.

1 medium carrot, cubed
1 medium potato, cubed
7 or 8 cauliflower florets
6 to 8 haricots verts, cut into 1-inch (2½-cm) pieces
2 tablespoons coconut oil
2 bay leaves
2 (1-inch/2½-cm) cinnamon sticks
4 whole cloves
2 star anise
10 to 12 fresh curry leaves
4 green chiles, stemmed and slit
2 medium red onions, chopped
1 teaspoon fresh ginger paste (page 12)
1 teaspoon fresh garlic paste (page 12)
2 cups (400 ml) coconut milk
1 teaspoon table salt
Pinch of *garam masala* (spice mix; page 27)

1. Place a nonstick saucepan over high heat and add 2½ cups (500 ml) water. When the water comes to a boil, add the carrot and cook for 3 to 4 minutes. Remove with a slotted spoon and set aside. Repeat with the potato, cauliflower, and haricots verts separately.

2. Place a nonstick saucepan over medium heat and add the coconut oil. When small bubbles appear at the bottom of the pan, add the bay leaves, cinnamon, cloves, star anise, curry leaves, chiles, and onions. Sauté for 2 minutes or until the onions are translucent.

3. Add the ginger paste and garlic paste, and stir. Cook for 1 minute.

4. Add the carrot, potato, cauliflower, and coconut milk. Cook for 2 to 3 minutes. Add the salt and haricots verts, and stir. Lower the heat to low and cook for 4 to 5 minutes or until the haricots verts are tender.

5. Stir in the *garam masala*. Immediately remove from the heat and serve hot.

Karela Andhra Style

····❖⟪ **Sweet, sour, and spicy bitter gourd** ⟫❖···································

Generally, if you see the word *andhra* in the name of a dish, you can expect it to be sweet and sour with the flavor of an oil seed—in this case, sesame. Bitter gourd is widely used in Indian kitchens, and recipes for it vary from state to state. In fact, the bitterness is enjoyed to the hilt in the northern part of the country, where bitter gourds are cooked without the addition of sugar or jaggery.

Serves 4.

5 medium bitter gourds
1 teaspoon table salt
1-inch (2½-cm) piece fresh ginger, peeled
5 cloves garlic
4 dried red chiles, stemmed
1 tablespoon coriander seeds
1 teaspoon cumin seeds
1 teaspoon white sesame seeds
3½ tablespoons vegetable oil
2 medium red onions, chopped
¼ cup (70 grams) fresh tomato purée
2 tablespoons grated cane jaggery
2 tablespoons tamarind pulp

1. Wash and peel, the bitter gourds and cut them in half lengthwise. Remove the seeds and thinly slice. Sprinkle with ½ teaspoon of the salt and set aside for 10 to 15 minutes. Wash with plenty of water, drain, and squeeze out the excess water.

2. Put the ginger and garlic in a spice grinder with 1 tablespoon water and grind to a fine paste.

3. Place a small nonstick sauté pan over medium heat. Let it heat for 2 minutes, then add the chiles, coriander, cumin, and sesame seeds, and dry-roast, stirring continuously, for 2 minutes or until lightly browned. Let cool, then transfer to a spice grinder and grind to a fine powder.

4. Place a medium nonstick sauté pan over medium heat and add 1½ tablespoons of the oil. When small bubbles appear at the bottom of the pan, add the bitter gourds and sauté for 4 to 5 minutes or until lightly browned. Transfer to a bowl and set aside.

5. Add the remaining 2 tablespoons oil to the heated pan. When small bubbles appear at the bottom of the pan, add the onions and sauté for 3 to 4 minutes.

6. Add the ginger-garlic paste and sauté for 1 minute. Add the tomato purée and cook for 3 minutes.

7. Add the ground spices, jaggery, tamarind pulp, and remaining ½ teaspoon salt. Stir well, add ½ cup (100 ml) water, and bring to a boil. Add the bitter gourds and stir well. Lower the heat to low, cover, and simmer for 3 minutes. Serve hot.

Khadkhade

······ ⊱{ Lentil-and-vegetable medley }⊰ ···

This is another wonderful Goan vegetarian specialty. The taste of the radish is an excellent palate cleanser. I suggest that steamed rice accompany this mix of vegetables and *dal*.

Serves 4.

½ cup (100 grams) *toor dal/arhar dal* (split pigeon peas)
1¼ teaspoons table salt
3 tablespoons vegetable oil
½ teaspoon black mustard seeds
½ teaspoon cumin seeds
3 green chiles, stemmed and chopped
½-inch (1-cm) piece fresh ginger, chopped
¾ cup (100 grams) pie pumpkin, peeled and cut into 1-inch (2½-cm) cubes
1 medium potato, peeled and cut into 1-inch (2½-cm) cubes
15 thin green beans, strings removed, finely chopped
1¼ medium white daikon radishes, peeled and finely chopped
½ teaspoon ground turmeric
1½ teaspoons red chile powder
½ cup (60 grams) grated fresh coconut (or frozen unsweetened coconut)
½ teaspoon *garam masala* (spice mix; page 27)
1 tablespoon chopped fresh cilantro
8 to 10 fresh radish leaves, shredded
8 to 10 fresh spinach leaves, shredded

1. Put the *dal* in a large bowl, wash in plenty of water 2 or 3 times, and drain. Add 2 cups (400 ml) water and soak for 30 minutes. Drain in a colander.

2. Place a nonstick saucepan over high heat and add 1 quart (800 ml) water. When the water comes to a boil, add the *dal*. Lower the heat to medium, add ½ teaspoon of the salt, and cook, covered, for 10 to 12 minutes or until tender but still firm. Drain the *dal* in a colander set over a large bowl; set the *dal* and the cooking liquid aside.

3. Place a nonstick saucepan over medium heat and add the oil. When small bubbles appear at the bottom of the pan, add the mustard seeds and cumin. When the seeds sputter, add the chiles and ginger. Sauté for 15 seconds. Add the *dal*, pumpkin, potato, green beans, and radishes, and stir briskly.

4. Add the reserved cooking liquid, the remaining ¾ teaspoon salt, the turmeric, and chile powder, and stir. Add the coconut, stir, and simmer for 10 to 12 minutes or until the vegetables are tender.

5. Add the *garam masala* and stir. Add the cilantro, radish leaves, and spinach leaves. Cook for 1 minute, then remove from the heat.

6. Serve hot.

Khatta Meetha Kaddu

Sour and sweet pumpkin

When my mother included this in her weekly menu, I used to complain and make a big fuss. So she began talking to me about the goodness of pumpkin. Back then there was no talk about beta-carotene in orange-colored vegetables; all she said was, "It's good for you, so eat it up." Well, I am getting a dose of my own medicine now, because my daughters also screw up their noses at pumpkin. But when I started calling this dish *khatta meetha* ("sour and sweet"), they suddenly were more interested in eating it.

Serves 4.

3 tablespoons vegetable oil
½ teaspoon fenugreek seeds
Pinch of asafetida
2 green chiles, stemmed and chopped
1 pound (500 grams) pie pumpkin, peeled and cut into 1-inch (2½-cm) cubes
½ teaspoon table salt
½ teaspoon ground turmeric
1 tablespoon ground coriander
1-inch (2½-cm) piece fresh ginger, julienned
1½ teaspoons red chile powder
2 tablespoons sugar
1½ tablespoons freshly squeezed lemon juice
2 tablespoons chopped fresh cilantro

1. Place a medium nonstick sauté pan over medium heat and add the oil. When small bubbles appear at the bottom of the pan, add the fenugreek, asafetida, chiles, and pumpkin, and stir well.

2. Add the salt, turmeric, coriander, ginger, and chile powder, and stir again. Add 1 cup (200 ml) water, cover, and cook for 10 to 15 minutes.

3. Add the sugar, lemon juice, and cilantro. Cover and cook over medium heat for 10 minutes or until the pumpkin is very soft and mashed.

4. Serve hot.

Kumro Chechki

{ Pumpkin with spices }

Bengalis enjoy a lot of vegetables that cook quickly, such as pumpkin. They prepare it like this, with a few spices, or they combine it with potatoes or mash it and temper it with mustard oil.

Serves 4.

¼ cup (50 ml) vegetable oil
2 large red onions, sliced
½ teaspoon *kalonji* (nigella; see Note page 231)
2 pounds (1 kg) pie pumpkin, peeled, seeded, and cut into 1½-inch (4-cm) sticks
6 green chiles, stemmed and slit
2 teaspoons table salt
1 teaspoon ground turmeric
2 teaspoons ground cumin
½ teaspoon sugar

1. Place a medium nonstick sauté pan over medium heat and add the oil. When small bubbles appear at the bottom of the pan, add the onions and sauté for 4 to 5 minutes or until lightly browned.

2. Add the *kalonji* and sauté for 15 seconds.

3. Add the pumpkin and sauté for 3 to 4 minutes.

4. Add the chiles, salt, turmeric, and cumin and sauté for 1 minute. Add ¼ cup (50 ml) water and stir. Cover and cook for 5 to 6 minutes or until the pumpkin is soft. Add the sugar and stir.

5. Serve hot.

Lauki Kofta

················⋅⋅{ **Bottle gourd and tamarind dumplings in a spicy sauce** }⋅⋅················

I grew up in a very Punjabi atmosphere where *koftas* were cooked at least once a week. This is one of my favorite dishes from childhood. I remember being excited by the surprising tamarind filling inside.

Serves 4.

~ **For the *kofta*:**
1½ small lauki (bottle gourd; see Note)
3½ tablespoons *besan* (chickpea/gram flour)
¼ teaspoon red chile powder
½ teaspoon table salt
8 pieces tamarind with seeds (see Note)
1 quart (800 ml) vegetable oil

~ **For the sauce:**
3 tablespoons vegetable oil
2 medium red onions, chopped
5 medium tomatoes, puréed
¾ teaspoon ground turmeric
¾ teaspoon red chile powder
1½ tablespoons ground coriander
¾ teaspoon table salt
½ teaspoon *garam masala* (spice mix; page 27)
2 tablespoons chopped fresh cilantro

1. Make the *koftas*: Peel the bottle gourd and then grate coarsely. Squeeze to remove the excess water. Put in a large bowl, add the *besan*, chile powder, and salt, and combine well. It will be sticky but manageable. Divide into 8 portions.

2. Stuff one piece of tamarind into each portion and shape into balls.

3. Place a nonstick wok over high heat and add the oil. When small bubbles appear at the bottom of the wok, add the *koftas*, a few at a time, and cook, stirring gently with a slotted spoon, until golden brown and crisp on the outside. Remove with the slotted spoon and drain on paper towels.

4. Make the sauce: Place a large nonstick sauté pan over medium heat and add the oil. When small bubbles appear at the bottom of the pan, add the onions and sauté for 2 to 3 minutes or until light golden brown. Add the tomatoes and cook for 12 minutes or until the oil comes to the top.

5. Add the turmeric, chile powder, and coriander. Cook for 1 minute, stirring continuously. Add 2 tablespoons water and cook for 3 minutes or until the oil comes to the top again.

6. Add 3 cups (600 ml) water and bring to a boil. Add the salt, lower the heat to low, and simmer for 10 minutes. Keep the sauce hot.

7. Arrange the *koftas* on a serving plate and pour the sauce over them. Sprinkle with the *garam masala* and cilantro, and serve hot.

······§ **Notes** §⁜ Smooth-skinned *lauki*, or bottle gourd, has a pale green flesh with a firm texture. Choose young bottle gourds (less than 1 foot, or 30 cm, long); young gourds have a thin, tender peel and smaller seeds that don't need to be removed.

Instead of tamarind pieces, you can stuff the *koftas* with dried plums.

Malai Kofta Curry

······§ Stuffed *paneer* and *khoya* dumplings in a rich white sauce §······

Everyone should occasionally indulge in this creamy curry. My mother stuffed small portions of frozen *malai* (the cream skimmed from the top of whole milk) into the center of each *kofta.* If you want to stuff them, do as my mother did and add a little mashed potato to the mixture.

Serves 4.

~ For the *koftas*:
1½ cups (100 grams) grated *paneer* (pressed fresh cheese; page 17)
⅓ cup (50 grams) grated *khoya/mawa* (solid unsweetened condensed milk; page 37)
1 green chile, stemmed, seeded, and finely chopped
1 tablespoon cornstarch
½ teaspoon table salt
2 tablespoons raisins
1 quart (800 ml) vegetable oil

~ For the sauce:
½ cup (70 grams) cashews, soaked in water for 30 minutes
¼ cup (35 grams) *kakdi magaz* (dried cucumber seeds), soaked in water for 30 minutes
2 tablespoons vegetable oil
4 green cardamom pods
2 green chiles, stemmed and slit
¾ cup boiled onion paste (page 13)
½ tablespoon fresh ginger paste (page 12)
½ tablespoon fresh garlic paste (page 12)
½ cup (125 grams) plain yogurt
2 tablespoons butter
¾ teaspoon ground green cardamom
1 teaspoon table salt
½ teaspoon ground white pepper
¼ cup (50 ml) heavy cream

1. Make the *koftas*: Combine the *paneer*, *khoya*, chile, cornstarch, and salt in a bowl. Divide into 8 portions. Stuff raisins into each portion and shape into balls.

2. Place a nonstick wok over high heat and add 1 quart (800 ml) oil. When small bubbles appear at the bottom of the wok, lower the heat to low and gently slide in the *koftas*. Cook for 4 to 5 minutes or until lightly colored. Remove with a slotted spoon and drain on paper towels. Keep warm.

3. Make the sauce: Drain the cashews and *kakdi magaz*, and transfer to a food processor. Add ¼ cup (50 ml) water and process to a smooth paste.

4. Place a nonstick sauté pan over medium heat and add the 2 tablespoons oil. When small bubbles appear at the bottom of the pan, add the cardamom pods and sauté for 30 seconds. Add the chiles and sauté for 30 seconds.

5. Add the onion paste and sauté for 1 minute. Add the ginger paste, garlic paste, and cashew–*kakdi magaz* paste, and sauté for 2 to 3 minutes. Add the yogurt and stir well. Add 2 cups (400 ml) water and stir well. When the mixture comes to a boil, add the butter and stir well. Add the ground cardamom, salt, and white pepper, and cook for 1 minute.

6. Pour the sauce through a strainer into a clean saucepan. Place over medium heat and bring to a boil. Add the cream, stir, and remove from the heat.

7. Place the *koftas* in a serving dish, pour the hot sauce on top, and serve immediately.

Chef's Tip Cook one *kofta*. If it breaks, add a little more cornstarch to the mixture. Also, make sure the oil is hot when you add the *koftas*.

Note *Kakdi magaz*, or dried cucumber seeds, are thinner and longer than most other melon seeds. They're used mostly to garnish select Indian desserts, sweet chutneys, and some savory snacks. They can be replaced with other melon seeds such as honeydew or cantaloupe.

Masaledar Karele

······⟨ **Bitter gourds stuffed with spicy masala** ⟩·····································

Look for small, tender gourds, as they are easier to handle. I use the gourds' rough peel here because that's where most of the nutrients lie. Some people tie up the stuffed gourds with kitchen string before cooking them, which helps to keep the filling in and maintain the shape of the gourd. (Removing the string at the table is nothing short of entertainment.)

Serves 4.

8 medium bitter gourds
2¾ teaspoons table salt
4 large red onions, peeled
3½ tablespoons fennel seeds
2 teaspoons ground coriander
2 teaspoons ground roasted cumin (page 32)
¾ teaspoon ground turmeric
1½ tablespoons *amchur* (dried mango powder)
¾ tablespoon red chile powder
½ tablespoon *garam masala* (spice mix; page 27)
¾ cup (150 ml) vegetable oil
1 tablespoon sugar
1 green chile, stemmed and slit

1. Peel the bitter gourds and reserve the peelings in a small bowl. Slit the gourds lengthwise, leaving the stem ends intact, and spoon out the seeds. Rub 1 teaspoon of the salt on both the outside and inside of the gourds. Set aside for 30 minutes. Squeeze gently and rinse under running water. (This removes much of the bitterness.) Pat dry.

2. Add ¼ teaspoon salt to the gourd scrapings and set side for 30 minutes. Squeeze well.

3. Finely chop 2 of the onions and slice the remaining 2.

4. Place a small nonstick sauté pan over low heat, add the fennel, and dry-roast for 30 seconds. Let cool, transfer to a spice grinder, and grind to a fine powder. Transfer to a small bowl and add the coriander, cumin, turmeric, *amchur*, chile powder, and *garam masala*, and stir well.

5. Place a medium nonstick sauté pan over medium heat and add 3 tablespoons of the oil. When small bubbles appear at the bottom of the pan, add the chopped onions and sauté for 6 to 8 minutes or until golden. Remove from the heat and add the spice mixture, the remaining 1½ teaspoons salt, and the sugar. Divide into 8 portions.

6. Stuff 1 portion into each of the slit gourds and set aside.

7. Place a nonstick sauté pan over medium heat and add the remaining oil. When small bubbles appear at the bottom of the pan, add the sliced onions, chile, and bitter gourd peelings, and sauté for 3 to 4 minutes.

8. Neatly arrange the stuffed gourds over this mixture. Lower the heat to low, cover, and cook, turning a few times, for 15 to 20 minutes or until the gourds are tender and evenly browned on all sides.

9. Serve hot.

Mirchi Ka Salan

······⊰{ **Sautéed chiles with peanuts and curry leaves** }⊱·······················

In India, chiles are the essence of the cuisine in all of the regions. Some like it hot and some like it mild, but in Hyderabad, where the spicy Andhra cuisine rules the roost, this hot chile preparation is a must with the area's famous Hyderabadi *biryani* (page 481); a *raita* or chutney might be served alongside the *biryani*. My version is mildly spiced.

Serves 4.

18 to 20 plump green chiles (2 inches/5 cm long)
1 quart (800 ml) plus 2 tablespoons vegetable oil
¼ cup (35 grams) sesame seeds
1 tablespoon coriander seeds
1 teaspoon cumin seeds
½ cup (75 grams) roasted peanuts
2 dried red chiles, stemmed and broken
1-inch (2½-cm) piece fresh ginger, chopped
6 to 8 cloves garlic, peeled
½ teaspoon brown mustard seeds
8 to 10 fresh curry leaves
1 medium red onion, grated
1 teaspoon ground turmeric
½ tablespoon tamarind pulp
¾ teaspoon table salt

1. Wash the green chiles under running water and drain well in a colander. Pat dry with a kitchen towel. Slit them in half lengthwise, keeping the stem ends intact, and remove the seeds.

2. Place a nonstick wok over medium heat and add 1 quart (800 ml) of the oil. When small bubbles appear at the bottom of the wok, add the chiles and cook for 2 minutes. Remove with a slotted spoon and drain on paper towels.

3. Place a nonstick sauté pan over medium heat. Add the sesame seeds, coriander, and cumin, and dry-roast for 5 minutes. Set aside to cool completely. Transfer to a mini food processor, add the peanuts, red chiles, ginger, garlic, and ½ cup (100 ml) water, and process to a smooth paste.

4. Place a nonstick sauté pan over medium heat and add the remaining 2 tablespoons oil. When small bubbles appear at the bottom of the pan, add the mustard seeds. When they sputter, add the curry leaves and sauté for 30 seconds. Add the onion and sauté for 4 to 5 minutes or until light golden brown.

5. Add the turmeric and stir well. Add the ground peanut paste and cook for 3 minutes, stirring continuously.

6. Stir in 1 cup (200 ml) water and bring to a boil. Lower the heat and cook for 10 minutes.

7. In a bowl, dissolve the tamarind pulp in ½ cup (100 ml) water, then add it to the pan. Add the fried green chiles and salt, and cook over low heat for 8 to 10 minutes.

8. Transfer to a serving bowl and serve hot.

Moolyachi Bhajee

························{ **Fresh and crunchy radish greens** }···

The greens of the radish are used effectively in most regional cuisines of India, especially in the west. Maharashtrians favor a lot of leafy greens in their cuisine—some of which are alien to most North Indians. Since settling down in Mumbai, I have learned a lot of creative uses for greens, and this dish is an example.

Serves 4.

14 ounces (400 grams) white daikon radish with leaves
¼ cup (25 grams) *besan* (chickpea/gram flour)
1 tablespoon vegetable oil
¼ teaspoon brown mustard seeds
¼ teaspoon asafetida
1½ teaspoons *dhuli urad dal* (split skinless black gram)
4 green chiles, stemmed and chopped
¼ teaspoon ground turmeric
1 teaspoon table salt
½ teaspoon grated cane jaggery
2 tablespoons chopped fresh cilantro

1. Peel and chop the radish. Put in a large bowl. Finely chop the radish leaves and set aside.

2. Place a nonstick sauté pan over low heat, add the *besan*, and dry-roast, stirring continuously, for 3 to 4 minutes or until fragrant. Set aside.

3. Place a nonstick sauté pan over medium heat and add the oil. When small bubbles appear at the bottom of the pan, add the mustard seeds. When they begin to sputter, add the asafetida and *dal*, and sauté for 30 seconds.

4. Add the chiles, turmeric, radish, radish leaves, salt, and jaggery. Stir. Cover and cook, stirring occasionally, for 6 to 7 minutes or until the radish is tender and the excess moisture has evaporated.

5. Sprinkle in the *besan* and stir. Cook over medium heat for 2 minutes, stirring occasionally. Add ½ cup (100 ml) water and stir well. Cook for 5 minutes or until the water has evaporated.

6. Garnish with the cilantro and serve hot.

Mushroom Shagoti

······⁘{ **A vegetarian version of Chicken Xacuti** }⁘······

This dish comes from my Goan repertoire and goes best with the Goan bread called *pav*, but it also goes very well with steamed rice or *sannas* (page 161). The spongy mushrooms absorb the marinade quickly. The spices are preroasted to shorten the cooking time so that the mushrooms don't overcook.

Serves 4.

8 whole cloves
10 whole black peppercorns
¼ teaspoon *ajwain*
½ teaspoon fennel seeds
½ teaspoon cumin seeds
1½ tablespoons coriander seeds
1-inch (2½-cm) cinnamon stick, broken
2 star anise
4 dried red chiles, stemmed and broken
¼ teaspoon freshly grated nutmeg
1 blade mace
1 tablespoon white poppy seeds
1 cup (120 grams) grated fresh coconut (or frozen unsweetened coconut)
4 to 6 cloves garlic, chopped
3 tablespoons vegetable oil
3 large red onions, finely chopped
35 to 40 white mushrooms, quartered
1½ teaspoons table salt
1 tablespoon tamarind pulp

1. Place a nonstick wok over medium heat and add the cloves, peppercorns, *ajwain*, fennel, cumin, coriander, cinnamon, star anise, chiles, nutmeg, mace, and poppy seeds. Cook until fragrant. Add the coconut and dry-roast for 2 to 3 minutes or until the coconut is lightly browned. Let cool completely. Transfer to a mini food processor with the garlic and 1 cup (200 ml) water and process to a smooth paste. Transfer to a small bowl.

2. Place a medium nonstick sauté pan over medium heat and add the oil. When small bubbles appear at the bottom of the pan, add the onions and sauté until well browned. Add the mushrooms and salt, and stir. Add the ground paste and stir well. Add ½ cup (100 ml) water and the tamarind pulp, and simmer for 3 to 4 minutes.

3. Serve hot.

Nadru Yakhni

·······⁂{ Lotus root }⁑···

Lotus root is an exotic vegetable in most parts of India and not readily available outside the state of Kashmir, which has huge bodies of fresh water that contain lotus plants in massive quantities. Kashmiri food, especially the Kashmiri Pandit cuisine, also uses yogurt as a base for many curries. Yogurt not only adds sourness but also gives the curries body.

Serves 4.

1¼ pounds (500 grams) lotus root
2 teaspoons table salt
1 quart (800 ml) vegetable oil
2 medium red onions, sliced
2 cups (500 grams) plain yogurt
1 teaspoon ground fennel seeds
1 teaspoon ground ginger
2 tablespoons ghee (page 37)
½ teaspoon caraway seeds
4 to 6 green cardamom pods
2 black cardamom pods
4 to 6 whole cloves
2 (1-inch/2½-cm) cinnamon sticks
Generous pinch of *kasoori methi* (dried fenugreek leaves), crushed

1. Peel the lotus root, wash it thoroughly under running water, and cut it on the diagonal into ¾-inch (2-cm) rounds.

2. Place a nonstick saucepan over high heat and add 6 cups (1.2 liters) water. When the water comes to a boil, add the lotus root and ½ teaspoon of the salt, and lower the heat to medium. Cover and cook for 50 minutes or until tender.

3. Place a nonstick wok over medium heat and add the oil. When small bubbles appear at the bottom of the pan, add the onions and cook, stirring with a slotted spoon, until brown and crisp. Remove with the slotted spoon and drain on paper towels. Set aside to cool completely.

4. Transfer the onions to a food processor, add 3 tablespoons water, and grind to a smooth paste.

5. Put the yogurt in a small bowl and add ½ cup (100 ml) water. Whisk thoroughly.

6. Place a nonstick sauté pan over medium heat and add the yogurt mixture. Cook, stirring continuously, for 2 to 3 minutes or until the mixture changes color. Remove from the heat.

7. Put the fennel and ginger in a bowl, and stir in 1 cup (200 ml) water. Add the onion paste and whisk until well blended.

8. Place a nonstick saucepan over medium heat and add the ghee. When the ghee melts and small bubbles appear at the bottom of the pan, add the caraway, green and black cardamom, cloves, and cinnamon, and sauté until fragrant.

9. Stir in the onion mixture, then the yogurt mixture and the lotus root. Add the remaining 1½ teaspoons salt and stir. Cook for 5 to 7 minutes or until the sauce thickens.

10. Stir in the *kasoori methi* and serve hot.

Navratan Korma

Navratan means "nine jewels." In this *korma* there are a few vegetables, a few mushrooms, *paneer*, and the rarely used *makhana* (puffed lotus seeds), nine ingredients in all. Artists in the royal courts of the Mughal emperors were called *navratan* and the emperors' gorgeous jewelry was made of nine different gleaming gems.

Serves 4.

¼ cup (40 grams) cashews
1 medium carrot, cut into ½-inch (1-cm) cubes
4 cauliflower florets
3 thin long beans, strings removed, cut into ½-inch (1-cm) pieces
1 medium potato, cut into ½-inch (1-cm) cubes
¼ cup (40 grams) shelled green peas
¾ teaspoon table salt
2 tablespoons vegetable oil
2 whole cloves
2 whole black peppercorns
1-inch (2½-cm) cinnamon stick
2 green cardamom pods
½ cup (125 grams) boiled-onion paste (page 13)
½ tablespoon fresh ginger paste (page 12)
½ tablespoon fresh garlic paste (page 12)
2 tablespoons plain yogurt
2 green chiles, stemmed and chopped
5 white button mushrooms, halved
15 grams *makhana* (puffed lotus seeds; optional; see Note), fried in 1 cup vegetable oil until golden
¼ cup (40 grams) *paneer* cut into ½-inch (1-cm) cubes
¼ cup (50 ml) heavy cream
½ tablespoon raisins

1. Soak half of the cashews in ¼ cup (50 ml) warm water for 10 minutes. Drain, put in a spice grinder, and grind to a smooth paste. Transfer to a bowl. Chop the remaining cashews.

2. Place a nonstick saucepan over medium heat and add 1½ cups (300 ml) water. Bring to a boil and add the carrot, cauliflower, beans, potato, and peas. Add ¼ teaspoon of the salt. Cook over medium heat for 10 minutes or until the vegetables are tender, and drain in a colander. Refresh in cold water and drain again.

3. Place a nonstick sauté pan over medium heat and add the oil. When small bubbles appear at the bottom of the pan, add the cloves, peppercorns, cinnamon, and cardamom, and sauté for 30 seconds or

until fragrant. Add the onion paste and sauté for 5 to 8 minutes or until the raw flavors disappear.

4. Add the ginger paste, garlic paste, and yogurt, and stir well. Lower the heat to low, add the chiles and cashew paste, and cook, stirring, for 5 minutes.

5. Add the mushrooms and blanched vegetables. Cook for 2 to 3 minutes and add the remaining ½ teaspoon salt and ¾ cup (150 ml) water. Stir well and add the *makhana* (if using) and *paneer*. Stir and cook for 30 seconds.

6. Bring to a boil, add the cream, and remove from the heat.

7. Transfer to a serving dish and garnish with the chopped cashews and raisins. Serve hot.

········⦅ **Note** ⦆ *Makhana*, a plant belonging to the water lily family that's cultivated for its white seeds, is available at Indian grocery stores.

Papad Ka Shaak

......•} *Papads* **with yogurt,** *boondi,* **and spices** }•...

When it comes to vegetarian food, Rajasthani cuisine is very ingenious. Rajasthani cooks use chickpea flour with great élan—and pulses and sun-dried vegetables too. The first time I had this *papad* preparation, at a Marwari friend's place, I was a bit taken aback by the film of oil and hot red chiles floating on top. Being a good guest, I ate it up and, believe me, I enjoyed it. In this adaptation, the oil and chile powder have been reduced somewhat.

Serves 4.

2 large *papads* (thin crackers made with lentil flour)
1 cup (250 grams) sour plain yogurt (see page 513)
1 tablespoon *besan* (chickpea/gram flour)
½ cup (40 grams) plain savory *boondi* (page 587)
3 tablespoons vegetable oil
½ teaspoon cumin seeds
Generous pinch of asafetida
3 dried red chiles, stemmed and broken in half
¼ teaspoon ground turmeric
½ teaspoon red chile powder
1 teaspoon ground coriander
1 teaspoon *garam masala* (spice mix; page 27)
¾ teaspoon table salt
2 tablespoons chopped fresh cilantro

1. Hold one *papad* at a time with tongs and roast it over an open gas flame until crisp. Break into medium-size pieces. You can also microwave on high for 1 minute or until the *papad* is cooked.

2. Put the yogurt and *besan* in a large bowl. Add 1 cup (200 ml) water and whisk well. Set aside.

3. Put 2 cups (400 ml) warm water in a large bowl and add the *papad* pieces and *boondi*; soak for 1 to 2 minutes. Drain in a colander and set aside.

4. Place a medium nonstick sauté pan over medium heat and add the oil. When small bubbles appear at the bottom of the pan, add the cumin. When it begins to change color, add the asafetida and chiles, and sauté for 15 seconds.

5. Add the yogurt mixture, turmeric, and chile powder, and stir briskly. Reduce the heat to low, add the coriander and *garam masala*, and cook, stirring continuously. When the mixture comes to a boil, add the *papads* and *boondi*. Boil for 2 minutes, add the salt, and stir gently.

6. Remove from the heat and sprinkle with the cilantro. Serve hot.

Papri Nu Shaak

This is one of the winter vegetable dishes that are famous in Gujarat. My wife, Alyona, who is from Gujarat, introduced this recipe to our table and sometimes uses eggplant instead of sweet potato. If you can't find Indian broad beans, you can use green beans. Traditionally, green garlic would be used in this preparation instead of garlic paste, but it is only available in winter. Serve this dish with *roti* (page 18).

Serves 4.

3 tablespoons vegetable oil
½ teaspoon *ajwain*
2 medium red onions, diced
1 teaspoon fresh garlic paste (page 12)
1 pound (500 grams) Indian broad beans (hyacinth beans), strings removed, cut in half crosswise
2 medium sweet potatoes, peeled and diced
1 large tomato, diced
¾ teaspoon table salt
3 green chiles, stemmed and chopped
¼ teaspoon ground turmeric

1. Place a nonstick wok over medium heat and add the oil. When small bubbles appear at the bottom of the wok, add the *ajwain*. When it begins to change color, add the onions and garlic paste, and sauté over medium heat for 2 minutes.

2. Add the beans and 1 cup (200 ml) water, and bring to a boil. Lower the heat to low, cover, and cook for 2 to 3 minutes.

3. Add the sweet potatoes, tomato, and salt. Cover and cook for 15 minutes or until the sweet potatoes and beans are almost tender and the liquid has reduced.

4. Add the chiles and turmeric, and cook, uncovered, for 5 to 6 minutes or until the excess liquid has evaporated and the oil comes to the top.

5. Serve hot.

Pittla

Pittla is a classic Marathi dish. This is to be eaten with *roti* (page 18). The coconut gives this dish a nice texture and flavor. It's best served right off the stove; once it cools down, the consistency changes.

Serves 4.

1⅓ cups (135 grams) *besan* (chickpea/gram flour)
¼ cup (30 grams) grated fresh coconut (or frozen unsweetened coconut; optional)
1 tablespoon ghee (page 37)
1 teaspoon brown mustard seeds
3 green chiles, stemmed and minced
Pinch of asafetida
½ teaspoon ground coriander
¼ teaspoon ground turmeric
½ teaspoon ground roasted cumin (page 32)
½ teaspoon red chile powder
1¼ teaspoons table salt
2 tablespoons minced fresh cilantro

1. Sift the *besan* into a large bowl. Add 2 cups (400 ml) water and stir to make a smooth batter. Set aside.

2. If using the coconut, place a small nonstick sauté pan over medium heat and add the coconut. Dry-roast, stirring continuously, until light brown and fragrant. Set aside in a small bowl.

3. Place a nonstick saucepan over medium heat and add the ghee. When the ghee melts and small bubbles appear at the bottom of the pan, add the mustard seeds. When they sputter, add the chiles and asafetida, and cook for 1 minute.

4. Add the *besan* batter, coriander, turmeric, cumin, chile powder, salt, and 1 cup (200 ml) water, and stir well.

5. Cook, stirring continuously so that the mixture does not stick or burn, for 7 minutes or until the *besan* is cooked and the mixture is thick enough to coat the back of the spoon. Remove from the heat.

6. Taste and add salt if needed. Garnish with the coconut and cilantro, and serve hot.

Olan

·······⁜{ **Pumpkin curry** }⁜···

It is a misconception that all Indian curries are hot. This flavorful but mild *olan* from Kerala is a perfect example of how gentle a curry can be.

Serves 4.

1⅓ teaspoons table salt
1⅓ cup (240 grams) pie pumpkin, peeled and cubed
1⅓ cup (240 grams) white pumpkin, peeled and cubed
2 tablespoons coconut oil
½ teaspoon brown mustard seeds
3 green chiles, stemmed and slit
10 to 12 fresh curry leaves
1 tablespoon grated cane jaggery
¼ cup grated fresh coconut

1. Place a nonstick saucepan over medium heat and add 1 cup (200 ml) water, the salt, the pie pumpkin, and the white pumpkin. Bring to a boil and cook, stirring frequently, for 10 to 12 minutes or until the pumpkin is soft.

2. Remove from the heat and mash lightly with the back of a ladle.

3. Place a nonstick sauté pan over medium heat and add the coconut oil. When small bubbles appear at the bottom of the pan, add the mustard seeds. When they sputter, add the chiles and curry leaves.

4. Add the mashed pumpkin and stir. Add the jaggery and cook, stirring, until it is dissolved.

5. Sprinkle with the coconut and serve hot.

Puzhanikkai More Kozhambu

····· Ash gourd in a spicy yogurt-and-coconut sauce ·····

Here, ash gourd (also called winter melon) is cooked in sour yogurt, yielding a curry that greatly resembles North Indian *kadhi*. Incidentally, the "z" in *kozhambu* is pronounced like "l." In Tamil homes, where the dish is often made for the festival of Pongal, okra is sometimes added to the curry.

Serves 4.

14 ounces (400 grams) ash gourd (page 586), peeled, seeded, and cut into 2-inch (5-cm) sticks

3½ teaspoons table salt

1 teaspoon *toor dal/arhar dal* (split pigeon peas)

2 teaspoons *chana dal* (split Bengal gram)

2 teaspoons raw rice

6 green chiles, stemmed and chopped

½ teaspoon cumin seeds

1 teaspoon coriander seeds

1½ cups (180 grams) grated fresh coconut (or frozen unsweetened coconut)

30 fresh curry leaves

3 cups (750 grams) sour plain yogurt (see page 513)

¼ cup (15 grams) chopped fresh cilantro

¼ cup (50 ml) vegetable oil

1 teaspoon brown mustard seeds

4 dried red chiles, stemmed and broken in half

½ teaspoon fenugreek seeds

½ teaspoon *ajwain*

1. Place a nonstick saucepan over medium heat and add 1 quart (800 ml) water. When the water comes to a boil, add the ash gourd and 1 teaspoon of the salt, and boil for 5 minutes. Drain in a colander and set aside.

2. Put the *dals* and rice in a bowl, wash in plenty of water 2 or 3 times, and drain. Add 1 cup (200 ml) water and soak for 15 minutes. Drain and put in a food processor with the green chiles, cumin, coriander, coconut, and 15 of the curry leaves. Add ¼ cup (50 ml) water and process to a smooth paste.

3. Put the yogurt in a large bowl and add 1 cup (200 ml) water. Whisk well. Add the remaining 2½ teaspoons salt and the ground paste, and whisk thoroughly.

4. Place a nonstick saucepan over medium heat, add the yogurt mixture, and cook, stirring continuously, until it comes to a boil. Lower the heat to low, add the cilantro and the remaining 15 curry leaves, and simmer for 4 to 5 minutes or until the mixture thickens.

5. Add the ash gourd and stir.

6. Place a small nonstick sauté pan over medium heat and add the oil. When small bubbles appear in the bottom of the pan, add the mustard seeds. When they begin to sputter, add the red chiles, fenugreek, and *ajwain*. When the seeds change color, pour the oil over the yogurt curry and cover immediately with a lid to trap the flavors.

7. Let rest off the heat for 3 to 4 minutes, then stir well and serve.

········⊰{ **Chef's Tip** }⊱ Use slightly sour yogurt (see page 513) for an especially tasty and tangy curry.

Pyaaz Ki Tarkari

·······⊰{ Onions with tamarind }⊱···

Not only does it not take much time to prepare, the taste and texture of this typical Hyderabadi onion dish is so lovely that I had to share it with you. No tears here: These onions will make you smile.

Serves 4.

3½ tablespoons vegetable oil
8 medium red onions, sliced
1 teaspoon fresh ginger paste (page 12)
1 teaspoon fresh garlic paste (page 12)
½ teaspoon table salt
½ teaspoon ground turmeric
1 teaspoon red chile powder
2 tablespoons tamarind pulp

1. Place a nonstick sauté pan over medium heat and add the oil. When small bubbles appear at the bottom of the pan, add the onions and cook until light golden.

2. Add the ginger paste and garlic paste, and sauté for 1 minute or until the raw flavors disappear.

3. Add the salt, turmeric, and chile powder, and sauté for 2 minutes. Sprinkle in ¼ cup (50 ml) water. Lower the heat, cover, and simmer for 4 to 5 minutes.

4. Add the tamarind pulp and cook for 2 to 3 minutes or until the oil comes to the top.

5. Serve hot.

Senai Roast

······ ❧ **Roasted marinated yams** ❧ ·····································

I get many inquiries from vegetarians about meat substitutes, and I often suggest yams, which are dense and especially meaty when roasted like this.

Serves 4.

½ teaspoon ground turmeric
1½ teaspoons table salt
1¾ pounds (800 grams) yams, peeled and cut into 3-inch (7½-cm) fingers
8 dried red chiles, stemmed and broken in half
1 teaspoon cumin seeds
1 tablespoon fennel seeds
5 or 6 whole black peppercorns
10 to 12 fresh curry leaves
1 tablespoon *chana dal* (split Bengal gram)
1 tablespoon raw rice
Small ball seedless tamarind (or ½ teaspoon tamarind pulp)
1 cup (200 grams) *rawa/suji* (semolina flour)
½ cup (100 ml) vegetable oil
2 tablespoons freshly squeezed lemon juice

1. Place a nonstick saucepan over high heat and add 2 cups (400 ml) water, the turmeric, and 1 teaspoon of the salt, and bring to a boil. Lower the heat to medium, add the yams, and cook for 3 to 4 minutes or until half cooked. Drain in a colander and then pat dry with an absorbent kitchen towel.

2. Place a nonstick sauté pan over medium heat. Add the chiles, cumin, fennel, peppercorns, curry leaves, *dal*, rice, and tamarind ball (if using), and dry-roast for 3 to 4 minutes or until fragrant. Set aside to cool.

3. Transfer to a food processor with ¾ cup (150 ml) water (and the tamarind paste, if using instead of the tamarind ball), and process to a smooth paste. Transfer to a large bowl, add the remaining ½ teaspoon salt, and stir well. Add the yams and stir to coat them with the masala paste. Cover the bowl with plastic wrap and put in the refrigerator for about 30 minutes.

4. Spread the semolina on a plate and roll the masala-coated yam pieces in it. Shake off the excess semolina and put the yams on a plate.

5. Place a nonstick sauté pan over medium heat and add the oil. When small bubbles appear at the bottom of the pan, lower the heat to low, gently slide in the yam fingers, in small batches, and cook for 8 to 10 minutes or until crisp and golden brown. Remove with a slotted spoon and drain on paper towels. Sprinkle with the lemon juice and serve hot.

······ ❧ **Chef's Tip** ❧ Try this with potatoes or sweet potatoes. Breadfruit prepared this way is also delicious.

Shukto

······❦{ Mixed vegetables with bitter gourd }❦···

Bengalis enjoy a variety of mixed-vegetable preparations like *shukto* and *chorchori* (page 259) that make good use of small bits of vegetables that might otherwise go to waste. *Shukto* is a treat for those who love bitter gourd and strong mustard. Serve it with steamed rice and *cholar dal* (page 490).

Serves 4.

1¼ teaspoons black mustards seeds

2 tablespoons vegetable oil

1 medium bitter gourd, peeled and cut into ½-inch (1-cm)-thick rounds

1 medium radish, cut into 1-inch (2½-cm) sticks

2 drumstick vegetables (see page 588), peeled and cut into 1½-inch (4-cm) pieces (optional)

1 medium long eggplant, cut into 1-inch (2½-cm) sticks

2 medium potatoes, peeled and cut into 1-inch (2½-cm) sticks

2 medium green unripe bananas, peeled and cut into 1-inch (2½-cm) sticks

½ teaspoon ground turmeric

1 teaspoon fresh ginger paste (page 12)

1 teaspoon table salt

¼ teaspoon sugar

1. Put 1 teaspoon of the mustard seeds in a spice grinder, add 2 teaspoons water, and grind to a smooth paste.

2. Place a medium nonstick sauté pan over medium heat and add the oil. Add the bitter gourd and sauté for 5 to 6 minutes or until golden brown. Remove with a slotted spoon and set aside on a plate.

3. Add the remaining ¼ teaspoon mustard seeds to the hot oil remaining in the pan. When the seeds sputter, add the radish, drumsticks, eggplant, potatoes, and bananas, and sauté for 7 to 8 minutes or until light golden brown.

4. Add the turmeric, ginger paste, and salt, and sauté for 2 minutes. Add the bitter gourd and stir. Add the mustard-seed paste and sauté for 2 minutes.

5. Add 1 cup (200 ml) water and stir well. Add the sugar and stir. Cover and cook for 8 to 10 minutes or until the drumsticks are soft.

6. Serve hot.

Undhiyu

······⁕§ Mixed vegetables with dumplings §⁕·······

One of the most exotic vegetable medleys that Gujarati cuisine has to offer, this dish is made especially in winter when all the various beans are in season. It gets its name from the word *oondhu*, which means "upside down" in Gujarati. Traditionally, the vegetables were cooked in an earthenware pot placed upside down in a fire of fresh herbs and leaves. Feel free to substitute any other similar vegetables for the beans and yams. Serve with fresh *puris* (page 21).

Serves 4.

9 ounces (250 grams) small *surti papdi* (see Note)
½ cup (75 grams) green peas
2 pinches of baking soda
1½ teaspoons table salt
5 small eggplants
4 medium potatoes, halved
1 small purple yam, cut into ¾-inch (2-cm) cubes
1 small orange yam, cut into ¾-inch (2-cm) cubes
1 medium green banana, cut into ¾-inch (2-cm) cubes
1 cup (120 grams) grated fresh coconut (or frozen unsweetened coconut)
1 cup (30 grams) green garlic, with tops, chopped
2 cups (120 grams) chopped fresh cilantro
1 teaspoon ground coriander
¾ teaspoon ginger paste (page 12)
¾ teaspoon green chile paste (page 13)
½ cup (75 grams) shelled green peas
3 tablespoons vegetable oil
1 teaspoon *ajwain*

~ For the *muthiyas*:
1 cup (40 grams) chopped *methi* (fresh fenugreek leaves)
Pinch of baking soda
½ teaspoon table salt
¼ cup (25 grams) *besan* (chickpea/gram flour)
½ cup (75 grams) *atta* (whole-wheat flour)
½ teaspoon ginger paste (page 12)
½ teaspoon green chile paste (page 13)
2 teaspoons ground coriander
¼ teaspoon ground turmeric
1 teaspoon red chile powder
2 teaspoons plus 1 quart (800 ml) vegetable oil
¼ cup (65 grams) plain yogurt

1. String the *surti papdi* and slit them open. Put in a bowl and add the green peas. Sprinkle with a pinch of baking soda and ¼ teaspoon of the salt, and set aside.

2. Slit the eggplants into quarters from the bottom, leaving the stem ends intact, and put them in a bowl. Add the potatoes, yams, banana, 1 teaspoon of the salt, and a pinch of baking soda, and set aside.

3. Make the *muthiyas*: Put the *methi* in a bowl, add the baking soda and ¼ teaspoon of the salt, and rub it in. Set aside for 5 minutes.

4. Add the *besan*, *atta*, ginger paste, green chile paste, coriander, turmeric, chile powder, the remaining ¼ teaspoon salt, and 2 teaspoons of the oil, and combine well. Add the yogurt, and knead to make a stiff dough. Divide into 12 to 16 portions, and shape each into 1-inch-long (2½-cm-long), ½-inch-thick (1-cm-thick) rolls.

5. Place a nonstick wok over high heat and add 1 quart (800 ml) oil. When small bubbles appear at the bottom of the wok, lower the heat to medium, slide in the dough rolls, and cook, stirring with a slotted spoon, until golden and crisp. Remove with the slotted spoon and drain on paper towels. Set the *muthiyas* aside.

6. Combine the coconut, green garlic, cilantro, coriander, ginger paste, green chile paste, and the remaining ¼ teaspoon salt. Transfer half of this mixture to a food processor. Add the green peas and process coarsely. Transfer to a bowl, add the remaining coconut mixture, and combine well.

7. Add half of the coconut mixture to the beans and stir. Add the remaining coconut mixture to the other vegetables and stir.

8. Place a nonstick saucepan over medium heat and add 3 tablespoons oil. When small bubbles appear at the bottom of the pan, add the *ajwain* and sauté for 15 seconds.

9. Add 2 cups (400 ml) water and bring to a boil. Arrange alternating layers of the bean mixture and the other vegetable mixture in the pan. Lower the heat to low, cover, and cook for 35 to 40 minutes or until the vegetables are almost tender. Occasionally stir the vegetables gently.

10. Add the *muthiyas* and cook for 5 minutes. Serve hot.

······⟨ **Note** ⟩⁕ *Surti papdi* are a special type of Indian green beans available frozen at Indian grocery stores. You can use regular green beans as a substitute, though they will alter the taste.

Vegetable Dhansaak

······*{ Parsi vegetable stew }*·····································

The *dals* give this stew body and increase the nutritional content, and the vegetables provide little pockets of interesting flavors. This hearty dish is perfect with brown rice (page 15) for a quiet family dinner.

Serves 4.

¼ cup (50 grams) *toor dal/arhar dal* (split pigeon peas)
2 tablespoons *masoor dal* (split red lentils)
2 tablespoons *dhuli moong dal* (split skinless green gram)
2 tablespoons *chana dal* (split Bengal gram)
4 ounces (125 grams) pie pumpkin, peeled and cut into ½-inch (1-cm) cubes
2 medium eggplants, cut into ½-inch (1-cm) cubes
1 large potato, peeled and cut into ½-inch (1-cm) cubes
¼ medium bunch *methi* (fresh fenugreek leaves), trimmed and chopped
10 to 15 fresh mint leaves, chopped, plus 1 sprig
½ teaspoon ground turmeric
2⅛ teaspoons table salt
1-inch (2½-cm) piece fresh ginger, chopped
5 or 6 cloves garlic, chopped
4 or 5 green chiles, stemmed and chopped
1 teaspoon cumin seeds
2 tablespoons ghee (page 37)
2 tablespoons vegetable oil
2 medium red onions, chopped
1 teaspoon red chile powder
2 tablespoons *dhansaak masala* (spice mix; page 26)
2 medium tomatoes, chopped
2 tablespoons freshly squeezed lemon juice
2 tablespoons chopped fresh cilantro

1. Put the *dals* in a bowl, wash in plenty of water 2 or 3 times, and drain. Add 2 cups (400 ml) water and soak for 1 to 2 hours. Drain in a colander.

2. Place a nonstick saucepan over high heat and add 1 quart (800 ml) water. When it comes to a boil, add the *dals*, pumpkin, eggplant, potato, *methi*, chopped mint, turmeric, and 1 teaspoon of the salt. Lower the heat to low, cover, and cook, stirring occasionally, for 45 minutes or until the *dals* and vegetables are soft. Mash well with an immersion blender. The mixture should be homogenous. Add 2 cups (400 ml) water and stir well.

3. Put the ginger, garlic, chiles, cumin, and ⅛ teaspoon salt in a spice grinder with 2 tablespoons water and grind to a fine paste. Transfer to a small bowl.

4. Place a nonstick saucepan over medium heat and add the ghee and oil. When small bubbles appear at the bottom of the pan, add the onions and sauté over low heat for about 7 minutes or until golden.

5. Add the ground paste, chile powder, and *dhansaak masala* and stir. Add the tomatoes and sauté until they are soft. Add the *dal* mixture and stir well. Add the remaining 1 teaspoon salt and simmer for 5 minutes.

6. Add the lemon juice and cilantro, and stir.

7. Garnish with the mint sprig and serve hot.

Zunka Bhakar

·······⋇⟩ **Chickpea flour porridge** ⟨⋇···

Served with *bhakri* (also known as *bhakar*), an Indian griddle bread (page 453) made from sorghum flour (*jawari*), this combination is a low-glucose meal that provides sustained energy for hardworking Maharashtrian farmers.

Serves 4.

1 cup (100 grams) *besan* (chickpea/gram flour)
⅛ teaspoon asafetida
¼ teaspoon ground turmeric
1 teaspoon red chile powder
½ teaspoon ground roasted cumin (page 32)
1 teaspoon ground coriander
½ teaspoon sugar
1 teaspoon table salt
3 tablespoons vegetable oil
½ teaspoon brown mustard seeds
½ teaspoon cumin seeds
8 fresh curry leaves
1 green chile, stemmed and slit
2 medium red onions, chopped
2 tablespoons chopped fresh cilantro

1. In a large bowl, combine the *besan*, half of the asafetida, the turmeric, chile powder, ground cumin, coriander, sugar, salt, and 1 cup (200 ml) water.

2. Place a nonstick saucepan over medium heat and add 2 tablespoons of the oil. When small bubbles appear at the bottom of the pan, add the mustard seeds. When the seeds sputter, add the cumin seeds, the remaining asafetida, the curry leaves, and chile, and sauté for 30 seconds. Add the onions and sauté for 5 minutes or until golden brown.

3. Add the *besan* mixture and stir well. Drizzle 1 tablespoon of the oil around the sides of the pan. Cover and cook for 8 minutes, stirring occasionally.

4. Sprinkle with the cilantro and serve hot.

·······⋇❳ **Chef's Tip** ❲⋇ Shredded cabbage or chopped green bell peppers can also be added to the *zunka*.

Vatana Nu Leelu Shaak

·······⋇❳ **Freshly shelled green peas** ❲⋇···

In the Gujarati language the name of this dish means "peas in green curry," and it is one of the simplest and smartest ways to capture the sweetness of fresh green peas in a side dish. It's especially good with *roti* (page 18) and *raita*.

Serves 4.

1-inch (2½-cm) piece fresh ginger, roughly chopped
2 green chiles, stemmed and roughly chopped
2 tablespoons vegetable oil
¼ teaspoon asafetida
½ teaspoon brown mustard seeds
1½ cups (225 grams) shelled fresh green peas
2 teaspoons ground coriander
1 teaspoon ground roasted cumin (page 32)
½ teaspoon red chile powder
1 teaspoon table salt
½ teaspoon *garam masala* (spice mix; page 27)

1. Put the ginger and chiles in a spice grinder with 1 tablepoon water, and grind to a fine paste.

2. Place a nonstick sauté pan over medium heat and add the oil. When small bubbles appear at the bottom of the pan, add the asafetida and mustard seeds, and sauté until the seeds begin to sputter. Add the ginger-chile paste and peas, and sauté for 2 minutes, stirring continuously.

3. Add the coriander, cumin, and chile powder, and cook over medium heat for 1 minute, stirring continuously.

4. Stir in 1 cup (200 ml) water and bring to a boil. Lower the heat to low and simmer, stirring occasionally, for 10 minutes or until the peas are tender.

5. Add the salt and *garam masala*, and stir.

6. Transfer to a serving bowl and serve hot as a side dish.

Kadai Paneer

······· ❀⟩ *Paneer* cooked in a wok ⟨❀ ·································

This is the quintessential *paneer* dish found on most Indian restaurant menus. The flavor of coriander is dominant, so make sure that the coriander seeds you use are fragrant and of good quality. Check to ensure that they are not too brown and woody: A little green hue on the seeds means they are young and will have a stronger aroma.

Serves 4.

2 dried red chiles, stemmed

1 tablespoon coriander seeds

1 teaspoon cumin seeds

¼ cup (50 ml) vegetable oil

1 teaspoon fresh garlic paste (page 12)

2 medium red onions, sliced

2 green chiles, stemmed and chopped

1-inch (2½-cm) piece fresh ginger, chopped, plus ¼-inch (½-cm) piece fresh ginger, julienned

6 medium tomatoes, chopped

2 teaspoons table salt

1 pound (500 grams) *paneer* (pressed fresh cheese; page 17), cut into 1-inch (2½-cm) triangles

2 small green bell peppers, seeded and julienned

1 teaspoon *garam masala* (spice mix; page 27)

1 tablespoon *kasoori methi* (dried fenugreek leaves), crushed

2 tablespoons chopped fresh cilantro

1. Place a small nonstick sauté pan over medium heat. Let it heat for 2 minutes, then add the red chiles, coriander, and cumin, and dry-roast for 1 to 2 minutes or until fragrant. Set aside to cool. Transfer to a mortar and pound with a pestle to a coarse powder.

2. Place a medium nonstick sauté pan over medium heat and add the oil. Add the garlic paste and sauté for 10 seconds. Add the onions, green chiles, and chopped ginger, and sauté for 3 to 4 minutes.

3. Add the tomatoes and sauté for 5 minutes or until the oil comes to the top. Add the roasted and pounded spices and the salt, and sauté for 2 to 3 minutes. Add 1½ cups (300 ml) water and stir. When the water comes to a boil, cover and cook for 8 to 20 minutes.

4. Increase the heat to high, add the *paneer* and bell peppers, and sauté for 2 to 3 minutes or until the *paneer* pieces are fully coated with the mixture.

5. Add the *garam masala*, *kasoori methi*, and cilantro, and stir.

6. Transfer to a serving bowl, garnish with the julienned ginger, and serve hot.

Palak Paneer

······•※⟩ **Pressed fresh cheese with spinach** ⟨※··

Palak paneer is one of the most common everyday Punjabi dishes. Spinach is a winter green in India, but thanks to advanced technology, fresh spinach is available almost all year round. However, you can also use frozen spinach in this recipe. I'm of the opinion that *palak paneer* tastes best without too many spices and herbs, hence the simplicity of this version. Serve this dish with *parathas* (page 18).

Serves 4.

3 large bunches fresh spinach, stemmed
1¾ teaspoons table salt
4 green chiles, stemmed and chopped
¼ cup (50 ml) vegetable oil
¾ teaspoon cumin seeds
12 to 14 cloves garlic, chopped
10 ounces (300 grams) *paneer* (pressed fresh cheese; page 17), cut into 1-inch (2½-cm)
   cubes
1½ tablespoons freshly squeezed lemon juice
⅓ cup (60 ml) heavy cream

1. Wash the spinach thoroughly under running water. Drain well in a colander.

2. Place a nonstick saucepan over medium heat, add 10 cups (2 liters) water and 1 teaspoon of the salt, and bring to a boil. Add the spinach and blanch in the salted boiling water for 2 minutes. Refresh under running water. Drain well in a colander.

3. Transfer to a food processor, add the chiles, and process to a fine paste.

4. Place a nonstick sauté pan over medium heat and add the oil. When small bubbles appear at the bottom of the pan, add the cumin. When it begins to change color, add the garlic and sauté for 30 seconds. Add the spinach purée and stir. Add ½ cup (100 ml) water.

5. Bring to a boil, then add the *paneer* and stir gently. Add the remaining salt and the lemon juice, and stir gently. Add the cream and remove from the heat. Taste and add more salt if needed.

6. Serve hot.

······•※⟩ **Chef's Tip** ⟨※ To retain the bright green color of the spinach—not to mention its flavor—do not overcook it.

Paneer Makhni

····· *❋❴ **Paneer** in a silky tomato sauce ❵❋* ·······································

Makhni can mean two things when it comes to food: that the sauce is as smooth as butter, or that there is a lot of butter in the sauce. In this case, it means both. Here, in one of the best-selling dishes in restaurants in India, *paneer* gets the royal treatment: The curry is as smooth as butter, and there is plenty of it in the sauce as well. The sourness of the tomatoes is cleverly tempered by the honey, and the dried fenugreek leaves add a heady aroma. Serve the dish with *naan* (page 20) or *parathas* (page 18).

Serves 4.

2 tablespoons vegetable oil
12 green cardamom pods
½ blade mace
3 cloves garlic, unpeeled, roughly chopped
2½ teaspoons *deghi mirch* (red chile) powder (page 587)
18 large tomatoes, roughly chopped
1¾ teaspoons table salt
1 cup (240 grams) butter
2 teaspoons ground roasted *kasoori methi* (dried fenugreek leaves)
1 tablespoon honey
½ cup (100 ml) heavy cream
12 ounces (350 grams) *paneer* (pressed fresh cheese; page 17), cut into 1-inch (2½-cm) triangles

1. Place a nonstick saucepan over medium heat and add the oil. When small bubbles appear at the bottom of the pan, add the cardamom and mace. Sauté for 1 minute or until fragrant. Add the garlic and sauté for 1 minute.

2. Stir the chile powder into 3 tablespoons water to make a paste. Add this paste to the pan and sauté for 30 seconds.

3. Add the tomatoes and salt, and cook for 15 minutes or until the tomatoes are pulpy. Pour through a strainer into a nonstick saucepan. Transfer the solids to a blender and blend to a smooth paste. Push the solids through the strainer into the strained liquid. Add ¾ cup (150 ml) water and stir well.

4. Place a nonstick griddle over medium heat and place the pan with the sauce over it. Add the butter and simmer, stirring occasionally, for 10 minutes or until the raw flavors of tomato disappear.

5. Add the *kasoori methi* and honey. Stir and cook for 5 minutes. Add the cream and cook for 2 minutes.

6. Add the *paneer* and stir gently.

7. Serve hot.

Paneer Piste Ka Salan

······⊹⟩ *Paneer* and pistachio curry ⟨⊹······

Get ready for a pleasant journey: When you try this dish, your taste buds will travel from the nuttiness of the pistachios to the cleansing effect of the green chutney. When I was researching this recipe, I added *paneer* instead of the typical chicken or meat. I did that because I wanted to increase the choices for vegetarians when it comes to royal cuisine, and I believe that this rich and silky curry is a great addition.

Serves 4.

2 cups (400 ml) vegetable oil

2 large red onions, sliced

1¼ cup (150 grams) shelled pistachios, blanched and peeled (see Note page 40)

½ cup (125 grams) plain yogurt

1 pound (500 grams) *paneer* (pressed fresh cheese; page 17)

¼ cup (50 grams) *pudina aur dhaniya* chutney (mint-and-cilantro chutney; page 22)

1 tablespoon fresh garlic paste (page 12)

½ tablespoon fresh ginger paste (page 12)

¼ cup (50 grams) ghee (page 37)

5 green cardamom pods

5 whole cloves

1-inch (2½-cm) cinnamon stick

2 blades mace

7 or 8 saffron threads, crushed

½ teaspoon *garam masala* (spice mix; page 27)

2 teaspoons table salt

2 or 3 drops *kewra* (screw pine) water (page 588)

1. Place a nonstick wok over medium heat and add the oil. When small bubbles appear at the bottom of the wok, add half of the onions and cook, stirring with a slotted spoon, until browned. Remove with the slotted spoon and drain on paper towels.

2. Reserve 1 tablespoon of the pistachios for garnish. Put the remaining pistachios in a food processor. Add the remaining sliced onions, 2 tablespoons of the browned onions, and the yogurt, and process to a smooth paste.

3. Cut the *paneer* into 1-inch (2½-cm) triangles. Put in a bowl, add the chutney, and stir gently. Cover the bowl with plastic wrap and set aside to marinate for 15 minutes.

4. Put the garlic paste and ginger paste in a small bowl, add 2 tablespoons water, and stir well.

5. Place a nonstick sauté pan over medium heat and add 2 tablespoons of the ghee. When the ghee melts and small bubbles appear at the bottom of the pan, add the cardamom, cloves, cinnamon, and mace, and sauté for 30 seconds or until fragrant. Add the garlic and ginger paste mixture, and sauté for 15 seconds. Add the pistachio paste, stir, and cover. Simmer for 2 to 3 minutes. Add the saffron, *garam masala*, salt, and 1 cup (200 ml) water, and simmer for 4 to 5 minutes.

6. Place another nonstick sauté pan over medium heat and add the *paneer*. Sauté over high heat for 2 minutes, stirring gently so that the *paneer* pieces do not break. Transfer to a serving dish.

7. Add the *kewra* water to the simmering pistachio sauce and stir. Immediately pour the sauce over the *paneer* pieces.

8. Garnish with the reserved pistachios and the remaining browned onions, and serve hot.

Paneer Tamatar Ka Khut

······⁂⟩ *Paneer* cooked with tomatoes ⟨⁂······

Hyderabadi royal cuisine has been strongly influenced by the Andhra style of South India, hence the use of typically Andhran ingredients like tamarind, coconut, and sesame oil here. The roasted *chana dal* acts as a thickening agent. Serve with *parathas* (page 18).

Serves 4.

½ lemon-size ball tamarind
15 medium tomatoes, chopped
2-inch (5-cm) piece fresh ginger, chopped
10 to 12 cloves garlic, crushed
6 to 8 dried red chiles, stemmed and broken in half
1 tablespoon sesame oil
1 teaspoon brown mustard seeds
1 teaspoon cumin seeds
20 fresh curry leaves
3 (1-inch/2½-cm) cinnamon sticks
1 teaspoon ground turmeric
2 teaspoons ground coriander
1 teaspoon ground roasted cumin (page 32)
1½ teaspoons table salt
2 tablespoons ground roasted *chana dal*
½ cup (100 ml) coconut milk
9 ounces (250 grams) *paneer* (pressed fresh cheese; page 17), cut into 1-inch (2½-cm) fingers

1. Put the tamarind in a bowl, add 1 cup (200 ml) warm water, and soak for 30 minutes. Squeeze out the pulp, push through a strainer, and set aside.

2. Place a nonstick saucepan over medium heat and add ½ cup (100 ml) water, the tomatoes, ginger, garlic, and chiles, and bring to a boil. Lower the heat to low, cover, and simmer for 20 to 25 minutes or until the tomatoes are pulpy. Set aside to cool.

3. Push the cooled mixture through a strainer and set aside in a bowl. Transfer the solids to a food processor and process to a smooth paste. Push the paste through a strainer into the same bowl.

4. Place a nonstick saucepan over medium heat and add the sesame oil. When small bubbles appear at the bottom of the pan, add the mustard seeds and cumin seeds, and sauté until the mustard seeds begin to sputter. Add the curry leaves, cinnamon, turmeric, coriander, and ground cumin, and sauté for 1 minute.

5. Add the tomato mixture and bring to a boil. Stir in the tamarind pulp and salt.

6. Add the ground *dal* and stir thoroughly. Lower the heat to low and stir in the coconut milk and *paneer*. Simmer for 2 to 3 minutes.

7. Serve hot.

Shaam Savera

·······•⟩ *Koftas* made of *paneer* coated with spinach in a creamy tomato sauce ⟨•·······

Shaam savera is my best-known signature dish and one of my first creations on national TV. I had not planned to make this on the day of the shoot, but creativity took over and this is what I came up with!

Serves 4.

~ For the *koftas*:
5 medium bunches fresh spinach, trimmed
2 tablespoons plus 1 quart (800 ml) vegetable oil
1 teaspoon cumin seeds
10 to 12 cloves garlic, finely chopped
6 or 7 green chiles, stemmed and minced
1⅛ teaspoons table salt
¼ teaspoon ground turmeric
¼ cup (25 grams) *besan* (chickpea/gram flour)
½ cup (70 grams) grated *paneer* (pressed fresh cheese; page 17)
⅛ teaspoon ground green cardamom
¼ cup (30 grams) cornstarch

~ For the *makhni* sauce:
2 tablespoons vegetable oil
12 green cardamom pods
½ blade mace
20 cloves garlic, roughly chopped
2½ teaspoons *deghi mirch* (red chile) powder (page 587)
18 large tomatoes, roughly chopped
1¾ teaspoons table salt
1 cup (240 grams) butter
2 teaspoons ground roasted *kasoori methi* (dried fenugreek leaves)
1 tablespoon honey
½ cup (100 ml) heavy cream

1. Make the *koftas*: Wash the spinach leaves under running water.

2. Place a nonstick saucepan over medium heat, add 8 cups (1.6 liters) water, and bring to a boil. Add the spinach and blanch for 2 to 3 minutes. Drain in a colander and refresh under cold water. Squeeze out the excess water, let cool, and finely chop. Transfer to a large bowl.

3. Place a nonstick sauté pan over medium heat and add 2 tablespoons of the oil. When small bubbles appear at the bottom of the pan, add the cumin, garlic, and chiles, and sauté for 1 minute. Add 1 teaspoon of the salt and the turmeric, and stir. Add the *besan* and sauté for 1 to 2 minutes. Add the spinach and sauté, stirring continuously, until the mixture is dry and begins to leave the sides of the pan. Set aside to cool. Divide into 8 portions.

4. In a bowl, mash the *paneer* together with the remaining ⅛ teaspoon salt and the cardamom. Divide into 8 portions and shape into balls.

5. Take a spinach portion, flatten it on your palm, and place a *paneer* ball in the center. Gather the edges and shape into a ball. Repeat with the remaining spinach and paneer portions.

6. Spread the cornstarch on a plate and roll the stuffed spinach balls in it. Shake off the excess.

7. Place a nonstick wok over high heat and add 1 quart (800 ml) oil. When small bubbles appear at the bottom of the wok, lower the heat to low and gently slide in the stuffed spinach balls. Cook for 2 to 3 minutes or until golden brown. Remove with a slotted spoon and drain on paper towels. Set aside.

8. Make the *makhni* sauce: Place a nonstick saucepan over medium heat and add the oil. When small bubbles appear at the bottom of the pan, add the cardamom and mace. Sauté for 1 minute or until fragrant. Add the garlic and sauté for 1 minute.

9. Stir the chile powder into 3 tablespoons water to make a paste. Add this paste to the pan and sauté for 30 seconds.

10. Add the tomatoes and salt, and cook for 15 minutes or until the tomatoes are pulpy. Pour through a strainer into a nonstick saucepan. Transfer the solids to a food processor and process to a smooth paste. Push the paste through the strainer into the strained liquid. Add ¾ cup (150 ml) water and stir well.

11. Place a nonstick griddle over medium heat and place the pan with the sauce over it. Add the butter and simmer, stirring occasionally, for 10 minutes or until the raw flavors of tomato disappear.

12. Add the *kasoori methi* and honey. Stir and cook for 5 minutes. Add the cream and cook for 2 minutes.

13. Pour the sauce into a serving bowl, halve the *koftas*, place them in the sauce, and serve immediately.

·······⊰ **Chef's Tip** ⊱ Before cooking the *koftas*, cook one and check to see if it holds its shape. If it breaks, add some more sautéed *besan* to the spinach mixture to bind it.

Shahi Paneer

·······⊰ **A rich *paneer* curry** ⊱···

The food of the Mughals, who ruled ancient India for centuries, gets its flavors from the use of whole spices, well-cooked onion and tomato pastes, aromatic spices such as saffron, *garam masala*, and a heavy dose of luscious cream. The end product? An aromatic, smooth curry. This is my favorite *paneer* dish.

Serves 4.

6 medium tomatoes, roughly chopped
14 ounces (400 grams) *paneer* (pressed fresh cheese; page 17)
2 large red onions, quartered
2 tablespoons vegetable oil
3 whole cloves
2 (1-inch/2½-cm) cinnamon sticks
1 bay leaf
2 green chiles, stemmed and slit
1 teaspoon fresh ginger paste (page 12)
1 teaspoon fresh garlic paste (page 12)
1 teaspoon red chile powder
2 teaspoons ground coriander
½ teaspoon ground turmeric
½ teaspoon ground black pepper
¼ cup cashew paste (page 12)
1 cup (100 ml) heavy cream
Pinch of saffron threads
½ teaspoon *garam masala* (spice mix; page 27)
1 teaspoon table salt
¼ teaspoon ground green cardamom

1. Put the tomatoes in a blender and blend to a smooth purée. You should have about 2 cups of purée.

2. Cut the *paneer* into ½-inch-by-1-inch (1-cm-by-2½-cm) pieces.

3. Place a small nonstick saucepan over medium heat and add ½ cup (100 ml) water. Add the onions and boil for 5 to 7 minutes. Drain and let cool. Transfer to a food processor and grind to a fine paste. Set aside.

4. Place a nonstick sauté pan over medium heat and add the oil. When small bubbles appear at the bottom of the pan, add the cloves, cinnamon, and bay leaf, and sauté for 30 seconds or until fragrant.

5. Add the chiles and onion paste, and lower the heat to low. Sauté for 3 to 4 minutes but do not let the mixture brown. Add the ginger paste and garlic paste, and sauté for 30 seconds.

6. Add the tomato purée and sauté for 5 to 7 minutes or until the oil comes to the top. Add the chile powder, coriander, turmeric, and black pepper, and sauté for 1 minute.

7. Add the cashew paste and sauté for 2 minutes. Stir in the cream, saffron, *garam masala*, salt, and 1 cup (200 ml) water. Stir well and bring to a boil. Simmer for 3 minutes.

8. Add the *paneer* and stir gently until heated through.

9. Sprinkle with the cardamom and serve hot.

Vegetable and Paneer Jhalfrazie

·······⊰⊱ Spicy vegetables and *paneer* ⊰⊱·······

Quite popular in restaurants, this is one dish that will brighten up any party. The word *jhalfrazie* is a combination of *jhal*, meaning "spicy" or "pungent," and *frazie*, meaning "fried." This is an improvement on the Anglo-Indian *jhalfrazie* that was served in colonial times by servants who julienned the leftover roast from the previous night's dinner and stir-fried the meat with slices of bell peppers and chiles.

Serves 4.

1 large carrot, cut into 1-inch (2½-cm) sticks
10 thin long beans, strings removed, cut into 2-inch (5-cm) pieces
2 medium red onions, cut into thick slices
3 tablespoons vegetable oil
1 teaspoon cumin seeds
2 dried red chiles, stemmed and broken in half
1 medium red bell pepper, seeded and cut into 2-inch (5-cm) strips
1 medium yellow bell pepper, seeded and cut into 2-inch (5-cm) strips
1 medium green bell pepper, seeded and cut into 2-inch (5-cm) strips
½ teaspoon ground turmeric
1½ teaspoons red chile powder
1 teaspoon *garam masala* (spice mix; page 27)
1 teaspoon table salt
2 medium tomatoes, chopped
14 ounces (400 grams) *paneer* (pressed fresh cheese; page 17), cut into 2-inch (5-cm) sticks
2-inch piece fresh ginger, julienned
2 tablespoons chopped fresh cilantro
1½ tablespoons white vinegar
1 teaspoon sugar

1. Place a medium nonstick pan over medium heat and add 2 cups (400 ml) water. Bring to a boil and add the carrot and beans. Cook for 5 minutes, then drain in a colander. Refresh under running water and drain well.

2. Separate the onion slices into rings. Set aside.

3. Place a medium nonstick wok over medium heat and add the oil. When small bubbles appear at the bottom of the wok, add the cumin. When it begins to change color, add the chiles and onions, and sauté for 30 seconds.

4. Add the carrot, beans, and bell peppers, and sauté for 1 minute. Add the turmeric, chile powder, *garam masala*, and salt, and stir. Add the tomatoes and cook for 7 minutes or until they are pulpy.

5. Add the *paneer* and stir gently. Add the ginger and cilantro, and stir. Add the vinegar and sugar, and stir. Serve hot.

Main Courses: Fish, Shellfish, Lamb, and Chicken

The waters of the Arabian Sea, the Indian Ocean, and the Bay of Bengal lap at the coastline of India. The country also has a large network of waterways that teem with fish and shellfish that are quick and easy to cook. My favorite seafood dishes here are *karimeen pollichattu* (page 324) and the famous Goan shrimp *balchao* (page 342).

Indian cooks have perfected the art of tenderizing meat with marinades and slow cooking. Lamb and goat have been essential ingredients in the cooking of most regions in the country since the early days of Mughal rule. While royalty in Hyderabad feasted on *burrah masaledaar* (page 356), the average family slowly cooked *dal gosht* (page 358) and then stretched it with lentils. You can make the elaborate *lagan ka kheema* (page 381) as it would be served at a Parsi wedding or the simple *tariwala* meat (page 401) as it is made in the roadside eateries along the highways of Punjab.

Chicken is an incredibly versatile ingredient, and some of the most deliciously spiced Indian dishes use it. Chicken curries have become the mainstays of menus at Indian restaurants all over the world—from the robust *murgh zafrani do pyaza* of the Mughals to the spicy *kozhi thengai kozhambu* from the south. There are recipes for every taste, occasion, season, and budget in this chapter.

Bangda Udad Methi

Fried and ground rice adds a thickness and texture to this aromatic and fiery mackerel curry. If you cannot find fresh grated coconut, look in your Indian grocer's freezer aisle. Frozen grated coconut can be used instead; be sure to purchase the unsweetened variety. Serve with steamed rice.

Serves 4.

4 (3 ½-ounce/100-gram) mackerels, scaled and cleaned
2 teaspoons table salt
3 tablespoons oil
2 tablespoons raw rice
2 tablespoons *dhuli urad dal* (split skinless black gram)
½ teaspoon fenugreek seeds
5 whole black peppercorns
4 onions, sliced
1 cup (120 grams) grated fresh coconut
4 teaspoons tamarind pulp
8 dried whole red chiles, stemmed
2 teaspoons ground turmeric

1. Cut each fish horizontally into 4 pieces. Sprinkle the pieces with 1 teaspoon of the salt and put in the refrigerator for 15 minutes. Wash under running water and put in a colander to drain.

2. Place a medium nonstick sauté pan over medium heat and add 1 teaspoon of the oil. When small bubbles begin to appear at the bottom of the pan, add the rice and sauté until dark brown. Remove with a strainer and set aside on a paper towel to cool. To the oil remaining in the pan, add the *dal* and sauté until lightly browned. Drain and set aside with the rice to cool to room temperature.

3. Add the fenugreek and peppercorns to the oil remaining in the pan and sauté until fragrant. Drain and set aside.

4. Transfer the sautéed rice and *dal* to a spice grinder and grind to a coarse powder; set aside.

5. In a spice grinder, grind the sautéed fenugreek and peppercorns with 1 tablespoon water to a fine paste; set aside.

6. Return the pan to medium heat and add 2 teaspoons of the oil. When small bubbles begin to appear at the bottom of the pan, add ½ cup (100 grams) of the sliced onions and sauté until golden brown. Add the coconut and sauté until browned. Set aside to cool.

7. In a spice grinder, grind the cooled sautéed coconut and onions along with the tamarind, chiles, and turmeric to a coarse paste and set aside.

8. Place a medium nonstick saucepan over high heat and add the remaining 2 tablespoons oil. Add the remaining sliced onions, lower the heat to medium, and sauté until the onions are soft. Add the ground coconut paste, 5 cups (1 liter) lukewarm water, and the remaining 1 teaspoon salt, and stir. Add the fenugreek-peppercorn paste, stir, and bring to a boil.

9. Add the mackerels and the ground rice powder to the curry. Stir and lower the heat to low. Cook for 3 minutes or until the fish is cooked through (it should be flaky). Serve hot.

Bhapa Ilish

······ § Steamed fish § ···

Hilsa fish steamed with a tangy paste of mustard and green chiles is a Bengali specialty. Since *hilsa* is hard to find in the United States, you can use shad instead. Serve with steamed rice.

Serves 4.

2¼ pounds (1 kg) *hilsa* or shad, scaled and cleaned
1 teaspoon table salt
1 teaspoon ground turmeric
1 teaspoon yellow mustard seeds
1 teaspoon black mustard seeds
2 or 3 green chiles, stemmed
1-inch (2½-cm) piece fresh ginger
1 tablespoon refined mustard oil (see Note page 87)

1. Wash the fish well under running water. Cut horizontally into 1-inch-thick (2½-cm-thick) slices. Put in a bowl and sprinkle with ½ teaspoon of the salt and ½ teaspoon of the turmeric. Set aside for 5 minutes.

2. Combine the remaining ½ teaspoon turmeric, the yellow mustard seeds, black mustard seeds, chiles, ginger, and 2 tablespoons water in a spice grinder. Grind to a smooth paste. Add the remaining ½ teaspoon salt and grind again. Transfer to a bowl. Add the paste to the fish pieces, turning them to coat evenly, and put in the refrigerator for 30 minutes to marinate.

3. Put water in the bottom of a steamer over high heat. Place the fish in the top of the steamer, drizzle with the mustard oil, and cover. Steam for 8 to 10 minutes. Remove the steamer from the heat and let the fish stand, covered, for 3 minutes. Uncover, arrange the fish on a serving platter, and serve hot.

Chapa Pulusu

Fish curries in the South of India usually feature coconut or coconut milk, but this recipe uses the souring agents tomato and tamarind. While only tamarind is typically used with seafood in Andhra Pradesh, I added the tomato to give this dish a little bit of sweetness to take the edge off the sourness. Ideally, this fish should be cooked in an earthenware pot.

Serves 4.

14 ounces (400 grams) pomfret, cut into 8 fillets
1 teaspoon ground turmeric
3½ teaspoons fresh ginger paste (page 12)
3½ teaspoons fresh garlic paste (page 12)
1 tablespoon freshly squeezed lemon juice
1½ teaspoons table salt
2 tablespoons vegetable oil
½ teaspoon cumin seeds
½ teaspoon brown mustard seeds
¼ teaspoon fenugreek seeds
10 fresh curry leaves
2 dried red chiles, stemmed and broken in half
1 large red onion, chopped
2 medium tomatoes, chopped
1½ teaspoons red chile powder
¼ teaspoon ground roasted cumin (page 32)
½ teaspoon ground coriander
¼ cup (70 grams) tomato purée
1 tablespoon tamarind pulp

1. Wash the fish slices under running water and drain them well in a colander.

2. In a large bowl, combine 2 cups (400 ml) water, the turmeric, 2 teaspoons of the ginger paste, 2 teaspoons of the garlic paste, the lemon juice, and ½ teaspoon of the salt. Add the fish and set aside for 20 minutes.

3. Place a nonstick sauté pan over medium heat and add the oil. When small bubbles appear at the bottom of the pan, add the cumin seeds, mustard seeds, fenugreek, curry leaves, and chiles, and sauté for 30 seconds or until fragrant.

4. Add the onion and sauté for 4 minutes or until the onion is translucent. Add the remaining 1½ teaspoons ginger paste and garlic paste, and sauté for 1 minute.

5. Add the chopped tomatoes and sauté for 2 minutes. Add the remaining 1 teaspoon salt and stir. Add the chile powder, ground cumin, and coriander, and stir well. Add 3 cups (600 ml) water and cook for 3 minutes or until the tomatoes are pulpy. Add the tomato purée and bring to a boil. Simmer for 10 minutes.

6. Add the tamarind pulp and stir well. When it comes to a boil, cook, stirring occasionally, for 7 minutes or until the oil comes to the top.

7. Drain the fish and gently slide the slices into the sauce. Lower the heat to low, cover, and cook for 10 minutes or until the fish is cooked through.

8. Serve hot.

Chimborya Cha Kalwan

·······⊰❖ **Spicy crab with coconut masala** ❖⊱·································

The cuisine of Maharashtra is as diverse as the people and their culture. The dishes in this state range from purely vegetarian to an amazing array of highly spiced meat and seafood curries. This dish epitomizes the diversity of that cuisine. Serve the crabs with steamed rice.

Serves 4.

4 (9-ounce/250 gram) blue crabs
4 large red onions
8 tablespoons vegetable oil
5 cloves garlic, roughly chopped
2 (½-inch/1-cm) cinnamon sticks
4 whole cloves
2 green cardamom pods
12 whole black peppercorns
3 tablespoons coriander seeds
2 teaspoons fennel seeds
1 teaspoon white poppy seeds
1⅓ cups (110 grams) grated dried coconut
2 tablespoons table salt
1 tablespoon ground turmeric
2½ tablespoons red chile powder
1 star anise
4 fresh *kokum* petals (see Note page 588)

1. Separate the claws and cut each crab into 4 pieces. Wash and remove the gills and stomach sac from the underside. Crack the claws lightly, wash thoroughly under running water, and drain well in a colander.

2. Slice 3 of the onions and chop the remaining onion.

3. Place a nonstick sauté pan over medium heat and add 1 tablespoon of the oil. When small bubbles appear at the bottom of the pan, add the sliced onions and garlic, and sauté for 12 minutes or until well browned. Remove with a slotted spoon and set aside in a bowl.

4. To the same heated pan, add another 1 tablespoon of the oil. When small bubbles appear at the bottom of the pan, add 1 cinnamon stick, 3 cloves, the cardamom, and 8 peppercorns, and sauté for 30 seconds. Remove with a slotted spoon and add to the bowl with the onion mixture.

5. To the oil in the heated pan, add the coriander and fennel, and sauté for 1 minute. Remove with a slotted spoon and add to the bowl.

6. To the oil in the heated pan, add the poppy seeds and sauté for 30 seconds. Remove with a spoon and add to the bowl.

7. Finally, to the oil in the heated pan, add the coconut and sauté for 6 minutes or until well browned and fragrant. Add to the bowl. Let the mixture cool completely.

8. Transfer the sautéed ingredients to a food processor, add ½ cup (100 ml) water, and process to a fine paste.

9. Place the crabs in a large bowl. Add the salt, turmeric, and chile powder, and toss to coat. Set aside for 5 minutes.

10. Heat the remaining 6 tablespoons oil in a nonstick saucepan. When small bubbles appear at the bottom of the pan, add the remaining cloves, remaining peppercorns, remaining cinnamon, and the star anise, and sauté for 30 seconds. Add the chopped onion and sauté for 5 minutes or until well browned.

11. Add the crabs and sauté for 8 minutes or until the shells turn orange. Add 5 cups (1 liter) water. Increase the heat to high and bring to a boil. Add the coconut mixture and *kokum* petals and stir well. Lower the heat to medium and cook for 45 minutes.

12. Serve hot.

Chingri Macher Kofta Curry

······❋⟩ Delicious deep-fried shrimp *koftas* cooked in a coconut-onion gravy ⟨❋······

Shrimp is my favorite seafood. These succulent dumplings dunked in coconut sauce are a dream come true. Just try it once and you will understand why I think this dish is so tasty! Serve with steamed rice.

Serves 4.

30 to 40 small shrimp
3 large red onions
1 teaspoon table salt
4 green chiles, stemmed and chopped
2 tablespoons chopped fresh cilantro
1 egg, beaten
¼ cup (30 grams) breadcrumbs
1 quart (800 ml) plus 2 teaspoons vegetable oil
5 cloves
1-inch (2½-cm) cinnamon stick
6 green cardamom pods
1½ teaspoons ground turmeric
2-inch (5-cm) piece ginger
2 bay leaves
1 cup (200 ml) coconut milk

1. For the *koftas*: Peel, devein, and wash the shrimp thoroughly under running water. Finely chop 1 onion.

2. Place a nonstick heavy-bottomed saucepan over high heat, add 1½ cups (300 ml) water, and bring to a boil. Add the shrimp and cook for 2 minutes.

3. When the shrimp are fully cooked, drain in a colander and allow them to cool. Mince the boiled shrimp in a food processor, transfer the shrimp to a bowl, and add ½ teaspoon of the salt, the chopped onion, green chiles, and cilantro, and stir well. Divide this mixture into 12 portions and shape into balls.

4. Dip the balls in the beaten egg and roll in the breadcrumbs.

5. Place a medium nonstick wok over medium heat and add 1 quart (800 ml) of the oil. When small bubbles appear at the bottom of the wok, gently slide the *koftas* in and deep-fry for 2 to 3 minutes or until they are light golden. Remove with a slotted spoon, drain on paper towels, and set aside.

6. For the sauce: Roughly chop the remaining 2 onions and place them in a food processor. Add the cloves, cinnamon, cardamom pods, turmeric, and ginger, and process into a fine paste.

7. Place a nonstick saucepan over medium heat and add the 2 teaspoons oil. When small bubbles appear at the bottom of the pan, add the bay leaves and the spice mixture, and sauté for 4 to 5 minutes, stirring continuously. Add 1 cup (200 ml) water to prevent scorching.

8. Gradually add the coconut milk, stirring continuously. Add the remaining ½ teaspoon salt.

9. Add the *koftas* and lower the heat to low. Simmer for 10 minutes or until the sauce thickens a little.

10. Transfer to a serving bowl and serve hot.

Chingri Malai Curry

······· { Shrimp in a rich coconut-milk gravy } ·······································

India has an extensive coastline. There's a variety of fish available, but the best shrimp, in my opinion, are from the Bay of Bengal. This dish is typically prepared with shrimp with their heads on (the heads are considered a delicacy). You can, of course, remove the heads if you like. Serve with steamed rice.

Serves 4.

15 medium shrimp
1 teaspoon ground turmeric
1 teaspoon table salt
¼ cup (50 ml) filtered mustard oil (see Note page 87)
1 teaspoon sugar
1 teaspoon cumin seeds
1 teaspoon mustard seeds
2 tablespoons fresh ginger paste (page 12)
½ teaspoon red chile powder
1 tablespoon cumin paste (see Note)
5 or 6 green chiles, stemmed and slit
1 cup (200 ml) coconut milk
1 teaspoon *garam masala* (spice mix; page 27)

1. Peel and devein the shrimp and wash them thoroughly under running water. Drain well in a colander. Transfer to a bowl, add ½ teaspoon of the turmeric and ½ teaspoon of the salt, and stir well. Set aside to marinate for 15 minutes.

2. Place a medium nonstick sauté pan over high heat and add 2 tablespoons of the mustard oil. When small bubbles appear at the bottom of the pan, add the shrimp and sauté for 2 to 3 minutes. Transfer to a plate and set aside.

3. Put the remaining 2 tablespoons mustard oil in the same heated pan and place over medium heat. When small bubbles appear at the bottom of the pan, lower the heat to low, and add the sugar, cumin seeds, and mustard seeds. When the seeds begin to sputter, add the ginger paste, chile powder, cumin paste, and the remaining ½ teaspoon turmeric. Cook, stirring, for 5 to 6 minutes.

4. Add the shrimp and green chiles and cook, stirring, for 1 minute. Add the coconut milk and the remaining ½ teaspoon salt and simmer over low heat for 6 to 8 minutes. Do not let it boil.

5. Sprinkle with the *garam masala* and stir.

6. Transfer the curry to a serving bowl and serve hot.

······⋅⋅⊰ **Note** ⊱⋅ To make cumin paste, soak 1 tablespoon cumin seeds in 2 tablespoons water overnight. Grind in a spice grinder to a smooth paste.

Doi Mach

······⋅⊰ **Fish in a yogurt curry** ⊱⋅·······································

In this specialty from Bengal, *rohu* fish (a type of carp) is simmered in a spiced-yogurt curry. If you want to give it an even greater Bengali flavor, you can cook the dish in mustard oil instead of ghee. In order to do that, first heat the mustard oil to the smoking point. Remove from the heat and let cool. Then heat it again and proceed with step 2. Serve with steamed rice.

Serves 4.

1 (1⅓-pound/600-gram) *rohu* fish (or any freshwater fish), scaled and cleaned
1 cup (250 grams) plain yogurt
2 teaspoons table salt
2 tablespoons ghee (page 37)
2 bay leaves
4 to 6 whole cloves
3 or 4 green cardamom pods
2 onions, grated
3 green chiles, stemmed and slit
½ teaspoon red chile powder
¼ teaspoon ground turmeric

1. Cut the fish into 1-inch-thick (2½-cm-thick) slices. Whisk the yogurt and salt until smooth, then add to the fish, toss to coat, and put in the refrigerator for 20 minutes to marinate.

2. Place a medium nonstick saucepan over medium heat and add the ghee. When small bubbles appear at the bottom of the pan, add the bay leaves, cloves, and cardamom. Sauté for 15 seconds. Add the onions, chiles, chile powder, and turmeric, and sauté for 5 to 7 minutes.

3. Add the fish along with the yogurt and stir well. Bring to a boil, then lower the heat to low. Cover and cook for 7 to 8 minutes, until the fish is cooked through.

4. Transfer to a shallow serving dish and serve.

Fish in Coconut Gravy

·······⊰ Fish in a rich and creamy coconut-milk sauce ⊱·································

This simple fish curry is prepared with ingredients that are almost always found in Indian kitchens and is excellent served with steamed rice. I like the no-fuss method of preparation.

Serves 4.

1 teaspoon table salt
½ teaspoon fresh ginger paste (page 12)
½ teaspoon fresh garlic paste (page 12)
1 tablespoon tamarind pulp
½ teaspoon ground turmeric
1 pound (500 grams) pomfret, cleaned and cut crosswise into ½-inch-thick (1-cm-thick) pieces (see Note)
2 tablespoons vegetable oil
2 green chiles, stemmed and slit
1 medium red onion, diced
1 small tomato, diced
1½ teaspoons red chile powder
2 cups (400 ml) thick coconut milk
¼ teaspoon ground roasted cumin (page 32)
2 tablespoons chopped fresh cilantro

1. In a large bowl, stir together the salt, ginger paste, garlic paste, tamarind pulp, and turmeric. Add the fish and toss to coat. Set aside to marinate for 20 minutes.

2. Place a nonstick sauté pan over medium heat and add the oil. When small bubbles appear at the bottom of the pan, add the chiles and onion, and sauté for 7 to 8 minutes or until the onion is translucent.

3. Add the tomato and chile powder, and cook for 2 minutes or until the tomato is soft. Add 1 cup (200 ml) water and stir. Bring to a boil.

4. Add the fish and cook for 5 minutes or until the fish is cooked through.

5. Add the coconut milk and cumin, and bring to a boil. Remove from the heat and transfer to a serving bowl.

6. Garnish with the cilantro and serve hot.

·······⊰ **Note** ⊱· You can substitute pompano or butterfish for the pomfret.

Fish Moilee

This flavorful coconut-based curry is from Kerala, a magnificent state in South India with a rich culinary repertoire. The dish is very simple to prepare and can be served with steamed white rice. If you can't find pomfret or *rohu*, you can also use Florida pompano or any freshwater fish—or even prawns. Serve with steamed rice.

Serves 4.

2 (14-ounce/400-gram) whole pomfret or *rohu* fish (see Note)
1 teaspoon table salt
2 teaspoons freshly squeezed lemon juice
1 tablespoon vegetable oil
1 teaspoon brown mustard seeds
8 to 10 fresh curry leaves
2 onions, chopped
2 teaspoons fresh ginger paste (page 12)
2 teaspoons fresh garlic paste (page 12)
3 green chiles, stemmed and slit
1 teaspoon ground turmeric
1½ cups (300 ml) coconut milk

1. Trim the fins of the pomfret and clean the fish well. Cut each fish crosswise into 4 pieces. Wash under running water and drain in a colander. Sprinkle with ½ teaspoon of the salt and the lemon juice and set aside for 15 minutes.

2. Place a medium nonstick sauté pan over medium heat and add the oil. When small bubbles appear at the bottom of the pan, add the mustard seeds. When they sputter, add the curry leaves and sauté for 2 seconds. Add the onions, and cook until soft and translucent.

3. Add the ginger paste, garlic paste, chiles, turmeric, and fish. Stir well and cook over high heat for 30 seconds.

4. Add the coconut milk and the remaining ½ teaspoon salt. Lower the heat to low, cover, and cook for about 10 minutes or until the fish is just cooked through.

5. Transfer the curry to a shallow serving dish and serve hot.

·······⟨ **Note** ⟩⟨⟩ If using *rohu*, cut into 1-inch-thick (2½-cm-thick) slices.

Goan Shrimp Curry

This deliciously tangy shrimp curry, with fresh coconut and lots of ginger and garlic, is cooked in a style that is typical of Goan cuisine. Serve with steamed rice.

Serves 4.

20 shrimp
1½ teaspoons table salt
2 teaspoons cumin seeds
2 tablespoons coriander seeds
6 dried red chiles, stemmed
1 cup (120 grams) grated fresh coconut (or frozen unsweetened coconut)
2-inch (5-cm) piece fresh ginger, chopped
15 cloves garlic, chopped
2 tablespoons tamarind pulp
2 tablespoons vegetable oil
1 small onion, chopped
2 green chiles, stemmed and slit
1 tablespoon malt vinegar or cider vinegar

1. Peel and devein the shrimp. Wash thoroughly under running water. Drain in a colander for 15 minutes. Sprinkle with 1 teaspoon of the salt and set aside for 10 minutes.

2. Place a medium nonstick sauté pan over medium heat. Add the cumin, coriander, and dried chiles, and dry-roast for 5 to 8 minutes. Transfer to a bowl and set aside to cool.

3. Put the roasted spices, the coconut, ginger, garlic, tamarind pulp, and 1 cup (200 ml) water in a mini food processor, and process to a fine paste.

4. Place a medium nonstick sauté pan over high heat and add the oil. When small bubbles appear at the bottom of the pan, lower the heat to medium, add the onion, and sauté until golden brown. Add the green chiles and the remaining ½ teaspoon salt and sauté over medium heat for 3 minutes more, stirring continuously.

5. Add the ground paste and 1½ cups (300 ml) water. Bring to a boil, then lower the heat to low and add the shrimp. Cook for about 5 minutes or until the shrimp are cooked through.

6. Stir in the vinegar. Transfer to a serving bowl and serve hot.

Hara Masalewali Machchli

······❋{ **A whole fish cooked in green chutney** }❋······································

Fresh cilantro plays a key role in most regional cuisines of India. It is used not only as a garnish, but also as a main ingredient in chutney-type sauces like this one, in which it is treated almost as a green vegetable.

Serves 4.

4 (7½-ounce/220 gram) whole pomfrets, cleaned (see Note)
1 teaspoon table salt
½ teaspoon ground turmeric
6 tablespoons vegetable oil
1 teaspoon cumin seeds
2 teaspoons coriander seeds
10 cloves garlic, roughly chopped
1½-inch (4-cm) piece fresh ginger, roughly chopped
3 green chiles, stemmed and roughly chopped
½ cup (60 grams) grated fresh coconut (or frozen unsweetened coconut)
½ cup (30 grams) chopped fresh cilantro
2 tablespoons freshly squeezed lemon juice
½ cup (75 grams) rice flour
2 tablespoons *rawa/suji* (fine semolina flour)

1. Make 2 or 3 slits on both sides of the middle bone on each fish. Put them on a large plate. Rub the salt and turmeric all over them, and set aside to marinate for 15 minutes.

2. Place a nonstick sauté pan over medium heat and add 2 tablespoons of the oil. When small bubbles appear at the bottom of the pan, add the cumin, coriander, garlic, ginger, and chiles, and sauté for 1 to 2 minutes. Add the coconut and sauté for 2 minutes. Set aside to cool.

3. Transfer to a mini food processor, add the cilantro, lemon juice, and ¼ cup (50 ml) water, and process to a fine paste.

4. Using your fingertips, rub the paste all over the fish, including inside the slits.

5. Combine the rice flour and *rawa* on a plate.

6. Place a nonstick sauté pan over medium heat and add the remaining ¼ cup (50 ml) oil. While the oil is heating, coat the fish with the rice-*rawa* mixture. When small bubbles appear at the bottom of the pan, gently add the fish, one at a time, and cook for 3 to 4 minutes on each side or until the fish is cooked through and both sides are evenly done.

7. Serve hot.

······❋{ **Note** }❋ You can substitute pompano or small butterfish for the pomfret.

Iggaru Royya

This dish has a very thick sauce, but if you want to serve it with rice, add a little water to make the curry a little thinner.

Serves 4.

24 to 30 small shrimp
5 tablespoons vegetable oil
1 cup (120 grams) grated fresh coconut (or frozen unsweetened coconut)
4 dried red chiles, stemmed
1 teaspoon cumin seeds
½ teaspoon fenugreek seeds
10 to 12 whole black peppercorns
2 red onions, chopped
1 tablespoon fresh ginger paste (page 12)
1 tablespoon fresh garlic paste (page 12)
2 tomatoes, chopped
1 teaspoon table salt
10 to 12 fresh curry leaves
2 tablespoons chopped fresh cilantro

1. Peel and devein the shrimp. Wash thoroughly under running water. Drain in a colander for 15 minutes, then pat dry with a kitchen towel.

2. Place a medium nonstick sauté pan over medium heat and add 2 tablespoons of the oil. When small bubbles appear at the bottom of the pan, add the coconut, chiles, cumin, fenugreek, and peppercorns, and sauté for 2 to 3 minutes. Transfer to a bowl and set aside to cool to room temperature.

3. Transfer the mixture to a food processor with ¾ cup (150 ml) water and process to a coarse paste.

4. Place a medium nonstick saucepan over high heat and add the remaining 3 tablespoons oil. When small bubbles appear at the bottom of the pan, add the onions and sauté until golden brown. Add the ginger paste and garlic paste and sauté until all the moisture evaporates. Add the coconut-chile paste and sauté over medium heat for 3 minutes, stirring continuously.

5. Add the tomatoes, salt, and curry leaves, and sauté over low heat for 3 to 4 minutes.

6. Add the shrimp and toss well. Increase the heat to high and cook for about 5 minutes or until the shrimp are cooked through.

7. Transfer to a serving dish. Garnish with cilantro and serve hot.

Ilish Macher Sorse Jhol

······· ⁕{ **Mustard fish** }⁕ ···

This famous dish has its roots in eastern India. It is a pungent dish with a predominant mustard flavor. *Hilsa* fish (an oily fish that's the most popular fish of West Bengal), is hard to find in the United States, but you can substitute shad. Serve with steamed rice.

Serves 4.

1 (1⅓-pound/630-gram) whole *hilsa* fish, scaled and cleaned
1 teaspoon table salt
1 teaspoon ground turmeric
¾ teaspoon red chile powder
2 tablespoons mustard seeds
5 green chiles, stemmed
¼ cup (50 ml) refined mustard oil (see Note page 87)
2 medium red onions, chopped

1. Cut the fish horizontally into 1-inch-thick (2½-cm-thick) slices and wash well under running water. Drain in a colander and transfer to a bowl.

2. Sprinkle with ½ teaspoon of the salt, ½ teaspoon of the turmeric, and ¼ teaspoon of the chile powder. Set aside to marinate for 15 minutes.

3. Soak the mustard seeds in ¼ cup (50 ml) water for 15 minutes. Transfer to a spice grinder with 2 of the chiles and ¼ teaspoon of the salt, and grind to a fine paste.

4. Place a nonstick wok over medium heat and add the mustard oil. When the oil is hot, add the fish and fry, turning, until both sides are lightly browned. Drain on paper towels and set aside.

5. Combine the remaining ½ teaspoon turmeric, the remaining ½ teaspoon chile powder, the mustard paste, and 2 cups (400 ml) water.

6. Return the wok, with the oil remaining in it, to medium heat. Add the onions and stir. Slit the remaining green chiles, add to the wok, and sauté for 3 to 4 minutes or until the onions are browned. Add the turmeric–chile powder–mustard mixture and bring to a boil.

7. Add the fish and the remaining ¼ teaspoon salt, and simmer for 5 to 7 minutes or until the fish is cooked through.

8. Transfer to a serving dish and serve hot.

Jhinga Kalimirch

This is one of India's hottest dishes. But I always say that the cook is in control, and you can decrease the quantity of peppercorns if you like. The best peppercorns in India come from the verdant state of Kerala, where the air is full of heady aromas. The yellow chile powder used here is an ingredient from Benares and is a common spice used in the *chaats* sold by street vendors there.

Serves 4.

20 medium shrimp, peeled and deveined
1½ teaspoons table salt
2 tablespoons freshly squeezed lemon juice
4 medium red onions
5 medium tomatoes, roughly chopped
1 quart (800 ml) plus 3 tablespoons vegetable oil
½ cup (125 grams) plain yogurt
1-inch (2½-cm) cinnamon stick
3 green cardamom pods
2 teaspoons fresh garlic paste (page 12)
2 teaspoons fresh ginger paste (page 12)
¼ cup (75 grams) cashew paste (page 12)
1 teaspoon ground turmeric
½ teaspoon yellow chile powder (or cayenne)
25 black peppercorns, crushed, plus more for garnish if desired

1. Put the shrimp in a bowl, add the salt and lemon juice, and toss to coat. Cover the bowl with plastic wrap and set aside to marinate for 20 minutes.

2. Thinly slice 3 of the onions and chop the remaining onion.

3. Put the tomatoes in a blender and blend to a smooth purée. Transfer to a bowl and set aside.

4. Place a nonstick wok over high heat and add 1 quart (800 ml) oil. When small bubbles appear at the bottom of the wok, lower the heat to medium and add the sliced onions. Cook, stirring occasionally with a slotted spoon, until the onions are well browned. Remove with the slotted spoon and drain on paper towels. Let cool completely.

5. Transfer the onions to the blender, add the yogurt, and blend to a fine paste.

6. Place a nonstick sauté pan over medium heat and add 2 tablespoons of the oil. When small bubbles appear at the bottom of the pan, add the cinnamon and cardamom, and sauté for 30 seconds or until fragrant. Add the garlic paste and ginger paste, and sauté for 30 seconds. Add the cashew paste and sauté for 2 minutes. Add the tomato purée and cook, stirring, for 15 minutes. Add the turmeric and chile powder, and cook, stirring, for 1 minute.

7. Add the onion paste and stir well. Bring to a boil, then remove from the heat and let cool slightly. Pour through a strainer into a bowl; discard the solids.

8. Place a nonstick sauté pan over medium heat and add the remaining 1 tablespoon oil. When small bubbles appear at the bottom of the pan, add the peppercorns and chopped onion, and sauté for 4 to 5 minutes or until the onion is browned.

9. Add the shrimp and stir. Add the tomato mixture and 1 cup (200 ml) water. Stir and cook until the mixture comes to a boil and the shrimp are cooked through.

10. Garnish with a few more crushed peppercorns, if you wish. Serve hot.

Karimeen Pollichattu

········· ⁕{ **Fish steamed in banana leaf** }⁕ ···

The pearl spot fish is similar to pomfret, which you may be more familiar with. The first time I tasted this fish was in Bangalore in a restaurant at Taj Gateway. Some people get passionate about Norwegian salmon or sea bass from Chile; I feel the same way about pearl spot fish, which comes from the state of Kerala. Once you have tasted it, you will not mind flying it in or traveling to Kerala to try it. If you can't find pearl spot, use mackerel, silver pomfret, or tilapia.

Serves 4.

4 (5-ounce/150 grams) whole *karimeen* (pearl spot)
1 banana leaf (see Notes)
1 cup (140 grams) *sambhar* onions (similar to red pearl onions), peeled
9 tablespoons coconut or vegetable oil
½ teaspoon fenugreek seeds
½ teaspoon black mustard seeds
½ teaspoon fennel seeds
15 or 16 whole black peppercorns
16 dried red chiles, stemmed
¼ cup (12 grams) coriander seeds
2-inch (5-cm) piece fresh ginger, peeled
16 cloves garlic
6 green chiles, stemmed
25 to 30 fresh curry leaves, chopped
2 teaspoons tamarind pulp (see Notes)
1 tablespoon table salt

1. Scale the fish and clean the insides well. Wash under running water. Make deep slits on either side of each fish with a sharp knife and leave the fish in a colander to drain.

2. Wash the banana leaf and wipe it dry. Remove the center core and cut the leaf into 4 pieces. Holding them with tongs, singe the pieces over an open flame to make them malleable.

3. Peel all the onions and chop half of them. Leave the remaining onions whole.

4. Place a medium nonstick pan over medium heat and add 2 tablespoons of the oil. When small bubbles appear at the bottom of the pan, add the whole onions, fenugreek, mustard seeds, fennel, peppercorns, red chiles, coriander seeds, ginger, garlic, green chiles, half of the curry leaves, the tamarind pulp, and salt, and sauté for 2 to 3 minutes or until the onions are translucent.

5. Spread the mixture on a plate and set aside to cool to room temperature. Transfer to a food processor with ¼ cup (50 ml) water and process to a fine paste.

6. Spread half of the the paste liberally all over the fish, stuffing it into the slits. Set aside for 30 minutes to marinate.

7. Place a shallow nonstick sauté pan over medium heat and add 4 tablespoons of the oil. When small bubbles appear at the bottom of the pan, place the fish in a single layer and cook for 2 minutes on each side or until the fish are half cooked.

8. Place another nonstick sauté pan over medium heat and add 1 tablespoon oil. When small bubbles appear at the bottom of the pan, add the chopped onions, the remaining curry leaves, and the remaining ground paste, and cook, stirring continuously, for 2 minutes.

9. Spread half of the onion mixture over the banana leaf pieces and place one fish on each piece. Spread the remaining mixture over the fish and fold in the sides of the banana leaf pieces to wrap the fish completely.

10. Place the nonstick sauté pan from step 7 over medium heat and add the remaining 2 tablespoons oil. When small bubbles appear at the bottom of the pan, add the fish parcels and cook for 3 to 4 minutes on each side or until the fish are cooked through, making sure that the leaves do not burn during cooking.

11. Serve hot in the parcels.

·······⊰ **Notes** ⊱⁕ While banana leaf is preferable, you can wrap the fish in aluminum foil or parchment paper instead.

For sourness, *kodumpuli,* also called "fish tamarind," is traditionally used here. Since it is not readily available, I call for regular tamarind pulp in the recipe; you can also use *amchur* (dried mango powder).

Kesari Bharwan Jhinga

······⁕⦘ **Stuffed shrimp in a saffron curry** ⦗⁕······

This impressive dish of shrimp stuffed with chicken will have your guests exclaiming in delight.

Serves 4.

~ **For the shrimp:**
8 tiger shrimp
1 teaspoon fresh ginger paste (page 12)
1 teaspoon fresh garlic paste (page 12)
½ teaspoon table salt
1 tablespoon freshly squeezed lemon juice
2 ounces (60 grams) ground chicken

~ **For the sauce:**
¼ tablespoon cashew paste (page 12)
½ tablespoon boiled-onion paste (page 11)
Generous pinch of saffron threads
¾ teaspoon ground green cardamom
4 teaspoons vegetable oil
3 green cardamom pods
3 whole cloves
1-inch (2½-cm) cinnamon stick
8 whole black peppercorns, plus ¾ teaspoon crushed black peppercorns
¾ teaspoon *ajwain*
¾ teaspoon fresh garlic paste (page 12)
¾ teaspoon fresh ginger paste (page 12)
2 green chiles, stemmed and slit
½ teaspoon table salt

1. Make the shrimp: Peel the shrimp but leave the shells on the tails. Devein, wash thoroughly under running water, and drain well in a colander. Carefully slit each shrimp lengthwise without cutting all the way through. Flatten each shrimp just enough to make it look like a butterfly. Pat dry and put in a bowl.

2. Add the ginger paste, garlic paste, salt, and lemon juice and rub them in well. Cover the bowl with plastic wrap and put in the refrigerator to marinate for 30 minutes.

3. Preheat the oven to 300°F/150°C.

4. Divide the chicken into 8 portions. Take a shrimp, point the head side toward you, place 1 portion of the chicken on the wide end of the shrimp, and roll the shrimp up until you reach the tail. Fasten the loose end with a toothpick. Wrap up each shrimp in a small piece of aluminum foil and put them all on a baking sheet. Bake on the middle rack of the oven for 5 to 6 minutes. Remove from the oven.

5. Make the sauce: Whisk the cashew paste and boiled-onion paste together in a bowl. Crush the saffron, dissolve it in 1 tablespoon lukewarm water, add it to the paste mixture along with the ground cardamom, and set aside.

6. Place a nonstick saucepan over medium heat and add the oil. When small bubbles appear at the bottom of the pan, add the cardamom pods, cloves, cinnamon, and whole peppercorns, and sauté for 15 seconds. Add the *ajwain* and sauté for 30 seconds.

7. Add the ginger paste and garlic paste, and sauté for 2 minutes. Add the onion-paste mixture and sauté until the oil comes to the top. Add 1½ cups (300 ml) water and bring to a boil. Lower the heat to low and simmer, stirring occasionally, for 2 minutes. Remove from the heat, pass the sauce through a strainer into another nonstick saucepan, and discard the solids.

8. Place the pan with the sauce over medium heat, and as it begins to boil, lower the heat to low and add the chiles, crushed peppercorns, and salt.

9. Unwrap the shrimp and add them to the sauce. Transfer to a serving bowl and serve hot.

Kolambi Bharleli Vangi

······❧{ Eggplant stuffed with shrimp }❧······

There are many versions of this recipe in India. In this particular version, eggplants are stuffed with spicy shrimp and cooked in an onion-tomato mixture.

Serves 4.

7 ounces (200 grams) medium shrimp
1½ teaspoons table salt
¾ teaspoon ground turmeric
¼ cup (50 ml) vegetable oil
4 medium red onions, chopped
2 medium tomatoes, chopped
4 green chiles, stemmed and chopped
1 teaspoon ground coriander
1 teaspoon ground roasted cumin (page 32)
1 teaspoon freshly squeezed lemon juice
¼ cup (15 grams) chopped fresh cilantro
9 baby eggplants
1 tablespoon fresh ginger paste (page 12)
1 tablespoon fresh garlic paste (page 12)
½ teaspoon red chile powder
2 teaspoons tamarind pulp

1. Peel and devein the shrimp and wash thoroughly under running water. Sprinkle with ½ teaspoon of the salt and ½ teaspoon of the turmeric. Set aside for 10 to 15 minutes to marinate.

2. Place a medium nonstick saucepan over medium heat and add 2 tablespoons of the oil. When small bubbles appear at the bottom of the pan, lower the heat to low and add half of the onions. Sauté for 3 to 4 minutes or until translucent.

3. Add half of the tomatoes and cook, stirring continuously, for 4 minutes or until the oil comes to the top.

4. Add the chiles, coriander, cumin, lemon juice, half of the cilantro, ½ teaspoon of the salt, and the shrimp. Sauté for 3 to 4 minutes. Transfer to a bowl and let cool to room temperature.

5. Slit the eggplants into quarters from the bottom, keeping the stem end intact. Stuff the shrimp mixture into the eggplants.

6. Place a medium nonstick sauté pan over high heat and add the remaining 2 tablespoons oil. When small bubbles appear at the bottom of the pan, lower the heat to medium and add the remaining onions. Sauté for 3 to 4 minutes or until light golden brown.

7. Add the ginger paste and garlic paste, and sauté for 1 minute. Add the remaining tomatoes and sauté for 3 to 4 minutes or until the oil comes to the top. Add 1 cup (200 ml) water, the remaining ¼ teaspoon turmeric, the chile powder, tamarind pulp, and the remaining ½ teaspoon salt. Stir well.

8. Place the stuffed eggplants in the pan, lower the heat to low, cover, and cook for 25 minutes, turning the eggplants occasionally.

9. Transfer to a serving bowl, garnish with the remaining cilantro, and serve hot.

Kolambi Kaju Curry

There is a special dish cooked in Maharashtra that is made using cashews and the flesh of tender coconut. But tender coconut is not readily available in all parts of the world, so I replaced the coconut with an ingredient that is also flavorful and tender: shrimp.

Serves 4.

20 medium shrimp, peeled and deveined
15 cloves garlic, peeled
2-inch (5-cm) piece fresh ginger, peeled
8 whole black peppercorns
4 whole cloves
2-inch (5-cm) cinnamon stick, broken
¼ cup (15 grams) chopped fresh cilantro
2 green chiles, stemmed
¼ cup (50 ml) vegetable oil
2 large red onions, chopped
2 teaspoons red chile powder
½ teaspoon ground turmeric
4 teaspoons tamarind pulp
2 teaspoons table salt
20 cashews

1. Wash the shrimp thoroughly under running water and drain well in a colander.

2. Put 8 cloves garlic, the ginger, peppercorns, cloves, cinnamon, half the cilantro, and the chiles in a food processor. Add ¼ cup (50 ml) water and process to a fine paste.

3. Crush the remaining 7 cloves garlic.

4. Place a nonstick sauté pan over medium heat and add the oil. When small bubbles appear at the bottom of the pan, add the crushed garlic and sauté for 3 minutes. Add the onion and sauté for 5 minutes.

5. Add the ground garlic–spice mixture and sauté for 5 minutes. Add the chile powder and turmeric, and sauté for 30 seconds. Add the tamarind pulp, salt, and 1½ cups (300 ml) water. Stir well and bring to a boil.

6. Add the shrimp and cashews, and simmer for 8 minutes.

7. Garnish with the remaining cilantro and serve hot.

Kolmi No Patio

In this popular Parsi dish, shrimp (*kolmi*, as the Parsi call them) are cooked in a strong, tangy, garlic-flavored sauce. This dish is usually accompanied by steamed rice and a plain lentil dish on the side.

Serves 4.

14 ounces (400 grams) medium shrimp, peeled and deveined
2 teaspoons fresh ginger paste (page 12)
2 teaspoons fresh garlic paste (page 12)
1½ teaspoons table salt
¼ teaspoon ground turmeric
1 teaspoon red chile powder
2 tablespoons vegetable oil
5 green cardamom pods
1-inch (2½-cm) cinnamon stick
3 medium red onions, sliced
2 medium tomatoes, chopped
1 tablespoon white vinegar
1 tablespoon sugar

1. Wash the shrimp thoroughly under running water and drain well in a colander.

2. Put the shrimp in a bowl and add the ginger paste, garlic paste, 1 teaspoon of the salt, the turmeric, and chile powder. Stir well, cover the bowl with plastic wrap, and put in the refrigerator to marinate for 1 hour.

3. Place a nonstick saucepan over medium heat and add the oil. When small bubbles appear at the bottom of the pan, add the cardamom and cinnamon, and sauté until fragrant.

4. Add the onions and sauté for 5 minutes or until lightly browned. Add the tomatoes and sauté for 5 to 7 minutes or until soft.

5. Add the marinated shrimp and stir. Cover and cook for 15 minutes.

6. Add the vinegar and sugar, and stir until the sugar dissolves.

7. Transfer to a serving dish and serve hot.

Machchli Tak-A-Tak

······⁕{ **A fish curry cooked on a griddle** }⁕······

The *tawa* (griddle) in Indian homes is usually reserved for making *rotis* and *parathas*. Other foods cooked on a *tawa* are often made in restaurants and at wedding banquets where food is prepared to order. This dish's name, *tak-a-tak*, is explained in the recipe. *Rawas*, the fish used here, is called the Indian salmon. It is very different from American salmon. For this recipe, you can use rockfish or grouper if *rawas* is unavailable. Crabmeat is a good addition to this dish; substitute it for some of the shrimp and fish if you'd like.

Serves 4.

5 to 6 ounces (150 grams) shrimp, shelled and deveined
5 to 6 ounces (150 grams) *rawas* (Indian salmon), cut into 1-inch (2½-cm) cubes
2 teaspoons table salt
1 tablespoon coriander seeds
4 dried red chiles, stemmed and broken
5 tablespoons vegetable oil
1 tablespoon fresh garlic paste (page 12)
4 green chiles, stemmed and chopped
2-inch (5-cm) piece fresh ginger, chopped
1 large tomato, chopped
½ teaspoon roasted and crushed *kasoori methi* (dried fenugreek leaves)
1 teaspoon *garam masala* (spice mix; page 27)
1 medium red onion, chopped
4 cloves garlic, chopped
1 large potato, boiled, peeled, and chopped
1 tablespoon freshly squeezed lemon juice
2 tablespoons chopped fresh cilantro

1. Wash the shrimp and fish under running water and drain well in a colander. Transfer to a bowl, add 1 teaspoon of the salt, and toss.

2. Place a small nonstick sauté pan over medium heat. Add the coriander and red chiles, and dry-roast for 1 to 2 minutes. Transfer to a plate and set aside to cool completely. Transfer to a spice grinder and grind to a coarse powder.

3. Place a small sauté pan over medium heat and add 2 tablespoons of the oil. When small bubbles appear at the bottom of the pan, add the garlic paste and sauté for 1 minute. Add half of the coriander-chile powder and sauté for 30 seconds. Add half of the green chiles and half of the ginger, and sauté for 30 seconds.

4. Add the tomato and sauté for 7 minutes or until the oil comes to the top. Add ½ cup (100 ml) water and ½ teaspoon of the salt, and stir. Add the *kasoori methi* and ½ teaspoon of the *garam masala*. Stir well and remove from the heat. Set the sauce aside.

5. Place a large iron *tawa* (griddle) over medium heat and add the remaining 3 tablespoons oil. When small bubbles appear, add the shrimp and fish, and sauté for 2 minutes, stirring with a stainless-steel spatula. Shift the seafood from the center of the griddle toward the periphery.

6. Add the onion to the oil in the center of the griddle along with the remaining chiles, the remaining ginger, and the chopped garlic. Lower the heat to low and sauté for 2 to 3 minutes. Add the remaining coriander-chile powder and shift the seafood from the periphery to the center of the griddle.

7. Add the potato and sauté for 30 seconds. Using two stainless-steel spatulas held upright, begin to chop the seafood and potato. (This makes a "tak-a-tak" noise—hence the name of the dish.)

8. After every few strokes, stir the mixture. Cook in this manner for 4 to 5 minutes, then add the sauce and stir well. Sauté for 2 to 3 minutes or until the excess moisture has completely evaporated.

9. Add the remaining ½ teaspoon salt. Add the lemon juice and the remaining ½ teaspoon *garam masala*.

10. Transfer to a serving bowl and garnish with the cilantro. Serve hot.

Macher Jhol

····· A typical Bengali fish curry cooked in mustard oil ·····

A Bengali meal is highlighted by the fish preparation, and this is one of the most popular curries in the region. It is a thin curry, but the flavor of the mustard oil is striking. If you replace the mustard oil with vegetable oil, remember that the dish will loose its traditional flavor. Serve this with steamed rice.

Serves 4.

1⅓ pounds (600 grams) *rohu* (or any other freshwater fish; page 316), cut into 8 pieces
1 teaspoon table salt
½ teaspoon ground turmeric
¼ cup (50 ml) filtered mustard oil (see Note page 87)
2 medium potatoes, each cut into 6 pieces
1 bay leaf
1 medium red onion, finely chopped
2 tablespoons ginger-garlic paste (page 13)
1 teaspoon ground cumin
1 teaspoon red chile powder
2 medium tomatoes, puréed

1. Wash the fish pieces thoroughly under running water and drain in a colander. Place them in a bowl, add ½ teaspoon of the salt and ¼ teaspoon of the turmeric, and stir well. Put in the refrigerator to marinate for 15 minutes.

2. Place a nonstick sauté pan over high heat and add the mustard oil. When the oil starts to smoke, reduce the heat to medium, add the potato pieces, and sauté until browned. Drain and set aside.

3. To the same oil, add the fish pieces, two at a time, and sauté until lightly browned. Drain and set aside.

4. To the oil remaining in the pan, add the bay leaf and onion, and sauté until well browned. Add the ginger-garlic paste and sauté for 1 minute.

5. Add the cumin, chile powder, and the remaining ¼ teaspoon turmeric, and sauté for 30 seconds. Add the tomato purée and simmer until the oil comes to the top.

6. Add 1 cup (200 ml) water and the remaining ½ teaspoon salt, and stir. When it comes to a boil, add the fish and potatoes, and simmer for 3 to 4 minutes.

7. Transfer to a bowl and serve hot.

Malabar Chemeen Kari

·········≈{ **Shrimp and drumstick vegetable curry** }≈··

In this South Indian curry, which is traditionally cooked in a clay pot, drumsticks provide the main flavor. They are long, slender vegetable pods that grow on the *moringa* tree. Drumsticks are very popular in the southern parts of India and are commonly used to make stews, *dals*, and curries. You can find them canned and frozen in most Indian grocery stores. If you can't find them, you can use green beans, but please note that the taste will be different.

This curry is excellent with steamed rice; keep the sauce a little thin in consistency if you plan to serve it that way. You can use any kind of fish or any other seafood here instead of the shrimp.

Serves 4.

1 pound (500 grams) small shrimp
1 teaspoon ground turmeric
1½ teaspoons table salt
2 medium green mangoes
1½ cups (180 grams) grated fresh coconut (or frozen unsweetened coconut)
5 tablespoons vegetable oil
10 to 12 small shallots, halved
1 tablespoon red chile powder
1 tablespoon ground coriander
2 green chiles, stemmed and slit
4 curd chiles, stemmed and slit (see Note)
10 to 12 fresh curry leaves
1 tablespoon tamarind pulp
1 tablespoon coconut oil
1 teaspoon fenugreek seeds, lightly crushed
4 dried red chiles , stemmed
2 drumstick vegetables, stemmed

1. Peel, devein, and wash the shrimp thoroughly under running water. Drain in a colander for 10 minutes, then pat dry with paper towels and transfer to a bowl. Add the turmeric and 1 teaspoon of the salt, and stir. Cover the bowl with plastic wrap and put in the refrigerator for 30 minutes to marinate.

2. Peel and pit the mangoes and cut them into wedges.

3. Soak the coconut in 1 cup (200 ml) warm water for 15 minutes. Transfer to a food processor and process into a fine paste.

4. Place a nonstick saucepan over medium heat and add 3 tablespoons of the vegetable oil. When small bubbles appear at the bottom of the pan, add the shallots and sauté for 2 minutes or until translucent. Add the chile powder and coriander, and cook, stirring continuously, for a few seconds.

5. Add the green chiles, curd chiles, curry leaves, and tamarind pulp. Sauté for 1 minute. Add the coconut paste and 3 cups (600 ml) water. Bring to a boil and cook until reduced by half.

6. Pour the sauce through a strainer into a deep bowl, pressing well to extract all the flavors. Set aside.

7. Place another medium nonstick saucepan over medium heat and add the remaining 2 tablespoons vegetable oil and the coconut oil. When small bubbles appear at the bottom of the pan, add the fenugreek and dried chiles, and stir well over medium heat.

8. Add the shrimp, drumsticks, and mangoes. Cook over medium heat, stirring continuously, until the shrimp are almost cooked through.

9. Add the sauce and simmer for 2 to 3 minutes or until the shrimp are cooked through and the sauce is well combined.

10. Transfer to a serving bowl and serve hot.

·······⟨ **Note** ⟩⁕ Curd chiles are chiles that have been soaked in yogurt and dried. They are available at Indian grocery stores. If you cannot find them, leave them out.

Malvani Fish Curry

·······⊰{ A rich and spicy fish curry }⊱·······

Malvan is a part of the Konkan coast—and coastal food highlights seafood. What distinguishes Malvani fish curries is not just the variety of gravies but also the variety of recipes for the same kind of fish using a dazzling number of combinations of spices and ingredients, as well as dry and wet cooking styles. The most amazing and fiery fish curry I have ever eaten, like the one here, was at the table of Mrs. Samant, a family friend. Malvani food has loads of punch to it, which is just one of the reasons you will go back for a second helping. Serve with steamed rice. *Surmai* is a popular fish in India, but is hard to find in the United States. You can use pomfret or mackerel instead.

Serves 4.

1 pound (500 grams) whole *surmai* (kingfish), pomfret, or mackerel
1 tablespoon freshly squeezed lemon juice
1 teaspoon ground turmeric
1 teaspoon table salt
1 teaspoon cumin seeds
2 teaspoons coriander seeds
4 or 5 dried red chiles, stemmed
¾ cup (90 grams) grated fresh coconut (or frozen unsweetened coconut)
2 medium onions, chopped
6 to 8 whole black peppercorns
1 tablespoon tamarind pulp
2 tablespoons vegetable oil
1 medium tomato, chopped
2 green chiles, stemmed and slit

1. Cut off the head of the fish and clean the insides. Wash thoroughly under running water. Cut the fish horizontally into 1-inch-thick (2½-cm-thick) slices and put in a bowl. Add the lemon juice, ½ teaspoon of the turmeric, and the salt, and stir well. Cover the bowl and put it in the refrigerator for 15 to 20 minutes to marinate.

2. Place a small nonstick sauté pan over medium heat. Add the cumin and coriander, and dry-roast for 2 minutes or until fragrant. Let cool, then transfer to a food processor with the dried chiles, the remaining ½ teaspoon turmeric, the coconut, half of the onions, the peppercorns, tamarind pulp, and 1 cup (200 ml) water, and process to a smooth paste.

3. Place a medium nonstick saucepan over medium heat and add the oil. When small bubbles appear at the bottom of the pan, add the remaining onion and sauté for 3 to 4 minutes or until lightly browned. Add the tomato and green chiles and sauté for 2 to 3 minutes or until the oil comes to the top. Add the coconut paste and cook over high heat for 1 minute. Add 1½ cups (300 ml) water and bring to a boil. Lower the heat to medium, add the marinated fish, and cook for 5 to 6 minutes or until the fish is cooked through. Transfer to a serving bowl and serve hot.

Mamallapuram Kal Erra

·····⋅⋅{ Tamil-style *masala* shrimp in banana leaves }···

Chennai, formerly known as Madras, is one of the major metropolitan cities of India. Some miles away on a well-built state highway is Mamallapuram, which is also known as Mahabalipuram. This place is famous for its ancient carved stone temples. I once drove down there on a day trip after doing a show in Chennai to relish a bit of India's rich heritage. This shrimp preparation is a souvenir of that short visit years ago.

Serves 4.

16 large shrimp
8 teaspoons brown mustard seeds
2-inch (5-cm) piece fresh ginger, sliced
4 green chiles, stemmed and chopped
1 teaspoon tamarind pulp
½ teaspoon ground turmeric
1 teaspoon red chile powder
1¼ teaspoons table salt
2 teaspoons anise seeds
½ teaspoon fenugreek seeds
2 teaspoons cumin seeds
2 tablespoons vegetable oil
2 banana leaves

1. Preheat the oven to 350°F/175°C.

2. Peel the shrimp, but keep the tails intact. Devein and wash thoroughly under running water. Drain well in a colander.

3. Put 6 teaspoons of the mustard seeds, the ginger, chiles, and tamarind pulp in a spice grinder. Add 2 tablespoons water and grind to a smooth paste. Transfer to a bowl, add the turmeric, chile powder, and salt, and stir.

4. Put the anise, fenugreek, cumin, and the remaining 2 teaspoons mustard seeds in a spice grinder and grind to a powder. Transfer to another small bowl.

5. Place a nonstick sauté pan over medium heat and add the oil. When small bubbles appear at the bottom of the pan, add the spice powder. Sauté for 15 seconds, then quickly pour it over the ground paste and stir well.

6. Rub this paste liberally on the shrimp. Wrap them up neatly in the banana leaves, half in each leaf, and fold the leaves into tight parcels.

7. Place the parcels on a baking sheet and bake for 20 to 30 minutes.

8. Unwrap and serve immediately.

Meen Nirappiyathu

······❧ Mackerel stuffed with coconut masala and shallow-fried ❧······

We have used mackerel here because it is a nice oily fish. But you can use any oily fish, preferably one with a single center bone. And instead of pan-frying, you can broil them. Traditionally, the fish is roasted directly over a charcoal fire.

Serves 4.

8 (3-ounce/85-gram) mackerels, heads removed, cleaned
¼ cup (30 grams) grated fresh coconut (or frozen unsweetened coconut)
1-inch (2½-cm) piece fresh ginger, chopped
4 green chiles, stemmed and chopped
4 dried red chiles, stemmed
2 tablespoons chopped fresh cilantro
2 tablespoons chopped fresh mint
15 fresh curry leaves, chopped
1 tablespoon tamarind pulp
1 teaspoon table salt
2 tablespoons vegetable oil
2 lemons, cut into wedges

1. Trim off the fish fins with scissors, wash well, and drain. Slit each fish from the side and remove the center bone without damaging the fish, if possible. Make ¼-inch-deep (½-cm-deep) cuts on both sides of each fish.

2. Put the coconut, ginger, green chiles, dried chiles, cilantro, mint, curry leaves, tamarind pulp, salt, and 3 tablespoons water in a mini food processor, and process to a fine paste.

3. Stuff most of the paste into the fish and rub the rest on the outside. Arrange the fish on a plate, cover with plastic wrap, and put in the refrigerator for at least 1 hour to marinate.

4. Place a medium nonstick sauté pan over medium heat and add the oil. When small bubbles appear at the bottom of the pan, gently place the fish, two at a time, in the pan and cook each side for 3 to 4 minutes or until both sides are evenly golden brown. Drain on paper towels.

5. Arrange the fish on a platter, garnish with the lemon wedges, and serve hot.

Meen Vattichattu

Kerala is famous for its exotic *payasam* (rice dessert) as well as for its banana wafers and a vast variety of fish preparations such as this mildly tangy and spicy curry. Serve it with steamed rice.

Serves 4.

1 pound (500 grams) *surmai* (kingfish), cut into 2-inch-thick (5-cm-thick) fillets
Lemon-size ball of tamarind
1 tablespoon ground coriander
¼ teaspoon ground turmeric
¼ teaspoon ground fenugreek
5 tablespoons red chile paste (see Note page 13)
2 teaspoons table salt
2 teaspoons coconut oil
½ teaspoon brown mustard seeds
½ teaspoon *dhuli urad dal* (split skinless black gram)
10 to 12 fresh curry leaves
2 dried red chiles, stemmed and broken in half

1. Wash the fish under running water and drain well in a colander.

2. Soak the tamarind in 1 cup (200 ml) warm water for 15 minutes. Squeeze to remove the pulp, then strain it into a nonstick saucepan and discard the seeds and stringy solids. Add 2 cups (400 ml) water and stir well.

3. Place over medium heat and bring to a boil.

4. Meanwhile, combine the coriander, turmeric, and fenugreek in ¼ cup (50 ml) water and stir to make a smooth paste. Add this paste to the boiling tamarind water along with the chile paste and stir until all the ingredients are thoroughly combined. Simmer for 6 minutes or until the liquid is reduced by half.

5. Add the fish and cook for 7 minutes or until the fish is cooked through.

6. Place a small nonstick sauté pan over medium heat and add the coconut oil. When small bubbles appear at the bottom of the pan, add the mustard seeds. When they sputter, add the *dal*, curry leaves, and chiles. Sauté for 15 seconds, then add to the fish. Cover immediately to trap the flavors.

7. Serve hot.

Podichapa

Crisp pieces of fish briefly marinated in garlic and ginger are perfect for a quick snack. In Andhra Pradesh, this is enjoyed as a side with *dal* and rice.

Serves 4.

1 pound (500 grams) *rawas* (Indian salmon; see Note page 167) or regular salmon fillets, cut into 2½-inch (6-cm) pieces
1½ teaspoons table salt
⅝ teaspoon ground turmeric
2 teaspoons red chile powder
4 teaspoons fresh garlic paste (page 12)
1 tablespoon fresh ginger paste (page 12)
2 teaspoons ground coriander
1½ teaspoons ground black pepper
1 tablespoon freshly squeezed lemon juice
1 quart (800 ml) vegetable oil

1. Put 5 cups (1 liter) water in a deep bowl, add ½ teaspoon of the salt and ⅛ teaspoon of the turmeric, and stir. Wash the fish pieces in the seasoned water and drain well in a colander.

2. Pat the fish pieces with an absorbent towel and put them in a bowl. Add the remaining 1 teaspoon salt, remaining ½ teaspoon turmeric, the chile powder, garlic paste, ginger paste, coriander, pepper, and lemon juice, and stir well. Let stand for 10 minutes.

3. Place a nonstick wok over high heat and add the oil. When small bubbles appear at the bottom of the wok, slide in the fish pieces, a few at a time. Cook, stirring with a slotted spoon, for 4 minutes. Remove with the slotted spoon and drain on paper towels.

4. Serve hot.

Rawas Ambotik

······{ Hot-and-sour salmon curry }······

Ambotik is a combination of two words: *ambot*, meaning "sour," and *tik*, meaning "spicy." *Ambotik* preparations are Portuguese in origin, and the strong influence of that cuisine in India is evident in Goan cooking. Serve this dish with steamed rice.

Serves 4.

1¾ pounds (800 grams) *rawas* (Indian salmon; see Note page 167), or regular salmon fillets, cut into ½-inch-thick (1-cm-thick) slices
1½ teaspoons table salt
1 teaspoon ground turmeric
1 tablespoon coriander seeds
1 teaspoon cumin seeds
1 cup (120 grams) grated fresh coconut (or unsweetened frozen coconut)
2 large red onions, chopped
8 to 10 dried red chiles, stemmed and broken
1-inch (2½-cm) piece fresh ginger, chopped
8 to 10 cloves garlic, chopped
5 whole cloves
2-inch (5-cm) cinnamon stick
1½ tablespoons white vinegar
3 tablespoons vegetable oil
4 or 5 green chiles, stemmed and slit
1½ tablespoons tamarind pulp

1. Put the fish in a large bowl, add 1 teaspoon of the salt and the turmeric, toss to coat, and set aside to marinate for 20 minutes.

2. Place a nonstick sauté pan over medium heat, add the coriander and cumin, and dry-roast for 2 minutes. Transfer to a plate and set aside to cool completely.

3. Put the coconut, half of the chopped onions, the red chiles, the roasted coriander and cumin, ginger, garlic, cloves, cinnamon, and vinegar in a food processor with 1 cup plus 2 tablespoons (230 ml) water, and process to a fine paste. Set aside.

4. Place a nonstick sauté pan over medium heat and add the oil. When small bubbles appear at the bottom of the pan, add the remaining onions and sauté for 4 to 5 minutes or until golden brown.

5. Add the ground paste and cook over high heat for 3 to 4 minutes, stirring continuously.

6. Add 2½ cups (500 ml) water and bring to a boil. Add the green chiles and stir. Add the fish and simmer for 5 minutes.

7. Add the tamarind pulp and the remaining ½ teaspoon salt. Stir gently and cook over low heat for 5 minutes. Serve hot.

Shrimp Balchao

········❧{ Shrimp in a sweet-and-sour gravy }❧·································

This dish from coastal Goa is essentially a pickled shrimp dish, but its sweet-and-sour taste makes it unique. I also make a vegetarian version using *paneer*. Serve with steamed rice.

Serves 4.

40 medium shrimp, shelled and deveined
1 teaspoon table salt
2-inch (5-cm) piece fresh ginger, chopped
10 cloves garlic
1 teaspoon cumin seeds
15 dried red chiles, stemmed and broken in half
10 to 12 whole cloves
2-inch (5-cm) cinnamon stick, broken
1 teaspoon black mustard seeds
1 cup (200 ml) malt vinegar or cider vinegar
¾ cup (150 ml) vegetable oil
2 large onions, finely chopped
2 large tomatoes, chopped
2 tablespoons sugar

1. Put the shrimp in a bowl and sprinkle with the salt. Toss once and set aside for 10 minutes.

2. Put the ginger, garlic, cumin, chiles, cloves, cinnamon, mustard seeds, and vinegar in a food processor, and process to a paste.

3. Place a medium nonstick sauté pan over medium heat and add the oil. Add the shrimp and fry until they turn pink. Remove with a slotted spoon and set aside.

4. Add the onions to the oil remaining in the pan and sauté over medium heat for 4 to 5 minutes or until lightly browned.

5. Add the tomatoes and sauté for 3 to 4 minutes or until the tomatoes turn pulpy.

6. Add the ground paste and sauté for 3 to 4 minutes or until the oil begins to come to the top and the vinegar evaporates. The final mixture should be wet but not runny.

7. Add the shrimp and stir well. Add the sugar and cook over low heat for 5 minutes.

8. Transfer to a serving dish and serve hot.

Shrimp Ghassi

{ Shrimp curry }

Frying the spices and then grinding them is the traditional way to prepare this dish, which originates from Karnataka. Serve with steamed rice.

Serves 4.

24 medium shrimp
1¼ teaspoons table salt
2 tablespoons vegetable oil
2 teaspoons coriander seeds
1 teaspoon cumin seeds
8 to 10 whole black peppercorns
¼ teaspoon fenugreek seeds
4 dried red chiles, stemmed
1 cup (120 grams) grated fresh coconut (or frozen unsweetened coconut)
1 medium onion, chopped
5 cloves garlic
½ teaspoon ground turmeric
1½ tablespoons tamarind pulp

1. Peel and devein the shrimp. Wash them thoroughly under running water and drain in a colander. Transfer to a bowl and sprinkle with 1 teaspoon of the salt; toss well and put in the refrigerator for 15 minutes.

2. Place a medium nonstick sauté pan over high heat and add 1 teaspoon of the oil. Lower the heat to low, add the coriander, cumin, peppercorns, fenugreek, and chiles, and sauté for 5 minutes. Transfer to a bowl and let cool to room temperature. Transfer the mixture to a food processor with the coconut, half of the onion, the garlic, turmeric, tamarind pulp, and 1 cup (200 ml) water, and process to a fine paste.

3. Place a deep nonstick saucepan over high heat and add the remaining 1 tablespoon plus 2 teaspoons oil. When small bubbles appear at the bottom of the pan, lower the heat to low, add the remaining onion, and sauté for 3 to 4 minutes or until translucent. Add the ground paste and sauté for 5 to 6 minutes over medium heat.

4. Add the shrimp and stir well. Add ½ cup (100 ml) water and the remaining ¼ teaspoon salt. Increase the heat to medium and bring to a boil. Cover and cook until the shrimp are cooked through.

5. Transfer to a serving bowl and serve hot.

Shrimp Peri Peri

······✳{ **A Portuguese-style spicy shrimp curry** }·······································

Peri peri is what the Portuguese call small red bird's-eye chiles. The Portuguese influence is strong in the food of Goa, the most popular beach getaway in India. I have replaced the fresh chiles in this recipe with lots of dried ones and have mellowed the edge by adding red bell pepper instead of more of the fiery-hot chiles.

Serves 4.

24 medium shrimp, peeled and deveined
½ teaspoon table salt
1 teaspoon crushed black peppercorns
6 tablespoons vegetable oil
6 cloves garlic, chopped
1-inch (2½-cm) piece fresh ginger, chopped
1 medium red onion, chopped
1 medium red bell pepper, seeded and cut into 1-inch (2½-cm) cubes
10 dried red chiles, stemmed and seeded
1 medium tomato, chopped
¼ cup (50 ml) white vinegar

1. Wash the shrimp thoroughly under running water and drain well in a colander. Put in a bowl. Add the salt and peppercorns, and toss well. Cover the bowl with plastic wrap and put in the refrigerator to marinate for 30 minutes.

2. Place a nonstick sauté pan over medium heat and add 4 tablespoons of the oil. When small bubbles appear at the bottom of the pan, add the garlic and ginger, and sauté for 1 to 2 minutes or until browned.

3. Add the onion and sauté for 2 to 3 minutes or until translucent. Add the bell pepper, chiles, and tomato, and cook until the tomato is pulpy. Add the vinegar and stir. Remove from the heat and set aside to cool.

4. Transfer to a food processor and process to a fine paste. Add the paste to the shrimp and rub it in well.

5. Place the same nonstick sauté pan over medium heat and add the remaining 2 tablespoons oil. When small bubbles appear at the bottom of the pan, add the shrimp and cook for 5 to 6 minutes or until cooked through. Remove the shrimp from the sauce and set aside on a plate. Place the pan over medium heat and cook for 5 to 6 minutes or until the sauce is almost dry.

6. Return the shrimp to the pan and cook for 1 minute. Serve hot.

Sungta Ani Torache Hooman

········❧{ **Shrimp and green-mango curry** }⁂··

This simple green-mango and shrimp preparation comes from the state of Goa. Serve it with steamed rice.

Serves 4.

11 ounces (330 grams) shrimp, peeled and deveined
¼ teaspoon ground turmeric
1 teaspoon fresh ginger paste (page 12)
1 teaspoon fresh garlic paste (page 12)
1 teaspoon table salt
1 medium green mango
1 cup (120 grams) grated fresh coconut (or frozen unsweetened coconut)
1 tablespoon coriander seeds
5 dried red chiles, stemmed and broken
15 whole black peppercorns
¼ cup (50 ml) vegetable oil
2 green chiles, stemmed and slit
1 large red onion, chopped
1 cup (200 ml) coconut milk

1. Put the shrimp in a large bowl. Add the turmeric, ginger paste, garlic paste, and ½ teaspoon of the salt, and stir well. Set aside to marinate for 15 minutes.

2. Peel the mango and cut it in half. Discard the pit, then cut the mango into 8 equal pieces.

3. Put the coconut, coriander, red chiles, and peppercorns in a food processor with 1 cup (200 ml) water, and process to a smooth paste.

4. Place a nonstick saucepan over medium heat and add the oil. When small bubbles appear at the bottom of the pan, add the green chiles and sauté for 1 minute. Add the onion and sauté for 3 to 4 minutes or until lightly browned.

5. Add the shrimp and sauté for 1 minute. Add the coconut paste, mango, remaining ½ teaspoon salt, and ½ cup (100 ml) water, and cook for 2 minutes or until the shrimp are cooked through.

6. Stir in the coconut milk and simmer for 2 minutes.

7. Serve hot.

Tandoori Pomfret

······· ⁂⟩ **Pomfret cooked tandoor style** ⟨⁂ ·······

Pomfret cooked in a tandoor oven is the most popular fish dish in any good seafood restaurant in Mumbai. But for ease of preparation, I've given instructions for cooking it in a conventional oven. The best way to enjoy this fish is with lots of lemon juice.

Serves 4.

4 (7½ -ounce/220-gram) small whole pomfrets, cleaned and washed (you can also use
    butterfish or pompano)
1¾ teaspoons table salt
2 tablespoons freshly squeezed lemon juice
1 teaspoon fresh ginger paste (page 12)
1 teaspoon fresh garlic paste (page 12)
1½ cups (375 grams) plain yogurt
2½ teaspoons red chile powder
2 teaspoons *garam masala* (spice mix; page 27)
2 tablespoons vegetable oil
½ teaspoon *ajwain*
¼ cup (20 grams) *besan* (chickpea/gram flour)
¾ teaspoon ground turmeric
¼ cup (50 ml) butter, melted
1 lemon, cut into wedges

1. Pat the fish dry with an absorbent towel. Make incisions on both sides of each fish. Combine 1 teaspoon of the salt, the lemon juice, ginger paste, and garlic paste, and rub it all over the fish. Put the fish on a platter, and set aside for 20 minutes.

2. Combine the yogurt, the remaining ¾ teaspoon salt, the chile powder, and *garam masala* in a bowl, and set aside.

3. Place a nonstick sauté pan over medium heat and add the oil. When small bubbles appear at the bottom of the pan, add the *ajwain* and *besan*, and sauté for 4 to 5 minutes or until fragrant. Remove from the heat and stir in the turmeric. Add to the yogurt mixture and whisk well. Rub this mixture all over the fish and into the incisions. Cover the platter with plastic wrap and put in the refrigerator to marinate for 1 hour.

4. Preheat the oven to 350°F/175°C.

5. Put the fish on a greased baking sheet and bake on the middle rack of the oven for 8 to 10 minutes, watching carefully that the fish do not overcook.

6. Baste with the butter and cook for another 5 minutes or until the fish have a golden and crisp crust, again watching carefully that the fish do not overcook.

7. Serve hot with the lemon wedges.

Tisryache Kalvan

The Malvanis of western India like to cook clams in this flavorful fashion. Be sure to clean the clams well before using and discard any clams that do not open after steaming in step 2. Serve with steamed rice.

Serves 4.

2³⁄₄ **pounds (1.3 kg) clams**
1 **teaspoon table salt**
½ **tablespoon freshly squeezed lemon juice**
2 **red onions**
3 **tablespoons vegetable oil**
5 **whole cloves**
5 **or 6 whole black peppercorns**
2-**inch (5-cm) cinnamon stick**
½ **teaspoon caraway seeds**
1 **teaspoon coriander seeds**
5 **or 6 dried red chiles, stemmed**
½ **cup (40 grams) dried grated coconut**
2 **tablespoons tamarind pulp**
1 **tablespoon fresh ginger paste (page 12)**
1 **tablespoon fresh garlic paste (page 12)**
¼ **teaspoon ground turmeric**
½ **cup (100 ml) coconut milk**
1 **tablespoon chopped fresh cilantro**

1. Soak the clams in 5 cups (1 liter) water for 15 minutes, scrub lightly, and rinse thoroughly under running water.

2. Place a deep nonstick saucepan over high heat and add 2 cups (400 ml) water. Cover and bring to a boil. Add the clams and cover again. Open the lid after 1 minute and check to see if the clams have opened slightly. If they have, drain the clams in a colander set over a large bowl; reserve the water. Refresh the clams under running water and drain in the colander.

3. Remove one shell of each clam, keeping the meat on the other shell. Sprinkle the clams with salt and the lemon juice. Refrigerate for 15 minutes.

4. Slice 1 onion and chop the other.

5. Place a medium nonstick sauté pan over high heat and add 1 tablespoon of the oil. When small bubbles appear at the bottom of the pan, lower the heat to medium and add the sliced onion. Sauté for 3 to 4 minutes or until golden brown. Transfer to a food processor and set aside.

6. Place the sauté pan from step 5 over medium heat and dry-roast the cloves, peppercorns, cinnamon, caraway, coriander, chiles, and coconut for 10 minutes or until fragrant. Add to the food processor with the browned onions and add the tamarind pulp and 1 cup (100 ml) water. Process to a fine, smooth paste.

7. Place a deep nonstick saucepan over high heat and add the remaining 2 tablespoons oil. When small bubbles appear at the bottom of the pan, lower the heat to medium, add the chopped onion, and sauté for 3 to 4 minutes or until light golden brown.

8. Add the ginger paste and garlic paste and sauté for 30 seconds. Lower the heat to low, add the ground spice mixture, and sauté for 5 minutes. Add ½ cup (100 ml) water and bring to a boil.

9. Add the clams, turmeric, and coconut milk. Check the seasoning and cook for 5 minutes. Remove from the heat and transfer to a serving bowl.

10. Garnish with the cilantro and serve hot.

Yera Poondu Masala

·······⋇❴ Garlic shrimp curry ❵⋇···

Another gem from the South Indian state of Kerala, this shrimp curry's predominant flavor is that of garlic. Of course, you can reduce (or increase) the garlic to suit your palate. Be sure to use fresh garlic here, as that will provide the best taste.

Serves 4.

20 to 24 medium shrimp
1 tablespoon freshly squeezed lemon juice
1½ teaspoons table salt
6 dried red chiles, stemmed
1 tablespoon coriander seeds
1 tablespoon cumin seeds
10 to 12 whole black peppercorns
20 cloves garlic, crushed
6 tablespoons sesame oil
½ teaspoon black mustard seeds
1 teaspoon *dhuli urad dal* (split skinless black gram)
10 to 12 fresh curry leaves
1 medium onion, chopped
2 green chiles, stemmed and slit
1 medium tomato, chopped

1. Peel and devein the shrimp and wash them thoroughly under running water. Drain in a colander for 10 minutes. Transfer to a bowl, add the lemon juice and salt, and stir well. Cover the bowl with plastic wrap and put in the refrigerator for 20 minutes to marinate.

2. Heat a medium nonstick sauté pan over medium heat and dry-roast 4 dried chiles, the coriander, cumin, peppercorns, and 15 cloves garlic. Transfer the mixture to a bowl and let cool to room temperature. Transfer to a food processor with ¼ cup (50 ml) water and process to a smooth paste.

3. Place a wide nonstick saucepan over high heat and add the oil. When small bubbles appear at the bottom of the pan, lower the heat to medium and add the mustard seeds, *dal*, the remaining dried chiles, and the curry leaves.

4. Add the remaining garlic, the onion, green chiles, and the ground paste. Sauté over high heat for 2 to 3 minutes or until the oil comes to the top.

5. Add the tomato and cook until the mixture becomes thick and dry.

6. Add the shrimp, toss well, and cover with a tight-fitting lid. Cook over low heat, stirring frequently, for about 10 minutes. Uncover and cook over high heat to thicken the sauce. Serve hot as a side dish.

Aab Gosht

······❊⟫ Lamb with *chana dal*, green chiles, and coconut milk ⟨❊······

The secret of a smooth flavor in this gravy is the timing—especially the addition of the coconut milk, which can curdle and make the dish look unappetizing. Follow the recipe instructions carefully and don't let the mixture boil after you add the coconut milk. Serve with *rotis* (page 18).

Serves 4.

¼ cup (50 grams) *chana dal* (split Bengal gram)
1⅔ pounds (750 grams) boneless lamb, cut into 1-inch (2½-cm) cubes
8 green chiles, stemmed
1-inch (2½-cm) piece fresh ginger
5 cloves garlic
¼ cup (50 ml) vegetable oil
4 medium red onions, chopped
3 medium tomatoes, chopped
¼ teaspoon ground turmeric
1½ teaspoons table salt
½ teaspoon *garam masala* (spice mix; page 27)
½ teaspoon ground black pepper
2 teaspoons ground coriander
2 teaspoons ground roasted cumin (page 32)
1 cup (200 ml) coconut milk

1. Put the *chana dal* in a bowl, wash it in plenty of water 2 or 3 times, and drain. Add 1 cup (200 ml) water and soak for 20 minutes. Drain the *dal* in a colander.

2. Trim off the excess fat from the lamb. Set aside.

3. Slit 4 of the chiles and reserve for garnish. Put the remaining chiles, the ginger, garlic, and 2 tablespoons water in a spice grinder, and grind to a fine paste.

4. Place a medium nonstick saucepan over high heat and add the oil. When small bubbles appear at the bottom of the pan, lower the heat to medium, add the onions, and sauté for 2 to 3 minutes or until they are translucent. Add the tomatoes, ginger-garlic-chile paste, turmeric, and salt, and stir. Sauté for 2 minutes. Add the cubes of lamb and stir so that it is well coated. Sauté for about 15 minutes or until the lamb is well browned.

5. Add the *chana dal* and 2½ cups (500 ml) water and stir. Bring to a boil over high heat, then lower the heat to medium, cover, and cook for 35 minutes or until the lamb is almost done.

6. Add the *garam masala*, pepper, coriander, and cumin. Lower the heat to low, cover, and cook for 20 minutes or until the lamb is tender.

7. Add the coconut milk and cook to just heat through; do not let the curry come to a boil.

8. Transfer the curry to a serving bowl, garnish with the slit green chiles, and serve hot.

Aattu Kari Podimas

······•{ Peppery-hot ground lamb with coconut and onions }•·····················

I have eaten ground lamb and goat cooked in a variety of ways, but the robust flavor of this dish is unforgettable: It lingers in the mind for days. Serve with *parathas* (page 18).

Serves 4.

20 to 25 whole black peppercorns
2 teaspoons cumin seeds
1 teaspoon fennel seeds
1-inch (2½-cm) piece fresh ginger
12 cloves garlic
1 pound (500 grams) freshly ground lamb
1 teaspoon red chile powder
2 teaspoons ground coriander
2 medium red onions, chopped
3 tablespoons vegetable oil
½ cup grated fresh coconut (or frozen unsweetened coconut)
1 large tomato, chopped
½ cup (30 grams) chopped fresh cilantro
10 to 12 fresh curry leaves
1½ teaspoons table salt

1. Place a small nonstick sauté pan over medium heat. Add the peppercorns, cumin, and fennel, and dry-roast for 3 to 4 minutes or until the seeds are fragrant. Let cool to room temperature, then transfer to a spice grinder and grind to a fine powder.

2. In the same spice grinder, add the ginger and garlic, and grind to a smooth paste. Transfer to a small bowl and set aside.

3. Put the lamb in a large bowl and add the ginger-garlic paste, freshly ground spices, chile powder, coriander, and onions, and stir well. Cover the bowl with plastic wrap and put it in the refrigerator for about 30 minutes to marinate.

4. Place a medium nonstick sauté pan over medium heat and add the oil. When small bubbles appear at the bottom of the pan, add the lamb mixture, increase the heat to high, and cook, stirring continuously, until the excess liquid evaporates. When the lamb is nearly cooked and reduced in quantity, lower the heat to low and add the coconut, tomato, cilantro, and curry leaves. Add the salt and stir well.

5. Cover and cook for 5 minutes more or until the lamb is fully cooked. Transfer to a serving dish and serve hot.

Achari Gosht

······⁕{ **Lamb cooked with pickling spices** }⁕··

This dish tastes best when it is allowed to sit for a while after cooking. This allows all the souring agents to release their true flavors. So cook it, let it cool to room temperature, cover, and refrigerate for at least a few hours, preferably overnight. When you are ready, reheat and serve with your favorite Indian bread.

Serves 4.

1¾ pounds (800 grams) bone in lamb, cut into 1½-inch (4-cm) cubes
2 tablespoons fresh ginger-garlic paste (page 13)
1 tablespoon malt vinegar
2 teaspoons table salt
¼ teaspoon yellow mustard seeds
¼ teaspoon fenugreek seeds
1½ teaspoons cumin seeds
½ cup (100 ml) filtered mustard oil (see Note page 87)
½ teaspoon asafetida
2 bay leaves
½ teaspoon *kalonji* (nigella; see Note page 231)
4 medium red onions, sliced
6 to 8 green chiles, stemmed and slit
1 teaspoon red chile powder
1 tablespoon ground coriander
½ teaspoon ground turmeric
¼ teaspoon ground fennel seeds
¼ teaspoon black salt
1 cup (250 grams) plain yogurt
1 teaspoon *garam masala* (spice mix; page 27)

1. Put the lamb in a large bowl. Add the ginger-garlic paste, vinegar, and 1 teaspoon of the salt, and rub them in. Cover the bowl with plastic wrap and put in the refrigerator for 1 hour to marinate.

2. Place a small nonstick sauté pan over medium heat. Add the mustard seeds, fenugreek, and 1 teaspoon of the cumin seeds, and dry-roast for 30 seconds. Set aside to cool completely. Transfer to a spice grinder and grind to a fine powder. Set aside in a small bowl.

3. Place a nonstick saucepan over medium heat and add the mustard oil. When small bubbles appear at the bottom of the pan, add the asafetida, bay leaves, the remaining ½ teaspoon cumin, and the *kalonji*, and sauté for 30 seconds.

4. Add the onions and cook for 3 to 4 minutes or until the onions are translucent.

5. Add the lamb and chiles, and stir. Cover and cook for 30 minutes or until the lamb is half done.

6. Add the chile powder, coriander, turmeric, fennel, and the roasted spice powder, and stir well. Add the black salt, cover, and cook for 10 minutes or until the lamb is almost done.

7. Add the yogurt and cook for 10 minutes or until the lamb is very tender. Add the *garam masala* and stir. Cool to room temperature and refrigerate.

8. Serve hot the next day.

Aloobukhara Kofta

······{ **Ground-lamb meatballs stuffed with dried plums in a flavorful sauce** }······

In the early nineteenth century, the Sikh empire had a stronghold in Punjab, the Land of Five Rivers. The king captured Lahore (Pakistan) and annexed Kashmir (in northern India). So you can imagine the goings-on in the royal kitchen, where cooks from these three regions competed to put the best before the king! This plum-filled dumpling is a perfect example of the blending of these cuisines.

Serves 4.

8 prunes, pitted (dried plums; see Note)
8 almonds, blanched and peeled (see Note page 40)
14 ounces (400 grams) finely ground lamb
½-inch (1-cm) piece fresh ginger, chopped
3 green chiles, stemmed and minced
¼ teaspoon *anardana* (dried pomegranate seeds), roasted and ground
1¼ teaspoons table salt
½ teaspoon *garam masala* (spice mix; page 27)
2½ tablespoons vegetable oil
2 or 3 whole cloves
2 green cardamom pods
½-inch (1-cm) cinnamon stick
2 medium red onions, diced
2 teaspoons fresh garlic paste (page 12)
1½ teaspoons fresh ginger paste (page 12)
2 teaspoons ground coriander
1 teaspoon red chile powder
½ teaspoon ground turmeric
1 cup (240 grams) fresh tomato purée
½ teaspoon ground green cardamom
½ teaspoon ground mace
2 tablespoons chopped fresh cilantro

1. Stuff the prunes with the almonds and set aside.

2. Put the meat in a large bowl, add the chopped ginger, chiles, *anardana*, ½ teaspoon of the salt, and the *garam masala*, and combine well. Divide into 8 portions and shape into balls.

3. Flatten each ball between your palms and place a stuffed prune in the center. Gather the edges to enclose the prune and shape back into a ball. Place the balls on a plate, cover with plastic wrap, and put in the refrigerator for 15 minutes.

4. Place a nonstick saucepan over medium heat and add the oil. When small bubbles appear at the bottom of the pan, add the cloves, cardamom, and cinnamon, and sauté for 1 minute.

5. Add the onions and sauté for 4 to 5 minutes. Add the garlic paste and ginger paste, and sauté for 1 minute.

6. Combine the coriander and chile powder in 1 tablespoon water and add it to the pan, along with the turmeric and the remaining ¾ teaspoon salt, and sauté for 1 minute.

7. Add the tomato purée and cook for 3 to 4 minutes or until the oil comes to the top.

8. Add 1¼ cups (250 ml) water, bring to a boil, and cook for 10 minutes or until the sauce thickens.

9. Remove from the heat and pour the sauce through a fine sieve into a clean saucepan. Discard the solids. Place the pan over medium heat. Add the cardamom and mace, stir well, and cook for 1 minute.

10. Add the stuffed meatballs and cook for 8 to 10 minutes or until cooked through.

11. Garnish with the cilantro and serve hot.

········⁕⟨ **Note** ⟩⁕ You can use dried apricots instead of dried plums.

Bhindi Ka Shorva

Okra lovers will adore this rich dish. Meat adds body to the dish, but the flavor of okra dominates it.

Serves 4.

1 pound (500 grams) bone-in lamb, cut into 1½-inch (4-cm) pieces
8 ounces (250 grams) okra, trimmed
1 tablespoon *amchur* (dried mango powder)
1¾ teaspoons table salt
1½ teaspoons red chile powder
1 teaspoon *garam masala* (spice mix; page 27)
3 tablespoons vegetable oil
6 cloves garlic, chopped
3 medium red onions, sliced
½ teaspoon fresh ginger paste (page 12)
½ teaspoon fresh garlic paste (page 12)
½ teaspoon ground turmeric
2 tablespoons plain yogurt, whisked
1 tablespoon tamarind pulp
¼ cup (15 grams) chopped fresh cilantro

1. Trim the excess fat from the lamb and put the pieces in a large bowl.

2. Slit the okra in half from the bottom, leaving the stem ends intact.

3. Combine the *amchur*, ¼ teaspoon of the salt, ½ teaspoon of the chile powder, and ¼ teaspoon of the *garam masala*, and stuff the okra with this mixture. Set aside.

4. Place a medium nonstick saucepan over medium heat and add 1 tablespoon of the oil. When small bubbles appear at the bottom of the pan, add the okra and garlic, and sauté gently for 2 to 3 minutes. Transfer to a bowl and set aside.

5. Add the remaining 2 tablespoons oil to the pan. When small bubbles appear at the bottom of the pan, add the onions and sauté for 2 to 3 minutes or until golden brown. Add the ginger paste and garlic paste, and sauté for 2 minutes. Add the remaining 1½ teaspoons salt, the turmeric, the remaining 1 teaspoon chile powder, and the yogurt, and stir. Cook, stirring the masala, for 3 minutes more.

6. Add the lamb and sauté for 5 minutes or until the masala is dry. Add 2½ cups (500 ml) water and bring to a boil. Cover and cook for 10 to 15 minutes or until the lamb is tender.

7. Add the tamarind pulp, okra, and 1 cup (200 ml) water, and bring to a boil. Lower the heat to low, cover, and cook for 5 minutes or until the okra is tender.

8. Remove from the heat and sprinkle with the remaining ¾ teaspoon *garam masala* and the cilantro. Transfer to a serving bowl and serve hot.

Burrah Masaledaar

⋯⋯⋯ ⋇{ Spicy lamb chops }⋇ ⋯⋯⋯⋯⋯⋯⋯⋯⋯⋯⋯⋯⋯⋯⋯⋯⋯⋯⋯⋯⋯⋯⋯

This recipe uses browned-onion paste, which gives a rich sweetness and an appetizing reddish brown color to the curry. This paste is best made fresh before you use it. Since the onions also add sweetness, we balance that by adding a souring agent, in this case yogurt.

Serves 4.

1½ pounds (700 grams) lamb chops
2 teaspoons fresh ginger paste (page 12)
2 teaspoons fresh garlic paste (page 12)
2 tablespoons malt vinegar
2 teaspoons table salt
1 quart (800 ml) plus 6 tablespoons vegetable oil
4 medium red onions, sliced
4 to 6 whole cloves
2 black cardamom pods
1 blade mace
5 or 6 whole black peppercorns
1-inch (2½-cm) cinnamon stick
½ cup (125 grams) plain yogurt
½ teaspoon caraway seeds
1 quart (800 ml) lamb stock (page 35)
4 medium tomatoes, chopped
1 tablespoon red chile powder
1 teaspoon ground cumin
1 tablespoon ground coriander
2 tablespoons chopped fresh cilantro

1. Put the chops in a bowl. Add the ginger paste, garlic paste, vinegar, and 1 teaspoon of the salt, and toss. Cover the bowl with plastic wrap and put in the refrigerator to marinate for 30 minutes.

2. Place a nonstick wok over high heat and add 1 quart (800 ml) of the oil. When small bubbles appear at the bottom of the wok, lower the heat to medium, add the onions, and cook for 7 to 8 minutes or until well browned and crisp. Remove with a slotted spoon and drain on paper towels until cooled. Transfer to a food processor and process to a paste.

3. Place a small nonstick sauté pan over medium heat. Add the cloves, cardamom, mace, peppercorns, and cinnamon, and dry-roast for 30 seconds or until fragrant. Let cool completely, then transfer to a spice grinder and grind to a fine powder.

4. Put the yogurt in a small bowl, add the onion paste, and whisk until well blended.

5. Place a nonstick sauté pan over medium heat and add the remaining oil. When small bubbles appear at the bottom of the pan, add the caraway and sauté for 15 seconds. Add the chops and sauté for 7 to 8 minutes or until lightly browned. Add the yogurt mixture and sauté for 7 to 8 minutes or until the oil comes to the top.

6. Add the stock and bring to a boil. Lower the heat to low and simmer for 15 minutes or until the chops are half done.

7. Add the tomatoes, chile powder, cumin, and coriander, and cook for 20 minutes or until the tomatoes are completely mashed and the sauce is smooth.

8. Add the roasted spice powder and the remaining 1 teaspoon salt, and cook for 12 minutes or until the chops are cooked through.

9. Garnish with the cilantro and serve hot.

Dahi Kheema

·······⁘⟩ Ground lamb cooked with spices in a yogurt sauce ⟨⁘·············

I love how the yogurt in this dish not only softens the meat (yogurt is a great tenderizer) but also envelops the meat in a tangy flavor.

Serves 4.

2 tablespoons vegetable oil
5 whole cloves
1-inch (2½-cm) cinnamon stick
3 green cardamom pods
1 black cardamom pod
1 blade mace
2 bay leaves
2 medium red onions, finely chopped
6 or 7 green chiles, stemmed and chopped
2 teaspoons fresh garlic paste (page 12)
2 teaspoons fresh ginger paste (page 12)
14 ounces (400 grams) ground lamb
1 teaspoon table salt
2 teaspoons red chile powder
1 tablespoon ground coriander
½ teaspoon ground turmeric
1⅓ cups (335 grams) plain yogurt, whisked
¼ cup (15 grams) chopped fresh cilantro

1. Place a nonstick saucepan over medium heat and add the oil. When small bubbles appear at the bottom of the pan, add the cloves, cinnamon, green and black cardamom, mace, bay leaves, and onions, and sauté for 2 minutes or until fragrant.

2. Add the chiles and sauté for 1 minute. Add the garlic paste, ginger paste, and ½ cup (100 ml) water, and stir well.

3. Add the lamb and stir. Add the salt and sauté for 5 minutes or until the water evaporates.

4. Add the chile powder, coriander, and turmeric, and stir. Cook until the lamb is almost cooked and dry.

5. Add the yogurt and stir. Lower the heat to low, cover, and cook for 10 to 15 minutes or until the lamb is well done.

6. Transfer to a serving dish, garnish with the cilantro, and serve hot.

Dal Gosht

······⋇{ **Lamb cooked with lentils and spices** }⋇·····································

Hyderabadi cuisine is known for a lot of dishes that combine vegetarian foods with meat. This dish of pulses with meat is a fine example. In some homes, only one type of *dal* is used, but I like this richer version. Enjoy it with steamed rice.

Serves 4.

¼ cup (50 grams) *chana dal* (split Bengal gram)
2 tablespoons *arhar dal/toor dal* (split pigeon peas)
2 tablespoons *masoor dal* (split red lentils)
2 tablespoons vegetable oil
½ teaspoon cumin seeds
¼ tablespoon fresh ginger paste (page 12)
½ tablespoon fresh garlic paste (page 12)
2 green chiles, stemmed and slit
1 large red onion, chopped
1 medium tomato, chopped
1 teaspoon table salt
1 teaspoon red chile powder
1 teaspoon ground coriander
1 teaspoon ground roasted cumin (page 32)
¼ teaspoon ground turmeric
¼ teaspoon *garam masala* (spice mix; page 27)
10 ounces (300 grams) boneless lamb, trimmed and cut into 1-inch (2½-cm) cubes
½ tablespoon freshly squeezed lemon juice
2 tablespoons chopped fresh cilantro

1. Put the *dals* in a large bowl, wash in plenty of water 2 or 3 times, and drain. Add 2 cups (400 ml) water and soak for 30 minutes. Drain the *dals* in a colander.

2. Place a medium nonstick saucepan over medium heat and add the oil. When small bubbles appear at the bottom of the pan, add the cumin seeds. When they change color, add the ginger paste, garlic paste, and chiles, and sauté for 1 minute.

3. Add the onion and sauté for 3 to 4 minutes or until golden brown. Add the tomato and salt, and sauté for 2 minutes.

4. Add the chile powder, coriander, ground cumin, and turmeric, and sauté for 1 minute.

5. Add the *garam masala*, lamb, and *dals*, and sauté for 2 minutes.

6. Add 1 quart (800 ml) water and bring to a boil. Lower the heat to low, cover, and cook for 50 minutes or until the lamb is tender. Add the lemon juice and stir well.

7. Transfer the curry to a serving bowl, garnish with the cilantro, and serve hot.

Egg Nargisi Kofta

····⁕⁕{ Hard-boiled eggs wrapped in ground lamb in a spicy tomato sauce }⁕⁕····

The word *nargisi* is a derivative of the word *nargis*, which means "daffodil." Daffodils are beautiful, with sunshine-yellow centers and spikey white petals—a color combination that is revealed when the eggs are cut in half! This is an Awadi dish from Lucknow, in the state of Uttar Pradesh. Awadh has been greatly influenced by Mughal cooking.

Serves 4.

6 large eggs
8 ounces (250 grams) ground lamb or chicken
4 slices bread
1 teaspoon fresh ginger paste (page 12)
1 teaspoon fresh garlic paste (page 12)
6 green chiles, stemmed and chopped
2 teaspoons table salt
1 tablespoon red chile powder
2 teaspoons ground coriander
½ teaspoon ground roasted cumin (page 32)
3 tablespoons chopped fresh cilantro
2 tablespoons chopped fresh mint
½ cup (55 grams) bread crumbs
1 quart (800 ml) plus 2 tablespoons vegetable oil
4 medium red onions, chopped
4 medium tomatoes, chopped
1 teaspoon *garam masala* (spice mix; page 27)
½ teaspoon ground black pepper

1. Place a nonstick sauté pan over high heat and add 5 cups (1 liter) water. When the water comes to a boil, add 4 of the eggs and cook for 8 to 10 minutes. Remove from the heat and let the eggs cool in the water. Peel them and set aside.

2. Beat the remaining 2 eggs in a small bowl and set aside.

3. Put the lamb, bread, ginger paste, garlic paste, 3 of the chiles, and 1 teaspoon of the salt in a food processor and process to a smooth paste. Transfer to a bowl and stir in 1½ teaspoons of the chile powder, the coriander, cumin, half of the cilantro, and the mint. Combine well and divide the mixture into 4 portions.

4. Completely cover each egg with 1 portion of the lamb mixture. Smooth the surface with moistened hands. Spread the bread crumbs on a plate.

5. Place a nonstick wok over high heat and add 1 quart of the oil. When small bubbles appear at the bottom of the wok, lower the heat to medium. Dip each covered egg in the beaten eggs, roll it in the bread crumbs, and slide it into the hot oil. Cook for 8 minutes or until golden and crisp on the outside. Remove with a slotted spoon and drain on paper towels. Cut each egg ball in half vertically. Place in a shallow serving dish.

6. Make the tomato sauce: Place a nonstick sauté pan over medium heat and add the remaining 2 tablespoons oil. When small bubbles appear at the bottom of the pan, add the onions and cook for 5 minutes or until lightly browned.

7. Add the tomatoes, the remaining chiles, the remaining cilantro, the *garam masala*, the remaining 1½ teaspoons chile powder, the remaining 1 teaspoon salt, and the pepper. Add 6 cups (1.2 liters) water and simmer for 15 minutes.

8. Pour the sauce over the stuffed eggs and serve hot.

Erachi Olathiyathu

·······⋗§ **Super-spicy lamb with fennel and peppercorns** §⋖·······

A good Kerala curry, like this one, should be infused with red-hot chile—but you are the boss in your kitchen and can vary the heat to your taste. I would not compromise on the amount of black pepper or curry leaves, however.

Serves 4.

1¾ pounds (800 grams) bone-in lamb, cut into 1½-inch (4-cm) pieces
2 (2-inch/5-cm) cinnamon sticks
6 whole cloves
2 black cardamom pods
1 star anise
1 teaspoon fennel seeds
1 tablespoon red chile powder
2 tablespoons ground coriander
1 teaspoon ground turmeric
½ teaspoon ground black pepper
2 teaspoons table salt
2-inch (5-cm) piece fresh ginger
6 to 8 cloves garlic
20 fresh curry leaves
5 tablespoons vegetable oil
¼ cup (30 grams) thinly sliced fresh coconut (or frozen unsweetened coconut)
5 or 6 dried red chiles, stemmed
1 large red onion, peeled and thinly sliced

1. Put the lamb in a large bowl.

2. Place a small nonstick sauté pan over medium heat. Add the cinnamon, cloves, black cardamom, star anise, and fennel, and dry-roast for 2 minutes or until fragrant. Transfer to a plate and let cool. Transfer into a mortar and pound to a fine powder with a pestle.

3. Add the roasted spice powder to the lamb in the bowl. Add the chile powder, coriander, turmeric, pepper, and salt, and stir well. Set aside for 30 minutes to marinate.

4. Put the ginger, garlic, and 6 of the curry leaves in a mortar and crush with a pestle to a coarse paste.

5. Place a nonstick saucepan over medium heat and add 4 tablespoons (60 ml) of the oil. When small bubbles appear at the bottom of the pan, add the crushed ginger mixture along with the lamb and stir. Lower the heat to low and cook, adding 2½ cups (500 ml) water at regular intervals, for 50 to 55 minutes or until the lamb is cooked.

6. Place a small nonstick sauté pan over medium heat and add ½ tablespoon oil. When small bubbles appear at the bottom of the pan, add the coconut and sauté until lightly browned. Set aside.

7. Place another nonstick saucepan over medium heat and add the remaining ½ tablespoon oil. When small bubbles appear at the bottom of the pan, add the remaining 14 curry leaves, the red chiles, and onion, and sauté for 2 to 3 minutes or until the onion is translucent.

8. Add the lamb and lower the heat to low. Cook for 2 minutes or until the mixture is semidry. Add the browned coconut slices. Stir and cook for 30 seconds.

9. Serve hot.

Goan Lamb Curry

You can use beef, goat, or pork in this dish instead of the lamb. This curry, redolent with cinnamon and coriander, will taste better if it is allowed to sit in the refrigerator overnight. This allows the flavors to meld and the spices to do their magic. Serve with steamed rice.

Serves 4.

1⅔ pounds (750 grams) boneless lamb
1 teaspoon ground turmeric
1½ teaspoons table salt, or more if needed
1 tablespoon fresh ginger paste (page 12)
1 tablespoon fresh garlic paste (page 12)
1 tablespoon freshly squeezed lemon juice
1 tablespoon vegetable oil
6 whole cloves
2 green cardamom pods
10 to 12 whole black peppercorns
4 dried red chiles, stemmed
1-inch (2½-cm) cinnamon stick
1 tablespoon coriander seeds
1 bay leaf
2 onions, peeled and sliced
1½-inch (4-cm) piece fresh ginger, crushed
6 cloves garlic, crushed
1 cup (120 grams) grated fresh coconut (or frozen unsweetened coconut)
1 tablespoon white vinegar

1. Trim off the excess fat from the lamb. Cut into 1-inch (2½-cm) pieces.

2. Put the lamb in a deep bowl, add the turmeric, salt, ginger paste, garlic paste, and lemon juice, and stir well. Cover the bowl and put it in the refrigerator for 2 hours to marinate.

3. Place a medium nonstick sauté pan over high heat and add the oil. When small bubbles appear at the bottom of the pan, lower the heat to medium and add the cloves, cardamom, peppercorns, chiles, cinnamon, coriander, and bay leaf and sauté for 2 to 3 minutes or until fragrant.

4. Add the onions, ginger, and garlic, and sauté until the onions are browned. Add the coconut and sauté until the coconut is browned. Transfer to a plate and let cool to room temperature.

5. Transfer the cooled sautéed mixture to a food processor with 1 cup (200 ml) water and process to a fine paste; set aside.

6. Put the lamb in a nonstick saucepan, add 4 cups (800 ml) water, and place the pan over high heat. When the mixture comes to a boil, lower the heat to medium and cook, uncovered, for 1 hour or until the lamb is three quarters done.

7. Add the onion-coconut paste and stir well. Adjust the salt, if necessary, and cook over medium heat for 30 minutes or until the lamb is tender.

8. Add the vinegar and stir. Cover and let the curry stand for 15 minutes. Serve hot.

Gosht Korma

····❖{ **Lamb stewed in a rich coconut-and-cream sauce** }❖····

This is a rich dish with saffron, cream, coconut, and poppy seeds. It is an ideal main course for special occasions. Serve with fluffy steamed basmati rice on the side.

Serves 4.

14 ounces (400 grams) boneless lamb, cut into 1-inch (2½-cm) cubes
2 tablespoons plain Greek yogurt
1½ teaspoons table salt
1 tablespoon poppy seeds
5 or 6 saffron threads
2 medium red onions, peeled
2 tablespoons grated fresh coconut (or frozen unsweetened coconut)
3 green chiles, stemmed and roughly chopped
4 cloves garlic, crushed
1-inch (2½-cm) piece fresh ginger, grated
20 to 24 cashews
¼ cup (50 ml) vegetable oil
2½ tablespoons ground coriander
1 tablespoon ground roasted cumin (page 32)
½ teaspoon ground green cardamom
⅛ teaspoon ground cinnamon
1 tablespoon crushed black peppercorns
½ cup (100 ml) heavy cream

1. Put the lamb in a large bowl and stir in the yogurt and 1 teaspoon of the salt. Cover the bowl with plastic wrap and put in the refrigerator to marinate for 2 hours.

2. Soak the poppy seeds in ⅓ cup (65 ml) water for 30 minutes.

3. Soak the saffron in 2 tablespoons warm water.

4. Roughly chop 1 of the onions and thinly slice the other.

5. Place the roughly chopped onion in a food processor with the poppy seeds and the water they were soaked in. Add the coconut, chiles, garlic, ginger, and cashews, and process to a paste.

6. Place a nonstick saucepan over medium heat and add the oil. When small bubbles appear at the bottom of the pan, add the sliced onion, and sauté for 3 to 4 minutes or until golden brown.

7. Add the ground paste and sauté for 5 minutes or until the oil comes to the top.

8. Add the lamb, coriander, cumin, cardamom, cinnamon, and peppercorns, and sauté over high heat for 8 to 10 minutes or until the lamb is well browned on all sides.

9. Add 2½ cups (300 ml) water and the remaining ½ teaspoon salt, and simmer for 50 minutes or until the lamb is tender.

10. Stir in the saffron water and cream. Transfer to a serving dish and serve hot.

Gosht Pasanda

······❋⟨ **Yogurt-marinated lamb in a flavorful gravy** ⟩❋······························

Good-quality meat is the key ingredient here. Choose a leg or shoulder cut and then cut it into pieces yourself.

Serves 4.

1⅓ pounds (630 grams) boneless lamb, trimmed and cut into 1½-inch (4-cm) cubes
1 cup (250 grams) plain yogurt, whisked
2 teaspoons table salt
2 teaspoons fresh ginger paste (page 12)
2 teaspoons fresh garlic paste (page 12)
1 teaspoon red chile powder
1 teaspoon ground green cardamom
¼ cup (50 ml) vegetable oil
2 green cardamom pods
3 whole cloves
½-inch (1-cm) cinnamon stick
5 whole black peppercorns
1 bay leaf
4 medium red onions, sliced
2 green chiles, stemmed and chopped
1 tablespoon ground coriander
½ cup (140 grams) tomato purée

1. Flatten the lamb cubes with the flat side of a knife or a meat mallet.

2. Put the lamb in a large bowl, add the yogurt, salt, ginger paste, garlic paste, chile powder, and ground cardamom, and stir well. Cover the bowl with plastic wrap and put it in the refrigerator for about 2 hours to marinate.

3. Place a medium nonstick saucepan over medium heat and add the oil. When small bubbles appear at the bottom of the pan, add the cardamom pods, cloves, cinnamon, peppercorns, and bay leaf, and sauté for 1 minute or until fragrant. Add the onions and sauté for 3 to 4 minutes or until golden brown.

4. Add the chiles, coriander, and lamb, and cook, stirring, for 1 minute. Add 1 cup (200 ml) water and stir. Bring to a boil, then lower the heat to low, cover, and cook over low heat for 45 minutes or until the lamb is almost done.

5. Add the tomato purée and stir. Cook, covered, over low heat for 5 minutes or until the lamb is tender.

6. Transfer to a serving dish and serve hot.

Kaleji Ka Salan

····· ❧ **Liver curry** ❧ ···

In my early years of chef training, I was taught about "tandoor garnish," which is basically a fresh salad that contains some mint sprigs. The salad varies from restaurant to restaurant, but it usually has slices of tomato, onion, and cucumber or a mixture of shredded cabbage, carrot, and other vegetables. But the mint sprig is in all of them, and there's a reason why. Mint cleans the palate while you enjoy your meaty kebabs or tandoori chicken. It readies the taste buds for the next bite, and it is also a digestive aid. I have used the same principle in garnishing this dish, as liver tends to linger on the palate and the mint will be a welcome refreshment between bites. Serve with *roti* (page 18) or *parathas* (page 18).

Serves 4.

14 ounces (400 grams) lamb or chicken livers
1 teaspoon ground turmeric
2 teaspoons table salt
1 teaspoon fresh ginger paste (page 12)
1 teaspoon fresh garlic paste (page 12)
1 teaspoon red chile powder
¾ cup (190 grams) plain yogurt
½ cup (100 ml) vegetable oil
2 medium red onions, thinly sliced
1½ teaspoons ground coriander
A few sprigs fresh mint

1. Cut the liver into ½- to 1-inch (1- to 2½-cm) pieces.

2. Place a nonstick saucepan over high heat and add 3 cups (600 ml) water. When the water comes to a boil, add the liver, ½ teaspoon of the turmeric, and 1 teaspoon of the salt. Cook over high heat for 10 minutes, skimming the foam from the surface with a slotted spoon occasionally. Drain in a colander and let cool.

3. Combine the ginger paste, garlic paste, chile powder, the remaining ½ teaspoon turmeric, the remaining 1 teaspoon salt, the yogurt, and liver in a large bowl and set aside to marinate for 15 minutes.

4. Place a nonstick sauté pan over medium heat and add the oil. When small bubbles appear at the bottom of the pan, add the onions and cook for 6 to 8 minutes or until well browned.

5. Add the liver with the marinade and sauté for 8 to 10 minutes or until the excess water has evaporated. Add the coriander and sauté for 2 to 3 minutes.

6. Add 2 cups (400 ml) water. Bring to a boil, then lower the heat to low and simmer for 15 to 20 minutes or until the liver is cooked through.

7. Garnish with sprigs of mint and serve hot.

Kashmiri Gushtaba

······❧ **Meatballs in yogurt curry** ❧······

Most Indian regional cuisines have at least one dish of *koftas*—meatballs or vegetarian versions. This particular recipe is from the state of Kashmir and forms the concluding part of an exclusive ceremony called the Wazwan, a feast that can have up to thirty-six courses. This dish is served piping hot, and no one ever refuses it. It is often the last savory bite of the meal, followed by dessert and Kashmiri tea.

Serves 4.

1 quart (800 ml) vegetable oil
3 small red onions, sliced
1½ cups (375 grams) plain yogurt
1 teaspoon fresh garlic paste (page 12)
10 ounces (300 grams) boneless lamb from leg, fat reserved, cut into small pieces
1 teaspoon ground green cardamom
1 teaspoon table salt
3 tablespoons ghee (page 37)
3 cups (600 ml) lamb stock (page 35)
4 or 5 green cardamom pods
2 black cardamom pods
6 whole cloves
3½ teaspoons ground fennel seeds
1 tablespoon ground ginger
¼ teaspoon dried mint

1. Place a wok over high heat and add the oil. When small bubbles appear at the bottom of the wok, add the onions and cook until browned. Remove with a slotted spoon and drain on paper towels. Let cool, then transfer to a food processor with 3 tablespoons water and process to a fine paste.

2. Put the yogurt in a bowl and whisk until smooth. Add ½ cup (100 ml) water and whisk again.

3. Place a nonstick saucepan over medium heat and add the yogurt mixture. Lower the heat to low and cook, stirring continuously, for 5 minutes.

4. Put the garlic paste in a small bowl, add ¼ cup (50 ml) water, and stir. Let stand for 10 minutes.

5. Put the lamb, 3 ounces of the reserved fat, the ground cardamom, and ¼ teaspoon of the salt on a cutting board, and pat with a meat mallet until the mixture becomes very soft and smooth.

6. Dip your hands in chilled water and divide the lamb mixture into 12 equal portions. Shape them into round balls.

7. Place a nonstick saucepan over high heat. Add the yogurt mixture, the meatballs, ghee, and stock, and bring to a rapid boil. Lower the heat to medium, add the green and black cardamom pods, cloves, fennel, and ground ginger. Cover and boil for 10 to 12 minutes.

8. Add the garlic water and remaining ¾ teaspoon salt, and boil for 8 minutes. The mixture should have a souplike consistency.

9. Add the browned onion paste and cook until the meatballs are tender to the touch and the sauce has thickened.

10. Sprinkle with the mint and serve hot.

Khade Masale Ka Gosht

·······⋇⎨ Lamb curry with whole spices ⎬⋇·········

This is a basic lamb recipe that would be a good introduction for someone who is unfamiliar with Indian cooking. It uses most of the important spices (*khade masale* means "whole spices"), and the base is the onion-tomato sauce that is so essential to master when learning to cook Indian food.

Serves 4.

14 ounces (400 grams) boneless lamb, cut into 1-inch (2½-cm) cubes
2 teaspoons table salt
¼ teaspoon ground turmeric
2 teaspoons coriander seeds
3 dried red chiles, stemmed and broken
10 whole black peppercorns
3 tablespoons vegetable oil
½ teaspoon cumin seeds
2 green cardamom pods
1 black cardamom pod
2 whole cloves
1-inch (2½-cm) cinnamon stick
1 bay leaf
1 medium red onion, chopped
1½-inch (4-cm) piece fresh ginger, chopped
7 or 8 cloves garlic, chopped
3 green chiles, stemmed and chopped
Small pinch of ground mace
½ cup (125 grams) plain yogurt
1 medium tomato, chopped
2 tablespoons chopped fresh cilantro

1. Place a nonstick saucepan over high heat and add 2½ cups (500 ml) water. Add the lamb, 1 teaspoon of the salt, and the turmeric. When the water comes to a boil, lower the heat to medium, cover, and cook for 45 minutes or until the lamb is cooked through.

2. Put the coriander, red chiles, and peppercorns in a spice grinder and grind to a coarse powder.

3. Place a nonstick saucepan over medium heat and add the oil. When small bubbles appear at the bottom of the pan, add the cumin, green and black cardamom, cloves, cinnamon, and bay leaf. Sauté for 1 minute or until fragrant.

4. Add the onion and sauté for 3 to 4 minutes or until golden brown.

5. Add the ginger, garlic, and green chiles, and sauté for 2 minutes. Add the lamb, the remaining 1 teaspoon salt, the ground spices, and the mace.

6. Lower the heat to low and sauté, stirring continuously, for 6 to 8 minutes or until the lamb is browned. Remove from the heat, add the yogurt, and stir well. Return the pan to low heat and sauté for 6 to 8 minutes.

7. Add the tomato and sauté for 5 to 6 minutes or until the oil comes to the top.

8. Add 1 cup (200 ml) water, stir, and bring to a boil. Lower the heat, cover, and simmer, stirring occasionally, for 10 to 12 minutes or until the lamb is tender and the sauce becomes semidry.

9. Garnish with the cilantro and serve hot.

Kheema Hara Dhania

····•⊰{ Ground lamb cooked with cilantro and served with hard-boiled eggs }⊱•·····

I remember my dad making this when I was as young as seven years old. He would sauté the ground lamb very patiently until it was aromatic and then he would tap the spatula on the side of the pan, giving us a signal that dinner was just about ready. Mom would proceed into the kitchen and quickly make a batch of hot *rotis* (page 18). Fresh, wonderful food made lovingly—these are my fondest memories.

Serves 4.

2-inch (5-cm) piece fresh ginger, chopped
4 cloves garlic, chopped
3 tablespoons ghee (page 37)
1 teaspoon cumin seeds
3 or 4 green cardamom pods
1-inch (2½-cm) cinnamon stick
4 to 6 whole cloves
3 medium red onions, chopped
5 green chiles, stemmed and chopped
14 ounces (400 grams) ground lamb
1 tablespoon ground coriander
1½ teaspoons table salt
¼ teaspoon ground turmeric
7 or 8 black peppercorns, crushed
1 teaspoon *garam masala* (spice mix; page 27)
1 cup (60 grams) chopped fresh cilantro
4 eggs, hard-boiled, peeled, and quartered

1. Put the ginger and garlic in a spice grinder with 1 tablespoon water and grind to a paste.

2. Place a nonstick saucepan over medium heat and add the ghee. When small bubbles appear at the bottom of the pan, add the cumin seeds, cardamom, cinnamon, and cloves, and sauté for 30 seconds or until fragrant. Add the ginger-garlic paste and sauté for 30 seconds.

3. Add the onions and chiles, and sauté for 4 to 5 minutes or until the onions are golden brown.

4. Add the lamb and increase the heat to high. Cook, stirring continuously, for 10 minutes.

5. Add the coriander, salt, and turmeric, and stir well. Stir in 1½ cups (300 ml) cups water and bring to a boil. Lower the heat to medium, cover, and simmer, stirring occasionally, for 40 minutes or until the lamb is cooked through.

6. Add the peppercorns and *garam masala*, and stir. Add the cilantro and stir well. Cook until the excess liquid has evaporated.

7. Transfer to a serving bowl. Garnish with the eggs and serve hot.

Kheema Kaleji

Kaleji is Urdu for "liver." Liver is a rich source of iron and combines well with ground lamb. I like to prepare this as a dry dish with hardly any curry.

Serves 4.

7 ounces (200 grams) lamb liver or chicken liver
2 teaspoons ground turmeric
3 tablespoons melted butter or vegetable oil
1 teaspoon cumin seeds
2 medium red onions, chopped
1 tablespoon fresh ginger paste (page 12)
1 tablespoon fresh garlic paste (page 12)
3 or 4 green chiles, stemmed and chopped
14 ounces (400 grams) ground lamb
2 teaspoons ground coriander
1 teaspoon red chile powder
4 medium tomatoes, chopped
½ teaspoon black salt
1 teaspoon table salt
2 tablespoons chopped fresh cilantro

1. Clean, wash, and boil the liver in 3 cups (600 ml) water with 1 teaspoon of the turmeric for 5 minutes. Drain and let cool. Chop the liver into ½-inch (1-cm) pieces.

2. Place a heavy-bottomed sauté pan over medium heat and add the butter. When small bubbles appear at the bottom of the pan, add the cumin. When the seeds begin to change color, add the onions and cook, stirring continuously, for 5 to 6 minutes or until the onions are golden brown. Add the ginger paste, garlic paste, and chiles. Cook for 30 seconds.

3. Add the ground lamb and increase the heat to high. Cook, stirring frequently, until the lamb is nicely browned. Lower the heat to medium, add the coriander, the remaining 1 teaspoon turmeric, and the chile powder, and cook for 1 minute or until the spices are roasted well. Add the tomatoes and cook until the fat separates and becomes visible along the edges of the lamb.

4. Add the liver and 1 cup (200 ml) water. Bring to a boil, lower the heat to low, and simmer for 15 to 20 minutes or until the lamb and liver are cooked through.

5. Add the black salt, table salt, and half of the cilantro. Cook for 3 to 4 minutes, stirring frequently.

6. Garnish with the remaining cilantro and serve hot.

Kheema Matar

········❀⟩ **Ground lamb and green peas cooked with spices** ⟨❀·······································

I like to serve this with warm bread—a flatbread like *roti* (page 18) or *naan* (page 20)—and a side of onions doused in lemon and salt. A perfect meal for a lazy Sunday.

Serves 4.

½ cup (75 grams) green peas
2 tablespoons vegetable oil
2 medium red onions, chopped
1 teaspoon fresh garlic paste (page 12)
1 teaspoon fresh ginger paste (page 12)
1 pound (500 grams) ground lamb
2 green chiles, stemmed and minced
1 teaspoon ground coriander
1 teaspoon ground roasted cumin (page 32)
¾ teaspoon red chile powder
3 medium tomatoes, puréed
3 tablespoons chopped fresh cilantro
1½ teaspoons table salt
1 teaspoon *garam masala* (spice mix; page 27)
1½ tablespoons freshly squeezed lemon juice

1. Place a medium nonstick saucepan over medium heat. Add 2 cups (400 ml) water and bring to a boil. Add the peas and blanch them for 2 to 3 minutes. Drain in a colander. Refresh the peas with cold water and set aside in a small bowl.

2. Place a medium nonstick saucepan over medium heat and add the oil. Add the onions and sauté until they are lightly browned. Add the garlic paste and ginger paste, and sauté for 1 minute.

3. Add the lamb, chiles, coriander, cumin, and chile powder, and stir-fry for 5 minutes, breaking up any lumps. Add the tomatoes and sauté for 3 minutes.

4. Add ¾ cup (150 ml) water and bring to a boil. Cover, reduce the heat to low, and simmer for 30 minutes.

5. Add the blanched peas, cilantro, salt, *garam masala*, and lemon juice, and stir for 2 minutes. Add ½ cup (100 ml) water and stir well. Cover and simmer for about 10 minutes or until the peas are cooked well.

6. Transfer to a serving dish. Serve hot.

Kheema Par Eeda

·······**{** Eggs cooked on a bed of spicy ground lamb **}**·······

Give yourself time to savor this dish: The slightly runny yolk along with a bit of spicy meat spooned onto a warmed *roti* (page 18) is just heavenly. You could also serve the *kheema* with steamed rice.

Serves 4.

2 medium tomatoes, chopped
4 green chiles, stemmed and seeded
2½ tablespoons ghee (page 37)
1-inch (2½-cm) piece fresh ginger, chopped
6 cloves garlic, chopped
2 medium red onions, chopped
1 teaspoon ground turmeric
1 tablespoon ground roasted cumin (page 32)
1½ teaspoons red chile powder
1½ teaspoons plus ⅛ teaspoon table salt
1 pound (500 grams) ground lamb
1½ teaspoons sugar
2 tablespoons distilled white vinegar
4 small eggs
⅛ teaspoon ground black pepper
2 tablespoons chopped fresh cilantro

1. Put the tomatoes and chiles in a blender and blend to a smooth paste. Transfer to a bowl and set aside.

2. Place a nonstick saucepan over medium heat and add the ghee. When small bubbles appear at the bottom of the pan, add the ginger and garlic, and sauté for 1 minute. Add the onions and sauté for 2 minutes or until the onions are lightly colored. Add the turmeric, cumin, and chile powder, and stir. Add the tomato-chile paste and 1½ teaspoons of the salt, and sauté until the ghee comes to the top.

3. Add the lamb and sauté for 2 to 3 minutes. Add 1 cup (200 ml) water and stir. When the water comes to a boil, cover and cook for 15 minutes.

4. Add the sugar and vinegar, stir well, and cook for 5 more minutes or until the lamb is cooked through.

5. Break 1 egg at a time over the lamb mixture, spacing them evenly and keeping the yolks intact.

6. Sprinkle the remaining ⅛ teaspoon salt and the black pepper over the eggs, cover, lower the heat, and cook for 4 to 5 minutes or until the egg whites are set.

7. Sprinkle with the cilantro and serve hot.

Khichra

Khichdi is a simple dish of rice, *dals*, and sometimes vegetables that inspired the Anglo-Indian dish kedgeree. This dish from Hyderabad is the father of all *khichdis*, and features rice, *dals*, lamb or goat, and broken wheat with an array of spices. Nutritious to the core, this one-dish meal warrants a good postfeast nap!

Serves 4.

2 tablespoons *masoor dal* (split red lentils)
2 tablespoons *toor dal/arhar dal* (split pigeon peas)
2 tablespoons *chana dal* (split Bengal gram)
2 tablespoons *dhuli moong dal* (split skinless green gram)
½ cup (100 grams) *lapsi* (fine broken wheat)
¼ cup (50 grams) basmati rice
6 tablespoons vegetable oil
4 medium red onions, peeled and sliced
4 whole cloves
6 green cardamom pods
2-inch (5-cm) cinnamon stick
2 teaspoons fresh ginger paste (page 12)
2 teaspoons fresh garlic paste (page 12)
14 ounces (400 grams) boneless lamb, cut into ½-inch (1-cm) pieces
2½ teaspoons table salt
2 teaspoons red chile powder
½ teaspoon ground turmeric
2 tablespoons chopped fresh mint
2 tablespoons chopped fresh cilantro
2 tablespoons freshly squeezed lemon juice

~ For the tempering:
2 teaspoons ghee (page 37)
1 teaspoon red chile powder
1 teaspoon *garam masala* (spice mix; page 27)

~ For garnish:
A few sprigs fresh mint
4 green chiles, stemmed and slit
3 lemons, cut into wedges

1. Put the *dals* in a large bowl, wash in plenty of water 2 or 3 times, and drain. Add 3 cups (600 ml) water and soak for 2 hours. Drain and set aside.

2. Soak the *lapsi* in a separate bowl in 1½ cups (300 ml) water for 1 hour.

3. Wash and soak the rice in another bowl in 1 cup (200 ml) water for 30 minutes. Drain and set aside.

4. Place a medium nonstick sauté pan over medium heat and add 2 tablespoons of the oil. When small bubbles appear at the bottom of the pan, add the onions and sauté for 5 to 6 minutes or until golden brown. Set aside.

5. Place a nonstick saucepan over medium heat and add the remaining 4 tablespoons oil. Add the cloves, cardamom, and cinnamon, and sauté until fragrant. Add the ginger paste and garlic paste, and sauté until the raw flavors disappear.

6. Add the lamb and sauté until browned. Add half of the sautéed onions and stir to combine. Add the salt, chile powder, and the drained *dals*. Sauté for 2 to 3 minutes.

7. Add the *lapsi* and turmeric, and stir.

8. Add 5 cups (1 liter) water. Increase the heat to high, cover, and bring to a boil. Lower the heat to medium and simmer for about 1 hour or until all the *dals*, the *lapsi*, and the lamb are completely cooked.

9. Add the rice and cook for 30 minutes. Continue stirring and adding up to 2 cups (400 ml) water as the mixture becomes dry.

10. When the rice is cooked, mash the mixture with the back of a ladle to make a porridgelike consistency.

11. Add the mint, cilantro, and lemon juice, and stir. Set the *khichra* aside.

12. Make the tempering: Place a small nonstick sauté pan over medium heat and add the ghee. When the ghee melts and small bubbles appear at the bottom of the pan, remove from the heat and add the chile powder and *garam masala*. Add this immediately to the *khichra* and cover the pan to trap the flavors. Let stand for about 5 minutes.

13. Stir and transfer to a serving dish. Garnish with the mint sprigs, the remaining sautéed onions, the chiles, and lemon wedges. Serve hot.

Kolhapuri Pandhra Rassa

{ Lamb-flavored curry }

Kolhapur, an ancient city in southwest Maharashtra, boasts a bold and aromatic cuisine. Some of the most famous Kolhapuri dishes are meat preparations, including *sukka* lamb (page 378), *tambda rassa* (red lamb curry), and the recipe here.

Serves 4.

1 tablespoon sesame seeds
2 tablespoons white poppy seeds
¾ cup (90 grams) grated fresh coconut (or frozen unsweetened coconut)
2 medium red onions, quartered
1-inch (2½-cm) piece fresh ginger
6 to 8 cloves garlic
¼ cup (50 ml) vegetable oil
Pinch of freshly grated nutmeg
1-inch (2½-cm) cinnamon stick
4 or 5 green cardamom pods
1 black cardamom pod
5 or 6 whole cloves
1 blade mace
2 bay leaves
2 green chiles, stemmed and slit
5 cups (1 liter) lamb stock (page 35)
1 teaspoon table salt
1 tablespoon ground white pepper
A few sprigs fresh cilantro, finely chopped

1. Place a small nonstick sauté pan over medium heat. Add the sesame seeds and dry-roast for 2 to 3 minutes. Transfer to a small bowl and set aside to cool.

2. Put the poppy seeds in a small bowl, add ¼ cup (50 ml) warm water, and soak for 15 to 20 minutes. Drain in a fine sieve.

3. Place a small nonstick saucepan over medium heat and add ½ cup (100 ml) water. Add the roasted sesame seeds and the soaked poppy seeds. Boil for 2 to 3 minutes. Drain in a fine sieve and set aside to cool. Transfer to a food processor. Add the coconut and 5 tablespoons (75 ml) water, and process to a fine paste. Transfer the paste to a small bowl and set aside.

4. Place a deep nonstick saucepan over medium heat, add 1 cup (200 ml) water, and bring to a boil. Add the onions and boil for 3 to 4 minutes. Drain in a colander, transfer to a spice grinder, and grind to a fine paste. Transfer the paste to a small bowl and set aside.

5. Put the ginger and garlic and 1 tablespoon water in a spice grinder, and grind to a fine paste. Transfer to a small bowl and set aside.

6. Place a nonstick saucepan over medium heat and add the oil. When small bubbles appear at the bottom of the pan, add the nutmeg, cinnamon, green cardamom, black cardamom, cloves, mace, and bay leaves. Sauté for 1 minute.

7. When the spices change color and are fragrant, add the onion paste and sauté over medium heat, stirring continuously, for 5 to 6 minutes or until most of the moisture has evaporated but the onions are not browned.

8. Add the ginger-garlic paste and green chiles, and cook for 30 seconds. Add the sesame–poppy seed–coconut paste and cook for 3 to 4 minutes, stirring continuously.

9. Add the stock and increase the heat to high. When the mixture comes to a boil, lower the heat to medium and simmer for 3 to 4 minutes. Stir the white pepper into 1 tablespoon water and add it to the pan. Add the salt and stir well. Simmer for 10 to 15 minutes.

10. Garnish with the cilantro and serve hot.

Kolhapuri Sukka Lamb

·······❧ **Spicy coconut lamb** ☙·······

Most lamb dishes from the city of Kolhapur, in the Indian state of Maharashtra, lean heavily toward the fiery end of the heat spectrum. They mostly use *sankeshwari* chiles or *lavangi* chiles, which have quite a bite. However, if you cannot lay your hands on either of those varieties, use any red chile powder. Here we have used *bedgi* chile powder, which is slightly less spicy than cayenne but lends a beautiful red color to the dish.

Serves 4.

1¾ pounds (800 grams) bone-in lamb, cut into 12 pieces
2 teaspoons table salt
½ teaspoon ground turmeric
1¼ cups (100 grams) grated dried unsweetened coconut
5 medium red onions
¼ cup (50 ml) plus 1 quart (800 ml) vegetable oil
1 tablespoon fresh ginger paste (page 12)
1 tablespoon fresh garlic paste (page 12)
4 medium tomatoes, chopped
1 tablespoon red chile powder, preferably *bedgi* (see Note page 234)
½ teaspoon ground green cardamom
1 teaspoon *garam masala* (spice mix; page 27)

1. Put the lamb in a large bowl, add 1 teaspoon of the salt and the turmeric, and stir well. Set aside for 20 minutes.

2. Place a nonstick saucepan over high heat and add 3 cups (600 ml) water. Add the lamb. When the water comes to a boil, lower the heat to low, cover, and cook for 45 minutes or until the lamb is cooked through.

3. Uncover, increase the heat to high, and cook until the water is reduced to about 1 cup (200 ml). Drain in a colander set over a large bowl (reserve the stock), then transfer to a large bowl and set aside.

4. Place a medium nonstick sauté pan over medium heat. Add the coconut and dry-roast until light golden brown, stirring continuously to ensure that it does not burn. Transfer to a small bowl and set aside to cool.

5. Slice half of the onions and chop the rest.

6. Place a nonstick wok over high heat and add 1 quart (800 ml) oil. When small bubbles appear at the bottom of the wok, add the sliced onions and cook, stirring with a slotted spoon from time to time, until crisp and golden brown. Remove with the slotted spoon and drain on paper towels. Set aside to cool.

7. Transfer the coconut and browned onions to a food processor and add ½ cup (100 ml) warm water. Process to a fine paste.

8. Place a nonstick saucepan over medium heat and add the remaining ¼ cup (50 ml) oil. When small bubbles appear at the bottom of the pan, add the chopped onions and sauté until golden brown. Add the ginger paste and garlic paste, and sauté for 1 minute. Add the tomatoes and sauté for 5 minutes.

9. Add the chile powder and the coconut-onion paste and cook over high heat for 8 minutes or until the oil comes to the top.

10. Add the lamb and the remaining 1 teaspoon salt. Cook, stirring, for 2 minutes. Add the reserved stock and cook, stirring continuously, for 10 minutes or until the sauce is thick and the lamb is well coated.

11. Sprinkle with the cardamom and *garam masala*. Serve hot.

Laal Maas

Laal means "red" and *maas* means "meat." But do not be tempted to make it too red by using more chiles—it has plenty already (though some of my chile-loving friends would probably use more). Serve with steamed rice.

Serves 4.

1 teaspoon cumin seeds
2 tablespoons coriander seeds
15 to 20 dried red chiles, stemmed and seeded
1 cup (250 grams) plain yogurt
¼ teaspoon ground turmeric
1 teaspoon table salt, or more if needed
1¾ pounds (800 grams) lamb leg, cut into 1-inch (2½-cm) pieces
¼ cup (50 grams) ghee (page 37)
1 bay leaf
2 black cardamom pods
4 green cardamom pods
2 (1-inch/2½-cm) cinnamon sticks
10 cloves garlic, sliced
4 medium onions, sliced
2 tablespoons chopped fresh cilantro

1. Place a medium nonstick sauté pan over medium heat. After 2 minutes, add the cumin and coriander, and dry-roast for 2 minutes or until fragrant. Transfer to a plate and set aside to cool.

2. Transfer to a spice grinder with the dried chiles and grind to a powder.

3. Put the yogurt in a medium bowl and add the ground cumin-coriander-chile mixture, the turmeric, and 1 teaspoon salt. Add the lamb and stir well. Cover the bowl with plastic wrap and put in the refrigerator for 30 minutes to marinate.

4. Place a medium nonstick saucepan over medium heat and add the ghee. When small bubbles appear at the bottom of the pan, add the bay leaf, black and green cardamom, and cinnamon, and sauté for 30 seconds or until fragrant. Add the garlic and sauté for 1 minute or until light golden. Add the onions and sauté for 8 minutes or until the onions are golden.

5. Add the lamb along with the marinade and sauté for 15 minutes.

6. Add 2 cups (400 ml) water and bring to a boil. Lower the heat to low, cover tightly, and simmer, stirring occasionally, for 1 hour or until the lamb is tender. Adjust the seasoning.

7. Transfer to a serving dish, garnish with the cilantro, and serve immediately.

Lagan Ka Kheema

······{ A ground lamb or goat dish served during weddings }·········

The Parsi community is small in India, but their cuisine has some big stories to tell. The multicourse formal dinners at weddings feature *saas ni machchi* (pomfret in sweet-and-sour sauce) or the famous banana leaf–wrapped fish called *patrani machchi*, along with this festive ground-lamb dish smoked with charcoal, a kebab-studded goat *pulao*, and a thick *dal*. The meal would end with *kulfi* or *lagan nu* custard (a close cousin of crème caramel).

Serves 4.

1 quart (800 ml) vegetable oil
4 medium red onions, sliced
2 tablespoons white poppy seeds
2 tablespoons *chironji/charoli* (melon seeds)
¼ cup grated dried coconut
15 whole cloves
2 (1-inch/2½-cm) cinnamon sticks
8 green cardamom pods
4 black cardamom pods
8 to 10 saffron threads
2 tablespoons warm milk
¼ cup (50 grams) ghee (page 37)
1½ teaspoons caraway seeds
2 tablespoons fresh ginger paste (page 12)
2 tablespoons fresh garlic paste (page 12)
4 teaspoons ground coriander
1½ teaspoons ground roasted cumin (page 32)
1 tablespoon red chile powder
1 pound (500 grams) ground lamb or goat
1¼ teaspoons table salt
1 cup (250 grams) plain yogurt, whisked
¼ cup (15 grams) chopped fresh cilantro
¼ cup (15 grams) chopped fresh mint, plus 2 sprigs for garnish
2 tablespoons freshly squeezed lemon juice
1 onion skin
1 lemon, cut into wedges

1. Place a nonstick wok over medium heat and add the oil. When small bubbles appear at the bottom of the wok, add the onions and cook, stirring with a slotted spoon, for 7 to 8 minutes or until they are golden and crisp. Remove with the slotted spoon, drain on paper towels, and set aside to cool completely.

2. Transfer to a food processor and process into a smooth paste. Transfer to a small bowl and set aside.

3. Place a small nonstick sauté pan over medium heat and add the poppy seeds, melon seeds, and coconut, and dry-roast until lightly browned. Transfer to a plate and set aside to cool completely. Transfer to a spice grinder, add ¼ cup (50 ml) water, and grind to a smooth paste.

4. Return the pan to medium heat, add 5 of the cloves, the cinnamon, green cardamom, and black cardamom, and dry-roast until lightly colored. Transfer to a plate and set aside to cool completely. Transfer to a spice grinder and grind to a fine powder.

5. Combine the saffron with the warm milk in a small bowl.

6. Place a heavy-bottomed nonstick sauté pan over medium heat and add 3 tablespoons of the ghee. When small bubbles appear at the bottom of the pan, add the caraway seeds, ginger paste, and garlic paste, and sauté for 2 to 3 minutes or until the raw flavors disappear. Add the browned onion paste and sauté for 1 minute.

7. Add the coriander, cumin, and chile powder, and sauté for 2 to 3 minutes.

8. Add the meat and sauté over low heat, stirring continuously. Add the poppy seed paste. Cook for 4 to 5 minutes. Add the salt and stir.

9. Add the yogurt and simmer for 4 to 5 minutes. Add the cilantro and chopped mint, stir, and cook for 2 minutes. Add 1 cup (200 ml) water and cook for 30 minutes.

10. Add the roasted spice powder and stir well. Add the lemon juice and stir. Check for seasoning and remove from the heat.

11. Push the meat to the sides of the pan and make a hollow in the center. Place an onion skin in the center like a bowl. Hold a piece of natural charcoal with tongs and heat it over an open flame until red hot. Place the hot charcoal in the onion skin. Pour the remaining 1 tablespoon ghee over the charcoal and place the remaining 10 cloves over it. Cover immediately and set aside for 5 minutes so that the flavors are well absorbed. Uncover, remove the onion skin and charcoal, and transfer the meat to a serving dish.

12. Garnish with mint sprigs and lemon, and serve hot.

Maamsam Koora

This Andhra-style curry has to be one of the greatest lamb curries ever. It has the perfect blend of spices, and despite the quantity of black pepper used, it is not too spicy.

Serves 4.

14 ounces (400 grams) boneless lamb, cubed
2 teaspoons table salt
¼ teaspoon ground turmeric
1 teaspoon poppy seeds
½ teaspoon fennel seeds
4 whole black peppercorns
1 teaspoon coriander seeds
1 teaspoon cumin seeds
1-inch (2½-cm) cinnamon stick
2 whole cloves
2 green cardamom pods
¼ cup (50 ml) vegetable oil
10 fresh curry leaves
3 medium red onions, chopped
1 teaspoon fresh ginger-garlic paste (page 13)
½ teaspoon red chile powder
2 teaspoons ground black pepper
1 large tomato, chopped
2 tablespoons chopped fresh cilantro

1. Place a nonstick saucepan over high heat. Add the lamb and 3 cups (600 ml) water, 1 teaspoon of the salt, and the turmeric. Bring to a boil, then lower the heat to low, cover, and cook for about 45 minutes. Drain in a colander set over a large bowl; reserve the stock.

2. Place a small nonstick sauté pan over medium heat. Add the poppy seeds, fennel, peppercorns, coriander, cumin, cinnamon, cloves, and cardamom and dry-roast for 2 to 3 minutes or until fragrant. Set aside to cool. Transfer to a spice grinder and grind to a fine powder. Set aside.

3. Place a nonstick saucepan over medium heat and add the oil. When small bubbles appear at the bottom of the pan, add the curry leaves and onions. Sauté until the onions are browned. Add the ginger-garlic paste, chile powder, and 1 teaspoon of the ground black pepper, and sauté for 1 minute.

4. Add the tomato and the lamb, increase the heat to high, and cook for 5 minutes or until the tomato is soft.

5. Lower the heat to medium, add the remaining 1 teaspoon salt and the ground spices, and simmer for 5 minutes. Add the reserved stock and 1½ cups (300 ml) water and bring to a boil. Cover and simmer for 10 to 15 minutes or until the lamb is well coated with thick sauce.

6. Add the remaining 1 teaspoon ground black pepper and stir well.

7. Transfer to a serving dish, garnish with the cilantro, and serve hot.

Malvani Lamb

......·⁎⦃ **Lamb or goat dish with roasted spices** ⦄⁎··

Malvani food uses the roasting of spices to good effect. Roasting not only releases the aromatic oils in the spices but also gives a well-rounded finish to the sauce. This dish is full flavored and goes well with steamed rice.

Serves 4.

1¾ pounds (800 grams) bone-in lamb or goat, cut into 1-inch (2½-cm) cubes
1½ teaspoons table salt
1½ tablespoons fresh ginger paste (page 12)
1½ tablespoons fresh garlic paste (page 12)
12 dried red chiles, stemmed and broken in half
1 tablespoon coriander seeds
6 to 8 whole cloves
7 or 8 whole black peppercorns
¾ teaspoon cumin seeds
¾ teaspoon caraway seeds
6 green cardamom pods
4 black cardamom pods
¾ cup (60 grams) grated dried coconut
1½ teaspoons white poppy seeds
5 tablespoons vegetable oil
4 medium red onions, thinly sliced
¾ teaspoon ground turmeric
2 tablespoons chopped fresh cilantro

1. Put the meat in a bowl, add the salt, ginger paste, and garlic paste, and combine well. Cover the bowl with plastic wrap and put in the refrigerator to marinate for 30 minutes.

2. Place a nonstick sauté pan over medium heat and roast, one at a time, the chiles, coriander seeds, cloves, peppercorns, cumin, caraway, green and black cardamom, coconut, and poppy seeds. Transfer to a plate and set aside to cool completely. Transfer to a spice grinder and grind to a fine powder.

3. Place a heavy-bottomed nonstick sauté pan over medium heat and add the oil. When small bubbles appear at the bottom of the pan, add the onions and sauté for 5 minutes or until light golden brown.

4. Add the meat and turmeric, and sauté for 15 minutes. Add 5 cups (1 liter) water and stir. Cover and cook over low heat for 50 minutes or until the meat is tender.

5. Add the ground spices and stir well. Add ½ cup (100 ml) water and simmer for 5 minutes.

6. Garnish with the cilantro and serve hot.

Mangshor Curry

······⁂{ **Bengali lamb curry** }⁑··

While Bengalis are known for their amazing fish curries, their lamb curries are excellent too. This recipe uses only the basic ingredients, but the result is wholesome and steeped in flavor. Serve with *luchi* (page 19) or steamed rice.

Serves 4.

14 ounces (400 grams) bone-in lamb, cut into 1-inch (2½-cm) pieces
2 teaspoons fresh ginger paste (page 12)
1½ teaspoons fresh garlic paste (page 12)
1½ teaspoons red chile powder
1 teaspoon ground roasted cumin (page 32)
½ teaspoon ground turmeric
1 teaspoon table salt
6 tablespoons vegetable oil
5 medium potatoes, cut into 1-inch (2½-cm) cubes
2 bay leaves
4 medium red onions, sliced

1. Put the lamb in a large bowl.

2. Add the ginger paste, garlic paste, chile powder, cumin, turmeric, and salt, and stir well. Cover the bowl with plastic wrap and set aside for 20 minutes.

3. Place a nonstick saucepan over medium heat and add the oil. When small bubbles appear at the bottom of the pan, add the potatoes and sauté for 5 minutes or until lightly browned. Remove with a slotted spoon and place in a bowl.

4. To the oil remaining in the pan, add the bay leaves and onions, and sauté for 3 to 4 minutes or until the onions are golden brown. Increase the heat to high, add the lamb, and sauté for 5 minutes. Add 2 cups (400 ml) water and the sautéed potatoes, and stir. When the water comes to a boil, lower the heat to low, cover, and cook for 45 minutes or until the lamb is cooked through and tender.

5. Serve hot.

Lamb Do Pyaza

······❋{ **Lamb cooked with plenty of onions** }❋······

In this dish, lamb is cooked with loads of onions prepared in different styles. Some of the onions are cooked with ginger and garlic and the rest are browned to perfection.

Serves 8.

4 dried red chiles, stemmed and broken
8 medium red onions
6 green chiles, stemmed
1 cup (200 grams) ghee (page 37)
1 tablespoon cumin seeds
2 tablespoons freshly squeezed lemon juice
2½ teaspoons table salt
2 green cardamom pods
2 whole cloves
1-inch (2½-cm) cinnamon stick
1 tablespoon fresh garlic paste (page 12)
1 tablespoon fresh ginger paste (page 12)
1¾ pounds (800 grams) lamb chops
2 tablespoons ground coriander
1½ teaspoons red chile powder
1 teaspoon ground turmeric
1 cup (250 grams) plain yogurt
1 teaspoon *garam masala* (spice mix; page 27)
2 tablespoons chopped fresh cilantro

1. Put the red chiles in a bowl and soak in ½ cup (100 ml) hot water for 20 minutes. Drain well.

2. Slice 5 of the onions and dice the remaining 3.

3. Chop 2 of the green chiles and slit the remaining 4.

4. Place a small nonstick sauté pan over medium heat and add 1 tablespoon of the ghee. When it melts, add the slit green chiles and sauté for 1 minute. Drain and set aside.

5. Put the cumin and soaked red chiles with 1 tablespoon of the lemon juice in a spice grinder or a mini food processor and grind to a paste. Transfer to a bowl and stir in 1 teaspoon of the salt. Rub the paste all over the lamb chops, cover with plastic wrap, and put in the refrigerator to marinate for 1 hour.

6. Place a nonstick sauté pan over medium heat and add the remaining ghee. When small bubbles appear at the bottom of the pan, add the diced onions and sauté for 3 to 4 minutes or until lightly browned. Remove with a slotted spoon, transfer to a bowl, and set aside to cool.

7. Pour the ghee through a strainer and return the ghee to the pan over medium heat. When small bubbles appear at the bottom of the pan, add the cardamom, cloves, and cinnamon and sauté for 30 seconds. Add the sliced onions and sauté for 6 to 8 minutes or until well browned.

8. Add the chopped green chiles, ginger paste, and garlic paste, and sauté for 2 minutes. Add the lamb chops and sauté, stirring continuously, for 5 to 6 minutes or until all the excess moisture evaporates.

9. Add the coriander, chile powder, turmeric, and the remaining 1½ teaspoons salt, and sauté for 2 minutes.

10. Add the yogurt and stir. Cover and cook for 30 to 40 minutes or until the meat is completely cooked and tender.

11. Add the sautéed diced onions and simmer for 10 minutes. Add the *garam masala* and cilantro, and stir.

12. Transfer to a serving bowl and serve hot.

Lamb Ishtew

·······⟨ **A Kerala-style lamb stew** ⟩·······

For a long time the list of foods people associated with South India didn't extend beyond the typical *dosas* and *idlis* (served in most South Indian restaurants worldwide), but today the rich tapestry of the south is gaining wider recognition as more people become aware of the differences between the various regional cuisines of South India. This mildly spiced curry, replete with coconut, is a fine example of Kerala's diverse cuisine. Serve it with *appams* (page 14).

Serves 4.

5 or 6 whole black peppercorns
¼ teaspoon cumin seeds
2 teaspoons *chana dal* (split Bengal gram)
½ teaspoon coriander seeds
1¾ pounds (800 grams) bone-in lamb, preferably from the leg, cut into 1½-inch (4-cm) pieces
¼ cup (50 ml) vegetable oil
2 star anise
1-inch (2½-cm) cinnamon stick
4 green cardamom pods
2 medium potatoes, each cut into 6 to 8 pieces
10 to 12 fresh curry leaves
4 or 5 green chiles, stemmed and slit
2 cups (400 ml) coconut milk
1 teaspoon table salt

1. Place a nonstick griddle over medium heat, add the peppercorns, cumin, *dal*, and coriander, and dry-roast over medium heat for 3 to 4 minutes. Transfer to a plate and let cool completely. Transfer to a spice grinder and grind to a powder.

2. Place a nonstick saucepan over high heat and add 1 quart (800 ml) water. When it comes to a boil, add the lamb and lower the heat to medium. Cover and cook for 45 minutes, or until the lamb is cooked through. Drain in a colander set over a large bowl and set aside. Reserve the cooking water—lamb broth—for another use.

3. Place a heavy-bottomed nonstick sauté pan over medium heat and add the oil. When small bubbles appear at the bottom of the pan, add the star anise, cinnamon, and cardamom, and sauté for 15 seconds. Add the lamb, potatoes, curry leaves, and chiles. Sprinkle with the ground spices, stir, and cook, stirring continuously.

4. Pour ½ cup (100 ml) of the coconut milk in a cup and dilute it with ¾ cup (150 ml) water. Add to the lamb and bring to a boil. Lower the heat, cover, and cook over medium heat for 10 to 12 minutes or until the potatoes are almost cooked. Pour another ½ cup (100 ml) of the coconut milk in a cup and dilute with ½ cup (100 ml) water. Add to the lamb, cover, and cook for 7 minutes or until both the lamb and potatoes are tender.

5. Remove from the heat and stir in the remaining 1 cup (200 ml) coconut milk and the salt. Return to the heat and simmer for 2 to 3 minutes.

6. Serve hot.

Lamb Razala

Lamb, shallots, prunes, and nuts in a simple curry

This is the sort of lamb curry that you will find if you travel the byways of Hyderabad.

Serves 4.

14 ounces (400 grams) boneless lamb, cut into 1½-inch (4-cm) cubes
1 tablespoon fresh ginger paste (page 12)
1 tablespoon fresh garlic paste (page 12)
1 cup (250 grams) plain yogurt
1½ teaspoons table salt
¼ cup (50 ml) vegetable oil
10 shallots, peeled
2 medium red onions, chopped
6 dried red chiles, stemmed
2 teaspoons ground coriander
1 teaspoon red chile powder
4 pitted prunes
5 pistachios, chopped
5 almonds, chopped
5 cashews, chopped

1. Put the lamb in a large bowl. Add the ginger paste, garlic paste, yogurt, and 1 teaspoon of the salt, and stir well. Cover the bowl with plastic wrap and put in the refrigerator to marinate for 1 hour.

2. Place a small nonstick sauté pan over medium heat and add 1 tablespoon of the oil. Add the shallots and sauté for 3 to 4 minutes. Set aside.

3. Place a nonstick saucepan over medium heat and add the remaining 3 tablespoons oil. When small bubbles appear at the bottom of the pan, add the onions and sauté for 5 to 6 minutes. Add the chiles and sauté for 30 seconds.

4. Add the coriander, chile powder, and the remaining ½ teaspoon salt, and stir. Add the lamb and sauté for 5 to 6 minutes or until the oil comes to the top.

5. Add the prunes, pistachios, almonds, and cashews, and stir. Add 3 cups (600 ml) water and bring to a boil. Cover and cook for 40 minutes or until the lamb is almost tender. Add the shallots and cook for 10 minutes or until the lamb is tender.

6. Serve hot.

Lamb Rogan Josh

······ ⋇⟨ Brilliant red lamb curry ⟩⋇ ·······

Rogan josh is a classic rich red curry from Kashmir. Here I present a modern version that is a top seller in our restaurants. Fragrant spices like fennel and ginger dominate and give the curry a touch of the exotic. Make sure you use good-quality meat with plenty of fat for this dish. The final look of the curry is eye-catching, with a thin film of oil on top. Serve it with steamed rice and *naan* (page 20) or *parathas* (page 18).

Serves 4.

∽ **For the garnish:**
1 quart (800 ml) vegetable oil
1 large red onion, sliced

∽ **For the curry:**
1¼ cups (250 ml) vegetable oil
20 green cardamom pods
8 whole cloves
6 black cardamom pods
1 teaspoon anise seeds
2 bay leaves
15 to 20 whole black peppercorns
11 large red onions, sliced
2 tablespoons ginger-garlic paste (page 13)
1¾ pounds (800 grams) bone-in lamb (preferably with shanks), cut into 1-inch (2½-cm) pieces
1 tablespoon table salt
2 tablespoons ground fennel seeds
1 teaspoon ground green cardamom
5 tablespoons red chile paste (see Note page 13)
1 cup (250 grams) plain yogurt
12 cups (2.5 liters) lamb stock (page 35)
2 teaspoons *garam masala* (spice mix; page 27)
4 teaspoons ground coriander
2 teaspoons ground roasted cumin (page 32)
Atta dough (whole-wheat flour dough; page 36)

1. Make the garnish: Place a nonstick wok over high heat and add the oil. When small bubbles appear at the bottom of the wok, lower the heat to medium, add the onion, and cook, stirring occasionally with a slotted spoon, until well browned. Remove with the slotted spoon and drain on paper towels. Set aside.

2. Make the curry: Place a nonstick saucepan with a tight-fitting lid over medium heat and add the oil. When small bubbles appear at the bottom of the pan, add the green cardamom pods, cloves, black cardamom, anise, bay leaves, and peppercorns, and sauté for 30 seconds or until fragrant.

3. Add the onions and sauté for 15 minutes or until tari. Add the ginger-garlic paste and sauté for 1 minute. Add the lamb and stir well.

4. Add the salt, fennel, ground cardamom, and chile paste, and stir. Sauté for 2 to 3 minutes, stirring so that all the lamb pieces are well coated.

5. Add the yogurt and stir. Cover and cook for 15 minutes.

6. Add the stock, *garam masala*, coriander, and cumin, and stir. Cover and seal the edges with *atta* dough or aluminum foil. Lower the heat to low and cook for 1 hour or until the lamb is tender.

7. Remove the lamb from the sauce and strain the liquid into another nonstick saucepan. Pick out and discard the cardamom pods, cloves, bay leaves, and peppercorns from the strainer, then transfer the remaining solids to a food processor. Process until smooth, and add to the pan with the liquid.

8. Return the lamb to the sauce and place the pan over medium heat. Simmer for 4 to 5 minutes.

9. Garnish with the browned onions and serve hot.

Nalli Nihari

····›{ Lamb shanks }‹··

Nihari means "fasting." This dish can be prepared at night so that it's ready to eat at the crack of dawn. This is especially handy during the month of Ramadan when Muslims eat this for their *sehri* before starting their day-long fast. The history of this dish reveals that it was a favorite breakfast of the Mughal royalty in Agra and that it was served with *roti*. It remains a favorite dish in the land of the Taj Mahal.

Serves 4.

1 quart (800 ml) vegetable oil
2 medium red onions, sliced
2 tablespoons ghee (page 37)
1¾ pounds (800 grams) lamb shanks
2½ tablespoons *nihari masala* (spice mix for *nihari*; page 29)
1½ teaspoons table salt
½-inch (1-cm) piece fresh ginger, julienned
2 tablespoons *atta* (whole-wheat flour)
1 teaspoon freshly squeezed lemon juice
2 tablespoons chopped fresh cilantro

1. Place a nonstick wok over high heat and add the oil. When small bubbles appear at the bottom of the wok, lower the heat to medium, add the onions, and cook, stirring constantly with a slotted spoon, until browned and crisp. Remove with the slotted spoon and drain on paper towels.

2. Place a nonstick saucepan over medium heat. Add the ghee and when small bubbles appear at the bottom of the pan, add the lamb and *nihari masala* and sauté for 8 minutes.

3. Add 6 cups (1.25 liters) water and 1 teaspoon of the salt. Cover and cook for 45 minutes or until the lamb is tender.

4. Add half of the browned onions and half of the ginger, and simmer for 2 minutes.

5. Combine the *atta* and 6 tablespoons (90 ml) water in a small bowl, ensuring that there are no lumps. Add to the lamb and simmer for 10 minutes or until the gravy thickens.

6. Add the remaining ½ teaspoon salt and the lemon juice, and stir.

7. Transfer to a serving dish, garnish with the remaining fried onions, the remaining ginger, and the cilantro, and serve hot.

Nawabi Korma

·······∗⟨ Lamb with dried fruit and nuts ⟩∗·······

Cooking meat or poultry with nuts and dried fruit is a fine example of the royal cuisine of India. Though it would probably be difficult to find food like this served on a regular basis at home, it is common at Indian weddings and parties. Serve it as part of a special meal for any big celebration.

Serves 4.

10 dried apricots, pitted
1½ cups (410 grams) plain Greek yogurt
½ teaspoon ground roasted cumin (page 32)
½ teaspoon ground turmeric
½ teaspoon ground black pepper
1½ teaspoons table salt
1-inch (2½-cm) piece fresh ginger, chopped
½ cup (60 grams) shaved fresh coconut
10 almonds, blanched and peeled (see Note page 40)
10 pistachios, blanched and peeled (see Note page 40)
14 ounces (400 grams) boneless leg of lamb, cut into 1½-inch (4-cm) cubes
Generous pinch of saffron threads
2 tablespoons lukewarm milk
5 whole cloves
3 or 4 green cardamom pods
1-inch (2½-cm) cinnamon stick
4 dried red chiles, stemmed and broken
1 blade mace
¼ teaspoon freshly grated nutmeg
2 teaspoons white poppy seeds
3 tablespoons ghee (page 37)
2 large red onions, diced

1. Soak the apricots in ½ cup (100 ml) water for 15 minutes. Drain and reserve the water. Chop the apricots roughly.

2. Put the yogurt in a large bowl. Add the cumin, turmeric, black pepper, and 1½ teaspoons of the salt, and whisk well.

3. Put the ginger, the apricots and their soaking water, the coconut, almonds, and pistachios in a food processor, and process to a smooth paste. Add to the yogurt mixture and stir well.

4. Add the lamb to the yogurt mixture and stir. Cover the bowl with plastic wrap and put in the refrigerator to marinate for 2 hours.

5. Combine the saffron and the lukewarm milk in a small bowl.

6. Place a nonstick sauté pan over medium heat and add the cloves, cardamom, cinnamon, chiles, mace, nutmeg, and poppy seeds, and dry-roast for 2 minutes or until fragrant. Set aside to cool completely. Transfer to a spice grinder and grind to a fine powder.

7. Place a nonstick sauté pan over medium heat and add the ghee. When the ghee melts and small bubbles appear at the bottom of the pan, add the onions and sauté for 8 minutes or until golden brown.

8. Add the lamb along with the marinade and cook over high heat until the mixture comes to a boil. Add the ground spices and stir well. Add 1 cup (200 ml) water and bring to a boil, lower the heat to low, cover, and simmer for 50 minutes or until the lamb is tender and the sauce is thick.

9. Add the saffron milk and simmer for 2 minutes.

10. Transfer to a serving bowl and serve hot.

Saag Wala Gosht

····§{ **Lamb with spinach and spices** }§····································

This is a popular dish in many restaurants. Frozen spinach can be substituted for fresh spinach, or you can use mustard greens.

Serves 4.

1¾ pounds (800 grams) bone-in lamb, cut into 1½-inch (4-cm) pieces
1-inch (2½-cm) cinnamon stick
6 green cardamom pods
2 black cardamom pods
4 whole cloves
¼ teaspoon ground turmeric
1½ teaspoons table salt
2 medium bunches spinach, stemmed
5 green chiles, stemmed
¼ cup (50 ml) vegetable oil
1 teaspoon cumin seeds
1 tablespoon fresh ginger paste (page 12)
1 tablespoon fresh garlic paste (page 12)
3 medium red onions, sliced
1-inch (2½-cm) piece fresh ginger, julienned

1. Put the lamb in a large bowl.

2. Place a nonstick saucepan over high heat and add 3 cups (600 ml) water. Add the cinnamon, green cardamom, black cardamom, cloves, turmeric, and 1 teaspoon of the salt, and bring to a boil. Add the lamb. Lower the heat to low, cover, and cook for 1 hour. Drain in a colander set over a large bowl; reserve the stock.

3. Place a medium nonstick saucepan over medium heat. Add 5 cups (1 liter) water. When the water comes to a boil, add the spinach and blanch for 1 to 2 minutes. Drain in a colander. Transfer to a food processor. Add the chiles and process to a smooth purée. Set aside.

4. Place a nonstick saucepan over medium heat and add the oil. When small bubbles appear at the bottom of the pan, lower the heat to low, add the cumin, ginger paste, and garlic paste, and sauté for 1 minute. Add the onions and sauté for 6 minutes or until the onions are well browned.

5. Add the lamb and half of the reserved stock. Stir well, cover, and cook for 15 minutes. Add the remaining stock and ½ teaspoon salt, and cook for 3 minutes.

6. Add the spinach purée, stir well, and bring to a boil.

7. Transfer to a serving dish, garnish with the julienned ginger, and serve hot.

Salli Ne Jardaloo Ma Gos

·······⊰ **A rich lamb curry with apricots, garnished with fried potato shreds** ⊱·······

The flavor of the apricot intensifies as it dries—it's sweet and tart. I suggest that you use small brown dried apricots for this recipe rather than pitted golden apricots.

Serves 4.

¾ cup (75 grams) dried apricots, with pits
2 tablespoons distilled white vinegar
2 tablespoons sugar
1¾ pounds (800 grams) boneless lamb, cut into 1½-inch (4-cm) cubes
2 teaspoons fresh ginger paste (page 12)
2 teaspoons fresh garlic paste (page 12)
1½ teaspoons table salt
¼ teaspoon ground turmeric
1 teaspoon red chile powder
2 tablespoons vegetable oil
5 green cardamom pods
1-inch (2½-cm) cinnamon stick
3 medium red onions, sliced
2 medium tomatoes, chopped
Potato *salli* (fried potato shreds; see Note)

1. Soak the apricots in ¾ cup (150 ml) water, the vinegar, and sugar until soft. Drain, reserving the liquid, and remove the pits.

2. Put the lamb in a large bowl, add the ginger paste, garlic paste, 1 teaspoon of the salt, the turmeric, and chile powder, and stir to coat. Cover the bowl with plastic wrap and put in the refrigerator to marinate for 1 hour.

3. Place a nonstick saucepan over medium heat and add the oil. When small bubbles appear at the bottom of the pan, add the cardamom and cinnamon, and sauté until fragrant.

4. Add the onions and sauté for 5 minutes or until lightly browned.

5. Add the lamb and sauté for 5 minutes. Add the tomatoes and sauté for 5 to 7 minutes or until they soften. Add the apricot-soaking liquid and 1 cup (200 ml) water, and stir. Cover and cook for 30 minutes.

6. Add the apricots and stir. Cover and cook for 30 minutes.

7. Transfer to a serving dish, garnish with the potato *salli*, and serve hot.

·······⊰ **Note** ⊱ To make potato *salli*, slice 2 small potatoes into thin rounds, then julienne the strips. Soak in salted water for 15 minutes. Drain and pat dry with an absorbent towel. Deep-fry in hot oil, stirring continuously, until golden and crisp. Remove with a slotted spoon and drain on paper towels.

Saoji Lamb

······❈{ **A spicy lamb curry** }❈······

In the heart of the state of Maharashtra lies the affluent city of Nagpur. It is often called the "Orange City," because it is a major trade center for oranges. Nagpur has many restaurants that serve the tribal Saoji cuisine, which leans toward thick curries. This lamb dish has a gravy that is best sopped up with little square freshly baked white breads called *pav*, or warm dinner rolls. Serve with steamed rice.

Serves 4.

6 tablespoons vegetable oil
6 medium onions, sliced
2 tablespoons coriander seeds
1 teaspoon caraway seeds
4 to 6 whole cloves
20 whole black peppercorns
3 or 4 green cardamom pods
4 or 5 black cardamom pods
2 (1-inch/2½-cm) cinnamon sticks
4 or 5 bay leaves
8 to 10 dried red chiles, stemmed
1 tablespoon poppy seeds
½ cup (40 grams) dried grated coconut
1 tablespoon *dagad phool* (lichen stone flower; optional; see Note)
1 tablespoon fresh ginger paste (page 12)
1 tablespoon fresh garlic paste (page 12)
1¾ pounds (800 grams) bone-in lamb, cut into 1½-inch (4-cm) pieces
1½ teaspoons table salt

1. Place a medium nonstick sauté pan over medium heat and add 4 tablespoons of the oil. When small bubbles appear at the bottom of the pan, add the onions, coriander, caraway, cloves, peppercorns, green cardamom, black cardamom, cinnamon, bay leaves, chiles, poppy seeds, coconut, and *dagad phool* (if using). Lower the heat to low and sauté for 10 minutes or until fragrant. Set aside to cool.

2. Transfer the cooled spices to a food processor with 1¾ cups (350 ml) water and process to a paste. Set aside.

3. Place a nonstick saucepan over medium heat and add the remaining 2 tablespoons oil. When small bubbles appear at the bottom of the pan, add the ginger paste and garlic paste, and sauté for 2 minutes. Add the onion-spice paste and sauté for 1 minute. Add the lamb and stir well. Sauté, stirring continuously, for 4 to 5 minutes. Add 3 cups (600 ml) water and the salt, and bring to a boil. Cover and cook, stirring from time to time, for 45 minutes or until the lamb is tender. Transfer to a serving bowl and serve hot.

······❈{ **Note** }❈ *Dagad phool* is a fungus that lends a dark color and musky flavor to dishes.

Shaan E Raan

This dish is very popular in restaurants in India. Choose a leg from a young lamb because the meat is tender and will cook faster.

Serves 6 to 8.

1 (3-pound/1.5-kg) whole leg of lamb, skinned, fat trimmed
2 tablespoons fresh garlic paste (page 12)
2 tablespoons fresh ginger paste (page 12)
1 tablespoon table salt
¼ teaspoon ground cinnamon
1 teaspoon ground green cardamom
¼ teaspoon ground cloves
1 teaspoon ground anise
1 tablespoon fresh green chile paste (page 13)
2 tablespoons fresh red chile paste (see Note page 13)
½ teaspoon ground turmeric
¼ teaspoon freshly grated nutmeg
½ cup (100 ml) vegetable oil
6 large red onions, chopped, plus 1 large red onion sliced into rings
4 large tomatoes, chopped
2 tablespoons ground coriander
1 tablespoon ground roasted cumin (page 32)
3 to 4 teaspoons red chile powder
½ tablespoon *garam masala* (spice mix; page 27)
1 cup (250 grams) plain yogurt, whisked
2 tablespoons chopped fresh cilantro
Sprig fresh mint

1. Trim the excess fat from the lamb and make small incisions all over the meat with a sharp knife.

2. Combine the garlic paste, ginger paste, 2 teaspoons of the salt, the cinnamon, cardamom, cloves, anise, green chile paste, red chile paste, turmeric, and nutmeg in a small bowl. Rub this mixture all over the lamb. Put the lamb on a rimmed baking sheet, cover with plastic wrap, and put in the refrigerator to marinate for at least 2 hours and up to overnight.

3. Preheat the oven to 350°F/175°C.

4. Place a medium nonstick saucepan over medium heat and add the oil. When small bubbles appear at the bottom of the pan, add the chopped onions and sauté for 9 to 10 minutes or until light golden.

5. Add the tomatoes and sauté for 10 minutes or until the oil comes to the top. Add the coriander, cumin, and chile powder, and sauté for 2 minutes. Add the *garam masala* and stir well. Stir in the yogurt, cilantro, and the remaining 1 teaspoon salt. Sauté for 1 minute, then remove from the heat and set aside.

6. Grease another rimmed baking sheet with nonstick cooking spray and place the marinated leg of lamb on it.

7. Pour the masala over the lamb. Cover with aluminum foil and roast for 1 hour. Lower the oven temperature to 325°F/160°C and continue to roast for 40 to 45 minutes or until tender.

8. Transfer the lamb to a serving platter. Cut into slices, garnish with the onion rings and mint, and serve hot.

Taar Korma

······ }{ Lamb in an almond-and-yogurt sauce }{ ························

This is an interesting mix: saffron and almonds that are reminiscent of Mughal cooking, and curry leaves with coconut milk, which are typical of South Indian cuisine.

Serves 4.

1 quart (800 ml) plus 6 tablespoons vegetable oil
3 large red onions, sliced
10 to 12 saffron threads
1 tablespoon warm milk
4 green cardamom pods
4 whole cloves
2-inch (5-cm) cinnamon stick
2 bay leaves
1²⁄₃ pounds (750 grams) lamb shoulder, cut into 1¹⁄₂-inch (4-cm) cubes
1¹⁄₂ teaspoons fresh garlic paste (page 12)
1 teaspoon fresh ginger paste (page 12)
1¹⁄₂ teaspoons table salt
¹⁄₂ cup (125 grams) plain yogurt, whisked
20 almonds, blanched and peeled (see Note page 40) and ground to a paste
¹⁄₄ cup red chile paste (see Note page 13)
1 teaspoon red chile powder
6 cups (1.2 liters) lamb stock (page 35)
10 black peppercorns, roasted and crushed
¹⁄₄ teaspoon ground green cardamom
¹⁄₄ teaspoon ground cloves
Pinch of ground mace
Pinch of freshly grated nutmeg
1 cup (200 ml) coconut milk
10 to 12 fresh curry leaves
2 green chiles, stemmed and slit

1. Place a nonstick wok over high heat and add 1 quart of the oil. When small bubbles appear at the bottom of the wok, lower the heat to medium and add the onions. Cook, stirring continuously with a slotted spoon, until browned and crisp. Remove with the slotted spoon, drain on paper towels, and set aside to cool. Transfer to a food processor, add 4 teaspoons water, and process to a paste.

2. Put the saffron in a small bowl and soak in the warm milk for 10 minutes. Transfer to a small mortar and crush the saffron threads with a pestle.

3. Place a nonstick sauté pan over medium heat and add 5 tablespoons of the oil. When small bubbles appear at the bottom of the pan, add the cardamom pods, whole cloves, cinnamon, and bay leaves, and sauté until they are lightly colored.

4. Add the lamb, increase the heat to high, and sauté for 2 minutes to sear it.

5. Lower the heat to medium, add the garlic paste, ginger paste, and salt, and sauté for 1 minute. Add ⅔ cup (135 ml) water, cover, and cook for 10 minutes.

6. Uncover and cook until the excess moisture has completely evaporated. Remove from the heat and stir in the yogurt. Return to the heat and sauté, stirring continuously, until the oil comes to the top.

7. Add the browned-onion paste, almond paste, and red chile paste, and sauté for 2 minutes. Add the chile powder and the stock. Stir and bring it to a boil. Cover and cook for 50 minutes or until the lamb is tender.

8. Add the crushed peppercorns, ground cardamom, ground cloves, mace, and nutmeg, and stir. Remove from the heat. Add the coconut milk and stir well.

9. Place a small nonstick sauté pan over medium heat and add the remaining 1 tablespoon oil. When small bubbles appear at the bottom of the pan, add the curry leaves and chiles, and sauté for 1 minute. Add to the lamb and stir well.

10. Serve hot.

Tariwala Meat

......⟨ **Lamb or goat in a thin sauce** ⟩..

This dish has been a favorite in my family ever since I can remember. The color is an appetizing deep red, and it is fun to mop up the spicy gravy with hot *rotis* (page 18). If we ran out of *rotis*, we would raid the bread box and continue eating the meat with regular bread.

Serves 4.

6 tablespoons vegetable oil
1-inch (2½-cm) cinnamon stick
2 green cardamom pods
2 black cardamom pods
6 whole black peppercorns
1 star anise
4 large red onions, sliced
2 bay leaves
1 tablespoon fresh ginger paste (page 12)
1 tablespoon fresh garlic paste (page 12)
2 large tomatoes, chopped
2 tablespoons red chile powder
2 teaspoons *garam masala* (spice mix; page 27)
1 tablespoon ground coriander
1¾ pounds (800 grams) bone-in lamb or goat, cut into 1-inch (2½-cm) pieces
2 cups (400 ml) lamb stock (page 35)
1 tablespoon table salt
2 large potatoes, cut into 1-inch (2½-cm) cubes

1. Place a nonstick sauté pan over medium heat and add the oil. When small bubbles appear at the bottom of the pan, add the cinnamon, green and black cardamom, peppercorns, and star anise, and sauté for 1 minute.

2. Add the onions and sauté for 4 minutes or until lightly browned. Add the bay leaves and sauté for 30 seconds.

3. Add the ginger paste and garlic paste, and stir. Add the tomatoes and sauté for 2 to 3 minutes.

4. Add the chile powder, *garam masala*, and coriander. Sauté for 3 to 4 minutes or until the oil comes to the top.

5. Add the meat and sauté for 7 to 8 minutes or until lightly browned.

6. Add the stock and salt, and stir. Cover and cook for 40 minutes.

7. Add the potatoes and simmer for 11 to 12 minutes or until the potatoes are tender and the sauce has thickened slightly. Serve hot.

Akhrot Murgh

······•§{ **Walnut chicken** }§•······

Indian cuisine uses lots of nuts and oily seeds. Typically, cashew paste is used to thicken and flavor curries, and almonds are used to garnish many sweet and savory dishes. This dish, an example of the royal cuisine of India, is a little different because it uses walnuts, which impart an especially strong nuttiness to the chicken.

Serves 4.

14 ounces (400 grams) boneless, skinless chicken, cut into ½-inch (1-cm) pieces
1 tablespoon fresh ginger paste (page 12)
1 tablespoon fresh garlic paste (page 12)
1½ teaspoons table salt
1 teaspoon ground roasted cumin (page 32)
¼ cup (60 grams) plain yogurt
½ cup (60 grams) walnuts
1 tablespoon vegetable oil
1 medium red onion, grated
1 large tomato, puréed
4 green chiles, stemmed and chopped
1 teaspoon ground coriander
2 tablespoons heavy cream
¼ teaspoon *garam masala* (spice mix; page 27)

1. Put the chicken in a large bowl. Add the ginger paste, garlic paste, salt, ½ teaspoon of the cumin, and the yogurt, and stir well. Cover the bowl with plastic wrap and set aside to marinate for 30 minutes.

2. Place a nonstick saucepan over medium heat and add 1½ cups (300 ml) water. Add the walnuts and boil for 3 minutes. Drain and peel them. Transfer to a spice grinder, add 2 tablespoons water, and grind to a coarse paste.

3. Place a nonstick sauté pan over medium heat and add the oil. When small bubbles appear at the bottom of the pan, add the onion and sauté for 2 to 3 minutes or until lightly browned.

4. Add the tomato, stir well, and sauté for 2 minutes or until the oil comes to the top.

5. Add the chiles and cook for 2 minutes. Add the coriander and the remaining ½ teaspoon cumin, and stir well. Cook for 1 minute.

6. Add the chicken and ¼ cup (50 ml) water, and stir well. Cover and cook for 5 to 6 minutes or until the chicken is cooked through.

7. Add the walnut paste and simmer for 2 to 3 minutes. Add the cream and *garam masala*, and stir well. Simmer for 2 minutes.

8. Transfer to a serving bowl and serve hot.

Anjeer Murgh

····•} Chicken with figs {•···

Dried figs, plums, and apricots were essential ingredients in the meat and poultry dishes made in the royal kitchens of India. While chicken takes especially well to figs, lamb is lovely with prunes and apricots.

Serves 4.

10 dried figs
1½-inch (4-cm) piece fresh ginger, chopped
6 cloves garlic, peeled
2 green chiles, stemmed and minced
1 cup (250 grams) plain yogurt
¼ cup finely ground cashews
1 teaspoon red chile powder
2 teaspoons ground coriander
1 teaspoon *garam masala* (spice mix; page 27)
2 tablespoons ground *dalia* (roasted *chana dal*, storebought)
2 teaspoons table salt
¼ cup (50 ml) vegetable oil
1 pound (500 grams) boneless, skinless chicken, cut into 1-inch (2½-cm) cubes
1 teaspoon caraway seeds
3 dried red chiles, stemmed and broken in half
1-inch (2½-cm) cinnamon stick
2 large red onions, diced
6 or 7 saffron threads
2 tablespoons heavy cream
Chandi ka varq (edible silver foil; see page 188)

1. Put the figs in a bowl and soak in 1 cup (200 ml) water for 30 minutes. Drain in a colander.

2. Put the ginger and garlic in a mini food processor with 2 tablespoons water, and process to a fine paste.

3. In a large bowl, combine the ginger-garlic paste, green chiles, yogurt, cashews, chile powder, coriander, *garam masala*, ground *dal*, salt, and 2 tablespoons of the oil, and stir well. Add the chicken and figs, and stir to coat. Cover the bowl with plastic wrap and put in the refrigerator to marinate for 1 hour.

4. Place a nonstick sauté pan over medium heat and add the remaining 2 tablespoons oil. When small bubbles appear at the bottom of the pan, add the caraway, red chiles, and cinnamon, and sauté until fragrant. Add the onions and sauté for 4 minutes or until golden brown.

5. Add the chicken and figs. Stir gently, increase heat to high, and cook for 3 minutes.

6. Add 2 cups (400 ml) water and the saffron. Stir well and cook for 5 minutes or until the liquid has thickened and the chicken is tender and cooked through. Stir in the cream.

7. Remove from the heat and transfer to a serving bowl. Garnish with the *chandi ka varq* and serve hot.

Bharwan Pistewala Murgh

······⊰ **Pistachio-stuffed chicken rolls with green sauce** ⊱······

Cook this when you are in the mood to have something exotic made with chicken. It is especially worth the effort when you want to present your guests with an elaborate dish at a party.

Serves 4.

½ small bunch fresh cilantro
2 medium red onions, roughly chopped
2-inch (5-cm) piece fresh ginger, roughly chopped
7 or 8 cloves garlic
2 or 3 green chiles, stemmed
½ cup (65 grams) pistachios, blanched and peeled (see Note page 40)
2 boneless, skinless chicken breasts
1½ teaspoons table salt
4 ounces (120 grams) ground chicken
1 teaspoon fresh green chile paste (page 13)
½ teaspoon ground green cardamom
3 tablespoons vegetable oil
1-inch (2½-cm) cinnamon stick
4 green cardamom pods
6 whole cloves
¼ cup (65 grams) plain yogurt, whisked
½ teaspoon *garam masala* (spice mix; page 27)
¼ cup (50 ml) heavy cream
1 fresh red chile, stemmed, thinly sliced on the diagonal

1. Put the cilantro, onions, ginger, garlic, green chiles, and 1 tablespoon of the pistachios in a food processor, and process to a fine paste. Transfer to a small bowl and set aside.

2. Trim off the excess fat from the chicken breasts. Using a sharp knife, split the chicken breasts horizontally from one side without cutting all the way through. Sprinkle with ½ teaspoon of the salt and rub it evenly over both sides of the breasts. Set aside for 15 minutes.

3. Put the ground chicken, the remaining pistachios, ½ teaspoon of the salt, the chile paste, and ground cardamom in a bowl, and stir well.

4. Open the split chicken breasts on a clean work surface. Using the back of the knife or a mallet, gently flatten the chicken breasts. Divide the stuffing evenly among the breasts, placing it in the center. Roll the chicken breasts into cylinders and wrap in aluminum foil.

5. Place a deep nonstick pan over high heat and add 2 cups (400 ml) water. When the water comes to a boil, lower the chicken cylinders into the water and poach for 2 to 3 minutes. Drain and set aside until cool enough to handle. Unwrap the rolls.

6. Place a medium nonstick sauté pan over medium heat. Add 2 tablespoons of the oil. When small bubbles appear at the bottom of the pan, add the chicken rolls. Increase the heat to high and cook for 2 minutes. Set aside.

7. Place a medium nonstick saucepan over medium heat. Add the remaining 1 tablespoon oil. When small bubbles appear at the bottom of the pan, add the cinnamon, cardamom pods, and cloves, and sauté until fragrant. Lower the heat to low, add the cilantro mixture, and sauté for 2 to 3 minutes. And 1 cup (200 ml) water and bring to a boil.

8. Add the yogurt and stir. Add the remaining ½ teaspoon salt and the *garam masala*, and cook for 3 to 4 minutes. Add the cream and stir. Remove from the heat and pour the sauce through a strainer into a bowl, discarding the solids.

9. Slice the chicken rolls on the diagonal. Pour the sauce onto a serving platter and arrange the chicken-roll slices over it. Garnish with red chile slices and serve hot.

Butter Chicken

······⊰ **Chicken in a rich tomato-and-cream gravy** ⊱·····················

Butter chicken is a popular Punjabi dish, and one that characterizes the essence of the region's cooking. The greatness of the dish, also called chicken *makhni*, comes from the immersion of roasted chicken in a curry that is as smooth as butter. This velvety texture, and the mingling of the sour and the sweet and the spices, is what gives the dish its name. Serve the chicken with fresh *naan* (page 20).

Serves 4.

14 ounces (400 grams) boneless chicken, cut into 1½-inch (4-cm) pieces
1 teaspoon red chile powder
1 tablespoon freshly squeezed lemon juice
½ teaspoon table salt

~ For the marinade:
½ cup (140 grams) Greek yogurt
2 teaspoons fresh ginger paste (page 12)
2 teaspoons fresh garlic paste (page 12)
½ teaspoon red chile powder
½ teaspoon *garam masala* (spice mix; page 27)
1 teaspoon table salt
2 teaspoons refined mustard oil (see Note page 87)

~ For roasting:
2 tablespoons butter, melted

~ For the sauce:
1 teaspoon *kasoori methi* (dried fenugreek leaves)
2 tablespoons butter
4 green cardamom pods
½ teaspoon ground mace
1 teaspoon red chile powder
5 cloves garlic, roughly chopped
½-inch (1-cm) piece fresh ginger, chopped
12 medium tomatoes, roughly chopped
1 teaspoon table salt
1 tablespoon honey
3 tablespoons plus 1 teaspoon heavy cream

1. Prick the chicken pieces all over with a fork. Put them in a large bowl and add the chile powder, lemon juice, and salt, and stir well. Cover the bowl with plastic wrap and put in the refrigerator for 30 minutes.

2. Make the marinade: Put the yogurt in a large bowl. Add the ginger paste, garlic paste, chile powder, *garam masala*, salt, and mustard oil, and stir well with a wooden spoon.

3. Add the chicken to this yogurt mixture and stir well to coat. Cover the bowl with plastic wrap and put in the refrigerator to marinate for 3 to 4 hours.

4. Roast the chicken: Preheat the oven to 400°F/200°C. Soak wooden skewers in water.

5. Thread the chicken pieces onto the wooden skewers, arrange them on a baking sheet, and bake for 10 to 12 minutes or until almost cooked through. Baste the chicken pieces with the butter and cook for 2 minutes more. Remove the chicken from the skewers onto a plate and set aside.

6. Make the sauce: Place a small nonstick sauté pan over medium heat. Add the *kasoori methi* and toss for 2 minutes to make it crisp. Transfer to a bowl and let cool, then crush it with your hand to a powder. Set aside.

7. Place a nonstick saucepan over low heat and add 1 tablespoon of the butter. When it melts, add the cardamom and mace, and cook until fragrant.

8. Stir the chile powder and 1 tablespoon water together to make a smooth paste. Add it to the pan and stir. Add the garlic, ginger, and tomatoes, and stir well. Cook for 20 minutes or until the tomatoes become pulpy.

9. Pour the mixture through a strainer into a bowl. Transfer the solids to a food processor and process until smooth. Strain into the bowl and discard any remaining solids in the strainer.

10. Place another nonstick saucepan over low heat and add the remaining 1 tablespoon butter. When it melts, add the strained mixture and cook, stirring occasionally, for 15 minutes.

11. Add the *kasoori methi* and cook for 5 minutes. Add the salt, honey, and cream, and stir well. Cook for 2 minutes.

12. Add the chicken pieces and cook for 3 minutes.

13. Serve hot.

Chandi Korma

........∗⟩ **Chicken cooked in a silvery gravy** ⟨∗........

Chandi means "silver," a reference to the rich and silky gravy that coats this chicken dish. The effect is enhanced by a layer of silver *varq*, or edible silver foil. It is a regal sight, indeed, one that pretties up many a party table in my home. Serve this with hot *parathas* (page 18).

Serves 4.

30 almonds, blanched and peeled (see Note page 40)
3 tablespoons *kharbooja* seeds (melon seeds)
1 tablespoon fresh ginger paste (page 12)
1 tablespoon fresh garlic paste (page 12)
1 (1¾-pound/800-gram) chicken, cut into 12 pieces
1 cup (250 grams) plain yogurt
1¼ teaspoons table salt
1 teaspoon ground white pepper
¾ teaspoon ground green cardamom
1½ teaspoons crushed dried untreated rose petals
¼ cup (50 grams) ghee (page 37)
3 medium red onions, chopped
2 or 3 green chiles, stemmed and crushed
½ cup (90 grams) grated *khoya/mawa* (solid unsweetened condensed milk; page 37)
20 pistachios, blanched and slivered (see Note page 40)
¼ cup (50 ml) heavy cream
Dash of rosewater
2 sheets of *chandi ka varq* (edible silver foil; see page 188)

1. Cut 15 of the almonds into slivers and set aside. Put the remaining 15 almonds in a spice grinder, grind to a smooth paste, and set aside in a small bowl.

2. Soak the melon seeds in ½ cup warm water for 15 minutes. Drain, put them in a spice grinder, and grind to a fine paste. Set aside.

3. In a large bowl, stir together the ginger paste, garlic paste, chicken, yogurt, 1 teaspoon of the salt, the white pepper, cardamom, and ½ teaspoon of the rose petals. Cover the bowl with plastic wrap and put in the refrigerator to marinate for 2 hours.

4. Place a nonstick saucepan over high heat and add the ghee. When small bubbles appear at the bottom of the pan, lower the heat to medium and add the onions. Sauté the onions for 3 to 4 minutes or until translucent.

5. Add the chiles and *khoya*, and sauté for 10 minutes.

6. Add the melon-seed paste and the almond paste, and sauté for 5 to 7 minutes, stirring continuously, over medium heat.

7. Add the chicken and sauté for 3 minutes over high heat. Add ¾ cup (150 ml) water and bring to a boil. Lower the heat to low and simmer for 10 minutes.

8. Add half of the slivered almonds and pistachios and ½ teaspoon of the rose petals, and stir. Cover and cook for 5 to 6 minutes or until the chicken is tender.

9. Add the cream and rosewater, and stir well.

10. Place the chicken pieces on a serving plate and spoon the sauce over them. Cover with the silver *varq* and garnish with the remaining rose petals and almond and pistachio slivers. Serve immediately.

Chettinadu Kozhi Sambhar

········{ Spicy chicken with *dal* }·····································

This is one of the curries that we enjoy at home with a bowl of brown rice, especially on a lazy Sunday. The kids get their chicken and my wife, Alyona, is satisfied that she has given them healthy lentils.

Serves 4.

1 (2-pound/1 kg) chicken, skinned and cut into 12 pieces
½ teaspoon ground turmeric
½ teaspoon table salt
¼ cup *toor dal/arhar dal* (split pigeon peas)
6 tablespoons (90 ml) sesame oil
1 tablespoon coriander seeds
½ teaspoon whole black peppercorns
1 tablespoon *chana dal* (split Bengal gram)
1-inch (2½-cm) piece fresh ginger
8 cloves garlic
8 dried red chiles, stemmed
4 green chiles, stemmed
2 star anise
4 whole cloves
2-inch (5-cm) cinnamon stick
10 to 12 fresh curry leaves
2 medium red onions, finely chopped
1 tablespoon tamarind pulp
2 tablespoons chopped fresh cilantro

1. Trim the excess fat from the chicken and put the pieces in a large bowl.

2. Add the turmeric and salt, and stir well. Cover the bowl with plastic wrap and put in the refrigerator to marinate for 3 hours.

3. Put the *toor dal* in a bowl, wash in plenty of water 2 or 3 times, and drain. Add 1 cup (200 ml) water and soak for 30 minutes. Drain the *dal* in a colander.

4. Place a medium nonstick saucepan over medium heat. Add 2 cups (400 ml) water and the soaked *dal*. When the water begins to boil, lower the heat to low, cover, and cook for 15 to 20 minutes or until the *dal* is soft and fully cooked. Transfer the *dal* and cooking water to a bowl, and set aside.

5. Place a medium nonstick sauté pan over medium heat. Add 2 tablespoons of the sesame oil. When small bubbles appear at the bottom of the pan, add the coriander, peppercorns, *chana dal*, ginger, garlic, 6 of the red chiles, and the green chiles, and sauté for 2 minutes or until lightly browned. Remove from the heat and let cool.

6. Transfer to a mini food processor with ¼ cup (50 ml) water, and process to a paste. Set aside.

7. Place a medium nonstick saucepan over medium heat and add the remaining 4 tablespoons sesame oil. When small bubbles appear at the bottom of the pan, add the star anise, cloves, cinnamon, remaining 2 red chiles, and the curry leaves, and cook, stirring, for 1 minute.

8. When the spices begin to change color and are fragrant, add the onions and fry until lightly browned. Add the marinated chicken pieces and stir again. Add the ground paste and sauté for 2 minutes, stirring to coat the chicken.

9. Add the tamarind pulp and stir. Cover and cook over low heat for 15 to 20 minutes or until the chicken is cooked through and tender.

10. Add the cooked *dal* and cooking water, and cook until the chicken and *dal* combine well and the mixture thickens to a curry consistency.

11. Transfer the curry to a serving dish. Garnish with the cilantro and serve hot.

Chicken Curry

····· ·{ Chicken cooked in a simple onion–tomato masala }· ·····

You will find this curry at practically all the *dhabas* (roadside eateries) in North India. Economical and tasty, this dish gives you a taste of simple Punjabi home cooking. Serve it with steamed rice, *parathas* (page 18), or *naan* (page 20).

Serves 4.

1 (1¾-pound/800-gram) chicken, skinned and cut into 12 pieces
¼ cup (50 ml) vegetable oil
1-inch (2½-cm) cinnamon stick
4 or 5 cloves
4 or 5 green cardamom pods
4 medium red onions, grated
1 tablespoon fresh ginger paste (page 12)
1 tablespoon fresh garlic paste (page 12)
½ teaspoon ground turmeric
1½ tablespoons ground coriander
1½ teaspoons ground roasted cumin (page 32)
1 teaspoon red chile powder
4 medium tomatoes, puréed
1½ teaspoons table salt
1 teaspoon *garam masala* (spice mix; page 27)
1 tablespoon chopped fresh cilantro

1. Trim the excess fat from the chicken and put the pieces in a large bowl.

2. Place a medium nonstick saucepan over medium heat and add the oil. When small bubbles appear at the bottom of the pan, add the cinnamon, cloves, and cardamom, and sauté for 1 minute. When the spices change color and are fragrant, add the onions and sauté for 3 to 4 minutes or until golden brown. Add the ginger paste and garlic paste, and sauté for 2 to 3 minutes, stirring continuously.

3. Add the turmeric, coriander, cumin, and chile powder. Stir well.

4. Add the tomatoes and sauté for 3 to 4 minutes, stirring continuously. Cook for 7 to 8 minutes or until the oil comes to the top.

5. Add the chicken and salt, and stir. Increase the heat to high and sauté for 5 minutes or until the chicken pieces are well coated with the sauce. Add 1½ cups (300 ml) water and bring to a boil. Lower the heat to low, cover, and cook for 10 minutes or until the chicken is cooked through.

6. Transfer to a serving bowl. Sprinkle with the *garam masala* and garnish with the cilantro. Serve hot.

Chicken Kandhari Kofta

····· ·❋❭ Ground-chicken balls in a pomegranate gravy ❬❋· ·····································

I have made this recipe for as long as I can remember and it is always a hit. An authentic Mughlai preparation, it sells like hotcakes in most good restaurants in New Delhi. The pomegranate syrup is the life and soul of the gravy. Serve with *naan* (page 20) or *parathas* (page 18).

Serves 4.

8 ounces (250 grams) ground chicken
½ teaspoon ground cinnamon
1½ teaspoons table salt
3 tablespoons vegetable oil
¾ cup (190 grams) boiled-onion paste (page 11)
½ tablespoon fresh ginger paste (page 12)
½ tablespoon fresh garlic paste (page 12)
1 teaspoon red chile powder
1 tablespoon ground coriander
⅔ cup (150 grams) cashew paste (page 12)
½ cup (120 grams) tomato purée
½ teaspoon *garam masala* (spice mix; page 27)
2 tablespoons pomegranate molasses
½ cup (100 ml) heavy cream

1. Put the chicken in a medium bowl, add the cinnamon and 1 teaspoon of the salt, and stir thoroughly. Divide into 8 equal portions and shape the mixture into balls. Place them on a platter, cover with plastic wrap, and put it in the refrigerator for 30 minutes.

2. Place a medium nonstick saucepan over high heat and add the oil. When small bubbles appear at the bottom of the pan, add the onion paste and sauté for 15 minutes or until light golden. Add the ginger paste and garlic paste and sauté for 1 minute. Add the chile powder and coriander, and sauté for 3 minutes.

3. Dilute the cashew paste in ¼ cup (50 ml) water and add it to the pan along with the tomato purée. Sauté over high heat, stirring constantly, for 5 minutes. Lower the heat to medium, add ½ cup water and the remaining ½ teaspoon salt, and bring to a boil. Add the chicken balls and cook for 10 minutes. Give it a gentle stir, cover, and cook for 5 minutes.

4. Add the *garam masala* and pomegranate molasses. Stir gently and check for seasoning. Simmer for 5 minutes. Stir in the cream and remove from the heat.

5. Transfer the curry to a serving dish and serve hot.

Chicken Xacuti

Rui Madre, a chef from Goa, taught me to make this extremely popular dish while I was in Varanasi. Rui now manages a hotel in Goa, and every time I visit, no matter where I am staying, I insist that he cook it for me. Serve with steamed rice.

Serves 4.

1 (1¾-pound/800-gram) chicken, skin removed, cut into 12 pieces on the bone
½ teaspoon ground turmeric
2 teaspoons table salt
1 tablespoon freshly squeezed lemon juice
⅓ cup (65 ml) plus 2 tablespoons oil
2 (1-inch/2½-cm) cinnamon sticks
6 whole cloves
4 dried red chiles, stemmed
2 tablespoons white poppy seeds
1 teaspoon *ajwain*
1 teaspoon cumin seeds
10 to 12 whole black peppercorns
1 teaspoon fennel seeds
4 star anise
1½ tablespoons coriander seeds
1 bay leaf
¼ teaspoon freshly grated nutmeg
4 to 6 cloves garlic
¾-inch (2-cm) piece fresh ginger, crushed
2 medium red onions, chopped
1½ cups (180 grams) grated fresh coconut (or frozen unsweetened coconut)
1 tablespoon malt vinegar or cider vinegar
1 tablespoon chopped fresh cilantro

1. Put the chicken in a bowl. Add the turmeric, 1½ teaspoons of the salt, and the lemon juice, and stir well. Cover the bowl with plastic wrap and put in the refrigerator for 30 minutes to marinate.

2. Place a medium nonstick saucepan over high heat and add the ⅓ cup (65 ml) oil. When small bubbles appear at the bottom of the pan, lower the heat to low. Add the cinnamon, cloves, chiles, poppy seeds, *ajwain*, cumin, peppercorns, fennel, star anise, coriander, bay leaf, nutmeg, garlic, ginger, and onions, and sauté for 5 to 7 minutes or until the onions are browned.

3. Add the coconut and sauté for 5 to 7 minutes more or until the coconut is browned.

4. Transfer to a plate and set aside to cool to room temperature.

5. Transfer to a food processor with 1 cup (200 ml) water, and process to a fine paste.

6. Place a medium nonstick saucepan over medium heat and add the remaining 2 tablespoons oil. When small bubbles appear at the bottom of the pan, lower the heat to medium, add the chicken, and sauté for 3 to 4 minutes.

7. Add the spices and coconut mixture and stir well. Add 1 cup (200 ml) water and stir. When the mixture comes to a boil, lower the heat to medium and cook for 25 minutes or until the chicken is cooked through.

8. Add the vinegar, the remaining ½ teaspoon salt, and the cilantro, and stir.

9. Transfer to a serving bowl and serve hot.

Dum Murgh

······⊰ **Chicken cooked in its own steam with flavorful spices** ⊱······

This dish uses a slow-cooking method that was introduced to India by the Mughals in the early sixteenth century. Traditionally, a special pot called a *handi* is used. It is covered with a tight-fitting lid and sealed using a whole-wheat dough to ensure that not a wisp of steam escapes from the pot and the food cooks in its own juices with all the flavors intact.

Serves 4.

2-inch (5-cm) piece fresh ginger
6 to 8 cloves garlic
3 or 4 green chiles, stemmed
1 (1¾-pound/800-gram) chicken, skinned and cut into 12 pieces
1½ cups (375 grams) plain yogurt
1 teaspoon table salt
20 almonds
3 cups (600 ml) vegetable oil
2 medium red onions, sliced
4 teaspoons ghee (page 37)
2 bay leaves
1 tablespoon ground coriander
1 teaspoon ground roasted cumin (page 32)
¼ teaspoon ground mace
¼ teaspoon ground green cardamom
½ teaspoon ground black cardamom
¼ teaspoon ground cinnamon
½ cup (100 ml) heavy cream

1. Put the ginger, garlic, and chiles in a spice grinder with 1 tablespoon water, and grind to a fine paste. Set aside.

2. Trim the excess fat from the chicken, put the pieces in a large bowl, and add the yogurt, ginger-garlic-chile paste, and salt. Stir well, cover the bowl with plastic wrap, and put in the refrigerator to marinate for 2 hours.

3. Soak the almonds in 1 cup (200 ml) warm water for 15 to 20 minutes. Peel the soaked almonds and transfer to a food processor. Process to a fine paste. Set aside.

4. Place a medium nonstick wok over high heat and add the oil. When small bubbles appear at the bottom of the wok, add the onions and cook until golden brown. Remove with a slotted spoon and drain on paper towels; set aside to cool.

5. Transfer the onions to a food processor and process to a fine paste. Set aside.

6. Place a medium nonstick saucepan over medium heat and add the ghee. When the ghee melts and small bubbles appear at the bottom of the pan, add the bay leaves and sauté for 30 seconds. Add the chicken and cook for 8 to 10 minutes or until the gravy starts boiling and reducing. Add the coriander, cumin, onion paste, and almond paste dissolved in ½ cup (100 ml) water. Stir well.

7. Cover with a tight-fitting lid or aluminum foil so that the steam does not escape. (Alternatively you can cover the pan and seal the edges using *atta* dough; see page 36.) Cook over low heat for 15 to 20 minutes.

8. Uncover and add the mace, green cardamom, black cardamom, and cinnamon. Stir in the cream.

9. Transfer to a serving dish. Serve hot.

Hara Masala Murgh

This is one of my favorite dishes, a green curry that is different from most traditional Indian curries such as tomato-onion or coconut.

Serves 4.

35 almonds
1 (1¾-pound/800-gram) chicken, skinned and cut into 12 pieces
1 cup (60 grams) chopped fresh cilantro
½ cup (30 grams) chopped fresh mint
4 green chiles, stemmed
½ cup (60 grams) grated fresh coconut (or frozen unsweetened coconut)
5 whole cloves
1-inch (2½-cm) piece fresh ginger
6 to 8 cloves garlic
1½ teaspoons table salt
3 tablespoons vegetable oil
4 green cardamom pods
2 medium red onions, peeled and chopped
1½ cups (375 grams) plain yogurt, whisked
1 tablespoon ground coriander
1 tablespoon ground roasted cumin (page 32)
¼ cup (50 ml) heavy cream

1. Soak the almonds in 1 cup (200 ml) warm water for 15 to 20 minutes. Peel the soaked almonds and transfer to a spice grinder. Grind to a fine paste. Set aside.

2. Put the cilantro, mint, chiles, coconut, cloves, ginger, and garlic in a food processor with 1 teaspoon of the salt and 1 cup (200 ml) water, and process to make a smooth chutney. Transfer the chutney to a large bowl.

3. Add the chicken to the chutney and stir well to coat. Cover the bowl with plastic wrap and put in the refrigerator to marinate for 30 minutes.

4. Place a medium nonstick saucepan over medium heat and add the oil. When small bubbles appear at the bottom of the pan, pound the cardamom and add it to the oil. Add the onions and sauté for 5 minutes or until golden brown.

5. Add the chicken and sauté for 2 to 3 minutes or until the extra moisture dries up and the sauce coats the chicken well.

6. Add the almond paste and yogurt, and cook, stirring, for 2 minutes.

7. Add the coriander, cumin, and the remaining ½ teaspoon salt, and stir well. Increase the heat to high, cover, and cook for 2 minutes. Lower the heat to medium and cook for 15 to 20 minutes or until the chicken is cooked through and tender.

8. Add the cream and stir.

9. Transfer to a serving dish. Serve hot.

Kachchi Mirchi Ka Murgh

······ ❊〰 **Stuffed chiles with chicken marinated in spiced yogurt** 〰❊ ······

Stuffing chiles with the spice mix may be laborious, but the results are spectacular. Do try this recipe.

Serves 4.

1 (1¾-pound/800-gram) whole chicken, skinned and cut into 12 pieces
2 green chiles, stemmed
2 teaspoons yellow mustard seeds
10 to 12 small *bhavnagri mirchi* (large green chiles; see Note)
2 teaspoons ground fennel seeds
½ teaspoon ground fenugreek
2 teaspoons ground roasted cumin (page 32)
½ teaspoon *kalonji* (nigella; see Note page 231)
1½ teaspoons table salt
1 cup (250 grams) plain yogurt, whisked
2 tablespoons vegetable oil
2 medium red onions, sliced
1 tablespoon fresh ginger paste (page 12)
1 tablespoon fresh garlic paste (page 12)
1 tablespoon ground coriander
½ teaspoon ground turmeric
½ teaspoon red chile powder

1. Trim off the excess fat from the chicken.

2. Put the green chiles in a mortar and crush, using a pestle. Transfer to a small bowl and set aside. Crush the mustard seeds in the mortar, transfer them to another bowl, and set aside.

3. Slit the *bhavnagri* chiles on one side and remove and discard the seeds. Set aside.

4. In a small bowl, combine the fennel, fenugreek, cumin, crushed mustard seeds, *kalonji*, and ½ teaspoon of the salt. Stuff this mixture into the slit *bhavnagri* chiles and set aside.

5. Put the chicken in a large bowl. Add the remaining 1 teaspoon salt, the yogurt, and crushed chiles, and stir. Let the chicken marinate for about 15 minutes.

6. Place a medium nonstick saucepan over medium heat and add the oil. When small bubbles appear at the bottom of the pan, add the onions and sauté for 2 to 3 minutes or until soft. Add the stuffed chiles and stir.

7. Add the ginger paste, garlic paste, coriander, turmeric, and chile powder, and sauté for 2 to 3 minutes. Lower the heat to low, cover, and cook for 10 minutes or until the chiles are soft.

8. Add the marinated chicken and cook, stirring, for 7 minutes. Increase the heat to medium, cover, and cook for 5 to 7 minutes. Stir once, then lower the heat to low, cover, and cook for 10 minutes or until the chicken is cooked through.

9. Transfer to a serving dish and serve hot.

Note *Bhavnagri mirchi* chiles are large, plump chiles, 4 to 4½ inches long, that are not very spicy. They are ideal for stuffing. You can use Anaheim chiles as a substitute.

Kadai Chicken

Spicy chicken cooked in a wok

Kadai is Hindi for "wok," and I remember that my mother had quite a collection of them in various metals—iron and brass especially. This chicken is ideally cooked in an iron wok, which lends its color to the dish, but these are rare in modern kitchens, and a nonstick wok works just fine here.

Serves 4.

2 teaspoons cumin seeds
2 teaspoons coriander seeds
8 whole black peppercorns
5 dried red chiles, stemmed
3 tablespoons vegetable oil
2 large red onions, chopped
1 tablespoon fresh ginger paste (page 12)
1 tablespoon fresh garlic paste (page 12)
5 green chiles, stemmed and chopped
2 large tomatoes, chopped
2 teaspoons table salt
1 (1¾-pound/800-gram) chicken, cut into 12 pieces
¼ cup cashew paste (page 12)
¼ teaspoon *garam masala* (spice mix; page 27)
2 tablespoons chopped fresh cilantro

1. Place a small nonstick sauté pan over medium heat. After 2 minutes, add the cumin, coriander, peppercorns, and red chiles, and dry-roast for 3 minutes. Let cool, then transfer to a mortar and pound to a coarse powder with a pestle.

2. Place a nonstick wok over medium heat and add the oil. When small bubbles appear at the bottom of the wok, add the onions and sauté for 4 to 5 minutes or until browned. Add the ginger paste, garlic paste, and green chiles, and sauté for 2 minutes.

3. Add the tomatoes and salt, cover, and cook for 2 minutes. Add the roasted spice powder and sauté for 1 minute.

4. Add the chicken and stir. Cover and cook for 15 minutes. Add the cashew paste and ½ cup (100 ml) water. Cook for 3 minutes.

5. Add the *garam masala* and stir. Garnish with the cilantro and serve hot.

Kairi Murgh

······⟨ Tart green mango and chicken ⟩······

I have tried making this with boneless chicken, but the look of the dish and its flavor are much more appealing with bone-in chicken.

This dish uses a unique method to impart the taste of outdoor charcoal grilling to the chicken: a red-hot piece of charcoal doused with ghee and cloves is placed in a bowl along with the chicken.

Serves 4.

1 (1¾-pound/800-gram) chicken, cut into 12 pieces
2 medium green mangoes
1½ teaspoons fresh ginger paste (page 12)
1½ teaspoons fresh garlic paste (page 12)
1½ teaspoons green chile paste (page 13)
1 teaspoon table salt
2 teaspoons *garam masala* (spice mix; page 27)
4 or 5 whole cloves
1 teaspoon ghee (page 37), melted
2 tablespoons vegetable oil
2 medium red onions, sliced
¼ teaspoon ground turmeric
1½ teaspoons red chile powder
2 teaspoons ground coriander
2 tablespoons chopped fresh cilantro

1. Trim the excess fat from the chicken and put the pieces in a large bowl.

2. Peel and cut the mangoes into small pieces. Place half of them in a food processor and process to a purée. Transfer to a small bowl and set aside. Set the remaining mango pieces aside.

3. To the chicken, add ¾ teaspoon of the ginger paste, ¾ teaspoon of the garlic paste, ¾ teaspoon of the chile paste, ½ teaspoon of the salt, 1 teaspoon of the *garam masala*, and the mango purée, and stir to coat. Cover the bowl with plastic wrap and put in the refrigerator to marinate for 1 hour.

4. Hold a natural charcoal piece with kitchen tongs directly over a gas flame. When it is red hot, put it in a small stainless-steel bowl and place the bowl in the center of the marinated chicken pieces. Put the cloves on the coal, pour the ghee on it, and immediately cover the bowl with a lid. Let stand for 10 minutes so that the flavor of the coal and cloves are absorbed by the chicken.

5. Place a medium nonstick saucepan over medium heat and add the oil. When small bubbles appear at the bottom of the pan, add the onions and sauté until translucent. Add the remaining ¾ teaspoon ginger paste, ¾ teaspoon garlic paste, and ¾ teaspoon chile paste, and sauté for 2 minutes.

6. Add the chicken, turmeric, chile powder, coriander, remaining 1 teaspoon *garam masala*, and ½ teaspoon salt, and the reserved mango pieces. Stir well to coat.

7. Increase the heat to high and cook for 5 to 6 minutes. Add the cilantro and ¾ cup (150 ml) water. Cover and cook for 10 to 12 minutes or until the chicken is cooked through.

8. Transfer to a serving dish. Serve hot.

Kheema Bhari Hari Mirch

······*} Green chiles stuffed with spiced ground chicken {*······

The traditional version of the recipe, from the South Indian city of Hyderabad, uses ground goat, but here I use chicken, which is healthier.

Serves 4.

6 tablespoons vegetable oil
½ teaspoon cumin seeds
2 large red onions, chopped
1 teaspoon fresh ginger paste (page 12)
1 teaspoon fresh garlic paste (page 12)
2 green chiles, stemmed and slit
2 tablespoons red chile paste (see Note page 13)
3 medium tomatoes, puréed
¼ teaspoon ground turmeric
1 tablespoon ground coriander
14 ounces (400 grams) ground chicken
1½ teaspoons table salt
½ teaspoon *garam masala* (spice mix; page 27)
2 teaspoons freshly squeezed lemon juice
¼ cup chopped fresh cilantro
12 *bhavnagri mirchi* (large green chiles; see page 418)

1. Place a nonstick wok over medium heat and add 3 tablespoons of the oil. When small bubbles appear at the bottom of the wok, add the cumin seeds and sauté until they change color. Add the onions and sauté for 5 minutes.

2. Add the ginger paste, garlic paste, green chiles, and red chile paste, and sauté for 2 minutes. Add the tomatoes and cook for 5 minutes. Add the turmeric and coriander, and sauté for 1 minute.

3. Add the chicken and 2 tablespoons water, and cook for 8 minutes. Add the salt and *garam masala*, and stir well. Add the lemon juice and cilantro, and stir well. Remove from the heat and set aside to cool slightly.

4. Slit the *bhavnagri* chiles on one side and remove the seeds and the white pith, keeping the stem intact.

5. Stuff the chicken mixture into the chiles.

6. Place a nonstick saucepan over medium heat and add the remaining 3 tablespoons oil. When small bubbles appear at the bottom of the pan, add the stuffed chiles and any leftover ground chicken mixture. Cover and cook for 8 minutes.

7. Serve hot.

Kori Ajadina

······⊰ **Chicken with fresh coconut** ⊱··

Centuries ago, a group of Roman Catholics fled Portugal and settled in Mangalore along the western coast of India. They adopted the local cuisine and created a fusion of Portuguese and traditional Mangalorian styles. Mangalore Catholic cuisine has chicken and pork specialties as well as an array of chutneys, including dried-prawn chutney and *brinjal* chutney. Their chicken curry *kori gassi* (page 424) is famous, and so is this dry preparation.

Serves 4.

1 (1¾-pound/800-gram) chicken, cut into 12 pieces
2 tablespoons freshly squeezed lemon juice
1½ teaspoons table salt
1 teaspoon ground turmeric
3 tablespoons vegetable oil
1-inch (2½-cm) cinnamon stick
4 or 5 whole cloves
1 bay leaf
10 fresh curry leaves
2 medium red onions, chopped
1-inch (2½-cm) piece fresh ginger, chopped
5 or 6 cloves garlic, chopped
3 medium tomatoes, chopped
1 cup (120 grams) grated fresh coconut (or frozen unsweetened coconut)
2 tablespoons chopped fresh cilantro

~ For the masala powder:
1-inch (2½-cm) stick cinnamon
3 whole cloves
3 green cardamom pods
5 or 6 whole black peppercorns
1 teaspoon cumin seeds
1 tablespoon coriander seeds
½ teaspoon fenugreek seeds
1 teaspoon white poppy seeds
6 dried red chiles, stemmed

1. Put the chicken in a large bowl.

2. Add the lemon juice, 1 teaspoon of the salt, and ½ teaspoon of the turmeric, and stir. Set aside for 20 minutes.

3. Make the masala powder: Place a medium nonstick sauté pan over medium heat. Add the cinnamon, cloves, cardamom, peppercorns, cumin, coriander, fenugreek, poppy seeds, and chiles, and dry-roast for 3 to 4 minutes or until fragrant. Transfer to a plate and set aside to cool. When cooled, transfer to a spice grinder and grind to a fine powder. Set aside.

4. Place a nonstick saucepan over medium heat and add the oil. When small bubbles appear at the bottom of the pan, add the cinnamon, cloves, and bay leaf. Sauté for 1 minute or until fragrant. Add the curry leaves and onions, and sauté for 2 to 3 minutes.

5. Add the ginger and garlic, and sauté for 5 minutes. Add the tomatoes and the remaining ½ teaspoon salt. Stir well. Add the remaining ½ teaspoon turmeric and the freshly ground masala powder, and stir for 2 to 3 minutes or until the oil comes to the top.

6. Add the coconut and stir for 2 to 3 minutes. Add the cilantro and stir. Add the chicken and stir. Sauté until the chicken pieces are well coated with the mixture.

7. Add 1½ cups (300 ml) water and bring to a boil. Lower the heat to low, cover, and cook for 10 to 15 minutes or until the chicken is cooked through.

8. Transfer to a serving dish and serve hot.

Kori Gassi

The food of the Bunt community in Karnataka offers dishes that use a delicate combination of red chiles, coconut milk, and curry leaves. This *kori gassi* is their signature dish. Serve it with rice *wade* (page 463).

Serves 4.

1 (1¾-pound/800-gram) chicken, cut into 1½-inch (4-cm) pieces
1 tablespoon fresh ginger paste (page 12)
1 tablespoon fresh garlic paste (page 12)
1 teaspoon table salt
3 medium red onions
3 tablespoons vegetable oil
2 tablespoons coriander seeds
2 whole cloves
1-inch (2½-cm) cinnamon stick
1½ teaspoons fennel seeds
⅛-inch (3- to 4-mm) piece nutmeg
1 blade mace
8 dried red chiles (preferably *bedgi* chiles, see page 234), stemmed
2 or 3 cloves garlic
½ teaspoon ground turmeric
1 tablespoon tamarind pulp
¾ cup (150 ml) coconut milk
2 tablespoons chopped fresh cilantro

1. Put the chicken in a large bowl, add the ginger paste, garlic paste, and salt, and stir well. Cover the bowl with plastic wrap and put in the refrigerator to marinate for 1 hour.

2. Thinly slice 2 of the onions. Place the remaining onion over an open gas flame and roast until the outer skin is charred. Set aside to cool, then remove the charred skin.

3. Place a small sauté pan over medium heat and add 1 tablespoon of the oil. When small bubbles appear at the bottom of the pan, add the coriander and sauté until lightly browned. Remove with a slotted spoon and put in a bowl. To the oil in the heated pan, add the cloves, cinnamon, fennel, nutmeg, mace, and red chiles, and sauté until fragrant. Add to the coriander seeds and set aside to cool completely.

4. Transfer to a food processor, add the garlic, roasted onion, and 7 tablespoons water, and process to a paste.

5. Place a deep nonstick sauté pan over medium heat and add the remaining 2 tablespoons vegetable oil. When small bubbles appear at the bottom of the pan, add the sliced onions and sauté for 4 to 5 minutes or until well browned.

6. Add the chicken, turmeric, and 1 cup (200 ml) water, and stir. Cover and cook for 10 minutes or until the chicken is almost cooked through.

7. Add the ground paste and stir well. Add the tamarind pulp diluted in ½ cup (100 ml) water, stir, and simmer for 3 to 4 minutes.

8. Add the coconut milk and simmer for 2 to 3 minutes.

9. Transfer to a serving dish, garnish with the cilantro, and serve hot.

Koyla Chicken

······※{ Chicken smoked with charcoal }··

The Indian name of this dish sounds poetic to me, but the literal translation, "charcoal chicken," does not sound very appetizing. This recipe uses a special technique for smoking indoors: A bowl containing a glowing piece of charcoal is nestled in a plate of chicken, some ghee is poured over the coal, and everything is immediately covered with a large bowl to smoke. The dish is really superb, especially served with fresh *naan* (page 20), and will always impress your family and friends.

Serves 4.

1 (1¾-pound/800-gram) chicken, cut into 12 pieces
2 teaspoons fresh ginger-garlic paste (page 13)
1 teaspoon *garam masala* (spice mix; page 27)
1½ teaspoons red chile powder
2 teaspoons table salt
6 medium tomatoes
10 to 15 cashews
3 tablespoons butter
4 or 5 green chiles, stemmed and slit
1 tablespoon freshly squeezed lemon juice
1 tablespoon chopped fresh cilantro
½ cup (100 ml) heavy cream
1 tablespoon ghee (page 37), melted

1. Remove the skin from the chicken and put the pieces in a large bowl. Add the ginger-garlic paste, *garam masala*, chile powder, and 1 teaspoon of the salt, and stir to coat. Cover the bowl with plastic wrap and put in the refrigerator to marinate for 1 hour.

2. Place a medium nonstick saucepan over high heat, add 5 cups (1 liter) water, and bring to a boil. Add the tomatoes and blanch for 2 to 3 minutes. Drain in a colander and let cool. Peel the tomatoes and purée them in a blender. Transfer the tomato purée to a bowl and set aside.

3. Place a small nonstick sauté pan over medium heat. Add the cashews and dry-roast for 2 to 3 minutes. Let cool, then transfer to a mortar and coarsely grind with a pestle. Set aside.

4. Place a medium nonstick saucepan over medium heat and add the butter. When the butter melts, add the chicken and sauté for 2 minutes. Add the chiles and sauté for 1 minute.

5. Add the tomatoes and sauté for 2 to 3 minutes. Add 1 cup (200 ml) water and the remaining 1 teaspoon salt, and stir. Lower the heat to low, cover, and cook for 15 minutes or until the chicken is almost done.

6. Add the cashews, cover, and simmer for 3 to 4 minutes or until the chicken is cooked through and tender.

7. Add the lemon juice and cilantro, and cook for 1 minute or until the oil comes to the top. Gently stir in the cream. Remove from the heat.

8. Hold a piece of natural charcoal with tongs over an open gas flame and heat until red hot. Place it in a small stainless-steel bowl. Place the bowl on the cooked chicken. Pour the ghee over the coal. Immediately cover the pan with a lid so that the flavor of the smoke will be absorbed by the cooked chicken. Open the lid after 2 minutes and remove the steel bowl with the coal.

9. Transfer the chicken to a serving dish and serve hot.

Kozhi Ishtew

······❧{ **Chicken and potato cooked in coconut milk** }❦······

This lovely stew comes from Kerala, in South India. Coconut milk, if heated beyond a certain temperature, curdles and becomes unpalatable, but if it's added in stages and diluted, the mixture will turn out smooth and velvety. Serve the stew with *appams* (page 14) or *parathas* (page 18).

Serves 4.

10 to 12 whole black peppercorns
¼ teaspoon cumin seeds
2 teaspoons *chana dal* (split Bengal gram)
½ teaspoon coriander seeds
¼ cup (50 ml) vegetable oil
2 star anise
1-inch (2½-cm) cinnamon stick
4 green cardamom pods
1 (1¾-pound/800-gram) chicken, cut into 12 pieces
1 large potato, peeled and cut into 8 pieces
10 to 12 fresh curry leaves
4 green chiles, stemmed and slit
2 cups (400 ml) thick canned coconut milk
1 teaspoon table salt

1. Place a small nonstick sauté pan over medium heat and add the peppercorns, cumin, *dal*, and coriander. Dry-roast for 2 minutes or until the *dal* is lightly browned. Set aside to cool completely. Transfer to a spice grinder and grind to a powder.

2. Place a medium nonstick sauté pan over medium heat and add the oil. When small bubbles appear at the bottom of the pan, add the star anise, cinnamon, and cardamom, and sauté for 1 minute. Add the chicken, potato, curry leaves, and chiles. Sprinkle with the ground spices and sauté for 1 minute.

3. Put 1 cup (200 ml) of the coconut milk in a bowl and set aside. Put ½ cup (100 ml) of the remaining coconut milk in a second bowl and dilute with ½ cup (100 ml) water. Put the remaining ½ cup (100 ml) coconut milk in a third bowl and dilute with ¾ cup (150 ml) water.

4. Add the contents of the third bowl to the curry and simmer for 5 minutes. Add the contents of the second bowl and cook for 10 minutes or until both the chicken and potatoes are cooked through.

5. Remove from the heat and add the contents of the first bowl and the salt. Return to low heat and simmer for 5 minutes but do not boil.

6. Serve immediately.

Kozhi Thengai Kozhambu

·······{ **Chicken in a coconut curry** }························

Three Cs—chicken, coconut, and curry leaves—make this dish! This classic dish from Tamil Nadu, in South India, uses shallots instead of red onions.

Serves 4.

1 (1¾-pound/800-gram) chicken, cut into 20 to 24 pieces
½ teaspoon ground turmeric
1¾ teaspoons table salt
¼ cup (50 ml) vegetable oil
1 cup (120 grams) grated fresh coconut (or frozen unsweetened coconut)
10 shallots, peeled
1-inch (2½-cm) piece fresh ginger, chopped
6 cloves garlic, chopped
10 green chiles, stemmed and chopped
2 dried red chiles, stemmed and broken in half
2 tablespoons coriander seeds
2 star anise
2 bay leaves
10 to 12 fresh curry leaves

1. Make the chicken: Put the chicken in a bowl and rub in the turmeric and ¾ teaspoon of the salt. Cover the bowl with plastic wrap and put in the refrigerator to marinate for 30 minutes.

2. Make the masala: Place a nonstick sauté pan over medium heat and add 2 tablespoons of the oil. When small bubbles appear at the bottom of the pan, lower the heat to low and add the coconut, shallots, ginger, garlic, green chiles, red chiles, and coriander seeds. Sauté until fragrant and lightly browned. Set aside to cool completely. Transfer to a food processor with 1¼ cup (250 ml) water and process to a smooth paste.

3. Place a nonstick sauté pan over medium heat and add the remaining 2 tablespoons oil. When small bubbles appear at the bottom of the pan, add the star anise and bay leaves, and sauté for 30 seconds.

4. Add the curry leaves and chicken. Increase the heat to high and sauté until the chicken is lightly browned.

5. Lower the heat to medium, add the masala paste, and combine well. Add 1½ cups (300 ml) water and the remaining 1 teaspoon salt and simmer for 11 to 12 minutes or until the chicken is cooked through and the sauce has thickened.

6. Serve hot.

·······{ **Chef's tip** }· Instead of the grated coconut, try making the dish with coconut milk—it will give it a smoother and richer finish.

Kozhi Urundai Kozhambu

····❈{ Chicken meatballs in a sour-and-spicy sauce }❈····

Here, delicate chicken meatballs are cooked in a smooth tomato sauce with Indian spices. This dish does not reheat well, so serve it right away. It's delicious with steamed rice.

Serves 4.

~ For the meatballs:
7 ounces (200 grams) ground chicken
1 tablespoon vegetable oil
4 or 5 cashews
1 tablespoon *chana dal* (split Bengal gram)
½ tablespoon white poppy seeds, soaked for 15 minutes and drained
¼ teaspoon fennel seeds
1 or 2 whole cloves
3 or 4 green chiles, stemmed and broken
1 or 2 dried red chiles, stemmed and chopped
1 medium red onion, roughly chopped
4 cloves garlic, roughly chopped
¼ cup (60 grams) grated fresh coconut (or frozen unsweetened coconut)
½ large egg, whisked
½ teaspoon table salt

~ For the sauce:
¼ cup (50 ml) vegetable oil
8 to 10 dried red chiles, stemmed and broken
3 tablespoons coriander seeds
½ teaspoon ground turmeric
1 teaspoon fennel seeds
1 teaspoon cumin seeds
2 tablespoons white poppy seeds, soaked for 15 minutes and drained
10 whole black peppercorns
4 whole cloves
3 medium red onions, roughly chopped
6 cloves garlic
2 medium tomatoes, chopped
1 teaspoon table salt
¼ cup (60 grams) tamarind pulp

1. Make the meatballs: Put the chicken in a bowl.

2. Place a nonstick sauté pan over medium heat and add the oil. When small bubbles appear at the bottom of the pan, add the cashews, *dal*, poppy seeds, fennel, cloves, green chiles, red chiles, onion, garlic, and coconut, and sauté for 2 minutes or until fragrant. Set aside to cool. Transfer to a food processor with ¼ cup (50 ml) water and process to a fine paste.

3. Add the paste to the chicken. Add the egg and combine. Add the salt and combine well. Cover the bowl with plastic wrap and put in the refrigerator to marinate for 30 minutes.

4. Divide the chicken mixture into 12 portions, and shape into balls using dampened palms and fingers. Put the chicken balls on a plate, cover them with plastic wrap, and set aside in the refrigerator until needed.

5. Make the sauce: Place a nonstick sauté pan over medium heat and add 1 tablespoon of the oil. When small bubbles appear at the bottom of the pan, add the chiles, coriander, turmeric, fennel, cumin, poppy seeds, peppercorns, cloves, onions, and garlic, and sauté for 3 minutes or until fragrant. Set aside to cool. Transfer to a food processor with ½ cup (100 ml) water and process to a fine paste.

6. Place a nonstick saucepan over medium heat and add the remaining 3 tablespoons oil. When small bubbles appear at the bottom of the pan, add the tomatoes and ½ teaspoon of the salt and sauté for 7 minutes or until the tomatoes are pulpy.

7. Add the ground paste and sauté for 2 minutes or until the oil comes to the top. Add the tamarind pulp, 1 quart (800 ml) water, and the remaining ½ teaspoon salt, and combine well. Bring to a boil, then lower the heat to low, and add the meatballs. Simmer, without stirring, and shake the pan occasionally to prevent sticking for 12 minutes or until the meatballs are cooked through and the sauce has thickened.

8. Serve hot.

Kozhi Vartha Kari

····•{ **Tamil fried chicken** }•····

Here the chicken is evenly coated with a glaze that is sour, peppery, and infused with the aroma of curry leaves. Serve it with rice and *sambhar* (page 32) and maybe a small salad on the side.

Serves 4.

2 dried red chiles, stemmed
2-inch (5-cm) piece fresh ginger
6 to 8 cloves garlic
1 teaspoon red chile powder
1 tablespoon freshly squeezed lemon juice
1 teaspoon ground turmeric
2 teaspoons table salt
1 (1¾-pound/800-gram) chicken, cut into 12 pieces
5 tablespoons vegetable oil
12 to 15 fresh curry leaves
2 medium red onions, chopped
2 medium tomatoes, finely chopped
2 teaspoons ground coriander
1 tablespoon tamarind pulp
1 teaspoon *garam masala* (spice mix; page 27)
30 black peppercorns, crushed
2 tablespoons chopped fresh cilantro

1. Put the chiles, ginger, and garlic in a spice grinder and grind to a smooth paste. Transfer to a large bowl. Add the chile powder, lemon juice, turmeric, and 1 teaspoon of the salt, and stir. Add the chicken and stir to coat. Cover the bowl with plastic wrap and put in the refrigerator to marinate for 1 hour.

2. Place a medium nonstick saucepan over medium heat and add 2 tablespoons of the oil. When small bubbles appear at the bottom of the pan, add the chicken and sauté over high heat until dry and lightly browned. Drain the chicken on paper towels and set aside.

3. Place the same pan back over medium heat. Add the remaining 3 tablespoons oil. When small bubbles appear at the bottom of the pan, add the curry leaves and stir well. Add the onions and sauté until browned. Add the tomatoes, the remaining 1 teaspoon salt, and the coriander, and cook until the oil comes to the top.

4. Add the chicken and stir. Add 1 cup (200 ml) water. Cover and cook for 15 minutes or until the chicken is cooked through and the sauce coats the pieces.

5. Dissolve the tamarind pulp in 1 cup (200 ml) water, add it to the pan, and simmer for 10 minutes, stirring occasionally. Add the *garam masala* and stir gently. Add the peppercorns and stir.

6. Garnish with the cilantro and serve hot.

Kozhi Vartha Kozhambu

······⋅⊰ **Chicken curry from Kerala** ⊱⋅······

If you visit Kerala, the most verdant of the southern states of India, be sure to take a boat excursion and feast on beautiful, simple curries like this fragrant one featuring coconut milk. Serve it with steamed rice.

Serves 4.

2 tablespoons vegetable oil
1-inch (2½-cm) cinnamon stick
1 teaspoon fennel seeds
10 to 12 fresh curry leaves
3 medium red onions, thinly sliced
½ tablespoon fresh ginger paste (page 12)
½ tablespoon fresh garlic paste (page 12)
2 teaspoons ground coriander
½ teaspoon ground turmeric
1 tablespoon red chile powder
1½ teaspoons table salt
3 medium tomatoes, chopped
1 (1¾-pound/800-gram) chicken, cut into 12 pieces
1½ cups (300 ml) coconut milk
1 tablespoon tamarind pulp

1. Place a heavy-bottomed nonstick sauté pan over medium heat and add the oil. When small bubbles appear at the bottom of the pan, add the cinnamon and fennel, and sauté for 30 seconds or until fragrant. Add the curry leaves and onions, and sauté for 3 to 4 minutes or until the onions are golden brown.

2. Add the ginger paste and garlic paste, and sauté for 1 minute. Add the coriander, turmeric, chile powder, and salt, and sauté for 2 minutes.

3. Add the tomatoes and sauté for 5 to 6 minutes or until the tomatoes are pulpy.

4. Add the chicken and sauté for 3 to 4 minutes or until the oil comes to the top.

5. Add half of the coconut milk, lower the heat to low, and cook, covered, for 4 to 5 minutes or until the chicken is cooked through and tender.

6. Add the tamarind pulp, stir, and simmer for 1 minute. Add the remaining coconut milk and cook, covered, for 5 minutes.

7. Transfer to a serving bowl and serve hot.

······⋅⊰ **Chef's tip** ⊱⋅ You can use mixed vegetables instead of chicken to make the dish vegetarian.

Laziz Tikka Masala

·······⋅⊰ Boneless tandoori-style chicken in a spicy sauce ⊱⋅·······

Laziz is the Urdu word for "luscious." This is an elaborate recipe, but it will win a lot of hearts!

Serves 4.

~ **For the chicken *tikka*:**
14 ounces (400 grams) boneless chicken, cut into 1½-inch (4-cm) pieces
2 teaspoons red chile powder
2 tablespoons freshly squeezed lemon juice
1 teaspoon table salt
1 cup (275 grams) plain Greek yogurt
1 tablespoon fresh ginger paste (page 12)
1 tablespoon fresh garlic paste (page 12)
1 teaspoon *garam masala* (spice mix; page 27)
2 tablespoons refined mustard oil (see Note page 87)

~ **For the sauce:**
3 tablespoons vegetable oil
2 tablespoons butter
½ teaspoon cumin seeds
3 medium red onions, chopped
2 teaspoons fresh ginger paste (page 12)
2 teaspoons fresh garlic paste (page 12)
½ teaspoon ground roasted cumin (page 32)
1½ teaspoons ground coriander
4 medium tomatoes, chopped
½ teaspoon table salt
¼ cup (60 grams) tomato purée
1 teaspoon red chile powder
½ teaspoon *garam masala* (spice mix; page 27)
2 tablespoons chopped fresh cilantro
1 teaspoon roasted and crushed *kasoori methi* (dried fenugreek leaves)
¼ cup (50 ml) heavy cream

1. Make the chicken *tikka*: Put the chicken in a bowl, add 1 teaspoon of the chile powder, 1 tablespoon of the lemon juice, and the salt, and toss to coat. Cover the bowl with plastic wrap and place in the refrigerator to marinate for about 30 minutes.

2. Combine the yogurt, the remaining 1 tablespoon lemon juice, the ginger paste, the garlic paste, the remaining 1 teaspoon chile powder, and the *garam masala* in a large bowl. Add the chicken and mustard oil, and stir well. Cover the bowl with plastic wrap and put in the refrigerator to marinate for about 2 hours.

3. Preheat the oven to 400°F/200°C.

4. Thread the chicken onto skewers. Put the skewers on a baking sheet and bake on the middle rack of the oven for 15 to 20 minutes. Remove from the oven. Slide the chicken off the skewers onto a plate and set aside.

5. Make the sauce: Place a nonstick sauté pan over medium heat and add the oil and butter. When small bubbles appear at the bottom of the pan, add the cumin seeds. When they change color, add the onions and sauté for 5 minutes or until well browned.

6. Add the ginger paste and garlic paste and sauté for 2 to 3 minutes. Add the ground cumin and coriander and stir well.

7. Add the tomatoes and stir. Lower the heat to low and sauté for 15 minutes or until the tomatoes are completely cooked and the oil comes to the top. Add the salt and stir.

8. Add the tomato purée and sauté for 2 minutes. Stir in ½ cup (100 ml) water and cook for 2 to 3 minutes. Add the chicken *tikka* and simmer for 5 minutes. Add the chile powder, *garam masala*, and 1 tablespoon of the cilantro. Stir well and cook for 2 minutes.

9. Stir in the *kasoori methi* and cream. Remove from the heat and transfer to a serving bowl.

10. Garnish with the remaining 1 tablespoon cilantro and serve hot.

Makai Murgh

This recipe started out as a vegetarian dish with corn, tomatoes, and bell peppers, but my two girls expect a new chicken dish from me every week so I added the chicken in a creative moment. They are happy with it, and so am I, because some healthy vegetables are included in their diet this way. Serve this with hot *rotis* (page 18).

Serves 4.

1 cup (150 grams) fresh or drained canned corn kernels
1 teaspoon cumin seeds
5 or 6 whole black peppercorns
1 teaspoon coriander seeds
3 whole cloves
4 medium boneless, skinless chicken breasts
½ cup (125 grams) plain yogurt, whisked
1 teaspoon table salt
1 teaspoon red chile powder
½ teaspoon ground turmeric
1½ tablespoons vegetable oil
3 cloves garlic, chopped
1-inch (2½-cm) piece ginger, chopped
3 medium tomatoes, puréed
2 medium green bell peppers, seeded and chopped
2 tablespoons chopped fresh cilantro

1. Put ½ cup (75 grams) of the corn in a mini food processor and process to a paste.

2. Place a medium nonstick sauté pan over medium heat. Let it heat for 2 minutes, then add the cumin, peppercorns, coriander, and cloves, and dry-roast for 3 minutes or until fragrant. Transfer to a plate and set aside to cool. Lightly crush in a mortar with a pestle.

3. Cut the chicken into ½-inch (1-cm) pieces and put them in a bowl. Add the yogurt, salt, chile powder, and turmeric, and stir well. Set aside to marinate for 15 minutes.

4. Place a medium nonstick saucepan over medium heat and add the oil. When small bubbles appear at the bottom of the pan, add the garlic and ginger, and sauté for 1 minute. Add the corn kernels and the corn paste, and stir. Add ½ cup (100 ml) water and bring to a boil. Add the crushed spices and stir. Add the tomatoes and simmer for 3 to 4 minutes.

5. Add the chicken and stir. Simmer for 10 minutes or until the chicken is almost done.

6. Add the bell peppers, salt, and cilantro. Stir and cook for 1 minute.

7. Serve hot.

Malvani Chicken Hirwa Masala

····❈⟨ **Chicken in a green masala** ⟩❈···

Malvani cuisine is a delightful mix of Maharashtrian and Goan cuisines. The Malvan region boasts an extensive coastline, so coconut milk is prevalent in most of its dishes. The creaminess of the coconut is offset by red-hot chiles, and souring agents like tamarind and *kokum* fruit. Naturally, there is an abundance of seafood, but chicken is not uncommon.

Serves 4.

1 (1¾-pound/800-gram) chicken
1 teaspoon table salt
1¼ cups (75 grams) chopped fresh cilantro
½ cup (60 grams) grated fresh coconut (or frozen unsweetened coconut)
½-inch (1-cm) piece fresh ginger, chopped
4 cloves garlic, peeled
6 green chiles, stemmed and chopped
2 tablespoons vegetable oil
1-inch (2½-cm) cinnamon stick
2 black cardamom pods
2 green cardamom pods
1 bay leaf
2 or 3 whole cloves
½ teaspoon cumin seeds
3 medium red onions, chopped
½ cup (100 ml) thick coconut milk
¼ teaspoon *garam masala* (spice mix; page 27)

1. Clean the chicken, remove the skin, and cut into 16 pieces. Transfer to a bowl and rub the salt all over the chicken. Cover the bowl with plastic wrap and set aside.

2. Reserve 2 tablespoons of the cilantro for garnish. Place the remaining cilantro in a food processor with the coconut, ginger, garlic, chiles, and ¼ cup (50 ml) water, and process to a paste. Add this paste to the chicken and stir well to coat.

3. Place a nonstick sauté pan over medium heat and add the oil. When small bubbles appear at the bottom of the pan, add the cinnamon, black and green cardamom, bay leaf, cloves, and cumin, and sauté until fragrant. Add the onions and cook for 3 minutes or until soft and translucent.

4. Add the chicken and sauté over low heat for 5 to 6 minutes. Add 2 cups (400 ml) water and cook for 4 to 5 minutes or until the chicken is cooked through.

5. Add the coconut milk and *garam masala*. Stir well.

6. Garnish with the reserved cilantro and serve hot.

Murgh Zafrani Do Pyaza

·······⟨ **A saffron-flavored chicken curry loaded with onions** ⟩·········

Saffron adds a depth to certain curries that cannot be identified at first bite. If you really want to understand how saffron affects this dish, try making it once without the saffron. Serve the curry with *parathas* (page 18).

Serves 4.

25 almonds, roasted
1 tablespoon *chironji/charoli* (melon seeds; page 587), roasted
1 tablespoon white poppy seeds, roasted
½ cup (100 ml) vegetable oil
2 medium red onions, sliced
1 tablespoon fresh ginger paste (page 12)
1 teaspoon fresh garlic paste (page 12)
1 tablespoon red chile powder
1 teaspoon ground turmeric
1⅔ pounds (850 grams) bone-in chicken, cut into 1-inch (2½-cm) pieces
1¼ teaspoons table salt
½ cup (125 grams) plain yogurt
3 cups (600 ml) chicken stock, (page 34)
½ teaspoon *garam masala* (spice mix; page 27)
Generous pinch of saffron threads

1. Put the almonds, melon seeds, and poppy seeds in a spice grinder, and grind to a fine powder.

2. Place a nonstick sauté pan over medium heat and add the oil. When small bubbles appear at the bottom of the pan, add the onions and sauté for 2 to 3 minutes or until lightly browned.

3. Add the ginger paste and garlic paste, and sauté for 2 minutes. Add the chile powder and turmeric, and stir well.

4. Add the chicken and sauté for 5 minutes. Add the salt and stir.

5. Add the yogurt and cook for 1 to 2 minutes. Add the ground almond mixture and cook for 5 minutes, stirring continuously.

6. Add the stock and bring to a boil. Lower the heat to low, cover, and simmer for 20 minutes or until the chicken is cooked through.

7. Add the *garam masala* and saffron, stir, and remove from the heat.

8. Transfer to a serving bowl and serve hot.

Murtabak

This is a masterful construction of thin *chapatis* (Indian griddle breads) and a saffron-flavored egg, cheese, and chicken mixture, a great example of the royal Nizami cuisine of Hyderabad. Treat it like a one-dish meal, as it is quite filling.

Serves 4.

~ **For the *chapatis*:**
Scant 1 cup (120 grams) *maida* (refined flour) or pastry flour, plus extra for dusting
1 tablespoon vegetable oil
½ teaspoon table salt

~ **For the filling:**
6 large eggs
A few saffron threads
2 tablespoons warm milk, plus ½ cup (100 ml) milk
2 tablespoons vegetable oil
2 medium red onions, chopped
1 teaspoon fresh ginger paste (page 12)
1 teaspoon fresh garlic paste (page 12)
1 teaspoon red chile powder
½ teaspoon ground turmeric
9 ounces (270 grams) ground chicken
1 teaspoon table salt
1 teaspoon *garam masala* (spice mix; page 27)
2 teaspoons freshly squeezed lemon juice
About ½ cup (120 grams) ghee (page 37), for brushing the pans
1½ cups (150 grams) grated mild white cheese
¼ cup (15 grams) chopped fresh cilantro
¼ cup (15 grams) chopped fresh mint
10 green chiles, stemmed and chopped

1. Make the *chapatis*: Put the *maida* in a large bowl. Add the oil and salt. Rub with your fingers until the mixture resembles bread crumbs.

2. Add ¼ cup (50 ml) water and knead to make a soft dough. Cover with a damp cloth and set aside for 30 minutes.

3. Divide the dough into 9 portions. Dust a work surface with a little flour and roll out each portion into a thin 8-inch round.

4. Place a nonstick griddle over medium heat and add a dough round. Cook, turning, until lightly browned on each side. Set aside. Repeat with the remaining dough rounds.

5. Make the filling: Place a nonstick saucepan over medium heat, add 2½ cups (500 ml) water, and bring to a boil. Add 5 of the eggs and boil for 12 minutes. Remove from the heat, drain, and plunge the eggs into a bowl of cold water. Peel and chop the eggs and set aside in a bowl.

6. Beat the remaining egg in a bowl and set aside.

7. In a small bowl, soak the saffron in the 2 tablespoons warm milk.

8. Place a nonstick sauté pan over medium heat and add the oil. When small bubbles appear at the bottom of the pan, add the onions and sauté for 4 minutes or until lightly browned.

9. Add the ginger paste and garlic paste, and sauté for 2 minutes or until the raw flavors disappear. Add the chile powder and turmeric, and sauté for 3 to 4 minutes.

10. Add the chicken and salt, and cook for 8 minutes, stirring continuously. When the excess moisture has evaporated, add the *garam masala* and lemon juice. Transfer to a plate and let cool. Transfer to a food processor and process to a coarse paste.

11. Preheat the oven to 350°F/175°C.

12. Brush a round cake pan with a little ghee and line the bottom with 1 *chapati*. Sprinkle with a little milk and top it with 2 tablespoons of the chicken mixture, a little chopped egg, grated cheese, cilantro, mint, and chiles. Brush with a little beaten egg. Cover with another *chapati* and repeat the layering again until you have used all of the dough rounds.

13. Gently brush the top with the saffron mixture and bake for 35 minutes or until golden brown and set.

14. Unmold onto a plate and cut into wedges.

15. Serve hot.

Naattu Kozhi Curry

······⋇⦃ **Countryside chicken curry from Kerala** ⦄⋇······

Kozhi means "chicken," and this is a slightly modified and updated version of a rural dish from Kerala in all its spicy, thick, saucy glory. It's nice to mop up the sauce with *roti* (page 18). Use two Cornish game hens if you can't find a young spring chicken.

Serves 4.

1 (1¾-pound/800-gram) spring chicken
½ cup (100 ml) vegetable oil
½ cup (60 grams) grated fresh coconut (or frozen unsweetened coconut)
6 dried red chiles, stemmed and broken in half
3 tablespoons *chana dal* (split Bengal gram)
¼ cup (25 grams) coriander seeds
1 tablespoon whole black peppercorns
2 teaspoons cumin seeds
2-inch (5-cm) cinnamon stick, broken
2 whole cloves
4 green cardamom pods
2 tablespoons white poppy seeds
2 bay leaves
10 to 12 fresh curry leaves
2 star anise
2 medium red onions, peeled and chopped
1 tablespoon fresh ginger paste (page 12)
2 tablespoons fresh garlic paste (page 12)
½ teaspoon ground turmeric
2 medium tomatoes, puréed
2 teaspoons table salt

1. Cut the chicken into 12 to 16 pieces and set aside.

2. Place a small nonstick sauté pan over medium heat and add 2 tablespoons of the oil. When small bubbles appear at the bottom of the pan, add the coconut, chiles, *dal*, coriander, peppercorns, cumin, cinnamon, cloves, and cardamom. Sauté for 5 minutes or until fragrant. Transfer to a bowl and set aside to cool.

3. To the same hot pan, add the poppy seeds and place over low heat. Roast for 3 to 4 minutes, then add to the other sautéed spices and stir. When the mixture cools completely, transfer it to a mini food processor and process to a coarse powder.

4. Place a medium nonstick sauté pan over medium heat and add the remaining 6 tablespoons (90 ml) oil. When small bubbles appear at the bottom of the pan, add the bay leaves, curry leaves, and star anise, and stir. Add the onions and sauté for 3 to 4 minutes or until lightly browned.

5. Add the ginger paste and garlic paste, and sauté for 1 minute. Add the chicken and turmeric, and toss for 2 to 3 minutes.

6. Add the tomatoes and the spice powder, and stir well. Add 2½ cups (500 ml) water and the salt, and stir again. Cover and cook for 15 minutes or until the chicken is cooked through and the oil comes to the top.

7. Check the seasoning and serve hot.

Palak Chicken

·······*{ **Chicken with spinach** }*··

Cooking meat and poultry with spinach is very popular in North India. My girls love this simple dish with hot *rotis* (page 18) on a cool day.

Serves 4.

2 cups (335 grams) frozen blanched and chopped spinach
6 tablespoons vegetable oil
8 whole black peppercorns
2 bay leaves
8 whole cloves
5 green cardamom pods
2 medium red onions, chopped
1-inch (2½-cm) piece fresh ginger, chopped, plus 1-inch (2½-cm) piece fresh ginger, julienned
4 cloves garlic, chopped
1 (1¾-pound/800-gram) chicken, cut into 12 pieces
2 teaspoons ground roasted cumin (page 32)
1 teaspoon ground coriander
½ teaspoon ground turmeric
2 teaspoons table salt
2 green chiles, stemmed and slit
5 tablespoons (75 grams) plain yogurt
¼ teaspoon *garam masala* (spice mix; page 27)

1. Thaw the spinach, put in a food processor, and process to a fine purée. Set aside.

2. Place a nonstick saucepan over medium heat and add the oil. When small bubbles appear at the bottom of the pan, add the peppercorns, bay leaves, cloves, and cardamom, and sauté for 1 minute. Add the onions, chopped ginger, and garlic, and sauté, stirring continuously, for 4 minutes or until the onions are lightly browned.

3. Add the chicken, cumin, coriander, turmeric, 1 teaspoon of the salt, and the chiles, and sauté for 6 minutes. Add 1 tablespoon of the yogurt and stir. Sauté for 1 minute, then add 1 more tablespoon yogurt. Repeat until all of the yogurt has been added. Cook for 10 minutes more, stirring continuously. Add ½ cup (100 ml) water and stir.

4. Add the spinach and julienned ginger, and cook for 2 minutes. Add the remaining 1 teaspoon salt and the *garam masala* and stir.

5. Serve hot.

Paneer Anda

········⊰ *Paneer* and eggs ⊱···

When I was growing up in Delhi, fresh *paneer* used to be sold at vegetable stalls along with the fresh produce. Today, it is sold in the freezer section of stores, but I always prefer it fresh. I made up this recipe when my kids, as they are wont to do, demanded something new.

Serves 4.

2 medium tomatoes
4 large eggs
2 tablespoons ghee (page 37)
1 medium red onion, minced
4 cloves garlic, minced
½ teaspoon ground turmeric
½ teaspoon red chile powder
½ teaspoon ground black pepper
1 teaspoon table salt
7 ounces (200 grams) *paneer* (pressed fresh cheese; page 17), cut into 1-inch (2½-cm) cubes
¾ teaspoon *garam masala* (spice mix; page 27)
1 tablespoon chopped fresh cilantro

1. Put the tomatoes in a saucepan with 3 cups (600 ml) hot water for 5 minutes. Drain, let cool, and peel. Dice the tomatoes and set aside.

2. Place a nonstick saucepan with 2 cups (400 ml) water over high heat, add the eggs, and bring to a boil. Boil for 10 minutes. Drain and set the eggs aside on a plate to cool. When cooled, peel them and cut into quarters.

3. Place a small nonstick sauté pan over medium heat and add the ghee. When the ghee melts and small bubbles appear at the bottom of the pan, add the onion and garlic, and sauté for 3 minutes or until

golden brown.

4. Add the turmeric, chile powder, black pepper, and salt, and sauté for 30 seconds. Add the tomatoes and cook for 7 minutes or until the oil comes to the top.

5. Add 1 cup (200 ml) water and cook until the excess liquid has evaporated. Mash to a smooth paste with a wooden spoon.

6. Add 1 cup (200 ml) water and stir. Bring to a boil, lower the heat, and add the *paneer* and boiled eggs. Simmer gently for about 7 minutes.

7. Sprinkle with the *garam masala* and cilantro, and serve hot.

Quick Jeera Chicken

········⋅⦃ **Chicken flavored with cumin** ⦄⋅⦂ ··

This is an ideal dish to make when in a hurry, because chicken is not only good to eat but also fast to cook. I take advantage of that fact and dish this up as an Indian stir-fry. The mint and cilantro create magic with the cumin and pepper… I can actually smell the aroma even as I write this!

Serves 4.

1 (1¾-pound/800-gram) chicken, cut into 12 pieces
1 tablespoon freshly squeezed lemon juice
2 teaspoons table salt
2 tablespoons vegetable oil
2 teaspoons cumin seeds
8 to 10 green chiles, stemmed and cut in half
½ teaspoon ground turmeric
½ cup (125 grams) plain yogurt, whisked
¼ cup (15 grams) chopped fresh cilantro
7 or 8 black peppercorns, crushed
2 tablespoons chopped fresh mint

1. Put the chicken in a large bowl. Add the lemon juice and 1 teaspoon of the salt, and stir well. Cover the bowl with plastic wrap and put in the refrigerator to marinate for 30 minutes.

2. Place a medium nonstick saucepan over medium and add the oil. When small bubbles appear at the bottom of the pan, add the cumin. When the cumin begins to change color, add the chiles and turmeric, and sauté for 10 seconds.

3. Add the chicken and sauté for 8 to 9 minutes or until well browned. Add the yogurt, cilantro, peppercorns, and the remaining 1 teaspoon salt. Stir well and add ½ cup (100 ml) water. Cover, lower the heat to low, and cook for 20 minutes or until the chicken is cooked through.

4. Transfer to a serving dish, sprinkle with the mint, and serve hot.

Thengenkai Kori

I first tasted this in Mangalore, a beautiful coastal town in the South Indian state of Karnataka. I found this mildly spiced chicken curry absolutely delicious, and it's a simple preparation that works well at home.

Serves 4.

4 medium bone-in chicken breasts
2 teaspoons fresh garlic paste (page 12)
1 teaspoon fresh ginger paste (page 12)
1½ teaspoons table salt
¾ cup (190 grams) plain yogurt
1 teaspoon red chile powder
½ teaspoon ground turmeric
3 tablespoons vegetable oil
3 whole cloves
1-inch (2½-cm) cinnamon stick
2 medium red onions, chopped
1½ cups (300 ml) chicken stock (page 34)
1 cup (200 ml) thick coconut milk
¼ teaspoon ground green cardamom

1. Put the chicken in a bowl, add 1 teaspoon of the garlic paste, ½ teaspoon of the ginger paste, and 1 teaspoon of the salt, and rub in well. Cover the bowl with plastic wrap and set aside to marinate for 15 minutes.

2. Put the yogurt in a small bowl. Add the chile powder and turmeric, and whisk well.

3. Place a nonstick sauté pan over medium heat and add the oil. When small bubbles appear at the bottom of the pan, add the cloves and cinnamon, and sauté for 30 seconds. Add the onions and sauté for 4 to 5 minutes or until lightly browned. Add the remaining 1 teaspoon garlic paste and the remaining ½ teaspoon ginger paste, and sauté for 30 seconds.

4. Remove from the heat and stir in the yogurt mixture. Return the pan to low heat and cook, stirring continuously, for 5 to 6 minutes or until the oil comes to the top.

5. Add the stock and bring to a boil. Add the chicken and the remaining ½ teaspoon salt, and stir. Cover and cook for 15 to 20 minutes or until the chicken is cooked through.

6. Remove from the heat. Remove the chicken with a slotted spoon and put in a bowl. Push the gravy through a strainer into another nonstick sauté pan and place over low heat. Add the chicken and coconut milk, and cook for 2 minutes.

7. Transfer to a serving bowl, sprinkle with the cardamom, and serve hot.

Wafer Per Eda

····•{ **Eggs with potato chips** }•··

This unusual method of cooking eggs is native to the Parsi community in India. Parsis came to India from Persia and settled in the Indian state of Gujarat. Their cooking skills are legendary, and even in this simple dish, you will notice their innovative and delightful approach.

Serves 4.

1 tablespoon vegetable oil
½ teaspoon cumin seeds
1 medium red onion, sliced
2 green chiles, stemmed and chopped
1 medium tomato, chopped
1 cup (200 grams) potato chips
1 teaspoon table salt
4 medium eggs
1 tablespoon chopped fresh cilantro

1. Place a medium nonstick saucepan over medium heat and add the oil. When small bubbles appear at the bottom of the pan, add the cumin and onion, and sauté for 2 to 3 minutes or until light golden. Add the chiles and tomato, and cook for 3 minutes or until the tomatoes are soft.

2. Add the potato chips, salt, and 2 tablespoons water. Cover and cook for 1 minute. Uncover and spread the mixture evenly in the pan.

3. Crack the eggs, one at a time, on top of the potato chip mixture to cover completely.

4. Lower the heat to low, cover, and cook for about 5 minutes or until the eggs are set.

5. Garnish with the cilantro and serve immediately.

Zafrani Dum Murgh

Chicken that is cooked in a coal-fired clay oven called a *tandoor* is probably the most common Indian dish available outside India. Here, I've added a hint of saffron and then roasted the chicken in a conventional oven.

Serves 4.

1 (1¾-pound/800-gram) chicken
1 cup (250 grams) plain yogurt
1½ teaspoons table salt
1 teaspoon red chile powder
¾ teaspoon fresh ginger paste (page 12)
¾ teaspoon fresh garlic paste (page 12)
1 quart (800 ml) vegetable oil
3 medium red onions, sliced
½ cup (30 grams) chopped fresh cilantro
½ cup (30 grams) chopped fresh mint
5 green chiles, stemmed and chopped
2 tablespoons freshly squeezed lemon juice
5 whole cloves
2 green cardamom pods
2-inch (5-cm) cinnamon stick
3 or 4 saffron threads
2 tablespoons grated fresh coconut (or frozen unsweetened coconut)
10 almonds, blanched and peeled (see Note page 40), ground
¼ cup (60 grams) butter, melted

1. Pat the chicken dry. Prick it all over with a fork.

2. Put the yogurt in a bowl and stir in 1 teaspoon of the salt, the chile powder, ginger paste, and garlic paste. Rub the mixture generously on the chicken, inside and out. Put the chicken in a large bowl, cover with plastic wrap, and put in the refrigerator to marinate for 5 to 6 hours.

3. Place a nonstick wok over high heat and add the oil. When small bubbles appear at the bottom of the pan, lower the heat to medium, add the onions, and cook, stirring constantly with a slotted spoon, until they are browned and crisp. Remove with the slotted spoon and drain on paper towels. Set aside to cool completely. Crumble lightly with your fingers.

4. Preheat the oven to 325°F/160°C.

5. Put the cilantro, mint, chiles, lemon juice, remaining ½ teaspoon salt, the cloves, cardamom, and cinnamon in a mini food processor, add 1 tablespoon water, and process to a smooth paste. Transfer to a bowl and stir in the browned onions, saffron, coconut, and almonds. Rub the mixture all over the chicken and prick it all over with a fork again.

6. Grease a baking sheet with a little melted butter. Brush the chicken with some melted butter and place it on the baking sheet. Bake on the middle rack of the oven for 15 minutes.

7. Baste with the remaining melted butter and bake for 20 minutes more or until cooked through.

8. Remove from the oven and let rest for 5 minutes. Carve the chicken and serve hot.

Breads

India is the country of golden wheat. We use other grains, such as rice, corn, and millet, but wheat, semolina, and whole-wheat flour rule. People around the world are switching from highly refined grains to those that are closer to their natural state—white bread to whole wheat, white rice to brown—but India has been eating what is essentially whole-wheat bread for centuries: the simple, humble, everyday *roti* (page 18) and *chapati* (page 438), an unleavened griddle bread.

A puffed-up *roti* called a *phulka* always fascinates travelers from abroad, and I demystify the process here. Knead the dough with water, and as the *roti* is exposed to high heat, the water begins to evaporate rapidly. This creates steam, which is what causes the bread to balloon. *Rotis* are best rolled out with a light hand that evenly distributes the pressure over the expanding surface (a long, thin Indian-style rolling pin is best for this). Dusting with flour once or twice can help you to prevent folds in the rolled-out *roti* and thus ensure perfect puffing.

But the world of Indian breads does not stop at the *roti*, *naan* (page 20), and *paratha* (page 18) that you might order in your local Indian restaurant to sop up saucy curries. In this chapter you'll find intriguing breads like the Rajasthani *bati* (page 462), a whole-wheat bread enriched with plenty of ghee, and breads that can be served as substantial dishes in and of themselves. The chicken *kheema kulcha* (page 454), for example, can be cut up and served as a hot starter, and the many layers of *pudina paratha* (page 461) can be separated and served with chicken, meat, or *dal*.

Aloo Anardana Kulcha

A Punjabi stuffed bread with potato and dried pomegranate seeds

Dried pomegranate seeds, or *anardana*, are the star attraction here. They share their tartness only when crushed or ground and are rarely used whole. They are readily available at Indian grocery stores.

This *kulcha* pairs very well with *chole*. With *khajoor aur imli ki* chutney (sweet date-and-tamarind chutney; page 22), sliced onions, and green chiles, it's simply irresistible.

Makes 8.

2 cups (240 grams) *maida* (refined flour) or pastry flour
¾ teaspoon table salt
¼ teaspoon baking soda
2 tablespoons plain yogurt
2 tablespoons milk
3 tablespoons vegetable oil
1 teaspoon *anardana* (dried pomegranate seeds)
2 medium potatoes, boiled, peeled, and grated
½ medium onion, diced
¼ medium bunch fresh cilantro leaves, finely chopped
8 to 10 fresh mint leaves, finely chopped
2 green chiles, stemmed and minced
½ tablespoon red chile powder
½ tablespoon ground roasted cumin (page 32)
¾ teaspoon *kalonji* (nigella; see Note page 231)
2 tablespoons butter

1. Sift the *maida*, ½ teaspoon of the salt, and the baking soda into a large bowl. Gradually add the yogurt and milk, and stir well. Add ½ cup (100 ml) water and knead to make a soft and smooth dough. Cover with a wet cloth and let rest for 10 minutes.

2. Add 2 tablespoons of the oil and knead the dough well. Cover and set aside for at least 1 and up to 3 hours.

3. Divide the dough into 8 equal portions and shape them into smooth balls.

4. Heat a nonstick sauté pan over medium heat. Add the *anardana* and dry-roast them for 2 minutes. Cool and grind to a coarse powder in a spice grinder.

5. In a large bowl, combine the potatoes, onion, cilantro, mint, green chiles, *anardana*, chile powder, cumin, and the remaining ¼ teaspoon salt. Divide the potato mixture into 8 equal portions and set aside.

6. Flatten a portion of dough, place a portion of the potato mixture in the center, and fold the dough over to form a ball. Place the stuffed dough on a lightly floured work surface and roll gently into a 4- to 5-inch (10- to 12½-cm) round. Brush lightly with oil, sprinkle *kalonji* on the surface, and press with your palm.

7. Place a nonstick *tawa* (griddle) over medium heat. Let it heat for 2 minutes, then place a dough round on it and cook until the underside has light golden specks. Flip over and cook until the second side has light golden specks.

8. Brush the hot *kulchas* with butter and serve immediately.

Aloo Paratha

·······⊰ **An Indian bread stuffed with potato** ⊱···

This is comfort food for Punjabis, especially the children, and is served for breakfast, lunch, teatime, and dinner. Glistening with ghee (page 37) and served piping hot with yogurt and Indian-spiced pickle, it is a signature bread of rural as well as urban Punjab.

Makes 8.

2 cups (300 grams) *atta* (whole-wheat flour)
¾ teaspoon table salt
1 teaspoon *anardana* (dried pomegranate seeds)
2 medium potatoes, boiled, peeled, and grated
1 teaspoon red chile powder
1 green chile, stemmed and chopped
½ cup (120 grams) butter, melted

1. Sift the *atta* and ½ teaspoon of the salt into a large bowl. Gradually add ¾ (150 ml) cup water and knead to make a smooth dough. Cover with a damp cloth and let rest for 15 minutes.

2. Heat a nonstick sauté pan over medium heat. Add the *anardana* and dry-roast for 2 minutes. Cool and grind to a coarse powder in a spice grinder.

3. Combine the potatoes, *anardana*, chile powder, green chile, and the remaining ¼ teaspoon salt in a large bowl. Stir well.

4. Divide the dough into 8 equal portions and shape into smooth balls. Cover with a wet cloth and set aside for 5 minutes.

5. Take a dough ball and flatten it by pressing it between your palms. Place a portion of the potato mixture in the center, bring in the edges to enclose it, and shape into a ball again. Seal the edges completely so that the potato stuffing does not come out. Repeat with the remaining dough and filling.

6. Flatten the balls, sprinkle with a little flour, and roll them with a rolling pin into 6-inch (15-cm) rounds.

7. Place a nonstick *tawa* (griddle) over medium heat. Let it heat for 2 minutes, then place a *paratha* on it and cook for 3 minutes. Turn the *paratha*, drizzle ½ tablespoon of the butter on it, spreading it to cover the entire surface. Reduce the heat to low and cook until golden brown. Turn again and drizzle the other side with ½ tablespoon butter. Cook over low heat until golden brown. Repeat with the remaining *parathas*.

8. Serve hot.

Bakharkhani

······❊⟩ **A rich bread fit for a king** ⟨❊······

Legend has it that this bread is the creation of Nawab Bakhar Khan, after whom it is named. A sweet bread with nuts, seeds, and essences, this is wonderful with kebabs.

Makes 8.

2 cups (240 grams) *maida* (refined flour) or pastry flour
½ teaspoon baking powder
1 teaspoon table salt
¾ cup (150 ml) milk
2½ teaspoons sugar
12 to 14 raisins (optional)
1 tablespoon *chironji/charoli* (melon seeds; see page 587)
½ tablespoon active dry yeast
1 teaspoon *kewra* (screw pine) water
5 tablespoons (75 grams) ghee (page 37), melted
10 almonds, blanched (page 40) and sliced

1. Sift the *maida*, baking powder, and salt together into a deep bowl.

2. Place a nonstick saucepan over medium heat. Add the milk and heat. Add the sugar and stir until it dissolves. Remove from the heat and let cool to room temperature.

3. Soak the raisins, if using, and the *chironji* in ½ cup (100 ml) warm water for 5 minutes, drain, and set aside.

4. Put the dry yeast in a small bowl, add ¼ cup (50 ml) lukewarm (not hot) water, and set aside for 3 minutes to dissolve.

5. Make a well in the center of the *maida* mixture, add the milk mixture, *kewra* water, and dissolved yeast, and gradually stir to make soft dough. Cover with a damp cloth and set aside for 10 minutes.

6. Gradually add 3 tablespoons of the ghee to the dough and knead until it is incorporated. Add the almonds, raisins, and *chironji*. Knead the dough, cover, and set aside in a warm place for 30 minutes to rise.

7. Preheat the oven to 475°F/250°C.

8. Divide the dough into 8 equal portions, make balls, cover, and set aside for 10 minutes.

9. Flatten the balls and roll them out into 5-inch (12½-cm) rounds. Prick the entire surface of each round with a fork.

10. Arrange the rounds on an ungreased baking sheet and bake for 10 to 12 minutes, until the bread is fully cooked.

11. Remove from the oven, brush with the remaining ghee, and serve hot.

Besan Ki Masala Roti

·······⋙❧ **A spicy gram-flour bread** ☙⋘···

This spicy bread is a traditional breakfast in parts of India. The two different flours used, gram flour and whole-wheat flour, are good sources of energy and protein.

Makes 8.

1 cup (100 grams) *besan* (chickpea/gram flour)
½ cup (75 grams) *atta* (whole-wheat flour)
½ teaspoon *amchur* (dried mango powder)
1½ teaspoons ground roasted cumin (page 32)
½ teaspoon ground coriander
½ teaspoon red chile powder
¼ teaspoon ground turmeric
2 green chiles, stemmed and chopped
2 tablespoons chopped fresh cilantro
2 tablespoons plus 4 teaspoons ghee (page 37), melted
1 teaspoon table salt

1. Put the *besan* in a bowl. Add the *atta*, *amchur*, cumin, coriander, chile powder, turmeric, green chiles, cilantro, 2 tablespoons of the ghee, the salt, and ¼ cup (50 ml) water, and knead to make a soft dough. Cover with a damp cloth and let rest for 10 to 15 minutes.

2. Divide the dough into 8 equal portions and roll into balls. Roll each ball into an 8-inch (20-cm) round.

3. Place a nonstick *tawa* (griddle) over high heat. Let it heat for 2 mintues, then lower the heat to medium. Place the dough rounds, one at a time, on the *tawa* and cook, drizzling ½ teaspoon ghee on each *roti*. Turn over a few times to ensure even cooking on both sides. Cook each *roti* for 4 minutes or until crisp on both sides. Serve hot.

Bhakri

A nutritious and wholesome millet bread

This rustic bread is thought of as a high-energy food by farmers of Maharashtra. They eat it with salt, green chiles, and sometimes a red onion—not chopped or sliced, but simply smashed with the fist and peeled.

Makes 8.

1¼ cups (300 grams) *jawar* (sorghum) or millet flour
2 teaspoons table salt
2 teaspoons sesame seeds
3 tablespoons ghee (page 37)

1. Place the *jawar* flour and salt in a large bowl. Knead, gradually adding enough water to make a stiff dough. Divide the dough into 8 equal portions.

2. Place a small piece of plastic wrap on a flat work surface. Take one portion of the dough, roll it into a ball, and place it on the plastic. Wet your fingers with water and pat the ball into a thick 6-inch (15-cm) round.

3. Place a nonstick *tawa* (griddle) over medium heat. Let it heat for 2 minutes, then place a dough round on it and sprinkle a few sesame seeds on top. Brush some water on the entire surface of the *bhakri* so that the sides do not crack. Cook over medium heat for 1 minute on each side, then place the *bhakri* over an open gas flame until it puffs up, about 30 seconds. Turn and cook until it puffs up again. Repeat with the remaining dough rounds.

4. Remove from the heat, spread with ghee, and serve hot.

Chicken Kheema Kulcha

·······⋇{ **A bread stuffed with spicy chicken** }⋇·······

Kulchas are soft breads that are baked in clay ovens.

Makes 8.

4 cups (480 grams) *maida* (refined flour) or pastry flour
3 teaspoons table salt
½ teaspoon baking soda
¼ cup (50 ml) milk
¼ cup (60 grams) plain yogurt
2 tablespoons vegetable oil
1-inch (2½-cm) piece fresh ginger, chopped
3 or 4 garlic cloves, crushed
1½ medium red onions, chopped
1 pound (500 grams) ground chicken
½ teaspoon ground turmeric
1½ teaspoons red chile powder
1 teaspoon *garam masala* (spice mix; page 27)
¼ cup (15 grams) chopped fresh cilantro, chopped
3 tablespoons butter, melted

1. Sift the flour, 2 teaspoons of the salt, and the baking soda into a large bowl. Add the milk and yogurt, and stir. Add ½ cup (100 ml) water and knead into a soft dough. Cover with a damp cloth and set aside for 15 minutes.

2. Divide the dough into 8 equal portions.

3. Place a nonstick sauté pan over medium heat and add the oil. When small bubbles appear at the bottom of the pan, add the ginger, garlic, and onions, and sauté until lightly browned. Add the chicken and cook, stirring, until all the moisture evaporates and the chicken is cooked through.

4. Add the remaining 1 teaspoon salt, the turmeric, chile powder, *garam masala*, and cilantro, and stir well. Divide this mixture into 8 equal portions and set aside to cool.

5. Roll out each portion of dough into a 3-inch (7½-cm) round. Place a portion of the chicken mixture in the center of each, gather the edges to enclose the filling, and shape into a ball. Using a rolling pin, roll out into as thin a disk as possible.

6. Place a nonstick *tawa* (griddle) over medium heat and let it heat for 2 minutes. Place a dough round on it and cook, turning once or twice, until both sides are lightly browned. Repeat with the remaining dough rounds. (Alternatively, cook the *kulchas* in the oven: Preheat the oven to 400°F/200°C. Place the *kulchas* on a greased baking sheet and bake for 10 to 15 minutes.)

7. Brush with the butter and serve hot.

Garlic Naan

······⊰{ **A North Indian baked flatbread infused with garlic** }⊱······

I have had many versions of garlic *naan*, some mild and some highly flavored. This version is right in the middle, and it is great on its own or with any thick lentil curry or chicken curry. *Naan* takes quite a lot of practice to master but is well worth the effort.

Makes 8.

2 cups (240 grams) *maida* (refined flour) or pastry flour
½ teaspoon baking powder
¼ teaspoon baking soda
½ teaspoon table salt
30 cloves garlic
1 teaspoon confectioners' sugar
¾ cup (150 ml) milk
1 tablespoon plain yogurt
1 tablespoon chopped fresh cilantro
1 tablespoon vegetable oil
3 tablespoons butter, melted

1. Set a couple of tablespoons of the *maida* aside for dusting and sift the remaining *maida*, the baking powder, baking soda, and salt into a large bowl.

2. Put 20 of the garlic cloves in a food processor with 1 tablespoon water, and process to a fine paste. Mince the remaining 10 cloves and set aside.

3. To the sifted *maida* mixture, add the confectioners' sugar, milk, garlic paste, half of the minced garlic, the yogurt, and cilantro, and knead to make a medium-soft dough. Rub the oil over the surface, cover with a damp cloth, and set aside for at least 1 hour.

4. Punch the dough with your hands to make it soft and pliable, then divide it into 8 equal portions. Cover the dough with a damp cloth and let it rest for 1 hour more.

5. Flatten each dough ball between your palms, coat with a little melted butter, and dust with the reserved *maida*. Roll into a ball again, cover, and set aside for 15 minutes.

6. Preheat the oven to 475°F/250°C.

7. Roll each dough ball on a floured work surface into a 5- to 6-inch (12½- to 15-cm) round. Pull it from one end to shape it into an elongated oval. Sprinkle with the remaining minced garlic.

8. Bake (on baking sheets) for 7 minutes or until brown spots appear on the surface of the *naan*. (Alternatively, cook in a tandoor oven. Or cook on a preheated *tawa* or griddle, moistening the *naan* on either side with a little water as they cook.)

9. Drizzle with melted butter and serve hot.

Khaari Puri

Khaari puri means "bread with salt," but there's much more going on here. These breads are wonderful for a Sunday brunch with a pot of freshly made plain yogurt and a glass of hot masala tea (page 48).

Makes 16.

½ teaspoon cumin seeds
½ teaspoon coriander seeds
1¾ cups (110 grams) *atta* (whole-wheat flour)
2 tablespoons *besan* (chickpca/gram flour)
2 tablespoons ground coriander
1 tablespoon red chile powder
¼ teaspoon ground turmeric
½ teaspoon *garam masala* (spice mix; page 27)
1½ teaspoons table salt
1 tablespoon chopped fresh cilantro
2 tablespoons ghee (page 37) melted
2 green chiles, stemmed and chopped
1 quart (800 ml) plus 4 teaspoons vegetable oil, plus more for the dough

1. Place a small nonstick sauté pan over medium heat. Let it heat for 2 minutes, then add the cumin and coriander seeds, and dry-roast until light golden and fragrant. Set aside to cool, then transfer to a mortar and crush with a pestle (you can use a spice grinder here if your grinder can accomodate such a small quantity).

2. Place the *atta* in a large bowl. Add the *besan*, ground coriander, chile powder, turmeric, *garam masala*, salt, cilantro, crushed cumin and coriander seeds, ghee, and ¼ cup (50 ml) water, and knead to make a stiff dough. Cover with a damp cloth and let rest for 10 minutes.

3. Divide the dough into 16 portions and roll into balls. Lightly coat each ball with a little oil and roll out into 3-inch (7½-cm) rounds.

4. Place a nonstick wok over high heat and add the 1 quart (800 ml) oil. When small bubbles appear at the bottom of the wok, lower the heat to medium. Gently slide in the dough rounds, one or two at a time, and cook, turning with a slotted spoon, for 4 to 5 minutes or until golden brown on both sides.

5. Remove with the slotted spoon and drain on paper towels. Serve hot.

Khasta Roti

Khasta means "crisp," and these *rotis* are just that. Is it this crispiness that endears them to me, or is it the pinch of sugary sweetness? Either way: They're delicious! If you'd like, serve these as they do in India: Let the *rotis* cool to room temperature, then tell your guests to crush each one delicately in the palms of their hands.

Makes 8.

1 teaspoon sugar
½ teaspoon table salt
1 cup (120 grams) *maida* (refined flour) or pastry flour
2 tablespoons coarse *rawa/suji* (semolina flour)
¼ cup (50 grams) ghee (page 37), melted
½ teaspoon *ajwain*

1. Put the sugar and salt in a small bowl, add ¼ cup (50 ml) water, and stir until dissolved.

2. Put the *maida*, semolina flour, ghee, *ajwain*, and the salt and sugar water in a bowl, and knead to make a stiff dough. Cover with a damp cloth and set aside for 15 minutes.

3. Divide the dough into 8 portions and shape into balls. Flatten each ball and roll out into a 6-inch (15-cm) round.

4. Place a nonstick sauté pan or *tawa* (griddle) over medium heat. Let it heat for 2 minutes, then place a *roti* in the pan and cook, turning, until both sides are crisp. Repeat with the remaining dough rounds.

5. Serve hot.

Koki

This is a rich flatbread enjoyed at breakfast. The cream gives it its melt-in-your-mouth quality. A typical Sindhi *koki* is rather alarmingly large, but you can make them in any size. My mom flecks them with light knife marks in diamond shapes so that breaking the cooled bread into clean pieces is easy.

Makes 8.

2½ cups (375 grams) *atta* (whole-wheat flour)
2 small red onions, peeled and diced
2 teaspoons table salt
2 green chiles, stemmed and minced
1 teaspoon *ajwain*
1 teaspoon *anardana* (dried pomegranate seeds), crushed
2 tablespoons chopped fresh cilantro
¼ cup (50 grams) ghee (page 37), melted
¼ cup (50 ml) heavy cream

1. Put the *atta* in a large bowl. Add the onions, salt, green chiles, *ajwain*, *anardana*, cilantro, 1 tablespoon of the ghee, and the cream, and stir well. Add ¾ cup (150 ml) water and knead to make a stiff dough. Cover and let rest for about 15 minutes.

2. Divide the dough into 8 equal portions. Lightly dust with a little flour and roll out into a thick 5-inch (12½-cm) round.

3. Place a nonstick *tawa* (griddle) over medium heat. Let it heat for 2 minutes, then place a dough round on the *tawa* and cook for 2 to 3 minutes on each side or until evenly cooked on both the sides. Brush with a little of the remaining ghee and cook, pressing with a flat spoon, until both sides are light golden. Repeat with the remaining dough rounds.

4. Serve hot.

Makki Di Roti

Breads, in all their glorious variety, form the staple of an Indian meal. This bread uses cornmeal, which makes it the quintessential Punjabi bread. I would be remiss if I didn't mention this bread's soul mate, *sarson ka saag* (mustard greens; page 254), which it always seems to accompany. Served hot with a dollop of white butter and cane jaggery on cold wintry evenings, it is absolute manna.

When I first learned to make this *roti*, my mother gave me this little tip for shaping the dough: "Just put your ball of dough between two plastic sheets and then pat it into shape."

Makes 8.

1½ cups (200 grams) *makai ka atta* (cornmeal)
½ teaspoon table salt
¼ teaspoon *ajwain*
1 cup (200 ml) lukewarm water
8 teaspoons vegetable oil
Butter

1. Put the cornmeal in a large bowl. Add the salt, *ajwain*, and lukewarm water, and knead to make a medium-soft dough. Divide the dough into 8 equal portions and shape into balls. Pat each ball between moistened palms to make a 5-inch (12½-cm) round of medium thickness. (Alternatively, roll out each ball between two sheets of oiled plastic wrap.)

2. Place a nonstick *tawa* (griddle) over high heat and let it heat for 2 minutes. Reduce the heat to medium, place one dough round on the *tawa*, and cook until one side is half done. Turn over and drizzle ½ teaspoon of the oil over the top. Turn over again and drizzle 1 teaspoon oil over the second side. Cook until both sides are golden brown.

3. Repeat with the remaining dough rounds.

4. Serve hot with a dollop of butter on each *roti*.

Missi Roti

A spiced Indian bread

Missi roti is like a savory short-crust pastry; it's easy to break and melts in your mouth. I love to serve this with *dal* (pages 488–515).

Makes 8.

2 cups (300 grams) *atta* (whole-wheat flour)
½ cup (50 grams) *besan* (chickpea/gram flour)
1½ teaspoons salt
1 teaspoon red chile powder
½ teaspoon ground turmeric
2 teaspoons ground coriander
1 teaspoon *garam masala* (spice mix; page 27)
2 medium red onions, chopped
4 green chiles, stemmed and chopped
2 tablespoons chopped fresh cilantro leaves
1 tablespoon plus 8 teaspoons vegetable oil

1. Place the *atta*, *besan*, salt, chile powder, turmeric, coriander, *garam masala*, onions, green chiles, cilantro, and 1 tablespoon of the oil in a large bowl. Add ½ cup water and knead to make a soft dough. Divide the dough into 8 equal portions and roll into balls. Roll out each ball into a 6-inch (15-cm) round.

2. Place a nonstick *tawa* (griddle) over medium heat and let it heat for 2 minutes. Place one dough round on the *tawa* and cook for 30 seconds. Turn over and drizzle ½ teaspoon oil around it. Turn again and drizzle another ½ teaspoon oil around the *roti*. Cook until both sides are cooked and light brown specks appear on the surface. Repeat with the remaining dough rounds.

3. Serve immediately.

Pudina Paratha

Breads like _pudina paratha_ taste very different depending on whether they are cooked on a griddle or in the more traditional tandoor oven. This bread is delicious either way, but more adventurous cooks can rig up a makeshift tandoor at home. On the stovetop, heat a deep, heavy pan with a handle over medium-high heat while you roll out the dough (this works with _roti_ as well). Lightly dampen one side of a dough round. Carefully stick the wet side onto the inside wall of the pan, then quickly turn the pan upside down over the heat source—a gas flame works best. The heat will cook the bread until little black flecks appear on the top surface, just as it does in a tandoor. The bread will become unstuck as the water dries up, and you can easily pull it out of the pan and serve it. Our favorite dish to serve with _pudina paratha_ is _dal makhni_ (page 491).

Makes 8.

> 1 cup fresh mint leaves
> 2 cups (300 grams) _atta_ (whole-wheat flour)
> 1½ teaspoons table salt
> 1 tablespoon plus 8 teaspoons vegetable oil
> 3 tablespoons butter, melted
> 2 teaspoons _chaat masala_ (spice mix for _chaat_; page 24)

1. Wash and pat the mint leaves dry. Heat a nonstick griddle over medium heat and lightly roast half of the mint leaves on it. Cool and crush to a powder in a spice grinder. Chop the remaining mint leaves and set aside.

2. Put the _atta_ and salt in a bowl. Add the chopped mint, 1 tablespoon of the oil, and ¾ cup (150 ml) plus 1 tablespoon water, and knead to make a stiff dough. Cover and let rest for 20 to 25 minutes.

3. Divide the dough into 8 equal portions and shape into balls. Roll out each ball into a 6-inch (15-cm) round, brush with butter, and sprinkle with some flour. Roll the dough back into a ball. Let rest for 5 minutes, then roll out each ball again into a 5- to 7-inch (12½- to 17-cm) round.

4. Place the nonstick _tawa_ (griddle) over medium heat again and let it heat for 2 minutes. Place a dough round on the _tawa_ and cook, turning and drizzling ½ teaspoon oil on each side, until both sides are light golden brown. Repeat with the remaining dough rounds.

5. Spread butter on each _paratha_ while still hot.

6. Stir the roasted mint powder and _chaat masala_ together, and sprinkle over the hot _parathas_. Before serving, crush the _parathas_ lightly between your palms to open up the layers.

Rajasthani Bati

······⊱{ **A traditional Rajasthani baked bread** }⊰············

Many years ago, I attended a wedding in Rajasthan where the guests were treated to a lavish lunch; it was there that I tasted this bread (which is traditionally baked over a cow-dung fire) for the first time. The hosts were very hospitable and coaxed me to enjoy more of this *bati* soaked in ghee and served with a thick lentil *dal*. I still remember the extended nap afterward! Serve these with *Rajasthani panchmel dal* (page 506) and more ghee (page 37).

Makes 8.

2 cups (300 grams) *atta* (whole-wheat flour)
¼ teaspoon baking powder
2 teaspoons table salt
1 cup (200 grams) ghee (page 37), softened
½ teaspoon *ajwain*

1. Preheat the oven to 425°F/220°C.

2. Sift the *atta*, baking powder, and salt into a large bowl. Rub ⅔ cup (160 grams) of the ghee into the flour mixture until it resembles bread crumbs. Add the *ajwain* and ¾ cup (150 ml) water and knead to make a dough. Divide the dough into 8 portions and shape them into balls.

3. Transfer the balls to a baking sheet and bake for about 10 minutes or until they just begin to change color. Lower the oven temperature to 400°F/200°C and bake for 35 minutes more.

4. Put the remaining ⅓ cup (80 grams) ghee in a large microwave-safe bowl and melt it in a microwave oven for 1 minute on high.

5. Remove the *batis* from the oven, press them lightly, and soak them in the melted ghee for at least 1 and up to 2 hours.

6. Remove from the bowl and serve.

Rice Wade

The rice flour here is cooked first so that it can be kneaded into a malleable dough; otherwise rice-flour dough is too sticky to handle. This bread closely resembles the North Indian *puri* and is excellent with any lamb or chicken curry.

Makes 16.

1 tablespoon fenugreek seeds
2 tablespoons fennel seeds
1 teaspoon table salt
2 cups (300 grams) rice flour
1 small red onion, grated
1 quart (800 ml) vegetable oil

1. Place a deep nonstick saucepan over high heat and add 2¼ cups (450 ml) water. Add the fenugreek and fennel seeds. When the mixture comes to a boil, lower the heat to medium and simmer for about 5 minutes; the flavor of the seeds will infuse the water.

2. Pour through a fine strainer into another saucepan and reheat the water. Add the salt and stir. Add the rice flour in a steady stream and cook, stirring, for 5 minutes or until a dough forms and leaves the edges of the pan.

3. Transfer to a bowl, cool, and knead in the onion.

4. Apply a little oil to your hands and divide the dough into 16 portions. Roll each portion into a ball between your palms. Keeping the dough on one palm, spread it with the fingers of your other hand into a 3-inch (7½-cm) round.

5. Place a nonstick wok over high heat and add the oil. When small bubbles appear at the bottom of the wok, add the dough rounds, one by one, and cook, pressing lightly with a slotted spoon, until they puff up. Turn over and continue cooking until both sides are light golden brown. Remove with the slotted spoon and drain on paper towels.

6. Serve hot.

Sheermal

This is a soft and sweet bread that looks like a close cousin of *naan* and has the richness of saffron. Because of its sweetness, it is usually served with chicken *korma*.

Makes 16.

2 cups (240 grams) *maida* (refined flour) or pastry flour
1 teaspoon table salt
2 teaspoons sugar
¾ cup plus 3 tablespoons (195 ml) warm milk
A few saffron threads
2 or 3 drops *kewra* (screw pine) water
¼ cup (50 grams) ghee (page 37), melted
2 tablespoons butter, plus more for the baking sheets

1. Sift the *maida* and salt into a large bowl.

2. Put the sugar and ¾ cup (150 ml) of the warm milk in a medium bowl and stir until the sugar dissolves. Put the saffron and the remaining 3 tablespoons warm milk in a small bowl and stir until it dissolves; set aside.

3. Add the sugar and milk mixture and the screw pine water to the *maida* mixture. Stir well, then add 2 tablespoons water, and knead to make a soft dough. Cover with a damp cloth and set aside for 10 minutes.

4. Add the ghee to the dough and knead it in well. Knead again to a soft dough. Cover and set aside for 10 minutes.

5. Divide the dough into 16 portions and form into balls. Cover and set aside for 10 minutes.

6. Preheat the oven to 525°F/275°C. Flatten the balls on a lightly floured surface and roll out each ball into a 6-inch (15-cm) round. Prick the entire surface with a fork.

7. Grease baking sheets with butter, arrange the dough rounds on them, and bake for 8 minutes.

8. Remove, brush the *sheermals* with the saffron milk, and bake again for 3 to 4 minutes, until fully cooked.

9. Brush with butter and serve immediately.

Thepla

This is one Indian flatbread that has a fairly long shelf life. And because of its longevity, Gujaratis carry a pack of them when they travel and enjoy them as snacks with a sweet mango pickle called *chhunda*. My wife, Alyona, makes a variety of *theplas* that uses less oil. This is her recipe.

Makes 12.

1 cup (150 grams) *atta* (whole-wheat flour)
¼ cup (25 grams) *besan* (chickpea/gram flour)
½ cup (20 grams) chopped *methi* (fresh fenugreek leaves)
¼ teaspoon ground turmeric
½ teaspoon red chile powder
¼ teaspoon fresh ginger paste (page 12)
¼ teaspoon green chile paste (page 13)
1 teaspoon table salt
5 tablespoons (75 ml) vegetable oil
½ cup (125 grams) plain yogurt

1. Put the *atta*, *besan*, *methi*, turmeric, chile powder, chile-ginger paste, salt, and 1 tablespoon of the oil in a large bowl, and stir well. Add the yogurt and knead to make a semisoft dough. Cover with a damp cloth and set aside for 15 minutes.

2. Divide into 12 portions and shape into balls. Roll out each ball into a thin 6-inch (15-cm) round.

3. Place a nonstick *tawa* (griddle) over medium heat and let it heat for 2 minutes. Place a dough round on it and cook, turning and brushing ½ teaspoon oil on each side, until both sides are golden. Repeat with the remaining dough rounds.

4. Serve hot or let cool and store in airtight containers for up to 1 week and serve at room temperature.

Tikadia

······❊} **A crisp whole-wheat bread stuffed with spicy onion and tomato** {❊······

A simple, spice-filled bread that pairs well with vegetable sides.

Makes 4.

1½ cups (225 grams) *atta* (whole-wheat flour)
1½ teaspoons table salt
6 tablespoons ghee (page 37), melted, plus more for serving
1 teaspoon roasted cumin seeds (page 32)
½ teaspoon red chile powder
1 medium red onion, diced
½ medium tomato, diced
2 teaspoons chopped fresh cilantro

1. Place the *atta*, 1 teaspoon of the salt, and ¼ cup (50 grams) of the ghee in a large bowl. Add 1 cup plus 2 teaspoons (210 ml) water and knead to make a soft dough.

2. In a separate bowl, combine the cumin, chile powder, onion, tomato, and cilantro.

3. Divide the dough into 4 portions and shape into balls. Roll out each ball to a thick 3-inch (7½-cm) round and brush with 1½ teaspoons of the ghee. Place a portion of the onion-tomato mixture in the center. Sprinkle with a little salt. Gather the edges to enclose the filling and seal. Press and roll out into a thick 3-inch (7½-cm) round.

4. Place a nonstick *tawa* (griddle) over high heat and let it heat for 2 minutes. Lower the heat to medium and place one dough round on the *tawa*. Cook, turning, for 2 to 3 mintues or until golden brown on both sides. Repeat with the remaining dough rounds.

5. Serve hot, topped with a dollop of ghee.

CHAPTER 10

Pulaos, Biryanis, and Other Rice Dishes

The aroma of basmati rice as it cooks epitomizes the Indian *pulaos* and *biryanis*. Basmati rice originated in India, and rice is a staple in the diets of 50 percent of the Indian population. Many Indian festivals, such as Lohri in the north, Pongal in the south, and Bihu in Assam, are based around the rice harvest.

Pulaos and *biryanis* are appetizing and especially charming when cooked with spices, vegetables, pulses, or meats. *Biryanis*, of course, are some of the most popular and satisfying Indian dishes, and here is your chance to learn to make the famous Hyderabadi *kachche gosht ki biryani* (page 481), *murgh biryani* (page 486), and the Gujarati *ek handi nu dal bhaat* (page 470)—a delicious one-pot meal, as are many of these dishes.

Aloo Gobhi Ki Tahiri

This is a nutritious *pulao* that can be prepared quickly. It's perfect as a light Sunday dinner.

Serves 4.

1 cup (200 grams) raw rice
2 tablespoons ghee (page 37)
1 teaspoon cumin seeds
2 bay leaves
1-inch (2½-cm) cinnamon stick
1 black cardamom pod
3 or 4 whole black peppercorns
4 or 5 whole cloves
1 medium red onion, thinly sliced
1 medium potato, peeled and cut into ½-inch (1-cm) cubes
½ medium head cauliflower, separated into small florets
1 teaspoon ground turmeric
1½ teaspoons red chile powder
1 teaspoon *garam masala* (spice mix; page 27)
1 teaspoon table salt

1. Put the rice in a large bowl, wash in plenty of water 2 or 3 times, and drain. Add 3 cups (600 ml) water and soak for 20 minutes. Drain the rice in a strainer.

2. Place a medium nonstick saucepan over medium heat. Add the ghee, and when small bubbles appear at the bottom of the pan, add the cumin, bay leaves, cinnamon, cardamom, peppercorns, and cloves, and sauté for 1 to 2 minutes or until fragrant. Add the onion and sauté for 3 to 4 minutes or until lightly browned.

3. Add the potato and cauliflower, and sauté over medium heat for 2 minutes.

4. Add the soaked rice, turmeric, chile powder, *garam masala*, and salt, and stir. Add 2 cups (400 ml) hot water and stir again. Bring to a boil, then lower the heat to low, cover, and cook for 15 to 20 minutes or until the rice is tender.

5. Transfer to a serving dish. Serve hot.

Cauliflower and Lemon Rice

······§{ **An ideal way to use up leftover steamed rice** }§··

Mahabaleshwar is a favorite weekend getaway for people living in Mumbai. It is famous for its strawberries, but little did I know that the strawberries thrive in the shade of large green leaves that lovingly hold huge milky-white heads of cauliflower! So on one of my trips I picked up a cauliflower that was so massive I had to figure out what to do with it all. I needed to be innovative, and this rice dish is the result.

Serves 4.

11 ounces (330 grams) small cauliflower florets
2 tablespoons freshly squeezed lemon juice
1½ teaspoons table salt
Pinch of sugar
4 green chiles, stemmed and roughly chopped
3 dried red chiles, stemmed and broken in half
2 tablespoons coriander seeds
5 or 6 cashews, roughly chopped
¼ teaspoon ground turmeric
1 teaspoon vegetable oil
¼ teaspoon brown mustard seeds
½ teaspoon *dhuli urad dal* (split skinless black gram)
⅛ teaspoon fenugreek seeds
Pinch of asafetida
7 or 8 curry leaves
2 cups (300 grams) cooked basmati rice

1. Place a nonstick saucepan over medium heat, add 1 quart (800 ml) water, and bring to a boil. Add the cauliflower and cook for 5 to 6 minutes. Drain in a colander and set aside.

2. Put the lemon juice in a small bowl. Add the salt and sugar, and stir until dissolved. Set aside.

3. Put the green chiles, red chiles, coriander, cashews, and turmeric in a spice grinder with ¼ cup (50 ml) water, and grind to a fine paste.

4. Place a nonstick wok over medium heat and add the oil. When small bubbles appear at the bottom of the wok, add the mustard seeds, *dal*, and fenugreek, and sauté until the *dal* is lightly browned. Add the asafetida and curry leaves, and sauté for 30 seconds.

5. Add the ground paste and cauliflower, and stir well. Add the rice and lemon juice mixture and stir gently. Lower the heat to low, cover, and cook for 5 minutes.

6. Serve hot.

Ek Handi Nu Dal Bhaat

In this one-pot dish, lentils and rice are cooked together along with spices and puréed tomatoes.

Serves 4.

½ cup (100 grams) *toor dal/arhar dal* (split pigeon peas)
¾ cup (150 grams) raw rice
3 tablespoons ghee (page 37)
½ teaspoon cumin seeds
2 or 3 whole cloves
4 or 5 whole black peppercorns
1 bay leaf
1 medium red onion, sliced
¾ teaspoon fresh ginger paste (page 12)
¾ teaspoon fresh garlic paste (page 12)
1 large potato, peeled and cut into 1-inch (2½-cm) pieces
¼ teaspoon ground turmeric
¾ teaspoon red chile powder
¼ teaspoon *garam masala* (spice mix; page 27)
2 green chiles, stemmed and chopped
2 teaspoons table salt
1 large tomato, puréed
¼ cup (15 grams) chopped fresh cilantro

1. Put the *dal* and rice in a large bowl, wash in plenty of water 2 or 3 times, and drain. Add 4 cups (800 ml) water and soak for 20 minutes. Drain the *dal* and rice in a strainer.

2. Place a medium nonstick saucepan over medium heat and add the ghee. When small bubbles appear at the bottom of the pan, add the cumin, cloves, peppercorns, and bay leaf, and sauté for 1 to 2 minutes or until fragrant. Add the onion, ginger paste, and garlic paste, and sauté for 2 minutes or until the onion is lightly browned.

3. Add the potato and stir well. Add the drained *dal* and rice, and stir. Add the turmeric, chile powder, *garam masala*, and chiles, and stir well. Add 1 quart (800 ml) water and the salt. Bring to a boil, then lower the heat to low, cover, and cook for 7 minutes or until the *dal* and rice are almost tender.

4. Stir in the tomato purée and cilantro. Mash the mixture slightly with the back of a ladle. Cover and cook over low heat for 4 to 5 minutes.

5. Transfer to a serving dish. Serve hot.

Fodnicha Bhaat

······{ Tempered rice }···

This very simple dish is a delicious way of using up leftover white rice. Make sure the rice is at room temperature before adding it to the spices.

Serves 4.

3 tablespoons vegetable oil
½ teaspoon black mustard seeds
½ teaspoon cumin seeds
10 to 12 fresh curry leaves
4 green chiles, stemmed and chopped
½ teaspoon ground turmeric
3 tablespoons peanuts
3 cups (450 grams) cooked rice
½ teaspoon table salt
2 tablespoons chopped fresh cilantro

1. Place a medium nonstick sauté pan over medium heat. Add the oil and when small bubbles appear at the bottom of the pan, add the mustard seeds. When the seeds begin to sputter, add the cumin and curry leaves.

2. Add the chiles, turmeric, and peanuts, and sauté for 1 minute.

3. Add the rice and salt and stir well.

4. Transfer to a serving dish. Garnish with the cilantro and serve hot.

Gatte Ka Pulao

····•} *Besan* dumplings with rice {•····

This beautiful dish has many layers of flavors as the *besan* (chickpea flour) dumplings, or *gatte*, and the spiced rice come together. Making the dumplings requires practice and patience, but it's well worth it.

Serves 4.

~ **For the dumplings:**
1½ cups (150 grams) *besan* (chickpea/gram flour)
Pinch of asafetida
¼ teaspoon ground turmeric
1 teaspoon red chile powder
½ teaspoon table salt
Pinch of baking soda
½ teaspoon fresh ginger paste (page 12)
2 tablespoons plain yogurt
7 or 8 fresh mint leaves, chopped
1 quart (800 ml) vegetable oil

~ **For the rice:**
1½ cups (300 grams) raw basmati rice
¼ cup (50 grams) ghee (page 37)
1 teaspoon sesame seeds
2 bay leaves
5 or 6 whole cloves
3 green cardamom pods
2 black cardamom pods
2 (1-inch/2½-cm) cinnamon sticks
1 tablespoon fresh ginger paste (page 12)
½ cup (75 grams) fresh or frozen green peas, boiled
1 teaspoon table salt
1 teaspoon ground roasted cumin (page 32)
2 teaspoons *garam masala* (spice mix; page 27)
2 tablespoons chopped fresh cilantro

1. Make the dumplings: In a large bowl, combine the *besan*, asafetida, turmeric, chile powder, salt, baking soda, ginger paste, yogurt, and mint. Add ¼ cup (50 ml) water and stir to make a stiff dough. Divide the dough into 4 equal portions. Apply ½ teaspoon of the oil to your palms and roll each portion into a 6-inch (15-cm) long cylinder.

2. Place a medium nonstick saucepan over high heat, add 2 cups (400 ml) water, and bring to a boil. Lower the dough cylinders into the water, lower the heat to medium, and cook for 10 to 15 minutes. Drain in a large colander. Let cool slightly, then cut each cylinder into ½-inch (1-cm) lengths.

3. Heat the remaining oil in a deep-fryer to 375°F/190°C. Gently lower the dumplings in the oil and fry until golden. This should take 3 to 4 minutes. Remove the dumplings with a slotted spoon and drain on paper towels. Set aside.

4. Make the rice: Put the rice in a bowl and wash in plenty of water 2 or 3 times. Add 3 cups (600 ml) water and soak for 30 minutes. Drain the rice in a strainer.

5. Place a deep nonstick saucepan over high heat, add 6 cups (1.2 liters) water, and bring to a boil. Add the rice and stir once. Lower the heat to medium and cook, stirring occasionally, for 7 to 8 minutes. Take care that the rice grains do not become too soft. Drain in a strainer.

6. Place a nonstick saucepan over medium heat and add the ghee. When small bubbles begin to appear at the bottom of the pan, add the sesame seeds, bay leaves, cloves, green and black cardamom pods, and cinnamon, and sauté for 1 minute.

7. Add the ginger paste and sauté for 30 seconds. Add the peas, salt, and dumplings, and sauté for 1 minute. Add the rice, cumin, *garam masala*, and cilantro. Toss to mix well.

8. Lower the heat to low, cover, and cook for 2 minutes. Serve immediately.

Hare Aam Ke Chawal

······§ Green-mango rice §······

This delightfully tangy rice gets its sourness from green mangoes, which are balanced by the natural sweetness of the fresh coconut. I suggest using basmati rice for this.

Serves 4.

2 medium green mangoes, peeled and grated
1½ tablespoons roasted peanuts
¼ cup (30 grams) grated fresh coconut (or frozen unsweetened coconut)
Generous pinch of ground turmeric
1 tablespoon vegetable oil
¼ teaspoon black mustard seeds
¼ teaspoon cumin seeds
Generous pinch of asafetida
20 fresh curry leaves
2 dried red chiles, stemmed
3 cups (450 grams) cooked basmati rice
1 teaspoon table salt
1½ tablespoons ghee (page 37), melted

1. Put one quarter of the mangoes, half of the peanuts, 3 tablespoons of the coconut, and the turmeric in a food processor, and process to a coarse paste.

2. Place a medium nonstick sauté pan over medium heat and add the oil. When small bubbles appear at the bottom of the pan, add the mustard seeds. When the seeds begin to sputter, add the cumin, asafetida, curry leaves, and chiles, and sauté for 1 minute or until fragrant.

3. Add the paste and the remaining peanuts, and sauté for 1 minute. Add the rice and stir well. Add the remaining mango and the salt, and cook, stirring well, for 2 to 3 minutes.

4. Transfer to a serving dish. Drizzle with the ghee and garnish with the remaining coconut. Serve hot.

Imli Til Ke Chawal

······⋇{ Tamarind-and-sesame rice }⋇·······

This dish, from the South Indian state of Andhra Pradesh, is a great way to use leftover white basmati rice. The rice is combined with tamarind and sesame seeds in a quick stir-fry and topped with fried onions. This is a hearty and quick dish for a weeknight.

Serves 4.

½ cup (100 ml) plus 3 tablespoons vegetable oil
1 medium onion, sliced
1 teaspoon fresh ginger paste (page 12)
1 teaspoon fresh garlic paste (page 12)
¼ teaspoon ground turmeric
1 teaspoon red chile powder
2 tablespoons tamarind pulp
3 cups (450 grams) cooked basmati rice
½ teaspoon table salt
3 tablespoons roasted sesame seeds
2 tablespoons chopped fresh cilantro

1. Place a medium nonstick wok over medium heat and add ½ cup (100 ml) of the oil. When small bubbles appear at the bottom of the wok, add the onion and fry for 5 to 6 minutes or until golden brown. Remove with a slotted spoon and drain on paper towels; set aside.

2. Place a medium nonstick saucepan over medium heat and add the remaining 3 tablespoons oil. When small bubbles appear at the bottom of the pan, add the ginger paste and garlic paste, and sauté for 1 minute.

3. Add the turmeric and chile powder, and sauté for 1 minute more. Add the tamarind pulp. Cook for 2 to 3 minutes. Add the salt and stir. Add the rice and stir thoroughly. Add the sesame seeds and cook for 2 minutes. Sprinkle the cilantro and the fried onions onto the rice and stir.

4. Transfer to a serving bowl. Serve immediately.

Kathal Ki Biryani

············ ∗⦅ Jackfruit biryani ⦆∗ ··

A *biryani* is a delightful rice dish laden with spices and nuts, typically with chicken or lamb as its star ingredient. But this *biryani* is different. Here, the starring role goes to a lemon-yellow fruit called jackfruit. Believe it or not, when I have guests at home, this is the *biryani* that they are most likely to demand. Serve with *raita*.

Serves 4.

1½ cups (300 grams) raw basmati rice
2½ teaspoons table salt
4 green cardamom pods
3 black cardamom pods
3 whole cloves
2 (1-inch/2½-cm) cinnamon sticks
5 or 6 saffron threads
2 tablespoons warm milk
1 quart (800 ml) vegetable oil
2 pounds (1 kg) raw jackfruit
4 medium red onions, thinly sliced
¼ cup (50 grams) ghee (page 37)
½ teaspoon caraway seeds
1 tablespoon fresh ginger paste (page 12)
1 tablespoon fresh garlic paste (page 12)
1 teaspoon ground turmeric
1 teaspoon ground roasted cumin (page 32)
2 teaspoons ground coriander
1 tablespoon red chile powder
3 medium tomatoes, chopped
1½ cups (375 grams) plain yogurt, whisked
1 small bunch fresh cilantro, chopped
1 teaspoon *garam masala* (spice mix; page 27)
1 small bunch fresh mint, torn
1 tablespoon *kewra* (screw pine) water

1. Put the rice in a large bowl, wash in plenty of water 2 or 3 times, and drain. Add 3 cups (600 ml) water and soak for 20 minutes. Drain the rice in a strainer.

2. Place a medium nonstick saucepan over high heat and add 10 cups (2 liters) water, 1 teaspoon of the salt, 2 of the green cardamom pods, 1 of the black cardamom pods, the cloves, and 1 of the cinnamon sticks. When the water begins to boil, add the rice and cook over high heat until it is half done, about 12 minutes. Drain in a strainer and refresh in cold water. Drain well and spread out on a plate to cool to room temperature.

3. Soak the saffron in the milk and set aside.

4. Grease the blade of a sharp knife with oil. Use the knife to peel the jackfruit, remove the center core, and cut into 1½-inch (4-cm) cubes.

5. Place a large nonstick wok over high heat and add the oil. When small bubbles begin to appear at the bottom of the wok, add the jackfruit and sauté for 5 to 6 minutes or until browned. Remove with a slotted spoon and drain on paper towels.

6. In the same wok, sauté half of the onions for 4 to 5 minutes or until golden brown and crisp. Remove with the slotted spoon and drain on paper towels.

7. Place a medium nonstick sauté pan over high heat and add 3 tablespoons of the ghee. When small bubbles appear at the bottom of the pan, lower the heat to low and add the caraway and the remaining green and black cardamom pods. Crush the remaining cinnamon stick and add it to the pan. When the spices change color and are fragrant, add the remaining onions and sauté for 5 minutes or until lightly browned.

8. Add the ginger paste and garlic paste, and sauté for 2 minutes. Add the turmeric, cumin, coriander, chile powder, and tomatoes, and continue to sauté for 5 minutes more or until the tomatoes soften.

9. Add the jackfruit and stir. Add the yogurt, the remaining 1½ teaspoons salt, and the cilantro, and cook for 2 minutes or until the jackfruit is well coated with the sauce. Remove from the heat.

10. In a nonstick saucepan, arrange the *biryani* layers: First, spread half of the jackfruit mixture in the pan. Spread half of the rice over the jackfruit mixture. Sprinkle with the saffron milk, *garam masala*, half of the mint leaves, and a few drops of *kewra* water. Spread the rest of the jackfruit mixture evenly over the rice and cover it with the remaining rice, spreading evenly. Top with the fried onions, the remaining mint leaves, the remaining *kewra* water, and the remaining 1 tablespoon ghee. Cover the pan with aluminum foil. Place the pan over low heat and cook for 20 to 25 minutes.

11. Remove from the heat, remove the foil, and serve hot.

Narangi Pulao

As modern as this dish looks and sounds, it actually has roots in the Mughal empire! This highly aromatic dish is great served with a side of creamy lentils.

Serves 4.

1½ cups (300 grams) raw basmati rice
8 medium oranges
6 to 8 saffron threads
1 tablespoon warm milk
¼ cup (50 grams) ghee (page 37)
2 (1-inch/2½-cm) cinnamon sticks
2 whole cloves
2 green cardamom pods
1 teaspoon sea salt
¼ cup (50 grams) sugar
7 or 8 black peppercorns, coarsely crushed

1. Put the rice in a large bowl, wash in plenty of water 2 or 3 times, and drain. Add 3 cups (600 ml) water and soak for 20 minutes. Drain the rice in a strainer.

2. Cut each orange in half horizontally. Using a juicer, extract the juice from the oranges and set it aside. Reserve 8 of the juiced orange halves for serving. Cut the rind of 2 of the oranges into thin strips (be sure to scrape out the membranes left over after juicing).

3. Place a medium nonstick saucepan over medium heat, add ½ cup (100 ml) water and the sliced orange rind, and bring to a boil. Boil for 1 minute, then drain and set aside.

4. Soak the saffron in the milk and set aside.

5. Place the saucepan over medium heat and add the ghee. When small bubbles appear at the bottom of the pan, add the cinnamon, cloves, and cardamom, and sauté for 1 minute or until fragrant.

6. Add the rice and sauté for 2 minutes. Add 2 cups (400 ml) of the orange juice and 1 cup (200 ml) water. Add the sea salt, sugar, crushed peppercorns, and orange rind, and stir once.

7. Add the saffron milk and stir. Cover and cook over medium heat for about 20 minutes or until the rice is tender.

8. Spoon the rice into the reserved orange halves and serve immediately.

Paneer and Peas Pulao

·······•❧ *Paneer* and green-pea pilaf ❧•·······

This dish of rice, spices, and peas cooked together has an interesting twist: a bit of sugar. Just as salt brings out certain flavors in sweet baked goods, sugar can add another layer of flavor to a savory dish like this modified version of the Bengali *chanar pulao*.

Serves 4.

1½ cups (300 grams) basmati rice
3 tablespoons ghee (page 37)
2 teaspoons sugar
14 ounces (400 grams) *paneer* (pressed fresh cheese; page 17), cut into 1-inch (2½-cm) cubes
1 large red onion, thinly sliced
1 bay leaf
1-inch (2½-cm) cinnamon stick
2 whole cloves
2 green cardamom pods
2½ teaspoons table salt
½ cup (75 grams) shelled green peas, blanched

1. Wash and drain the rice and spread it out to dry on an absorbent towel. When completely dry, transfer to a large bowl and stir in 1 tablespoon of the ghee and the sugar.

2. Place a small nonstick sauté pan over medium heat and add 1 tablespoon of the ghee. When the ghee melts, add the *paneer* and toss so that the cubes are evenly browned on all sides. Remove with a slotted spoon and set aside.

3. To the same hot pan, add the remaining 1 tablespoon ghee and the onion, and place over medium heat. Sauté for 2 to 3 minutes or until the onion is crisp and browned. Remove with a slotted spoon and set aside.

4. Return the pan with the ghee to medium heat and add the bay leaf, cinnamon, cloves, and cardamom, and sauté for 30 seconds or until fragrant. Add the rice mixture and salt, and sauté for 2 to 3 minutes.

5. Add 3 cups (600 ml) hot water and bring to a boil. Lower the heat to low, cover, and cook for 8 to 10 minutes or until the rice is tender and all the water has been absorbed.

6. Add the *paneer* and peas, and stir gently.

7. Sprinkle with the browned onions and serve immediately.

Scallion Pulao

·······•⊰ **Scallions and rice** ⊱•···

There are hundreds of ways of taking steamed rice to an exotic level. It is not possible to list them all, because even while you are working on one innovation, ideas for new ones are jostling for attention. I love this *pulao* because it is simple and crunchy and delicious.

Serves 4.

1½ cups (300 grams) basmati rice
3 tablespoons vegetable oil
1 teaspoon cumin seeds
6 scallions, bulbs thinly sliced, green tops chopped
8 to 10 cloves garlic, sliced
2 teaspoons table salt
1 teaspoon *garam masala* (spice mix; page 27)
1 tablespoon freshly squeezed lemon juice

1. Put the rice in a large bowl, wash in plenty of water 2 or 3 times, and drain. Add 3 cups (600 ml) water and soak for 30 minutes. Drain in a fine strainer.

2. Place a nonstick saucepan over medium heat and add the oil. When small bubbles appear at the bottom of the pan, add the cumin. When it begins to change color, add the scallion bulbs and garlic, and sauté for 2 to 3 minutes or until browned.

3. Gently stir in the rice. Add 3 cups (600 ml) water, the salt, and *garam masala*, and stir. Lower the heat to low, cover, and simmer for 8 to 10 minutes or until the rice is tender and all the water is absorbed.

4. Remove from the heat and sprinkle with the lemon juice. Fluff the rice up with two forks, garnish with the scallion tops, and serve immediately.

Erachi Choru

Lamb *pulao*

This South Indian dish is an easy, one-pot dinner that contains both lamb and rice. The spice trio of cinnamon, cardamom, and cloves gives it a wonderful flavor.

Serves 4.

¼ cup (50 ml) vegetable oil
3 (1-inch/2½-cm) cinnamon sticks
6 green cardamom pods
6 whole cloves
4 large red onions, thinly sliced
6 green chiles, stemmed and slit
1½-inch (4-cm) piece fresh ginger, julienned
1 tablespoon fresh garlic paste (page 12)
14 ounces (400 grams) boneless lamb, cut into 1½-inch (4-cm) pieces
3 tablespoons chopped fresh cilantro
3 teaspoons table salt
1 tablespoon freshly squeezed lemon juice
1½ cups (300 grams) basmati rice, soaked

1. Place a nonstick saucepan over medium heat and add the oil. When small bubbles appear at the bottom of the pan, add the cinnamon, cardamom, cloves, and onions, and sauté until the onions are browned. Add the chiles, ginger, and garlic paste, and sauté until fragrant.

2. Add the lamb and sauté for 2 minutes. Add half of the cilantro and sauté for 2 minutes.

3. Stir in 1½ cups (300 ml) water, 2 teaspoons of the salt, and the lemon juice. Lower the heat to low, cover, and cook for 45 minutes or until the lamb is tender.

4. Drain and add the rice to the lamb, along with the remaining 1 teaspoon salt and 1 cup (200 ml) water. Cover and cook 15 to 20 minutes, or until the rice is done.

5. Garnish with the remaining cilantro and serve hot.

Kachche Gosht Ki Biryani

····· ❧ **Lamb _biryani_** ❧ ···

Many people find it difficult to believe that uncooked lamb can be combined and cooked with half-cooked rice and still come out perfectly tender. This dish proves that it can be done. Serve with _raita_.

Kewra (screw pine) water adds a lovely fragrance to this dish and is available in Indian grocery stores. If you can't find it, you can leave it out. Also, when using rose petals for this dish, be sure to use ones that haven't been chemically treated.

Serves 4.

1²⁄₃ pounds (750 grams) bone-in lamb
1 quart (800 ml) vegetable oil
4 large red onions, sliced
1½ cups (375 grams) plain yogurt
½ cup (30 grams) chopped fresh mint
½ cup (30 grams) chopped fresh cilantro
1½ tablespoons fresh ginger paste (page 12)
1 tablespoon fresh garlic paste (page 12)
1 green chile, stemmed and chopped
1½ teaspoons red chile powder
½ teaspoon ground turmeric
3 teaspoons table salt
2 tablespoons fresh untreated rose petals
1 teaspoon _garam masala_ (spice mix; page 27)
1½ cups (300 grams) raw basmati rice
½ teaspoon _kewra_ (screw pine) water
½ teaspoon rosewater
3 tablespoons ghee (page 37)
3 whole cloves
1-inch (2½-cm) cinnamon stick
3 green cardamom pods
1 black cardamom pod
7 or 8 whole black peppercorns
½ teaspoon caraway seeds
A few saffron threads
2 tablespoons warm milk
1-inch (2½-cm) piece fresh ginger, cut into thin strips
Atta (whole-wheat flour) dough to seal (see Note)

1. Trim the excess fat from the lamb. Cut into 2-inch pieces.

2. Place a nonstick wok over high heat and add the oil. When small bubbles appear at the bottom of the wok, lower the heat to medium, add the onions, and fry until well browned. Remove with a slotted spoon and drain on paper towels.

3. Put the lamb in a bowl. Add the yogurt, half of the fried onions, half of the mint leaves, half of the cilantro, the ginger paste, garlic paste, green chile, chile powder, turmeric, 2 teaspoons of the salt, 1 tablespoon of the rose petals, and ½ teaspoon of the *garam masala*, and stir well to coat all the lamb pieces. Cover the bowl with plastic wrap and put in the refrigerator for at least 30 minutes to marinate.

4. Put the rice in a medium bowl, wash in plenty of water 2 or 3 times, and drain. Add 4 cups (800 ml) water and soak for 20 minutes. Drain the rice in a strainer.

5. Place a nonstick saucepan over high heat and add 5 cups (1 liter) water. When it comes to a boil, add the rice and cook until the rice is half cooked, about 12 minutes. Drain in a strainer and transfer the rice to a bowl.

6. Sprinkle the rice with the *kewra* water, rosewater, 2 tablespoons of the ghee, the remaining ½ teaspoon *garam masala*, the cloves, cinnamon, green and black cardamom pods, peppercorns, caraway, and the remaining 1 teaspoon salt, and stir well.

7. Soak the saffron in the milk and set aside.

8. Spread the remaining 1 tablespoon ghee in the bottom of a nonstick saucepan. Spread the lamb in the pan and top it with the rice. Sprinkle with the remaining fried onions, the remaining mint and cilantro, the saffron milk, and the ginger.

9. Cover with a lid and seal the sides with a rope of the *atta* dough. Place the pan over low heat and cook for 15 minutes.

10. Place a griddle or heat diffuser under the pan and cook over low heat for 45 to 60 minutes or until both the lamb and rice are completely cooked.

11. Let stand for 5 to 10 minutes before opening the seal. Serve hot.

Note To make the *atta* dough, add just enough water to ½ cup (60 grams) *atta* to make a stiff dough. Roll the dough into a thin cylinder and arrange it on the rim of the pan. Place a lid on top and press so that it fits tightly into the dough. The dough helps to seal the pan and thus prevent steam from escaping. Alternatively, use a tight-fitting lid or a piece of aluminum foil.

Kesari Seafood Pulao

I call this dish my Indian paella.

Serves to 4 to 6.

1½ cups (300 grams) raw basmati rice
16 clams
2½ teaspoons table salt
15 to 20 medium shrimp
¾ cup (190 grams) plain yogurt, whisked
2 teaspoons fresh ginger paste (page 12)
2 teaspoons fresh garlic paste (page 12)
1 teaspoon green chile paste (page 13)
2 large pomfret fillets, cut into 1-inch (2½-cm) pieces
1 quart (800 ml) vegetable oil
4 medium red onions, sliced
2½ tablespoons ghee (page 37)
1 bay leaf
6 to 8 whole black peppercorns
3 or 4 green cardamom pods
2 black cardamom pods
1 star anise
2-inch (5-cm) cinnamon stick
½ teaspoon ground turmeric
1¼ teaspoons red chile powder
1 teaspoon *garam masala* (spice mix; page 27)
1 tablespoon ground coriander
7 or 8 saffron threads
1 tablespoon freshly squeezed lemon juice
2 tablespoons chopped fresh cilantro
10 to 12 fresh mint leaves, torn

1. Put the rice in a large bowl, wash in plenty of water 2 or 3 times, and drain. Add 3 cups (600 ml) water and soak for 20 minutes. Drain the rice in a strainer.

2. Soak the clams in 5 cups (1 liter) water for 15 minutes, scrub lightly, then drain. Wash the clams thoroughly under running water and drain.

3. Place a deep nonstick saucepan over high heat and add 2½ cups (500 ml) water and 1 teaspoon of the salt. Cover and bring to a boil. Add the clams and cover. Open the lid after 1 minute and check to see if the clams have opened slightly. If they have, drain the clams in a colander set over a bowl; reserve the water. Refresh the clams under running water and set aside in the colander to drain.

4. Remove one shell of each clam, keeping the meat on the other shell.

5. Peel and devein the shrimp. Wash them thoroughly under running water and drain in a colander.

6. Put the yogurt in a large bowl. Add half of the ginger paste, half of the garlic paste, half of the green chile paste, and the remaining 1½ teaspoons salt. Whisk well with a wire whisk. Add the clams, shrimp, and fish. Cover the bowl with plastic wrap, and put in the refrigerator for 20 minutes to marinate.

7. Place a medium nonstick wok over high heat and add the oil. When small bubbles appear at the bottom of the wok, add half of the onions and fry until browned and crisp. Remove with a slotted spoon and drain on paper towels.

8. Place a medium nonstick saucepan over medium heat and add the ghee. When small bubbles appear at the bottom of the pan, add the bay leaf, peppercorns, green and black cardamom, star anise, cinnamon, and the remaining onions. Sauté for 3 to 4 minutes or until the onions are golden brown.

9. Add the remaining ginger paste, garlic paste, and green chile paste, and stir well for 2 minutes. Add the rice and stir again. Sauté for 2 minutes, then add the reserved clam water.

10. Add the turmeric, chile powder, *garam masala*, coriander, and saffron, and stir well. Add the shrimp, fish, and clams, and stir again. Add the lemon juice, cilantro, and mint, and stir. Add the fried onions and stir again.

11. Lower the heat to low, cover, and cook for 10 minutes or until the rice is completely cooked.

12. Remove from the heat and let rest, covered, for 5 to 10 minutes. Serve directly from the cooking pan at the dining table in order to retain maximum flavor.

Kheema Pulao

This is a version made popular by my colleague Chef Harpal Singh Sokhi, who is a name to be reckoned with in regional South Indian cooking.

Serves 4.

1 cup (200 grams) raw basmati rice
1½ tablespoons vegetable oil
2 medium red onions, sliced
8 ounces (250 grams) ground lamb
1½ teaspoons table salt
1 teaspoon red chile powder
¼ teaspoon ground turmeric
¼ cup (60 grams) plain yogurt, whisked
1 teaspoon *garam masala* (spice mix; page 27)
1½ tablespoons ghee (page 37)
½ teaspoon cumin seeds
5 or 6 cloves garlic, chopped
1-inch (2½-cm) piece fresh ginger, chopped
2 green cardamom pods
2 whole cloves
1-inch (2½-cm) cinnamon stick
5 whole black peppercorns
4 green chiles, stemmed and slit
2 tablespoons chopped fresh mint
2 tablespoons chopped fresh cilantro

1. Put the rice in a large bowl, wash in plenty of water 2 or 3 times, and drain. Add 4 cups (800 ml) water and soak for 20 minutes. Drain the rice in a strainer.

2. Place a medium nonstick saucepan over high heat and add 4 cups (800 ml) water. When the water comes to a boil, add the rice. Lower the heat to medium and cook the rice for 12 to 15 minutes or until done. Drain in a strainer and set aside.

3. Place the saucepan over medium heat and add the oil. When small bubbles appear at the bottom of the pan, add the onions and sauté for 2 to 3 minutes or until pale golden. Add the lamb and sauté for 3 to 4 minutes.

4. Add the salt, chile powder, and turmeric, and stir. Cover and cook for 2 minutes.

5. Add the yogurt and stir. Add ½ cup (100 ml) water and cook until the lamb is cooked through. Stir in the *garam masala*.

6. Place another medium nonstick saucepan over medium heat and add the ghee. When small bubbles appear at the bottom of the pan, add the cumin. When the seeds begin to change color, add the garlic, ginger, cardamom, cloves, cinnamon, peppercorns, and chiles, and sauté for 1 minute.

7. Add the lamb mixture, stir, and cook for 2 minutes. Add the rice and stir well. Add the mint and cilantro, and toss to mix well.

8. Transfer to a serving dish and serve hot.

········⊰ **Chef's Tip** ⊱⊛ You can make this with ground chicken, which will take less time to cook than the lamb.

Murgh Biryani
········⊰ Spiced chicken layered with rice ⊱⊛·······································

In a perfectly cooked *biryani*, each rice grain is separate yet bound by flavor, succulent meat is infused with tantalizing flavors, and the entire dish exudes heady aromas. Overall it is a pot full of flavors and marvelous textures. Serve this with *burani* (page 68).

Serves to 4 to 6.

4-inch piece fresh ginger, peeled
1 cup (250 grams) plain yogurt
2½ teaspoons table salt
6 cloves garlic, chopped
3 teaspoons red chile powder
1⅓ pounds (600 grams) bone-in chicken, cut into 1½-inch (4-cm) pieces
6 green cardamom pods
8 whole cloves
2 (1-inch/2½-cm) cinnamon sticks
2 bay leaves
1½ cups (300 grams) basmati rice, soaked
1 quart (800 ml) plus 3 tablespoons vegetable oil
4 large red onions, sliced
1 tablespoon ground coriander
1 teaspoon ground turmeric
2 teaspoons *garam masala* (spice mix; page 27)
4 medium tomatoes, chopped
1 tablespoon chopped fresh cilantro
Generous pinch of saffron threads
½ cup (100 ml) warm milk
2 tablespoons chopped fresh mint
3 tablespoons butter
Atta (whole-wheat flour) dough to seal (see Note page 482)

1. Chop 2 inches of the ginger and julienne the remainider.

2. Put the yogurt in a bowl. Add 1 teaspoon of the salt, half of the garlic, half of the chile powder, and half of the chopped ginger, and stir well. Add the chicken and stir to coat. Cover the bowl with plastic wrap and put in the refrigerator to marinate for about 1 hour.

3. Place a nonstick saucepan over high heat and add 5 cups (1 liter) water. Add 3 of the cardamom pods, 4 of the cloves, 1 cinnamon stick, the bay leaves, and 1 teaspoon of the salt. When the water comes to a boil, drain the rice and add it to the pan. Cook until the rice is three quarters done. Drain and set aside.

4. Place a nonstick wok over high heat and add 1 quart (800 ml) oil. When small bubbles appear at the bottom of the wok, add 1 cup of the onions and cook, stirring occasionally with a slotted spoon, for 10 minutes or until the onions are golden. Remove with the slotted spoon and drain on paper towels. These browned onions will be used during the layering in step 9.

5. Place a nonstick saucepan over medium heat and add 3 tablespoons oil. Add the remaining cardamom, cloves, and cinnamon, and sauté for 1 minute or until fragrant. Add the remaining onions and sauté for 4 to 5 minutes or until light golden.

6. Add the remaining chopped ginger, the remaining garlic, the coriander, turmeric, the remaining chile powder, 1 teaspoon of the *garam masala*, the tomatoes, and the remaining ½ teaspoon salt. Sauté for about 5 minutes. Cover and cook for 2 minutes.

7. Add the chicken and cook over high heat for 5 minutes. Add ½ cup (100 ml) water and stir. Lower the heat and simmer for 10 to 15 minutes or until the chicken is cooked through and tender. Add the cilantro and stir well.

8. Dissolve the saffron in the warm milk.

9. Spread the rice evenly over the chicken. Sprinkle with the saffron milk, the remaining 1 teaspoon *garam masala*, the julienned ginger, mint, and browned onions, and dot with butter.

10. Cover with a lid and seal the sides with a rope of *atta* dough.

11. Place a nonstick griddle over medium heat and let it heat well. Put the pan with the chicken and rice on the griddle and lower the heat to low. Cook for 15 minutes.

12. Serve hot.

Dals, Kadhis, and Sambhars

The dishes in this chapter are Indian comfort food: lentil and bean *dals* or stews, yogurt-based *kadhis*, and lentil *sambhars*. They are also good sources of fiber and protein (along with calcium, phosphorus, vitamin B, and iron). Here you'll find authentic Punjabi *dals* like *dhaabay di dal* (page 492) and *maa chole di dal* (page 500).

Kadhis are blends of yogurt and herbs that are helpful digestive aids. Every region adds its own signature spices and herbs to its *kadhis*, and so a variety of dishes are enjoyed across the Indian subcontinent. A Punjabi *kadhi* will be thick, whereas a tangy-sweet Gujarati *kadhi* is as thin as soup. Accompany them with *roti*, rice, or both.

Lentil *sambhars* can also be made in many ways, and these recipes are great jumping-off points for concocting your own distinctive versions.

Amti

This sweet-and-sour lentil preparation originates from the Indian state of Maharashtra, and its secret lies in the *goda masala*, a spice mix that is very typical of that region. Serve with *chapatis* (page 438) or steamed rice.

Serves 4.

¾ cup (150 grams) *toor dal/arhar dal* (split pigeon peas)
¼ teaspoon ground turmeric
1½ tablespoons vegetable oil
1 teaspoon black mustard seeds
5 or 6 fresh curry leaves
½ teaspoon red chile powder
1 teaspoon table salt
2 tablespoons tamarind pulp
1 tablespoon grated cane jaggery
1 teaspoon *goda masala* (spice mix; page 28)

1. Put the *dal* in a deep bowl, wash it in plenty of water 2 or 3 times, and drain. Add 2 cups (400 ml) water and soak for 30 minutes. Drain the *dal* in a colander.

2. Put the *dal* in a nonstick saucepan. Add 3 cups (600 ml) water and the turmeric. Place over high heat and bring to a boil. Lower the heat to medium and cook for 20 minutes or until the *dal* is completely cooked and soft. Once it has cooled down a little, mix with a wire whisk or an immersion blender until smooth.

3. Place a medium nonstick wok over medium heat and add the oil. When small bubbles begin to appear at the bottom of the pan, add the mustard seeds, curry leaves, and chile powder. Lower the heat and when the seeds begin to sputter, add the *dal*. Stir briskly with a ladle to mix well.

4. As the *dal* begins to boil, add the salt, tamarind pulp, and jaggery, and stir. Add the *goda masala* and 1½ cups (300 ml) hot water and stir again. Simmer for 6 to 8 minutes. Remove from the heat and pour into a serving bowl. Serve immediately.

Cholar Dal

Coconut-flavored split Bengal gram

Some summer breaks during my school years were spent at my aunt's home in Kolkata (Calcutta). She always served me delicious Bengali food that she had learned to make while living there, and this dish was among my favorites. This *dal* was served with thin refined-flour breads called *luchis* (see Note page 19), and I remember we used to marvel at the elasticity of the *luchi* dough. I think this *dal* with *luchis* is an excellent brunch option, filling and simple to prepare. But steamed rice goes well with it too.

Serves 4.

1¼ cups (250 grams) *chana dal* (split Bengal gram)
¾ teaspoon ground turmeric
1 teaspoon table salt
2½ teaspoons sugar
3 tablespoons ghee (page 37), melted
¼ cup (65 grams) fresh coconut, diced
4 whole cloves
1-inch (2½-cm) cinnamon stick
1 black cardamom pod
½ teaspoon cumin seeds
2 bay leaves
2 dried red chiles, stemmed
2 green chiles, stemmed and slit
1 teaspoon fresh ginger paste (page 12)
1 teaspoon raisins

1. Put the *dal* in a deep bowl, wash it in plenty of water 2 or 3 times, and drain. Add 4 cups (800 ml) water and soak for 1 hour. Drain in a colander and set aside.

2. Place a medium nonstick saucepan over high heat. Pour 3 cups (600 ml) water in the pan and bring it to a boil. Add the drained *dal*. Bring to a boil, then lower the heat to medium, cover, and cook for 10 to 15 minutes or until the *dal* is just soft. Take care that the *dal* grains do not get mashed.

3. Add the turmeric, salt, and sugar, and simmer over low heat until most of the water is absorbed and the *dal* is thick.

4. Place a medium nonstick sauté pan over medium heat and add 2 tablespoons of the ghee. When small bubbles appear at the bottom of the pan, lower the heat to low, add the coconut, and sauté until golden brown. Drain on a paper towel and set aside.

5. Add the remaining 1 tablespoon ghee to the same pan and place over medium heat. When small bubbles appear at the bottom of the pan, lower the heat to low and add the cloves, cinnamon, black cardamom, cumin, bay leaves, red chiles, and green chiles, and sauté for 2 minutes or until fragrant. Remove from the heat and pour the spices over the *dal* in the saucepan. Stir well with a ladle.

6. Add the ginger paste, coconut, and raisins, and simmer for 5 minutes over low heat.

7. Pour the *dal* into a serving bowl and serve immediately.

·······⋇{ **Note** }⋇ *Luchis*, deep-fried breads, are similar to *puris*, but while *puris* are made with *atta* (whole-wheat flour), *luchis* are made with *maida* (refined flour).

Dal Makhni

·······⋇{ *Dal* **with butter and cream** }⋇···

It's a common misconception that the more butter and cream you use in this *dal*, the tastier it will be. The trick is actually in getting the right proportions of butter, cream, and ginger into the pot and cooking them with care. Serve with garlic *naan* (page 455) or *pudina parathas* (page 461).

Serves 4.

½ cup (125 grams) *sabut urad* (whole black gram)
1½ teaspoons table salt
1 teaspoon grated fresh ginger, plus ½-inch (1-cm) piece ginger, cut into thin strips
½ cup (15 grams) cooked red kidney beans (canned is fine)
1 tablespoon vegetable oil
3 tablespoons butter
1 teaspoon cumin seeds
1 large red onion, chopped
4 cloves garlic, minced
4 medium tomatoes, chopped
1 teaspoon *garam masala* (spice mix; page 27)
½ cup (100 ml) heavy cream
1 teaspoon red chile powder
1 tablespoon chopped fresh cilantro

1. Put the *sabut urad* in a large bowl, wash it in plenty of water 2 or 3 times, and drain. Add 3 cups (600 ml) water and soak for 10 to 12 hours. Drain the *dal* in a colander.

2. Place a medium nonstick saucepan over high heat and add 5 cups (1 liter) water. Bring to a boil, then add the *dal*, salt, and half the grated ginger, and bring to a boil again. Lower the heat to medium, cover, and cook for 1 hour and 15 minutes.

3. Add the kidney beans and stir well. Cook for 10 minutes or until well blended.

4. Place a medium nonstick saucepan over medium heat and add the oil and butter. When the butter melts and small bubbles appear at the bottom of the pan, add the cumin. When they begin to change color, add the onion and sauté for 3 to 4 minutes or until the onion is golden brown.

5. Add the remaining grated ginger, the garlic, and tomatoes. Sauté until the tomatoes are well mashed and the oil starts to come to the top. Add the *dal* and stir. Add 2 cups (400 ml) water, increase the heat to high, and bring to a boil.

6. Add the *garam masala* and stir. Lower the heat to low and simmer for 15 minutes.

7. Reserve 2 tablespoons of the cream for garnish and add the remaining cream along with the chile powder to the *dal* and stir. Simmer for 5 minutes over low heat.

8. Remove from the heat and pour into a serving bowl. Garnish with the sliced ginger, cilantro, and reserved cream, and serve immediately.

Dhaabay Di Dal

·······⋇{ Creamy, spicy lentils }⋇··

Dhaabas are the roadside eateries that dot most of the highways in India, and this *dal* is a favorite on their menus. Serve with steamed rice.

Serves 4.

½ cup (100 grams) *chilkewali urad dal* (split black gram with skin)
¼ cup (50 grams) *chana dal* (split Bengal gram)
½ cup (115 grams) cooked red kidney beans (canned is fine)
¼ cup (50 ml) vegetable oil
1-inch (2½-cm) piece fresh ginger, chopped
8 to 10 cloves garlic, chopped
1 medium red onion, chopped
2 green chiles, stemmed and chopped
½ tablespoon ground roasted cumin (page 32)
1 tablespoon red chile powder
2 medium tomatoes, chopped
3 tablespoons butter
1½ teaspoons table salt
2 tablespoons chopped fresh cilantro
1 tablespoon *kasoori methi* (dried fenugreek leaves)

1. Place the *dals* in a large bowl, wash them in plenty of water 2 or 3 times, and drain. Add 2 cups (400 ml) water and soak for at least 6 hours. Drain the *dals* in a colander.

2. Place a medium nonstick saucepan over high heat and add 6 cups (1.5 liters) water. When the water begins to boil, add the *dals* and bring to a boil again. Lower the heat to medium, cover, and cook for 1 hour.

3. Add the kidney beans, stir well, and cook for 10 minutes.

4. Place a medium nonstick saucepan over medium heat and add the oil. When small bubbles appear at the bottom of the pan, add the ginger and garlic, and sauté for 1 minute or until golden brown. Add the onion and chiles, and sauté for 4 to 5 minutes or until the onion is golden brown.

5. Add the cumin and chile powder, and sauté for 1 minute. Add the tomatoes and cook over high heat for 3 to 4 minutes, stirring continuously. Add the *dal* mixture and butter, and stir well.

6. Add the salt and cilantro, and stir. Lower the heat to low and cook for 10 minutes, stirring occasionally.

7. Crush the *kasoori methi* between your palms and sprinkle it over the *dal*.

8. Remove from the heat and pour the *dal* into a serving bowl. Serve immediately.

Ghugni

Chole (*chholay masala*; page 25) from the north of India could easily be a cousin to this *ghugni* from eastern India. In the states of West Bengal, Bihar, Orissa, and Assam, *ghugni* is a popular street food. In some places it is served topped with crisp shreds of fried potato.

Serves 4.

1 cup (220 grams) yellow *vatana* (whole dried peas)
1 teaspoon table salt
3 tablespoons vegetable oil
2 tablespoons thinly sliced fresh coconut
½ teaspoon cumin seeds
2 bay leaves
1 large red onion, sliced
1 teaspoon fresh ginger paste (page 12)
1 teaspoon fresh garlic paste (page 12)
4 or 5 green chiles, stemmed and chopped
2 medium tomatoes, puréed
1 tablespoon ground coriander
½ teaspoon ground roasted cumin (page 32)
½ teaspoon red chile powder
¾ teaspoon ground turmeric
½ teaspoon *garam masala* (spice mix; page 27)
1 medium red onion, diced
4 teaspoons tamarind pulp
2 tablespoons chopped fresh cilantro

1. Put the *vatana* in a large bowl, wash in plenty of water 2 or 3 times, and drain. Add 3 cups (600 ml) water and soak overnight. Drain in a colander.

2. Place a nonstick saucepan over high heat and add 6 cups (1.2 liters) water. When it comes to a boil, add the *vatana* and salt. When the mixture comes to a boil again, lower the heat to medium, cover, and cook for 1½ hours or until very soft.

3. Place a medium nonstick sauté pan over medium heat and add 1 tablespoon of the oil. When small bubbles appear at the bottom of the pan, add the coconut and sauté until golden brown. Remove with a slotted spoon and set aside.

4. Add the remaining 2 tablespoons oil to the same heated pan. When small bubbles appear at the bottom of the pan, add the cumin seeds, bay leaves, onion, ginger paste, garlic paste, and chiles, and sauté for 3 to 4 minutes or until the onions are lightly browned.

5. Add the tomatoes and sauté for 3 to 4 minutes or until the oil comes to the top.

6. Add the coriander, ground cumin, chile powder, and turmeric, and stir well. Add the cooked peas along with the cooking liquid and simmer for 4 to 5 minutes or until the liquid thickens.

7. Add the *garam masala* and stir well.

8. Ladle into individual serving bowls and top with the onion, tamarind pulp, coconut, and cilantro. Serve immediately.

Gongura Pappu

········❊{ Sorrel leaves with lentils }❊···

This tasty *dal* from Andhra Pradesh is a complete meal when served with rice. In some homes, the spice level of this dish is upped by many notches.

Serves 4.

½ cup (100 grams) *toor dal/arhar dal* (split pigeon peas)
2 green chiles, stemmed and chopped
¼ teaspoon fenugreek seeds
½ teaspoon ground turmeric
1 teaspoon red chile powder
¼ teaspoon grated cane jaggery
¾ teaspoon table salt
2 tablespoons ghee (page 37)
1 teaspoon brown mustard seeds
2 dried red chiles, stemmed and broken in half
1 teaspoon *dhuli urad dal* (split skinless black gram)
6 cloves garlic, crushed
8 to 10 fresh curry leaves
Pinch of asafetida
1 medium red onion, diced
1 cup chopped fresh sorrel leaves (see Note)
¼ cup (30 grams) grated fresh coconut (or frozen unsweetened coconut)

1. Put the *toor dal* in a large bowl, wash in plenty of water 2 or 3 times, and drain. Add 1½ cups (300 ml) water and soak for 2 hours. Drain in a colander.

2. Place a nonstick saucepan over high heat and add 3½ cups (700 ml) water. When it comes to a boil, add the *toor dal*, green chiles, fenugreek, and turmeric. Lower the heat to medium, cover, and cook for 35 minutes or until the *dal* is soft.

3. Purée the *dal* with an immersion blender or use a potato masher to mash it well. Add the chile powder and jaggery, and cook for 3 to 4 minutes. Add the salt and stir well.

4. Place a nonstick sauté pan over medium heat and add the ghee. When small bubbles appear at the bottom of the pan, add the mustard seeds. When they begin to sputter, add the dried chiles, *dhuli urad dal*, and garlic. Sauté for 30 seconds. Add the curry leaves and asafetida, and sauté for 15 seconds. Add the onion and sauté for 2 to 3 minutes or until lightly browned. Add the sorrel and sauté until it wilts.

5. Add the sautéed mixture to the *dal* and stir well. Add 1 cup (200 ml) water and stir. Bring to a boil.

6. Add the coconut and serve hot.

········⁕{ **Note** }⁕ Sorrel turns a dark greenish black after cooking.

Jain Osaman

········⁕{ **A thin green-gram soup** }⁕ ·······································

This lovely soup is simple to make and tastes terrific. Traditionally *osaman* is made with *toor dal* (split pigeon peas), but in my house it is made with *sabut moong*, which is equally good.

Serves 4.

1 cup (240 grams) *sabut moong* (whole green gram)
1 teaspoon table salt
½-inch (1-cm) piece fresh ginger, peeled
2 green chiles, stemmed
2 tablespoons ghee (page 37)
Generous pinch of asafetida
1 teaspoon black mustard seeds
1 teaspoon cumin seeds
3 or 4 whole cloves
1-inch (2½-cm) cinnamon stick
5 or 6 curry leaves
1 tablespoon ground coriander
½ teaspoon ground turmeric
1 teaspoon plain yogurt
1 teaspoon grated cane jaggery
2 teaspoons freshly squeezed lemon juice
1 tablespoon minced fresh cilantro

1. Put the *sabut moong* in a bowl, wash in plenty of water 2 or 3 times, and drain. Add 2 cups (400 ml) water and soak for about 30 minutes. Drain in a colander.

2. Put the *moong* in a nonstick saucepan, add 5 cups (1 liter) water and ½ teaspoon of the salt, and place over high heat. Bring to a boil, lower the heat to medium, and cook for 20 to 25 minutes or until the *moong* is soft.

3. Put the ginger, chiles, and ½ teaspoon water in a blender, and grind to a fine paste. Transfer to a small bowl, add 1 tablespoon water, and stir.

4. Drain the *moong* in a colander set over a bowl. Reserve the *moong* for use in another dish; set the liquid aside to use in this soup.

5. Place a nonstick saucepan over medium heat and add the ghee. When small bubbles appear at the bottom of the pan, add the asafetida, mustard seeds, cumin, cloves, cinnamon, curry leaves, diluted ginger–green chile paste, coriander, and the remaining ½ teaspoon salt. When the seeds sputter, add the *moong* cooking liquid and stir. Add the turmeric and stir again. When the mixture begins to boil, add the yogurt and stir.

6. Add the jaggery and stir. Let the mixture simmer for 2 to 3 minutes.

7. Just before serving, add the lemon juice and cilantro. Serve hot.

Khattu Mag

········⊰{ **Green gram cooked with sour yogurt and spices** }⊱·····················

I tasted this for the first time at my in-laws' home after I got married to Alyona. My mother-in-law had made it herself, and I was impressed: The combined flavors are both delightful and healthy.

Serves 4.

½ cup (100 grams) *sabut moong* (whole green gram)
1½ teaspoons table salt
1½ cups (375 grams) low-fat plain sour yogurt (see page 513), whisked
2 tablespoons *besan* (chickpea/gram flour)
¼ teaspoon ground turmeric
1 teaspoon fresh ginger paste (page 12)
1 teaspoon green chile paste (page 12)
1 teaspoon sugar
1 tablespoon vegetable oil
Pinch of asafetida
½ teaspoon black mustard seeds
½ teaspoon cumin seeds
3 or 4 whole cloves
1-inch (2½-cm) cinnamon stick
¼ teaspoon fenugreek seeds
8 to 10 fresh curry leaves

1. Put the *sabut moong* in a large bowl, wash it in plenty of water 2 or 3 times, and drain. Add 2 cups (400 ml) water and soak for 1 hour. Drain the *moong* in a colander.

2. Place a medium nonstick saucepan over high heat and add 2 cups (400 ml) water. Add the *moong* and 1 teaspoon of the salt and bring to a boil. Lower the heat to medium, cover, and cook for 15 to 20 minutes or until the *moong* is soft.

3. Put the yogurt in a large bowl and add the remaining ½ teaspoon salt, the *besan*, turmeric, ginger paste, and chile paste. Whisk until thoroughly combined. Add the sugar and 1 cup (200 ml) water and whisk again.

4. Place a second medium nonstick saucepan over medium heat and add the oil. When small bubbles appear at the bottom of the pan, add the asafetida, mustard seeds, cumin, cloves, cinnamon, fenugreek, and curry leaves and sauté for 2 minutes. Once the seeds sputter, add the yogurt mixture and cook for 5 minutes or until the *besan is* cooked and the yogurt mixture thickens.

5. Add the cooked *moong* and cook for 3 to 4 minutes over medium heat. Remove from the heat and pour the curry into a serving bowl. Serve immediately.

········⊰{ **Note** }⊱ You can also make this with the cooked *moong* left over after making *jain osaman* (page 496).

Lauki Chana Dal

·····⋊{ **Bottle gourd-and-lentil curry** }⋉·····

Bottle gourd is a very mild-tasting vegetable, and here it is paired with hearty *chana dal*. Serve this dish with steamed rice or hot *naan*.

Serves 4.

½ cup (100 grams) *chana dal* (split Bengal gram)
1 small bottle gourd, peeled and cut into 1-inch (2½-cm) pieces
1 teaspoon table salt
½ teaspoon ground turmeric
½ teaspoon red chile powder
2 teaspoons ground coriander
2 green chiles, stemmed and chopped
½-inch (1-cm) piece ginger, chopped
2 tablespoons ghee (page 37)
½ teaspoon cumin seeds
Generous pinch of asafetida
1 teaspoon sugar
2 teaspoons freshly squeezed lemon juice
2 tablespoons chopped fresh cilantro

1. Put the *chana dal* in a bowl, wash it in plenty of water 2 or 3 times, and drain. Add 2 cups (400 ml) water and soak for 1 hour. Drain the *dal* in a colander.

2. Place a medium nonstick saucepan over high heat. Add the *chana dal*, bottle gourd, salt, turmeric, chile powder, coriander, chiles, ginger, and 2 cups (400 ml) water and bring to a boil. Lower the heat to low, cover, and cook for 20 minutes or until the *dal* is soft and the bottle gourd is cooked. Mash slightly using the back of a spoon and stir well. Transfer the *dal* mixture to a bowl and set aside.

3. Place a medium nonstick sauté pan over medium heat. Add the ghee. When small bubbles appear at the bottom of the pan, add the cumin and asafetida, and cook for 1 to 2 minutes or until the seeds begin to change color.

4. Add the *dal* mixture and stir. Add the sugar and stir well again. Simmer for 2 minutes, stirring occasionally.

5. Add the lemon juice and stir. Remove from the heat and transfer the curry to a serving bowl. Garnish with the cilantro and serve immediately.

Maa Chole Di Dal

·······•{ **North Indian lentils** }•······································

This classic lentil preparation uses two types of lentils and is a favorite among North Indians. While the lentils provide a unique taste, the real secret of this dish is the tempered mixture of the spices, onions, and tomatoes.

Serves 4.

½ cup (100 grams) *chilkewali urad dal* (split black gram with skin)
½ cup (100 grams) *chana dal* (split Bengal gram)
1½ teaspoons table salt
¼ teaspoon ground turmeric
1-inch (2½-cm) piece fresh ginger, chopped
3 green chiles, stemmed and chopped
2 or 3 tablespoons ghee (page 37)
1 tablespoon butter
1 teaspoon cumin seeds
1 onion, chopped
2 tomatoes, chopped
½ teaspoon red chile powder
2 tablespoons chopped fresh cilantro

1. Put the *dals* in a large bowl, wash in plenty of water 2 or 3 times, and drain. Add 4 cups (800 ml) water and soak for 1 hour. Drain the *dals* in a colander.

2. Place a medium nonstick saucepan over medium heat, add 4 cups (800 ml) water, and bring to a boil. Add the *dals*, salt, turmeric, half of the ginger, and half of the chiles. When the mixture comes to a boil again, lower the heat to medium, cover, and cook for 35 minutes or until the *dals* are soft. Stir well with a ladle to make a homogenous mixture but without mashing the *dals*.

3. Place a small nonstick sauté pan over medium heat and add the ghee and butter. When the butter melts, add the cumin and the remaining ginger and chiles. When the seeds begin to change color, add the onion and sauté for 2 minutes or until the onion is lightly browned.

4. Add the tomatoes and sauté for 2 to 3 minutes or until the tomatoes are soft. Add the chile powder and sauté for 1 minute or until the ghee and butter come to the top.

5. Add the tomato mixture to the *dals* and stir well. Place the saucepan over medium heat and simmer for 5 minutes or until the tomato mixture blends well with the *dals*.

6. Transfer the *dal* to a serving bowl, garnish with the cilantro, and serve immediately.

Masaledar Chholay

Two eternal favorites of Punjabi home cooking are *masaledaar chholay* and *rajma* (spiced red kidney beans). When I was a child, we had them in our house at least once a week. This dish is always a good choice for Sunday lunch. Serve with steamed rice, *raita*, garlic *naan* (page 455), and salad.

Serves 4.

2 (1-inch/2½-cm) pieces fresh ginger
8 to 10 cloves garlic
2 green chiles, stemmed
2 tablespoons cumin seeds
6 tablespoons vegetable oil
3 large red onions, peeled and chopped
1 tablespoon ground coriander
1 teaspoon red chile powder
1 tablespoon coarsely ground *anardana* (dried pomegranate seeds)
4 medium tomatoes, chopped
1½ teaspoons table salt
2½ cups (560 grams) cooked chickpeas (canned is fine)
2 tablespoons chopped fresh cilantro

1. Put the ginger, garlic, and chiles in a spice grinder, and grind to a paste.

2. Place a small nonstick sauté pan over medium heat. Add the cumin and dry-roast for 2 minutes or until fragrant. Cool and grind to a powder in a spice grinder.

3. Place a nonstick saucepan over medium heat and add the oil. When small bubbles appear at the bottom of the pan, add the onions and sauté for 4 to 5 minutes or until browned. Add the ginger–garlic–green chile paste and sauté for 2 minutes. Add the coriander, cumin, chile powder, and *anardana*, and sauté for 1 to 2 minutes or until the oil comes to the top.

4. Add the tomatoes and salt. Cook for about 8 minutes or until the oil comes to the top.

5. Add the chickpeas and sauté for 2 minutes. Add 1 quart (800 ml) water and simmer for 10 minutes.

6. Garnish with the cilantro and serve hot.

Chef's Tip If you feel like it, you can add boiled and diced potatoes. You can also make this dish with dried chickpeas: Soak 1½ cups (300 grams) dried chickpeas in 1 quart (800 ml) water overnight. Drain and put in a saucepan with 1½ quarts (1.2 liters) water, 2 teaspoons tea leaves tied in a double layer of cheesecloth, and 1 teaspoon salt; cook for 60 minutes or until soft. Discard the tea-leaf bag and use the cooked beans as described in the recipe above.

Palakwali Dal

I can recall the appetizing aroma of this *dal* from when my mother used to make it for us on cold winter days in Delhi. She would bring it to the table piping hot, pour a generous portion on a pile of fluffy rice, and then drizzle some fragrant ghee over it.

Serves 4.

1 teaspoon ground turmeric
1¼ teaspoons table salt
¾ cup (150 grams) *dhuli moong dal* (split skinless green gram), well rinsed
2 tablespoons vegetable oil
1 teaspoon cumin seeds
Pinch of asafetida
2 medium red onions, diced
2 green chiles, seeded and diced
2 dried red chiles, stemmed and broken
1-inch (2½-cm) piece fresh ginger, chopped
4 cloves garlic, chopped
15 to 20 fresh spinach leaves, roughly shredded
1 teaspoon freshly squeezed lemon juice

1. Place a nonstick saucepan over medium heat and add 6 cups (1.2 liters) water, the turmeric, and salt, and bring to a boil. Add the *dal* and cook for 30 minutes or until it is tender.

2. Place another nonstick saucepan over medium heat and add the oil. When small bubbles appear at the bottom of the pan, add the cumin and asafetida. When the cumin begins to change color, add the onions and green and red chiles. Sauté for 3 minutes or until the onions are soft and translucent.

3. Add the ginger and garlic, and sauté for 30 seconds.

4. Add the *dal*, bring to a boil, and add the spinach and lemon juice. Simmer for 3 to 4 minutes.

5. Transfer to a serving bowl and serve hot.

Paruppu

Dal with rice is a favorite combination in most Indian homes. It could be any *dal*, but pigeon peas are popular in the southern states and in Gujarat. As my wife comes from Gujarat, this is her idea of an everyday *dal*.

Serves 4.

1 cup (200 grams) *toor dal/arhar dal* (split pigeon peas)
Pinch of asafetida
1 ½ tablespoons vegetable oil
½ teaspoon ground turmeric
1 teaspoon brown mustard seeds
1 teaspoon *dhuli urad dal* (split skinless black gram)
1 teaspoon cumin seeds
12 fresh curry leaves
1 large red onion, chopped
4 green chiles, stemmed and slit
3 cloves garlic, chopped
2 medium tomatoes, chopped
2 teaspoons table salt
2 tablespoons chopped fresh cilantro

1. Put the *toor dal* in a large bowl, wash in plenty of water 2 or 3 times, and drain. Add 3 cups (600 ml) water and soak for 2 hours. Drain in a colander.

2. Place a nonstick saucepan over high heat and add 6 cups (1.2 liters) water. Bring to a boil and add the *toor dal*, asafetida, 1 teaspoon of the oil, and the turmeric. Cook, uncovered, for 40 minutes or until the *dal* is soft. Let cool for a few minutes and mash it lightly. Return to medium heat and simmer for 5 to 6 minutes.

3. Place a nonstick sauté pan over medium heat and add the remaining oil. When small bubbles appear at the bottom of the pan, add the mustard seeds. When they begin to sputter, add the *dhuli urad dal*, cumin, and curry leaves, and sauté for 15 seconds. Add the onion and sauté until translucent. Add the chiles, garlic, and tomatoes, and sauté for 6 minutes or until the tomatoes are pulpy.

4. Add the sautéed mixture to the *dal* and bring to a boil. Add the salt and cook for 3 to 4 minutes.

5. Garnish with the cilantro and serve hot.

Puliseri

You can use rice powder as a substitute for the raw rice (this is used as a thickener). You can add different fruits such as papaya or pineapple for extra flavor. If you don't have fresh coconut, you can use frozen coconut, but be sure it is unsweetened.

Serves 4.

1 tablespoon raw rice
1 cup (120 grams) grated fresh coconut (or frozen unsweetened coconut)
1 quart (800 ml) buttermilk
1 teaspoon table salt
2 tablespoons peanut oil
1 teaspoon black mustard seeds
½ teaspoon fenugreek seeds
3 dried red chiles
1 teaspoon red chile powder
10 to 12 fresh curry leaves

1. Wash the rice, then soak it in ¼ cup (50 ml) water in a small bowl for 15 minutes.

2. Drain the rice in a small strainer. Transfer to a mini food processor and add the coconut and ¾ cup (150 ml) warm water, and process to a smooth, thick paste.

3. Put the buttermilk in a deep bowl. Add the rice-and-coconut paste and the salt, and whisk until well blended. Set aside.

4. Place a medium nonstick saucepan over medium heat and add the oil. When small bubbles appear at the bottom of the pan, add the mustard seeds, fenugreek, and chiles. When the seeds begin to sputter, add the chile powder and curry leaves. Stir well.

5. Add the buttermilk mixture and bring to a boil. Lower the heat to low and simmer for 10 minutes or until slightly thickened. Transfer to a serving bowl. Serve immediately.

Punjabi Rajma

········· § **A rich kidney-bean curry** § ··

This traditional hearty bean dish is very popular in North India and is typically served with steamed rice.

Serves 4.

3 tablespoons vegetable oil
2 bay leaves
2 red onions, chopped
1-inch (2½-cm) piece fresh ginger, chopped
2 or 3 cloves garlic, chopped
2 teaspoons red chile powder
1 tablespoon ground coriander
½ teaspoon ground turmeric
1 teaspoon ground roasted cumin (page 32)
3 tomatoes, chopped
1 teaspoon table salt
2½ cups (560 grams) cooked red kidney beans (canned is fine)
1 teaspoon *garam masala* (spice mix; page 27)
1 tablespoon chopped fresh cilantro

1. Place a medium nonstick saucepan over high heat and add the oil. When small bubbles appear at the bottom of the pan, lower the heat to medium, add the bay leaves, and sauté for 1 minute. Add the onions and sauté for 3 to 4 minutes or until the onions are golden brown.

2. Add the ginger and garlic and sauté for 1 minute. Add the chile powder, coriander, turmeric, and cumin, and stir. Add the tomatoes and salt, and cook until the tomatoes become pulpy and the oil leaves the sides and comes to the top of the mixture.

3. Add the beans and 1½ cups (300 ml) water and stir. Lower the heat to low and cook for 15 minutes, stirring occasionally. If the mixture is too thick, add another ½ cup (100 ml) water.

4. Add the *garam masala* and cook for 5 minutes. Remove from the heat and transfer to a serving bowl. Garnish with the cilantro and serve immediately.

Rajasthani Panchmel Dal

·······⁕{ **A five-lentil *dal* from Rajasthan** }⁕·······

Rajasthani food, or food of the desert, is robust and filling. One example is this combination of five pulses (*panchmel*) that blend together beautifully. By far the most popular accompaniment to this *dal* is the crisp wheat-flour cake called *bati* (page 462), which seems to soak up the *dal* like a sponge.

Serves 4.

¼ cup (50 grams) *chana dal* (split Bengal gram)
¼ cup (60 grams) *sabut moong* (whole green gram)
¼ cup (50 grams) *dhuli urad dal* (split skinless black gram)
¼ cup (50 grams) *toor dal/arhar dal* (split pigeon peas)
¼ cup (55 grams) *sabut masoor* (whole red lentils)
1½ teaspoons table salt
½ teaspoon ground turmeric
3 tablespoons vegetable oil
¼ teaspoon asafetida
½ teaspoon cumin seeds
4 or 5 whole cloves
2 dried red chiles, stemmed and broken in half
½ teaspoon fresh green chile paste (page 13)
½ teaspoon fresh ginger paste (page 12)
1 teaspoon ground roasted cumin (page 32)
1 teaspoon ground coriander
1 teaspoon red chile powder
3 medium tomatoes, chopped
½ teaspoon *garam masala* (spice mix; page 27)
2 tablespoons chopped fresh cilantro

1. Combine the *dals* in a bowl, wash in plenty of water 2 or 3 times, and drain. Add 3 cups (600 ml) water and soak for 2 hours. Drain.

2. Place a nonstick saucepan over high heat and add 1 quart (800 ml) water. Add 1 teaspoon of the salt and the turmeric, and bring to a boil. Lower the heat to medium, add the *dals*, and cook, uncovered, for 25 minutes or until the *dals* are tender.

3. Place another nonstick saucepan over medium heat and add the oil. When small bubbles appear at the bottom of the pan, add the asafetida, cumin seeds, cloves, and red chiles. When the cumin changes color, add the chile paste and ginger paste, and sauté for 1 minute. Add the ground cumin, coriander, and chile powder, and stir well. Add the tomatoes and cook for 8 to 10 minutes or until the oil comes to the top. Add the cooked *dals* with the cooking liquid, the remaining ½ teaspoon salt, and 1½ cups (300 ml) water. Cook for 10 minutes, stirring well.

4. Add the *garam masala* and stir. Transfer to a serving bowl, garnish with the cilantro, and serve hot.

Sambhar

······❋❴ A flavorful and spicy *dal* ❵❋······

I love this spicy lentil preparation that is native to South India and is usually served with *dosas* (page 122), *idlis* (page 120), or steamed rice. My father-in-law makes a point of correcting the pronunciation of the dish whenever and wherever he eats it: It's "sambhaar," not "sambar."

Serves 4.

½ cup (100 grams) *toor dal/arhar dal* (split pigeon peas)
¾ teaspoon ground turmeric
2 drumstick vegetables, cut into 2½-inch (6-cm) pieces
2 tablespoons tamarind pulp
2 tablespoons *sambhar* powder (spice mix for *sambhar*; page 32)
½ teaspoon asafetida
1½ teaspoons table salt
2 tablespoons vegetable oil
½ teaspoon black mustard seeds
¼ teaspoon fenugreek seeds
10 fresh curry leaves
2 dried red chiles, stemmed and broken in half
¼ cup (15 grams) chopped fresh cilantro

1. Place the *dal* in a large bowl, wash it in plenty of water 2 or 3 times, and drain. Add 1½ cups (300 ml) water and soak for 15 to 20 minutes. Drain the *dal* in a colander.

2. Place a large nonstick saucepan over high heat and add 4 cups (800 ml) water. When the water comes to a boil, lower the heat to medium. Add the *dal* and ½ teaspoon of the turmeric, and cook, covered, for 20 minutes or until the *dal* is soft. Mash the cooked *dal* slightly with a wooden spoon.

3. Place another nonstick saucepan over high heat, add 1 cup (200 ml) water, and bring to a boil. Lower the heat to medium and add the drumstick. Cover and cook for 5 minutes. Stir in the tamarind pulp, 2 cups (400 ml) water, the *sambhar* powder, ¼ teaspoon of the asafetida, the remaining ¼ teaspoon turmeric, and the salt, and cook over medium heat for 15 minutes or until the mixture is reduced by half. Add the mashed *dal*, along with the water it was cooked in, to the tamarind mixture. Lower the heat to low and cook for 10 minutes.

4. Meanwhile, place a small sauté pan over medium heat and add the oil. When small bubbles appear at the bottom of the pan, add the mustard seeds. When they begin to sputter, add the fenugreek, curry leaves, the remaining ¼ teaspoon asafetida, and the chiles, and sauté for 10 seconds. Add the tempering to the *dal* and cover to trap the flavors.

5. Remove from the heat. Garnish with the cilantro. Serve hot.

······ ❧ **Note** ❧ Drumstick vegetables are long and green, with ridges running lengthwise along them. They are available frozen and canned in Indian grocery stores.

······ ❧ **Chef's Tip** ❧ You can add different vegetables—white radish, okra, pumpkin, *brinjal* (small round eggplants), or *sambhar* onions (like red pearl onions or mini shallots)—either individually or in combination. In South India, every family has its own style of making *sambhar*.

Sookhi Dal Amritsari

······ ❧ **Lentils with ginger** ❧ ··

The city of Amrtisar lies in the state of Punjab. Punjabi cooking traditionally uses a lot of ginger and onion, and this lentil dish illustrates this. Ginger adds flavor, of course, but since the lentils used here can be a little hard to digest, it also acts as a digestive aid. In most of Punjab, this is a typical wintertime dish.

Serves 4.

1 cup (200 grams) *dhuli urad dal* (split skinless black gram)
1 teaspoon table salt
½ teaspoon ground turmeric
3 (1-inch/2½-cm) pieces fresh ginger, cut into thin strips
¼ cup (50 ml) vegetable oil
Pinch of asafetida
1½ teaspoons cumin seeds
2 small red onions, chopped
2 to 3 green chiles, stemmed and chopped
2 small tomatoes, chopped
1 teaspoon red chile powder
¾ teaspoon *garam masala* (spice mix; page 27)
2 tablespoons chopped fresh cilantro
4 teaspoons freshly squeezed lemon juice

1. Place the *dal* in a bowl, wash it in plenty of water 2 or 3 times, and drain. Add 2 cups (400 ml) water and soak for 1 hour. Drain the *dal* in a colander.

2. Place a medium nonstick saucepan over high heat. Add the *dal*, 2 cups (200 ml) water, ½ teaspoon of the salt, the turmeric, and half of the ginger. Bring to a boil over high heat, then lower the heat to low, cover, and cook for 10 minutes or until the *dal* is soft but the grains are separate. Drain the *dal* in a fine sieve and set aside.

3. Place a small nonstick sauté pan over medium heat and add the oil. When small bubbles appear at the bottom of the pan, lower the heat to medium and add the asafetida and cumin seeds. When the seeds begin to change color, add the onions and sauté for 3 to 4 minutes or until they are lightly browned. Add the remaining ginger, the chiles, and tomatoes, and sauté for 2 minutes. Add the chile powder and sauté until the oil comes to the top.

4. Add the drained *dal* to the tomato mixture and stir. Add the remaining ½ teaspoon salt, the *garam masala*, cilantro, and lemon juice, and stir again. Cook for 2 minutes.

5. Transfer the *dal* to a serving bowl and serve immediately.

Varan

········· A dish made of split pigeon peas ·········

The pure taste of comfort! This simple lentil curry is a staple in Maharashtrian homes in western India. To serve, press steamed rice into small round molds and turn the molds over onto serving plates. Remove the molds, and pour the hot *dal* over the rice with a generous drizzle of ghee.

Serves 4.

½ cup (100 grams) *toor dal/arhar dal* (split pigeon peas)
½ teaspoon table salt
¼ teaspoon ground turmeric
2 teaspoons ghee (page 37)
Pinch of asafetida
½ teaspoon cumin seeds

1. Place the *dal* in a bowl, wash it in plenty of water 2 or 3 times, and drain. Add 1 cup (200 ml) water and soak for 30 minutes. Drain the *dal* in a colander.

2. Place a medium nonstick saucepan over high heat. Add 2 cups (400 ml) water, the *dal*, salt, and turmeric, and bring to a boil. Lower the heat to medium, cover, and cook for 10 to 15 minutes or until the *dal* is completely cooked and soft. Purée thoroughly using an immersion blender.

3. Place a small nonstick sauté pan over medium heat. Add the ghee. When small bubbles appear at the bottom of the pan, add the asafetida and cumin. When the cumin seeds change color, add to the *dal* and cover to trap the flavors.

4. Serve hot.

Dal Dhokli

········⊰⊱ Strips of spicy dough cooked in flavorful lentils ⊰⊱ ········

My wife, Alyona, made this for me when we first got married. She grew up eating it and served it to me with much fanfare. While it was not love at first bite, over the years the dish has grown on me, and I have developed a great love for it.

Serves 4.

¾ cup (150 grams) *toor dal* (split pigeon peas)
¾ cup (100 grams) *atta* (whole-wheat flour)
2 tablespoons *besan* (chickpea/gram flour)
1 teaspoon table salt
¾ teaspoon ground turmeric
2 pinches of asafetida
½ tablespoon vegetable oil
1½ tablespoons peanuts
1 tablespoon ghee (page 37)
¼ teaspoon black mustard seeds
½ teaspoon cumin seeds
4 cloves garlic, finely chopped
4 fresh curry leaves
3 fresh *kokum* petals, or 2 dried (see page 588)
1½ teaspoons grated cane jaggery
2 tablespoons chopped fresh cilantro

1. Put the *toor dal* in a bowl, wash in plenty of water 2 or 3 times, and drain. Add 2 cups (400 ml) water and soak for 30 minutes. Drain the *dal* in a colander.

2. Put the *atta* and *besan* in another bowl. Add ½ teaspoon of the salt, ¼ teaspoon of the turmeric, a pinch of asafetida, the oil, and ¼ cup (50 ml) water, and knead to make a stiff dough.

3. Place a medium nonstick saucepan over medium heat. Add 1½ cups (300 ml) water and when it comes to a boil, add the *dal* and lower the heat to medium. Cover and cook for 10 minutes. Add the peanuts and the remaining ½ teaspoon turmeric, and stir. Cover and cook for 10 minutes or until the *dal* is tender and completely cooked.

4. Divide the dough into 4 portions and roll into balls. Using a rolling pin, roll out each ball into a thin *chapatti*. Using a sharp knife, cut 1½-inch (4-cm) diamond-shaped pieces. Set aside.

5. Place a medium nonstick sauté pan over medium heat and add the ghee. When small bubbles appear at the bottom of the pan, add the mustard seeds, cumin seeds, the remaining pinch of asafetida, the garlic, and curry leaves. When the seeds begin to sputter, remove from the heat and add the mixture to the *dal*.

6. Add 3 cups (600 ml) water, the remaining ½ teaspoon salt, and the *kokum* to the *dal* and bring to a boil. Add the jaggery and stir. Cook until the jaggery is completely dissolved and the *dal* is slightly thickened, then add the dough pieces and cook, stirring the *dal* occasionally and gently so that the dough pieces do not stick to the bottom of the pan.

7. When the dough pieces are cooked and the *dal* has thickened further, transfer to a serving bowl. Garnish with the cilantro and serve immediately.

Aamras Ki Kadhi

········⁂⟨ **Buttermilk-and-mango curry** ⟩⁂········

This lovely sweet-and-sour buttermilk curry is rich with the flavors of green and ripe mangoes. It is better to make the mango pulp yourself than to buy it, since most ready-made pulp is heavily sweetened.

Serves 4.

¾ **cup (210 grams) green mango pulp**
¾ **cup (210 grams) ripe mango pulp**
2 **tablespoons** *besan* **(chickpea/gram flour)**
¾ **teaspoon table salt**
¾ **cup (150 ml) buttermilk**
1 **tablespoon vegetable oil**
Pinch of asafetida
½ **teaspoon black mustard seeds**
¼ **teaspoon fenugreek seeds**
6 **to 8 fresh curry leaves**
2 **green chiles, stemmed and slit**
½ **cup (50 grams)** *boondi* **(see Note)**
Steamed rice

1. Place the green and ripe mango pulp, the *besan*, and salt in a large bowl, and whisk until smooth. Add the buttermilk and whisk again. Set aside.

2. Place a medium nonstick saucepan over medium heat and add the oil. When small bubbles appear at the bottom of the pan, add the asafetida, mustard seeds, and fenugreek seeds and sauté for 1 minute or until the seeds begin to sputter. Add the curry leaves and chiles and sauté for 2 minutes more; the curry leaves and chiles will turn slightly dark.

3. Add the mango mixture and stir slowly. Add 1½ cups (300 ml) water and stir until it blends well with the rest of the ingredients. Bring to a boil, then lower the heat to low and simmer for 10 to 15 minutes more, stirring occasionally.

4. Add the *boondi* and simmer for 5 minutes or until the *boondi* are soft and immersed in the curry. Remove from the heat and pour the curry into a serving bowl. Serve immediately with rice.

> **Note** *Boondi* are small deep-fried dumplings made from *besan* (chickpea/gram flour). They are available in Indian grocery stores.

Gujarati Kadhi

A simple yogurt curry

This yogurt-based curry can be served atop rice or on its own as a soup.

Serves 4.

¼ cup (25 grams) *besan* (chickpea/gram flour)
2 cups (500 grams) plain yogurt
3 tablespoons grated cane jaggery
2 green chiles, stemmed and chopped
1¼ teaspoons table salt
2 tablespoons vegetable oil
½ teaspoon black mustard seeds
½ teaspoon cumin seeds
8 to 10 fresh curry leaves
2 dried red chiles, stemmed and broken in half
3 or 4 whole cloves
1-inch (2½-cm) cinnamon stick
⅛ teaspoon asafetida

1. Put the *besan* in a large bowl, add the yogurt, and whisk until smooth. Add 1 quart (800 ml) water and stir well.

2. Add the jaggery and green chiles to the yogurt mixture, and stir well.

3. Place a nonstick saucepan over medium heat. Pour the yogurt mixture into the pan and cook, stirring continuously, for 10 to 15 minutes or until the *kadhi* is medium thick. Add the salt and stir well.

4. Place a small nonstick sauté pan over medium heat and add the oil. When small bubbles appear at the bottom of the pan, add the mustard seeds, cumin, curry leaves, red chiles, cloves, cinnamon, and asafetida. When the seeds begin to sputter, add the mixture to the *kadhi* and stir well.

5. Remove from the heat and pour the *kadhi* into a serving bowl. Serve hot.

Punjabi Kadhi

······⚬⟩ Chickpea-flour dumplings in a yogurt-based gravy ⟨⚬······

Forty years ago, many homes in India did not have refrigerators. So people used innovative recipes for ingredients that spoiled easily. One of those ingredients was yogurt. Without refrigeration, yogurt would often turn sour, and sour yogurt was the perfect excuse to make a comforting *kadhi*. If you have the patience, you can wait for your yogurt to sour, but you don't have to.

Be sure to mix the yogurt well with the *besan* before adding it to the pot or the yogurt will curdle. If you are in a hurry, you can omit the dumplings (*pakoras*) and just prepare this as a plain curry. Serve this with steamed rice.

Serves 4.

~ For the *pakoras*:
¾ cup (75 grams) *besan* (chickpea/gram flour)
1 red onion, chopped
½ cup (20 grams) chopped *methi* (fresh fenugreek leaves)
1-inch (2½-cm) piece fresh ginger, grated
1 teaspoon *ajwain*
1 teaspoon red chile powder
¼ teaspoon baking powder
½ teaspoon table salt
3 cups (600 ml) vegetable oil

~ For the *kadhi*:
1 cup (250 grams) plain whole-milk yogurt
¼ cup (25 grams) *besan* (chickpea/gram flour)
1 teaspoon ground turmeric
1½ teaspoons table salt
2 tablespoons vegetable oil
½ teaspoon fenugreek seeds
½ teaspoon cumin seeds
6 whole black peppercorns
2 dried red chiles, stemmed and broken into 2 or 3 pieces each
1 red onion, chopped
½-inch (1-cm) piece fresh ginger, chopped
1 teaspoon red chile powder
2 tablespoons chopped fresh cilantro

1. Make the *pakoras*: Place all the ingredients except the oil in a medium bowl and stir. Add ¼ cup (50 ml) water and stir to make a soft dough.

2. Place a medium nonstick wok over high heat and add the oil. When small bubbles appear at the bottom of the pan, drop in small portions (about 2 tablespoons) of the *besan* mixture and deep-fry for 7 to 8 minutes, stirring occasionally, until golden brown. Drain the *pakoras* on paper towels. Set aside.

3. Make the *kadhi*: Put the yogurt in a large bowl, add the *besan*, and whisk until smooth with no lumps. Add the turmeric, salt, and 3 cups (600 ml) water. Set aside.

4. Place a medium nonstick saucepan over medium heat and add the oil. When small bubbles appear at the bottom of the pan, add the fenugreek seeds, cumin, peppercorns, and red chiles. Sauté for 30 seconds. When the seeds begin to sputter, add the onion and ginger, and sauté for 1 minute. Pour the yogurt mixture into the pan. Bring to a boil, then lower the heat to low and simmer for about 15 minutes, stirring occasionally.

5. Add the chile powder and the *pakoras* and simmer for 4 to 5 minutes or until the *pakoras* are completely immersed in the *kadhi*.

6. Remove from the heat and transfer to a serving bowl. Garnish with the cilantro and serve hot.

Sindhi Kadhi

······{ Vegetables cooked in a chickpea-flour sauce }······

The recipes for *kadhis* and *dals* vary widely from home to home, and the older generation of cooks gets the proportions and measurements right by approximating. What follows is a dish I consider to be the perfect *sindhi kadhi*, which I first tasted at my mother's friend's home. I asked her for the recipe, and the darling woman told me just to add a pinch of this and handful of that! I have, of course, translated it all into standard measures for you. This curry served with steamed rice makes an ideal Sunday lunch.

Serves 4.

3 medium potatoes, peeled
¼ cup (50 ml) plus 1 tablespoon vegetable oil
1 teaspoon cumin seeds
1 teaspoon fenugreek seeds
¾ cup (75 grams) *besan* (chickpea/gram flour)
10 to 12 fresh curry leaves
2 green chiles, stemmed and chopped
1-inch (2½-cm) piece fresh ginger, grated
2½ teaspoons table salt
½ teaspoon ground turmeric
¼ cup (35 grams) shelled green peas
2 medium drumstick vegetables (see page 588), cut into 2-inch (5-cm) pieces
½ cup (75 grams) whole cluster beans, trimmed
1 cup (100 grams) whole okra, trimmed
2 large tomatoes, diced
2½ tablespoons tamarind pulp
1½ teaspoons red chile powder
3 tablespoons chopped fresh cilantro

1. Cut each potato in half vertically and then in half horizontally.

2. Place a nonstick saucepan over medium heat and add ¼ cup (50 ml) of the oil. When small bubbles appear at the bottom of the pan, add the cumin and fenugreek, and sauté for 15 seconds.

3. Lower the heat to low, add the *besan*, and sauté for 8 to 10 minutes or until the flour is browned and fragrant. Add 2 quarts (1.6 liters) water and bring to a boil. Add the curry leaves, chiles, and ginger, and stir. Add the salt and turmeric, and stir. Add the peas, drumsticks, and beans. Cover and simmer for 10 minutes. Add the potatoes and cook for 20 minutes.

4. Meanwhile, place a small nonstick sauté pan over medium heat and add the remaining 1 tablespoon oil. When small bubbles appear at the bottom of the pan, add the okra and sauté for 3 to 4 minutes.

5. To the pan with the other vegetables, add the tomatoes, tamarind pulp, and chile powder, and stir. Add the okra and stir. Cover and cook for 10 to 12 minutes. Garnish with the cilantro and serve hot.

Pickles, Chutneys, and *Morabbas*

No matter where you are in India, you will always see bottled pickles sitting on the dining table. Indian cooks take great pleasure in sharing their pickle recipes, and many of these recipes have been passed down for generations. Pickles are usually served with *rotis*, *parathas*, and *theplas*, and are often packed in lunchboxes for long journeys on the train.

In addition to pickle recipes, in this chapter you'll find the best recipes for *morabbas*, sweet pickles typically prepared with fruits and vegetables such as mangoes, carrots, or gooseberries; and homemade chutneys. Once, every Indian kitchen had a huge grinding stone with a heavy pestle, which was used to make chutney. These days, a mini food processor or blender most often replaces this traditional tool, but I think you'll find that the flavor is just as authentic.

Aloo Bukhare Ki Chutney

Sweet-and-sour plum chutney

Because plums are available for only a couple of months in India, plum season is a busy time for my wife, Alyona, as she bottles this chutney to use throughout the year. Serve this chutney with roast chicken or as a dip with any spicy starter.

Makes ¾ cup (225 grams).

8 to 10 medium ripe plums, pitted and puréed (see Note)
½ teaspoon table salt
½ cup grated cane jaggery
½ teaspoon black salt
1 teaspoon red chile powder
1 teaspoon ground roasted cumin (page 32)
6 to 8 dates, pitted and chopped

1. Heat a heavy-bottomed nonstick saucepan over medium heat and add the plum purée. When it comes to a boil, add the table salt, jaggery, black salt, and chile powder, and stir well. Simmer over medium heat for 10 minutes or until the mixture thickens.

2. Add the cumin. Stir and simmer for 2 to 3 minutes.

3. Stir in the dates and cook for 2 minutes, stirring continuously. Let cool completely and store in a sterilized, airtight container in the refrigerator for up to 15 days.

Note To purée the plums, place them in a food processor and process until smooth.

Amer Chatni

This sweet-and-sour mango relish is a great topping for plain grilled chicken or fish.

Makes 2½ cups (900 grams).

4 medium green mangoes
2 teaspoons vegetable oil
2 teaspoons *panch phoron* (see Note)
2 dried red chiles, stemmed
1 cup (250 grams) sugar
1 teaspoon table salt

1. Wash the green mangoes well and cut them, with the skin, into ¼-inch-thick slices; reserve the pits.

2. Place a medium nonstick saucepan over medium heat and add the oil. When small bubbles appear at the bottom of the pan, add 1 teaspoon of the *panch phoron* and the chiles. When the seeds sputter, add the mangoes and sauté for 1 minute. Add 2 cups (400 ml) warm water, the reserved mango pits, and sugar, and cook over medium heat, stirring continuously, for 10 to 15 minutes or until the mangoes are tender and the chutney is thick.

3. Add the salt and stir. Remove from the heat and set aside to cool.

4. Place a small sauté pan over medium heat and dry-roast the remaining 1 teaspoon *panch phoron* for 2 to 3 minutes or until fragrant. Remove from the heat, let cool, then transfer to a mortar and pound to a powder with a pestle. When the chutney has cooled, sprinkle the powder on top and serve as an accompaniment. Or, store in a sterilized, airtight container in the refrigerator for up to 15 days.

❊❳ **Note** ❲❊ *Panch phoron* is a mixture of equal parts mustard seeds, fenugreek seeds, *kalonji* (nigella seeds), cumin seeds, and fennel seeds.

Angoor Aur Khajur Ki Chutney

····§ **Grape-and-date chutney** §···

Creativity is an essential ingredient for good cooks, and this recipe is courtesy of my wife's mother, who loves making up new relishes. The chutney is chunky with plump raisins; it goes wonderfully with spicy *samosas* (page 154).

Makes 2 cups (600 grams).

25 to 30 seedless red grapes
1 cup (250 grams) dates, pitted and chopped
1 teaspoon red chile powder
1 teaspoon ground roasted cumin (page 32)
1½ tablespoons raisins
½ teaspoon table salt
¼ cup (50 grams) grated cane jaggery

1. Place a nonstick saucepan over medium heat. Add the grapes, dates, and ½ cup (100 ml) water, and cook for 12 minutes or until the grapes are completely broken down.

2. Add the chile powder, cumin, and raisins, and cook for 5 minutes.

3. Add the salt and jaggery, stir well, and cook for 1 minute or until the jaggery is completely dissolved and well blended.

4. Transfer to a serving bowl and let cool.

5. Serve at room temperature, or store in a sterilized, airtight container in the refrigerator for up to 15 days.

Chile Garlic Chutney

····§ **Fiery and flavorful garlic chutney** §···

If you think spice is nice, this red-hot chutney is for you. I love it with anything fried.

Makes 1 cup (300 grams).

10 dried red chiles, stemmed and seeded
12 large cloves garlic
2 teaspoons freshly squeezed lemon juice
1 teaspoon tamarind pulp
1 teaspoon sea salt
1 teaspoon ground roasted cumin (page 32)

1. Soak the chiles in 1½ cups (300 ml) water for 30 minutes. Drain in a colander.

2. Put the chiles and garlic in a food processor with the lemon juice, tamarind pulp, and ¼ cup (50 ml) water, and process to a fine paste.

3. Add the salt and cumin, and process again. Transfer to a sterilized, airtight container and store in the refrigerator for up to 2 weeks.

Nariel Aur Dhaniya Ki Chatni

······⁕⟨ Coconut cilantro chutney ⟩⁕······

This delicious chutney, a staple from South India, is ready in minutes. It keeps well in the fridge for up to a week. Serve it with *dosas* (page 122), *idlis* (page 120), or even *rotis* (page 18).

Makes 1½ cups (450 grams).

1 cup (120 grams) grated fresh coconut (or frozen unsweetened coconut)
3 green chiles, stemmed and chopped
¼ cup (75 grams) dry-roasted *chana dal* (split Bengal gram)
½ small bunch fresh cilantro, roughly chopped
½-inch (1-cm) piece fresh ginger, chopped
½ tablespoon freshly squeezed lemon juice
½ teaspoon sugar
¾ teaspoon table salt
1 teaspoon vegetable oil
¼ teaspoon brown mustard seeds
½ teaspoon *dhuli urad dal* (split skinless black gram)
Pinch of asafetida
5 fresh curry leaves

1. Put the coconut, chiles, *chana dal*, cilantro, ginger, and ½ cup (100 ml) water in a food processor, and process to a paste. Add the lemon juice, sugar, and salt, and process again. Transfer to a serving bowl.

2. Place a small sauté pan over medium heat and add the oil. When small bubbles appear at the bottom of the pan, add the mustard seeds. When they begin to sputter, add the *dhuli urad dal* and sauté for 30 seconds or until lightly browned. Add the asafetida and curry leaves, and immediately pour the tempering over the chutney. Stir well and serve, or let cool completely and store in a sterilized, airtight container in the refrigerator for up to 2 days.

Hirvi Mirchi Cha Thecha

·····{ **Spicy green-chile chutney** }··

This rustic accompaniment from the state of Maharashtra is neither a chutney nor a pickle. It is best made fresh and in a stone mortar, but in our modern kitchens, a food processor does just fine. As the chiles are sautéed in oil, their heat is tamed somewhat. For variety, use different types of chiles. Serve with *bhakris* (page 453).

Makes ¾ cup (225 grams).

1 tablespoon vegetable oil
1 teaspoon cumin seeds
8 cloves garlic, crushed
8 or 9 green chiles, stemmed and chopped
2 tablespoons sesame seeds
1 teaspoon sea salt
2 tablespoons grated fresh coconut (or frozen unsweetened coconut)
¼ medium bunch fresh cilantro, chopped

1. Place a medium nonstick sauté pan over medium heat and add the oil. When small bubbles appear at the bottom of the pan, add the cumin, garlic, and chiles, and sauté for 2 to 3 minutes.

2. Add the sesame seeds and sauté for 2 minutes. Add the sea salt, coconut, and cilantro, and cook for 3 to 4 minutes. Transfer the mixture to a plate and set aside to cool.

3. Transfer to a mortar and pound to a coarse paste with a pestle, or process in a food processor. Store in a sterilized, airtight container in the refrigerator. It will last for up to 1 week.

Keerai Chutney

······•⟨ Spinach chutney ⟩•······

Use fresh spinach to make this chutney. It has a certain palate-cleansing quality that remains true to the spinach's character. Serve the chutney with steamed rice.

Makes 1 cup (300 grams).

1 teaspoon vegetable oil
1 tablespoon *dhuli urad dal* (split skinless black gram)
1 tablespoon *chana dal* (split Bengal gram)
4 dried red chiles, stemmed
¼ teaspoon asafetida
1 medium red onion, finely chopped
1 large tomato, finely chopped
2 green chiles, stemmed and chopped
1 medium bunch spinach, roughly chopped
¼ cup (20 grams) grated fresh coconut (or frozen unsweetened coconut)
2 teaspoons tamarind pulp
1 teaspoon table salt

1. Place a nonstick wok over medium heat and add the oil. Add the *dals* and cook for 1 to 2 minutes or until golden brown.

2. Add the red chiles, asafetida, onion, tomato, and green chiles. Cook for 5 minutes.

3. Add the spinach, coconut, tamarind pulp, and salt. Stir well and cook for 2 to 3 minutes. Set aside to cool.

4. Transfer to a food processor and process to a fine paste.

5. Transfer to a serving bowl and serve, or store in a sterilized, airtight container in the refrigerator for up to 2 days.

Kele Ki Chutney

······· { **Ripe-banana relish** } ···

Here the humble banana is transported to new heights with tamarind and jaggery, and the ground ginger adds still more interesting notes.

Makes 1½ cups (450 grams).

4 to 5 tablespoons (80 to 100 grams) tamarind pulp
½ cup (100 grams) grated cane jaggery
1 dried red chile, stemmed and broken in half
½ teaspoon ground ginger
½ teaspoon red chile powder
½ teaspoon ground roasted cumin (page 32)
1 teaspoon fennel seeds
½ teaspoon table salt
1 large ripe banana, peeled and cut into rounds

1. Place a nonstick saucepan over high heat. Add the tamarind pulp, jaggery, and 2 cups (400 ml) water, and bring to a boil, stirring continuously.

2. Lower the heat to low, add the chile, ginger, chile powder, cumin, fennel, and salt, and cook for 15 to 20 minutes.

3. Add the banana. Cook for 4 to 5 minutes. Adjust the seasoning if necessary.

4. Let cool, then chill in the refrigerator and serve cold. Or, store in a sterilized, airtight container in the refrigerator for up to 2 days.

Khajur Ki Chutney

A Punjabi favorite, this chutney can be made in bulk and stored in the refrigerator, as the jaggery acts as a preservative. I like to serve this chutney (which I like to call India's ketchup) because it contains nutritious dates.

Makes 2½ cups (750 grams).

9 ounces (250 grams) dates, pitted and roughly chopped
¼ cup (50 grams) grated cane jaggery
½ teaspoon fennel seeds
½ teaspoon red chile powder
½ teaspoon black salt
2 bay leaves
4 whole cloves
2 black cardamom pods
1 teaspoon ground ginger
1 teaspoon ground roasted cumin (page 32)
1 tablespoon ghee (page 37)
½ teaspoon cumin seeds

1. Place a nonstick saucepan over medium heat and add the dates, jaggery, fennel, chile powder, black salt, bay leaves, cloves, cardamom, ginger, and ground cumin. Add 5 cups (1 liter) water and bring to a boil. Reduce the heat to low and cook for 20 minutes or until the mixture is thick.

2. Let cool to room temperature, then transfer to a food processor and process to a purée. Push through a fine strainer into a bowl and set aside.

3. Place a small nonstick sauté pan over medium heat and add the ghee. When small bubbles appear at the bottom of the pan, add the cumin seeds. When the seeds begin to change color, add this tempering to the chutney and stir.

4. Let cool and serve at room temperature, or store in a sterilized, airtight container in the refrigerator for up to 15 days.

Kharda

Traditionally, the chiles are ground in a mortar with a pestle. This relish is commonly made in the villages of Maharashtra, where it is eaten with *bhakri*, a type of thick Indian bread (page 453), and this makes a simple and unpretentious meal.

Makes 1 cup (300 grams).

1 tablespoon vegetable oil
1 teaspoon cumin seeds
20 green chiles, stemmed and roughly chopped
12 cloves garlic
1 small bunch fresh cilantro, roughly chopped
1 teaspoon table salt

1. Place a nonstick sauté pan over medium heat and add the oil. Add the cumin seeds and when they begin to change color, add the chiles and garlic. Sauté for 1 minute, then add the cilantro and stir. Lower the heat to low, add the salt, cover, and cook for 2 to 3 minutes.

2. Soften the chiles by pressing them with the back of a wooden spoon. Let cool.

3. Transfer to a food processor and process to a coarse paste. You should be able to see chile pieces. Store in a sterilized, airtight container in the refrigerator for up to 2 weeks.

Kolhapuri Dry Chutney

······*❊❳ **Spicy, hot, and flavorful chutney** ❲❊*······

Here, proper roasting of the individual spices is the most essential step. The roasting releases the aromatic oils and the blending gives this special chutney its authentic flavor. If you have leftover chutney, you can use it to make *kolhapuri sukka* lamb (page 378).

Makes 1 cup (300 grams).

2 tablespoons coriander seeds
1 tablespoon cumin seeds
1 tablespoon sesame seeds
½ tablespoon whole black peppercorns
½-inch (1-cm) cinnamon stick
5 whole cloves
1 teaspoon fennel seeds
20 cloves garlic, half left whole and half chopped
1 cup (60 grams) grated dried coconut
2 tablespoons vegetable oil
1 medium red onion, roughly chopped
1 cup (60 grams) finely chopped fresh cilantro
¼ cup (35 grams) red chile powder
1 teaspoon table salt

1. Place a medium nonstick sauté pan over medium heat. One by one, add the coriander, cumin, sesame seeds, peppercorns, cinnamon, cloves, fennel, and whole garlic cloves, and dry-roast each for 1 minute or until fragrant. Transfer to a bowl and set aside to cool.

2. In the same pan, dry-roast the coconut for 1 minute or until it turns reddish. Set it aside to cool.

3. Place a nonstick saucepan over medium heat and add the oil. When small bubbles appear at the bottom of the pan, lower the heat to low and add the onion, chopped garlic, and cilantro. Cook for 2 to 3 minutes or until well browned and crisp. Set aside to cool.

4. Combine all the ingredients from steps 1, 2, and 3, and process to a fine powder in a food processor. Stir in the chile powder and salt.

5. Transfer to a bowl and let cool to room temperature. Serve, or store in a sterilized, airtight container in the refrigerator for up to 1 month.

Papaya Chutney

A ripe-papaya relish

When you have a lot of papaya in the house, bottle it up! I made this chutney one Sunday afternoon when the smell of ripening papaya hung heavily in our home. My daughters complained about the smell so I started cooking. Now they praise this chutney, and it has become a regular preserve on our table. This goes well spread on bread.

Makes 3½ cups (1 kg).

1 pound (500 grams) sugar
1 large ripe papaya, peeled, seeded, and thinly sliced
1 teaspoon table salt
10 black peppercorns, crushed
1 teaspoon roasted *kale til* (black sesame seeds)
2 tablespoons *kakdi magaz* (dried cucumber seeds; page 588)
¼ cup (50 ml) malt vinegar
1 tablespoon vegetable oil
1 teaspoon cumin seeds
1-inch (2½-cm) piece fresh ginger, chopped
1 large red onion, peeled and cubed

1. Place a nonstick saucepan over medium heat. Add the sugar and 1 cup (200 ml) water, and bring to boil. Cook for 5 to 7 minutes or until you get a thin syrup.

2. Add the papaya and salt, and cook for 5 to 6 minutes or until the syrup thickens.

3. Add the black peppercorns, *kale til*, and *kakdi magaz*, and cook, stirring continuously, for 1 to 2 minutes.

4. Remove the pan from the heat, add the malt vinegar, and stir. Set aside to cool.

5. Place a nonstick sauté pan over medium heat and add the oil. When small bubbles appear at the bottom of the pan, add the cumin seeds. When they begin to change color, add the ginger and onion, and sauté until the onions are translucent.

6. Add to the cooked papaya and stir.

7. Let cool and serve. Or, store in a sterilized, airtight container in the refrigerator for up to 15 days.

Tamatar aur Adrak Ki Chutney

······ ❧ Ginger-and-tomato chutney ❧ ······

Chutneys are fun to serve as a dip, and this one pairs particularly well with Indian lentil wafers or *papads*, which you can purchase at any Indian grocery store. I suggest buying *papads* that can be micro-waved (as opposed to the ones that need to be deep-fried). Microwave one *papad* at a time, place on a platter, and serve with the chutney.

Makes 1½ cups (450 grams).

1 tablespoon vegetable oil
4 large ripe red tomatoes, roughly chopped
3-inch (7½-cm) piece fresh ginger, peeled
1 medium onion, finely chopped
1 tablespoon sesame seeds, roasted and ground
1 tablespoon peanuts, roasted and ground
1 teaspoon cumin seeds, ground
2 teaspoons red chile powder
1 tablespoon grated cane jaggery
½ teaspoon table salt
½ teaspoon black mustard seeds
10 to 12 fresh curry leaves

1. Place a nonstick saucepan over medium heat and add 2 teaspoons of the oil. When small bubbles appear at the bottom of the pan, add the tomatoes, ginger, and onion. Stir and cook for 20 minutes or until the mixture is brown and homogenous. Remove from the heat and set aside to cool.

2. Add the sesame seeds, peanuts, cumin, chile powder, jaggery, and salt, and stir. Transfer to a food processor and process to a smooth paste. Transfer to a bowl.

3. Place a small nonstick sauté pan over medium heat and add the remaining 1 teaspoon oil. When small bubbles appear at the bottom of the pan, add the mustard seeds and curry leaves. When the seeds begin to sputter, add this tempering to the chutney and stir.

4. Let cool completely and store in a sterilized, airtight container in the refrigerator for up to 2 weeks.

Cilantro Thokku

My colleagues who hail from Tamil Nadu claim this chutney is perfect with steamed rice and yogurt. And some insist that rice and *thokku* with ghee is also fantastic. This chutney can also be enjoyed with *roti* (page 18) or even with Western-style bread.

Makes 1 cup (300 grams).

1⅛ cup (250 grams) roughly chopped fresh cilantro
½ cup (100 grams) *dhuli urad dal* (split skinless black gram)
18 to 20 dried red chiles, stemmed and broken
4 teaspoons table salt
⅛ teaspoon asafetida
2 tablespoons tamarind pulp

1. Wash the cilantro and drain. Spread out on an absorbent kitchen towel until the water has completely evaporated.

2. Place a nonstick sauté pan over medium heat. Add the *dal* and dry-roast for 5 minutes or until fragrant. Transfer to a plate.

3. Add the chiles to the same heated pan and dry-roast for 2 minutes. Return the *dal* to the pan, add the salt, asafetida, and cilantro, and sauté for 1 to 2 minutes or until fragrant.

4. Add the tamarind pulp and stir. Set aside to cool completely.

5. Transfer to a mini food processor and process until smooth.

6. Serve, or store in a sterilized, airtight container in the refrigerator for up to 1 week.

Gajar Gobhi Shalgam Ka Achar

·······⁕} Punjabi-style winter-vegetable pickle {⁕·······

This pickle becomes more delicious as it ages and the flavors gain more depth. In Punjab, people in the city live in bungalows with kitchen gardens, and this pickle is a tribute to their gardens' winter produce.

Makes 60 ounces (1.7 kg).

12 tablespoons filtered mustard oil (see Note page 87)
6 tablespoons coarsely ground ginger
¼ cup coarsely ground garlic
1½ tablespoons mustard seeds, ground
1½ tablespoons red chile powder
1½ tablespoons *garam masala* (spice mix; page 27)
1 cup (200 grams) grated cane jaggery
1½ to 2 tablespoons table salt
1 pound (500 grams) carrots, cut into 1½-inch (4-cm) pieces
1 pound (500 grams) cauliflower, separated into medium florets
1 pound (500 grams) turnips, peeled and cut into 1½-inch (4-cm) pieces
3 tablespoons malt vinegar

1. Place a nonstick wok over medium heat and add the mustard oil. When small bubbles appear at the bottom of the wok, add the ginger and garlic and sauté until light golden.

2. Add the mustard seeds, chile powder, and *garam masala* and sauté for 15 seconds. Add the jaggery and salt, and stir well.

3. Add the carrots, cauliflower, and turnips, stir, and cook for 3 to 4 minutes. Remove from the heat and set aside to cool completely.

4. Stir in the vinegar.

5. Store in sterilized, airtight containers. This pickle will keep for up to 1 year at room temperature.

Garlic Pickle

······⋙❴ Sweet-and-sour garlic pickle ❵⋘······

This pickle is made differently throughout India. Some cooks pickle the garlic whole. I find that it is rather overwhelming to ingest a whole clove of spiced garlic, so I use crushed garlic in my recipe. This pickle has a very strong character, but perking up the palate is the job of a good pickle.

Serves 4.

3 cups (500 grams) garlic cloves
2-inch (5-cm) piece fresh ginger, peeled
1½ teaspoons black mustard seeds
1 teaspoon fenugreek seeds
1 teaspoon cumin seeds
1½ cups (300 ml) vegetable oil
1 teaspoon table salt
½ cup (120 grams) tamarind pulp
1½ teaspoons red chile powder
½ cup (100 grams) grated cane jaggery

1. Peel, wash, and pat dry the garlic. Process half of the garlic with the ginger in a mini food processor and crush the remaining cloves.

2. Place a medium nonstick sauté pan over medium heat and let it heat for 2 minutes. Add 1 teaspoon of the mustard seeds, the fenugreek, and cumin, and dry-roast for 2 minutes or until fragrant. Let cool, then grind to a coarse powder in a spice grinder.

3. Place a nonstick saucepan over medium heat and add 1 cup (200 ml) of the oil. When small bubbles appear at the bottom of the pan, add the remaining ½ teaspoon mustard seeds and the crushed garlic. Lower the heat to low and cook for 3 to 4 minutes.

4. Increase the heat to high, add the salt, the roasted and ground spices, and the tamarind pulp, and cook for 5 to 6 minutes.

5. Add the chile powder, garlic-ginger paste, and jaggery, and cook over medium heat for 1 minute or until the jaggery is dissolved.

6. Add the remaining ½ cup (100 ml) oil and cook until the pickle thickens a bit.

7. Let cool, then transfer to a dry, sterilized, airtight container and store in a cool, dry place for up to 3 months.

Ginger Pesarel

This is a terrific treat for ginger lovers. Use young rhizomes for this pickle, as woody ginger will not taste the same.

Makes ½ cup (150 grams).

12-inch (30-cm) piece fresh ginger
¼ cup (50 ml) vegetable oil
1 tablespoon (40 grams) black mustard seeds
½ teaspoon asafetida
1 teaspoon table salt
6 green chiles, stemmed and slit
2 tablespoons freshly squeezed lemon juice

1. Wash and peel the ginger. Pat dry with an absorbent cloth and finely julienne.

2. Place a nonstick sauté pan over medium heat and add the oil. When small bubbles appear at the bottom of the pan, add the mustard seeds. When they begin to sputter, add the asafetida and salt.

3. Stir in the ginger and chiles, toss well, and cook for 2 to 3 minutes.

4. Remove from the heat and drizzle with the lemon juice; stir well. Set aside for 1 hour before serving. The pickle can be stored in a sterilized, airtight container in the refrigerator for up to 6 days.

Sour and Spicy Eggplant Pickle

····❧{ **Eggplant spread** }❧··

I use this pickle more like a sandwich spread than a relish. I prefer to use eggplants that are lightweight for their size and have small round marks at the bottom, because the ones that are heavy and have oval marks are likely to have more seeds.

Makes 1½ cups (450 grams).

2-inch (5-cm) piece fresh ginger, peeled
4 cloves garlic
1½ cups plus 1 tablespoon (300 ml) vegetable oil
¼ cup (50 grams) dried red chiles, stemmed
2 teaspoons cumin seeds
2 teaspoons brown mustard seeds
2 teaspoons fenugreek seeds
4 small eggplants, each cut into 8 pieces
¼ cup (60 grams) table salt
1 tablespoon tamarind pulp
1 teaspoon ground turmeric
1 cup (200 ml) distilled white vinegar

1. Put the ginger and garlic in a mini food processor, and process to a paste. Set aside in a small bowl.

2. Place a small nonstick sauté pan over medium heat and add 1 tablespoon of the oil. When small bubbles appear at the bottom of the pan, add the chiles and sauté for 2 minutes. Remove with a slotted spoon and drain on paper towels; set aside to cool.

3. Place the same pan with the remaining oil over medium heat. When small bubbles appear at the bottom of the pan, add the cumin, mustard seeds, and fenugreek, and sauté for 2 minutes or until fragrant. Drain the oil using a small sieve and save the spices. Set aside to cool.

4. Add the ginger-garlic paste to the remaining hot oil in the pan and sauté for 1 minute.

5. Transfer the chiles and the sautéed spices to a spice grinder and grind to a powder. Set aside in a small bowl.

6. Place a nonstick wok over high heat and add 1¼ cups (250 ml) of the remaining oil. When small bubbles appear at the bottom of the wok, slide in the eggplant and cook for 6 to 7 minutes or until golden. Remove with a slotted spoon and place in a bowl. Add the salt, tamarind pulp, turmeric, ground sautéed spices, sautéed ginger-garlic paste, and vinegar, and stir.

7. Place a nonstick sauté pan over high heat and add the remaining ¼ cup (50 ml) oil. Heat until warmed through. Add to the bowl with the eggplant mixture. Stir well.

8. Let the pickle cool to room temperature before serving, or transfer to a sterilized, airtight container and store in a cool, dry place for up to 2 months.

Kachche Papite Ka Morabba

····❊} **A sweet relish of green papaya** {❊····································

Morabbas are sweet preserves that are made using either fruits or vegetables. Carrot *morabba* and *amla* (Indian gooseberry) *morabba* are readily available in Indian grocery stores, but until some enterprising individual mass-produces this special green-papaya *morabba*, it will have to be made at home.

Makes 1 cup (300 grams).

9 ounces (250 grams) green papaya, cut into 1-inch (2½-cm) cubes
1¼ cups (250 grams) sugar
Pinch of citric acid
1 teaspoon roasted *magaz* (melon seeds; optional)

1. Wash the papaya and drain well in a colander. Prick the cubes all over with a fork and set aside.

2. Place a nonstick saucepan over high heat and add 5 cups (1 liter) water. When the water comes to a boil, add the papaya and cook for 18 minutes or until soft. Drain and set aside.

3. Place a nonstick saucepan over medium heat and add 1 cup (200 ml) water and the sugar. Cook, stirring, until the sugar dissolves. Add the citric acid, stir, and cook for 5 minutes.

4. Add the papaya and stir. Cook for 2 to 3 minutes or until thick and syrupy.

5. Add the melon seeds and remove from the heat. Let cool completely, then store in a sterilized, airtight container in the refrigerator for up to 3 weeks.

Papaya Ki Launj

Green papaya chutney

This intriguing combination of seeds transforms something as simple as raw papaya into an interesting chutney. This chutney pairs well with Indian breads like *paratha* (page 18) and *thepla* (page 465).

Makes 2½ cups (750 grams).

11 ounces (300 grams) green papaya, peeled and seeded
1 tablespoon ghee (page 37)
Pinch of asafetida
¼ teaspoon *kalonji* (nigella; see Note page 231)
½ teaspoon black mustard seeds
½ teaspoon cumin seeds
5 or 6 whole cloves
1 teaspoon red chile powder
½ teaspoon ground turmeric
½ cup (100 grams) sugar
½ teaspoon table salt
1 teaspoon anise seeds, coarsely ground

1. Thinly slice the papaya.

2. Place a medium nonstick saucepan over high heat and add 1½ cups (300 ml) water. As the water starts to boil, lower the heat to medium, add the papaya, and cook for 4 to 5 minutes. Drain and set aside.

3. Place a nonstick saucepan over medium heat and add the ghee. When small bubbles appear at the bottom of the pan, lower the heat to low, add the asafetida, *kalonji*, mustard seeds, cumin, cloves, chile powder, and turmeric, and cook until the seeds sputter.

4. Add 2 cups (400 ml) water and stir. Add the sugar and stir until it dissolves. Continue to cook until syrupy. Add the salt and cook for 4 to 5 minutes.

5. Add the papaya and cook for 10 minutes or until the papaya is tender.

6. Add the anise and stir.

7. Let cool completely, then store in a sterilized, airtight container the refrigerator for up to 15 days.

CHAPTER 13

Food for Fasts and Festivals

Indian culture is a tapestry woven out of many diverse communities and faiths. People pray to many gods, and every religion has its own set of rules and rituals that govern prayers and eating habits.

This is a special section of recipes for fasting days, when the use of certain cereals, pulses, and greens is not allowed. It is heartening to know that a day of fasting becomes a day of feasting on unusual delights such as these. A *sabudana thalipeeth* (page 540) is a filling meal, especially when followed by a lovely dessert of *dudhi halwa* (page 544) or *kaju katli* (page 546).

Kele Wafers

During my trips to Cochin, in South India, I make a point of visiting the street carts where the locals fry banana wafers in coconut oil. It's a wonderful experience watching these being made and seeing the pale banana slices change to bright yellow as they're fried—but eating them absolutely fresh is even better!

Nendra bananas are big yellow-skinned bananas, a speciality of coastal Kerala. They're hard to find in the United States, but you can substitute green plantains.

Makes about 2 cups (400 grams).

1 tablespoon vegetable oil
4 medium raw *nendra* bananas or green plantains
1 quart (800 ml) coconut oil (see Note)
4 teaspoons table salt

1. Grease your palms with a little vegetable oil. This makes it easy to handle and peel the raw bananas (since the skin of these bananas oozes a resin). Peel all the bananas with a vegetable peeler and set aside.

2. Place a nonstick wok over high heat and add the coconut oil. When small bubbles appear at the bottom of the wok, lower the heat to medium. Holding a good-quality, heat-resistant vegetable slicer over the hot oil, thinly slice 1 banana directly into the fryer. Fry until the wafers become light yellow.

3. Put 1 tablespoon water in a small bowl, add 1 teaspoon salt, and stir to dissolve the salt. Sprinkle over the oil and wait until the water evaporates.

4. Remove the wafers with a slotted spoon and drain on paper towels.

5. Repeat steps 3 and 4 for the remaining 3 bananas.

6. Transfer the wafers onto another plate and serve hot. Or let cool to room temperature and store in an airtight container. These will keep for 1 week.

·······⊰ **Note** ⊱ If you do not like the flavor of coconut oil, you can use any other oil instead; the flavor will be different but still good.

Rajgire Ka Thepla

As wheat is verboten during fasting in India, breads such as *rotis* and *parathas* are off limits. But *rajgira* flour solves the problem. The flour is gluten free and so the dough is rather delicate, but the addition of mashed potatoes helps tremendously. Make the breads ⅛ inch (3 to 4 mm) thick, and serve them with a bowl of plain yogurt.

Makes 12.

3 cups (400 grams) *rajgira atta* (see Note)
1½ teaspoons black salt
1-inch (2½-cm) piece fresh ginger, grated
1 teaspoon white sesame seeds
2 green chiles, stemmed and chopped
2 medium potatoes, boiled, peeled, and mashed
2 tablespoons plain yogurt
7 tablespoons ghee (page 37)
2 tablespoons chopped fresh cilantro

1. Put 2½ cups of the *rajgira atta* in a bowl. Add the black salt, ginger, sesame seeds, and chiles, and stir. Add the potatoes, yogurt, 3 tablespoons of the ghee, and the cilantro, and stir. Add ½ cup (100 ml) water and knead to make a semisoft dough. Cover and set aside for 30 minutes.

2. Divide the dough into 12 portions and shape into balls. Dust each ball with some of the remaining *rajgira atta* and pat into a 5-inch (12½-cm) round.

3. Place a nonstick griddle over medium heat. Let it heat for 2 to 3 minutes, then place a dough round on it. Cook for 1 minute, then flip with a spatula and cook the other side for 1 minute.

4. Drizzle ½ teaspoon of the remaining ghee all around and cook until it is light golden and crisp around the edges. Flip again and drizzle ½ teaspoon ghee around it. Cook until the second side is light golden and crisp around the edges.

5. Transfer to a serving plate and repeat with the remaining dough rounds.

6. Serve hot.

·······⋇{ **Note** }⋇· *Rajgira atta* is flour made from the seeds of the amaranth plant. It is gluten free and rich in lysine, an essential amino acid that is hard to find in vegetarian protein sources.

Sabudana Khichdi

There are many versions of this snack, but the most interesting one is sold at roadside carts in Indore, a bustling business center in the heart of Madhya Pradesh. You buy the plain cooked sago by weight and then top it with lemon juice and crunchy fried peanuts.

Serves 4.

1½ cups (300 grams) sago
3 tablespoons ghee (page 37)
1 teaspoon cumin seeds
4 or 5 green chiles, stemmed and broken into 4 pieces
1 medium potato, boiled, peeled, and cut into ½-inch (1-cm) cubes
3 tablespoons grated fresh coconut (or frozen unsweetened coconut)
¾ cup (110 grams) roasted peanuts, coarsely chopped
1 teaspoon table salt
1 teaspoon sugar
2 tablespoons chopped fresh cilantro

1. Put the sago in a large bowl, wash it in plenty of water 2 or 3 times, and drain. Add 1½ cups (300 ml) water and soak for 3 to 4 hours; after 2 hours, stir once. The sago grains should be separate and moist.

2. Place a medium nonstick sauté pan over medium heat and add the ghee. When the ghee melts and small bubbles appear at the bottom of the pan, add the cumin and chiles. When the cumin seeds begin to change color, add the potato and cook for 1 minute.

3. Add the sago, coconut, and peanuts, and cook for 4 to 5 minutes, stirring well.

4. Add the salt and sugar, and stir gently. Remove from the heat.

5. Sprinkle with the cilantro and serve hot.

····· ❈❳ **Note** ❳❈ Sago, or tapioca pearls, are made from the starch extracted from sago palm trees. In India, it is a very popular ingredient.

Sabudana Thalipeeth

The Navratri fasts (which precede the festival of Dassera in India) allow for the consumption of sago, potatoes, peanuts, and coconut, and this rich bread, served with any chutney, is filling—a good choice for those who are eating only one meal a day.

Serves 4.

½ cup (100 grams) sago
¼ cup (40 grams) roasted peanuts
1 medium potato, boiled, peeled, and mashed;
1 medium raw potato, peeled and grated
3 green chiles, stemmed and chopped
¼ teaspoon red chile powder
2 tablespoons chopped fresh cilantro
¼ cup (45 grams) sago flour
1 teaspoon table salt
1 teaspoon vegetable oil
1 teaspoon ghee (page 37)

1. Put the sago in a large bowl, add 1 cup (200 ml) water (almost enough to cover it), and soak for about 2 hours. Drain in a colander.

2. Put the peanuts in a spice grinder and grind coarsely. Transfer to a large bowl and add the drained sago, peanuts, mashed and raw potatoes, chiles, chile powder, cilantro, sago flour, and salt, and stir thoroughly.

3. Divide into 4 portions and shape into balls.

4. Grease a thick plastic or polyethylene sheet with ¼ teaspoon oil and place one sago ball on it. Flatten the ball into a thick 6-inch (15-cm) round with moistened or greased fingers.

5. Place a nonstick griddle over medium heat and add ¼ teaspoon of the ghee.

6. Gently transfer the sago round onto the griddle and peel the plastic off. Cook, turning, until evenly golden brown on both sides. Repeat with the remaining sago balls and ghee.

7. Serve immediately.

Sabudana Vadas

····· Sago snacks ·····

Here sago is combined with mashed potatoes and fried in oil. The outside is golden and crisp while the inside is soft and moist. Typically, it is served with coconut chutney. If you want to serve this as an appetizer, make smaller balls and serve them with toothpicks. Have a tomato sauce or dip ready.

Makes 16.

1 cup (200 grams) sago
½ cup (75 grams) roasted peanuts
1-inch (2½-cm) piece fresh ginger
3 green chiles, stemmed and chopped
3 medium potatoes, boiled, peeled, and mashed
2 tablespoons chopped fresh cilantro
1 tablespoon freshly squeezed lemon juice
2 teaspoons table salt
1 quart (800 ml) vegetable oil

1. Put the sago in a large bowl, add 2 cups (400 ml) water (almost enough to cover it), and soak for about 2 hours. Drain in a colander.

2. Put the peanuts in a spice grinder and grind coarsely. Transfer to a large bowl and set aside.

3. Place the ginger and chiles in a spice grinder, add 2 tablespoons water, and grind to a paste. Add to the peanuts, along with the drained sago, potatoes, cilantro, lemon juice, and salt, and stir well. Divide into 16 portions and shape into balls. Flatten slightly between your palms to make *vadas*.

4. Place a nonstick wok over high heat and add the oil. When small bubbles appear at the bottom of the wok, lower the heat to medium and gently slide in 4 *vadas* at a time. Cook, turning a few times with a slotted spoon, until golden brown and crisp all over. Remove with the slotted spoon and drain on paper towels.

5. Serve immediately.

Vrat Ki Kadhi

····· ⊰ **Water chestnut–flour curry** ⊱ ·····································

This unusual dish, prepared with water chestnut flour, is served during periods of fasting in India. You can find the flour at your local Indian grocery store.

Serves 4.

2 tablespoons *singhare ka atta* (water chestnut flour)
¼ teaspoon black salt
1 teaspoon red chile powder
¼ teaspoon ground cinnamon
1¾ cups (440 grams) plain yogurt, whisked
2 tablespoons ghee (page 37)
1 teaspoon cumin seeds
3 dried red chiles, stemmed and broken in half
10 to 12 fresh curry leaves
½ teaspoon sugar
1 teaspoon table salt
1 tablespoon chopped fresh cilantro

1. Put the *singhare ka atta* in a large bowl. Add the black salt, chile powder, cinnamon, and yogurt, and whisk until well blended. Add 1 quart (800 ml) water and whisk again. Set aside.

2. Place a medium nonstick saucepan over medium heat and add the ghee. When small bubbles appear at the bottom of the pan, add the cumin seeds, chiles, and curry leaves. Sauté until the cumin seeds begin to change color. Add the yogurt mixture and cook until the mixture is slightly thick.

3. Add the sugar and table salt, and stir. Lower the heat to low and simmer for 2 minutes.

4. Remove from the heat and transfer to a serving bowl. Garnish with the cilantro and serve immediately.

Badam Doodh

·······ঃ{ **Almond milk** }ঃ···

This rich milk gets its character from the almonds and spices used to flavor it. Be sure to use the best-quality almonds that you can find for this warm drink.

Makes 4 cups.

40 almonds
5 cups (1 liter) milk
Generous pinch of saffron threads
½ teaspoon ground green cardamom (see Note page 559)
Pinch of freshly grated nutmeg
½ cup (100 grams) sugar

1. Soak the almonds in 2 cups (400 ml) boiling water for 5 to 10 minutes. Drain, then rub off the skins. Slice 15 of them and set aside. Put the remaining almonds in a food processor, and process to a paste.

2. Place a nonstick saucepan over high heat and add the milk. When it comes to a boil, lower heat to medium, add the almond paste, and simmer over low heat for 15 to 20 minutes.

3. Add the saffron, cardamom, and nutmeg, and stir. Add the sugar and stir until it dissolves.

4. Remove from the heat and pour into individual heatproof glasses. Garnish with the sliced almonds and serve hot.

Badam Halwa

·······ঃ{ **Rich almond pudding with saffron** }ঃ···

It's delicious, I'll admit, especially on a cold winter evening, but this pudding is absolutely laden with fat! Do try it, but eat only a very small portion if you are watching your calories.

Serves 4.

1½ cups (150 grams) almonds
10 cups (2 liters) milk
¾ cup (175 ml) ghee (page 37)
1 cup (200 grams) sugar
8 to 10 saffron threads

1. Place a nonstick saucepan over high heat. Add 3 cups (600 ml) water and bring to a boil. Add ¾ cup (75 grams) of the almonds and bring to a rolling boil. Remove from the heat and set aside for 5 minutes. Drain well, then rub off the skins.

2. Transfer the blanched and unblanched almonds to a food processor, and process coarsely.

3. Place the saucepan over high heat. Add the milk and bring to a boil, stirring continuously. Lower the heat to medium and cook, stirring continuously, until the milk is reduced by three quarters. Set aside.

4. Place another nonstick saucepan over medium heat and add the ghee. When small bubbles appear at the bottom of the pan, add the ground almonds and lower the heat to low. Sauté for 5 minutes or until lightly browned.

5. Add the sugar, reduced milk, and saffron, and cook for 20 minutes or until all the liquid is absorbed and the mixture thickens. Serve warm.

Dudhi Halwa

······⋅⁂{ **Bottle gourd sweet** }⁂··

Dudhi halwa always seems to be overshadowed in India by the popularity of *gajar halwa* (page 563), a dessert prepared with carrots. But not anymore! This *halwa* does not require as much cooking time as *gajar halwa* and is also an allowed food on fasting days in India. I like the way my mother-in-law sets it in a flat dish until it solidifies and then cuts it into neat squares and serves it with style.

Serves 4.

1 medium bottle gourd
3 cups (600 ml) milk
3 tablespoon ghee (page 37)
½ cup (100 grams) sugar
1 teaspoon ground green cardamom (see Note page 559)
10 raisins
10 almonds, chopped
5 cashews, chopped
5 pistachios, chopped

1. Peel and halve the bottle gourd and scrape out the seeds. Grate it finely and transfer to a bowl.

2. Place a nonstick saucepan over medium heat, add the milk, and cook for 8 to 10 minutes or until it is reduced to about 2 cups (400 ml).

3. Place another nonstick saucepan over medium heat and add the ghee. When the ghee melts and small bubbles appear at the bottom of the pan, add the grated gourd and sauté for 12 to 15 minutes.

4. Add the reduced milk and cook, stirring continuously, for 10 minutes or until all the excess liquid has evaporated.

5. Add the sugar and cardamom. Stir well and remove from the heat.

6. Garnish with the raisins, almonds, cashews, and pistachios, and serve hot or at room temperature.

Kaju Katli

···········⊰ A nutty and flavorful sweet with cashews ⊱···

Katli means "a thin layer." The best *kaju katli* will be the one that is ⅛ to ¼ inch (4 to 5 mm) in thickness, and expert *halwais* (cooks skilled in making Indian sweetmeats) think nothing about rolling it out that thin. Homemade *kaju katli* is strongly cashew flavored, but since cashews are expensive, commercial makers sometimes use cashew essence and solidified milk products to fortify it.

Makes 20.

1⅓ cups (275 grams) sugar
2 tablespoons liquid glucose
1½ tablespoons ghee (page 37)
4¼ cups (900 grams) finely ground cashews
Chandi ka varq (edible silver foil; see page 188)

1. Place a nonstick saucepan over medium heat. Add 1⅓ cups (265 ml) water and the sugar, and cook for 12 minutes or until the syrup reaches 245°F/118°C, or until it has a multi-string consistency (see Note page 570).

2. Stir in the liquid glucose and ghee.

3. Remove from the heat and add the cashews, stirring continuously. Knead lightly to make a soft dough.

4. Grease an aluminum pan and spread the dough on it. Smooth the surface by pressing with your hands onto a sheet of waxed paper. Gently spread the silver *varq* over the top and cut the *kaju katli* into diamonds. Serve at room temperature.

5. Store in an airtight container for up to 2 days.

CHAPTER 14

Indo-Chinese

China is a neighbor to most of the northeastern states of India, and much of its food culture has trickled down into the subcontinent. In fact, Chinese food is the most popular choice when Indians dine out. Indian cooks have begun to experiment and create exotic foreign dishes. The strong Indian palate, however, means that many dishes are tweaked to suit our tastes. This has created a special category of fusion foods that have become so ubiquitous that it would not be unusual for *chile paneer* (page 549) and crunchy Chinese *bhel* (page 550) to make an appearance at a traditional Indian wedding feast.

Chicken Chow Mein

······{ **A chicken-and-noodle dish** }······

A decade or so ago, it was fashionable in India to serve Indo-Chinese dishes at parties and wedding banquets. Things are changing now as the Indian palate moves on to Indo-Mexican, Indo-Italian, and so on. But chicken chow mein remains a favorite dish on many restaurant menus and at many parties.

Serves 4.

1 teaspoon table salt
¼ cup (50 ml) vegetable oil
7 ounces (200 grams) egg noodles (spaghetti shaped)
8 baby corn cobs, halved lengthwise
1 large egg, beaten
2 or 3 cloves garlic, sliced
1-inch (2½-cm) piece fresh ginger, chopped
1 medium red onion, sliced
6 fresh button mushrooms, halved
1 medium red bell pepper, seeded and julienned
1 (4-ounce/125-gram) boneless, skinless chicken breast, cooked and shredded
2 teaspoons light soy sauce
1 teaspoon sesame oil
1 tablespoon toasted sesame seeds

1. Place a nonstick saucepan over medium heat, add 6 cups (1.2 liters) water, ½ teaspoon of the salt, and 1 tablespoon of the vegetable oil, and bring to a boil. Add the noodles and cook for 8 minutes or until almost done. Drain in a colander. Refresh in cold water, drain again, and spread on a large plate to cool.

2. Place a nonstick saucepan over medium heat, add 1 cup (200 ml) water, and bring to a boil. Add the baby corn and blanch for 2 minutes. Drain in a colander, refresh in cold water, drain again, and set aside.

3. Place a nonstick sauté pan over medium heat and add 1 teaspoon of the oil. Add the egg and stir to scramble it. When it is set, transfer to a small bowl and set aside.

4. Place a nonstick wok over medium heat and add the remaining vegetable oil. When small bubbles appear at the bottom of the wok, add the garlic, ginger, and onion, and sauté for 2 to 3 minutes.

5. Add the baby corn, mushrooms, and bell pepper, and sauté for 2 to 3 minutes. Add the chicken and sauté for 1 minute. Add the soy sauce and remaining ½ teaspoon salt, and stir well.

6. Add the noodles and sesame oil, and toss. Add the scrambled egg and toss again. Lower the heat to low and cook for 2 to 3 minutes or until the noodles are heated through.

7. Transfer to a serving bowl. Garnish with the sesame seeds and serve hot.

Chile Chana

I created this on a Sunday when the kids wanted something different—something that happens a lot, let me tell you! Thinking quickly, I turned some chickpeas into a special Indo-Chinese dish and served it with steamed rice. The kids were happy, and so was I.

Serves 4.

2 tablespoons vegetable oil
2-inch (5-cm) piece fresh ginger, chopped
3 or 4 cloves garlic, crushed
1 medium red onion, sliced
3 or 4 green chiles, stemmed and sliced
2 medium green bell peppers, seeded and julienned
½ teaspoon red chile powder
1 teaspoon red chile paste
1 tablespoon soy sauce
½ teaspoon table salt
2 cups (300 grams) cooked chickpeas

1. Place a nonstick wok over medium heat and add the oil. When small bubbles appear at the bottom of the wok, add the ginger and garlic, and sauté for 1 to 2 minutes or until lightly browned.

2. Add the onion, chiles, and bell peppers, and sauté for 3 to 4 minutes. Add the chile powder and chile paste, and sauté for 30 seconds. Add 2 tablespoons water and the soy sauce. Stir well and add the salt.

3. Add the chickpeas and stir. Sauté for 4 to 5 minutes.

4. Serve hot.

Chile Paneer

Steamed rice is the best partner for this dish, a lovely mix of Indian and Chinese styles of cooking. You can replace the *paneer* with tofu, but if you do, skip steps 1 and 2. If you want to serve this as a starter, decrease the amount of stock so that there is no extra sauce.

Serves 4.

11 ounces (300 grams) *paneer* (pressed fresh cheese; page 17), cut into 1-inch (2½-cm) fingers
3 tablespoons cornstarch
1 quart (800 ml) plus 2 tablespoons vegetable oil
3 or 4 cloves garlic, crushed
1 medium red onion, halved and thickly sliced
2 medium green bell peppers, seeded and cut into thick strips
6 to 8 green chiles, stemmed and sliced
1 cup (200 ml) vegetable stock
¾ teaspoon table salt
2 tablespoons soy sauce

1. Put the *paneer* in a bowl and sprinkle with 1 tablespoon of the cornstarch. Toss gently to coat.

2. Place a medium nonstick wok over high heat and add 1 quart (800 ml) oil. When small bubbles appear at the bottom of the wok, lower the heat to medium, add the *paneer*, and cook for 1 minute or until the edges start to turn brown. Remove with a slotted spoon and drain on paper towels.

3. Place the remaining 2 tablespoons cornstarch in a small bowl and add ½ cup (100 ml) water. Whisk well and set aside.

4. Place a nonstick wok over medium heat and add 2 tablespoons oil. When small bubbles appear at the bottom of the wok, add the garlic and sauté for 30 seconds.

5. Add the onion, bell peppers, and chiles, and sauté for 2 to 3 minutes.

6. Add the *paneer* and stir in the stock. Add the salt and soy sauce, and stir.

7. Add the cornstarch mixture and cook over high heat, stirring, until the sauce is thick enough to coat the *paneer* and vegetables.

8. Serve immediately.

Chinese Bhel

······❋⟨ **A popular street food with an Indo-Chinese treatment** ⟩❋······

I call this the "scrunch, munch, and it's gone" *bhel*. No matter how large a serving I make for friends, it's gone in no time. It is rather difficult to trace the origin of any Indo-Chinese dish, but kudos to the unknown inventor of this tasty dish. I use noodles without eggs because they fry better than egg noodles.

Serves 4.

7 ounces (200 grams) eggless noodles
1 quart (800 ml) plus 1 tablespoon vegetable oil
1¼ teaspoons table salt
3 scallions, bulbs and greens sliced separately
½ cup (70 grams) bean sprouts
¼ cup (40 grams) roasted peanuts, crushed
2 tablespoons Sichuan sauce (page 23)
2 tablespoons ketchup

1. Place a nonstick wok over medium heat and add 6 to 8 cups (1.2 to 1.6 liters) water, 1 tablespoon oil, and 1 teaspoon of the salt. Bring to a boil, add the noodles, and cook for 7 to 8 minutes or until almost done. Drain, refresh in cold water, drain again, and spread on a large plate to cool.

2. Place a nonstick wok over medium heat and add 1 quart (800 ml) oil. When small bubbles appear at the bottom of the wok, gently slide in the noodles in small batches and cook for 5 to 6 minutes or until crisp and golden brown. Remove with a slotted spoon and drain on paper towels. Set aside to cool.

3. Crush the noodles lightly and put them in a bowl. Add the scallion bulbs, bean sprouts, and peanuts, and toss well.

4. Add the Sichuan sauce and ketchup, and toss again. Taste and add the remaining ¼ teaspoon salt if needed.

5. Transfer to individual serving plates and garnish with the scallion tops. Serve immediately.

Spring Dosas

Lentil-and-rice pancakes with Sichuan sauce

Fusion food like this—a South Indian *dosa* filled with a Sichuan-style sauce—has taken the Indian street-food scene by storm.

Serves 4.

2 tablespoons plus 2 teaspoons vegetable oil
1 medium red onion, thinly sliced
2 medium carrots, grated
1 medium green bell pepper, seeded and julienned
1 cup (90 grams) finely shredded cabbage
½ tablespoon light soy sauce
½ teaspoon ground white pepper
5 tablespoons Sichuan sauce (page 23)
1 teaspoon table salt
½ cup (70 grams) bean sprouts
½ cup (50 grams) finely chopped scallion greens
2 cups *dosa* batter (page 122)
2 teaspoons butter, softened

1. Place a nonstick wok over medium heat and add 2 tablespoons oil. When small bubbles appear at the bottom of the wok, add the onion, carrots, and bell pepper, and stir-fry for 30 seconds. Add the cabbage and stir-fry for 1 minute. Add the soy sauce, white pepper, 1 tablespoon of the Sichuan sauce, and the salt. Add the bean sprouts and scallions, and stir-fry for about 30 seconds. Set the mixture aside to cool completely. Divide into 4 portions.

2. Place a nonstick griddle or flat sauté pan over medium heat. Wipe it clean with a lightly oiled cloth. Let it heat for 1 to 2 minutes. Pour ¼ cup of the *dosa* batter on the pan and spread it evenly with the back of the ladle to make a 9-inch (23-cm) disk. Drizzle ½ teaspoon of the oil around the *dosa* and cook over low heat for 1 minute.

3. Spread 1 tablespoon of the Sichuan sauce over the *dosa*. Then spread ½ teaspoon butter over it. Place one portion of the filling on one side of the *dosa* and gently roll the *dosa* along with the filling. Cook until the roll is golden on all sides. Cut into pieces on the bias, repeat with the remaining batter and filling, and serve immediately.

Chicken Lollipops

······§ Fried marinated chicken wings §······

In some restaurants red food coloring is added to this marinade to make the "lollipops" more attractive, but I choose not to use any additive. Serve them with Sichuan sauce (page 23) right after cooking, when the crust is still crisp.

Serves 4.

24 whole chicken wings
2 tablespoons fresh garlic paste (page 12)
2 tablespoons fresh ginger paste (page 12)
2 tablespoons red chile paste (see Note page 13)
1 teaspoon light soy sauce
1½ teaspoons distilled white vinegar
½ teaspoon ground white pepper
1½ teaspoons table salt
¼ cup (30 grams) *maida* (refined flour) or pastry flour
¾ cup (90 grams) cornstarch
2 large eggs
6 tablespoons plus 1 quart (800 ml) vegetable oil

1. Cut off the wing tips (discard them or save them for stock). Cut the wings in half at the joint. Remove the thin bone from each flat section, and pull the flesh to one end of the thick bone to make a "lollipop."

2. Put the chicken in a large bowl. Add the garlic paste, ginger paste, 1 teaspoon of the chile paste, the soy sauce, vinegar, white pepper, and salt. Stir so that all the wings are well coated. Cover the bowl with plastic wrap and put it in the refrigerator to marinate for 2 hours.

3. Combine the *maida*, cornstarch, eggs, 6 tablespoons (90 ml) oil, and the remaining chile paste in a bowl, and whisk thoroughly with a wire whisk. Add 1 tablespoon water and whisk again to make a thick batter of pouring consistency. Let the batter rest for 15 to 20 minutes.

4. Place a nonstick wok over high heat and add 1 quart (800 ml) oil. When small bubbles appear at the bottom of the wok, lower the heat to medium, dip the marinated wings in the batter, and gently slide them into the hot oil, a few at a time. Cook, turning frequently with a slotted spoon, for 3 to 4 minutes or until crisp and golden brown. Remove with the slotted spoon and drain on paper towels.

5. Serve hot.

Chicken Manchurian

······•} **Chicken dumplings in a spicy Chinese-style sauce** {•······

This is one of the most popular dishes in the Indo-Chinese repertoire. Kids love it as much as adults do. It is typically served with hot garlic fried rice (page 554).

Serves 4.

8 ounces ground chicken
½-inch (1-cm) piece fresh ginger, minced
5 cloves garlic, minced
1 green chile, stemmed and minced
½ teaspoon table salt
1 large egg, whisked
Pinch of ground white pepper
⅓ cup (40 grams) cornstarch
1 quart (800 ml) vegetable oil

~ **For the Manchurian sauce:**
3 tablespoons cornstarch
3 medium scallions with green tops
1 tablespoon vegetable oil
1-inch (2½-cm) piece fresh ginger, minced
4 to 6 cloves garlic, minced
1 green chile, stemmed and minced
2-inch (5-cm) rib celery, minced
2½ cups (500 ml) chicken stock (page 34)
1½ tablespoon dark soy sauce
1 teaspoon table salt
½ teaspoon sugar
¼ teaspoon ground white pepper
½ tablespoon white vinegar

1. Put the chicken in a bowl. Add the ginger, garlic, chile, salt, egg, white pepper, and cornstarch, and stir well. Divide into 12 portions and shape into balls.

2. Place a nonstick wok over high heat and add the oil. When small bubbles appear at the bottom of the wok, lower the heat to medium and gently slide in the chicken balls. Cook, stirring gently with a slotted spoon, for 6 minutes or until lightly browned. Remove with the slotted spoon and drain on paper towels.

3. Make the Manchurian sauce: Put the cornstarch in a bowl. Add 1 cup (200 ml) water and whisk until well mixed. Set aside.

4. Finely chop the scallion bulbs and greens separately.

5. Place a nonstick saucepan over medium heat and add the oil. When small bubbles appear at the bottom of the pan, add the ginger, garlic, chile, and celery, and sauté for 30 seconds. Add the scallion bulbs and sauté for 30 seconds. Add the stock, soy sauce, salt, and sugar. Stir well, add the white pepper, and stir again. When the mixture comes to a boil, add the cornstarch mixture and stir. Simmer for 3 to 4 minutes or until the sauce thickens. Add the vinegar and stir again.

6. Add the chicken balls and scallion greens, and simmer for 1 minute.

7. Serve hot.

Hot Garlic Fried Rice

·······⋇{ Spicy rice with garlic }⋇·······

This is a fine example of Indo-Chinese food, which is big business for restaurants in India—roadside eateries in particular. While a far cry from authentic Chinese, Indo-Chinese fusion has its own charms.

Serves 4.

1½ tablespoons vegetable oil
10 cloves garlic, finely chopped
6 scallions, bulbs sliced, green tops minced
1 medium carrot, diced
1 medium green bell pepper, seeded and diced
2 teaspoons red chile paste (see Note page 13)
2 dried red chiles, stemmed and broken into 4 pieces
1½ teaspoons table salt
1½ cups (300 grams) raw rice, cooked and chilled
¼ teaspoon soy sauce
1 teaspoon white vinegar

1. Place a medium nonstick sauté pan over medium heat and add the oil. When small bubbles appear at the bottom of the pan, add the garlic and stir-fry for 30 seconds. Add the scallion bulbs, carrot, bell pepper, chile paste, red chiles, and salt. Stir-fry over high heat for 3 minutes.

2. Add the rice, scallion tops, soy sauce, and vinegar, and stir-fry over high heat for 3 minutes.

3. Serve hot.

CHAPTER 15

Sweets and *Mithais*

In India, sweets and *mithais* (milk-based desserts) are used as religious offerings and as a way to show hospitality. They are made and served to celebrate auspicious occasions, such as the birth of a baby, receiving an excellent grade at school, or getting a new job. If you meet someone in India who is celebrating something, it is likely you will be told "*muh meetha kijiye*" (have a sweet).

Anaarase

····· ·{ **Rice-and-cane jaggery sweets with poppy seeds** }· ·····

This is an exotic cookie that is quite labor intensive to make. *Anaarase* is a traditional sweet made by Maharashtrians for Laxmi Puja (a special prayer to Laxmi, the goddess of wealth) during the Diwali festival. It is also prepared in Karnataka with ready-made rice flour. Some tips: Do not make the *anaarase* too thin or they will be hard. And be sure you cook them with the poppy-seed side up so the seeds don't fall off.

Makes 16.

1½ cups (250 grams) short-grain rice
About 6 ounces (165 grams) grated cane jaggery
¼ cup (50 grams) white poppy seeds
4½ cups (900 grams) ghee (page 37)

1. Wash and soak the rice in 1 quart (800 ml) water for 3 days, taking care to change the water daily. On the fourth day, drain the rice, spread on an absorbent towel, and let dry for 1 hour. Grind to a fine powder and weigh it; there should be about 6 ounces (175 grams).

2. Add an equal weight of jaggery and stir. Let rest, covered, for 2 days, then knead it into a dough. Divide the dough into 16 portions and shape into balls.

3. Spread the poppy seeds on a plate. Roll out each ball to a 3-inch (7½-cm) round and press one side into the poppy seeds to coat.

4. Place a nonstick wok over medium heat and add the ghee. When the ghee melts and small bubbles appear at the bottom of the wok, lower the heat to low and gently slide in one round at a time, keeping the poppy seed–coated side up. Cook for 2 to 3 minutes without turning.

5. Remove with a slotted spoon and drain on paper towels. Set aside to cool completely, then store in an airtight container for up to 1 week.

Balushahi

These round doughnutlike desserts are coated with a thick sugar syrup. I prefer to make them bite-size, but in *mithai* (sweet) shops you can expect to see large ones.

Makes 12.

1½ cups (180 grams) *maida* (refined flour) or pastry flour
¼ teaspoon baking soda
6 tablespoons plus 3 cups (675 grams) ghee (page 37), softened
6 tablespoons (115 grams) plain yogurt, whisked until smooth
2½ cups (500 grams) sugar
2 tablespoons milk
4 or 5 pistachios, finely chopped

1. Sift the flour and baking soda into a large bowl. Add 6 tablespoons (75 grams) of the ghee and rub it into the flour mixture until it resembles bread crumbs. Add the yogurt and knead to make a soft dough. Cover with a damp cloth and let rest for 45 minutes.

2. Divide the dough into 12 portions and shape into smooth balls. Take care not to overwork the dough. Make a slight dent in the center of each ball with your thumb. Keep the balls covered.

3. Place a nonstick wok over medium heat and add the 3 cups (600 grams) ghee. When the ghee melts and small bubbles appear at the bottom of the wok, lower the heat to low and gently slide in the dough balls, two or three at a time, and cook. If necessary, carefully place a griddle underneath the wok so that the ghee does not get too hot. The *balushahis* will gradually start floating to the top. Turn them gently with a slotted spoon and cook on the other side until golden. The entire process will take 30 to 45 minutes. Remove with the slotted spoon and drain on paper towels. Set aside to cool to room temperature, about 45 minutes.

4. Place a nonstick saucepan over high heat and add 1 cup (200 ml) water. Add the sugar and cook, stirring occasionally, until the sugar dissolves. Add the milk; the scum will rise to the surface. Carefully scoop out the scum and discard. Continue to cook until the syrup reaches a two-string consistency (see Note page 570).

5. Remove from the heat and add the cooled *balushahis*; soak them in the syrup for 2 hours.

6. Gently remove the *balushahis* from the syrup with a slotted spoon and place them on a serving plate. Sprinkle with the pistachios and set aside for 2 to 3 hours or until the syrup hardens into a thin white layer. Serve.

Badam Pista Kulfi

······=ξ **Frozen dessert with almonds and pistachios** {=······································

My earliest memories of *kulfi* (similar to ice cream) have always been about the traditional version served with its faithful partner, *falooda* (thick vermicelli made of cornstarch, available at Indian groceries). For some strange reason, my elder brother, Rajeev, who isn't a chef but a strategy consultant, perfected the art of making *falooda* long before I did. You can serve this recipe with or without *falooda*, which you can purchase at the Indian grocery store.

Serves 4.

7½ **cups (1.5 liters) milk**
Pinch of saffron threads
1 **can (400 grams) sweetened condensed milk**
¼ **cup (35 grams) almonds, coarsely ground**
¼ **cup (35 grams) pistachios, coarsely ground**
1 **cup (150 grams) grated *khoya/mawa* (unsweetened solid condensed milk; page 37)**
  (see Notes)

1. Place a nonstick saucepan over medium heat, add the milk, and bring to a boil. Add the saffron, lower the heat to low, and simmer for 30 minutes or until the milk is reduced by half.

2. Add the sweetened condensed milk, almonds, and pistachios, and stir well. Remove from the heat and set aside to cool to room temperature.

3. Add the *khoya* and stir well. Pour into individual *kulfi* molds (see Notes) and place them in the freezer to set.

4. When firm, unmold and serve immediately.

······=ξ **Notes** {=· You can use ¾ cup (100 grams) dry milk powder instead of the *khoya*. Some Indian stores now sell *khoya* in the refrigerated section.

Kulfi molds are available in Indian grocery stores. Or you can use ice-pop molds and sticks.

Besan Ke Laddoo

·······❦ **A very popular *besan* sweet** ❦··

Diwali is a festival of lights and is celebrated with loads of sweets and savories that are all made at home. My wife, Alyona, makes these *laddoos* every year for this holiday.

Makes 24.

12 to 15 cashews
12 to 15 almonds
1¼ cups (225 grams) ghee (page 37)
4 cups (400 grams) *jada besan* (coarse chickpea/gram flour)
1 teaspoon ground green cardamom (see Note)
2½ cups (250 grams) confectioners' sugar

1. Put the cashews and almonds in a spice grinder, and coarsely grind them. Transfer to a large bowl and set aside.

2. Place a nonstick wok over medium heat and add the ghee. When the ghee melts, lower the heat to low and add the *besan*. Cook, stirring continuously, for 15 to 20 minutes or until the *besan* is fragrant and light brown.

3. Add the cardamom and ground nuts. Stir well, then remove from the heat. Let cool for about 15 minutes.

4. Add the confectioners' sugar and stir well. You may use your hands to do this.

5. Shape into walnut-size round *laddoos* and arrange on a serving plate. Serve. Store leftover cooled *laddoos* in an airtight container in the refrigerator.

·······❦ **Chef's Tip** ❦ *Laddoos* that have been kept for a few days in the refrigerator should be warmed for 15 to 20 seconds in a microwave oven to soften and refresh them.

·······❦ **Note** ❦ To grind cardamom for sweet dishes: Grind a few green cardamoms (whole pods) with a little sugar. You can store the ground mixture in an airtight jar for use in sweet dishes and desserts.

Bhapa Doi

························ ·❊{ **Bengali steamed yogurt** }❊· ··

This is one of my favorite desserts—a traditional festive sweet, but one of the easiest to make when you're in a hurry. *Bhapa* in Bengali means "steamed." And *doi* means "yogurt."

Serves 4.

1 can (400 grams) sweetened condensed milk
1 cup (250 grams) thick plain yogurt, whisked
1 cup (200 ml) milk
15 raisins
10 almonds, blanched (see Note page 40) and slivered
15 pistachios, blanched (see Note page 40) and slivered

1. Put the sweetened condensed milk in a bowl. Add the yogurt and whisk. Add the milk and whisk again until well blended.

2. Add the raisins, almonds, and pistachios, and stir well.

3. Transfer to the top part of a steamer. Cover with aluminum foil and place the top on the steamer. Place the steamer over high heat and add 2 cups (400 ml) water. When the water comes to a boil, place the container with the milk mixture in the steamer, cover, and steam for 20 to 25 minutes.

4. Remove from the steamer, remove the foil, and set aside to cool to room temperature. Place the *bhapa doi* in the refrigerator to chill. Slice and serve chilled.

Chhenar Payesh

························ ·❊{ *Chhena*-and-nut dessert }❊· ···

I adore this delicious, very easy dessert from the eastern Indian state of Bengal. You can find *chhena*, a fresh cheese, at Indian grocery stores, or you can make it yourself as described in the Notes.

Serves 4.

5 cups (1 liter) milk
¼ cup (65 grams) sugar
½ cup (50 grams) cow's milk *chhena* (fresh cheese; see Notes)
5 or 6 almonds, blanched (see Note page 40) and chopped
7 or 8 pistachios, blanched (see Note page 40) and chopped

1. Place a nonstick saucepan over high heat and add the milk. When it comes to a boil, lower the heat to medium and simmer, stirring frequently, for 20 minutes or until the milk is reduced by half.

2. Add the sugar and cook until it dissolves.

3. Mash the *chhena* in a bowl, then add it to the milk mixture. Simmer for 2 minutes. Transfer to a serving bowl and set aside to cool.

4. Sprinkle with the almonds and pistachios, and serve.

> **Notes** ❈ If cow's milk *chhena* is not available, *chhena* made from buffalo's milk is fine. I recommend *chhena* made from cow's milk because it is lower in fat.
>
> To make *chhena*, put 2½ cups (500 ml) milk in a deep saucepan and bring it just to a boil. Squeeze the juice of 1 lemon into the milk and stir until it curdles. Drain away the whey and transfer the solids to a double layer of cheesecloth. Weight it down with a plate and something heavy so that all the excess liquid is drained away. This will yield ½ cup *chhena*.

Chocolate Walnut Burfi

❈ **Chocolate-and-walnut dessert** ❈

In India, it is customary to give your friends desserts during festivals. In my opinion, homemade *mithais* (sweet, milk-based desserts) are much better than store-bought for gifts, and I would be flattered if someone made this *burfi*—which is not found in sweet shops—and gave some to me on Diwali, the Indian festival of lights.

Makes 16.

3½ cups (500 grams) grated *khoya/mawa* (unsweetened solid condensed milk; page 37)
½ cup (60 grams) roughly chopped walnuts
⅔ cup (125 grams) sugar
3 tablespoons whole milk
11 ounces (300 grams) dark chocolate, chopped
Vegetable oil for greasing

1. Place a nonstick sauté pan over medium heat. Add the *khoya* and sauté for 4 to 5 minutes.

2. Reserve a few chopped walnuts and add the rest to the pan, along with the sugar and milk. Stir well and cook for 15 minutes or until the mixture thickens.

3. Melt the chocolate in the top of a double boiler over simmering water. Pour the chocolate through a fine sieve if there are any lumps, then let it cool to room temperature.

4. Divide the *khoya* mixture into 2 equal parts. To one part, add the melted chocolate and stir well.

5. Grease a 9-by-13-inch (23-by-33-cm) baking pan with oil.

6. Pour the plain *khoya* mixture into the baking pan and shake it so that the mixture spreads evenly (this should give you a ½ inch (1-cm) thickness). Spread the chocolate *khoya* mixture over the first layer. Sprinkle with the reserved walnuts. Set aside to cool for 45 minutes to 1 hour. When completely cooled, cut into squares or diamonds and serve. This sweet does not have a long shelf life and therefore should be consumed within a day.

Double Ka Meetha

······⁛{ **A rich bread pudding** }⁛······

I do not know exactly why, but in North India, bread is known as "double roti." One explanation is that the yeast-leavened bread dough doubles in size. *Double ka meetha* is an Indian version of bread-and-butter pudding. Serve this after a fairly light meal.

Serves 4.

1 loaf white bread, cut into thick slices
2½ cups (450 grams) ghee (page 37)
1 tablespoon *kakdi magaz* (dried cucumber seeds)
1 tablespoon *chironji / charoli* (melon seeds)
1 tablespoon chopped cashews
1 tablespoon slivered almonds
1 tablespoon slivered pistachios
1¼ cups (250 grams) sugar
1 cup (200 ml) milk
Generous pinch of saffron threads
¼ teaspoon ground green cardamom (see Note page 559)
Heavy cream

1. Trim the edges of the bread slices.

2. Place a small nonstick sauté pan over medium heat and add 2 tablespoons of the ghee. When the ghee melts, add the *kakdi magaz*, *chironji*, cashews, almonds, and pistachios and cook until golden brown. Set aside.

3. Place a nonstick wok over high heat and add the remaining ghee. When the ghee melts, lower the heat to medium, slide in the bread slices, and cook until golden brown. Remove with a slotted spoon and drain on paper towels.

4. Place a nonstick saucepan over medium heat. Add the sugar and 1 cup (200 ml) water and cook, stirring until the sugar dissolves. Add ¼ cup (50 ml) of the milk and cook. When the scum rises to the top, scoop it off carefully with a spoon and discard.

5. Add the cardamom and saffron to the syrup and stir. Add the fried bread and stir. Add the remaining ¾ cup (150 ml) milk and cook until all the syrup is absorbed and the bread is very soft.

6. Add the nut mixture and stir to combine.

7. Serve hot, drizzled with cream.

Gajar Halwa

·······{ **Warm carrot pudding** }·······

Gajar halwa, or *gajrela*, as it is sometimes fondly called, is a famous sweet made in all Punjabi homes during winter. Some like it hot, some like it cold, some even like it nine days old! It refrigerates well, and some families always have a large tin of *gajar halwa* on hand.

Serves 4.

1½ tablespoons ghee (page 37)
4 medium carrots, grated
½ cup (100 grams) sugar
Pinch of ground green cardamom (see Note page 559)
½ cup (75 grams) grated *khoya/mawa* (unsweetened solid condensed milk; page 37)
1 cup (200 ml) milk
2 or 3 cashews, chopped
2 or 3 almonds, blanched (see Note page 40) and sliced
6 to 8 raisins
1 sheet *chandi ka varq* (edible silver foil; see page 188)

1. Place a nonstick heavy-bottomed pan over medium heat and add the ghee. When small bubbles appear at the bottom of the pan, add the carrots and sauté for 10 minutes or until the carrots are soft.

2. Add the sugar and cook for 1 minute more. Add the cardamom and stir well. Add the *khoya* and cook for 1 minute or until it melts and mixes with the rest of the ingredients in the pan.

3. Add the milk and stir. Lower the heat to low and cook for 12 minutes or until the mixture is thick.

4. Add the cashews, almonds, and raisins, and stir. Remove from the heat and transfer the *halwa* to a serving bowl.

5. Decorate with the silver foil and serve hot or at room temperature.

Gil-E-Firdaus

········ ᐧ{ **Bottle gourd cooked in milk** }ᐧ ····································

This is one of the best-selling desserts at our Yellow Chilli restaurants, where we make it with a sugar substitute.

Serves 4.

5 tablespoons (75 grams) raw rice
1¼ cups (250 grams) grated bottle gourd
2 tablespoons ghee (page 37)
5 cups (1 liter) milk
⅔ cup (100 grams) grated *khoya/mawa* (unsweetened solid condensed milk, page 37)
⅔ cup (125 grams) sugar
A few drops of rosewater
10 almonds, sliced
A few untreated rose petals

1. Put the rice in a bowl, wash it in plenty of water 2 or 3 times, and drain. Add 1 cup (200 ml) water and soak for about 1 hour. Drain the rice in a colander and spread out to dry for 1 hour.

2. Put the rice in a spice grinder, and coarsely grind to a semolina consistency.

3. Place a nonstick saucepan over high heat and add 1 cup (200 ml) water. When the water begins to boil, add the bottle gourd and cook for 3 minutes or until soft. Drain well and set aside.

4. Place a nonstick saucepan over medium heat and add the ghee. When the ghee melts and small bubbles appear at the bottom of the pan, add the rice and sauté for 10 seconds.

5. Add the milk and bring to a boil. Lower the heat to low and cook, stirring continuously, for 25 minutes or until the rice is soft.

6. Add the bottle gourd and simmer for 5 minutes. Add the *khoya* and sugar, and cook until the mixture is thick enough to coat the back of a spoon. Stir in the rosewater.

7. Pour into individual serving bowls and set aside to cooled to room temperature. Place the bowls in the refrigerator to chill.

8. Sprinkle with the almonds and rose petals, and serve chilled.

Gulab Jamun

·······⁕} **Deep-fried sweet dumplings dipped in sugar syrup** {⁕··

A *gulab* is a rose and *jamun* is a fruit. However, this dessert contains neither! I am not quite sure how it got its name, but this is one of the most beloved (and sweetest) of all Indian desserts. In my restaurant I serve a very special version called *gulab-e-gulkand*, which is stuffed with candied roses.

Serves 4.

1 cup (130 grams) dry milk powder
2 tablespoons *maida* (refined flour) or pastry flour
¼ teaspoon baking soda
¼ cup (60 grams) plain yogurt, whisked
1¼ cups (250 grams) sugar
1 teaspoon milk
¼ teaspoon ground green cardamom (see Note page 559)
Pinch of saffron, threads
2¼ cups (450 grams) ghee (page 37)

1. Put the milk powder in a bowl. Add the *maida* and baking soda, and stir well. Add the yogurt and stir to make a soft dough. Divide into 16 equal portions and shape them into round, smooth balls. Set aside.

2. To make the sugar syrup, place a nonstick saucepan over high heat and add 1 cup (200 ml) water. Add the sugar and cook, stirring continuously, until the sugar is dissolved. Add the milk and stir. The scum containing the impurities in the sugar will rise to the top. Gently gather it with a spoon and discard. You will get a clear syrup. Add the cardamom and saffron, and stir. Cook until the syrup reaches 130°F/54°C. Remove from the heat and cover to keep the syrup warm.

3. Place a nonstick wok over medium heat and add the ghee. Heat until the ghee reaches a temperature of 160°F/71°C or until it is fragrant.

4. Gently slide in four dough balls at a time and cook, gently spooning hot ghee over the balls with a slotted spoon, until the balls are deep golden, about 2 minutes.

5. Drain the balls in the slotted spoon and transfer them to the sugar syrup. Repeat with the remaining balls. Soak the dumplings in the syrup for at least 15 minutes before serving warm or at room temperature.

·······⁕} **Chef's Tip** {⁕ The temperature of the ghee should be low or the *jamuns* will cook only on the outside and will remain raw on the inside. You may stuff *gulab jamuns* with saffron and pistachio nuts, sugar crystals, or *gulkand* (candied rose petals, available at Indian grocery stores).

Jalebi

These syrupy spirals are the most popular fresh *mithai* (dessert) in most of northern and western India. I have seen them being made at sweet shops, and now they are even cooked in front of guests at weddings. *Jalebis* might be common and innocuous, but they tug at the strings of many hearts.

Makes 30.

1½ cups (195 grams) plus 2 tablespoons *maida* (refined flour) or pastry flour
¼ teaspoon yellow or orange food coloring
2½ cups (500 grams) sugar
½ teaspoon ground green cardamom (see Note page 559)
2¼ cups (450 grams) ghee (page 37)

1. Put 1½ cups (195 grams) of the *maida* in a bowl, add 1½ cups (300 ml) water, and knead the batter, with your hands, until completely smooth. This will take some elbow grease. The batter should not have any lumps at all. Cover the bowl and set aside in a warm place to ferment for 20 hours.

2. Knead the batter again for 15 minutes. Add the food coloring and the remaining 2 tablespoons *maida*, and knead again for 10 minutes.

3. Place a nonstick saucepan over high heat and add 2 cups (400 ml) water. Add the sugar and cook, stirring continuously, until the sugar is dissolved. Add the cardamom and cook, stirring, until the syrup reaches a one-string consistency (see Note page 570). Let the syrup cool to lukewarm.

4. Place a wide nonstick sauté pan over medium heat and add the ghee. Pour some of the batter into a squeeze bottle. When the ghee melts and small bubbles appear at the bottom of the pan, lower the heat to medium. Hold the bottle over the hot ghee and gently squeeze the batter in round 4-inch (10-cm) spirals, starting from the outside and working to the inside.

5. Cook, gently turning with a slotted spoon, for 8 minutes on each side or until the spirals are evenly golden and crisp. Remove with the slotted spoon to the sugar syrup and soak for 2 to 3 minutes.

6. Drain and serve hot.

······❊❧ **Chef's Tip** ❧❊ Traditionally the *jalebis* are fried in a special pan called a *jalebi tawi*, which is wide and not too deep, and the batter is squeezed through a *jalebi* cloth, which is a piece of thick cloth with a ⅛ inch (3-mm) hole in the center. *Jalebi* making takes some practice and patience. To start, make one at a time, and when you have perfected that, try making several at a time. To make crisp *jalebis*, add a little rice flour to the *maida*.

Kalakand

Milk is God's gift to mankind and a cook's dream ingredient. For Indians, it is the basis for many sweets, *kalakand* being just one of them. A good-quality *kalakand* will be a little grainy on the palate and not cloyingly sweet. One tip: *Kalakand* does not have a long shelf life, so it's best to make only as much as you can consume in a day.

Makes 16.

10 cups (2 liters) buffalo milk (or cow's milk)
¼ teaspoon alum, crushed (see Note)
¼ cup (50 grams) sugar
½ tablespoon ghee (page 37)
20 pistachios, thinly sliced
1 sheet *chandi ka varq* (edible silver foil; see page 188)

1. Place a deep, heavy-bottomed nonstick saucepan over medium heat, add the milk, and bring to a boil. Boil, stirring continuously, for 8 minutes or until the milk thickens slightly.

2. Add the alum and cook over medium heat, stirring continuously, for 20 minutes or until the milk becomes grainy.

3. Cook for 20 minutes more or until most of the moisture evaporates and a solid mass remains.

4. Add the sugar and stir well. Cook for 5 to 10 minutes or until the mixture thickens again.

5. Grease a 9-by-13-inch (23-by-33-cm) baking pan with the ghee. Pour the milk mixture into the pan and smooth the surface. Sprinkle the pistachios on top. Set aside in a cool, dry place for 1 hour or until firm.

6. When completely set, decorate with the silver foil, cut into squares or diamonds, and serve.

·······•} **Note** {• Alum is often used in processing pickles, and as a flocking agent.

Kheer Kadam

This is as exotic as it can get: one dessert combined with another! Bengalis, from the eastern part of India, are indeed masters at making milk-based sweets. These will not keep well for more than a day—nor will they need to.

Makes 16.

16 mini *rasgullas* (Indian pressed fresh cheese dessert; store-bought)
2 cups (300 grams) plus 3 tablespoons finely grated *khoya/mawa* (unsweetened
    solid condensed milk; page 37)
¼ cup (25 grams) confectioners' sugar
½ teaspoon rose essence or rosewater

1. Remove any excess sugar syrup from the *rasgullas* by draining them.

2. Put 2 cups (300 grams) of the *khoya* in a bowl and stir in the confectioners' sugar. Knead to make a smooth dough.

3. Place a nonstick sauté pan over high heat, add the *khoya*-sugar mixture, and cook for 4 to 5 minutes. Transfer to a bowl and set aside to cool.

4. Add the rose essence or rosewater and knead well. Divide into 16 portions and shape into balls. Lightly flatten the balls by pressing in the center with your thumb and thinning the edges. Place a *rasgulla* in each. Gather the edges of the dough to enclose the *rasgulla*. Roll into a ball.

5. Put the remaining 3 tablespoons *khoya* in a mini food processor and grind to a powder. Roll the balls in the powder.

6. Chill in the refrigerator and serve cold.

Khubani Ka Meetha

·······⟩ **A rich and delicate dish with dried apricots** ⟨·········

Peaches and cream, strawberries and cream, apricots and cream . . . fresh fruit and cream seem to create magic. The doyennes of Hyderabadi cuisine did it a bit differently, using dried apricots (*khubani*) to create a masterpiece that wowed the royal Nizami household. These days it is traditionally served at weddings.

Serves 4.

1 pound (500 grams) dried, pitted whole apricots
1 cup (200 grams) sugar
¼ cup (50 ml) *malai* (see Note) or heavy cream
10 to 12 almonds, blanched (see Note page 40), peeled, and sliced

1. Put the apricots in a large bowl, add 3 cups (600 ml) water, and soak overnight. Drain the apricots and reserve the water.

2. Place a large nonstick saucepan over high heat and add the reserved apricot water. When the water comes to a boil, add the apricots and cook for 9 minutes. Add the sugar and boil until the sugar is dissolved. Remove from the heat and set aside to cool slightly. Reserve some of the apricots and transfer the rest into a food processor, and process to a purée.

3. Transfer the apricot purée to a medium nonstick saucepan. Add the reserved whole apricots and place the pan over medium heat. Simmer for 2 to 3 minutes.

4. Transfer to a serving dish, drizzle with the cream and garnish with the almonds, and serve hot or let cool to room temperature and then serve.

·······⟩ **Note** ⟨· *Malai* is the cream that forms on the top of boiled milk. To prepare it, boil whole milk, let it cool, then skim off the cream.

Malpua

This gooey, rich, sweet pancake is a real treat on a Sunday morning! Don't skimp on the ghee here, as it really adds to the richness of the dish.

Serves 4.

5 cups (1 liter) milk, or more if necessary
1½ cups (300 grams) sugar
6 to 8 saffron threads
¼ cup plus 1 teaspoon (30 grams) *maida* (refined flour) or pastry flour
1 tablespoon *rawa/suji* (semolina flour)
2¼ cups (450 grams) ghee (page 37)

1. Place a nonstick saucepan over high heat. Add the milk and bring to a boil. Lower the heat to medium and simmer, stirring frequently, until the milk reduces and is thick enough to coat the back of a wooden spoon. Set aside to cool to room temperature.

2. Reserve 2 tablespoons of the sugar. Put the remaining sugar in a saucepan, add ½ cup (100 ml) water and cook over medium heat, stirring occasionally. Add 2 teaspoons of the milk and stir. The scum containing the impurities in the sugar will rise to the top. Gently gather it with a spoon and discard. You will get a clear syrup. Cook until the sugar syrup reaches one-string consistency (see Note). Remove from the heat and cover to keep warm.

3. Dissolve the saffron in 1 teaspoon of warm milk. Add it to the sugar syrup.

4. To the cooled reduced milk, add the *maida* and *rawa* and the reserved 2 tablespoons sugar. Stir well to make a batter of pouring consistency, adding a little more milk if needed. Set aside at room temperature for 3 hours; do not keep the batter in the refrigerator.

5. Place a wide nonstick sauté pan over high heat and add the ghee. When small bubbles appear at the bottom of the pan, lower the heat to medium and pour in a ladleful of batter to form a pancake. Gently spoon hot ghee over the pancake for 1 minute, then turn the pancake over. Cook, turning, until both sides are golden brown. Drain with a slotted spoon and immerse in the warm sugar syrup for 15 minutes. Repeat with the remaining batter.

6. Remove with a slotted spoon and serve warm.

······ ❧ **Note** ❧ To check if the sugar syrup has reached a one-string consistency, place a drop of slightly cooled syrup between your thumb and forefinger, and slowly pull them apart. If the syrup forms a single string, the syrup is ready.

Meethe Chawal

This delicately flavored dish is typically served on special occasions. It gets its oomph from the cardamom and saffron combination. You can adjust the level of sweetness by reducing the sugar.

Serves 4.

2 cups (400 grams) raw basmati rice
3 tablespoons ghee (page 37)
20 almonds
12 cashews
3 whole cloves
1-inch (2½-cm) cinnamon stick
5 or 6 whole black peppercorns
1 black cardamom pod
3 green cardamom pods
1¾ cups (375 grams) sugar
25 saffron threads

1. Put the rice in a large bowl, wash it in plenty of water 2 or 3 times, and drain. Add 4 cups (800 ml) water and soak for 20 minutes. Drain the rice in a fine colander.

2. Place a medium nonstick saucepan over medium heat and add the ghee. When small bubbles appear at the bottom of the pan, add the almonds and cashews, and fry for 2 to 3 minutes. Remove with a slotted spoon and drain on paper towels. Let cool, then thinly slice the almonds and split the cashews in half and put them in a small bowl.

3. Return the pan with the ghee to medium heat and add the cloves, cinnamon, peppercorns, black cardamom, and green cardamom, and sauté for 1 minute or until fragrant.

4. Add the rice and sauté gently for 2 to 3 minutes. Add 3½ cups (700 ml) warm water and bring to a boil. Lower the heat to low, cover, and cook until all the water is absorbed.

5. Put the sugar in a medium bowl, add 1 cup (200 ml) warm water, and stir until the sugar dissolves. Add the saffron and stir. Add this syrup to the rice, stirring gently to mix well. Cover and continue to cook the rice over low heat until it is cooked and almost all the liquid is absorbed.

6. Remove from the heat and let stand for 5 minutes. Transfer the rice to a serving platter, garnish with the almonds and cashews, and serve.

Naralachi Karanjis

······❈} Crescent-shaped pastries filled with sweetened coconut {❈······

Karanjis are sweet-filled pastries that celebrate auspicious moments in any Maharashtrian household. They are made with many different fillings, but this is the one I have tasted most often since I made Mumbai my home. The festivals of Ganpati and Diwali are incomplete without *karanjis*.

Makes 8.

~ For the dough:
½ cup (60 grams) *maida* (refined flour) or pastry flour
¾ tablespoon fine *rawa/suji* (semolina flour)
1½ tablespoons ghee (page 37)
¼ cup (50 ml) milk
1 quart (800 ml) vegetable oil

~ For the filling:
½ cup (60 grams) grated fresh coconut (or frozen unsweetened coconut)
15 to 20 raisins, chopped
1¼ cups (125 grams) confectioners' sugar
½ teaspoon ground green cardamom (see Note page 559)
¼ cup (50 ml) milk

1. Make the dough: Sift the *maida* into a bowl. Add the semolina and ghee, and stir with your fingertips until the mixture resembles bread crumbs. Add the milk and knead to make a semisoft dough. Cover with a damp cloth and set aside for 30 minutes.

2. Make the filling: Place a nonstick sauté pan over medium heat. Add the coconut and dry-roast until lightly browned.

3. Add the raisins, confectioners' sugar, cardamom, and milk, and stir well. Remove from the heat and let cool completely.

4. Knead the dough once again and divide into 8 portions. Roll out each portion into a 4-inch (10-cm) round. Place one round on a work surface. Place one portion of the filling on one half of the round. Brush a little water on the edges of the dough, fold the empty half over, and press the edges to seal. Trim with a pastry wheel. Repeat with the remaining dough and filling.

5. Place a nonstick wok over high heat and add the oil. When small bubbles appear at the bottom of the wok, lower the heat to medium and slide in two *karanjis* at a time. Cook, gently turning with a slotted spoon, until crisp and golden brown all over. Remove with the slotted spoon and drain on paper towels.

6. Let cool completely, then store in an airtight container for up to 3 days. Serve at room temperature.

Phirni

···⊰{ Chilled rice pudding with nuts }⊱·····································

Kheer (made with whole rice) is probably a better-known rice pudding than *phirni* (made with ground rice), but in my opinion *phirni* tastes equally good—and it can be made with one third the effort of *kheer*.

Serves 4.

6 tablespoons (90 grams) raw rice
5 cups (1 liter) milk
Generous pinch of saffron threads
1 cup (200 grams) sugar
½ teaspoon ground green cardamom (see Note page 559)
15 pistachios, blanched (see Note page 40) and sliced

1. Put the rice in a small bowl, wash it in plenty of water 2 or 3 times, and drain. Add 1 cup (200 ml) water and soak for 30 minutes. Drain the rice in a colander and transfer to a spice grinder. Grind to a coarse paste. Stir in a little water or some of the milk.

2. Place a nonstick saucepan over medium heat, add the milk, and bring to a boil. Add the rice paste and stir well. Lower the heat to low and simmer, stirring continuously, for 5 minutes or until the rice is completely cooked. Add the saffron and stir well. Add the sugar and cardamom, and cook until the sugar is dissolved.

3. Spoon into earthenware or china serving bowls and garnish with the pistachios. Put in the refrigerator to chill for 1 hour before serving.

Rabdi

···⊰{ Thickened milk with pieces of cream }⊱·····························

Cooks called *halwais* labor in local sweet shops all over India, reducing milk in gargantuan woks by stirring the hot liquid continuously. The result of their hard work is either this thick, sweet dessert with large bits of cream in it or the dry, crumbly cake called *khoya* or *mawa*, which is the basis of countless other sweets.

Serves 4.

8 to 10 almonds
8 to 10 pistachios
1 quart (800 ml) whole milk
2 tablespoons sugar
1 teaspoon rosewater
¼ teaspoon ground green cardamom (see Note page 559)

1. Place a nonstick saucepan over medium heat, add ½ cup (100 ml) water, and bring to a boil. Add the almonds and pistachios, and remove from the heat. Let the almonds and pistachios blanch in the hot water for 2 to 3 minutes. Drain and set aside to cool. Peel and thinly slice them.

2. Place a nonstick saucepan over medium heat, add the milk, and bring to a boil. Lower the heat to low and cook, stirring frequently, for 40 minutes. As the cream forms, it will stick to the sides of the pan.

3. Add the sugar and stir until it is dissolved. Simmer for 5 minutes or until the milk is reduced to one quarter of its original volume.

4. Scrape off the cream from the sides of the pan and return it to the thickened milk. Remove from the heat and stir in the rosewater.

5. Transfer to a serving bowl and decorate with the almonds, pistachios, and cardamom. Serve warm or chilled.

Raghavdas Laddoo

·······⊰ Sweet semolina balls with roasted coconut ⊱···

There's a special, much-loved type of Indian sweet called *laddoos*. The more common ones are the chickpea flour–based *laddoos* of the north and the semolina-based ones of Maharashtra. During the festival of Ganapati, these coconut-and-semolina *laddoos* are prepared as *naivedyam* (offerings to the Almighty).

Makes 25.

½ cup (60 grams) grated fresh coconut (or frozen unsweetened coconut)
6 tablespoons ghee (page 37)
1½ cups (300 grams) coarse *rawa/suji* (semolina flour)
½ teaspoon ground green cardamom (see Note page 559)
2 tablespoons raisins
1¾ cups (375 grams) sugar

1. Place a nonstick wok over medium heat. Let it heat for 2 minutes, then lower the heat to low, add the coconut, and cook for 6 minutes or until reddish brown. Transfer to a bowl and set aside.

2. Put the ghee in the same hot wok over low heat. Add the semolina and cook for 15 minutes or until lightly browned. Remove from the heat, add the browned coconut, and stir well.

3. Add the cardamom and stir well. Reserve a few raisins for garnish and stir the rest into the semolina mixture.

4. Place a nonstick saucepan over medium heat. Add the sugar and ¾ cup (150 ml) water, and cook until a syrup of one-string consistency is formed (see Note page 570).

5. Add the semolina mixture and stir well. Cover and remove from the heat; set aside for 15 minutes or until the mixture cools a little.

6. Grease your palms with a little ghee, take a little of the semolina mixture into your palms and shape into a round ball. Decorate each ball with a raisin. Repeat with the remaining semolina mixture and raisins.

7. When the *laddoos* are completely cooled, store in an airtight container for up to 2 days.

Rasmalai

······∗⦃ **Soft cheese patties soaked in sweetened milk** ⦄∗······

Juicy and *creamy*: two words that do not go together except when used to describe this traditional Indian dessert. It is available in *mithai* (sweet) shops across the country, but making it from scratch at home is an exhilarating experience. The results are superb, and you are bound to get some pats on the back.

In this recipe, the first syrup is used for cooking the cheese patties. Since this syrup has a bit of flour, it cannot be used for soaking the patties once they are cooked. So we prepare another syrup, this time without the flour.

Makes 12.

~ For the *chenna:*
5 cups (1 liter) whole milk
1½ tablespoons distilled white vinegar

~ For the first syrup:
1¼ cups (250 grams) sugar
2 tablespoons whole milk
1 teaspoon *maida* (refined flour) or pastry flour

~ For the second syrup:
2½ cups (500 grams) sugar
2 tablespoons whole milk

~ For the *rabdi*:
5 cups (1 liter) whole milk
3 tablespoons sugar
Pinch of saffron threads

1. Make the *chenna*: Place a heavy-bottomed pot over high heat and add the milk. When it comes to a boil, lower the heat to low, add the vinegar, and stir until the liquid whey separates from the solid curds.

2. Line a strainer with a double layer of cheesecloth and pour in the whey and curds; drain, then gather the curds up in the cloth and dip the *chenna*, in the cloth, in a bowl of cold water until it is completely chilled. Squeeze out any excess water and press with your palms until all the water drains away. The *chenna* should form a ball.

3. Transfer the *chenna* to a plate and divide into 12 portions. Take each portion between your palms and press and roll to form a flat patty. Set aside.

4. Make the first syrup: Place a nonstick saucepan over high heat. Add the sugar and 3 cups (600 ml) water and cook, stirring until the sugar is dissolved. When the syrup comes to a boil, add the milk. The scum will rise to the top. Gently spoon off the scum and discard.

5. Bring the syrup to a rolling boil. Lower the *chenna* patties into the syrup. In a small cup, stir the *maida* into ¼ cup (50 ml) water to make a slurry. Add this to the syrup and stir. Cover and cook for 20 minutes, adding ½ cup (100 ml) water every 5 minutes so that the syrup does not thicken. Remove from the heat and set aside.

6. Make the second syrup: Place a nonstick saucepan over high heat. Add the sugar and 2 cups (400 ml) water, and cook, stirring continuously, until the sugar is dissolved. When the syrup comes to a boil, add the milk. The scum will rise to the top. Gently spoon off the scum and discard. Let the syrup cool slightly; it should be warm, not hot.

7. With a slotted spoon, remove the *chenna* patties from the first syrup and put them in the second syrup to soak.

8. Make the *rabdi*: Place a nonstick saucepan over high heat and add the milk. When it comes to a boil, lower the heat to medium and cook, stirring continuously, until the milk is reduced by one quarter. Scrape off the cream that collects on the sides of the pan and drop it back into the milk.

9. Add the sugar and saffron, and cook for 5 minutes more. Transfer to a large bowl.

10. Remove each *chenna* patty from the second syrup, gently press to remove excess syrup, and add into the *rabdi* to soak.

11. Chill in the refrigerator for at least 2 hours so the *chenna* patties absorb the *rabdi*. Serve cold.

Rosogulla

This masterpiece of sweets is the basis for many other Bengali desserts. People are often hesitant to make these at home, thinking that there is some secret to making them well. The secret is practice!

Makes 16.

~ **For the *chenna*:**
5 cups (1 liter) whole milk
1½ tablespoons distilled white vinegar

~ **For the first syrup:**
1¼ cups (250 grams) sugar
2 tablespoons whole milk
1 tablespoon *maida* (refined flour) or pastry flour

~ **For the second syrup:**
1¼ cups (250 grams) sugar
2 tablespoons whole milk

1. Make the *chenna*: Place a nonstick saucepan over high heat and add the milk. When it comes to a boil, lower the heat to low, add the vinegar, and stir until the liquid whey separates from the solid curds.

2. Line a strainer with a double layer of cheesecloth and pour in the whey and curds; drain, then gather the curds up in the cloth and dip the *chenna*, in the cloth, in a bowl of cold water until it is completely chilled. Squeeze out any excess water and press with your palms until all the water drains away. The *chenna* should form a ball. Transfer the *chenna* to a plate and divide into 16 portions. Take each portion between your palms and press and roll into a ball. Set aside.

3. Make the first syrup: Place a nonstick saucepan over high heat. Add the sugar and 2 cups (400 ml) water and cook, stirring continuously, until the sugar is dissolved. When the syrup starts boiling, add the milk. The scum will rise to the top. Gently spoon off the scum and discard.

4. Bring the syrup to a rolling boil. Lower the *chenna* balls into the syrup. In a small bowl, stir the *maida* into 1 cup (200 ml) water to make a slurry. Add half of this to the syrup and stir. Cover and cook for 25 minutes. Add ½ cup (100 ml) water every 5 minutes so that the syrup does not thicken. Add the remaining slurry after 10 or 15 minutes. Remove from the heat and set aside.

5. Make the second syrup: Place a nonstick saucepan over high heat. Add the sugar and 2 cups (400 ml) water, and cook, stirring continuously, until the sugar is dissolved. When the syrup comes to a boil, add the milk. When the scum rises to the top, gently spoon it off and discard. Let the syrup cool slightly; it should be warm, not hot.

6. With a slotted spoon, remove the *chenna* balls from the first syrup and put them in the second syrup to soak. Chill in the refrigerator for at least 2 hours so the *chenna* balls absorb the syrup. Serve cold.

Sakkarai Pongal

The festival of Pongal in Tamil Nadu celebrates the harvest and marks a period of prosperity and plenty. *Ponga* literally means "overflowing," and it is customary to cook this sweet in small pots and allow it to boil over as a mark of thanksgiving.

Serves 4.

3 green cardamom pods
1 tablespoon sugar
¼ cup (50 grams) *dhuli moong dal* (split skinless green gram)
¾ cup (150 grams) short grain rice, soaked for 30 minutes
3 cups (600 ml) milk
1 cup (200 grams) grated cane jaggery
¼ cup (50 grams) plus 1 tablespoon ghee (page 37)
1 tablespoon chopped fresh coconut
2 tablespoons raisins
7 or 8 cashews

1. Break the cardamom pods and put the seeds in a spice grinder. Add the sugar and grind to a fine powder.

2. Place a nonstick saucepan over medium heat. Add the *dal* and dry-roast for 2 to 3 minutes or until fragrant. Transfer to a bowl and set aside.

3. Drain and add the rice to the same heated pan and dry-roast for 1 minute. Transfer to another bowl and set aside.

4. Return the *dal* to the same heated pan. Add 2½ cups (500 ml) of the milk and 1½ (300 ml) cups water and bring to a boil. Cover and cook for 10 minutes or until the *dal* is three quarters done.

5. Add the rice, the remaining ½ cup (100 ml) milk, and 1 cup (200 ml) water. Cover and cook for 20 minutes or until both the *dal* and rice are cooked.

6. Add the jaggery and stir continuously until the jaggery is dissolved. Add ¼ cup (50 ml) of the ghee and stir.

7. Meanwhile, place a small nonstick sauté pan over medium heat and add the remaining 1 tablespoon ghee. When the ghee melts, add the coconut, raisins, and cashews, and sauté until lightly browned. Add to the *dal*-rice mixture.

8. Add the ground cardamom mixture and stir. Cook for 2 to 3 minutes.

9. Remove from the heat and serve hot.

Semiya Payasam

······*§ **Vermicelli pudding** §*···

Simple ingredients are used to create this remarkable dessert that is made on all auspicious occasions in South India. The trick to a perfect *payasam* is to use less *semiyan* and more milk than you might think you'd need. This pudding has a tendency to thicken as it cools, so you can add more milk to thin it.

Serves 4.

¼ cup (50 grams) ghee (page 37)
1 cup (130 grams) *semiyan* (wheat-flour vermicelli; see Note)
10 cashews
4½ cups (900 ml) milk
1 cup (200 grams) sugar
Generous pinch of saffron threads
½ teaspoon ground green cardamom (see Note page 559)

1. Place a medium nonstick sauté pan over medium heat and add the ghee. When the ghee melts, add the *semiyan* and sauté for 2 to 3 minutes or until light golden brown. Add the cashews, stir well, and set aside.

2. Place a heavy-bottomed nonstick saucepan over high heat and add the milk. Bring to a boil, then add the *semiyan* and cashews. Stir gently, lower the heat to medium, and simmer for 5 minutes, stirring frequently.

3. Add the sugar and continue to simmer, stirring frequently. Cook for 3 to 4 minutes.

4. Stir in the saffron and cardamom. Stir well and serve hot, chilled, or at room temperature.

······*§ **Note** §*· If using ready-roasted *semiyan*, you don't need to roast it further; just add it to the milk in step 2.

Sheer Kurma

······⁕{ Sweet vermicelli pudding }⁕ ···

If there is a *biryani* feast during the Muslim festival of Id, *sheer kurma* will not be far behind. The quantity and types of nuts used vary from home to home.

Serves 4.

A few saffron threads
2 tablespoons warm milk, plus 7½ cups (1.5 liters) milk
2 tablespoons ghee (page 37)
⅔ cup plus 2 tablespoons (100 grams) *semiyan* (wheat-flour vermicelli; see Note)
¼ teaspoon ground green cardamom (see Note page 559)
Pinch of freshly grated nutmeg
2 tablespoons *chironji/charoli* (melon seeds, page 587)
8 to 10 almonds, blanched (see Note page 40), peeled, and slivered
8 to 10 pistachios, blanched (see Note page 40), peeled, and slivered
⅔ cup (125 grams) sugar

1. Soak the saffron in the 2 tablespoons warm milk.

2. Place a heavy-bottomed nonstick saucepan over medium heat and add the ghee. When it melts, add the vermicelli and sauté for 3 to 4 minutes or until light golden.

3. Add the milk, increase the heat to high, and bring to a boil. Lower the heat to medium and simmer for 20 minutes or until the milk thickens and turns light pink.

4. Add the cardamom, nutmeg, saffron mixture, melon seeds, almonds, pistachios, and sugar, and simmer for 10 minutes.

5. Serve hot.

······⁕{ **Note** }⁕ If using ready-roasted *semiyan*, you don't need to roast it further; just add it with the milk in step 3.

Shrikhand

Many North Indians might not be aware of this dessert until they visit Gujarat or Maharashtra. When I first tasted it, I did not like it and coaxed my wife, Alyona, to finish off my bowl so that my mother-in-law would not be offended. Anyway, time is a great leveler; I like *shrikhand* now, and as a chef, I have created many desserts using it as a base.

Serves 4.

3 cups (750 grams) plain yogurt
2 cups (250 gms) confectioners' sugar
Generous pinch of saffron threads
1 tablespoon warm milk
2 teaspoons *chironji*/*charoli* (melon seed, page 587)
¼ teaspoon ground green cardamom (see Note page 559)
8 to 10 pistachios, blanched (see Note page 40), peeled, and sliced

1. Pour the yogurt into a double layer of cheesecloth and hang it for 4 to 5 hours in the refrigerator to drain out the whey.

2. Transfer the drained yogurt to a large bowl. Add the confectioners' sugar and stir until the sugar is completely dissolved.

3. Put the warm milk in a small bowl, add the saffron, and stir until well blended. Add the saffron milk to the yogurt mixture and stir well.

4. Add the melon seeds and cardamom, and stir well.

5. Chill in the refrigerator. Garnish with the pistachios and serve cold.

····❖{ **Chef's Tip** }❖ Add 1 cup mango purée to this *shrikhand* to make *amrakhand*, a delightful summer dessert.

Sooji Ka Halwa

A semolina dessert subtly flavored with saffron

This is practically an instant dessert and one of the most popular in North Indian homes. Every cook makes *sooji ka halwa* a bit differently, but however it's made, it is a true comfort food.

Serves 4.

A few saffron threads
1 tablespoon milk
1¼ cups (250 grams) ghee (page 37)
5 or 6 almonds, slivered
5 or 6 cashews, chopped
5 or 6 raisins
1 cup (200 grams) coarse *rawa/suji* (semolina flour)
1¼ cups (250 grams) sugar
½ teaspoon ground green cardamom (see Note page 559)

1. Soak the saffron in the milk.

2. Place a nonstick wok over medium heat and add the ghee. When small bubbles appear at the bottom of the wok, add the almonds, cashews, and raisins, and cook for 2 to 3 minutes or until lightly browned. Remove with a slotted spoon and drain on paper towels.

3. Add the semolina to the same ghee and sauté until golden brown. Set aside.

4. Place a nonstick saucepan over high heat and add 1 quart (800 ml) water. When the water comes to a boil, add the semolina.

5. Lower the heat to medium and cook, stirring continuously, for a few minutes or until the semolina is cooked and most of the water is absorbed.

6. Add the saffron mixture, sugar, and cardamom. Stir well and cook until all the liquid has been absorbed.

7. Garnish with the almonds, cashews, and raisins. Serve hot.

Sweet-Potato Kheer

······*{ Mashed-sweet-potato-and-milk dessert }*······································

The fasting days of Navratri that precede the festival of Dassera call for a variety of dishes that can be prepared without wheat, rice, pulses, and certain spices. One can use tubers, ginger, chiles, and herbs such as curry leaves and cilantro, but no green vegetables. So potatoes, yams, *colocassia*, and sweet potatos are used often. Sweet potato is lovely in this sweet milk-based dessert.

Serves 4.

3 tablespoons ghee (page 37)
2 medium sweet potatoes, boiled, peeled, and mashed
½ cup (100 grams) sugar
3½ cups (700 ml) whole milk
¼ teaspoon ground green cardamom (see Note page 559)
10 to 12 cashews, broken into pieces
10 to 12 almonds, thinly sliced
10 to 12 pistachios, thinly sliced

1. Place a nonstick saucepan over medium heat and add the ghee. When the ghee melts and small bubbles appear at the bottom of the pan, add the sweet potatoes and cook, stirring frequently, for 6 minutes.

2. Add the sugar and stir. Stir in the milk and cook for 4 to 5 minutes.

3. Add the cardamom and cook for 8 minutes or until the mixture thickens.

4. Add the cashews, almonds, and pistachios, and stir well.

5. Transfer to a serving bowl and serve hot or chilled.

Vrindavan Peda

·······⊰ **A sweet, ball-shaped dessert** ⊱·······

Lord Krishna's love for milk and dairy products is legendary. This *peda* is made specifically as a *naivedya* (offering) to him at Mathura Vrindavan, his birthplace.

Makes 12.

2 cups (300 grams) grated *khoya/mawa* (unsweetened solid condensed milk; page 37)
¼ cup (50 grams) granulated sugar
¼ teaspoon liquid glucose (see Note)
¼ cup (30 grams) superfine sugar

1. Place a nonstick sauté pan over medium heat and add the *khoya*. Sauté, stirring continuously, for 8 to 10 minutes. Remove from the heat and set aside to cool.

2. Place another nonstick sauté pan over medium heat. Add the granulated sugar and ¼ cup (50 ml) water and cook, stirring continuously, until it forms a syrup of one-string consistency (see Note page 570). Add the liquid glucose and stir well. Remove from the heat.

3. Add the *khoya* mixture to the sugar syrup and stir well. Transfer the mixture to a bowl and allow to cool at room temperature.

4. Divide the mixture into 12 portions and shape into balls. Press the balls to flatten them slightly.

5. Spread the superfine sugar on a plate and the roll the *pedas* lightly in it.

6. Arrange the *pedas* on a serving dish and serve.

·······⊰ **Note** ⊱ Liquid glucose is added so that the *pedas* remain soft and the sugar does not crystallize. If you can't find it, light corn syrup can be substituted.

ACKNOWLEDGMENTS

I WOULD LIKE TO THANK all of my teammates who have helped me create this book. I wish to acknowledge the content team led by Rajeev Matta and Chef Anupa Das, who have been thoroughly involved in coordinating everything. Throughout the process, I received expert input from Chef Harpal, who helped to finalize the recipes. I also want to mention the eager beavers in our test kitchen: our team of young chefs who have helped with the research, testing, tasting, measuring, and plating up of all this food. They have done the trials and retrials with a smile and exhibited super efficiency in spite of all the pressure put on them. Thanks to Neena Murdeshwar and Tripta not only for the editorial support and meeting all the deadlines, but also for chipping in with the trials. And my special thanks to my wife, Alyona. She has been overseeing things all along and even cooked some of the dishes that she knows better than I do!

I would also like to thank two very important people, without whom this book would not have happened: Monica Bhide and Michael Psaltis. They have been captaining this ship with vision and clarity, and my sails are full with the winds of enjoyment and sheer pleasure that working with them has given me.

And thank you to Natalie Kaire, who has been incredibly supportive, helpful, and passionate since the start, and to the entire team at Stewart, Tabori & Chang.

COMMON INGREDIENTS

Ajwain: Also known as carom seeds, *ajwain* smells almost exactly like thyme because it contains thymol. However, it is more aromatic and less subtle in taste as it is slightly bitter and pungent. Even a small amount can dominate the flavor of a dish, so use it sparingly. *Ajwain* is also valued for its antiflatulence properties.

Amchur: Dried unripe green mango, *amchur* is usually ground into a fine powder, but it is sometimes available in large pieces. *Amchur* features the acidic, tart, and slightly spicy flavor of unripe mangoes, and it is added to curries, vegetable dishes, *dals*, and *paratha* fillings, and sprinkled over *chaats*. A little goes a long way, and cooks should remember to use *amchur* in moderation.

Anardana: Made of dried pomegranate seeds or arils, this spice is used in Indian and Pakistani cuisines to add tartness to dishes, and sometimes it replaces pomegranate syrup or molasses in Middle Eastern and Persian dishes. The dried seeds are usually lightly dry-roasted and ground just before being used in curries such as *chole* (chickpea curry). Be sure to grind the seeds well before adding them to a dish; otherwise they can add a gritty texture to the food.

Anise seeds: These crescent-shaped seeds of a flowering plant in the parsley family are used in sweet and savory dishes. The flavor resembles that of licorice, fennel, and tarragon. Anise seeds are used as a digestive and in after-dinner candied-spice mixtures much like the more commonly used fennel.

Asafetida: This gummy resin, usually sold as a fine powder, has a strong, heady aroma. A pinch is enough to make its presence known in a dish. Essential in many *dals*, asafetida also adds its garlicky zing to meat dishes and pickles.

Ash gourd: A mottled pale green squash with a chalky white fuzz coating the outside, ash gourd is the fruit of *Benincasa hispida*, a vine. It is also called winter melon.

Atta (whole-wheat flour): Indian *atta* flour is finely milled whole-wheat flour—that is, it contains not only the endosperm but the germ and bran of the flour, and is therefore somewhat more healthful than white or all-purpose flour. It is also finer than U.S.-style whole-wheat flour. If you can't find *atta* (which is available from any Indian grocer), either substitute half fine whole-wheat flour (preferably not "stone-ground," as those flours tend to be quite coarse) and half all-purpose flour, or sift your whole-wheat flour through a fine-mesh sieve before measuring it, to remove some of the larger pieces of bran.

Banana leaves: The large, wide leaves of the banana tree are commonly used in India and Southeast Asia both as a natural serving plate and as a wrapper for steamed or grilled foods. Frozen, folded leaves are widely available in Indian and Asian markets and in many general supermarkets as well.

Bay leaves: The leaves of the laurel tree are usually sold dried, and they add a gentle, sweet flavor to dishes.

Besan (chickpea/gram flour): Made from finely ground chickpeas, *besan* is gluten free and high in protein. It is available from Indian grocers and can sometimes be found in the bulk section of health food stores.

Bitter gourd: Also called bitter melon, this lumpy, warty green gourd with pointed ends (*Momordica charantia*) can be found in Indian and Asian markets. To tame the bitterness a bit, the gourd can be sliced, salted, and rinsed before using, much like eggplant.

Black cardamom: These seed pods have a smoky character, a strong camphorlike flavor, and a pleasant aroma. The seeds inside the pods are used for flavoring vegetable and meat dishes, and the whole pod is often added to stewed dishes and removed before serving.

Black pepper: This popular spice is made from dried ripe berries and is used ground or as whole peppercorns. Most Indian cooks use black peppercorns in *pulaos* along with cardamom, cloves, and bay leaves. In South India, black peppercorns are the basis of the hot curries and are ground into masala pastes.

Black salt: A pinkish or purplish salt whose particular mineral impurities give it its distinctive color, flavor, and sulfurous aroma. It is sometimes labeled or referred to as "rock salt," but do not substitute regular rock salt—the salt sprinkled on sidewalks and roads to melt ice—or "ice cream salt," as these are inedible and not the same as Indian black salt, *kala namak*.

Black sesame seeds: These small, flat seeds are dark in color and used in cooking for their medicinal properties. They are high in calcium, iron, copper, magnesium, and phosphorus, which help to maintain healthy bones, muscles, and blood.

Boondi: These fried chickpea-flour puffs are about the size of green peas. Look for packages of them in the snacks and *chaat*-ingredient sections of Indian grocery stores.

Caraway seeds: Caraway is smaller, darker, and more expensive than its close relative, cumin. It is grown in Kashmir and is used in *pulaos* and meat dishes.

Chironji/charoli: Not melon seeds (but regularly translated as such), *chironji* are round, light brown seeds from a small tree fruit (*Buchanania lanzan*). They are soft and nutlike, and their flavor is reminiscent of almonds (blanched almonds can be substituted for *chironji*). They should be refrigerated for long-term storage because of their high oil content.

Cilantro: This herb has wide, delicate, lacy green leaves and a pungent flavor. The seeds are known as coriander and are also used as a spice. Although fresh cilantro and coriander seeds come from the same plant, their flavors are very different and they cannot be used interchangeably. Fresh cilantro is used extensively in Indian cuisine as a garnish.

Cinnamon: The bark, wood, leaves, buds, flowers, fruits, and roots of the cinnamon tree are used for different purposes, but the bark is the most commonly used, either in pieces or ground to a fine powder. It adds a delicious woody flavor to desserts and is widely used in savory dishes. Kerala, a state in South India, is the country's major producer of the cinnamon used in Indian kitchens.

Cloves: These unopened dried flower buds look like snails. Cloves have a sweet and strongly minty flavor, and can be purchased whole or finely ground. India is one of the largest consumers of cloves in the world. Full-grown flower buds are picked green and dried in the sun until they become dark brown. With a fine aromatic flavor and warming qualities, cloves integrate well with other spices in sweet and savory dishes.

Coriander: The seeds of the cilantro plant are sold whole or ground. Coriander is mild, with an aroma similar to lemon, sage, and caraway. It is used in curry powder spice mixes, pickling, and soups. When young, the cilantro plant is used fresh for chutneys and sauces, and for flavoring curries and soups.

Cumin: These long, dark brown seeds are very aromatic and are sold whole or finely ground. Cumin is widely used in spice mixes, curry powders, and in vegetable dishes, pickles, soups, meat dishes, and even in cheeses, sausages, breads, cakes, and biscuits.

Curry leaves: This spice, which has a distinct lemon flavor, is used extensively in Southeast Asian cooking to add a very distinct flavor and aroma to dishes. Curry leaves are not related to curry powder at all. They are the leaves of the curry plant or tree, *Murraya koenigii*. They are used in a variety of soups, stews, chutneys, and sauces. Although they vaguely resemble bay leaves, curry leaves can be eaten and need not be removed from the dish before serving.

Dagad phool: Also known as lichen stone flower, this fungus lends its dark color and musky flavor to many dishes, although it is rarely used outside the Himalayan and mountain regions of western and central India. An excessive amount can make curries very bitter.

Dal: Dried beans, lentils, and peas all fall under the category of *dal*, and are used in myriad ways: as the main ingredients in soups and stews; soaked and fermented and ground for various pancakes; as a crunchy textural element in tempering with spices; and as a binding agent in meat and vegetable mixtures for ground-meat patties and kabobs. Following are commonly used *dals* that appear throughout this book:

>*chana dal* (split Bengal gram): Dried small chickpeas split in half, tan colored and larger than other *dals*.

>*dalia* (roasted *chana dal*): *Dalia* is often ground and used to thicken sauces, in marinades, and to add texture to chutneys.

>*dhuli moong dal* (split skinless green gram): Mung beans that have been husked to remove the skins, and split in half. They are yellow.

>*dhuli urad dal* (split skinless black gram): Small lentil-like beans that have been husked to remove the black skins, and split in half. They are creamy white in color.

>*masoor dal* (split red lentils): These skinned and halved red lentils, are salmon-colored and cook very quick.

>*sabut masoor* (whole red lentils): Red lentils with their brown skins left on. They are light brown, flat, and round.

>*sabut moong* (whole green gram): Whole mung beans with their skins. They are green.

>*toor dal/arhar dal* (split pigeon peas): Skinned and split yellow lentils.

Deghi mirch chile powder: Similar to paprika, this mild red chile powder is more sweet than hot. It is used in Indian food primarily for its color.

Dried red chiles: These hot red peppers are sun-dried before use. Different regions of India grow and use their own type of red chiles—Kashmiri chiles in Kashmir, *begdi* in Karnataka, *guntur* in Andhra Pradesh, etc. We have used Kashmiri dried red chiles in most of our recipes because they are not too spicy and they impart an appetizing color to dishes.

Dried rose petals: These are used to flavor and scent many *biryanis* and sweet dishes. If you dry your own, be sure to use roses that have not been treated with chemicals.

Drumstick vegetable: The young, mild-tasting fruit of the *Moringa oleifera* plant, drumstick is used extensively in Indian cooking, almost as commonly as green beans or asparagus in the United States, but is fairly scarce here. Drumstick vegetables are long and green, with ridges running the length of the vegetable.

Edible sandalwood powder: The dried wood of the sandalwood tree in powder form.

Fennel: These oval, greenish brown seeds are from the fennel plant. They are aromatic, with a slight licorice flavor. They are similar to anise seeds, but are larger. Fennel seeds are available whole or ground. Fennel is an effective digestive aid, and raw fennel seeds are often chewed after rich meals in India.

Fenugreek: These hard, yellowish brown, angular seeds are available whole, crushed, or roasted and ground. Fenugreek has a strong, aromatic, and bittersweet flavor. The leaves are used as an herb (*kasoori methi*). Fenugreek is cultivated worldwide in semi-arid areas. Fenugreek seeds are often paired with mustard seeds in tempering oil and are much in demand during pickling season.

Ganthia: Crunchy fried chickpea-flour sticks about the width and length of your little finger. They are sold in the snack and *chaat*-ingredient section of Indian grocery stores. See page 16 for a recipe.

Ghee: Ghee is butter that has been slowly cooked, skimmed, and clarified.

Ginger: The rhizome of the ginger plant is available fresh or dried; the latter is usually finely ground.

Green cardamom: This queen of Indian spices is the second-most important spice in India after cumin seeds. Green cardamom is an ancient and extremely flavorful spice that is native to India. Either the pods are used whole or the small black seeds are ground to a powder. Cardamom is widely used throughout the world, and nearly every food culture has its own distinctive way of using it in sweet and savory dishes.

Green chiles: Fresh hot capsicums. Indian green chiles that are most commonly used in the dishes in this book are very similar to serrano chiles in flavor and heat level, and finger-size serranos are a good substitute.

Indian broad beans (hyacinth beans): These are wide, long, flat green pods with beans inside. Their flavor is more pronounced than that of regular green beans, and is often likened to the flavor of lima beans. To use, remove the strings from the outside of the pods, then cut the pods crosswise into small pieces. Hyacinth beans, called *sem ki phalli* in India, are also available already chopped in the frozen-foods section of Indian grocery stores.

Jaggery: This is an unrefined dark brown cane (sometimes palm) sugar, sold in hard, solid cones or blocks that can be chopped with a heavy knife or grated on the coarse holes of a box grater. Jaggery is similar to Mexican *piloncillo*, or *panela*, and either of those may be used in place of jaggery. In a pinch, you could also use turbinado or natural cane sugar.

Kakdi magaz (dried cucumber seeds): Kakdi magaz are dried cucumber seeds. They are thinner and longer and also have a sweeter taste than most melon seeds. Used mostly to garnish select Indian desserts, sweet chutneys, and some savory snacks, they can be substituted with other melon seeds, such as cantaloupe and honeydew.

Kalonji (nigella): Small black seeds of the *Nigella sativa* plant, *kalonji* are also sometimes labeled "black sesame," "onion seeds," or "black cumin," though the seed is related to none of these. They lend their distinctive, slightly bitter flavor to *naan* and other breads.

Kashmiri red chile powder: Kashmiri red chiles are grown in Himachal Pradesh, Jammu, and Kashmir, and also in subtropical regions of North India, and are harvested from November to February. The chiles are long and fleshy, with a very deep red color and mild flavor that makes the ground dried chiles much prized, especially in North Indian dishes. Paprika is a good substitute for these chiles.

Kasoori methi: These dried fenugreek leaves taste like a combination of celery and fennel, and have a slightly bitter bite. The leaves are usually crumbled and sprinkled over meat and vegetable curries just before serving.

Kewra (screw pine) water: This aromatic water made from distilled screw pine flowers, also known as *pandanus* or *kewra* in Hindi, is used to flavor *biryanis* and sweets.

Kokum: *Kokum* (*Garcinia indica*), also known as gamboge, is a native fruit of India and is grown abundantly in Konkan, Karnataka, and Kerala along the western coast of

India. It is found in the United States in Indian grocery stores in dried form.

Kurmura (puffed rice): Also often labeled "murmura," this is basmati rice that has been steamed at high pressure so that it puffs, much like puffed wheat. It is used in *chaats* and sweets.

Lapsi (fine broken wheat): Like bulgur or cracked wheat, but finer, *lapsi* is used in snacks and *dal* dishes, and can be cooked with ghee and sugar and garnished with nuts as a sweet treat for the festival of Diwali.

Lauki (bottle gourd): The smooth-skinned bottle gourd (*Lageneria siceraria*) has pale green flesh with a firm texture. Choose young bottle gourds (less than a foot long) rather than older, larger ones; young gourds have a thin, tender peel and undeveloped seeds that do not need to be removed. *Lauki* is also known as *doodhi*.

Lemongrass: The lower pale yellow and white part of this long, thick grass is sliced or pounded, and is used to add a lovely, vibrant citrus flavor to dishes.

Mace: This spice is derived from the fleshy red aril surrounding the nutmeg seed. Its flavor is similar to that of nutmeg, but with a hint of pepper. It should be used sparingly.

Maida (refined flour): Indian *maida* flour is a highly refined white flour. It is finer and softer than the all-purpose flour found in the United States. If you can't find *maida*, which, like the other flours used in this book, is available at any Indian grocer, substitute a white (not whole-wheat) pastry flour.

Malai burfi (condensed-milk *mithai*): Cubes of condensed-milk sweets readily available at Indian grocery stores.

Mangodi (dried *dal* dumplings): These large, grape-size dried dumplings made from puréed cooked *dhuli moong dal* (sometimes other *dals*) are available readymade at Indian grocery stores.

Mint: An excellent remedy for digestive problems, mint is well known for its fragrance and cool, refreshing flavor. It is usually used fresh, but retains much of its flavor when dried.

Mustard oil: Mustard oil is available in two varieties: filtered and refined. If you are using filtered mustard oil, you will need to first heat it until it reaches its smoking point, then let it cool completely before using. If you are using the refined variety, you can use it straight away. In either case, please use mustard oil that is labeled specifically for cooking. If you cannot find it, regular vegetable oil will work just as well.

Mustard seeds: These small, round seeds varying in color from black to brown to yellow are ubiquitous in southern Indian cooking, where the tempering of the oil in countless recipes begins with the addition of them. They pack a punch that is intensified in hot oil.

Nagkesar: Also known as cobra's saffron, this astringent herb is used to treat respiratory problems and as a digestive aid. The leaves are dried and used for their mild and slightly sweet flavor.

Nutmeg: A hard, oval, dried seed of an East Indian tree, nutmeg is widely cultivated in the tropics and is used as a spice in sweet and savory dishes either in grated or ground form.

Panch phoron: This mixture of five whole spices is made of cumin seeds, fenugreek seeds, *kalonji* (nigella), mustard seeds, and caraway seeds.

Paneer: Paneer is a fresh cheese that is pressed until solid enough to slice or cut into cubes. See page 17 for a recipe.

Poppy seeds: The ivory-colored variety is widely used in Indian cooking to add a hint of nutty flavor to dishes. The seeds are also soaked and ground to a paste, and used to thicken sauces.

Rawa/suji (semolina flour): Coarsely ground (sand-textured) wheat flour, *rawa/suji* contains the wheat's endosperm and germ, but not the bran, and is available in fine, medium, and coarse grinds. You can substitute farina (Cream of Wheat cereal), which is made from soft wheat; or semolina flour, which is made from harder durum wheat.

Red button chiles: These small dried red chiles that look like little balls are fried in oil to lend a mild smoky flavor to food. They should be removed before serving.

Ridged gourd: A vegetable in the cucumber family (*Luffa acutangula*), ridged gourd is long and dark green, with raised ridges running the length of the vegetable. Try to select younger ones; very mature ridged gourds can be tough and fibrous. Look for them in Indian markets and Asian grocery stores.

Rosewater and rose syrup: Indian stores sell rosewater and rose syrup. Rosewater is a clear, thin liquid distilled from rose petals, and is sprinkled on sparsely to provide a lovely aroma to savory and sweet dishes. Rose syrup is a thick, red, sugar-sweetened liquid with rose flavorings. It is used to add sweetness, color, and aroma to a dish.

Saffron: Thousands of individual threadlike strands of the stigma from the crocus flower are hand-plucked and dried to make a single ounce of this very expensive spice.

Saffron is used to flavor *biryanis* and sweet dishes, and also in some soups and curries and baked goods. It adds both its bright yellow color and a subtle flavor to dishes.

Sesame seeds: These tiny oily seeds impart a nutty flavor and texture to chutneys, desserts, and vegetable dishes. Their color ranges from ivory to light brown to black; white sesame seeds are used in most of the recipes in this book.

***Sev* (chickpea-flour vermicelli):** Very thin deep-fried chickpea-flour strands that look like broken-up vermicelli or angel-hair pasta, *sev* can be found in the snack and *chaat*-ingredients section of Indian grocery stores.

Star anise: Known as *phool chakri* or *badiyan* in India, this star-shaped spice has a flavor that resembles that of anise seeds. Star anise is usually used whole, valued for its beautiful form as well as its flavor.

Tamarind: The fruit of the tamarind tree, *Tamarindus indica*, these pods are about five inches long and contain seeds and a pulp that becomes extremely sour when dried. Tamarind is widely used in Indian, Middle Eastern, Mexican, and Southeast Asian cooking. See page 9 for more information about buying and using tamarind pulp and concentrate.

***Tirphala*:** The sun-dried fruit of the *tirphala* tree (which grows wild in the rain forests of Maharashtra and Karnataka in western India) looks like a Sichuan peppercorn except that the former is blackish brown and the latter is red in color. The husk of the dried berries is the actual spice, and it has a strong, woody, pungent aroma and a sharp and biting flavor. The husks are dry-roasted before being used in fish dishes or with pulses or in dishes of peas and beans. Because it is exclusive to this part of India, there is no English word for *tirphala*.

Turmeric: This spice is made from the intense yellow-orange rhizome of a tropical plant related to ginger. Dried and ground turmeric is used to flavor and color food. It is used in curry powder blends and plays an important role in imparting an appetizing golden color to *dals* and vegetable dishes.

White pepper: This comes from the same plant as black pepper, but the berries are picked when fully ripe rather than green. White pepper is not as hot as black.

Appam chetti: A concave iron griddle with a heavy lid used to make *appams* (special breads from South India). A heavy cast-iron or nonstick wok can be used instead, as long as it has a tight-fitting lid.

Chakli or ganthia press: This metal press comes with different dies (much like a cookie press) through which you can push various doughs into different shapes for frying. With it you can make *chakli*, *ganthia*, *murukku*, *sev*, and *idiappam*.

Coconut scraper: This ingenious tool consists of a set of crank-operated rounded serrated blades that can be mounted on a tabletop (or secured via suction). With it you can finely grate a halved coconut by holding the coconut half over the blades while you turn them with the crank; there is no need to shell and peel the coconut flesh. If you don't have a scraper like this, carefully remove the shell and brown peel from the white flesh with a paring knife and grate the coconut in a food processor.

Dosa griddle: This flat metal plate, usually made of iron or heavy-gauge aluminum, has an anodized surface. The surface is scratch resistant and does not crack or peel, allowing the use of metal spoons, spatulas, etc. You can use a nonstick griddle instead, but don't use metal utensils on it.

Double boiler: This stove-top pan is used to melt chocolate without burning or seizing, or to cook any other thick liquid, sauce, or porridge that would normally burn if cooked over direct heat. It consists of an upper vessel (containing the food) situated above a lower pot of water. When the water is brought to a boil, the steam produced in the lower pot transfers the heat to the upper pot.

Food processor: An electric kitchen appliance with a closed container and interchangeable blades that can chop, blend, shred, purée, or otherwise process food at high speed. I use a mini food processor to grind up small quantities of wet mixtures.

Idli steamer: This deep vessel with a lid has a vent that allows steam to escape and special plates with dents into which the *idli* batter is poured and then steamed. They are readily available at Indian grocery stores.

Kadai: A thick, deep, circular cooking pot that resembles a wok.

Kulfi molds: Aluminum or plastic individual-size molds in which the milk-and-nut mixture is frozen to make *kulfi* desserts. Ramekins, custard cups, or even ice-pop molds make good *kulfi* molds.

Paniyaram tawa: Mainly used in South India, this is an iron griddle with golf ball–size dents into which batter is poured to make *paniyaram*.

Pickle jars: Glass or porcelain pickle jars are sterilized (by submerging in boiling water for at least ten minutes) and allowed to dry thoroughly before being used to store homemade pickles; Indian pickle jars are available at Indian markets, or you can use American- or European-style canning jars.

Tawa: This is a large, flat, or slightly concave disk-shaped griddle made from cast iron, steel, or aluminum, used to cook *rotis* and *parathas*. Nonstick *tawas* are also now available. Any large, flat griddle or even a cast-iron skillet can be used instead.

SOURCES

Indian Grocery Stores

Indian Grocery Store Locator
Type in your zip code to find Indian grocery stores near you
www.diggsamachar.com/grocery/grocery.htm

Indian Supermarket Guide
Indian grocery stores and restaurants listed by state
www.videsh.com

Utensils

Amazon
Idli steamers, food steamers, spice grinders, and more
www.amazon.com

I Shop Indian
A good selection of Indian utensils
www.ishopindian.com

Ingredients

Amazon
Amazon carries a very good selection of Indian spices and herbs
www.amazon.com

India Foods Company
Great prices on herbs and spices
www.indianfoodsco.com

India Plaza
An online store offering herbs, spices, ready-to-eat meals, and much more
www.indiaplaza.com

My Spice Sage
An excellent collection of global spices
www.myspicesage.com

Penzeys
Very good quality spices
www.penzeys.com

Rani Foods (formerly Kundan Foods)
Spices and other ingredients
www.qualityspices.com
www.kundanfoods.com

Spices Galore
A good collection of spices and marinades from around the world
www.spicesgalore1.com

·······✺{ INDEX }✺·······